all decided to take the necessary precautions and to sleep in the safest place.

A typical incident happened just before lunch to-day. The P.M. had invited Cross, his Minister of Shipping, to lunch and was showing him great affability. Suddenly he charged back into the room at NO 10., where I was telephoning, and whispered hoarsely in my ear: "What is the name of the Minister of Shipping?". 'Cross', I whispered back furtively, because the Minister was standing in the doorway. "Oh", said the P.M, "Well what's his Christian name?". Cross must have heard the whole conversation!

John Peck and I dined at Down St. Station (the burrow, Winston calls it) where we fed excellently, and slept there in great comfort. The P.M. spent the night at the C.W.R. to await the "Moonlight Sonata", and became so impatient that he spent much of the time on the Air Ministry Roof.

Friday, November 15th

London had a quiet night but Coventry was subjected to violent bombardment — possibly the First Movement of the Sonata, which may continue throughout the moon period.

The P.M. has sent a real snorter to Lampson, in Egypt, who in a private telegram to Eden stigmatised one of the decisions of the Cabinet as "crazy".

P.T. Grigg, whom I saw this morning, was loud in his condemnation of his master, Eden. 'Complete Funk', he called him.

Moyra lunched with me at Prunier's, and after eating oysters

Sunday. 11/May/1941

10, Downing Street,
Whitehall,

I walked out into Downing Street at 8.0 a.m. on my way to the early service at Westminster Abbey. It was really a summer day with blue skies, but the smoke from many fires lay thick over London and obscured the sun. Burnt paper, from some demolished paper mill, was falling like leaves on a windy autumn day.

Whitehall was thronged with people, mostly sight-seers but some of them civil defence workers with blackened faces and haggard looks. One of them, a boy of 18 or 19, pointed towards the Houses of Parliament and said: "Is that the sun?" But the great orange glow at which we were looking was the light of so many fires south of the river. At Westminster Abbey there were fire-engines and the Policeman at the door said to me: "There will not be any services in the Abbey to-day, Sir", exactly as if it was closed for spring cleaning. I turned towards Westminster Hall on the roof of which I could see flames still leaping. Smoke rose from some invisible point in the pile of Parliament buildings beyond. I talked to a fireman. He shewed me Big Ben, the face of which was pocked and scarred, and told me a bomb had gone right through the Tower. The

Saturday, March 5th

CHEQUERS
BUTLER'S CROSS · AYLESBURY
BUCKS

At dinner this evening there were present, besides the Prime Minister, General de Gaulle, General Spears, Mr Menzies (Prime Minister of Australia), Duncan and Diana Sandys, Tommy Thompson and myself.

We talked of Germany and the Germans.

De Gaulle said that the important thing for people living in occupied territory was to remain aloof and superior. The Germans knew that they were inferior beings and were susceptible on the point. Moreover, this being so, it was important to show that the war was a world war. The Germans could see themselves as lords of Europe, but the idea of the world gave them vertigo. As for Hitler, he said: "Vous ne le prendrez pas, et cette fois il n'y aura pas un Doorn".

Duncan Sandys was very blood-thirsty. He wanted to destroy Germany by laying the country waste and burning towns and factories so that for years the German people might be occupied in reconstruction. He wanted to destroy their books and libraries so that an illiterate generation might grow up.

Louis Spears replied that this would make the Germans more hardy and virile, while their western conquerors would be growing effete on the fruits of victory. In his view Richelieu was the greatest of modern European statesmen. He had answered that he had been told she was off her head (I corrected him); at any rate what she obviously needed was............!

There were various nocturnal prowls before we went to bed. During one of them Eden, while holding forth on some topic, took a step backwards and disappeared head over heels into the deep ha-ha and barbed wire fence at the edge of the lawn.

Sunday, June 22nd

Awoken by the telephone with the news that Germany had attacked Russia. I went a round of the bedrooms breaking the news and produced a smile of satisfaction on the faces of the P.M. Eden and Winant. Winant, however, suspects it may all be a put up job between Hitler and Stalin (later the P.M. and Cripps laughed this to scorn).

Eden rushed off to the F.O. for the day; the P.M. decided to broadcast and actually came down to the Hawtrey Room at 11.0 a.m. to prepare it; Sir Stafford and Lady Cripps motored over to

The Fringes of Power

THE
FRINGES
OF
POWER

———

The Incredible Inside Story of
Winston Churchill During World War II

———

JOHN COLVILLE

THE LYONS PRESS

Guilford, Connecticut

An imprint of The Globe Pequot Press

Four individual pages from Sir John Colville's diaries are reproduced.

The Lyons Press is an imprint of The Globe Pequot Press.

First Lyons Press edition 2002
First American edition 1986

Printed in Canada

2 4 6 8 10 9 7 5 3 1

The Library of Congress Cataloging-in-Publication Data is available on file.

ISBN 1-58574-508-1

Dedicated to Mary Soames with affection and with penitence
for some of the less complimentary references to her in the
early part of this diary.

Contents

Acknowledgments

I am indebted to Messrs David Higham Associates, who act for the owners of the copyright of Miss Dorothy Sayers' books and papers, for permission to reproduce the hitherto unpublished poem, "The Burden of Ireland", which she sent to Winston Churchill at the beginning of January 1941.

I also thank the Society of Authors, on behalf of the Estate of Bernard Shaw, for permission to publish his letter to Winston Churchill on p. 171, the executors of the estate of the late Miss Helen Waddell for the reproduction of her verse on p. 524 and Sir John Peck for allowing me to include his "spoof" minute written on October 31st, 1940.

Miss Sheila Legat kindly typed the many thousand words of my manuscript diaries twenty-five years ago and I am grateful to her, as I am to Miss Joyce Macleod who with unfaltering accuracy retyped them for publication together with the narrative and the notes included in this volume. I am also much indebted to Mr Hilary Rubinstein of A. P. Watt & Co., to Mr Thomas C. Wallace of W. W. Norton & Co. and by no means least to Mr Ion Trewin of Hodder and Stoughton whom I have discovered to be the eighth Pillar of Wisdom.

Illustrations

Between pages 624 and 625

Princess Elizabeth and Prince Philip on their visit to the Paris Opera, May 1948.

Lady Margaret Egerton.

The Churchills at the author's wedding, October 1948.

The christening of Harriet Colville, February 1953.

King George VI's comment on the appointment of the author as joint principal Private Secretary to the Prime Minister, November 1951.

The Prime Minister greets the Italian Prime Minister, June 1953.

Preface

In the England of my youth primogeniture held sway, as indeed it still does in families with real estate to maintain and bequeath. My father and mother both came from well-known and by no means indigent families, but they were younger children and therefore, thanks to primogeniture, comparatively poor. I say comparatively, for in the twenty years between the two world wars we wanted for none of life's essentials, always had six or seven domestic servants, owned a fleet of small boats in the Isle of Wight and had a house in one of London's less fashionable squares. We had no motor-car (for my parents, both born long before the motoring era, equated a car with a carriage, complete with coachman and groom), we had no country house and we had no fine possessions. We always travelled about London by bus or underground; we never fed in restaurants, only went to a theatre on the last night of the school holidays and were constantly admonished to turn out the electric light. I remember going to the Opera at Covent Garden in full evening dress, my mother wearing her tiara and a large diamond brooch; and we travelled there and back in a Number 11 bus, covering the first and last few hundred yards on foot.

However, the money saved by my parents' carefulness (which never verged on meanness) went on providing their three sons with the best and most expensive education available; and though they were far from being cadgers, they had enough devoted friends and relations to provide their children with pheasants to shoot, horses to ride, yachts in which to race and pleasant country houses in which to stay.

Thus in 1936, when I came down from Trinity College, Cambridge, at the age of twenty-one, I had not been stinted of pleasures and had even, in the days when travel was still an adventure, been to the Soviet Union, steamed down the Danube in a barge, crossed Asia Minor in a third-class railway carriage, spent ten days as a guest in the monasteries of Mount Athos and learned to speak both French and German with fluency. I had also won two scholarships. However, I was well aware that I must soon earn my living with greater urgency than some of my university friends. This provided an incentive for hard work.

My two elder brothers had gone in to the City of London, one as a banker, the other as a stockbroker. To me, fascinated by political history and current affairs, the Foreign Office beckoned, though in those days the honour of belonging to the Diplomatic Service was thought to outweigh the need for reasonable remuneration and my father doubted if I could afford such a career.

The first problem was to get in: the entrance exam consisted of eighteen three-hour papers and four interviews. The competition was formidable. I was remarkably lucky: contrary to all expectations I succeeded at the age of twenty-two and at the first attempt.

In September 1937, after a memorable tour of Italy with my American friend Henry B. Hyde who, stimulated by a visit we made to the famous sage, Bernard Berenson, introduced me to the greatest of the Florentine and Venetian paintings (showing a sensitivity I shall never forget), I presented myself at the Foreign Office in Whitehall and was allotted to the Eastern Department.

The important problems confronting that department related to Palestine, where a plan to partition the territory between Arabs and Jews had succeeded in infuriating both parties, where the Mufti of Jerusalem was believed to be in the pay of the Germans and where the British Government was viciously attacked by Zionists who wanted more entry permits granted to Jews, and by Arabs who wanted all immigration stopped.

It is strange, on looking back, to remember that in the other territories over which we kept a watchful eye, peace reigned in Iraq under the firm rule of King Feisal's trusted old adviser, Nuri Pasha, not a ripple of commercial interest stirred the sandy wastes of Saudi Arabia and the Gulf States, and the few apparently insoluble problems related to an Iraqi claim to some date-gardens belonging to the Sheikh of Kuwait and to that of some distant heirs of Sultan Abdul Hamid to the Mosul oil fields.

My parish, with of course a senior First Secretary in charge, was Turkey and Persia. Persia was just a little tiresome, as the Shah, Reza Pahlevi, was a temperamental despot. We had to be particularly polite to him because of the enormous interests of the Anglo-Persian Oil Company (now British Petroleum) in the country, and there was an administrative complication in that the seven or eight British consular posts in the country reported (for some obscure nineteenth-century reason) to the Viceroy of India, though the Foreign Office were sent copies of their despatches.

Turkey was more exciting. Standing at the cross-roads joining Russia to the Mediterranean and Europe to the Middle East, and by no means remote from the route to India, the country was of political importance to both Britain and Germany. It was ruled dictatorially by Kemal Ataturk, the Grey Wolf, whose early inclination to the Germans had been sapped by the diligence of the British Ambassador, Sir Percy Loraine, able to stay up night after night gambling and drinking with Ataturk and becoming, in the process, an intimate friend and counsellor. The Germans tried to counter Loraine's influence by sending as their Ambassador the notorious Franz von Papen, more slippery than any eel; but they were too late, Loraine had landed the Turkish fish.

I was living with my parents at 66 Eccleston Square, immersed in all this oriental intrigue, and especially in coaxing unwilling supply departments to provide arms for Turkey and Persia in competition with German and Italian offers, when the world almost went to war over Czechoslovakia. It was September 1938, exactly a year after I joined the Foreign Office, that Britain and France stepped back from the brink of the precipice and signed the Munich Agreement with Hitler. Neither Britain nor France was ready for war. The French had a vast army; the British had the world's largest navy; but the Germans already had a powerful air force whereas by then the Royal Air Force had only received two or three operational Spitfires: not even two or three squadrons. The French Air Force was in a lamentable state.

In those last days of September 1938, trenches were dug in Hyde Park, plans were made to evacuate school children, gas-masks were prepared for distribution and every young man I knew, not already a soldier or sailor, joined a "Supplementary Reserve". However, after the signing of the Munich Agreement Neville Chamberlain assured us that there would be peace in our time; and he really believed it. So I returned to my middle-oriental ploys, to be rudely shaken when on March 15th, 1939, Hitler, contrary to the solemn promises he had given at Munich, sent his troops to seize Prague and, shortly afterwards, Danzig. On Good Friday Mussolini invaded Albania and Hitler began to make menacing threats to Poland.

On August 22nd, 1939, came the signature of the Molotov–Ribbentrop non-aggression pact between the Soviet Union and Germany, secretly partitioning Poland and agreeing to hand over the prosperous little Baltic States to Russia. It meant that short of a miracle war was certain.

On August 23rd I had been due to sail to New York on my first visit to the U.S.A. for a month's holiday in Wyoming where some close Anglo-American friends had rented a ranch. I looked forward with excitement to seeing America; and I had a strong emotional incentive, which had been growing throughout the summer. Hitler put a stop to all that, for all leave was cancelled just before my ship was due to sail, so at the beginning of September 1939 I was waiting at my desk in Whitehall for war to be declared, twenty-four years old, a Third Secretary in the Diplomatic Service of two years' standing and tempted to resign before, on my twenty-fifth birthday, my employment should become a reserved occupation from which there would be no escape while the war lasted. Unsure of what was going to happen next, I decided to keep a diary.

I have used extracts from it in several books I have written, and I lent a large part of it to Martin Gilbert for background information and quotation in the concluding volumes of his official life of Winston Churchill. Now, a long time after it was written, I present it in consecutive form, having eliminated a high proportion of the trivial entries which are of no general interest, but leaving in a few which may perhaps help to recapture the "atmosphere" of the time.

Since there are many for whom memories of those distant years are blurred, and at least two generations who had no first-hand experience of them, I thought it might be helpful to insert from time to time brief explanations and comments on people and events which, if familiar to my contemporaries, are scarcely so now.

In order to reduce the number of footnotes, which some may find informative but others distracting, I have compiled a series of biographical notes, inserted at the end of the book, and have marked the names in the text with an asterisk *.

Part One

September 1939–September 1941

1

The War Begins

The British and French Governments, rapidly followed by all four of Britain's self-governing Dominions, declared war on Germany on September 3rd, 1939, as soon as Hitler's forces invaded Poland. He had already recovered the Rhineland, seized Austria and Czechoslovakia and proclaimed that "Today Germany is ours; tomorrow the whole world".

It was a warm and bright Sunday morning, on which the early services in all the churches were packed with worshippers, many of whom had not been seen in church for a long time. When, after following their example, I arrived at the Foreign Office I was informed that I had been assigned to the Ministry of Economic Warfare which was in the course of being established in the vacant lecture rooms of the London School of Economics. It was to be a primary instrument in imposing an economic blockade on Germany, a policy which, combined with our control of the seas, many deluded optimists believed would bring Germany rapidly to her knees.

On reporting to this new and bewildering organisation I was given an empty desk and nothing whatever to do. I sat contemplating the green leather desk-tops until somebody switched on a wireless set (the word "radio" was not then much in use) and we listened to Neville Chamberlain announcing we were at war. We knew it was coming, but all the same Chamberlain's broadcast, made with slow, solemn dignity, induced a numbness from which we were rudely revived by the sirens moaning out the war's first air-raid warning.

I say we, for there were others sitting equally unemployed in the London School of Economics. It was widely believed that London would be reduced to rubble within minutes of war being declared, as recently depicted to an alarmed populace in the film of H. G. Wells' book called *Things to Come*; and it seemed that this was indeed about to happen. So we scuttled, preserving what semblance of nonchalance we could, to the air-raid shelter. There I played bridge with David Eccles,[1] Rufus Smith[2] and another new conscript to the Ministry. After the first rubber the all-clear sounded, for the sirens had been set off on account of a single unidentified aircraft spotted miles to the east of the Thames estuary.

We returned to our empty desks and at lunch-time, being assured that I should have nothing to do or even to read that day, I went home reflecting that we seemed remarkably ill-prepared for Armageddon. It was a lovely afternoon and so my brother Philip,* awaiting his call-up to the Grenadiers, motored me to Trent Park,[3] formerly the home of Sir Philip Sassoon and now owned by his close friend and cousin, Mrs Gubbay. It had an excellent private twelve-hole golf course on which my brother and I peacefully spent the first afternoon of war. A few days afterwards I went to the Foreign Office and pleaded, successfully, to be restored to my familiar and reasonably busy occupation in its Eastern Department.

On September 10th I began my diary. I wrote copiously in the first, undramatic months of the war; but I have drastically curtailed the extracts from the early pages and have excised many of the references to my private life and social activities. I have not, however, tampered with the text of the Diaries themselves even when they contain views on people and events which now seem to me dubious.

Sunday, September 10th

From the point of view of the civilian this war has hardly begun in earnest, and only the black-out at night, and the barrage balloons by day, remind one that Europe has finally toppled over the brink of the precipice upon which it has been balancing precariously for the last twelve months. Doubtless there is much in store for us that will dispel our cherished illusions of peace; but for the moment the war seems very unreal.

Ever since war was declared the sun has shone with unremitting splendour, and there is nothing about the gaily dressed, smiling

---

[1] Subsequently 1st Viscount Eccles. Holder of several ministerial offices and eventually Chairman of the Trustees of the British Museum.
[2] Later 2nd Lord Bicester and Chairman of Morgan Grenfell Ltd.
[3] Near Cockfosters. A splendid Queen Anne House.

crowds in the streets to remind us of this great catastrophe – except perhaps for the gas-masks slung across their backs and the number of men in uniform.

Monday, September 11th
Getting up at 7.30 I read the colourless newspapers in the sun on the balcony outside the back drawing-room, and walked to Coutts' after breakfast. Many of the bank clerks were wearing special constables' uniforms instead of their usual sober frock-coats.

I arrived at the F.O. just before 11.00 and spent a busy day there. The most interesting work I had was to assess the claims of Persia to receive support in armaments and flying instruction as compared with other countries. Persia has every intention of remaining neutral, but her goodwill is essential to us both on account of imperial communications and because of the Anglo-Iranian Oil Company, on which the navy to a large extent depend for their oil supplies. It is therefore important to please the Shah[1] by supplying him with aeroplanes and instructors, even if our effort in so doing will be wasted on incorrigibly neutral soil.

In general the impression to be gained at the F.O. is not as encouraging as that which the newspapers give. It seems likely that Mussolini's neutrality is very much of a put-up job and that he is still on the best and most intimate terms with Hitler. Italian neutrality is, however, clearly the wisest policy for the Axis powers: as far as Hitler is concerned it ensures Turkish neutrality and thus makes it less easy for the Allies to help Poland from the East, as well as introducing complications about the passage of warships, etc., through the Straits; from Mussolini's point of view it is eminently desirable, because the Italian people are at present violently opposed to war and Mussolini is bound to increase his prestige by keeping them out of it.

Russia remains the most uncertain factor. From reports that I have seen in telegrams, I have formed a shrewd suspicion that she is preparing to seize the eastern districts of Poland if and when Germany subdues that country.

Stalin's latest double-cross has been at the expense of the Poles. He promised them arms a short time ago, and now he says that the entry of Great Britain and France into the war has altered the situation and he can no longer supply any armaments at all. I begin

---

[1] Reza Pahlevi. Brigade commander who overthrew the effete Qajar dynasty and was proclaimed Shah in 1925. In 1941 he was deposed by the British and Russians, acting jointly, on account of his pro-German sympathies.

to think he is more villainous than Hitler, and even Marshal Voroshilov[1] and M. Molotov[2] are said to be ashamed of this continuous duplicity.

Tuesday, September 12th

For the first time there was a feeling of autumn in the air, and it was unpleasantly chilly as I sat on the balcony in my dressing-gown reading in the papers that the British Expeditionary Force had landed in France. It is as if one of those war films was being acted again in real life, only one misses the secure feeling of sitting in a comfortable armchair at the Curzon Cinema.

I had an interesting day at the F.O. trying to arrange for railway material to be shipped to Persia so that the Shah's susceptibilities may not be ruffled. I spent a good deal of thought on the subject, and was rewarded by being told that the action I proposed, and the drafts I submitted, were admirable. I shall probably be abashed before long by being told quite the opposite.

Mother[3] came up from Badminton for the day with Queen Mary.* She is furious at being marooned in the country and talks as though she were Ovid eating her heart out at Tomi. She was extremely funny about the effect of the air-raid alarms on the Queen. Apparently they so upset the old lady that she had acute and urgent stomach trouble, with disastrous and undignified results on the motor-drive from Sandringham to Badminton. They were forced to stop at a lonely inn, where the inn-keeper was most helpful. The Queen sent him a small silver knife as a thank-offering, and he replied by sending her a beautiful little carved silver chain (which, as Philip remarked, was a most suitable souvenir!). When they reached Badminton the Queen, who had spent three sleepless nights owing to air-raid warnings and thunderstorms, looked forward to a welcome rest, but was aroused the next morning at 6.00 a.m. because the kitchen-maid turned on the private air-raid warning in mistake for the electric light.

Wednesday, September 13th

At the F.O. I wound up the affairs of Turkey and Persia before transferring my attention to Palestine and Arabia. Of war news there was little, except for the fact that Poland has exhausted nearly all her resources of aerial defence, and that our comparative inactivity on the Western Front is causing general uneasiness. Why

---

[1] Marshal K. E. Voroshilov. Red Army leader in the Civil War. Eventually head of the Russian state.

[2] V. M. Molotov.* Soviet Foreign Minister.

[3] Lady Cynthia Colville.*

not bomb military objectives instead of scattering pamphlets is the question everybody is asking about the R.A.F. (Incidentally that body has not begun too well: it has violated Dutch neutrality, bombed a Danish town, and fought some Belgian planes over Belgian territory. Moreover, in the air-raid warning on September 5th the only casualty was one of our own planes falling to one of our A.A. guns.)

Encouraged by the postponement of petrol rationing for a week, so that enough coupons could be printed, I went for twenty-four hours to stay with my father's sister at Kenswick near the village of Broadheath in Worcestershire.

Sunday, September 17th

I went to the early service at Broadheath. After breakfast, when the others went to church, I walked through the fields for about an hour, and returned to the house in time to hear, on the 12.00 p.m. wireless bulletin, the harrowing news of Russia's invasion of Poland. The announcement by which the Soviet Government attempted to justify their act of unequalled greed and immorality is without doubt the most revolting document that modern history has produced. For the first time since the war began I felt really depressed, and frantic at the impossibility of our taking any effective action to prevent this crime. And yet I remember thinking, less than a year ago, that the Poles deserved the darkest fate in view of the way they treated the Czechs and that nobody could feel sorry for them if their turn came next.

After lunch and a game of billiards I motored Philip to Middleton via Stratford and Banbury. The house is occupied by a horde of Roman Catholic children, in the charge of a dozen nuns, and the family are living in the cottages. Old Lady Jersey (ninety years old now), Ronnie and Cynthia Slessor,[1] Ann Elliot,[2] David[3] and Joan,[4] and Grandie[5] and Virginia[6] were there, all with their respective children.

It was a glorious September evening and we sat about in the garden trying to concentrate on the peaceful sound of church bells

[1] Daughter of the 4th Earl of Kilmorey. Married first the 8th Earl of Jersey and then Ronald, formerly her children's tutor and brother of Marshal of the R.A.F. Sir John Slessor.

[2] Younger daughter of the 8th Earl of Jersey, married to Alexander Elliot.

[3] My eldest brother.*

[4] Elder daughter of the 8th Earl of Jersey, married to my brother David.

[5] 9th Earl of Jersey, owner of Middleton Park near Bicester and of Osterley.

[6] Lord Jersey's second wife. Formerly Virginia Cherrill; played the part of the blind girl in Charlie Chaplin's *City Lights*.

and to forget Russia and Poland and the rest of Europe's infected plague spots. Virginia returned from America yesterday in the *Manhattan* and was so frightened by the thought that she and her fellow passengers might be the incident to bring America into the war that she developed a temperature, as a result of which she walked about the sunlit garden looking like a ghost.

Monday, September 18th
The Foreign Office was less depressed by the Russian monstrosity than I had expected. Turkey seems to be standing firm, at the cost of our promising financial support on a scale vaster than we had ever contemplated. With such momentous news on everybody's lips, I find it difficult to concentrate on minor Palestinian or Arabian problems.

I lunched at the Travellers, which has fortunately reopened, and learned that the *Courageous* [large aircraft-carrier] had been sunk – our first naval disaster.

On leaving the office I called on Mary Roxburghe,[1] and found Middy Gascoigne[2] already there. We discussed the situation heatedly, and condemned the Government's inactivity severely (though one can but hope they are in reality doing more than they seem. But if they are, the Ministry of Information should give some indication of the fact, or the public will begin to lose confidence). Middy was looking lovely; Mary rather ill (she is to have an operation tomorrow).

Tuesday, September 19th
I rode through Wimbledon Common to Richmond Park on a horse incongruously called "Peaceful". Riding is an agreeable sedative and I find it easy to dream placidly and forget the slings and arrows of outrageous fortune.

The Poles are still gallantly resisting, though their government has fled; but the Russian invasion has been decisive and the Polish campaign is now over. The German people are unfortunately elated by their series of rapid successes, and Hitler evidently hopes that he can now conclude a generous peace settlement. He made a speech at Danzig this afternoon in which he threatened that if we carried on the blockade, the Germans had a terrible weapon in store, which could not be used against them, but which they had no wish to employ. This is probably meant to intimidate, but it does

[1] Youngest daughter of Lord Crewe. My mother's half-sister. Married to 9th Duke of Roxburghe.
[2] Hon. Mrs Gascoigne. Daughter of Lady Annabel Dodds, my mother's eldest sister, and mother of Bamber Gascoigne.

give one a slight feeling of uneasiness, because even Hitler and his satellites usually have something on which to base statements of this kind. For instance Ribbentrop[1] said last May or June that he was preparing the greatest diplomatic defeat that England had ever known, and though we laughed scornfully at the time we are now obliged to admit that the Russo-German pact does deserve that definition.

The war looks like being an immobile affair on the Western Front, with neither side bombing the other's civilian populations for some time to come, and the real test being whether Germany's economic resources and the morale of her people can defeat the navy's blockade and the morale of the Allies. This will be dangerous because it will be boring; and in wartime boredom is certain to breed discontent at home. However I do not think the Germans will begin their proverbial "frightfulness" until they feel they are losing or winning, so that London can probably sleep in peace for a good many weeks, or even months, to come.

Friday, September 22nd

At the Foreign Office I had very little to do except compose a few dreary letters to the Colonial Office about Palestine. In the morning, however, I attended a meeting of the Middle Eastern Sub-Committee of the Committee of Imperial Defence, to discuss means of gratifying the Sultan of Muscat. Except as a means of studying the psychology of elderly civil servants, such meetings are invariably tedious.

The most interesting telegram of the day was an explanation of why the Government has been doing so little lately, and is intended for the use of H.M. Representatives abroad who are met with the complaint that we have not lifted a finger to save Poland. The gist of the Government's argument is that "strategy is the art of concentrating decisive force at the decisive moment". The Poles knew we could give them no effective help and realised that we could only save them in the long run – when Germany has been defeated. "To have devoted hundreds of British planes to bombing raids in Germany would have meant spectacular successes, but the inevitable loss of machines which will be used more effectively on the Western Front." There may be something to be said for this policy, although its effect is exasperating to public opinion. Dr Brüning[2] told somebody I know – Eric Duncannon[3] I think – that the best way to treat Hitler is to keep him guessing, and perhaps

[1] Hitler's Foreign Minister, Joachim von Ribbentrop.*
[2] Dr Heinrich Brüning, German Chancellor 1930–32.
[3] Viscount Duncannon, subsequently 10th Earl of Bessborough.

our inactivity, if he thinks it hides some sinister purpose, may have that effect; but there is always the danger that he will take it for irresolution and degeneracy. In some circles it is thought that his first active move in the West will be a massed air-attack on the British navy and its bases.

In France there is calm but fixed determination: *"il faut en finir"*. The Consul at Rouen reports, however, that the French are showing some uneasiness about our declared intention to wage this war against Hitler and Nazism, and not against the German people. The French believe in the original sin of the German race and point out that in every major war from 1860 to the present day Germany has been the wanton aggressor and the disturber of European peace. The French consider that the leader and his ruling clique are of real insignificance: the character of the German people is such that they will always produce bellicose leaders with an ideology of force, and it does not matter if one calls the leader Frederick, Wilhelm or Hitler, or if his satellites are Junkers or Nazis. The German mentality is dangerous and incorrigible.

I do not believe this is true. If it were, there could be no alternative but to exterminate the whole German people, and such an act – even if it were possible – would be against the laws of God and man, besides being repugnant to the conscience of a world which claims to be civilised. If we win this war I am convinced that the only hope of a lasting peace, based on principles of justice and goodwill among men, will be to treat the Germans with the utmost generosity and to make a clean sweep of the past – whatever may be the feelings of bereaved wives and mothers. There must be no "guilt clause", no reparations and no public humiliation of Germany. Instead Germany must be placed on her feet economically, as far as it may be possible for us, in a devastated world, to do so. She must be disarmed; but so must the Allies. None of her rightful territories must be snatched from her, nor must she be partitioned; but she must be given free access to foreign and colonial markets. As far as possible the German people must be made to feel that they are not "pariahs", that they own and have produced much that is universally admired, and that their former enemies are willing to trust them, even to the extent of giving them colonies or mandates to govern. If this can be done, I believe they will respond and will appreciate such generosity; if they do not, then indeed the time will have come *pour en finir*. But it is going to be a task of unequalled difficulty to persuade the English and French peoples, hardened by years of war and suffering (and vitally affected in their pocket!) that this is the only wise and Christian course to pursue, and that it is the only chance of sparing future generations the curse of perpetually recurring wars. He who can convince the victorious side that such is the truth will deserve to be considered humanity's greatest benefactor; but he will need more than human powers to enable him to succeed.

Saturday, September 23rd

After lunch I went by train to Stansted[1] to spend the week-end with the Bessboroughs. They were just *en famille*, Lord and Lady Bessborough[2] and Moyra,[3] Eric [Duncannon] having joined his regiment. There were also sixty or more orphans, who played cricket happily on the lawn in front of the house but were carefully excluded from the main part of the house itself, which remains as cheerful and comfortable as ever.

We had an excellent dinner (nowhere is the food better than at Stansted) and afterwards Moyra and I alternately played backgammon and played with an unusually elaborate wireless set, from which we heard a German announcer broadcasting rather ineffectively, in English, about the wickedness of the English blockade measures. To be legal, he said, a blockade must be effective: let us hope that it may be, in every sense.

Sunday, September 24th

I woke up, in a very attractive bedroom, to see a powder-blue sky and the sun shining brilliantly on the lawns and borders. As I get older I very seldom have a feeling of present happiness: it is rather anticipation or reminiscence, and chiefly the former, which makes my heart swell with happiness. But this morning, as I lay in bed turning the pages at random of a sentimental novel, and contemplating the charm of my surroundings, I felt blissfully contented.

Wednesday, September 27th

Warsaw has surrendered after a heroic defence against overwhelming odds. Hitler is therefore free to turn his attention westwards, but it remains to be seen whether he will have the courage and stupidity to strike the first serious blow. For the moment the position can best be summed up in the words of the

---

[1] Stansted Park, Rowland's Castle, standing in a park laid out by Le Notre, some fifteen miles from Portsmouth.
[2] Vere, 9th Earl of Bessborough. Governor General of Canada, 1931–35. Married to Roberte de Neuflize.
[3] Lady Moyra Ponsonby. Afterwards married to the distinguished surgeon, Sir Denis Browne, and herself Superintendent in Chief of St John's Ambulance Brigade.

Italian Ambassador in Paris to Sir Eric Phipps:[1] "I have seen several wars waged without being declared; but this is the first I have seen declared without being waged."

I lunched with Charles Ritchie,[2] from Canada House, at La Coquille. He was in quite good spirits, and said what really got him down was the attempt to resurrect all the songs, scenes and emotions of 1914. It was like sitting in the dentist's waiting-room and turning over the pages of some twenty-five-year-old magazines.

It is, I think, essential that no gratuitous humiliations be heaped on the German people and that no reparations be taken. Moreover, purely German areas, like Danzig and the Sudetenland, should be included in the confederation. Of course the trouble will be that while many will agree that Germany should be treated with magnanimity, others, and especially the French, will be in favour of the harshest peace terms. I suppose the result will be a compromise, like Versailles, and in consequence discontent and resentment in Germany on which another Hitler will be able to build his diabolical system.

Thursday, September 28th

After breakfast I perused, with melancholy, the report of last night's budget – 7/6d income tax! [A fifty per cent increase.] Father is sunk in depression; personally I find it impossible to be really horrified by anything impersonal these days.

I am afraid the budget may have a chilling effect on public opinion which, unable to appreciate the essential merits of a waiting policy (waiting until we and the French are in a position to assert our mastery of the air), is already showing signs of impatience and is asking what we are fighting for. In some quarters this war has already been named "The Bore War". But it is clearly right to let Hitler take the initiative, both from a material and a psychological point of view: he will have to do so very soon (unless Russia takes some drastic and unexpected step) or else we and the French shall have won the mastery of the air and the blockade will have begun to take effect. But I am inclined to think Hitler's first move will be a gigantic air onslaught on the navy – and not on London.

On leaving the office I spent an hour talking to Mary Roxburghe, who is full of worries about the apathy being shown by the public (and also, not surprisingly, about the budget). We agreed that it

[1] British Ambassador in Berlin, 1933–37 and in Paris, 1937–39.
[2] Second Secretary at Canada House. Canadian High Commissioner in London, 1967–71.

would probably be a good thing if Chamberlain resigned soon and left the conduct of the war to some younger and forceful successor. Unfortunately I can see no Lloyd George on the horizon at present: Winston is a national figure, but is rather too old; and the younger politicians do not seem to include any outstanding personality. Halifax* would be respected, but he has not the drive necessary to keep the country united and enthusiastic.

Aunt Nancy[1] came to stay, and Brian O'Neill[2] dined with us. We talked incessantly of the war, and Brian, though he was in one of his silent and semi-sulky moods to begin with, was quite interesting when he discussed our war policy from the army point of view. Apparently the army think very highly of Ironside.

London, illuminated by the pale light of the harvest moon, looks more beautiful than ever before.

Friday, September 29th

So the Germans and Russians have consecrated their Unholy Alliance by a formal partition of Poland, a Gilbertian statement about responsibility for continuing the war, and an impressive but (hopefully) empty declaration about supplying Germany with raw materials.

Sunday, October 1st

We dined with Dorothy Cambridge[3] and heard Winston Churchill's inspiring speech on the wireless. He certainly gives one confidence and will, I suspect, be Prime Minister before this war is over. Nevertheless, judging from his record of untrustworthiness and instability, he may, in that case, lead us into the most dangerous paths. But he is the only man in the country who commands anything like universal respect, and perhaps with age he has become less inclined to undertake rash adventures.

Monday, October 2nd

Mallet,[4] one of the Private Secretaries, sent for me and asked me whether I should like to be one of the Assistant Private Secretaries to the Prime Minister. He said it was an interesting job, which would mean "being in the know" the whole time, but that it would

[1] Lady Annabel Dodds,* eldest daughter of the Marquess of Crewe.
[2] Hon. Brian O'Neill, adjutant, the Irish Guards, second son of Lady Annabel Dodds by her first husband, the Hon. Arthur O'Neill, M.P.
[3] Dorothy Hastings. Married George, 2nd Marquess of Cambridge, a nephew of Queen Mary.
[4] Sir Ivo Mallet. Second Private Secretary to the Foreign Secretary. Subsequently Ambassador in Belgrade and Madrid.

entail a good deal of drudgery. I said I would, because I knew that
to have such an appointment is likely to be an excellent stepping-
stone in the Diplomatic Service.

Consequently after lunching rather dully with John Cairncross[1]
(a very intelligent, though sometimes incoherent, bore) at the
Travellers, I went to the Treasury to interview a man called
Douglas and Rucker*, the Prime Minister's chief Private Secretary. The latter impressed upon me that my new job would
imply very long hours and a good deal that was utterly boring, but
it would also mean a certain amount of attendance at the House of
Commons and the control of appointments to bishoprics! There
are several other candidates in the field, so I shall not know for
certain whether I have been accepted at any rate until tomorrow.

After dinner we listened to a speech on the wireless by the
Archbishop of York,[2] which contained some wise words about the
peace to follow the war and even suggested European Federation.
What a glorious dream, but how difficult in practice when one
takes into consideration differences in language and prejudices
based on national pride or history.

Tuesday, October 3rd
I have been selected for the post at No. 10, which is most exciting,
and am to begin next week.

Wednesday, October 4th
Rode at Richmond before breakfast. It was cold and bright and
windy, and very exhilarating. There is little war news, but every
effort is being made by the Germans for their great peace offensive, which is almost certain to be launched this week. Meanwhile
Russia is systematically compelling the miserable Baltic states to
accept her suzerainty and, having got her booty, seems not indis-

---

[1] What I did not know about John Cairncross, so clever that in 1936 he passed first
into the Foreign Office a hundred marks ahead of a brilliant Fellow of All Souls,
Con O'Neill, was that he had been busy making notes about the opinions of his
Foreign Office and Civil Service contemporaries for the benefit of the Communist Party. When Guy Burgess fled to Russia with Donald Maclean in 1951,
these notes were found in a trunk he had left behind. Cairncross had ill-
advisedly dated each note and so, in 1953, by referring to my old 1939
engagement book, I was able to tell the security authorities, at a loss to identify
the hand-writing, with whom I had been lunching on the day a note about me
had been written. I asked them what Cairncross was then doing. They replied
that he was working in the Atomic Energy Division of the Ministry of Supply.
They said he had renounced his Soviet sympathies, but all the same I almost fell
off my office chair in astonishment.
[2] William Temple.

posed to take part in the peace moves. But Stalin's real intentions remain completely obscure: personally I suspect the worst and rather agrèe with Mother who says she feels Russia is a great "force of evil", which, long stationary, has now been set in motion by Ribbentrop's blind stupidity and is rolling gradually westwards. Mother has admirable faith and relies on the assistance of St Michael and All Angels against this disguised Beelzebub!

Thursday, October 5th

I spent most of the day wrestling with such problems as Ibn Saud's[1] desire to buy armaments from Germany, the Mufti's[2] not entirely disinterested wish to make a declaration to the Arabs in favour of the Allies, and the legal technicalities involved in deporting Foreign Legion deserters from Palestine to Syria (where, being Germans, their fate would probably be certain death).

There is little military activity: Hitler's peace proposals are expected tomorrow, and he seems to be having trouble with Italy. There is a sinister calm before the storm bursts and the war begins in fearful earnest. Herr Weizsäcker (of the German F.O.) is reported to have said that Germany will probably last till the New Year and then go Communist. Propaganda is said to be rife in the factories and to be likely to infect the army (who must be furious about the suspected murder of von Fritsch).[3]

Friday, October 6th

Went over to No. 10 for half an hour in the morning and was shown by Miss Watson[4] how some of my new duties are to be executed. She seems to be a kind, efficient, unassuming and rather wizened old thing (she tells me the Treasury are furious at my appointment – as being too young). I also met Captain Dugdale,[5] but could not see the Prime Minister or Sir Horace Wilson* as the Cabinet was meeting.

I was rather busy at the F.O. with the Mufti and other Palestinian questions. In the outside world the event of major importance was Hitler's long, overwhelming and slightly hysterical speech. Rather surprisingly he did not threaten us with destruction in its

---

[1] King Abdul Aziz of Saudi Arabia.
[2] The Mufti of Jerusalem. Pro-German and an incorrigible plotter.
[3] Werner, Baron von Fritsch. German Commander in Chief, 1934–38. He was opposed to Hitler's policies and was probably murdered by the Gestapo.
[4] Formerly typist, promoted to be a private secretary with responsibility for parliamentary Questions.
[5] Captain Thomas Dugdale, M.P. Created Lord Crathorne* in 1959.

most appalling form; but the terms he offered are, as was to be expected, unacceptable to all except a few intellectuals suffering from senility, like Bernard Shaw (whose article in this week's *New Statesman* is typical of a man whose particular form of exhibitionism is a constant wish to espouse lost causes in such a way as to irritate the majority of his fellow citizens. In this case his attitude will probably be genuinely harmful and be misrepresented abroad).

I dined with Diana Quilter[1] at Quaglino's. It was interesting, if macabre, to see all the khaki-clad dancers, but the place was miserably full, very smoky, and, of course, outrageously expensive. However Diana was, as ever, very agreeable and original, and it was pleasant to have a glimpse of "night life" in the new world.

Saturday, October 7th

I am indulging in an orgy of spending, in the belief that materials will grow worse in quality and more expensive. This morning I tried on a new suit and an overcoat at my tailor's, and two ruinous pairs of shoes at Peal's.[2]

After saying goodbye to Aunt Nancy, who is off to Nice, I caught the 1.50 to Stansted.

Sunday, October 8th

I looked from my bedroom window at the vistas which stretch away from Stansted, and saw the leaves of the trees, now turning yellow and red, perfectly still in the cold, windless and brilliantly sunny morning. I could not have enjoyed *Byron*[3] more (but I *am* being slow with it!) which shows how important it is to read in agreeable surroundings. Usually when I settle down to read the sun is shining too brightly, the fire is too hot, or somebody is being disturbing.

Hal Goodheart Rendel,[4] who never knows when to stop talking but certainly talks well, was loud in his denunciation of the German people as opposed to Hitler. He said that the Germans could never understand others (i.e. us) acting from principle instead of from interest. But are we? Surely it is at least convenient that for us the two coincide.

Lord Bessborough thinks we should have a War Cabinet, as in

---

[1] An agreeable and intelligent childhood friend. Later married Archibald Tennant.

[2] The "ruinous" shoes, hand-made and fitted on a last, cost £2.10.0. a pair.

[3] André Maurois' biography of Byron.

[4] Gifted and affluent architect, artistically erudite and a talented pianist. His face alternated between green and yellow in colour and was much commented on (behind his back).

the last war, with members freed from departmental duties. He points out that Lloyd George left the leadership of the House to Bonar Law, and only appeared there himself on rare and important occasions.

Monday, October 9th

Travelled up to London with Zara,[1] and discussed our late hosts very favourably. She looked very pretty, in black with an astrakhan hat, and has great vivacity.

At the F.O. I cleared up all the work I had left, and then took a rather sad leave of Lacy Baggallay (who was certainly the perfect Head of a Department) and the other members of my department. It is just over two years since I entered the F.O., and it seems an age. But it has been a pleasant "age", because I have had delightful people to work with, and plenty of free time with which to enjoy the vanished pomps of yesterday. Yet I think I have learned a lot. Miss Glasse, one of the typists, observed, when in saying goodbye I remarked that I should probably have a lot of work to do, "well that will be a change"!

---

[1] Younger daughter of Sir Harry and Lady Mainwaring. Married first Ronald Strutt (later Lord Belper) and secondly Peter Cazalet.

2

The Whitehall Scene

Even when I moved to 10 Downing Street, there was at first a monotony only sometimes varied by events or discussions worthy of record by one who saw all important papers and heard much political and military gossip, but was too junior to play any part in decision making. Nor, except in relation to Scandinavia, were a great number of notable decisions made in those dreary, depressing months of what was generally called the Phoney War. Only the war at sea was waged in earnest.

Once it was realised that the Germans had no immediate intention of bombing London or Paris, and that the expected offensive on the Rhine was delayed, there were lingering hopes in some breasts that the full impact of war might even yet be avoided for all but the unhappy Poles, whose spectacularly gallant but tragically ill-equipped army had been smashed, and whose country was being systematically devastated by Germans and Russians alike.

These hopes were expressed in the Cabinet by Lord Halifax and found a strong echo in the staff at 10 Downing Street, as indeed with many who had had personal experience of the First World War massacres. Neville Chamberlain was not anti-German, nor indeed was Winston Churchill; but Chamberlain, to whom the very thought of war was abhorrent, would have gone further than Churchill in making concessions to a new German Government, even if it had contained some of the Nazi leaders. On one point, however, he was adamant: nothing would ever induce him to deal with Hitler, whose supersession would be an essential prerequisite of any settlement. Mussolini might perhaps be tolerated, and might even be helpful in arranging a settlement: Hitler was beyond any conceivable pale.

This was because Chamberlain realised that Hitler's brutality was matched by his unreliability; but I think there was also an element of damaged vanity. At Munich, in September 1938, he had trusted Hitler in the face of strong remonstrances from the Foreign Office, but with encouragement from our gullible Ambassador in Berlin, Sir Nevile Henderson. Hitler had betrayed that trust and made a dupe of Chamberlain. One evening when I was returning with him from the House of Commons, he spoke angrily of some Opposition member who had been attacking Government policy. "I believe," said I, "that he is sincere in his views." "What of that?" replied the Prime Minister sharply. "I am sure Hitler was sincere at Munich, but he changed his mind a few days later." I thought that remark explained quite a lot about Chamberlain's ingenuous faith in the Munich agreement – and perhaps something about Chamberlain himself.

He was courteous to his staff, as were those close to him, like Sir Horace Wilson and the invariably delightful Parliamentary Private Secretary, Lord Dunglass.[1] The two senior Private Secretaries, Arthur Rucker and Cecil Syers,* were not only helpful to me and encouraging, but also men with a well-developed wit and sense of humour, so that the sound of laughter seldom failed to resound in the Private Secretaries' rooms and did much to relieve the gloom of those grey winter days.

The Prime Minister was encouraging to the young and inexperienced. The first time I was asked to prepare a memorandum, on a fairly complicated matter, for inclusion in the nightly Prime Ministerial box, it came back the following morning with a most complimentary red-ink note in Chamberlain's handwriting – far more complimentary than it deserved.

This was in marked contrast to the Chancellor of the Exchequer, Sir John Simon.* He also had a young, new Private Secretary, Burke Trend, who became many years later Secretary to the Cabinet. Trend was entrusted, at about the same time as I was, with the task of writing his first memorandum for the Chancellor. Since he is a man of exceptional ability, I have no doubt it was an admirable document; but on the following morning it was returned neatly torn into four pieces and without comment. To those who did not work under him, such as myself, Simon was friendly, forthcoming and often agreeably witty. I was one of a sadly restricted company who actually liked him.

Chamberlain was austere, and he seldom said to me anything not

[1] Alexander Douglas-Home, subsequently 14th Earl of Home, Sir Alec Douglas-Home and Lord Home of the Hirsel,* Prime Minister, 1963–64.

strictly related to business. At week-ends he retired to Chequers, where there was only one telephone (and that in the pantry). He disliked being disturbed, telephonically or otherwise, at week-ends or after dinner at 10 Downing Street. He never took a Private Secretary with him to Chequers; nor did he ever invite the members of his staff to lunch or dine with Mrs Chamberlain and himself. That was in marked contrast to Winston Churchill, who treated his Private Secretaries as part of the family, and indeed to Clement Attlee. Yet this austere man had such integrity, such devotion to duty and such high ideals and standards, that if it was at first difficult to feel affection for him it was impossible not to feel esteem.

The men of power in the Cabinet were Sir John Simon, Sir Samuel Hoare,[1] Lord Privy Seal (who invariably replied "m,yes, m,yes, m,yes" when one ventured to address him) and Lord Halifax, formerly Viceroy of India and now Foreign Secretary. Halifax was a sincerely religious, intelligent and by no means ingenuous man, who because of his political acumen and his deep love of both the Church and the hunting field was generally known as "the Holy Fox". To these was added on September 3rd, 1939, Winston Churchill, First Lord of the Admiralty and a stronger, more colourful personality than any of them. Many of his colleagues, and most senior civil servants, regarded him with suspicion, an attitude reflected by the staff at 10 Downing Street and one to which I was daily subjected.

There were also men of power behind the parliamentary screen. Of these Sir Horace Wilson* was the foremost, for Neville Chamberlain did little without his advice. It was not Wilson's fault that he was frequently required to advise on matters, such as foreign affairs and defence, of which he had scanty knowledge; for he had been brought to Downing Street from the Ministry of Labour by Chamberlain's predecessor, Stanley Baldwin, and he had been made indispensable. He was not ambitious: he was kind, high-principled and frequently wise; but being the Prime Minister's *alter ego*, he had come to believe himself as infallible as Chamberlain considered him to be. There were others – Sir Edward Bridges,* Secretary to the Cabinet, General Ismay,* Military Secretary to the Committee of Imperial Defence, Sir Alexander Cadogan,* Permanent Under-Secretary at the Foreign Office, to mention but a few – who were men of the highest character and calibre; and there was the attractive, extrovert Chief Whip, Captain David Margesson,* who saw the Prime Minister every morning at eleven

---

[1] Subsequently Viscount Templewood.*

o'clock and shared with Sir Horace Wilson a commanding influence on political appointments.

The leaders of the Labour Opposition were Clement Attlee and Arthur Greenwood; and the leader of the Liberal Party, Sir Archibald Sinclair,[1] had been Winston Churchill's second in command in the trenches during the First World War. All three were good and honourable men, Attlee being by far the most outstanding. Greenwood's value was impaired by his addiction to the bottle; and Sinclair, high-minded and patriotic, could seldom, when the time eventually came, stand up to the stronger personalities with whom it was his fate to contend.

While in the first months of the war Ministers and civil servants were striving to keep the administration on its competent, if unimaginative, track, the British Expeditionary Force, first two divisions, then four and after a few months ten (with an eventual target of fifty-five), disembarked in France. It contained the best professional soldiers in the British army and all the equipment which, after a shamefully late start, the country had been able to provide. It was led by a gallant hero of the First World War, Viscount Gort, V.C., D.S.O. and two bars, M.C.*, who had as his two Corps Commanders Sir Alan Brooke* and Sir John Dill.* Dill returned to London, to be Vice Chief of the General Staff, shortly before the Dunkirk campaign began.

The B.E.F. was subordinated to the French General Georges and, above him, to the Commander in Chief, General Gamelin,* who was mistakenly rated a military genius. The French, with some eighty divisions but a totally inadequate air force, had built what they believed to be an impregnable defence, the Maginot Line, stretching from Switzerland to the Belgian frontier. Behind this they were confident of their ability to resist any German onslaught, especially as leading military experts, such as Basil Liddell-Hart,* had declared that in modern war a defensive strategy must prevail. The main French objective, leading them to be enthusiastic exponents of Scandinavian adventures, and by contrast resolute opponents of bombing the Ruhr or mining the Rhine, was to keep the war off French soil. They felt they had suffered enough from previous Teutonic incursions.

Unfortunately, despite what had happened in 1914, the French Government had seen no need to extend the Maginot Line along the Franco-Belgian frontier which was only defended by an unimpressive ditch. This sector was allotted to Lord Gort and his B.E.F. who therefore had to spend the unusually icy winter of 1939/40

---

[1] Subsequently Viscount Thurso.*

building pill-boxes and constructing a somewhat more defensible line. It could never, in the time available, have been strong enough to resist a determined German attack by armoured divisions, of which the British themselves had only one and that not as yet ready to take its place in the line. Such was the position on December 31st, 1939.

Meanwhile I had moved my diary physically to a drawer in my writing-table at 10 Downing Street where succeeding volumes were kept locked and where I made daily entries or, when I was away for a day or two, hastened to record my activities as soon as I returned.

The following are extracts from what I wrote between October 10th and December 31st, 1939.

Tuesday, October 10th
My first day at No. 10. It began at 9.30 a.m. and finished at 6.30. In the course of it I met the Prime Minister, who was shy but welcoming, Mrs Chamberlain (who looks utterly vague), Sir Horace Wilson and Captain David Margesson. The latter said, "You know my daughters, I believe", with a rather penetrating stare!

> *The penetrating stare was due to his knowledge that I was deeply in love with his younger daughter, who was beautiful, gay and intelligent. Another of her suitors was Nicko Henderson,* later Ambassador in Bonn, Paris and Washington. He told me that if she did not finally say yes, he would never marry anybody else. I said the same applied to me. We both did marry somebody else and lived happily ever after. As for the delectable young lady, she married a third equally ardent suitor and also lived happily ever after.*

I sit in the same room as Miss Watson and Lord Dunglass. Miss Watson showed me how to deal with some of the enormous post which arrives every day now, and I also began looking into the question of the Ecclesiastical patronage with which I am to deal, and about which my predecessor, Jasper Rootham, came to talk to me in the morning.

I read with interest the various drafts, by the Prime Minister, Churchill, Cadogan, Vansittart[1] and Corbin,[2] suggested for the reply to Hitler's peace proposals. When the proposals are rejected

---

[1] Chief Diplomatic Adviser to the Government. See p. 162.
[2] French Ambassador in London.

it is thought likely that Hitler will launch a tremendous onslaught. For the moment calm reigns on land, sea and air.

Wednesday, October 11th

My appointment announced in *The Times*.

At No. 10 I made an effort to grasp the intricacies of the Ecclesiastical Patronage of the Crown, read the Cabinet minutes, etc., appointed one man to a Crown living, and answered a lot of irritating letters. One of the Prime Minister's correspondents said: "You may put this letter in the waste-paper basket; but remember you and I will meet face to face before the bar of judgment, and then it may be taken out of the waste-paper basket." A solemn thought if one is to spend one's time in purgatory dealing with neglected correspondence!

I left at about 6.00 p.m. and went to have a drink with the Stirlings (Margaret,[1] Bill[2] and Peter[3]). Peter leaves for Cairo tomorrow. Pam Berry[4] was there, obviously determined to lead a gay social life, war or no war. There was also a pretty girl, Prim Rollo,[5] and another not unattractive one, Lavinia Shaw-Stewart.

Dined with Lord and Lady Cambridge to meet the Duke of Beaufort. On the way there I fell headlong down an area, mistaking it for a porch in the black-out!

Thursday, October 12th

At No. 10 by 9.30, which is the disgustingly early hour we start work. Everybody was humming with excitement about the Prime Minister's statement in reply to Hitler, which is to be made this afternoon.

Mother and I dined with Grandfather[6] and Peggy[7] at Argyll House. We had a delightful, intimate evening, and it is clear that Grandfather, although he suddenly looks rather old, is still very alert mentally. When Mother and Peggy had left the dining-room, I sat a long time with him, sipping old brandy, and hearing him talk of his active political days. He told me that when at the India Office

---

[1] Afterwards Countess of Dalhousie.

[2] William Stirling of Keir, eldest of the family, leading figure in the Commandos and subsequently chairman of Keir and Cawdor.

[3] Entered the Foreign Office the same year as I did. A keen steeplechaser and one of the best shots in the kingdom.

[4] Daughter of Lord Kemsley. Later married the Marquess of Huntly. Not to be confused with Lord Birkenhead's daughter, Lady Pamela Berry.

[5] Later married David Niven and was killed by a fall downstairs.

[6] The Marquess of Crewe.*

[7] His second wife, born Lady Margaret Primrose.

and Colonial Office he had known every member of the staff and
had always considered it important that a Secretary of State should
be able to judge the individual capacities of those beneath him. He
spoke of the difficulty of forming a war cabinet of non-
departmental heads, because the Foreign Secretary must be included, and if you retain Lord Chatfield,[1] but dispense with the
Service Department heads, then what becomes of Winston? It
might, he thought, be possible to have a cabinet consisting only of
soldiers and sailors, but that would amount to martial law and
should only be resorted to if the prosecution of the war really
required it. He thought it most important that Winston should not
become Prime Minister, and considered that Chamberlain ought
to continue in office since he has both the necessary drive and the
confidence of the public. He agreed with me that there was no
younger man of outstanding ability on the political horizon.

After dinner I talked to Peggy (who has genius for using anti-
climax) and then Grandfather discoursed amusingly about family
history. He also said that as a small child he had been taken to
tea with a Lady Blakistone, aged 101 (born in 1759, the *Annus
Mirabilis*) who remarked how sorry she was that "her eldest boy
was not there to play with him". Her eldest boy turned out to be
eighty-one!

Friday, October 13th
The Germans are furious with Chamberlain's speech, but show no
signs of an immediate offensive. One cannot help wondering
whether Hitler really does want to start the war in earnest, or
whether all that has happened has been part of a gigantic bluff. It is
probably wishful thinking; but while there is life there is hope, and
I should not be surprised if Hitler now put forward further peace
proposals. However, short of a revolution in Germany, I do not see
what can stop it. The important thing is that every day's delay is so
much gain to us as far as war production is concerned.

Arther Rucker says he thinks Communism is now the great
danger, greater even than Nazi Germany. All the independent
states of Europe are anti-Russian, but Communism is a plague that
does not stop at national boundaries, and with the advance of the
Soviet into Poland the states of Eastern Europe will find their
powers of resistance to Communism very much weakened. It is
thus vital that we should play our hand very carefully with Russia,
and not destroy the possibility of uniting, if necessary, with a new
German Government against the common danger. What is needed

---

[1] Admiral of the Fleet and former First Sea Lord. Appointed by Chamberlain
Minister for Coordination of Defence with a seat in the War Cabinet.

is a moderate conservative reaction in Germany: the overthrow of the present régime by the army chiefs.

George Steward,[1] the Government press chief, tells me that Dugdale is much the ablest man in the junior ranks of the Government. The Whips are much the weakest spot in the present Government, and David Margesson's appointments (e.g. Sir J. Gilmour[2] today as Minister of Shipping) are usually deplorable.

Three German submarines sunk. As the B.B.C. announcer said, Friday the 13th has been a bad day for the Germans.

It was said in Whitehall that Sir John Gilmour's appointment was the worst since Caligula made his horse a Consul. This witticism has been repeated ad nauseam *since the war about numerous people; but it was the first time I had heard it.*

I repeated it to my Father[3] who smiled and said that when he was a young man he had heard it said of one of Disraeli's cabinet choices. Thinking it funny, and believing it to be original, he told his father (who was Derby's and Disraeli's Chief Whip in the House of Lords). His father replied: "When I was a young man, Lord Melbourne made an appointment. . . ." Where and when this now hackneyed joke originated I do not know – doubtless centuries ago.

Saturday, October 14th

It is a pity the B.B.C. were so boastful. This morning comes the news of the loss of the *Royal Oak*, at Scapa Flow and surrounded by the Fleet.

I was alone with Arthur Rucker all day at No. 10. He thinks it all-important that the war-mentality should not be aroused (he blames Winston with his submarine-hunts "not without relish") because he still hopes real war may be avoided.

In the afternoon, while I was alone in the room, Winston came in, carrying a large red box which he said was to be opened by the Prime Minister in person. He looked rather distraught, but said, as he went away, "Tell the Prime Minister we have got another submarine: that makes four yesterday." I had the red box before me for over half an hour, but managed to resist the temptation of opening it.

It has been a long day – 9.30 a.m. to 8.00 p.m. – and very tiring. What a drab world this is; especially when it rains all day.

[1] Press Officer at 10 Downing Street.
[2] Home Secretary, 1932–35. Not to be confused with the other Sir John (Jock) Gilmour, a much-respected stockbroker and father of Sir Ian Gilmour.
[3] The Hon. George Colville.*

Sunday, October 15th

Went to No. 10 for a few hours, to relieve Cecil Syers, about tea-time. Apparently a big offensive on the Western Front is thought imminent. Talked to Sir Walter Monckton* about the Ministry of Information, of which he is a part: he says all the best men are threatening to resign because of the chaos. Lord Macmillan[1] must go and we need some Northcliffe-like propagandist to put life into the place.

Monday, October 16th

Lunched with Milo Talbot,[2] who is at the Ministry of Economic Warfare. I like Milo provided I only see him once in six months.

Dined with the Kemsleys.[3] The party included the Aly Khans,[4] Sir Godfrey[5] and Lady Thomas, Beverley Baxter[6] and Lord Davidson[7]. We none of us dressed (to show it was war-time) but in every other respect it might have been a party of pre-war days; all the rooms were open, there was a galaxy of footmen, the dinner was vast and excellent, and wine flowed like water. Vulgar, perhaps, in these days; but certainly a pleasant relapse into the gilded past.

At dinner I sat between Sir Godfrey Thomas, whom I found most agreeable, and Pam Berry. Afterwards I talked to Lord Davidson who was interesting on the subject of Ribbentrop, whom he had known well and whose blindness about this country he had done his utmost to cure. He also spoke of the bad appointments recently made by the Government (e.g. Sir J. Gilmour to be Minister of Shipping) and said that Sir S. Hoare was largely to blame. He also thought David Margesson's advice bad. At the end of dinner Lord Kemsley read out a telegram he had received to the effect that the expected German offensive near Saarbrücken had begun.

Afterwards I played bridge with Beverley Baxter against Lord

---

[1] A distinguished judge, but far from distinguished Minister of Information.
[2] Lord Talbot de Malahide. A contemporary at Cambridge and in the Diplomatic Service.
[3] Lord Kemsley was owner of the *Sunday Times* and *Daily Sketch*. Brother of Lord Camrose (owner of *Daily Telegraph*). His second wife was Edith du Plessis.
[4] Son of the Aga Khan, married to the Hon. Joan Yarde-Buller.
[5] Seconded from the Foreign Office to be Secretary to the Prince of Wales (Edward VIII) and thereafter to Prince Henry, Duke of Gloucester.
[6] A Canadian who became a Conservative M.P. in 1935 and was editor of the *Daily Express*.
[7] Viscount Davidson. Private Secretary to a series of Prime Ministers and later Chairman of the Conservative Party.

Kemsley and Prince Aly Khan. It was amusing and at the same time quite good bridge. My partner is a talented bounder, and good company. I succeeded in winning £2.

Tuesday, October 17th

In the afternoon I went down to the House, heard Mr Hore-Belisha[1] having a rough time over Questions, and left after the P.M. had answered his (it was my duty to check what he said). Arriving back at No. 10 I found Lady Astor[2] on the doorstep having some raucous back-chat with the police about their wives. Interviewed the Bishop of Willesden.

Friday, October 20th

Not a very busy day. Received a delightful letter from Gay,[3] who still seems uncertain about coming back from America. Her father tells me he consulted Winston about the safety of returning on an American ship: "Perfectly safe," said Winston, "but of course there is a risk of their being torpedoed or mined!"

Caught the 5.30 train to Winchester, where I found Eddy Rothschild[4] and Peter Trehearne[5] awaiting me and looking very martial in their heavy military overcoats. We motored to Exbury[6] and arrived in time for dinner.

Saturday, October 21st

It was a day like summer, and although the leaves were by no means off the trees we could scarcely have had a better shoot. Pheasants were plentiful, the shooting was good, and we killed well over 250.

At lunch I sat next to an American girl called Gracia Nevill, who gave me a description of an hour's conversation she had had with Hitler at Berchtesgaden and described the complete difference in him when he was talking of politics and when he was talking of other matters. In the former case he was a fanatic, in the latter a quiet and very impressive conversationalist.

---

[1] Secretary of State for War.*

[2] Viscountess Astor. An American by birth and the first woman to take her seat in Parliament.

[3] Captain David Margesson's younger daughter.

[4] A close friend of mine at Harrow and Trinity. Later Senior Partner of N. M. Rothschild and Son.

[5] Another school and University friend, notable for his height, courage and good nature.

[6] Exbury, in the New Forest and on the Beaulieu River, has hundreds of acres of gardens devoted to rhododendrons, azaleas and the rarest of shrubs and trees.

Sunday, October 22nd

I walked round the garden, which was a sight of unparalleled beauty with its blaze of autumn red and gold, and talked to Lionel de Rothschild,[1] who was at his most agreeable. He suggested that our war aim should be to give Germany to the Jews, and divide up the Germans among the races of the world: in other words to make the two races change their position. But then, I said, the Jews in Germany will complain that the Germans control world finance!

Tuesday, October 24th

Went to the House in the afternoon. After Questions the P.M. saw Attlee and Greenwood, and afterwards Sir A. Sinclair, to harangue them about the disloyalty of the Opposition who, oblivious of the fact that we are at war, are seeking every opportunity to criticise the Government and increase their difficulties. Evidently the P.M.'s words were effective, because Attlee and Greenwood came out looking very chastened. Sir S. Hoare, with whom I had a short conversation, told me that in the last war the Opposition never made themselves unpleasant in this way: criticism of Haldane, etc., was always from outside the House. Probably the explanation is that the war seems scarcely to have begun, and nothing sufficiently drastic has happened to break the long-established traditions of party intrigue.

Wednesday, October 25th

In the morning I walked to Lambeth Palace to discuss Ecclesiastical matters with the Archbishop of Canterbury.[2] He was very charming and patriarchal, spoke charmingly of Mother ("one of the most excellent and distinguished members of the Church Assembly"), and every now and then introduced a sly sense of humour into his conversation which was most disarming. "That," he said, pointing to a barrage-balloon in the garden, "they call the Arch-blimp!"

Helped Arthur Rucker a little with the statement which the P.M. is to make in the House tomorrow, and which contains a forceful but dignified reply to Ribbentrop's fantastic speech at Danzig last night. It was said of Sir Stafford Cripps* that every time he opened his mouth he lost 100,000 votes for the Labour Party, and I begin to hope the same may be true of Ribbentrop and the Nazis. But then

---

[1] One of the two partners in Rothschilds. Creator of the magnificent gardens at Exbury.

[2] Cosmo Lang. Close friend of King George V. Widely, and in the main unjustly, criticised for his broadcast condemning Edward VIII's motives for abdicating.

it is probably easy to persuade the Germans that their cause is just, because they are so inherently stupid; and they will certainly fight, because they are so incontestably brave. When you get a cross between a Lion and an Owl, the result is a very curious phenomenon; but that is as close as I can get, biologically, to accounting for the German mentality.

Sunday, October 29th
The most interesting papers concerned a possible basis for peace. Two Englishmen, called Christie and Conwell-Evans, have been talking to high-placed Germans, of whom one is Prince Max von Hohenlohe, in Switzerland about the possibility of getting rid of Hitler and coming to terms with an anti-Nazi Government under Goering* on the basis of restoring independence to Poland and Bohemia, disarming all round, and agreeing to leave inviolate the unity and boundaries of Germany proper. It seems that the upper classes and high military authorities in Germany are anxious to avoid the outbreak of a real war, since they believe that Bolshevism in Germany would be the final and inevitable outcome. Prince Max produced nine points as a possible basis of negotiations. Lord Halifax proposed a rather cautious reply, to the effect that our war aims had already been clearly announced in the P.M.'s speeches (that we should declare our aims was considered by Prince Max indispensable, in order that the German people should abandon their conviction that we intend to partition and humiliate Germany) and that we could do nothing without consulting our French allies.

I am afraid the F.O. are rather defeatist about the possibility of procuring peace. The P.M., on the other hand, is in favour of a much more encouraging reply, and is prepared to accept eight out of the nine points, only stipulating that Hitler himself shall play no part in the proposed new order. In return for a change of régime (or at least a modification), restoration of frontiers and disarmament, the P.M. would be prepared to agree to economic assistance for Germany, to no demand for reparations, and to Colonial discussions. He wishes, however, to insert some safeguards for the Jews and the Austrians.

Monday, October 30th
On returning to the office after luncheon I found Lord Portal[1] waiting to see the P.M. He is anxious that business should return to London because of the disastrous effect decentralisation is having

---

[1] Viscount Portal of Laverstoke.*

on our economic life. He feels, as I do, that our greatest danger through the coming winter will be growing apathy, and he is seriously concerned at the poverty of our propaganda as a weapon to combat this.

Tuesday, October 31st

Sir Eric Phipps, in his last despatch, makes out the French case against Germany and supports that country's opposition to our theory that we are fighting against Hitlerism instead of against Germany. Much of what he says seems plausible, and no doubt his views represent very accurately those of the French; but in the interests of world peace I trust he is wrong, because there now seems just a chance of separating the German people from their leaders if we can convince the former of the purity of our intentions towards them. One can sympathise with the feelings of the French; but it was, after all, their intransigence which bred the bitterness and despair upon which Hitler rose to power.

The Government White Paper on German Concentration Camps is a sordid document calculated to appeal to people's lowest instincts, and reminiscent of the "Corpse Factory" propaganda in the last war. It does shed a lurid glow on the bestial sadism of the Germans at their worst; but after all most of the evidence is produced from prejudiced sources, and it is in any case undesirable to arouse passions before the war has begun in earnest. Lord Halifax, of all people, is said to have pressed for its publication, but I understand that the fanatically anti-German Kirkpatrick* is the man behind it all. Alec Dunglass, Cecil, Arthur and I all agreed in condemning its publication.

Thursday, November 2nd

I saw further papers about the Hohenlohe proposals. H. wants to come over to England, but this request has been refused and I gather Christie is going out to see him in Holland. Poor wretch, if Hitler should hear of his machinations! Van[1] and Halifax refuse to entertain seriously the idea of negotiating with Goering, but there seems reason to think that Hohenlohe and his friends, goaded by their fear that Hitler may turn Bolshevist, are only using Goering as a "stalking horse". One of Hohenlohe's more curious recommendations was that we should hastily start bombing military objectives in order to prove how serious are our intentions: pamphlets are not sufficiently impressive.

[1] Sir Robert Vansittart (see p. 162).

Saturday, November 4th

The Cabinet seem rather excited about the Russo-Finnish dispute. Personally I think that if the Finns stand firm the Russians, who are more hyaenas than bears, will not attack them.

David Margesson says he is in despair about the Cabinet. He would like to recommend the P.M. to get rid of Sam Hoare and Simon, who are egotistic intriguers; but the difficulty would be to find someone else to put in their place. Arthur Rucker thinks Sir Kingsley Wood[1]* would do as Chancellor of the Exchequer, but he is such an appalling speaker. Some people consider Reginald McKenna[2], of whom David had thought, dishonest. The trouble is that there are no promising young men on the horizon and it is necessary to fall back on such unattractive bureaucrats as Sir John Anderson.[3] David M. is even thinking of him as a possible Chancellor, but the appointment would be almost as unpopular as that of Gilmour as Minister of Shipping.

There is a first-class row in progress between Hore-Belisha [Secretary of State for War] and Kingsley Wood [Secretary of State for Air] about the provision of aircraft for the army; Belisha wants 250 bombers to be handed over to the exclusive control of the C. in C.; Kingsley Wood thinks that this would be disastrous in principle and in practice. It would mean the removal of nearly half our striking force of bombers from the R.A.F.

One feels some sympathy with David Margesson's anxiety to get rid of all the service ministers; but, as he says, it would be necessary to leave Winston in the Cabinet without portfolio, and heaven knows what that would presage.

The P.M. and Halifax are busy thinking out what reply can be sent to a communication from Daladier [French Prime Minister]* about war aims. The trouble is that any suggestion that Germany would be partitioned would unite everybody in Germany behind the Nazis, whereas a sensible moderate statement would dishearten the French. It will probably be necessary to confine any statement to the vaguest of generalisations, merely including something specific to the effect that the autonomy of the Poles,

---

[1] Beachcomber, the consistently funny columnist in the *Daily Express*, wrote at about this time:

Democracy gives us the men that we want,
And those that we chiefly adore
Are colourful, vital Kingsley Wood
And glamorous Samuel Hoare.

[2] Chancellor of the Exchequer in Mr Asquith's Liberal Government and subsequently Chairman of the Midland Bank.

[3] Later Viscount Waverley.*

Czechs and Slovaks will not be disregarded. Halifax and Chamberlain both think that one of the chief mistakes at Versailles was the establishment of small autonomous states which had not the strength to withstand the onslaught of ravening wolves. When Germany has been defeated it will be vital, Halifax thinks, to establish some form of federation in Central and South-Eastern Europe, at least in the financial and economic sphere. We ought to start working for that now. I am afraid, however, that the French tend to think these areas ought to be left to their hegemony.

Sunday, November 5th
The general situation now seems to be as follows. On the credit side, Germany has not yet attacked despite her armed superiority, and it seems incredible that if she really means to wage war in earnest she should have allowed these valuable months to slip by. The Empire, except perhaps for India, is solidly behind us, and the material support which Canada, for instance, can lend is as great as is her determination to do so. Neutral opinion is convinced of the justice of the Allies' cause and is disposed to be helpful when it safely can, e.g. the courageous decision of the Norwegian Government yesterday to intern the *City of Flint*'s German prize crew. Finally the U.S.A., as much no doubt for reasons of commercial profit as any other, has at last passed the new Neutrality Act, and the Germans are thoroughly disgruntled thereby.

On the debit side, I am alarmed to read in Cabinet papers how long it will be before our production of armaments, and particularly aeroplanes, is satisfactory. I am not impressed by our efficiency or ability to "get a move on". With the exception of the P.M., Halifax, Churchill and Kingsley Wood the Cabinet are not a striking collection, and the junior ministers do not seem to include any outstanding personalities. Our Intelligence Service seems very weak, despite the number of sympathisers we must have in Germany: we never seem to have accurate or certain information about German fleet and troop movements, whereas the Germans know all our movements within a few hours of their taking place – probably by means of very low-wave wireless transmitters in this country which it is difficult to detect. At home the public is inclined to boredom and apt to forget that a war calls for sacrifices. The press and the Opposition maintain an endless campaign of criticism and grumbling, which embarrasses the Government and provides the enemy with propaganda. The power of our propaganda in the U.S. and elsewhere does not seem very formidable. Finally trouble is brewing in India where Congress is attempting to blackmail us into constitutional concessions, as the price of its support, and is now threatening a campaign of non-cooperation.

Tuesday, November 7th
Went to the House for Questions. Hore-Belisha, as usual, was having a rather difficult time with questions about dependants' allowances, etc. The P.M. had arranged for a private notice question to be put down about the *News Chronicle*'s allegation that an "Inner Cabinet" existed which excluded the Service Ministers. He rebutted this false statement amidst universal applause.

After Questions Sinclair and Attlee came to see the P.M. and, after them, Sir P. Loraine.[1] Attlee said he was getting an enormous number of telegrams demanding the imposition of rationing: as Alec Dunglass remarked, it is astonishing that people grumble when one is doing one's best to let them live normally and to save them inconvenience.

Loraine, whom I had last seen in Istanbul in 1934, was full of conversation. He told me that he found Ciano[2] likeable, though conceited, and very quick. He also genuinely believed that C. was now disgusted with the Axis, largely because of the abominable way he was treated by Hitler and Ribbentrop at Salzburg. Loraine further said that it was a mistake to forget that Italy was fascist, and that being such she did not like democracies. On the other hand the King was determined not to fight against France, and throughout modern history Italy, when in danger, has always turned to the House of Savoy. The Crown Prince, he said, was anti-fascist, but he had not got the King's intelligence.

Wednesday, November 8th
Went down to the House for Questions. I waited to hear Winston Churchill make a statement about the loss of the *Royal Oak* and the naval situation. The best point he made was when, referring to the Nazi claims of destruction of our ships, he said that the British navy would be prepared to fight the whole German navy merely with those ships which the Germans claimed to have sunk.

The latest German claim is to have sunk H.M.S. *Kestrel*, which turns out to be a naval sea-plane base some miles inland.

---

[1] Successful Ambassador to Turkey before the war, winning Kemal Ataturk's friendship, and then Ambassador to Italy. A keen racehorse owner.
[2] Mussolini's son-in-law and Foreign Minister.

Thursday, November 9th

An attempt on Hitler's life unfortunately failed. It was probably genuine, but I should not be surprised if Hitler made use of the occasion for a great internal purge. He may even use it as a pretext for beginning the war in earnest. Let us hope it will not increase his popularity at home, as did the Rye House Plot that of Charles II.[1]

The P.M. has gout, rather badly. This may give a useful handle to those who think he is too old for the job and ought to retire. But there is really nobody to take his place: Halifax has not the forcefulness and Winston is too unstable.

The morning was spent in hectic preparations for the Mansion House speech, which Simon will now make in the P.M.'s place. Simon proved obstinate, unbelievably unhelpful, and ended by leaving half of the speech behind. Arthur Rucker pursued him with it to the Mansion House in a taxi.

The Cabinet and Chiefs of Staff think that an attack on Holland really is imminent, and the Dutch and the Belgians are in a state of terror. I rather doubt it: even Hitler would find this hard to justify, and there does not seem to have been any attempt to "prepare" German opinion. However, there is always a chance that Hitler may do something on November 11th – to wipe out the slur of twenty-one years ago – and it is conceivable he may choose the Low Countries for his gesture.

In any case, as Halifax said to the Cabinet, Hitler will find it difficult to remain inactive after the threatening speech he made in the Bierkeller at Munich yesterday. He said he would attack England and, in the words of the *Evening Standard*, one cannot count on his *always* telling lies!

Sunday, November 12th

Our secret reports claim that it would be a mistake to expect any collapse of German morale until serious military reverses have been suffered.

We listened to Winston Churchill's wireless speech, very boastful, over-confident and indiscreet (especially about Italy and the U.S.A.), but certainly most amusing.

Monday, November 13th

Winston's speech has made a very bad effect at No. 10 but the F.O. and the City take a favourable view (War-Loan rose a point!). The Italian and Dutch Representatives protested at the F.O.,

---

[1] Unsuccessful plot by disgruntled Whigs to kill Charles II on his way back to London from Newmarket. Its failure restored the King's waning popularity.

and Rab Butler* tells me he thought it beyond words vulgar. The Cabinet were evidently embarrassed; but Hankey* (who, I am told, always "sucks up") expressed great approval to Winston.

Tuesday, November 14th
The Belgo-Dutch crisis seems to be passing over. Alec Dunglass thinks that Hitler will take no drastic measures because the Germans think they can win a long war. I suspect he is right: there can surely be no other explanation for the waste of these precious ten weeks – unless Hitler really has got a "secret weapon", to which he can resort at any moment and with which he can make resistance impossible.[1] But that seems unlikely.

Cabinet meeting at the House at 6.00, which the P.M. did not attend (though he was carried down to this morning's meeting). I went down for the meeting, and sat there with Alec, helping him with parts of the speech which the P.M. is to make to the 1922 Committee.

Thursday, November 16th
The Cabinet are considering, very secretly, the possibility of bombing the Ruhr, which is the centre of German industrial life, if Belgium is attacked. They do not wish to do so because:
  (a) It would entail bombing the civilian population.
  (b) It would invite drastic retaliation.
  (c) We should lose a great many planes, which we can ill afford to lose.

Moreover the French are not anxious to take such a step before the spring, and do not think it would pay. The important question is whether an invasion of Belgium would be a decisive phase of the war. Our Chiefs of Staff think it would, and Gamelin* is prepared to use all his forces to stop a German advance on the Scheldt or on the line Antwerp–Namur. However he doubts whether an invasion of Belgium *would* be decisive. The British view is coloured by the fact that we do not want the Germans to be allowed tamely to occupy the Dutch and Belgian ports from which they could launch intensive attacks on England. The matter is to be discussed at a meeting of the Supreme War Council in London tomorrow.

Friday, November 17th
A hectic day. The Supreme War Council met in London to discuss the question of bombing the Ruhr, and I went to Victoria Station

---

[1] Hitler's secret weapon was the magnetic mine, which caused much damage to Allied shipping until it was neutralised by what was called "degaussing", a method devised in a comparatively short time by British scientists.

with Oliver Harvey[1] to welcome Daladier and Gamelin on the
P.M.'s behalf. They both look very undistinguished. The Council
met at No. 10, owing to the P.M.'s inability to move, and there was
a great deal of flurry in the morning with French A.D.C.s and camp
followers. The Council decided not to bomb the Ruhr if Belgium
was invaded, but only if French and English civilian or para-
military objectives were attacked. In case of invasion the Allied
armies will try to hold the Antwerp–Namur Line.

After lunch I saw the party off at Victoria and had a talk with
Oliver Harvey. He considers that Eden[2] has a first-rate brain
(contrary to No. 10 opinion) and is not merely a "glamour boy"
with a facility for speaking, but may easily be a future P.M. He
thinks that if anything happens to Chamberlain, Halifax would be
his successor if things remain quiet, but Churchill in the event of
serious military reverses (God forbid!).

Saturday, November 18th
I went to Chandos House[3] and was driven down to Farnham[3] by
Pam Berry and Ian Fleming.[4] Lord and Lady Kemsley were there,
and he was full of conversation. He thinks that Sam Hoare will slip
into the premiership if anything happens to N.C., but doubts his
holding it for long.

Sunday, November 19th
Lord Kemsley and Baxter are carrying on a journalistic war against
the *Sunday Pictorial* which has lately contained scurrilous attacks
on the P.M. (and which George Steward thinks is run by Winston's
supporters).

Tuesday, November 21st
Went down to the House where the P.M.'s statement about seizing
German exports was well received. He saw Kingsley Wood and
Lord Macmillan, and afterwards I drove back with him to No. 10.
He was quite conversational for once, but his favourite topic is the
weather.

Wednesday, November 22nd
The mine warfare continues with a vengeance and about a dozen
ships, including Italian and Japanese, have been sunk in the last

---

[1] Principal Private Secretary to Lord Halifax. Ambassador in Paris after the war.
    Created Lord Harvey of Tasburgh.
[2] Secretary of State for the Dominions till May 1940. Later Lord Avon, 1961.*
[3] The Kemsleys' London house in Queen Anne Street and country house at
    Farnham Royal.
[4] An officer in Naval Intelligence. Author of the James Bond stories.

few days. German aircraft have been dropping mines by parachute, and none of the waters on the south-east and east coasts can now be considered safe. The neutrals do not like our retaliatory measures, but the U.S. seem satisfied.

We are now dropping pamphlets over Germany in the form of a small newspaper called *Wolkiger Beobachter*[1], of which I saw a copy this morning. It is extremely well done, with cartoons (one *very* obscene), verses, and short facts about the war.

It has been decided to lay a mine barrage right across the North Sea, to prevent the egress of submarines and raiders, but this will cost much and will take a long time to put into effect.

Winston is agitating for an alleviation of the black-out and makes the silly proposal that street-lighting should be restored and switched off on receipt of the Yellow warning. As the P.M. points out, this would make the Yellow into a Red warning.

Saturday, November 25th
Simon looked in and said that his speech on the wireless, urging people to save, had been much criticised as damaging to trade and he hoped the P.M. would not mention the matter in his broadcast on Sunday. He wished, he said, that he had told people to go on shopping, but nevertheless to save all they could. "A Chancellor of the Exchequer expects to be cursed; but we must encourage National Savings in order to raise the money we require. Nobody realises yet what privations we have got to face."

Monday, November 27th
When I got home I found Lady Snowden[2] with Mother. She thinks a defeatist spirit is growing in the country (Alec Dunglass told me the other day he had the same impression and was afraid it might spread to the House).

Tuesday, November 28th
Lunched with Mariora Swinton[3] to meet Captain Troubridge,[4] lately Naval Attaché in Berlin. He says there is little anti-English

---

[1] Wolkiger meant coming from the clouds. A play on the title of the German newspaper *Völkischer Beobachter*.
[2] Ethel Snowden. Passionate teetotaller and social reformer. Wife of Philip Snowden, formerly Labour Chancellor of the Exchequer.
[3] Attractive wife of Lt-Col. Alan Swinton, Coldstream Guards, our next-door neighbour in Eccleston Square.
[4] Bluff and entertaining officer, subsequently a Vice-Admiral, who came of a family famous in naval history and had been naval attaché in Berlin. His father commanded the Mediterranean Cruiser Squadron in 1914; his grandson was the first husband of Princess Michael of Kent.

feeling in the south and that Goering is undoubtedly anxious for peace. Goering did not expect war: he had even ordered 600 young pheasants for delivery in October. He thinks the military leaders will soon get rid of Hitler and offer peace on their own terms – terms which we shall find it difficult to refuse in the face of popular opinion here. He also thinks it is silly to talk about making a martyr out of Hitler: he will in any case be a martyr to the Germans who will always revere him as the greatest figure in their history. Speaking of Hore-Belisha, Troubridge said women liked him because women always like Jews: they are both oppressed races!

I cannot help feeling that there is something very wrong with a code of honour which, as in the case of the *Rawalpindi*,[1] prescribes that a ship must go down with all hands fighting to the last when cornered by a bigger vessel and unable to escape. Why should not the crew scuttle their ship and take to the boats? The effect would be the same except that hundreds of lives might be saved from a fate of flames and impotent horror. Codes of honour are often relics of a barbarous age, and it is tragic that modern opinion should remain so obscurantist on these matters. But it is undeniably true that if the *Rawalpindi*'s crew had scuttled their ship and saved themselves, their action would have been represented as disgraceful at home and abroad.

Wednesday, November 29th

Dined with Dorothy Cambridge to meet the Duke of Beaufort,[2] who had been told (by the King, I think) that Mr Kennedy,* the American Ambassador, is talking about our inability to win the war. To the P.M. and the F.O. he poses as the greatest champion of our cause in the U.S.

Thursday, November 30th

Evidently the Russian threats were not bluff. Using the same technique as Hitler, a technique which does not gain in dignity for being second-hand, they invaded Finland this morning.

Arthur Rucker thinks this may ultimately be a good thing: it incontestably brands Russia, Germany and Japan as the wolves in the sheepfold and destroys any remaining illusions about the Soviet's altruistic intentions. He laments that after the last war the statesmen of Europe did not see Russia was the great menace and did not make friends with Germany on that basis. There might then

---

[1] The *Rawalpindi* was an armed merchant cruiser found and sunk by the German pocket-cruiser *Deutschland* against which she had no chance at all.

[2] Famous Master of the Beaufort Hounds. Master of the Horse. His wife, Mary, was a sister of Lord Cambridge and a niece of Queen Mary.

have been no Hitler; but now we are hopelessly divided in the face of a common foe and, as the Hungarian Regent said to our Minister in Budapest, it is on the fields of Europe ploughed up by German and Allied gunfire that the seed of Bolshevism will take root.

The Pope [Pius XII] put it all admirably in his recent encyclical, when he spoke of this "age of technical and civic progress tormented by spiritual emptiness and poverty". There lies the fundamental tragedy and the *fons et origo malorum*. Mankind has deposed God and deified the state, while substituting a kind of sentimental philanthropy (which stops at the barrier of self-interest) for a code of morality based on religious principle.

Went down to the House where the P.M. answered a Private Notice question about Finland, the references to the Russian invasion being greeted with cries of "shame". However, the P.M. privately thinks the invasion may not be a very serious matter.

The P.M. elaborated to Arthur his ideas for the future, after the war is over. He thinks there will have to be a World League, but its jurisdiction will only extend to economic and social questions. Within or beside that there would be a European League, the members of which would agree to bring their differences to a council table and would attempt to bring about disarmament by slow stages. He does not think an International Police Force is practical politics.

Sunday, December 3rd

At Cambridge I looked in for a short time at King's Chapel to hear the exquisite singing and generally to enjoy the unique beauty of the place. Afterwards I went to Newnham to see Janet Margesson,[1] with whom I walked along the sunlit "backs", ending up with sherry and a fervid political discussion in Alan Hodgkin's[2] rooms. Jan is an intelligent and agreeable companion, but is at present passing through the earnest undergraduate stage of finding nothing right with the world. Alan Hodgkin is a brilliant scientist and an unusually attractive personality – very unassuming.

Wednesday, December 6th

Returned to the House with the P.M. at 7.15 for the division on the socialist amendment to the loyal address. I listened to part of Herbert Morrison's* speech, fluent and moderate and rather impressive. He spoke of the World Revolution which had taken place in this century: a technical revolution which began in the

[1] Elder daughter of the Chief Whip, Captain David Margesson.
[2] Eminent physiologist. Master of Trinity College, Cambridge, 1978–84.

West and moved Eastwards. In the East it gained much; for instance the Russian experiment proved that collectivisation could work; but it also broke down disastrously in the East because it was accompanied by a doctrine which denied the Rights of Man (Liberal cheers). Eden replied for the Government, speaking easily and sometimes amusingly, but never descending from generalities to deal with the concrete facts for which the Opposition asked. As Alec Dunglass said, it was difficult to realise one was listening to a speech by a man who had been Foreign Secretary.

Thursday, December 7th
Awoken at 2 a.m. to deal with a letter to the P.M. from Winston, who has decided on the spur of the moment to proceed northwards to investigate the situation caused by the temporary disablement of the *Nelson* and the *Rodney*. The *Nelson* has struck a magnetic mine and will not be repaired for two months. This is not being divulged.

Lunched with Chips Channon* at his highly ornate house in Belgrave Square. Sat between Lady Cunard,[1] who is certainly most amusing, and Alice von Hoffmanstahl.[2] Lady Cunard spent her time trying to persuade me (as if I could help) that Archie Sinclair ought to be in the Government and that, despite the war, the Government ought to subvention music, possibly by diverting money from the Churches! Covent Garden, she tells me, is shut probably for good.

Friday, December 8th
Sir W. Seeds,[3] our Ambassador in Moscow, thinks Germany and Russia are now hand-in-glove and that there is little hope of a rift between them. He suspects that the Soviet intend to control all Scandinavia, and he thinks that the reasons against our declaring war on Russia are now less strong. Moreover he believes all the neutral states consider Russia more dangerous than Germany, and would welcome our changing our present state of undeclared war against Moscow into a real one. There are signs that when the League meets next week there will be strong support for Russia's expulsion from the League and for sanctions against her. Meanwhile Italy, Sweden, Great Britain and even Hungary are sending armed support to Finland, and Italy may be prepared to favour a Balkan bloc against Soviet aggression in that direction.

[1] American by birth. Scintillating conversationalist, indefatigable hostess and intimate friend of the celebrated orchestral conductor, Sir Thomas Beecham. Ardent supporter of King Edward VIII and Mrs Simpson.
[2] Alice Astor by birth. Married Raimond von Hoffmanstahl.
[3] Former Ambassador to Brazil, but only lasted a year in Moscow.

Lunched with Michael Grant[1] at the Travellers. He is working in Military Intelligence at the War Office, and is as good company, as brilliant and as egotistic as ever.

Wednesday, December 13th
Horace Wilson told me of the naval action being fought against the *Graf von Spee*. He and Edward Bridges were seeing the P.M. about a first-class row in progress between Hore-Belisha and Ironside [Chief of the Imperial General Staff]* on one side and Lord Gort on the other. The first two are, as usual, behaving disgracefully.

Thursday, December 14th
Tommy Dugdale tells me that Sinclair's speech last night was the best he had ever made. He showed, though not directly, that he knew a great many details about production, the number of divisions we propose to send to France, etc., which he could only have obtained from official sources. His speech must have been prepared either by Winston (who is quite capable of such a thing), or by Hore-Belisha via Sir Walter Layton.[2]

Friday, December 15th
The P.M., accompanied by Arthur, General Ismay and Alec Dunglass (in uniform, but looking very unmilitary) left by aeroplane for France, to inspect the troops and G.H.Q.

Consequently we had a quiet day at No. 10, with nothing but a large number of letters from boring members of the public to keep us busy. The only interesting paper that I saw was an account of a conversation between Alec Cadogan and the Duke of Würtemberg, who hopes for a military uprising in Germany soon (under two anti-Nazi Generals and with the support of three tank divisions) and thinks (optimistically, I fear) that the country will divide itself up into its former little states (though the Hohenzollerns would be excluded). He expects the new capital to be Munich, or possibly Stuttgart, and not Berlin. But he declares that the essential preliminary is that the generals shall be convinced the Allies will not make use of the occasion to crush Germany.

---

[1] A friend of mine at Harrow and Cambridge. Brilliant Classicist, successful author and expert from his early youth on Roman coins.

[2] Chairman of the *News Chronicle* and Editor of the *Economist*. A leading member of the Liberal Party. Made a peer in 1947.

Saturday, December 16th

Main papers of interest were:

(1) A memorandum by Winston on German iron ore supplies. He considers it essential to use drastic, and even illegal, methods to prevent ore being shipped from Norwegian ports, and he wants Cabinet authority to lay minefields in Norwegian territorial waters (with the justification that German U-boats are sinking ships in those waters) in order to drive ships carrying iron ore out of territorial waters into the hands of our contraband control.

(2) A Foreign Office appreciation of the situation in Scandinavia, weighing the possibilities of German intervention in the south if the Russians attack in the north. Sweden may very likely intervene on the side of Finland, but Norway and Denmark are determined on neutrality. Probably Germany will try to dissuade Russia from seizing Northern Norway and Sweden because in that case the iron ore, upon which Germany so much depends, would fall into Russian hands.

I have a feeling that Scandinavia may well end by being the chief theatre of war and that we may have to send troops there.

(3) A report on the Balkan situation, which has been changed by the Russian threat. Roumania is the weak spot, in danger of attack from three sides, from Russia, Bulgaria and Hungary, and susceptible to German pressure. Roumania (i.e. King Carol) would probably choose German domination rather than subjection to Russia.

Bulgaria is threatened by Bolshevisation, of which the King and ruling classes live in mortal fear. Her relations with Turkey are improving.

Yugoslavia is very cautious but, except for her Foreign Minister, very pro-Allies.

Turkey will not fight Russia if Bessarabia is seized, but would probably consider her vital interests threatened if the Russians tried to cross the Danube.

Hungary is increasingly anti-Nazi, terrified of Russia and looks to Italy as her mainstay. If the Bulgarians and Russians take their pound of flesh from Roumania, no Hungarian Government could prevent their people from going for Transylvania.

Greece, though pro-Allies, is becoming very anti-war as a result of commercial difficulties and a fall in the standard of living.

(4) A statement by the Chancellor on the financial situation. If the war begins in earnest, our military expenditure will amount to

half the national income. We must face the fact that there will be a great fall in the standard of living, that we shall not be able to obtain luxuries and even supplies to which we are used, that wages will not be able to rise in proportion to prices (without causing inflation), and that the burden will have to be borne equally by all classes. Even the confiscation of the incomes of all surtax payers would not solve the financial problem. A grim outlook, but I suppose these hardships will only make themselves felt gradually. The question is whether the morale on the home front is good enough to bear them. Judging from the raucous criticism of hitherto minor inconveniences, I am inclined to doubt this, unless the public's enthusiasm and determination is increased by sensational events in the war – which from a wider point of view is just what we want to avoid. From this angle Germany, and any totalitarian Government, is in a better position to wage war than we are.

Moreover I have no confidence in our propaganda.

Tuesday December 26th [On Christmas leave at Helperby in Yorkshire]
Anthony,[1] Philip and I hunted with the York and Ainsty (North) at Ripon, hiring horses as it was too far to hack. The country was lovely, much prettier than at Helperby, and the going good. After a somewhat ineffective morning, during which every time the fox tried to sally out into the open he was thwarted by zealous holiday-makers, we had two first-class runs in the afternoon. The first was short but with a lot of jumping, the second lasted over an hour and was finally ended by the death of the fox (everybody being in at the death, except the Master, the Whips and Anthony who got lost). At one stage I followed the wily Arthur Collins[2] and had a magnificent hunt alone with him, the hounds, the Master and the Whips.

Wednesday, December 27th
At Downing Street by 9.30 where I found Cecil Syers very disconsolate, having spent a depressing Christmas alone with Miss Watson at No. 10.

A dull day, the only excitement being the question whether or not we should take drastic steps to prevent Scandinavian iron ore

---

[1] Anthony Coates, younger son of my mother's twin sister Lady Celia Coates. Immensely popular, sincerely religious and possessor of a sparkling sense of humour. Joined the Coldstream Guards and was killed in Normandy in 1944.

[2] Later senior partner of Withers, the well-known solicitors.

reaching Germany. If we do, it may shorten the war, but it may mean our having to send an expeditionary force to Sweden. Winston, of course, is in favour of immediate action; but the Cabinet and the Chiefs of Staff are less enthusiastic.

Thursday, December 28th
The P.M. has another attack of gout, and is worried at the prospect of not being able to carry on if these attacks increase in number and violence. Meanwhile very secret soundings are being taken regarding the possibility of an enabling bill to allow a peer to speak, but not vote, in the Commons, so that Lord Stamp[1] can succeed Simon as Chancellor of the Exchequer.

> *The story of these negotiations was committed to paper by Lord Stamp. When his house was bombed, in 1941, and he killed, an envelope containing the account was blown into the street and found by an A.R.P. Warden who brought it to No. 10 Annexe. As I was on duty, it came to me. On reflection I did not show the paper to the Prime Minister, who had known nothing of the plot, but forwarded it directly to Sir Horace Wilson, then Secretary to the Treasury and, with the Governor of the Bank of England, Montagu Norman, one of the originators of the scheme.*

Friday, December 29th
There are signs of a renewed peace move. The Vatican and Mussolini are putting their heads together and may enlist the support of Roosevelt, to whom the R.C. vote is important.

Our (or rather Van's) conversations with German army leaders and Hohenlohe, through Conwell-Evans, are continuing and all hope of engineering an internal coup d'état does not seem to be abandoned. It is said that Hitler and his generals are at loggerheads over an invasion of Holland, which Hitler still favours (and which Ciano thinks probable).

A dull, but quite busy day. From conversations between Arthur and C. J. Harris[2] and Arthur and Horace Wilson, I gather Cabinet changes are under consideration, with a view to being rid of Hore-Belisha from the War Office. Kingsley Wood and others want him to go to the Ministry of Information, but Halifax opposes this (presumably because his brand of propaganda would be too

---

[1] Celebrated statistician, economist and expert on taxation. He had been ennobled in 1938.
[2] Secretary to successive Chief Whips at 12 Downing Street and a welcome habitué of No. 10.

vulgar) and it seems that the influence of Horace will also be wielded against this proposal.

Sunday, December 31st

Here at home, at the end of 1939, people seem to be resigned to the war without fully realising the hardships which it must, and the physical terror which it may, imply. Everybody is talking gaily about a changing world, a new social order, a complete revolution of national and international ideals; but do they realise what effect all this, if it comes to pass, will have upon them personally? It is easy to sit in the warmth, beautifully dressed, after an enormous meal, and talk academically about the inevitability of change and the charm of doing one's own housework; but it may be less easy to accommodate oneself to the grimness of reality.

At sea the war is going better for us. The *Graf Spee* affair, and the damaging of German warships by two of our submarines at about the same time, have greatly enhanced our prestige abroad and have given much-needed encouragement at home. The mine menace, the possibility of violent air onslaughts against our harbours or the Fleet at sea, and the slowing down of trade due to the convoy system are the major dangers and inconveniences with which we are now faced.

In Europe interest is, for the time being, centred on Finland, where the Russians are apparently meeting with unexpected and overwhelming setbacks. Germany may well be alarmed at the effect which the action of her new ally is likely to have on opinion both at home and abroad. The Italians are openly disgusted and frightened ("this monstrous aggression": shades of Abyssinia and Albania!), and it is increasingly clear that Ciano is now in the Allied camp. He even gives Loraine information which is obviously to the detriment of Germany, and he is a restraining influence on his father-in-law who hates democracies and cannot forgive or forget sanctions.[1] The newly cemented friendship of the Vatican and the Quirinal will probably strengthen the hands of both parties, who feel, I think, that the war should be stopped soon and that the belligerents should unite against Bolshevism.

As always throughout history, the situation in the Balkans is obscure, explosive and liable to change. The two most likely causes of trouble would be a Russian invasion of Bessarabia or a decision by the Germans that they must secure a firmer grasp on Roumania's oil supplies. The latter is not improbable as Germany's own

[1] The sanctions imposed by the League of Nations in 1935 when Italy invaded Abyssinia.

consumption, even during the present period of inactivity, far exceeds what she can import and what she can safely draw from her stocks.

The U.S. is aloof, and critical of what everybody in Europe is doing and thinking, without showing the least inclination to step in to redress the balance of the Old World.

In general, we seem to be floating on a sea of stagnant waters and in ships not built of the soundest timbers. Whether the much-advertised spring offensive will come off remains to be seen, but it is very doubtful whether we can reach next winter without something drastic happening, and I think the odds are fifty-fifty on peace or the real outbreak of war. The conditions in which the former could be made are at present unforeseeable; but at least each side is aware of its own shortages and weakness and both are afraid to begin the carnage. The consequences of the latter are only too easy to predict.

3

Indecision

January – March 1940

Monday, January 1st
The breakfast supplied by Mrs Chamberlain is really hardly edible, and so after sleeping at No. 10 I went across to the Travellers to feed well and in comfort. It is the Prime Ministerial coffee which is at fault: it tastes of strong burnt chicory and is, curiously enough, a source of pride to the Chamberlains and their staff who believe it to be unique in its excellence.

The Cabinet, instigated by Winston, are considering a daring offensive scheme in Northern Scandinavia, which they think might bring Germany to her knees but which also, to my mind, is dangerously reminiscent of the Gallipoli plan. Briefly, they have decided that if Germany could be denied her Scandinavian supplies of iron ore she would have to give up the struggle. They contemplate either (a) blockading Narvik, in Northern Norway, by means of destroyers and minefields, or (b) more boldly, landing a force in Northern Norway to take possession of the ore deposits and thus prevent shipments to Germany from the port of Lulea in Sweden. They hope to be able to force Norway and Sweden into the war on our side in order to put the major scheme into operation; if, as seems likely, this is not feasible then they might resort to the first and minor scheme, despite Scandinavian opposition. The effects are likely to be (i) a German invasion of Southern Scandinavia, (ii) a violent air-attack on this country by way of reprisal. The essential requisite is speed, and if the plan is adopted in either of its forms it will probably be put into execution before the spring. The Cabinet will debate the matter tomorrow.

Extensive Cabinet reconstruction is proposed: Macmillan to leave the Ministry of Information and become, eventually, a Lord of Appeal; Hore-Belisha to become Minister of Information (to the satisfaction of everybody connected with him in his present job); Oliver Stanley* to become Secretary of State for War; Lord Stamp to be made a Commoner by Act of Parliament (an unprecedented step) and be Chancellor of the Exchequer instead of Simon, who will be Lord President and do much of the Treasury work in the Commons. Arthur Rucker is doubtful about Stamp whom he considers the Sir James Jeans[1] of the economic world; David Margesson would secretly like Bob Brand[2] to be Chancellor, and hopes to have him in any case appointed to the Treasury in an advisory capacity. I suspect that the fact that he is a neighbour of the Margessons at Boddington, and a friend of David's, accounts for this whim of the Chief Whip.

Dined at the Travellers with Con O'Neill[3] and John Cairncross. The former says that the thing that he most dreads is a breach in the Russo-German alliance. If Germany turned against the Bolsheviks she would do so with the sympathy, and probably the active assistance, of all the neutrals, and her own crimes would be forgotten in an anti-Russian crusade. We and the French should be faced with the choice of coming to terms with Hitler, on a basis which left him in power in Germany, morally strengthened, or of attacking him when he himself was fighting against an enemy whom half our own people consider more venomous than the Nazis themselves. A great man, and perhaps Hitler is a great man, could use an opportunity such as this to re-establish himself in the eyes of his own people and of the world. And at the end of it all we should be faced with the same situation as we were in six months ago: a Germany armed to the teeth, loyal to its Government, and ruled by an unscrupulous clique whose word was not trustworthy and whose aggressive instincts were patent to the whole world.

Con, who is secretary to Grigg[4] at the Ministry of Information, has been invited to return to the F.O.; but Horace Wilson has apparently imposed his veto, inspired, of course thinks Con, by the memory of Con's resignation as a protest against the Munich policy. It seems an unlikely hypothesis: I cannot believe Horace

[1] Author of *The Mysterious Universe*. Considered to be a popular scientist rather than a profound one.

[2] Hon. Robert Brand, son of the 2nd Viscount Hampden and married to a sister of Lady Astor. Fellow of All Souls and eminent in the City of London. Treasury representative in Washington at the end of the war.

[3] Son of Sir Hugh O'Neill, M.P., later Lord Rathcaven. A Fellow of All Souls. Joined the Diplomatic Service in 1936 and resigned several times. Finally Ambassador to Finland and to the E.E.C.

[4] Sir Edward Grigg, M.P., formerly Secretary to Lloyd George and later Governor of Kenya. Parliamentary Secretary at the Ministry of Information, 1939–40. Created Lord Altrincham.

would bother his head about a twenty-five-year-old Third Secretary.

Tuesday, January 2nd
The most hectic morning I have had since being at No. 10. The Cabinet discussed the Scandinavian project and more or less agreed to adopt the proposal to stop the Narvik iron-ore trade, Winston hoping that this may lead to a German invasion of Norway and the consequent facilitation of our undertaking the major project of seizing the iron-ore fields with an armed force. The Cabinet decision will depend on the Chiefs of Staffs' consideration of the position if the Germans occupy the south Norwegian air-bases (from which aerial attacks on this country would be a grave menace).

The P.M. saw Stamp who was reluctant to become Chancellor. The curious constitutional suggestion of making him a Commoner has therefore been dropped and Sir J. Simon will maintain his position, blissfully unconscious of the schemes which have been evolved for his removal.

Wednesday, January 3rd
Miss Watson returned from her holiday which, nice as she is, rather disturbed the quiet and efficiency of No. 10.

Miss Watson, who had been a typist at No. 10 since the days of Lloyd George and Bonar Law, was promoted to the rank of Private Secretary and dealt conscientiously and well with the preparation of replies to Parliamentary Questions. She had an admirable character, loyal and affectionate, but she was not over-endowed with brain-power and her incurable tendency to make a fuss could be exasperating. She did not, however, lack acumen and one afternoon she assured me that the man at No. 10 with the greatest political sensitivity was Lord Dunglass. He was the only man round the Prime Minister who understood the House of Commons.

"He will be Prime Minister one day, Mr Colville."

"But, Miss Watson, he will be a peer before he reaches that seniority, and you couldn't have a Prime Minister in the House of Lords nowadays."

"That's as may be, Mr Colville. I shan't live to see it, but the day Lord Dunglass becomes Prime Minister, you just remember what Miss Watson said." I did.

There is now some doubt about the proposal to appoint Hore-Belisha Minister of Information, as the fact that he is a Jew would make him a target for the Nazis, who would represent all British propaganda as an inspiration of Judaism. This argument has impressed Horace Wilson and the P.M.

The Bishop of Lichfield (Woods)[1] came to see me to discuss Ecclesiastical appointments, with especial reference to the vacant see of Leicester. He wants Neville Talbot appointed, and also suggested the names of Canon Raven and Canon Barry, who are in his view two of the finest intellects in the C. of E., as men who should be given Bishoprics. Lord Halifax, last night, put forward the name of the Bishop of Willesden for Leicester.

The Cabinet seem disposed to go ahead with the Scandinavian plan, partly because they believe that the extension of the war would add to Germany's commitments and be definitely to her disadvantage. We are to prepare expeditions of a thousand men or so to seize Bergen, Trondhjem and Stavanger if, when we stop the Narvik traffic, the Germans invade Southern Norway. We cannot prevent them from taking Oslo and Christiansand, but the air menace to this country from German bases there will be incomparably less than Stavanger, etc. The chief dissentient in the Cabinet to the whole scheme is Hore-Belisha who, aptly I think, recalled that throughout history small military expeditions, like those contemplated at Bergen, Trondhjem and Stavanger, had been useless and had led to wider and more expensive undertakings, e.g. Walcheren in the Napoleonic Wars.

Thursday, January 4th

The Cabinet reshuffle is causing a lot of heartburning and proving very difficult. Halifax has come down so strongly against making Hore-Belisha Minister of Information that the idea has been dropped. Originally it had been decided that Malcolm MacDonald[2] should be President of the Board of Trade, "Shakes" Morrison[3] Secretary of State for the Colonies, Rob Hudson[4] Minister of Food. Now Hore-Belisha is to go to the Board of Trade and Sir

[1] Right Rev. E. S. Woods. Two of his sons became bishops.

[2] Son of Ramsay MacDonald. Secretary of State for the Colonies, 1935 and 1938–40. After the war served with great distinction overseas, in India as High Commissioner (1955–60) and in Kenya as Governor and later High Commissioner (1963–65).

[3] Held many ministerial posts but never reached the dizzy heights foretold for him. Chosen Speaker of the House of Commons in 1951.

[4] Former diplomat who became an M.P. in 1924 and was Minister for Agriculture for most of the war. Much disliked by most civil servants.

John Reith,* to the Ministry of Information. As Lady Oxford[1] writes regularly to her "Darling P.M." recommending Sir John Reith, she will probably think herself responsible for the appointment. But it may not be well received by the outside world who look upon Reith as the man who failed first at the B.B.C. and then at Imperial Airways.

After lunch Hore-Belisha came to see the P.M. and looked nervous and "on edge" (he had, I think, no idea that his resignation was to be demanded). As he went out I was alone in the room: he looked very worried, clapped his hands together gauchely and talked about the weather. Afterwards I heard that the interview had gone badly and Belisha had taken it all amiss. One cannot help sympathising with him: as President of the Board of Trade he will not even be in the War Cabinet, and after all he has in some ways done extremely well at the War Office and shown particular energy. But he has a way of antagonising people, very often just when he is trying to be at his best and most efficient. In him one sees very clearly those characteristics which inevitably, but inexplicably, make Jews unpopular.

Cecil Syers returned from leave, Miss Watson came to sit in the same room as me, and the peace of the last ten days vanished.

Friday, January 5th

After some hesitation Hore-Belisha has declined the Board of Trade and so will be out of the Government altogether. A businessman, said to be of considerable capacity, called Sir Andrew Duncan[2] is to have the Board of Trade. Rob Hudson will go to the Post Office and Tryon[3] will be given a peerage.

Lord Bledisloe[4] has written to ask the P.M. for the Governor-Generalship of Canada. It is extraordinary how shameless people can be.

The Cabinet have decided to give considerable assistance to the Finns (whose successes against the Russians continue to be astonishing) and it has been suggested that we should apply those "principles of non-intervention" so successfully followed by Germany and Italy in Spain.

---

[1] Margot, second wife of the Prime Minister Herbert Asquith. Born Margot Tennant.

[2] Chairman of the Iron and Steel Federation and of the Electricity Board.

[3] A gallant soldier. M.P. for Brighton from 1910. Minister of Pensions and later Postmaster General. Made a peer in 1940 and given the Office of Works, but died a few months later.

[4] Former Governor General of New Zealand. Nicknamed Lord Bloody-Slow by King George V.

Mother, who has taken frantically to knitting since war broke out, took me to buy some navy-blue wool for a pullover. It takes a war to domesticate some people!

Sunday, January 7th
Arrived at Downing Street at 6.00. Charles Peake,[1] who was there, thinks that the newspaper violence over Hore-Belisha's removal is a good thing, as there is now nothing left to say and the agitation must die down for lack of material.

Sir Walter Monckton* and Sir Kenneth Lee of the Ministry of Information also came in and gossiped. The latter told me that within a quarter of an hour of its being known that Lord Macmillan had resigned, the following notice was produced in the Ministry:

DEMISE OF LORD MACMILLAN

NO REITHS BY REQUEST.

Read a number of Cabinet and other papers. There are concentrations of troops at North German ports who are undergoing intensive training in embarking and disembarking, from which it seems possible that an attack on Southern Scandinavia may be imminent. On the other hand whenever a dramatic German move appears to be contemplated, and suitable precautions are taken, nothing seems to come of it: either Hitler and his advisers are continually changing their minds or, as Germans would be likely to do, they are making preparations for every conceivable move – an attack on Holland, an expedition to Scandinavia (to seize the aerodromes), an invasion of England or a move south-eastwards – so that there may be a large and carefully prepared choice of action available. It is also significant that the Germans are pressing on with the erection of fortifications in the east so that they may be ready for every contingency and may have an *Ostwall* as a bulwark against their present Russian allies.

Monday, January 8th
The Belisha excitement continues in the press, the *Daily Express* and other irresponsible pamphlets taking the line that Oliver Stanley's appointment is due to intrigues in "High Society". Hore-Belisha himself is obviously making mischief by having photographs published of himself at home, with little dog, etc.

---

[1] Witty member of the Diplomatic Service who was a friend and adviser of Lord Halifax. Ended his career as Ambassador in Athens.

Moreover Paramount Films have produced a pro-Belisha film, with an inflammatory commentary, which was shown in the cinemas last night and loudly applauded. All this may, as Charles Peake thinks, be a nine-days' wonder; but H.-B. is certainly experienced in the art of publicity and can probably be trusted to make all the capital he can out of the situation. It appears that the P.M. handled the affair rather badly and lost his temper when arguing with H.-B. (this is a report of Miss Watson, subsequently denied by Arthur Rucker).

Lunched with Michael Grant at Simpson's. He tells me the War Office is almost unanimous in favour of H.-B.'s resignation.

Tuesday, January 9th
Dullish day at No. 10. The Belisha storm seems to be settling and despite the prayers and supplications of David Margesson, the P.M. listened to Arthur Rucker and made no mention of the matter in his speech at the Mansion House.

Thursday, January 11th
The Finns are performing miracles against the Russians in their frozen forests, and attack after attack is being turned into a rout. The Soviets have succeeded in alienating the sympathies of the whole world and even if, by sheer weight of numbers, they finally succeed in overcoming Finnish resistance, it seems likely that the Finnish fiasco may have as unsteadying effect inside Russia as did Napoleon III's Mexican adventure in France. (What a poor historical analogy!)

The Cabinet now think of compromising about the Scandinavian plan, by using the threat of action at Narvik to induce the Norwegians and Swedes to give us what we want. The reaction of both countries to the notification of our intentions which we gave them was unexpectedly severe, and although Norway might not matter the P.M. feels we cannot afford to estrange Sweden. On the other hand both the Cabinet and the army feel that to extend the war to Scandinavia would be greatly to our advantage, and it seems that the most likely way of achieving this would be to incite and support Sweden in her assistance to Finland. The whole situation is very delicate: would the Germans dare attack Scandinavia, thereby risking the total loss of their iron-ore supplies if the attack failed or were too slow; on the other hand could they allow the Russians, when the snow melts in the spring, to smash their way through Finland and threaten Northern Scandinavia or even occupy the iron mines? Personally I am against our interference: (i) it would be dangerous and might involve disaster or withdrawal and the consequent blow to our prestige: (ii) the idea of wilfully extending the war to Scandinavia, and involving the Northern countries against their wishes, is a callous contradiction of those very principles for which we are fighting.

Met the famous Tom Jones,[1] who was a discovery of Lloyd George and has since devoted his life to "helping the under-dog". He has extraordinary natural charm and a Celtic quickness of mind. He told me of his meetings with Hitler, who he said was before all else an artist and whose *Weltanschauung* had in 1936 "paralysed him with terror". Ribbentrop he knew well, and said that the F.O. and particularly Eden had made a tremendous mistake in snubbing him so consistently. They had taken the line that R. was a stupid man with no humour and that that was the end of it; what they should have been considering was the way to deal with a stupid man who had the ear of Hitler. Snubs and laughter were unprofitable tactics.

Saturday, January 13th
Arthur and I alone at Downing Street. Fairly hectic morning. In view of the violent Swedish reactions, the Cabinet have more or less decided to drop the Narvik project (despite Winston's fulminations), but to prepare an expedition to Scandinavia in case the Swedes require help against the Russians or Germans in the spring. In the latter case we should be able to attempt our plan against the Gallivare iron-ore field with Norwegian and Swedish assistance.

The Cabinet has received information that an attack may be launched by the Germans against Holland and Belgium during the next few days while Europe is still frozen up.

Monday, January 15th
The Belgian crisis has intensified over the week-end and the Cabinet has decided to move troops into Belgium if the Belgians invite them, in order to seize the Wavre–Namur Line and forestall the Germans. Yesterday it seemed probable the Germans would advance at dawn on a line covering Holland, Belgium and Luxembourg; but today the situation is better and it looks as if an attack will at any rate be delayed. The German plans were divulged by some papers found in a German aeroplane which made a forced landing in Belgium, but the landing itself, the ostentatiously

---

[1] Valued adviser to Lloyd George. A wise Welshman, dedicated to social reform, at one time Deputy Secretary to the Cabinet.

ineffective efforts of the pilot to burn the papers, and subsequently to commit suicide, are suspiciously like a "put-up job", and it seems that the whole thing may have been arranged on purpose either: (a) in order to induce the Belgians to invite the Allies to enter the country, so that the Germans themselves may have good reason to attack, or (b) to forewarn the Allies, so that the plan of invasion may be abortive (i.e. a *coup de théâtre* on the part of the army who are thought to look unfavourably on Hitler's invasion project).

Tuesday, January 16th
The House met, and after Questions Hore-Belisha rose to make his resignation speech. The House was packed, even Lloyd George being in his place, and it was in a combative mood. Hore-Belisha spoke smoothly and well, with many soft phrases, and the feeling which his speech left on one was "Well, if he and the Generals, the Cabinet and the P.M. saw eye to eye on every question of policy, why was he forced to resign?" The P.M. rose to answer and did it, to my mind, very poorly. He categorically denied the rumours of why H.-B. had resigned and led everybody to believe that he was going to state the facts of the case; but he ended, amid a storm of questions and interruptions from the Opposition, by saying that there was no reason for him to give the House any explanation why he had taken such action. H.-B., in order to curry favour with the Opposition, had spoken much about the "democratisation" of the army, and I think his speech took the honours and made the P.M.'s seem lame. As Arthur Rucker said to me in the box, the trouble is that Belisha, while apparently playing the game and refusing to make mischief, is in fact intriguing behind the scenes.

After this affair the P.M. made a statement on the general situation which was too long and which seemed to bore the House with its dreary details about the help coming from the Dominions and Colonies. For some reason no subject is more boring to the average Englishman than the British Empire.

Wednesday, January 17th
Spent a good deal of the morning talking scandal with Alec Dunglass and the Chief Whip, who is certainly an unusually agreeable man. Talked also to the invariably and perhaps excessively cheerful George Townshend,[1] who is Ironside's A.D.C.

---

[1]   7th Marquess Townshend. A Harrow contemporary. Later Chairman of Anglia Television.

Went down to the House late in the afternoon and heard Cross,[1] the Minister of Economic Warfare, giving a review of his Department's not inconsiderable achievements. Dalton* replied for the Labour Party with a smooth but disobliging speech, which considerably annoyed the P.M. who confided to me afterwards how disgusted he was with the eternal carping and intrigue of the Opposition. He said that they only paid lip-service to the universally accepted doctrine that everything must be subordinated to the efficient prosecution of the war, and that in reality they were always searching for an opportunity to score off the Government and were saturated with the pettiness of party politics. I suggested that when air-raids or real fighting on land began in earnest (which one can still hope they may not), this attitude would change, and Mr Chamberlain agreed but said that even the blessings of peace at home could not make him wish for such a violent remedy.

He further told me that the Labour Party were angry with Attlee who yesterday made a speech on the Belisha issue which was sensible and sincere: his supporters argued that he should not have wasted such a splendid opportunity for attacking the P.M. Obviously the poor old man, who is doing his very best and is personally very sensitive in spite of his external coldness, feels these attacks deeply and, not without justice, considers them to show an incomprehensible lack of patriotism and common-sense in the face of an enemy who is the common enemy of all parties alike.

Thursday, January 18th

Had breakfast at the Travellers, where I read a good article on war aims in *The Contemporary Review* by Grandfather, called "Looking Ahead". He writes extremely well and has an attractive way of expressing himself but, like his grandson, is sometimes inclined to ramble.

I went down to the House for Questions and spent most of the time talking to Alec, Chips Channon and the Chief Whip. The P.M. is deciding against the publication of the Blue Book on our negotiations with Russia last summer, partly because the course of those negotiations would evoke criticism (of which there is too much at this time), and partly because there is no point in provoking the Russians before we actually go to war with them (if we do).

---

[1] Sir Ronald Cross. Later Minister of Shipping and High Commissioner in Australia, whither Churchill despatched him as he wanted his portfolio for Lord Leathers.

Our present relations with the Soviet Government are just about as bad as they could be.

Sweden is behaving badly about the despatch of volunteers to Finland across Swedish territory. I am glad to see we are going to send the Finns 100 aeroplanes and some volunteers.

Sunday, January 21st

Went to church with Father at St Peter's [Eaton Square]. Bitterly cold: it has been freezing now for a good many days, the temperature is as low as I can remember it, and it looks as if we may be in for a "cold spell" as acute as that of 1929 (when we skated at Harrow for six weeks on end).

After lunch Philip and I went down to Trent, now a camp for German prisoners. The house is surrounded by barbed wire and guarded by sentries, but we managed to force our way into the park and skated, unmolested by the military, for an hour on the large and deserted lake. It was snowing a little and all the surrounding country was white. The air was bitterly cold and we felt most exhilarated.

After tea went to Downing Street, were I found Cecil Syers who tells me that he has been appointed to a post in the Treasury and is leaving No. 10 shortly.

Monday, January 22nd

Miss Watson being ill, I had an agreeably busy day, most of which was taken up with Parliamentary Questions (her special preserve).

Another flotilla leader, the *Exmouth*, has been lost: the second in two days.

Lunched at home with Mother, who had come up from Badminton for the day and brought me a box of chocolates as a present from Queen Mary. The old lady is extraordinarily thoughtful and methodical, and is always fond of doing small things which give pleasure. She still continues to send me large packets of monograms, the envelopes addressed by herself – a practice she began when I was ten.

Wednesday, January 24th

An utterly hectic day, largely due to the continued absence of Miss W. It began with a scene. There has been a good deal of trouble over the proposed Blue Book on the Anglo-Soviet negotiations last summer. The French do not want it published; the Cabinet had decided to bow to the French demands. However the Opposition demand that it shall be published in spite of the French objections, and the P.M. could not persuade Attlee to the contrary. In a minute on a Parliamentary Question Frank Roberts[1] expressed himself rather tactlessly, said the P.M. "had failed" to do this and had "not succeeded" in doing that. When he saw this minute the P.M. was furious, called Frank Roberts insolent and impertinent, "damned his eyes", etc., etc. I could see that he resented it particularly as coming from the F.O., and I think he is unable to forget the opposition in that department to the Eden resignation in 1938, the Munich policy, and the whole influence of No. 10 as represented by himself and Horace Wilson. I was surprised at the violence of his fury which I could never have expected in such a cold man.

After lunching at No. 10 I went down to the House with the P.M. who had to answer nearly twenty Questions on behalf of the F.O. and himself. Some of these were embarrassing, including one about Unity Mitford's return from Germany, to which I had drafted the reply. Herbert Morrison alleged class distinction, etc., and was, as the P.M. said to me afterwards, "as poisonous as usual".

On the way back in the car we discussed a rumour, which Alec Dunglass has heard, that French morale is deteriorating, that an increasing section of French public opinion is for peace at any price, and that a number of politicians, including Bonnet[2] and Laval,* are intriguing for Daladier's downfall. The P.M. told me he considered Laval the most unscrupulous and unreliable of all French politicians – which is saying a lot!

Thursday, January 25th
The P.M. was again a bit acrimonious over Questions, but this time I was partly to blame because I had not insisted on the F.O. providing a really adequate reply to one of his marginal comments on a paper.

Friday, January 26th
So busy that by the end of the day I was almost blind with overwork. I was largely busy in compiling a complicated memorandum on the depressed state of the motor trade, and the efforts of the Government to remedy the matter, from evidence supplied by nine different departments. The main point seems to be that nothing can make up the loss suffered by garages, etc., owing to the

[1] One of the ablest and most dynamic members of the Diplomatic Service. Ambassador in Moscow, 1960–62 and in Bonn, 1963–68.
[2] Georges Bonnet held at one time or another almost every Government portfolio in France and was Daladier's Foreign Minister at the time of Munich.

withdrawal of so many private cars from the roads; and the necessary extra petrol allowance to attract these cars back cannot be supplied owing to shipping and foreign exchange difficulties. The question will be included in the debate on economic co-ordination next Thursday.

Mine is a curious job: sometimes, as today, I am dealing with matters of the greatest significance; at other times I have not enough to keep me occupied and am acting as little more than an office-boy. There are really too many of us for normal day-to-day work, and the difficulty is aggravated by Arthur (who otherwise has most of the known virtues) being so conscientious that he likes to keep everything in his own hands. Thus the remainder of us are often in the position of being mere spectators of events which are themselves of world-wide importance.

Saturday, January 27th

Another exhausting day, perfecting the memorandum, etc., and I had to go back to Downing Street in the afternoon.

Winston made a first-rate "fighting" speech at Manchester, which was broadcast. He is indeed an orator – perhaps the only one in the country today – and he does not read his speeches tamely like Halifax and the rest of them. Nevertheless he is a dangerous person unless kept well in control, as his Narvik-Lulea scheme shows.

Lady Maggy Bulkeley[1] died. She was a remarkable figure, rouged up to the eyes, short-sighted, witty and absurdly overdressed; and she certainly succeeded in remaining young in mind and in spirit long after she had, for all her paint and dyed hair, become very decrepit physically. She loomed so large in my childhood, presiding in state in the Squadron Garden, that her death symbolises a very definite break with the past. Of course Cowes, with its Edwardian tradition and atmosphere, was already merely a survival; but in many ways it was an historically interesting one, to which the personalities of Lady Maggy and her contemporaries contributed greatly. Father, who had known her for nearly seventy years, and I composed an obituary notice at the request of the *Sunday Times*.

Sunday, January 28th

Reached the mature age of twenty-five in a world covered with the deepest snow.

I spent the day at Tadworth, near Epsom Downs, with Pamela

[1] Daughter of 5th Earl of Hardwicke and wife of Sir Richard Williams-Bulkeley, Commodore of the Royal Yacht Squadron. Grandmother of Zara Mainwaring.

Foster[1] who has evacuated her children there. The snow was so deep that the railways were all out of working order and the journeys there and back were long, cold and tedious.

The return journey took three and a half hours instead of forty minutes, but it was enlivened by a brilliant fireworks display (caused by the ice on the electric cable) and by the entertaining and original conversation of two Austrian refugees, called Wassermann (he a Jewish chemist, she an Aryan doctor) who had been staying with Pamela's aunt. The husband tells me he expects a crack in Germany about next August – before a second winter sets in.

Monday, January 29th
Waded to No. 10 through drifts of snow and slush.

Cecil Syers goes to the Treasury today and an apparently delightful and estimable man in his forties, called Anthony Bevir* has arrived from the Cabinet offices to take his place.

The French are becoming excited about Finland and Scandinavia. They claim to have alarming evidence of energetic Russo-German collusion to force the issue in Finland. Consequently General Gamelin and Admiral Darlan* want to *prendre les devants* and to send a naval expedition to Petsamo,[2] followed by Chasseurs Alpins who can seize the iron-ore fields. They think this will mean war with Russia and thus an opportunity to bomb the Baku oilwells from Syria, to the discomfiture of all our enemies. The Supreme War Council will meet in Paris next week to discuss the question, although the French, impressed by the urgency of the matter, want the meeting to take place immediately.

A number of people seem to be thinking that Hitler will not take the offensive, but may even be in a position to win a long war of inactivity – or at least to ruin us economically and so, like Samson, to bring down the roof on himself and his enemies together. There is thus, for the first time, a feeling that we may have to start the fighting, and Winston even gave a hint to that effect in his speech on Saturday.

Dined with David and Joan, forcing my way miserably through slush and piled-up snow which formed itself into innumerable snares and pitfalls in the black-out. Father was there and Philip, who arrived just in time for dinner after an eight-hour journey by train from Kenswick. We drank champagne in honour of my

---

[1] Pamela Wilberforce, married to Anthony Foster, a childhood friend of my family. Her brother, Richard, became a distinguished Judge and Lord of Appeal.

[2] In the extreme north of Norway, close to the Russian frontier.

[twenty-fifth] birthday, and I departed reluctantly from a cheerful atmosphere to grope my snow-bound way back to bed at Downing Street.

Tuesday, January 30th

The newspapers point out that the year '40 has always been a bad year for Germany, or at least for the Hohenzollerns who represented it. Margraves, Electors and Kings, they died regularly in 1440, 1640, 1740 and 1840. Now Hitler has taken their place let us hope history will not let us down.

The Italians are already making good use of their neutrality and it looks as if we shall have to spend millions on unwanted imports, such as "horticultural produce" in order to get them to provide us with the few ships and guns we want and to buy coal from us instead of from Germany.

Wednesday, January 31st

The report of the West Indies Royal Commission shows such a deplorable state of affairs, with regard to health, housing and standard of living, that the Cabinet have decided not to publish it because of the outcry it would cause. However they propose to set about providing a remedy.

War with Russia seems now to be seriously contemplated, and we are examining methods of helping Finland which would include a naval expedition to Petsamo and the crushing of Russian resistance. If we do go to war, Germany and Italy are almost bound to become formally allied and Italy will then find it impossible even to use the threat of joining Germany as a bargaining counter.

M. Prytz, the Swedish Minister, wants us to go ahead with our Scandinavian project, whatever the apparent reactions of the Norwegian and Swedish Governments. Halifax says that Prytz's views are clearly far in advance of his Government's; it is a curious example of a diplomat working independently of and contrary to his orders. The present intention is that we shall stop the Narvik traffic and operate from a Norwegian fjord; however I think we have wasted too much time to make this worth while (unless we *want* to provoke a German invasion of Southern Scandinavia), because in a month or two Lulea will be free from ice.

Went to the House where the P.M. had rather a rough time from the Opposition, especially Shinwell,[1] about a Private Notice Ques-

---

[1] Emanuel Shinwell. First elected as a Labour M.P. in 1922. Served in Attlee's Government successively as Minister of Fuel and Power (1945–47), War (1947–50) and Defence (1950–51). Conscientious objector in the First World War. Created Life Peer 1970 and celebrated his 100th birthday in 1984.

tion on shipping. Afterwards I had a long talk with the Chancellor of the Exchequer (Sir John Simon), who explained that while the Government are now spending £50 million a year to stabilise prices, they will abandon this policy if the Opposition refuse to take the hint and the Trade Unions demand wage rises. Wages will rise to some extent, he says, but the workers must realise that we have got to export cheaply in order to meet foreign competition and that if wages rise inordinately this cannot be done. It is worth spending large sums to avoid "the vicious spiral of rising wages and prices", but if the Trade Unions refuse to co-operate (despite the fact that the Government have not tried to use their present policy as a bargaining factor) then the Chancellor will let prices rip and will try to reserve the money, now being spent on stabilisation, to meet the inflation which will inevitably follow.

Sir J. Simon said that we are going to make a tremendous effort to export, and so to earn foreign exchange by maintaining our normal exports (e.g. cloth) that we shall be able to afford to import steel, etc., from America and thus avoid diverting our present factories to war-manufactures for which they are unsuited and inexperienced. Moreover if we can keep our industry on a peace footing it will be less difficult to return to normal conditions after the war, and we shall have retained or even expanded our pre-war markets. One of our troubles, said Sir John, is due to the fact that in the last war countries such as Italy and Yugoslavia, which are now competing with us very strongly in the export market, were themselves belligerents and unable to compete. Moreover the American industrial machine was not then so developed and all-embracing as it is today.

George Steward pointed out that after 1931 our exchange position had been greatly eased by the fact that other currencies followed England off the Gold Standard and formed a sterling bloc. "Yes," said the Chancellor, "whereas today the sterling bloc consists of England, Scotland, Wales and doubtfully Ireland!"

Thursday, February 1st
Extremely bleary-eyed and depressed by the thaw.

Lunched at the Travellers with John Cairncross and subsequently talked to Sammy Hood,[1] who says that Reith is a fountain of energy at the Ministry of Information.

---

[1] 6th Viscount Hood. Joined the India Office on leaving Cambridge and was Private Secretary to Lord Zetland. Private Secretary to successive Ministers of Information in the early part of the war and then transferred to the Foreign Office where his wisdom and quiet efficiency were much esteemed.

Debate on economic co-ordination and on the demand for an overriding Economic Minister, responsible for all the departments concerned and representing them in the War Cabinet. The P.M. will turn down the proposal because he, and his advisers H.J.W. [Horace Wilson] and Lord Stamp, feel that the creation of such a minister would involve divided authority over departments and would not in the least add to the efficiency of our war effort. (The present agitation is partly aimed at the Chancellor, who resents it and is hurt. Great emphasis is laid on the fact that he has to represent both finance *and* economics in the Cabinet.)

The Cabinet have received a report to the effect that all Soviet ships have been ordered to return home, or to be in neutral ports, by a certain date. This looks ominous. Meanwhile M. Maisky [Soviet Ambassador] has had the impertinence to suggest that we should apply to Finland the same doctrine of strict non-intervention to which we adhered in Spain – which, when one thinks of Soviet policy in Spain, is an almost incredible proposal.

Friday, February 2nd
The Chancellor apparently made the speech of his life last night and I wish I had not felt too tired to go down to the House to hear him. Also Herbert Morrison was much less poisonous than usual, but the P.M. failed to respond or to pick up the olive branch. This is rather hard on Arthur Rucker who has been working behind the scenes to get Morrison to moderate his tone, but, as Arthur points out, the P.M. is incapable of being gracious at the right moment. He is a curious mixture of qualities and defects: I have nothing but admiration for his forcefulness, precision and capacity for hard work; and yet at the same time he is obstinate and vain. Vanity is a failing common to Prime Ministers – Ramsay MacDonald for instance (I remember his talking about himself to Mother and me for a solid hour and a half, before breakfast at Cowes one morning, at the time of the Schneider Cup); and I suppose it is natural in view of the adulation they receive but to which they are not, like Kings, accustomed. In N.C.'s case this vanity takes the form of resenting any kind of criticism or mockery. He feels it acutely when he is attacked personally in the press or in Parliament; his wrath against Frank Roberts the other day was due to a suspected lack of respect in the minute which offended him; and there is no surer way of gratifying him than to make some allusion to the exceptional importance of his position. In other words, he likes to be set on a pedestal and adored, with suitable humility, by unquestioning admirers.

General Ismay came in during the morning and gave an account of the Chiefs of Staff meeting in Paris, about Finland and Scandinavia, which is to be followed by a meeting of the Supreme War Council early next week. The French plan is for a landing at Petsamo, the consequent cutting-off of the Russian forces at Murmansk, and the movement of Finnish troops northwards against them, assisted by four divisions of Allied soldiers. Apparently the Petsamo expedition will involve our using a Norwegian fjord as a base, and the British view is that if we are going to violate Norwegian neutrality anyhow we may as well be hanged for a man as for a sheep and put the whole Narvik-Lulea project into effect. Our objections to the French plan include the points (i) that the Petsamo landing will necessitate the diversion from this country and the Western Front of anti-aircraft guns and aircraft which we can ill afford; (ii) that the four divisions which are to assist the Finns have got to be (a) raised and (b) equipped. The French talk vaguely about foreign subjects, living in France, who could be used. Both sides agree that if anything is to be done it must be done quickly, before the ice in the Gulf of Bothnia melts, the Germans can reach Lulea and the Russians can overwhelm Finland. Complete secrecy is also essential, but with the French "in the know" is it possible?

General Ismay thinks this French plan is political, sponsored by Daladier, etc., because of the ill effect of this continued inactivity on French morale. He says the French General Staff, and even Gamelin, are not really in favour of it, although Gamelin has now for the first time admitted the possibility of the Germans not attacking on the Western Front and says he thinks it is desirable to extend the war. Personally Ismay can see no point in all these risky proposals and thinks we should do better to stick to our original thesis that we can win a long-drawn-out siege by outstaying Germany. I agree with him except in so far as we may wreck our economy and ruin our prosperity in the process. Perhaps even that would be preferable to a real *guerre acharnée*.

Most of the morning was taken up listening to a long conversation between David Margesson, Arthur and Alec about the ineffectiveness of "Shakes" Morrison as Minister of Food and the possibility of removing him. Like Walter Elliot he is one of those exploded "future Prime Ministers".

Sunday, February 4th
Monty Sherman [Claims Adviser in the Foreign Office] died suddenly. Although not a brilliant person, he was certainly a remarkable one, as is proved by the affection felt for him by all sorts and conditions of men and by his friendship with such varying

personalities as D. H. Lawrence and T. E. Lawrence. Bon viveur, dilettante, collector of pictures and books, he was a wonderful host and a most sympathetic companion. He brought the secluded and academic charms of the university into the practical and hard-headed world of London and the Foreign Office. His boundless hospitality, made possible by a handsome fortune, was inspired by motives of genuine kindness and philanthropy. He will leave a gap in a lot of people's lives, and in particular in those of many members of the Foreign Office – where he held a position involving little work and enabling him to win the well-deserved affection of a great many people.

Monday, February 5th
The P.M. has gone to France for a meeting of the Supreme War Council about Scandinavia. Certain information about our project has inevitably leaked out owing to the necessity of enlisting volunteers from the army. Brian O'Neill told me yesterday that he would be going and he knew that Norway would be his destination. Others, less well-informed, imagine we are contemplating armed intervention on behalf of the Finns (because persons with ski-ing experience have been asked to volunteer).

There is trouble about two I.R.A. terrorists who are to be executed. Their death will make them martyrs in Ireland (where martyrdom is very coveted and very effective in its results) and will sway Irish opinion in the U.S.A. against this country. The Cabinet have discussed the matter, but seem disposed not to give way, despite the warning of Lord Lothian[1] and a personal letter from De Valera to the P.M. They are keeping no records of their long discussion on the subject, because a reprieve is not really a matter for them, but for the King's Prerogative, exercised through the Home Secretary.

Tuesday, February 6th
The I.R.A. executions continue to occupy everybody's mind. Cabinet Ministers are heavily guarded and the policeman outside No. 10 replaced his ordinary helmet by a tin one. De Valera is making a desperate effort to have the men reprieved as he feels that their deaths and martyrdom will strengthen the I.R.A. in Ireland and weaken his own position. Bomb outrages occurred in London, Birmingham and elsewhere.

[1] Philip Kerr, 11th Marquess of Lothian. One of "Milner's young men" in South Africa, Editor of *The Round Table*, Secretary to Lloyd George and Ambassador in Washington, 1939–40.

The P.M., Halifax, Winston, etc., returned from Paris where they have been for a meeting of the Supreme War Council. According to Arthur the discussions went very well and I presume our Scandinavian plans are finally determined.

I lunched with Jim Bowker[1] at the Wyndham,[2] but was called away very soon as the P.M. had scarcely set foot in London before he went down to the House to take Questions. His energy is remarkable; but he also hates to feel that anyone else is usurping his place as Prime Minister.

President Roosevelt is proposing to send Sumner Welles[3] over to Europe to visit the various capitals concerned and to examine the prospects of peace. This has been expected, because Hitler well knows how to play on neutral fears of an extension of the war and on the world-wide terror of Bolshevism. The P.M. thinks this move comes, very indirectly of course, from Germany, where Goering and others have long been posing as moderates and have been putting out peace feelers. The danger is that Welles' visit will give an opportunity to the peace-at-any-price minority here to raise their voices, while the controlled public opinion of Germany will present a united front. Moreover such an initiative, which could never really achieve anything since the destruction of the Nazi régime is, from our point of view, an essential prerequisite of peace, would open up endless possibilities of which the German propaganda machine would know only too well how to make use.

Wednesday, February 7th

Read the minutes of the Supreme War Council. It is now decided that we shall carry out our iron-ore plan on the pretext of sending help to Finland through Norway. The Finns will publicly appeal to the Norwegians and Swedes to allow foreign volunteers through their country, and we shall then demand permission to land our "volunteers" (in the approved "non-intervention" manner) at Narvik and Trondhjem, at the same time offering further troops to defend Norway and Sweden against any German invasion from the south. In the event – which Mr C. thinks *most* unlikely – of the Norwegians offering armed resistance to the Allies, and cutting the Narvik railway, we should probably be obliged to revert to the plan for a naval expedition to Petsamo in order to save our prestige and the Finns. Chamberlain and Daladier agree that the defeat of

---

[1] Diplomat of singular charm and cultivation. My immediate senior (and instructor) when I joined the Foreign Office in 1937. Subsequently Ambassador in Ankara and Vienna.

[2] The Wyndham Club, 4 St James's Square.

[3] Under Secretary in the State Department.

Finland would be a defeat for the Allied cause. Our expedition to Narvik will be ready by March 20th – orders to begin preparations were telephoned from Paris immediately the Supreme War Council had reached its decision – and it will consist of three British divisions (who were to have left for France today), some French Chasseurs Alpins, etc., and some Polish battalions. It will be under British command, and of course its primary objective will be, on its march to Finland, to seize the Gallivare iron-ore fields and occupy or incapacitate them.

Despite the serious foreign exchange position, the Supreme War Council also decided to order 3,000 aeroplane engines in the U.S.A., M. Daladier proclaiming that he would rather sell the art treasures of France than risk Germany maintaining preponderance in the air.

Friday, February 9th
Spent most of the day preparing for the P.M. a summary of the findings of the tribunal which investigated the *Thetis*[1] disaster. The Duke of Buccleuch[2] called and spent the morning trying to persuade Alec that peace was essential: in a year's time the same people would be in power in Germany and we should eventually have to make peace with them. Why not do so now, when comparatively little damage has been done and when there is still time to avert economic ruin?

Thursday, February 15th
The French cannot keep a secret: rumours of the Supreme War Council's decision have already permeated to Stockholm from Paris.

Went to the House for Questions. Had a long talk with Sir W. Citrine[3] (who is just back from Finland) about the economic interpretation of history and of other things. Citrine said that the Russians had even discovered an economic interpretation of Sex. We also discussed, with reference to Hitler, whether the man produces the hour or the hour the man, and agreed that neither was the case. Hitler could not have come into power without the peculiar circumstances that, in post-war Germany, gave him his opportunity; but it was the personal characteristics of the man who so came into power that made events take the course they have.

[1] The submarine H.M.S. *Thetis* sank in the Irish Channel in the summer of 1939 with great loss of life.
[2] Walter, 8th Duke of Buccleuch. As Lord Dalkeith an M.P. for twelve years. Entirely patriotic but an admirer of Hitler and strongly opposed to war.
[3] General Secretary of the T.U.C., 1925–46. Made a peer in 1946.

Citrine then talked for an hour to the P.M. about his impressions of Finland, while Alec and I discussed Munich and the attitude of the F.O. to the P.M. and Horace Wilson. Alec told me that our lack of armaments in September 1938 weighed very heavily with the P.M. during the Munich crisis, but that also it was only fair to admit that he and Horace believed that by the sacrifice of Czechoslovakia they could achieve permanent peace and that Hitler would be satisfied. The F.O. were equally mistaken in thinking Hitler was bluffing about war, and if the truth be told the only justification of Munich was *salus populi suprema lex*: war would have been disastrous to us and we had to sacrifice principle to security. This fact will probably be the salient one when future historians come to judge, but it should not be forgotten that the P.M. and Horace were prepared to use questions of principle as bargaining counters in the diplomatic game and looked on Munich as a permanent settlement, not as the postponement of an inevitable war. "Peace with Honour" was a blunder, but Mrs Chamberlain made him say that.

On the way back in the car the P.M. said that Citrine, like all the Labour Party, was very discursive and kept on going off the point (this is agony to the P.M.). Nevertheless he was very interesting about the deplorable morale of the Russians, who were shot and bullied from behind (he had talked to Russian prisoners), and the heroic resistance of the Finns. The P.M. thinks that once our Hurricane aircraft, and other foreign aircraft, are in action on the Finnish side "there won't be a Russian left in Finland". I am afraid he may be over-confident.

Saturday, February 17th
There was great excitement at No. 10 over the *Altmark*[1] affair, news of which reached us early in the morning. It is a perfect conclusion to the victory over the *Graf von Spee*.

I was going to Terling[2] for the week-end to stay with the Rayleighs and to see Sidney Cuthbert,[3] who has just returned from India. But

---

[1] The *Altmark*, a German merchant ship, was returning to Germany crammed with British prisoners taken from the ships the *Graf von Spee* had sunk. She took refuge in a Norwegian fjord, but H.M.S. *Cossack*, commanded by Captain Vian, entered the fjord, boarded the *Altmark* and freed the prisoners.

[2] Home of Lord and Lady Rayleigh in Essex.

[3] A great friend of mine and fellow traveller in the Balkans when we were both at Cambridge. Killed in action in Normandy in 1944 as a Major in the Scots Guards. He had had meetings with Gandhi by whom he was impressed and influenced – though not in the direction of pacifism.

at lunch-time I felt so unlike the journey, and so little inclined to the prospect of shooting pigeon in the deep snow, that I took my temperature and, finding it was nearly 103°, retired hurriedly to bed.

Sunday, February 18th–Monday, March 4th
Languished in bed with jaundice. Kind people came to see me and relièved the tedium.

For a few days it was pleasant to lie in bed with a cheerful fire, eating grapes and oblivious of all the world's cares, but it became exceedingly wearisome, and I was very glad when, after more than a fortnight, I was able to get up.

Friday, March 8th–Sunday, March 17th
Stayed at Uppark with Meg Fètherstonhaugh.[1]

It is the perfect country house, ideally situated in the loveliest country of the Sussex Downs and preserving much of the eighteenth century within its beautiful walls. There is nothing ugly inside or out, and at the same time it is very comfortable and pleasant to live in.

Uppark, near Petersfield, originally belonged to the Fetherstonhaugh family. Sir Matthew, last of the line and a notorious Regency rake, married a milkmaid at the end of his days. The house was left to the milkmaid's sister, who in accordance with Sir Matthew's will, took the name of Fetherstonhaugh. Many neighbours looked askance at this upstart; but the Commander-in-Chief at Portsmouth, Admiral of the Fleet the Earl of Clanwilliam, was kind to Miss Fetherstonhaugh. So, after a life tenancy for Lord Winterton's brother, who had also been kind to her, she bequeathed the estate to Lord Clanwilliam's second son with a proviso that the name Fetherstonhaugh be retained.

While still a Cambridge undergraduate I was invited for a week-end. The Meades had only just moved in. Little had changed in a hundred and fifty years: wallpapers, curtains, furniture were all much as Sir Matthew had left them.

A fellow guest was H. G. Wells whose mother had been old Miss Fetherstonhaugh's housekeeper. He had spent his childhood at Uppark, kept firmly in the housekeeper's apartment, well out of sight of Miss Fetherstonhaugh who, a milkmaid's younger sister

---

[1] Attractive wife of Admiral Sir Herbert Meade-Fetherstonhaugh, known to his friends as Jimmy.

though she might be, held firm views about keeping her own servants in their proper place.

He had not been back since he was a boy. At luncheon he told us that in the afternoons, when Miss Fetherstonhaugh went out driving in her carriage, he used to creep up to the library and read a book, his ears cocked for the sound of returning carriage wheels which necessitated a hasty departure. At the end of one shelf there had been a copy of Plato's Republic, *which he read and re-read and which had a profound influence on his thought, then and in later years.*

We left the dining-room and walked through the library. There, at the end of a shelf, untouched since he had hastily replaced it at the age of twelve, was the dusty and much-thumbed edition of Plato.

Meg was there, in excellent form, full of laughter and always charming so long as she can be prevented from talking on serious subjects, when she becomes fatuous. Jean Meade[1] was also there and I was very much struck by her cheerfulness, kindness, energy and competence. Nobody could be simpler or more anxious to help others or more ready to put herself out.

In order to keep Uppark going – which with its silver plate, its large rooms and its periodical repairs is no light task – they have taken some paying guests for the duration. This was all the more necessary as Jimmy Meade* has thrown up his job at the House of Lords and gone off to sea in command of a convoy, thus sacrificing a considerable amount of income. It is tragic that such courage and self-sacrifice should be wasted on something as futile as war: it ought to be possible to produce such qualities in peacetime and utilise them for a constructive purpose.

The P.G.s included Lady Mary Glyn,[2] a rather trenchant and occasionally quite interesting relic of another age, who knew Ruskin and remembers Garibaldi. There was also "A" Cecil,[3] nephew of the Prime Minister Salisbury, who is a little old-maidish but a very good talker and a man with great literary knowledge and experience. He was interesting as having known A. J. Balfour well and as being one of the "Souls". After dinner he read aloud to us, quite beautifully, short stories and fantasies by Oscar Wilde. By

---

[1] Sir Herbert and Lady Meade-Fetherstonhaugh's younger daughter. Married Michael Babington-Smith after the war.

[2] Meg Meade-Fetherstonhaugh's mother. Daughter of the 8th Duke of Argyll and widow of the Bishop of Peterborough.

[3] Algernon Cecil, a barrister and former President of the Oxford Union. Brother-in-law of Oliver Lyttelton.

way of contrast to this bearded blue-stocking there was Mr Charles Mead, whose interests centred on hunting and shooting. Lastly there was Audrey Paget,[1] aged seventeen, very attractive and refreshing with her enthusiasm for life and her passion for enjoyment. She has plenty of conversation and though strikingly "ingénue" is evidently not stupid.

I spent much of the time walking with Audrey or Jean on the lovely downs. Otherwise I read or played picquet. In the evenings, when "A" Cecil did not read to us, we played round games and laughed a great deal. Meg also showed me some interesting and amusing manuscripts, including letters from Lady Hamilton to Sir H. Fetherstonhaugh and eighteenth-century accounts of the estate.

Monday, March 18th
Returned to Downing Street. While I was away the Finnish resistance to Russia collapsed, despite the fact that we had been prepared up till the last to send the assistance we had promised. But Norway and Sweden proved recalcitrant and the Finns were exhausted. Probably it is all to the good: we have certainly lost prestige but we have reserved our strength to face Germany instead of dissipating it in the forests of Finland (and in all probability the Caucasus and Batum as well).

Tuesday, March 19th
Busy day. Big debate on Finland in the evening, during which the P.M. won great personal success. His birthday yesterday has caused us to be inundated with a flood of letters and telegrams.

Wednesday, March 20th
Daladier resigned.

News of our gigantic air-raid on Sylt, as a reprisal for a raid on Scapa Flow the other day, very well received by the public, which is otherwise rather depressed by the defeat of Finland. It looks as if this may be the beginning of a more active phase of the war, since the Germans will now probably undertake another raid by way of reprisal and so things will go on until somebody goes so far as to bomb civilians. Lord Hankey thinks that an intensive German attack on shipping is now to be expected, but doubts whether it will be extended to the ports as that would mean an attack on civilians and, as the Germans well know, immediate counter-attacks by us against the Ruhr, etc. The Pope has also hinted that considerable

---

[1] Seductively pretty daughter of Lord Queenborough by his second marriage.

air and naval activity is to be expected and thinks that in another month the Germans may begin land operations. However, he alludes darkly to the likelihood of certain unexpected events occurring in the meanwhile and has admitted to the French Ambassador that these would include the elimination of Hitler.

Thursday, March 21st

Lord Hankey has produced a strategical survey in which he emphasises the value to us of the present "static warfare" until such time as our war production has approached more nearly to its maximum. He doubts the Germans attacking Holland (which is of value to them economically) but believes they will concentrate on destroying our blockade (i) by heavy attacks on shipping, (ii) by attempting to establish their sway in the Balkans, if possible by peaceful methods. This second plan is probably the motive of the recent Brenner Pass conversations between Hitler and Mussolini. Italy is anxious to be friendly with the Allies, but Mussolini is personally hostile and he will certainly go as far as public opinion, the King and Ciano will let him in pursuing the old Axis pro-German policy. Loraine thinks that M. alone is responsible for this attitude and that he alone caused the recent breakdown of Anglo-Italian trade conversations. He cannot forget sanctions and he hates democracies.

Saw our Ambassador in Paris, Sir R. Campbell,[1] who told me that the political horizon in France was as bare as in this country. There is no sign of a new Clemenceau, with the possible exception of M. Dautry.

Friday, March 22nd

It is to be hoped that Hitler can resist the temptation to commit some nefarious act on Good Friday.

We, for our part, are debating the possibility of seizing Dr Schacht (Governor of the German Central Bank) at Gibraltar on his way to America in the *Conte di Savoia*. The F.O. are strongly opposed to this breach of international law, the advantages of which would be small. Winston, who is always for "action" in any form and at all costs, is pressing for Schacht's arrest.

Saw a paper by Boothby,* who has been travelling on the Continent. He paints a clever and lurid picture of young Germany, solid behind Hitler, confident in its role of an enthusiastic and virile

---

[1] Succeeded Sir Eric Phipps as Ambassador in Paris, 1939. On the fall of France he became Ambassador in Lisbon.

civilisation fighting against the decadent democracies of the West. He speaks of the new German moral code, according to which it is no disgrace to be dishonourable or brutal: the only unforgivable sin is to be weak (what a lesson for Good Friday!).

From all sides come disgusting accounts of the German terror in Poland: young men shot in hundreds, girls sterilised and conscripted for the soldiers' brothels, old people sent to hard labour in concentration camps or driven from their houses to die of exposure. At the same time the Germans continue their attacks on neutral ships, firing torpedos without warning and leaving the crews to their fate. I suppose there is a natural strain of brutality in the German character and as great an insensitivity to human suffering as there is a sensitivity to beauty. Certainly the Nazi doctrine has sublimated all that is most despicable in human nature, and it is difficult to see how this pernicious philosophy can be eradicated from the minds of the rising generation in Germany. However I still refuse to believe they are wholly abominable, and I think we ought sometimes to try and see ourselves reflected in their eyes: pharisaical, oblivious of the acts of aggression in our own history, rich and anxious to keep those riches for ourselves. Undoubtedly we are, as a nation, irritatingly self-righteous.

Motored Jean Meade down to Camfield Place [near Hertford] to stay with Lord Queenborough[1] for Easter. It is a comfortable modern house, part of the exterior covered with wood like a German or Swiss chalet, and it stands very well, looking across a valley to a distant horizon. Besides Lord Q. there was Audrey Paget, brimming over with life and good spirits and looking very attractive; Ann Paget (daughter of Peggy's friend Bridget Paget) who promises to be good looking but is at present shy, downtrodden and speechless; Mrs Stuart-Wortley, mother of Lady Loraine, who is pedantic and has a passion for high politics, about which she knows nothing, but is not disagreeable for all her self-assuredness; and finally a man called Kreck, effeminate, very talkative, intelligent and possessed of infuriating opinions about astrology, fortune-telling and Confucius which almost drove me to distraction. However he seemed to have a nice side to him.

---

[1] Almeric Paget. Conservative M.P., 1910–17. Married the rich Miss Pauline Whitney, by whom he had two handsomely endowed daughters (Olive Bailey and Dorothy Paget), and then another American, Edith Miller, by whom he had three exceptionally pretty daughters. He took little interest in them as he resented having no male heir.

Monday, March 25th

Sufficiently sunny and warm for us to sprawl in a heap in the middle of a field, on Audrey's coat, and laugh helplessly for the best part of an hour.

An interesting talk with William Teeling[1] who takes a gloomy view of post-war conditions in this country (owing to the fact that the middle classes are being ruined) and thinks that Conservatives, Liberals and Labour may have to combine against the extreme Left in order to fight revolution. We seem far from such a possibility today, but of course wars upset all calculations.

He agrees with me that our objective as far as Germany is concerned should be to smash her politically and militarily as a prelude to treating her with the utmost generosity.

Kreck told me that someone had once said: "Germany hates England with the love of a jealous woman."

Tuesday, March 26th

Politically there are two topics of importance: (i) a mooted change in the War Cabinet involving the removal of Chatfield, Hankey and Oliver Stanley from the Cabinet, the appointment of Winston as Minister for Co-ordination of Defence as well as First Lord, and, probably, the retention of Kingsley Wood in the Cabinet in some other capacity (because the P.M. and David Margesson put great trust in him), (ii) the approaching meeting of the Supreme War Council to debate the French thesis that the war should be prosecuted with greater vigour and that (a) Norwegian territorial waters should be violated, to stop the iron-ore traffic, and if possible Norwegian ports seized so as to make Germany retaliate and thus extend the war to Scandinavia, (b) Russia should be attacked and her oil sources at Batum destroyed by aerial attack from the Near East. With regard to (ii) the point is that Daladier fell because of criticism that the war was being prosecuted without energy or resolution, and M. Paul Reynaud,* D.'s successor, has therefore got to take, or try to take, some active measures. This, of course, suits the book of Winston whose policy is one of "action for action's sake"; personally I feel it would be very wrong to sacrifice lives merely in order to defend oneself from the accusation of irresolution unless there was some worthy objective for which those lives should be sacrificed. There is all the difference between being resolute, capable of seeing one's opportunities and able to use them, and taking some spectacular but valueless action merely in order to impress public opinion. To attack and to fail would be

[1] Elected M.P. for Brighton in 1944.

very serious in a war which is, at present, more psychological than military in character.

Wednesday, March 27th
While I was still in bed the Assistant Air Attaché in Paris rang up to ask about arrangements for the meeting of the Supreme War Council – oblivious of the fact that the cross-Channel telephone is almost sure to be tapped. When I suggested that he should ask the Embassy he implied that he had not thought of that!

The Cabinet undertook a thorough review of our strategy in view of the meeting of the Supreme War Council tomorrow and in particular of the new French Cabinet's wild proposals for drastic action. The Chiefs of Staff pointed out that we were not really in a position to take the offensive: our aircraft production was being built up on the basis of a three-year war and in consequence our immediate output was smaller than if we were budgeting for a *Blitzkrieg*; the Germans need only concentrate their defences on a short line from Luxembourg to Switzerland, whereas the Allies must be ready for an attack anywhere from the Channel to the Mediterranean; on the other hand if Germany were enabled to maintain her present inactivity she would, in six months' time, have remedied her present weak position in respect of oil by imports from Russia and Roumania.

So it seems that we shall have to be careful not to launch a major offensive and yet active in preventing the Germans from profiting by our waiting policy. A German attack on our ports and shipping by the new aerial torpedo, which they are thought to have devised, would mean the diversion of our trade to west coast ports and would seriously complicate our daily life. We can do the same to Germany by tightening the blockade (preventing the Germans using Norwegian territorial waters and "rationing" Italy more strictly for oil) and by putting into operation the mysterious ROYAL MARINE project about which there has lately been much talk, but which the French are frightened of our putting into effect. (It is a new river mine device.)[1]

The question of bombing Baku and of attacking Soviet oil ships in the Black Sea by means of submarines must depend on the attitude of Turkey. At present our Ambassador in Angora does not think the Turks would consent, although they might be ready

---

[1] It was a plan to drop mines from the air high up the Rhine so that they would float down and destroy German shipping in the river. It was finally implemented, far too late, after the German offensive on the Western Front had begun.

to do so later in the summer. We could bomb Baku by flying over Turkish or Persian territory, but there is danger of retaliation on the Anglo-Iranian Oil Company's refineries. There is also the question of public opinion in this country to be considered: the extension of the war to Russia without a *very* good cause would arouse much criticism. Personally I feel that if we were going to take these steps we ought to have done so before, while the Soviet Government had their hands full in Finland. But dilatoriness is inseparable from democracy, it appears.

The P.M. is anxious to do something spectacular – on the lines of the Sylt raid – which will help to keep public morale and interest high. The ROYAL MARINE operation would serve that purpose and it *might* make the Germans attack on the Western Front, which would be all to the good.

A report from the Vatican says that German conditions and morale have deteriorated in the last few weeks. In that case Hitler will be forced to show his hand.

The objects of the recent Brenner Meeting between Hitler and Mussolini remain obscure, but they probably related to the Balkans, especially Hungary (in which both the dictators have a lively interest) and Roumania.

The possibility of Cabinet changes is still in the air, and I think Lord Chatfield will almost certainly be dropped. David Margesson also wants to drop "Shakes" Morrison, who is a manifest failure, and appoint Rob Hudson Minister of Food. But apparently the latter is quite incapable of working with Civil Servants.

Talked to Sir John Reith who told me that he had given up smoking, because he regarded it as a "dirty, pernicious and childish habit", and had put on two stone as a result. He gives the impression of being a forceful personality.

Dined with Arthur Rucker at the Travellers and listened to an interesting exposition by him of the Fourth Dimension and the meaning of Time. My brain reels beneath such problems.

After dinner Charles Peake, who was in the Club, showed us an alarming communiqué to the effect that the French had "leaked" about the project of laying a minefield in Norwegian waters and stopping the iron-ore trade. Subsequently I saw a Secret Service report of a telephone conversation between M. Reynaud (who arrived in London this evening) and Paris. M. Reynaud was genuinely horrified, but it is clear that in France the most extraordinary things can be done, for internal political reasons, behind the back of the Government.

Thursday, March 28th

The Supreme War Council met at No. 10.

The Norwegian waters and ROYAL MARINE projects were agreed upon and are to take effect next week.

The Baku bombing scheme is to be carefully examined by the two staffs. If the Low Countries are invaded the Allies will march into Belgium without awaiting an invitation to do so.

Means of tightening the blockade are to be examined.

Cabinet reconstruction has now reached its final stage. Chatfield is to be dropped and to go to New Zealand as Governor General (if he will accept it). Sam Hoare is to go to the Air Ministry and Kingsley Wood to be Lord Privy Seal. Kingsley Wood is tired and is also a little out of his depth in the Air Ministry; Hoare is very much disliked by the H. of C., and David Margesson, Arthur (and I think Horace Wilson) would like to be rid of him altogether; but the P.M. refuses and so he is destined for the Air Ministry, where at least he will have to face open criticism and will be less easily able to intrigue. Rob Hudson is to go to the Ministry of Food, the discredited Morrison to the Board of Education and Lord De La Warr* to the Post Office. Hoare's appointment will be ill received.

4

Scandinavian Adventure

April 1940

Monday, April 1st
The French are making difficulties about the ROYAL MARINE operation and wish to postpone it, possibly because Daladier, who is now Minister for War, does not want Reynaud to get the credit, or possibly because the French fear instant retaliation which they are not in a position to withstand.

Tuesday, April 2nd
Whole Ministerial scheme changed again: Sam Hoare to Air, Kingsley Wood Lord Privy Seal, Morrison Post Office, Ramsbotham[1] (who is an educationist) Board of Education, Woolton* Food, Hudson Shipping, De La Warr Office of Works, Geoffrey Shakespeare[2] Department of Overseas Trade.

Thursday, April 4th
The Cabinet changes have met with a mixed reception in the country, being considered insufficiently drastic in some quarters. Sam Hoare is very much "in with" Beaverbrook and so his appointment was hailed with delight in the cheap press, but *The Times* was very disagreeable.

The chief centre of interest is the attempt to make the French revoke their refusal to let the R.M. operation take effect. The P.M. has written personally to Daladier and Winston is going over to Paris to do a little personal persuasion. We are trying to blackmail the French by maintaining that we may not undertake

---

[1] Created Lord Soulbury in 1941 and made a Viscount in 1954, after being the first Governor General of independent Ceylon.
[2] National Liberal M.P. Later Parliamentary Under-Secretary, Dominions Office.

the Norwegian territorial waters project unless we can combine it with the other.

Dined at the Travellers where I found Charles Ritchie, who was very good company and most amusing about Canadians. He says that all those who come to the top are sons of the Manse – from Mackenzie King to Beaverbrook. Perhaps that is why Lord Tweedsmuir[1] felt so much at home in Canada. Charles Ritchie is Private Secretary to the Canadian High Commissioner and is greatly exercised because he has to write a speech to the Youth of the Empire, and Lord Halifax, in his recent speech at Oxford, has stolen all the thunder.

On returning to No. 10 I had a talk with the Chancellor of the Exchequer, who is disgusted because the Ministry of Information have been trying to popularise themselves and persuaded Lord Stamp (who, says Simon, is not competent to talk about financial policy) to give a talk to journalists. As a result the Government have been declared by the press to be in favour of the Keynes Plan (which suggests forced loans, not bearing interest, and a capital levy at the end of the war to repay them). Simon was furious and became eloquent on the subject of Sir John Reith whom he described as "a self-advertising ass" who should never have been made Minister of Information. He told me he thought Lord Woolton a good choice as Minister of Food and that Lennox-Boyd[2] would do the Ministry of Food work well in the Commons as he knew the subject really well. He thought Sam Hoare would be good at the Air Ministry, as he is an excellent administrator, but the appointment had not been well received in the Conservative Party.

Friday, April 5th

Winston went over to Paris to try and convert Daladier to the ROYAL MARINE operation and then telephoned in the middle of the Cabinet to say that he had been converted by Daladier! This much amused the P.M. who said it was like the story of the pious parrot which was bought to teach good language to the parrot which swore, but ended by itself learning to swear. So now we shall proceed to lay a minefield in Norwegian waters but shall postpone

---

[1] John Buchan (1875–1940), author of *The Thirty-Nine Steps*. Governor General of Canada, 1935–40.

[2] After a gallant war record in the navy, held many responsible ministerial offices, ending as Secretary of State for the Colonies under Churchill, Eden and Macmillan. Loved and respected inside and outside Parliament, he was created Viscount Boyd of Merton in 1960. He was run over and killed in the King's Road in 1983.

the R.M. operation until the French have had time to remove their vulnerable aeroplane factories, etc., from places where they would be in danger from German retaliation.

Lunched with Arthur Rucker at the Athenaeum. Arthur says, with justice, that it is to the P.M. we owe our excellent case in the present war: if it had not been for Munich and the policy of appeasement our case would have lost half its strength, our desperate anxiety to maintain peace might have been questioned and, of course, we should in 1938 have been in a hopeless position of inferiority as regards armaments.

A young man called Anthony Gibbs (son of the writer Sir Philip Gibbs) came to see me and tell me of his discussions in Holland with the German General Wenninger about possible peace terms. The General said that the Nazi Party felt themselves hemmed in and would welcome a face-saving peace. He suggested terms including the reconstitution of Poland with the 1914 boundary (i.e. minus the corridor but with rights at Gdynia) and Czechoslovakia as at Munich. I took these terms to the Foreign Office where there have been other similar schemes put forward by people of this sort – all of whom claim that Goering is a moderate and would favour such proposals. The F.O. rightly regarded Goering with the deepest suspicion.

Saturday, April 6th
The laying of the minefield in Norwegian waters is timed for dawn on Monday. It may arouse some criticism, particularly as it will not now be accompanied by the spectacular ROYAL MARINE operation. A sharply worded note was sent yesterday, as a prelude, to the Norwegian and Swedish Governments, intended to justify the technically illegal action which we now propose to take. The Swedes have reacted violently, have asked what reason we have for the accusations we make against them, have talked about our previously friendly relations and have even said that we have brought the two countries near to war.

Rab Butler told me the F.O. were not very much in favour of this action and were definitely opposed to any project against Lulea (by laying mines from the air) on the ground that we had recently signed an agreement with Sweden allowing her to export a certain quantity of ore to Germany: we cannot thus violate a treaty we have signed. Rab said that this Norwegian project had gone through because the "Winston" policy of H.M.G. had gained a triumph over the "Halifax" policy. Halifax had only agreed to next Monday's move because of his loyalty to the P.M.

The P.M. for his part is not over-enthusiastic, but feels that after the expectations aroused by the meeting of the Supreme War Council the other day some effective action must be taken. He does not believe (like some people) in "action for action's sake", but he recognises the importance of the psychological factor in the present war and the necessity of throwing occasional sops to public opinion. The question is will it be only a sop? May not the Germans be stung to retaliate forcibly? Rab thinks not, on the ground that the German mind works like clockwork: they are now preparing to destroy our air force and shipping by concentrated attacks, and this activity on our part may, by destroying the clockwork precision of their plans, throw them into some confusion.

As regards Sweden, Rab thinks the key to their attitude is a determination to avoid fire and the sword at all costs. They would rather sell their souls and their country to the Nazis (provided the sale were effected without bloodshed) than stand up boldly for their beliefs and their independence. They would invite Germany to occupy their country peaceably rather than risk an armed invasion.

From Denmark comes a rumour that the Germans are proposing to invade Norway on Monday and to land troops at Narvik. It is also reported that German naval forces are moving northwards.

From the U.S. come reports of a conversation between Lothian, Roosevelt and Sumner Welles. Roosevelt is in favour of an Allied declaration to the heads of neutral states announcing that it is not the Allies' policy to partition Germany or destroy her sovereignty. Lothian thinks the difficulty would be that such a declaration would be taken as heralding a peace plan and might encourage the Germans to put up their terms (if they have any) by way of bargaining.

Lunched at the Travellers with Robert Cecil,[1] who gave me very secret figures intended to show that the Ministry of Supply is being mismanaged and our ammunition output utterly neglected.

Monday, April 8th
Arthur has 'flu, and so Tony Bevir and I are alone, in the very centre of the vortex.

At dawn British destroyers laid minefields in Norwegian waters. On the way back one of them, the *Glow-worm*, stopped to pick up a man who had fallen overboard and was intercepted by the Germans. At the time of writing no more signals are being received

---

[1] Intelligent and well-informed member of the Diplomatic Service, expert on German affairs. Director General of British Information Services, New York, 1959–61.

from her and she is thought to have gone down. Throughout the morning came rumours of an impending naval action and our ships were searching for a German force containing the *Gneisenau*. Then after lunch the Chancellor looked in and (with his liking for the sensational) told Tony and me that the Germans were "going into" South Sweden. We immediately set the wires buzzing, but the Chancellor's statement soon resolved itself into a Norwegian report that German ships were steaming across the Belt in the direction of Sweden. As a matter of fact such a possibility is not unexpected and we have an expedition to Narvik waiting to embark immediately information of a German move is received. Hence the tension.

Tuesday, April 9th
Woken early by a message to say that the Cabinet was meeting at 8.30. Got up in a hurry and rushed round to Downing Street to hear that Norway and Denmark had been invaded by the Germans. Meanwhile most of our fleet is busy chasing German ships towards the North Pole.

The morning was hectic (Tony and I were alone). Messages came to and from the Cabinet, which met again at 12.00, giving reports about the latest German moves or sending instructions for appropriate action on our part. The room was full of people, Sir John Reith, the Chief Whip, Alec Cadogan and various officials, and the question everyone was asking was why did our fleet allow the Germans to establish themselves at Bergen and Trondhjem. It seems that our ships were drawn off northwards by a well-executed feint, but certainly the result is unpleasant and I am not clear where the troops we are now despatching will be expected to land (unconfirmed reports say the Germans have taken Narvik too). However it is cheerful to remember that the last episode in which the British navy was drawn off by a feint ended in Trafalgar!

During the Cabinet "Pug" Ismay came out and said that as far as he could see the Cabinet were proposing to do the only thing that could lose us the war: namely *not* to take vigorous action. The measures at present envisaged are the sending of small naval units to clean up Bergen and other ports while the main fleet is chasing the *Scharnhorst* and *Gneisenau* northwards; the despatch of soldiers to occupy or recapture Narvik, Trondhjem, Bergen and, most important of all, Stavanger, which is the best Norwegian air-base; to take up once again with the French the R.M. operation and try to persuade them to agree to it; and to make fresh approaches to Holland and Belgium. Meanwhile it is not forgotten that this whole affair *may* be meant to occupy our attention while an attack is made on this country.

Lunch-time was spent drafting, with Rab Butler, Horace Wilson, Gladwyn Jebb[1] and Collier[2] (from the F.O.) the statement on the situation which the P.M. is to make in the House this afternoon. Generally speaking there seems to be a great deal of uncertainty as to what is happening, and my own impression is that the Germans have got a long start of us both in time (which is hard to explain as we knew that some violent reaction to our mining operations must be expected) and in decision. From our point of view the whole thing seems, as the Chief Whip said, to be "rather a fog". But, of course, if we can secure a naval victory the balance will be redressed in our favour. Bad visibility and a heavy sea have made things very difficult.

After the P.M. had made a statement in the House the Supreme War Council met, at 4.15, Reynaud, Daladier and Admiral Darlan having flown over from Paris. They decided to approach the Belgian Government with a view to the allied armies entering Belgium in order to man their lines: an attack on Holland and/or Belgium is expected in the course of the next few days and the French are anxious to forestall the Germans for once.

The situation is becoming clearer. The Germans have scored a considerable success by seizing the Norwegian ports despite our command of the sea, and we, who started the whole business, seem to have lost the initiative. Nevertheless the German hold on the northern ports must be precarious, we may be able to dislodge them without much difficulty and the operation may give us a chance of putting into action the original project for denying the Gallivare iron-ore fields to Germany. The First Lord (who at last sees a chance of action) is jubilant and maintains that our failure to destroy the German fleet up to the present is only due to the bad visibility and very rough weather in the North Sea, while if the German ships fly for home they will leave their garrisons exposed to our expeditionary forces. Horace Wilson is rather perturbed because he feels that now the Germans have got Denmark (and incidentally incarcerated our Legation), they will find it no difficult task to establish an overland line of communication with Bergen

[1] Private Secretary to Sir Alexander Cadogan and then adviser to Dr Dalton at the Ministry of Economic Warfare. Worked under Sir William Strang on plans for post-war Europe. Later British representative at the United Nations and Ambassador to France, 1954–60. Created Lord Gladwyn in 1960.

[2] Sir Laurence Collier. Head of the Foreign Office Northern Department. Subsequently Ambassador to Norway. Son of the Royal Academician John Collier.

and Trondhjem. Arthur Rucker is convinced that if this affair goes seriously wrong the Government will fall or be re-formed.

I dined with David. We listened to the news which was derived almost entirely from German sources: scarcely a word from our own. This is, I think, shocking and I know from his remarks this morning that Sir John Reith feels bitterly on the subject – but nobody will supply him with the necessary material.

When I got back to No. 10 the Chancellor confirmed the rumours I had heard from David that the Germans seized Narvik by a Trojan Horse manoeuvre: they congregated a lot of iron-ore ships in the harbour with soldiers disguised as seamen and hidden in the holds. "Very clever," said the Chancellor, "and we were ninnies, we were ninnies!"

About 10.00 news came through that our Wellingtons had returned safely from Bergen where they had scored a substantial hit on one German cruiser. I told the P.M. who seemed considerably cheered and said, "That is better than some of the news we have heard lately."

Wednesday, April 10th
Talked to the P.M. just before he set out on his morning walk.[1] He seemed rather depressed by the situation and admitted that the Germans had reason to be elated by their success. "The lesson to be drawn from it all is," he said, "not that the Allies are cowardly and slow-witted, but that it is impossible to help neutrals who will not help themselves. If the Norwegians and Swedes had agreed to our plans to help the Finns, we should now have been in possession of the Norwegian ports."

David Margesson says that the P.M. never expected the war to flare up as it now has.

News from the Air Ministry is not encouraging and the Admiralty are not cheered by the reports which have so far reached them. However the German air-attack on the fleet failed, though the *Rodney* was hit; and one of our submarines torpedoed a German cruiser last night. So far our naval expedition outside Narvik has failed to achieve anything. Apparently "things" are still happening in the North Sea.

The Supreme War Council conclusions show that we are to concentrate on occupying Narvik once the seas have been cleared. The ROYAL MARINE operation will be put into effect if the Germans attack on the Western Front or if Belgium is invaded.

[1] He and Mrs Chamberlain used to walk round the lake in St James's Park every morning acknowledging the greetings of passers-by as they went. Nobody was worried about security.

After lunch reassuring news came about our expedition to Narvik: far from failing to achieve anything we succeeded in doing a great deal of material damage, though we lost two destroyers in the process. The P.M. decided to make a statement to this effect in the House, and I went over to the Admiralty to get the details. I waited in the Private Secretaries' squalid little room while the First Lord toyed with a draft, and was shown a number of interesting telegrams from the fleet. Apparently there are still two large German squadrons at sea. Tonight aircraft from the *Furious* will make another attack, with aerial torpedos, on Bergen. I finally rushed the material for the statement back to No. 10, whence it was transmitted to the House with about two minutes to spare and read by the P.M. to an elated House.

Thursday, April 11th

Warm and summery weather at last.

A French mission arrived early at Downing Street to see the P.M. and Halifax. It is on its way to Stockholm to try to persuade the Swedes to come into the war, and is headed by M. Coulondre.

The press are full of extravagant and untrue stories about the recapture of Bergen and Trondhjem.

The Cabinet have indications that an attack on the Western Front is now imminent. It seems likely, therefore, that the Norwegian affair is really a diversion, especially as the generals commanding the German armies are insignificant men and the armies themselves are small. It is difficult to see why Hitler should be prepared to sacrifice his fleet for the sake of a diversion, because he certainly does seem to be sacrificing a large part of it. Possibly he thinks it is worth losing the navy in order to seize places, such as Stavanger, from which intensive aerial attacks can be made on this country. Meanwhile we are concentrating all our available troops for the seizure of Narvik and, if possible, the subsequent denial of the Gallivare ore mines to Germany.

In the afternoon I heard Winston make a speech in the House about the naval situation. He was witty, but less polished than usual. He caused much amusement by saying that Denmark had had most to fear from Germany of all the neutrals, because she had been the most recent to negotiate a non-aggression pact with her. He wisely damped down the absurd over-optimism of this morning's newspapers, but made a good case for the navy's achievements during the last three days.

The general atmosphere is one of nervous expectation. Where will the blow fall? Will it be Holland and Belgium, or the Maginot Line, or a great air attack on this country – or all together? The

Belgians have rejected the Anglo-French approach for an immediate entry into Belgium, but they may think better of it if we agree to move straight up to the Albert Canal–Meuse Line instead of merely halfway across the country to the Antwerp–Namur Line.

Mother and I dined with Grandfather and Peggy at Argyll House.[1] Grandfather is getting to look rapidly older but retains a great deal of his unrivalled charm. Peggy, with whom I gossiped for hours on a sofa, is at her best and most natural in conditions such as this. She often shows herself impractical, but is invariably witty in her conversation and shrewd in her judgments. It is amusing to hear both Grandfather and Peggy, who have always lived sumptuously and in state, expressing the most liberal and democratic theories. Peggy is sometimes quite revolutionary in her sentiments – but very aristocratic in her tastes.

Friday, April 12th
P. J. Grigg,* the Permanent Secretary to the War Office, came in and told us that many people in the War Office are pressing for us to concentrate on retaking Trondhjem instead of Narvik (the Norwegian Government is also asking us to do this). Grigg says that Ironside ("Tiny") and Stanley are not adopting a sensible attitude and he remarked to Arthur: "We must get the P.M. to take a hand in this before Winston and Tiny go and bugger up the whole war."

Then the Chancellor arrived and stayed most of the night. He wanted to talk to the P.M. about the Budget and the particular difficulties connected with the proposed Register of Wealth which is to help the Government assess war profits for subsequent taxation. The Governor of the Bank thinks that such a measure will cause general uneasiness: it will be thought to be the precursor to a Capital Levy – at any rate under a politically more advanced Government – and will discourage people from contributing to Government Loans. The Chancellor said his Budget was perfectly horrifying and he could only trust that the attack on the Western Front would coincide with Budget Day!

Then the Chancellor saw Tony's Homer, picked it up and insisted on reading to Arthur and me long passages from the *Iliad* about Priam begging Achilles for Hector's body. He went on interminably about the beauty of the passage, but I could not help being impressed by his erudition (which, of course, was what he intended). He is always quoting learnedly from the Classics.

---

[1] In the King's Road. The Crewes had moved there shortly before the war after selling Crewe House in Curzon Street to Messrs Thomas Tilling.

P. J. Grigg came back and the conversation turned to India. Simon was quite amusing in describing what he called "the masculine and simple view" adopted by Winston in the Cabinet. Winston rejoiced in the quarrel which had broken out afresh between Hindus and Moslems, said he hoped it would remain bitter and bloody and was glad that we had made the suggestion of Dominion status which was acting as a cat among the pigeons. Both Simon and Grigg agreed that this was not the moment to give anything away in India: we must remain firm as a rock, because British rule was today essential to India.

Monday, April 15th
Although I was busy all day with Ecclesiastical and other matters, there was very little happening. We are all waiting for a number of prospective operations in Norway, which go by such deceptive names as MAURICE, HENRY, PRIMROSE and ALPHONSE, to mature, and the centre of interest has shifted from Narvik to Trondhjem which, in order to keep up the spirits of the Norwegians, we are to make a rapid and determined effort to recapture. The destruction of half the German fleet has greatly improved the morale and recaptured the interest of the general public and, it appears, has had a correspondingly depressing effect in Germany. It is therefore to be presumed that another German coup is expected, and the general uneasiness about Italy, and in particular her designs on Dalmatia and Corfu, make it seem possible that some Italo-German coup is hatching in the Balkans. Mussolini's prestige is so great that he could probably carry an unwilling people into war or some perilous adventure if he so chose, though it would undoubtedly be his destruction in the end. Holland still languishes under the threat of invasion and sinister movements on the German side of the frontier.

Tuesday, April 16th
Little news of our fortunes in Norway, but there is still some reason for disquiet at Mussolini's sudden hatred for the Allies and all their works. He seems to be doing his best to work on Italian feeling and there is a fluttering in the Balkan dovecots.

In the evening the Chancellor came in, seized me by the shoulders and said: "Since we are quite alone I want to discuss a Classical matter with you: Aeneas was not the son of Priam but of Anchises." This was because the other night when he read to Arthur and me about Priam's plea for the body of Hector, the last of his numerous children, I, wishing to show an intelligent interest, interjected, "What about Aeneas?" "Oh," said the Chancellor,

"Priam was being effective, which is not necessarily the same as telling the truth." That he should remember and correct himself and me on such a small point shows what an amazing grasp of detail his remarkable brain possesses.

Hardly had I gone to sleep at No. 10 when I was informed that the P.M. wanted to see me. He was rather taken aback at seeing me in my dressing-gown, but told me that as a result of a conversation with the First Lord he wanted a meeting of the Military Co-ordination Committee summoned at 10 a.m. in the morning. I gather that our forces at Narvik, under Lord Cork,[1] are rather loth to make an attack because of the snow, but Winston feels that a long delay would be disastrous both for military and psychological reasons. There are signs that the Norwegians will lose heart if they are not quickly assured of substantial support.

Wednesday, April 17th

Plans for an attack by the Guards, Chasseurs Alpins, etc., on Trondhjem are being matured (Operation MAURICE). They will land after the enemy guns have been silenced by battleships and will be supported by a move southwards from Namsos by General Carton de Wiart[2] (Force HENRY). Lord Hankey hinted to me that he was a little worried by Winston's determination to direct the war: he remembers, he says, the operations at the Dardanelles all too clearly. He is going to warn the P.M. Ronald Harris,[3] who is Secretary to Sir E. Bridges, says that Winston has been presiding over innumerable committees, talking a lot and getting nothing done, but that now the P.M. has begun to preside over the Military Co-ordination Committee things are beginning to move, more practical plans are being made and there is a definite sign that the difficulties and opportunities of the situation are being handled in a realistic manner.

Went to the House for questions and met Major Astor,[4] who was

---

[1] Admiral of the Fleet the Earl of Cork and Orrery. Commanded H.M.S. *Repulse* in the First World War and the Home Fleet in the 1930s. Appointed to command the Norwegian expedition in 1940. Known in the navy as "Ginger Pop" on account of his red hair and occasionally explosive reactions; but highly esteemed by all ranks.

[2] Legendary hero of several wars who helped the Poles defeat the Red Army in 1920 and survived many severe wounds.

[3] Later held high rank in the Treasury and was eventually First Church Estates Commissioner.

[4] Afterwards 1st Lord Astor of Hever. Bought *The Times* in 1922 from the estate of Lord Northcliffe, but refrained from interfering with editorial control. M.P. for Dover, 1922–45. Not on good terms with his sister-in-law, Nancy Astor, nor by any means always with Winston Churchill.

waiting to be harangued by the P.M. about the unhelpful carping attitude which *The Times* has been adopting recently.

Thursday, April 18th

Went to the House where I met Sir J. Wardlaw Milne[1] who says that the public are beginning to believe, through constant repetition, the extravagant German communiqués which claim that the Germans have sunk half our fleet. He felt some authoritative dementi was required, but the P.M., to whom I mentioned this on the way back, disagreed on the grounds that there will always be people anxious to believe the worst but who do not represent the real feeling of the country.

Dined with Gordon Etherington-Smith[2] who, after varied and exciting adventures, has just returned from the Legation at Copenhagen. He described how the staff burned the last confidential paper as the Germans arrived at the Legation, how the Germans told him that he was a filthy Englishman and that if he wasn't careful he would be shot, and how, finally, after being paraded through the streets in drays, the staff were released by the Germans and treated very courteously.

Monday, April 22nd

The P.M. left for France to attend a meeting of the Supreme War Council. We have landed two forces successfully in Norway, one north of Trondhjem and one south, but partly owing to dangerously truthful prognostications in the press we have abandoned the difficult project of a landing from the sea under the guns of the navy and have adopted a pincer scheme instead. Strong forces will attack Trondhjem from Namsos in the north (if General Carton de Wiart can overcome transport and other difficulties which are increased by heavy German bombing) and from Aandalsnes in the south, where the railway is to be seized. Simultaneously a feint landing will be made and H.M. ships will bombard the town, which will thus be invested and not spectacularly stormed.

Dined with Herschel Johnson[3] (Minister at the American Embassy) at White's. He told me of his admiration for Lord Halifax whose mind, he felt, was always open to conviction and

---

[1] Senior backbench Conservative M.P. who later ran an unsuccessful campaign against Churchill's handling of the war.

[2] A former colleague in the Eastern Department of the Foreign Office.

[3] A friendly, hard-working and Anglophile member of the American Foreign Service who tried unavailingly to keep Joseph Kennedy on the right track, but was highly esteemed by Kennedy's successor, Gil Winant. American Ambassador in Stockholm at the end of the war.

who would never be afraid of yielding a point, if he believed he had been wrong, except on a question of basic principle. Afterwards we talked of Anglo-American relations and deplored the ignorance and misunderstanding on both sides and especially the increasing bitterness in England against America's attitude of critical and ineffective sympathy in the present war. He emphasised the real anxiety of the administration to be helpful.

Herschel Johnson spoke of the feeling in America that England was decadent and its ruling class effete. He himself realised that, whatever their external appearance, there was no tougher race than the English.

Tuesday, April 23rd

Represented the P.M. at a Memorial Service for H. A. L. Fisher (who was run over by a bus) at St Margaret's, Westminster. The Bishop of Winchester (Garbett)[1] gave a moving address and the Archbishop of Canterbury read, in his musical voice, the beautiful lesson from the Book of Wisdom. Immediately behind me sat Lloyd George: he paid little attention to the service, but when we reached the last hymn his Welsh blood got the better of his indifference and he shouted "For All the Saints who from their Labours Rest" in a high-pitched tenor which reached above the voices of the congregation.

Went to the luncheon of the St George's Society at Grosvenor House to celebrate St George's Day. Sat next to Audrey Paget and an attractive girl called Elspeth Ogylvie. Duff Cooper* spoke, in the place of Winston, and his eloquence was remarkable. He praised the absent First Lord (unduly, I thought – but then Winston is trying to get him back into the Government) and spoke of Germany with blood-curdling hatred. He castigated those who blamed the Nazis and whitewashed the Germans, maintaining that the German people as a whole were responsible for their repeated crimes. I thought of Burke's wiser statement: "I know no means of indicting a whole nation." After Duff Cooper the Canadian and Australian High Commissioners spoke.

Budget Day: it was less fearful than the Chancellor had led me to believe.

The P.M. returned from France and they all seemed rather elated. Here, on the other hand, gloom reigns (H.J.W. and the Chancellor) because of the difficulties which General Phillips'

---

[1] A deeply spiritual cleric who was Bishop of Winchester for ten years and from 1942 Archbishop of York. Brendan Bracken thought him a saint and tried hard to persuade Churchill to promote him to Canterbury when Archbishop Temple died.

brigade are meeting at Namsos. It appears that the snow is deep, that the men are obliged to keep to the roads and have no snow-shoes, that enemy aircraft attacks are bad and can be met with no adequate defence, that the Chasseurs Alpins (who are equipped for this sort of fighting) are remaining at the base and doing nothing.

Dined with Sidney Cuthbert at the Travellers. He is anxious to go to Norway because he says he would prefer to die, if die he must, in beautiful scenery!

Returned to No. 10 to sleep. The Military Co-ordination Committee met and discussed the situation. Edward Bridges said afterwards that Winston was being maddening, declaring that we had failed at Namsos, and making the most unreasonable proposals. As for Oliver Stanley, Bridges said that he hadn't an "ounce of guts".

The P.M. is depressed – more by Winston's rampages than by the inherent strategical difficulties with which we are confronted in Norway.

I gather that the Supreme War Council have decided to go all out for Trondhjem and Narvik (bearing in mind that stoppage of the iron-ore supplies is the main objective), to enter Belgium without an invitation if Holland is invaded (and incidentally to bomb the Ruhr), to pursue investigations about the bombing of Baku, and to take measures (such as naval movements in the Mediterranean, when ships can be spared, and military moves in North Africa) to prevent Mussolini doing anything rash and bellicose – a possibility which is now decreasing in likelihood.

Wednesday, April 24th

A large map of Scandinavia, studded with coloured pins, now stands in our room and groups of people cluster round it all the morning discussing the prospects of our adventure. General Ismay points out that we have only a small stake near Trondhjem and that it does not much matter if we lose it – a cold-blooded military way of looking at things. Actually I think the psychological cost would be considerable. Rob Hudson, Minister of Shipping, is chiefly interested in not losing the person of King Haakon, because while he is secured to us we can make use of 3,000,000 tons of Norwegian shipping.

I have an uneasy feeling that all is not being as competently handled as it might be. The failure to send snow-shoes for our men at Namsos (while the Germans have them) is unpleasantly reminiscent of the Crimean War. Moreover I do not put great faith in the judgment of the Chiefs of Staff or of our military pundits. There is not that appearance of thought-out, clockwork efficiency which I should like to see; but it may just be that the English way of doing things is superficially slipshod and unimpressive. Of one thing I am convinced: we make up our minds lamentably slowly and we do not insure against every eventuality like the Germans do. Time and again we have "missed the boat" (e.g. Finland, Norway) owing to excessive deliberation and fear of unnecessary extravagance.

Went back to Downing Street in time to greet the First Lord and take him into the P.M. The latter has been much less forbidding of late and has even taken to calling me Jock. His incredible capacity for hard work, and his apparent immunity from fatigue continue and seem even to increase as the problems become more difficult and the days heavier with work. His seventy-one years lie very easily upon his shoulders. I gather that his talk with Winston did not go too well: he is proving a difficult colleague.

Italy is moving still further from war. Mussolini is reported to have said, "Germany is trying to drag me into the war by the hair, but luckily I am bald." If Italy did come in, the Allies would probably send an expeditionary force to Salonica, provided Greece were complaisant.

Thursday, April 25th
The trouble about Winston, which has been brewing for the last few days, arises from his demand to be appointed Chairman of the Chiefs of Staff Committee. This would not only annoy the other service ministers but would also probably cause chaos among the Chiefs of Staff and planning experts because, as was shown when Winston presided over the Military Co-ordination Committee, his verbosity and restlessness make a great deal of unnecessary work, prevent any real practical planning from being done and generally cause friction. But if the P.M. refuses to acquiesce, Winston threatens to go down to the House and say he can take no responsibility for what is happening. To let this happen in wartime would be unthinkable: there would then be a first-class political crisis, because the country believes that Winston is the man of action who is winning the war and little realise how ineffective, and indeed harmful, much of his energy is proving itself to be. On the other hand if the P.M. gives in, Winston will have won his point by blackmail and he is likely to pursue the same tactics in order to get his way in future. Winston, for his part, professes absolute loyalty to the P.M. (and indeed they get on admirably), but complains that the Chiefs of Staff and the "Joint Planners" are making a hopeless muddle. A possible solution is to make Winston Minister for

Co-ordination of Defence and make somebody else (Alec suggests David Margesson) First Lord; but unfortunately Lord Chatfield was asked to resign only the other day on the grounds that the office is now superfluous.

Drove down to the House with the P.M. who is in an agreeable frame of mind, but obviously depressed and at a loss how to solve the Winston impasse. Stanley Baldwin lunched with him and he probably drew on his experience in dealing with such awkward problems.

At this point I should perhaps say something of Winston Churchill's views on Stanley Baldwin. At a later stage of the war, he showed him considerable magnanimity. However, he certainly believed that Baldwin, more than Chamberlain, was culpable of a neglect and an idleness which contributed much to the outbreak of the "most unnecessary war in history". I think, too, that there was a certain personal animosity based on the curious fact that Stanley Baldwin had once out-manoeuvred Churchill without the latter realising it until after the event. Few people ever did get the better of Winston Churchill and the case which I describe now is the only one which I ever heard him admit. It appears that after the famous Westminster Election, which Churchill just failed to win in 1923, Baldwin saw in him a menace to his own leadership and to the serene unanimity of the Conservative Party. He therefore skilfully offered him, in his 1924 Government, the great prize of the Chancellorship of the Exchequer. Churchill afterwards believed that Baldwin did this for two reasons: first because he knew that he would serve the Government loyally and that, being in one of its highest posts, there would be no likelihood of his giving trouble; and secondly because he did not think Winston would be a success at the Treasury and his political future would therefore be jeopardised. I do not know whether these were in fact Baldwin's motives, but Churchill believed them to have been so. It appears that during his Chancellorship of the Exchequer, lasting four years, he was only once asked inside 10 Downing Street other than on an official occasion, and he thought, probably rightly, that Baldwin had a personal antipathy to him.

In the evening I took down the record of a meeting of Ministers over which the P.M. presided. Nearly all the Ministers not in the War Cabinet were present and the P.M. gave them an account of the events of the previous week. He described the meeting of the Supreme War Council which had been entirely cordial, despite his anticipation of a quarrel with the French. The French Government had given way over the question of the control of French troops in Norway and had agreed to let us bomb the Ruhr and German military objectives in the event of an invasion of the Low Countries. The latter concession was unexpected in view of the French fears of retaliation on their aircraft factories, a consideration which had led them to veto the ROYAL MARINE operation.

The P.M. said that he had liked M. Reynaud on this occasion: he was a man who definitely improved on acquaintance. Turning to Norway, the P.M. painted a very black picture and said that we might well have to evacuate all our forces in the Trondhjem area. He told how the French anti-aircraft cruiser, which had been sent to cover the landing of the Chasseurs Alpins at Namsos, had been inexplicably withdrawn and the Germans had thus been enabled to bomb the French successfully and destroy their supplies. (This action of the French Admiral was not brought up at the Supreme War Council, a restraint which the French much appreciated.)

As faces round the table grew longer and longer (because even Ministers have been partially misled by the extravagant optimism of the press), the P.M. described the landing of German troops *by sea* at Trondhjem and the cutting off of Carton de Wiart's men. He told of the difficulties which snow and ice presented to Lord Cork at Narvik, of the exhaustion and the unhelpful attitude of the Norwegians (who could not even blow up a railway line) and the appalling problems caused by lack of air-bases and aircraft. The P.M. discounted the probability of Italy coming into the war, on the grounds that the army and air force were not ready, the people and the Pope wanted peace, and the country's resources were inadequate. He believed that at the Brenner meeting Mussolini had agreed to create a diversion while Hitler undertook his rapid and bloodless conquest of Scandinavia. Finally Mr C. spoke of the transports for German troops which were reported to be concentrated at German Baltic ports: he did not believe this portended an attack on Sweden (at any rate until the ice round Lulea melted) but thought the Germans might intend to seize the Aaland Islands.

The P.M. took the meeting admirably. He sat back in his chair, spoke slowly and rather colloquially, showed a certain sense of humour (which I had always doubted his possessing) and obviously commanded the undivided attention of all present. For my part I wrote more hectically than I had ever done since the days of lectures at Cambridge.

Friday, April 26th
The Military Co-ordination Committee (presided over by the P.M. and attended by the Service Ministers and Chiefs of Staff) decided

to evacuate our troops from Southern Norway, on the grounds that even if we captured Trondhjem we could not expect to hold it. We shall concentrate on Narvik, in order to be near the Swedish frontier and the iron-ore fields in the event of a German attack on Sweden. The Cabinet agreed, and the withdrawal will be effected slowly and be combined with a concentrated attack on Narvik. I fear the psychological effect will be deplorable: inside Germany Hitler will gain a much-needed triumph; and the effect on Italy may be dangerous. P. J. Grigg goes so far as to say it is a wrong decision and hints that it is a political manoeuvre of Winston, who sees that the P.M. will be discredited and his own position strengthened. Could he be quite so black?

One consideration which influenced the decision was the fact that our operations in Central Norway would involve a greater strain on our own resources than on those of the enemy, whose communications are so much easier.

The Winston problem is still much to the fore. The proposed solution, if W. accepts it, is that he should have a secretariat of his own, headed by General Ismay, who will be a member of the Chiefs of Staff Committee and there represent Winston's views. W. will become a kind of Deputy Prime Minister in matters connected with defence. The P.M. is wisely humouring Winston, whose position in the country is, quite unjustifiably, unassailable.

The French have heard of our proposed withdrawal from Norway and have gone up in smoke. The C.I.G.S. (Ironside, whom P. J. Grigg thinks the worst and most incompetent of men) was to have gone over to Paris today to explain matters, but the French seem to have obtained previous information and Gamelin has arrived this evening to harangue the P.M., Halifax and Winston. Meanwhile the Norwegian Minister in Brussels gloomily prophesies a second Gallipoli in Norway.

There must be something wrong with me: it is all so depressing and the Whitehall world is crowded with dark looks and knitted brows, but I just *cannot* take it tragically or feel nearly as depressed as I ought or, indeed, as I write.

Dined with Cynthia Keppel[1] at Luigi's where the food is delicious but the prices scandalous. We went to a propaganda film called *For England*, which was too long, and then proceeded to the Bierkeller in Leicester Square where, for the first time in the West End, I saw a group of bespectacled intellectuals remain firmly

[1] My second cousin, daughter of Lord Albemarle. In 1944 she married the distinguished historian, Professor Postan, whose first wife had been another well-known historian, Eileen Power.

seated while God Save the King was played. Everybody looked but nobody did anything, which shows that the war has not yet made us lose our sense of proportion or become noisily jingoistic.

Saturday, April 27th
A talk with Rab Butler who agrees that the Chiefs of Staff have an appalling lack of foresight (at least so it appears), that nobody can make a clear-cut decision, that everybody is unnecessarily rattled about Italy and that, in general, the Government and its advisers are not conducting themselves as creditably as could be wished.

The French are reported to have decided that if we withdraw our troops from Norway they will nevertheless keep theirs there. So it was decided to hold a meeting of the Supreme War Council and at 11.30 Ivo Mallet, from the F.O., and I motored down to Heston to meet Reynaud, Daladier, etc. Unfortunately the aeroplane arrived early and we missed them. I drove back with a French staff officer who told me that the French thought, like us, that Narvik and the iron ore was all-important but that for psychological reasons, and especially in order to stiffen the Swedes, we should at least maintain ourselves in Central Norway. The plain truth of the matter is that we have unadvisedly landed an insufficient number of troops without adequate equipment or support from the air, and we have met or are meeting with a serious reverse. Its political importance is greater than its military importance, for unless we can make some counter-stroke at Narvik or elsewhere the effect on public opinion at home and abroad will be serious. From what I can see the Chiefs of Staff are much to blame, also Winston who fusses but does nothing and Oliver Stanley who from all accounts is hopeless. Horace, David and Arthur seem to have got their knife into him, as they had it into Hore-Belisha before, and I suspect therefore that his days at the War Office are numbered. If Norway goes seriously wrong, then I suppose the popular outcry may force a reconstitution of the Government and Winston, to whom as much blame should attach as any other single individual, will ride triumphantly forward on the wave of undeserving national popularity.

One of Hitler's cleverest moves has been to make Winston Public Enemy Number One, because this fact has helped to make him Public Hero Number One at home and in the U.S.A.

The Supreme War Council met in the afternoon just after "that swine Rib", as Halifax calls him, had made a speech condoning German aggression in Norway on the grounds that the Allies were contemplating such action with Norwegian connivance. It was tragic to hear the conversation of the Polish Ambassador and

Norwegian Minister, who waited in our room to be summoned in at the end of the meeting. What, they asked each other, was it all about? Had some interesting news been received from Norway? Obviously they sensed that something was amiss and felt alarmed.

The Supreme War Council apparently reached agreement and decided to evacuate the Trondhjem area by degrees.

Monday, April 29th

At No. 10 gloom still prevails. We have lost most of General Morgan's brigade, Aandalsnes has been bombed to pieces and it is clear that nothing but a miracle can save us from evacuating the country south of Trondhjem. We may be able to hang on at Namsos until we can retire northwards to fortified positions and can reduce the German garrison in Narvik.

Among the P.M.'s visitors during the afternoon was Grandfather, as one of the leaders of the Liberal Opposition. I went and sat on the sofa with him in the hall and talked to him while he waited.

Arthur thinks we ought seriously to consider the possibility of a German invasion of the British Isles, first by air and then by sea, as in Norway: once German air-bases are established in Norway such an apparently fantastic scheme would be more feasible. Hankey has produced a book, written by a German military expert, according to which the Shetlands should be the next step after Norway: meanwhile we are hoping to adapt those unfortunate islands to aerial use.

Slept at No. 10, but was aroused in the early hours by General Dill[1] in connection with a telegram which showed that the Norwegians thought of capitulating unless they could be certain of more substantial help. I refused to awake the P.M. and Dill sent off a reply on his own account.

Tuesday, April 30th

Apart from adverse weather conditions and the lack of aerodromes from which British fighters can be operated, the two main sources of our troubles in Norway seem to be the following:
(i)   Cowardice, ineffectiveness and even treachery of the Norwegians. They fight half-heartedly (shades of the Finns last winter!) and they even refuse to allow their bridges, etc., to be blown up when our demolition squads arrive.
(ii) The lack of training of our troops, most of whom, in the

---

[1] Just back from commanding a Corps in France under Lord Gort to become Vice Chief of the Imperial General Staff.

Trondhjem sector at any rate, are inexperienced territorials or reservists called up on the outbreak of war. The French are averse to our removing regular divisions from France, but the Norwegian situation certainly calls for them – and for adequate supplies of equipment and A.A. protection.

Went with Betty Montagu[1] in the lunch-hour to hear one of the daily concerts at the National Gallery, where the admission is one shilling and various artists give their services free, in aid of charity. There was a large audience and we heard a performance of Mozart's Sonatas in E Flat, C Major and A Major by Eileen Ralph and Thomas Matthews. It was very enjoyable and a good relaxation. There was a buffet in an adjoining room where one could procure excellent sandwiches and coffee.

[1] Lady Elizabeth Montagu, daughter of the 9th Earl of Sandwich. She and her family were kind and hospitable friends with whom I frequently stayed at Hinchingbrooke, near Huntingdon. She was generally known as "Betts".

5

Change of Government and Dunkirk

May 1940

Wednesday, May 1st
Sir Roger Keyes* has written to Winston a letter condemning the pusillanimity of the Naval Staff, and has sent a copy to the P.M. He says that the navy have let down the army, that Trondhjem fjord could and should have been forced and the German positions bombarded by naval guns. He blames Pound* and maintains that the prestige of the Royal Navy is at stake (Charbonnière of the French Embassy tells me the same is true as far as French public opinion is concerned). Keyes ends by asking to be re-employed himself.

I feel it is most important to be rid of Ironside as C.I.G.S. and replace him by Dill. I have less and less confidence in the Chiefs of Staff, especially as far as the War Office is concerned, and Winston's unco-ordinated energy is not reassuring. "If I were the first of May, I should be ashamed of myself," Winston said this evening as he gazed at a sudden blight which had descended on the face of the earth. Personally I think he ought to be ashamed of himself in any case.

Friday, May 3rd
Our troops were safely evacuated from Namsos last night. This morning the press is full of the withdrawal from central Norway which is admitted to be a reverse, and there is a certain amount of criticism, though less than might have been expected. Sir John Reith says that "the situation is in hand, but not entirely restored". Berlin and Rome are jubilant and Sweden, that most lily-livered and defeatist of nations, has the cheek to be extremely critical of our action.

General Dill said this afternoon that militarily the situation was by no means precarious and that he did not think the German army was in really good fighting shape. Their soldiers were young and enthusiastic, but not steady. The only dangers to his mind were (i) the effect on Italy and the neutrals, (ii) the effect on the home-front and the intrigues to put in a more "active" Prime Minister, (iii) the effect on our Allies. He is a man who gives one confidence and who will, I hope, soon succeed Ironside as C.I.G.S.

Lord Portal, who also called at No. 10 this afternoon, told me that his information went to show that Winston himself was being loyal to the P.M., but his satellites (e.g. Duff Cooper, Amery,* etc.) were doing all in their power to create mischief and ill-feeling.

Sir A. Sinclair wrote a letter to the P.M. in the most unmeasured terms protesting against having the wires tapped during his tele-phone calls. Everything goes to show that he is a most untrustwor-thy person who is quite capable of passing on to the press what the P.M. tells him in confidence as an Opposition Leader.[1] In addition he is blinded by prejudiced hatred of the P.M., and gives frequent proof that his feelings are more powerful than his brains. To what depths of futility and even banefulness the Liberal Party has fallen, and what a dearth of brain-power there now is in a party which, in 1906, produced the most intellectually brilliant Cabinet in history.

Sir Victor Mallet, our Minister in Stockholm, has sent home an appalling description of our ineffectiveness and lack of defensive weapons in the Namsos area, which was provided by a man called Binney, of the British Steel Federation. Binney described a con-versation with French officers who said, "The British have planned this campaign on the lines of a punitive expedition against the Zulus, but unhappily we and the British are in the position of the Zulus, armed with bows and arrows against the onslaught of scientific warfare." Both Binney and Mallet sum up their criticisms in the complaint that "we have allowed the situation to develop instead of developing the situation".

There was also a somewhat alarming report from the Conserva-tive Central Office giving the observations of their agents in the provinces on the internal situation. It seems that the war is not popular among the lowest sections of the community, that there is a suspicion it is being fought in the interests of the rich, and that there is much discontent about the rising cost of living. This is but a slight foretaste of what we shall have to face after the war.

---

[1] Totally unjust to Sinclair who was wholly honest and patriotic even if he did detest Neville Chamberlain.

Monday, May 6th

At Downing Street all interest centres on tomorrow's debate on Norway. The P.M. is very depressed about the press attacks on him: he needs a tonic, says David Margesson; but in fact I think he suffers from a curious vanity and self-esteem which were born at Munich and have flourished, in spite of a good many wounds, ever since. David, Alec and Rab Butler think the position is good politically, even though strategically and diplomatically it may be precarious. Obviously the Government will win through tomorrow, but there will be many awkward points raised about Norway, and I am afraid that the confidence of the country may be somewhat shaken. But if we are to win this war we have got to be able to stand reverses and take them philosophically.

Tuesday, May 7th

Rode at Richmond before breakfast under cloudless skies and among trees in full bloom.

After lunch I went to the House for the keenly-awaited debate on the Norwegian contretemps. The P.M. spoke well, though he began unimpressively, and he put his arguments cogently, declining to be rattled by the constant interruptions from the Opposition benches. When he had finished speaking, it was generally agreed that the Government was going "to get away with it". Attlee made a savage attack on the ineptitude of the Government and declared that the confidence of the country would remain unshaken only provided the people were sure of good leadership.

Sinclair, for the Liberals, made an eloquent and venomous speech (though he was badly tripped up by the P.M. and by Winston on two occasions) in which he showed, as usual, a remarkable store of inside information, e.g. he knew all about the failure to send snow-shoes with our troops. He is a good debater, but his arguments, though often original (unlike Attlee's, which are commonplace) suffer from the petty-mindedness which is inherent in him. I was disappointed that L.G. did not rise to his feet. Sinclair made one telling point (at least it told with the Opposition) when he compared the policy of the Government to that of Lord Galway[1] at Almanza in 1707, as described by Macaulay: "He thought it more honourable to fail, according to rules, than to succeed by innovation."

---

[1] Henri de Massue de Ruvigny, 1st Earl of Galway (1648–1720), was a French soldier who settled in England, became a general in the British army, commanded the British forces in Portugal during the War of the Spanish Succession, won a number of battles, but was defeated by the French at Almanza in 1707.

Lord Hankey, who has got to open a similar debate in the Lords, complained to me that he would be addressing most of the members of the Fifth Column!

George Lansbury[1] died.

Reports received of a projected attack on the Western Front tomorrow.

Wednesday, May 8th

The debate took an unexpectedly unfavourable turn last night and as a result the Government is rocking. Sir Roger Keyes came down in full uniform and made a dramatic, if vulgar, oration about Trondhjem (based on Winston's justifiable refusal to re-employ him), Amery* made a slashing attack on the Government, and Oliver Stanley, winding up, was weak and ineffective. He impresses nobody and has obviously got to go.

So this morning everybody is at the nadir of gloom, lower than I have yet seen them. Alec, Rab Butler, David and Arthur are all talking about reconstituting the Government and seriously discussing schemes such as a bargain (to be put by Halifax to Morrison) whereby the Labour Party should be asked to come into the Government in return for the dropping of Sam Hoare, Kingsley Wood, Simon, etc., but on the condition that the P.M. retains the leadership. If, at their Whitsun conference next week, the Labour Party burn their boats and refuse co-operation, then the P.M. might have to resort to a Government of national figures (L.G., etc.).

What disgusts me is that everybody is concentrating their energies on an internal political crisis (*à la française*) instead of taking thought for the morrow about Hitler's next move. We must not be caught napping again; but I have the impression that an invasion of the Low Countries is the only German coup for which we are thoroughly prepared and to counter which we could take vigorous action.

Very soon after the beginning of the debate in the House, it became apparent that the fate of the Government hung in the balance, not that there can be any doubt they will win the division (which the Socialists today decided to force), but because all the attacks on the Government were personal attacks against the P.M. and it is clear that his position in the House is shaken. There were a series of venomous speeches by Herbert Morrison, Stafford Cripps, Lloyd George and Duff Cooper. In reply the Government could produce nobody of any power except Winston, who will wind

[1] Devoutly religious Leader of the Labour Party after 1931. A dedicated pacifist.

up tonight. Sam Hoare was ineffective and, indeed, Conservative backbenchers are more or less demanding his resignation as the price of their allegiance.

Lloyd George made probably the most forceful speech he has made for years: I could see that he held the House spellbound as he flung his arms about and denounced the incapacity of the P.M. and the Government. He said that our promissory notes to Czechoslovakia, Poland, Finland and Norway were so much waste paper and he expressed the hope that Winston would not allow himself to be used as an air-raid shelter beneath whom the Government could hide their blunders. The Opposition shouted themselves hoarse as L.G. became more and more vehement and less and less reasonable. Horace Wilson, who sat with me in the official gallery, said that the hatred written on their faces astonished him: it was the pent-up bitterness and personal animosity of years. Duff Cooper was vitriolic, but his oratory is certainly impressive.

Arthur, Kingsley Wood, George Steward and Alec Dunglass all seemed to think the P.M. would have to resign unless he could get a majority of a hundred votes; so much depends on whether the Conservative waverers can be induced by Amery, Duff Cooper, Spears,* Gunston,[1] Lady Astor, etc., to summon up the courage to go into the Opposition lobby to vote. Personally I feel that if the P.M. is firm he can win through: the pendulum is bound to swing back the other way, and all depends on how much his tough but sensitive personality is wounded by this terrific onslaught and manifest detestation of his enemies.

Horace said that what caused him the greatest anxiety was the encouragement this debate, with all its indiscretions, would give to the enemy and the opportunity they would have for launching a great attack (as is hourly possible in Holland) now that the whole vigour of the country is bent towards internal political strife.

A hurried dinner at Luigi's with Middy[2] (whose backbench friends think that the majority of Conservative waverers wish to give the Government a severe shock but not to overthrow it), Terence[3] and Jean Meade.

I went back to the House to hear Winston, but unfortunately the gallery was full and, despite Rab Butler's effort to smuggle me into a forbidden place, I failed to hear the speech. The Government got a majority of 81 – they had hoped for 100 – and were fairly satisfied. It had been a hard day, with the whole weight of opinion

[1] Long-serving Conservative M.P. who had been Parliamentary Private Secretary before the war to Neville Chamberlain and to Sir Kingsley Wood.
[2] Mary Gascoigne, formerly O'Neill.
[3] My first cousin, Terence O'Neill, later Lord O'Neill of the Maine.*

against the Government, and they will now be both obliged to reconstruct the Cabinet and to prosecute the war with greater vigour; so perhaps the shock they have received may be a healthy one. Slept at No. 10.

Thursday, May 9th

At 2 a.m. Mr Kennedy, the American Ambassador, rang me up to say that President Roosevelt had just telephoned to say that Germany had presented an ultimatum to Holland the previous afternoon. I rang up Sir E. Bridges, the F.O., etc., and caused a great deal of excitement but the report, as is so often the case in those from America, proved to be quite unfounded.

The Cabinet met at the House, which assembled in the morning. The air was full of rumours of impending resignation, etc., and in fact the P.M. spent the whole day discussing the future with Halifax, Winston, etc., and the Leaders of the Opposition. But I have not managed to glean much yet, except that the formation of a Coalition is not out of the question. But will Labour serve under the P.M.? The fundamental difficulty is that no alternative Prime Minister seems to be available, though it is possible that Mr C. might serve as Minister without Portfolio and right-hand man in a Government headed by Winston or Halifax. It is clear that if the freedom of the press is to be curbed, as is temporarily most desirable, and conscription of labour to be introduced, as may in the long run be inevitable, only a truly national Government could perform the task.

Dined with Mrs Henley[1] and went on afterwards to dance at the Savoy. Sat between Mrs H. and Mary Churchill (Winston's youngest progeny) and the others at dinner were Juliet Henley, Juliet Peel, Judy Montagu,[2] Mark Howard,[3] Julian Berry[4] and two Grenadiers whose names I missed. I thought the Churchill girl rather supercilious: she has Sarah's emphatic way of talking, and is better looking, but she seemed to me to have a much less sym-

---

[1] Daughter of the 4th Lord Stanley of Alderley, sister of Venetia Montagu and cousin of Clementine Churchill. A member of the Asquithian Liberal set. One daughter, Juliet, was a Principal in the Treasury during the war; another, Rosalind Pitt-Rivers, a brilliant scientist, was one of the first women to be a Fellow of the Royal Society.

[2] Daughter of Venetia Montagu.

[3] Eldest son of Hon. Geoffrey Howard of Castle Howard, former Liberal M.P. Killed in action in 1944 as was his youngest brother, Christopher. The second son, George, became Chairman of the B.B.C. and died in 1984.

[4] Youngest son of the 1st Viscount Camrose. Later Lieutenant Colonel commanding the Royal Horse Guards.

pathetic personality.[1] The Savoy was stuffy and I felt jaded, devitalised and utterly uninteresting.

Friday, May 10th

Rode at Richmond in summer heat. As I dismounted the groom told me that Holland and Belgium had been invaded.

At No. 10 the fog of war was too thick for me to gather very much of what was happening, but the Cabinet had met at 8.00 and things are obviously moving fast. The Government crisis will have to be postponed. Last night Attlee and Greenwood made it clear that they thought it unlikely their executive would agree to their serving under the P.M. In that case the P.M. may have to go to the Treasury and a Coalition be formed under Winston. The 1922 Committee have shown great animosity against Horace Wilson and he will probably have to retire upstairs in any case.

This morning Archie Sinclair apologised to the P.M. for any insolence or rudeness he had shown him; presumably he wants office.

Halifax is said to have declined to form a Government; so if the P.M. does go I am afraid it *must* be Winston. But the Belgian move has slowed matters up for the time being as the present moment would be a bad one for a change in departments.

Rab Butler tells me that the Secret Service told him yesterday that there was no chance of an invasion of the Netherlands: it was a feint. An attack on Hungary, on the other hand, was imminent. So much for our renowned foreign agents.

Since the above was written I have discovered that last night the P.M. told Winston and Halifax he would gladly serve under either of them. Halifax categorically refused to lead a Government; Winston licked his lips. This afternoon we all, Arthur, Alec, David and the whole gang of hangers-on, sat discussing the future form of the Government and weighing the unlikely chance of the King, who (remembering perhaps the Abdication) is understood not to wish to send for Winston, being able to persuade Halifax to recant his determination not to be P.M. We awaited the decision of the Labour Party, who, it was feared, might refuse to serve in any Government of which the P.M. was even a member. At about 4.45 Attlee rang up to say that they would agree to join a Government provided Neville Chamberlain was not P.M.; so now David's idea is that he should lead the House, as Lord President, like Bonar

---

[1] Mary Churchill, to whom I soon became and remain devoted, was not, at that particular time, feeling well disposed to Mr Chamberlain's Private Secretary and was also, quite understandably, much keener on her other neighbour at dinner, the attractive and intelligent Mark Howard.

Law in the last war, while Winston is the new Lloyd George. Provided the P.M. and Halifax remain in the War Cabinet there will at least be some restraint on our new War Lord. He may, of course, be the man of drive and energy the country believes him to be and he may be able to speed up our creaking military and industrial machinery; but it is a terrible risk, it involves the danger of rash and spectacular exploits, and I cannot help fearing that this country may be manoeuvred into the most dangerous position it has ever been in. One thing, however, is certain: if Winston thought the P.M. were trying to hold on to the reins of power he would create such mischief in the House of Commons that a really serious crisis would arise. Nothing can stop him having his way – because of his powers of blackmail – unless the King makes full use of his prerogative and sends for another man; unfortunately there is only one other, the unpersuadable Halifax.

Everybody here is in despair at the prospect. Personally I shall be sorry too, because I feel a greater loyalty towards the P.M. than I had supposed. And I shudder to think of Brendan Bracken* sitting in this room instead of the charming, inoffensive and extremely sensible Alec.

7.05 p.m.: The P.M. has come back from the Palace. Ministers not in the Cabinet have been sent for and told they will have to resign. The King has sent for Winston (fortunately, because Halifax, true to form, had gone off to the dentist!).

7.15.: Alec and I went over to the F.O. to explain the position to Rab, and there, with Chips, we drank in champagne the health of the "King over the Water" (not King Leopold, but Mr Chamberlain). Rab said he thought that the good clean tradition of English politics, that of Pitt as opposed to Fox, had been sold to the greatest adventurer of modern political history. He had tried earnestly and long to persuade Halifax to accept the Premiership, but he had failed. He believed this sudden coup of Winston and his rabble was a serious disaster and an unnecessary one: the "pass had been sold" by Mr C., Lord Halifax and Oliver Stanley. They had weakly surrendered to a half-breed American whose main support was that of inefficient but talkative people of a similar type, American dissidents like Lady Astor and Ronnie Tree.*

I went home to a solitary dinner and read *War and Peace*. At 9.00 I listened to the late P.M.'s broadcast which was well worded, although he is least effective when he raises his voice and tries to indulge in rhetoric.

On many subsequent occasions I heard Winston give an account of his talk with Mr Chamberlain and Lord Halifax, of which indeed he gives an account in his own history of the Second World War. He always believed, I think, that Mr Chamberlain would have liked Lord Halifax to be Prime Minister. Indeed, from the extracts already quoted from this diary it is clear that all at No. 10 Downing Street and many others, such as R. A. Butler, trusted that some miracle could achieve this. The King, although he gave Winston all the support in his power once the choice was made, certainly disliked the change and would have preferred Lord Halifax; and the feeling in Conservative, or at any rate old-fashioned, circles, was represented by a letter which Queen Mary wrote to my mother saying how much she hoped I would remain with Mr Chamberlain and not go on with the new Prime Minister.

At any rate Winston told me several times that when Chamberlain had summoned Lord Halifax and himself to the Cabinet Room he looked at him sharply and said, "Can you see any reason, Winston, why in these days a Peer should not be Prime Minister?" Winston saw a trap in this question. It would be difficult to say yes without saying frankly that he thought he himself should be the choice. If he said no, or hedged, he felt sure that Mr Chamberlain would turn to Lord Halifax and say, "Well, since Winston agrees I am sure that if the King asks me I should suggest his sending for you." Therefore Winston turned his back and gazed out on the Horse Guards Parade without giving any reply. There was an awkward pause, after which Halifax himself volunteered the suggestion that if the King were to ask Mr Chamberlain's opinion about his successor, he should propose Mr Churchill.

Saturday, May 11th

Rode early at Richmond. The balloons are all up again and London is looking as it did last September.

At No. 10 there is a prevailing air of uncertainty. Who will go and who will stay? "We are hanging," said Arthur, "suspended between Heaven and Hell." At about 10.30 N.C. received a letter from the new P.M. offering him the Lord Presidency of the Council, which he has accepted. It was pointed out that as Chancellor of the Exchequer, a post for which he is admirably equipped, he would have to bear the full brunt of socialist criticism on Treasury questions and the factor of personal animosity would assuredly be dragged in.

Lunched at the Travellers and talked to John Dashwood[1] and

---

[1] Owner of West Wycombe Park in Buckinghamshire and formerly a member of the Diplomatic Service. Married to an agreeable Canadian, Helen Eaton, who was a generous but discriminating hostess.

Nigel Ronald.[1] The latter, who represents one very definite section of opinion in the F.O., told me he thought Rab Butler a public danger, flabby in person and morally and mentally as well; a young man whose whole influence was that of an old one, whose inclination was to put a break on all initiative. He knew Kingsley Wood to be dangerous too: he had always advised the P.M. wrongly about the state of public opinion in the country, because he represented a small nonconformist world. At No. 10 both Rab and Kingsley are considered supermen, and so it is always refreshing to hear the other side of the case.

I cannot bear this indecision and idleness any longer and so have proposed myself to Hinchingbrooke for the night.

Sunday, May 12th, Whitsunday
Back in London I looked in at No. 10 and found Arthur looking very depressed. He is to go with Mr Chamberlain. Tony and I are to remain with Seal and Peck[2] from the Admiralty; Horace has been told bluntly that his services at No. 10 are no longer required; and Miss Watson is to be relegated to a back room to deal with "the post".

*　　*　　*

At this point in history one of the greatest administrations which has ever governed the United Kingdom was in the process of formation. It is therefore appropriate to attempt a character sketch of the man who led it, not in the light of what I knew or felt on May 12th, 1940, but of what I learned by personal experience in the subsequent twenty-five years. It is a formidable task because few public figures in all history have assumed so many mantles, displayed such an unlikely mixture of talents, experienced over so wide a span of years such a variety of triumphs and disasters, and been successively so suspected and so trusted, so disliked and so admired by his fellow countrymen.

I hope that in the pages of this diary some aspects of his character will by degrees unfold themselves. For the moment I will merely list those which, in retrospect, seem most striking to me. In his judgment, no less than in his activities, he was entirely unpredictable. A Private Secretary who works intimately with his master

---

[1] Foreign Office Wykehamist, all but mortally wounded in the First World War. Close to infallible in all matters relating to art, literature and gardening. I served on his staff when he was Ambassador to Portugal after the war. The only Ambassador Dr Salazar saw regularly.

[2] See p. 129.

over a long period can usually say with little risk of error what the reaction to a given proposition is likely to be. With Winston this was impossible, as even his wife found and admitted. I was often asked what the Prime Minister would feel about something and there were occasions on which I thought I knew the answer for a certainty. Sometimes I was right, but just as often I was wrong. There were none of his associates who would have claimed to do better. This was due to some strange intuitive power which he held and which might induce him to take a line contrary, as it appeared, to logic and contrary to the normal mental workings of everybody else.

Perhaps examples of this will appear in these pages and it is certainly true that his unaccountable attitude to apparently reasonable proposals was a frequent source of irritation as well as of astonishment to his Cabinet colleagues and to the Chiefs of Staff.

He always retained unswerving independence of thought. He approached a problem as he himself saw it and of all the men I have ever known he was the least liable to be swayed by the views of even his most intimate counsellors. Many people made the mistake of thinking that somebody – it might be General Ismay or Professor Lindemann – for whom the Prime Minister had the utmost respect and affection, would be able to "get something through". Unless the Prime Minister was himself impressed by the argument, pressure by others seldom had any effect. If a subject bored him he would pass it, however important, to somebody else for a decision and would scarcely pause to consider the grounds on which that decision had been reached. But once his personal attention was engaged he had to be convinced that his initial reaction was wrong before he would agree to change his line. He was open to persuasion, although it often needed courage to press the point, but he was never persuaded by the fact that those who argued a certain course were people whom he liked and respected. There were indeed a number of occasions when he showed a quite inexplicable facility for reaching the right decision on faulty logic and against all the best advice.

He had an unusual capacity for affection and an intense loyalty to those whom he had known long or who had served him well. Sometimes this loyalty went too far, as in the case of Sir Roger Keyes, and sometimes his affection for his children and his friends led him to take actions which gave rise to mutterings of nepotism. He had great compassion which he combined with personal generosity and his sympathy for those in misfortune was particularly marked in the case of humble people whose unhappiness was somehow drawn to his attention. Although he had a few enduring

dislikes, his magnanimity was a far more remarkable characteristic and he hated vindictiveness above all things. When the
bloodhounds were on the scent of Robert Boothby about charges
relating to some Czech gold, he said to me that he could not endure
"a man hunt".

His anger was like lightning and sometimes terrifying to see, but
it lasted a short time. He could be violently offensive to those who
worked for him and although he would never say he was sorry, he
would equally never let the sun go down without in some way
making amends or showing that he had not meant to be unkind.
His sarcasm could be biting, but it was often accompanied by an
engaging smile which seemed to say that no harm was really
intended. He had a great liking for young people, of either sex, and
he treated his Secretariat as if they were his children.

He was not easy to work for, particularly during the anxious days
of the war. Patience is a virtue with which he was totally unfamiliar.
As soon as he had ordered something to be done he expected that it
had been completed. Many was the time when he told me to do
something and before I had had time to get back to my telephone
he had rung the bell to enquire the result. He would ask for a draft,
either from his Private Office or from one of the departments, and
would expect it to be ready long before it was humanly possible.
His own rapidity of thought and expression was partly responsible
for this, together with the fact that having been in a position to give
orders all his life, and seldom obliged to execute them, he had no
conception of the practical difficulties of communication and of
administrative arrangements.

He also possessed, to an unusual degree, the ability to assimilate
quickly the main points in a complicated story. He would read a
long Cabinet Paper and pick out one or two aspects of the case,
frequently those which did not seem the most important. He would
pursue them with the utmost vigour. It was strange how often they
turned out in the end to be the principal points at issue.

Lovable though he was, and indeed an object of affection to
everybody who came in close contact with him, he was at the same
time curiously inconsiderate. In the war years, when feeding was
difficult, he thought nothing of keeping the Cabinet in their seats
until, for them, all hope of getting any food had passed, because he
himself had only to walk upstairs to lunch or dinner. Equally, it
never occurred to him to suppose that anybody might be tired or
over-worked. He thought nothing of sending for one in the temporary sanctuary of one's bath about some trivial point which could
well have waited until one was dressed. During meals at Chequers I
used often to be sent to the telephone half a dozen times and even

when I knew him well enough to suggest that a call might wait until after dinner, or that indeed the answer was already available, no excuse was accepted. Yet what would have been resented from any other man was accepted with almost complete equanimity from him; and this went not merely for his Private Secretaries, but also for the typists who might be kept up until three or four in the morning even when there was no work to do, and for the servants who might have to wait till after midnight before they could clear the dining-room table.

He often made impetuous remarks, both about people and events, and I have doubtless recorded some of these without realising, till I knew him much better, that a statement made with fiery vehemence, which few would dare contradict on the spot, was often modified on reflection. His reputation was for impetuosity, but that was, at least by the time he became Prime Minister, partly due to the forcefulness with which he expressed himself. He usually thought deeply about the matter afterwards and seldom acted without careful consideration. This applied, most strikingly, to his relationship with General de Gaulle.

He digested the more important of his decisions slowly. Sometimes it took him weeks of cogitation before he reached an answer which satisfied him. He would talk half aloud, half under his breath, about some matter which was occupying his mind. He might address apparently inconsequential remarks to his family or his staff, or even to the yellow cat, while under his breath you could hear him preparing some Minute to the Chiefs of Staff Committee or speech to the House of Commons. He would repeat again and again some phrase or quotation which would appear, most appositely, in a speech a few weeks later.

His interests were predominantly defence, foreign affairs and party politics. He cared less for domestic problems or the home front except when he was aroused for sentimental reasons, but he would wax furious, and send fiery minutes to his Ministers, over some apparent miscarriage of justice reported in the newspapers.

To matters of defence he gave the deepest thought, based on years of study and experience, and nothing influenced him more in a man's favour than an act of gallantry on the field of battle. It was at least partly to this that Lord De L'Isle, V.C.,* owed the Secretaryship of State for Air in 1951 and that Lord Louis Mountbatten owed his promotion to be Director of Combined Operations in 1941, though he subsequently lost favour because Churchill doubted his judgment and disliked his overt support of the Labour Party.

As far as foreign affairs went, he was more interested in events than in trends and he was in the main oblivious to the growth of nationalism as a force in British imperial affairs. For him India, Egypt and Africa were and should remain as they had been at the time of Omdurman. He mistrusted the Foreign Office whose members he regarded as defeatist and prone to socialism. It was, however, a source of regret to him that he had held every great office except that of Foreign Secretary and during Anthony Eden's absences he usually contrived to be the acting Secretary of State, much to the chagrin of Eden who would have preferred a more compliant *locum tenens*. There were even occasions on which he said to me that he would take over the Foreign Office and run it from 10 Downing Street. No word of this ever reached the corridors across the way, but I think that he seriously considered it.

Finally, in politics and indeed all his life, he was as strange a mixture of radical and traditionalist as could anywhere be found. He was certainly not conservative by temperament, nor indeed by conviction a supporter of the Conservative Party. On the other hand he was, as Lady Churchill once said to me, the only surviving believer in the divine right of Kings and his respect for the monarchy amounted almost to idolatry. He disliked the abolition of anything which had colour or tradition behind it. As regards religion he was an agnostic who, as the years went by, and I think more particularly as a result of the Battle of Britain, slowly began to conceive that there was some overriding power which had a conscious influence on our destinies. He seldom went to church and, curiously enough, only enjoyed christenings; but he unquestionably developed in his later years a conviction that this life was not the end. Once, driving back from Aldermaston, where he had been awed by the apocalyptic forecast of nuclear devastation, he told me that he thought he would soon die. He went on to say he could not help wondering whether the government above might not be a constitutional monarchy, in which case there was always a possibility that the Almighty might have occasion to "send for him".

*   *   *

Monday, May 13th
Winston is still in his lair at the Admiralty, but will begin to work at No. 10 this afternoon. He looks like keeping a double establishment until the Chamberlains move out of No. 11 as they will do in about a month's time. Neville Chamberlain sent for me to say goodbye and told me he would watch my career with interest.

Winston Churchill brought with him from the Admiralty his principal private secretary, Eric Seal, and also John Peck. Seal, who was a man of intelligence and integrity, was not fully on Churchill's "wavelength", though he understood him well. He remained at No. 10 for a little less than a year before leaving to take up an important defence assignment in the U.S.A.

John Peck, brilliant, a master of light verse and parody and invariably a pleasant companion, was at No. 10 until the end of the Coalition Government in 1945 and stayed on for a time with Mr Attlee before transferring to the Foreign Service. He was Ambassador in Dublin when a mob burned his embassy to the ground.

Went down to the House with Seal to hear the new P.M. ask for a vote of confidence in his Government. He made a brilliant little speech. Maxton[1] denounced the Coalition with wit and vehemence: he is a great idealist and not ashamed of being so. He sees no way of putting his ideals into practice at present and is not ashamed of admitting the fact. Lloyd George also spoke and was afterwards invited into the P.M.'s room and offered the Ministry of Agriculture (for which the cheap press has always tipped him). He refused it because he thinks the country is in a hopeless position and he is generally despondent.

I spent the day in a bright blue new suit from the Fifty-Shilling Tailors, cheap and sensational looking, which I felt was appropriate to the new Government. But of course it must be admitted that Winston's administration, with all its faults, has drive; and men like Duff Cooper, Eden, Lord Lloyd* and Herbert Morrison should be able to get things done. Moreover the Government has the complete confidence of the country.

Seal and Peck arrived at No. 10. From what they tell me of the First Lord's ways I am going to be much harder worked than of late.

Another crisis is brewing in the Mediterranean, and it begins to look as if Italy really may come in against us. Winston apparently thinks so, but I feel sure that much will depend on events in the Low Countries.

---

[1] James Maxton. Eloquent Leader of the Independent Labour Party. M.P. for the Bridgeton district of Glasgow. His honesty, sense of humour and independence of judgment won the admiration of his opponents and of few more than Winston Churchill.

Tuesday, May 14th

Rode at 7.30 in glorious weather.

There is still a certain air of "malaise" about No. 10, which is largely due to the contrast between the fixity of the late P.M.'s habits and the inconsequential nature of Winston's. I suppose we shall get used to it; but the prospect of constant late nights – 2.00 a.m. or later – is depressing.

Went with Mother, David and Joan to see Philip off to the front. He looked very happy and extremely well, and I feel sure he will be an admirable soldier. Father could not face the scene at Waterloo and did not come.

Some of Winston's correspondence today was entertaining. The Duke of Windsor wrote to congratulate him and spoke of his "great measure of practical and sympathetic support in the past"; Randolph Churchill spoke of the caucus which had kept him out of office for nine years and hoped it was not now too late; Oliver Stanley refused an offer of the Dominions' Office in view of the contemptuous way it had been offered and referred to Winston's blunt accusation that he lacked drive – why then had he been offered the post?

In the evening the military news was disturbing. Holland is to all intents and purposes lost, the French are being pressed on the Meuse, the Germans look like breaking through at Sedan, and we are besought to send more fighter squadrons to France if the enemy advance is to be checked. The French speak ominously of the lack of defences between Sedan and Paris.

The ROYAL MARINE Operation has now been put into force and mines have been placed in the Rhine and Moselle; but the Cabinet have decided not to bomb the Ruhr yet, until the position is clearer, because it may be necessary to conserve our long-range bombers for use in the land battle or against Italy if, as becomes increasingly likely, she comes in.

After dinner I went to Admiralty House, where Winston proposes to work at night. He has fitted up the ground floor for this purpose: the dining-room in which the private secretary and one of Winston's specially trained night-women-typists sit; the lovely drawing-room with its curious ugly dolphin furniture, which is used as a kind of promenade; and an inner room in which the Great Man himself sits. At the side of his desk stands a table laden with bottles of whisky, etc. On the desk itself are all manner of things: toothpicks, gold medals (which he uses as paper-weights), special cuffs to save his coatsleeves from becoming dirty, and innumerable pills and powders.

Peck and I arrived at about 9.15 and waited till 10.30 before

anything happened. In the meanwhile I read some of W.'s correspondence which we had ready for him. There was a letter from the
King, two or three days old, urging that Lord Beaverbrook* should
not be made Minister of Aircraft Production in view of the effect
likely to be produced in Canada. Also a large number of letters
suggesting various appointments. A note by Brendan Bracken*
referred to a number of "our friends" disliked by "the parachutist", by whom he meant David Margesson (who, owing to the
reconstruction, has landed in the enemy camp, I suppose).

At about 10.30 Winston came down, and then by degrees a
motley gathering appeared. David Margesson, Sinclair, Eden,
Beaverbrook, the American Ambassador (who told me the most
disquieting evidence of Italy's intention to enter the war) and Pug
Ismay. Strange bedfellows indeed! They walked about talking to
each other while Winston popped in and out first through one door
and then through the next, appointing Under Secretaries with
David, talking about the German thrust at Sedan with Eden and
listening to the alarmist and, I think, untrustworthy opinions of Mr
Kennedy. Eventually Tony Bevir came in to relieve me, Peck
having gone home early, and I walked home through the warm
night at about 1 a.m.

Wednesday, May 15th
A day of great trivial activity for me: incessant appointments,
telephone calls, etc. Most of the afternoon was spent offering
Under Secretaryships to various politicians and it was my difficult
job to explain on the telephone to Kenneth Lindsay, the Duke of
Devonshire, Lord Denham and Captain McEwen that their services were no longer required.

Pug Ismay is not too happy about the military situation. He says
the French are not fighting properly: they are, he points out, a
volatile race and it may take them some time to get into a warlike
mood. Pray Heaven not too long!

Dined at Bucks with Pat Hancock[1] who has just returned from
H.M. Legation at The Hague, where he was in constant danger
from snipers, parachutists and bombs. We had a most agreeable
dinner (which did not begin till 9.00 as Winston was busy drafting a
message, which was intended to be both strong and conciliatory, to
the Duce) and both the food and drink were delicious. But I
noticed a curiously worn and strained look about Pat which was no

---

[1] A contemporary at Trinity who passed the Diplomatic Service examination in
the same year as I did. A first-class brain coupled with an engaging touch of
eccentricity. Afterwards Ambassador in Oslo, Tel Aviv and Rome.

doubt partly due to physical weariness and partly to having had the meaning of war really brought home to him, an experience which is still in store for us.

Thursday, May 16th
Apparently the French are still not putting their best leg forward and a serious German incursion into French territory has taken place in the direction of Laon [north-west of Rheims]. I have always been a little afraid of the unbounded confidence placed in the quality of the French army, but now that the soil of France has been invaded they may show their traditional toughness. However for the moment things are serious, the air situation is bad (we have lost too many machines, although we have inflicted far more serious losses on the Germans), and our troops in Belgium may have to fall back in order to maintain a line with the French.

During the afternoon the operational news became increasingly alarming and it was evident that the German breakthrough was jeopardising not only Paris but the whole French army. Winston was away and so we could sit in the garden at No. 10 and enjoy the sun; but none of us felt like enjoying anything. Gossiped with the Chief Whip.

The Cabinet met at 11.00 p.m. to discuss a terrifying telegram Winston had sent from Paris and to decide whether seriously to weaken our defences by sending out fighters from this country. I will not describe the situation: it will be in every history book of the future; but evidently there has been lamentable staff work on the French side and Paris has been left undefended by reserves. We had hoped that only armoured divisions had penetrated the French defences, but it now seems that infantry divisions are pouring through the gap on a fifty-kilometre front.

Winston's telegram was decyphered in driblets and I rushed it into the Cabinet by instalments. W. wants us to mass all our air strength to stop the advance in order to save the collapsing French morale. He speaks of "the mortal gravity of the hour" – which made Arthur Rucker say "He is still thinking of his books" and Seal talk of his "blasted rhetoric". Everybody is on edge, except the soldiers.

W. wants a reply from the Cabinet by midnight and Cornwall-Jones, of the Cabinet Offices, is to give it to Ismay, who is with Churchill, in Hindustani.[1]

---

[1] In the First World War Lloyd George and Tom Jones used a similar deceptive device, but spoke in Welsh, which must have puzzled the Germans even more than Hindustani.

The Cabinet's decision was to send the ten fighter squadrons for which the French asked. That means denuding this country of a quarter of its first-line fighter defence. The reply was telephoned by Cornwall-Jones and I could not help laughing when he referred to "Lord President Sahib" and "C. A. S. Sahib". But it is dangerous, this Hindustani trick. It has been done too often now and I suspect the Germans know what language we use. Slept at No. 10.

Friday, May 17th
Rose at 6.00 to go down to Hendon to meet the P.M. on his return from France. He looked quite cheerful, having slept and breakfasted well at the Embassy. However Dill, Ismay and the rest of the unfortunate staff had had a miserable time. Winston had told them to be ready by 5.45, and it then transpired that he did not wish to leave until 7.00 and he had gone on sleeping while they wandered about aimlessly and could get no breakfast. He is very inconsiderate with his staff.

I drove back from Hendon with Ismay and two other officers, who were all heavy with sleep and had eaten nothing but a rusk. Ismay was very pessimistic and said the French were not merely retreating but were routed. Their nerves were shattered by this armoured warfare and by the German air superiority, and the French Government were upended by this sudden shattering of their faith in the invincible French army. Another General in the car – his Christian name was Otto, but that was all I could discover – was more optimistic. He thought that if we and the French could concentrate our air strength on the battle front so that the French can, as Winston puts it, fight "under a clean sky", the French troops might sit down, have a cigarette and turn round and fight. If they do, there is a good chance the present dark prospect may brighten into a major success.

The P.M. and Mrs Churchill lunched at the Japanese Embassy and I was asked too. It is a charming house in Grosvenor Square with attractive Japanese furniture and decoration. Corbin, Rob Hudson, Grigg[1] and Geoffrey Shakespeare were there. I sat next to the inscrutable First Secretary, who was polite but not sufficiently oriental to be attractive, and after lunch I talked to Geoffrey Shakespeare (the new Under-Secretary for the Dominions) who is longing for Italy to declare war on us.

Heard from the War Office that Brian O'Neill was among the soldiers killed on the troopship *Chobry* which was sunk off the Norwegian coast yesterday. This is the first casualty of this horrible

[1] Sir Edward Grigg, Parliamentary Secretary at the Ministry of Information.

war that has really brought the full meaning of it home to me. He had great charm and was, I believe, a most efficient soldier. He also had considerable brain-power of which he might one day have been able to make real use.

Winston is depressed. He says the French are crumpling up as completely as did the Poles (I hope and believe this to be an exaggeration) and that our forces in Belgium will inevitably have to withdraw in order to maintain contact with the French. There is, of course, a risk that the B.E.F. may be cut off if the French do not rally in time.

Saturday, May 18th

The position is still critical, and Admiral Phillips,[1] the best brain in the navy, observes to the P.M. that the Cabinet have now got to take a fundamental decision. They can either send most of the fighters from this country in the hope of turning the scale on the Western Front, in which case the war might be appreciably shortened; or they can maintain them here for defensive purposes, on the assumption that even if France's resistance is overcome we shall still carry on the war from here. If we send the fighters and lose them, then this country will be left at the mercy of concentrated German air attack and can hardly avoid destruction. It would be a terrifying gamble, but I am afraid it is one we ought to take.

Back to work by 3.30 and, after dining at home, went to Admiralty House. Winston was in excellent humour. He first of all dragooned the Chiefs of Staff and Ismay in the War Room upstairs, and then came downstairs, turned me out of my room and started dictating. So I repaired to his room and discussed with Brendan Bracken and Professor Lindemann* why, if we had a large number of unused aircraft in this country, we could not increase the quantity of our fighter squadrons. Apparently the wastage, especially in training, is something appalling. Bracken is a cad, "slick" and amusing, and quite likeable in his way; but rather too talkative and apt to make the most ridiculous pronouncements. Lindemann is supremely unattractive but has an air of competence and efficiency.[2]

Winston, who is full of fight and thrives on crisis and adversity, dictated a few brief notes, containing questions on strategical

[1] Vice Chief of the Naval Staff. Small in stature, but outstandingly clever and disarmingly simple in his tastes. Drowned in the *Prince of Wales* when she and the *Repulse* were sunk off the coast of Malaya in December 1941.

[2] I soon became great friends with them both and admired their respective abilities. Professor Lindemann was created Lord Cherwell in 1941.

points for the people concerned to answer, and then wrote a letter to General Georges[1] about the situation in France. Referring to the rapid advance of the German army he said, "The tortoise is thrusting his head very far beyond his carapace." In reality I think we are the tortoise, and Germany the hare. The tortoise will win in the end, but the hare is "making the going". I hope – but perhaps it is wishful thinking – that the present position is comparable to March 1918, with the Germans carrying all before them but with November 11th not very far ahead.

A. V. Alexander,* the new First Lord, came in and W. showed him the sharp and uncompromising reply Mussolini today sent to his firm but very polite telegram on becoming P.M. Alexander thought that as Italy's participation in the war was now virtually certain (which I do not believe) we should seize the initiative and occupy Crete. Winston answered that our hands were too full elsewhere to enable us to embark on adventures: such is the change that high office can work in a man's inherent love of rash and spectacular action.

Sunday, May 19th

Heavenly weather again. It has been cloudless for at least three weeks now and we can none of us really profit by it.

At No. 10 by 9.45 where I met and talked with Amery, the new Secretary of State for India. After the Cabinet I went to Admiralty House and found Mrs Churchill who said that the preacher at St Martin-in-the-Fields had preached such a pacifist sermon that morning that she got up and left. "You ought to have cried 'Shame'," said Winston, "desecrating the House of God with lies!" Then he came back and said to me, "Tell the Minister of Information with a view to having the man pilloried." It is refreshing to work with somebody who refuses to be depressed even by the most formidable danger that has ever threatened this country.

After lunch came the astounding and, if true, nerve-racking news that the French army south of the B.E.F. has melted away and left a vast gap on the British right. Winston was summoned back from Chartwell, where he had gone for a few hours' sunshine and to write his broadcast speech for tonight. At the moment Lord Gort's choice seems to be to retire to the sea, forming a bridgehead round Dunkirk or to fight his way south-eastwards, leaving the Belgians to their fate, in order to rejoin the French. Lord Gort has asked for a Cabinet decision on the action he is to take.

---

[1] In command of all the armies in north-east France, from the Channel to the Swiss frontier, 1939–40.

Our fortunes are at a low ebb, but I am still confident we shall win in the end and perhaps a shock to our self-esteem and feeling of security is not unwholesome. In any case, whatever Winston's shortcomings, he seems to be the man for the occasion. His spirit is indomitable and even if France and England should be lost, I feel he would carry on the crusade himself with a band of privateers. Perhaps my judgements of him have been harsh, but the situation was very different a few weeks ago.

The Cabinet met at 4.30 and decided that the B.E.F. must fight its way southwards towards Amiens to make contact with the French. Winston decided to fly to G.H.Q. to see Gort and to visit the front line, and I was to have gone with him. To my bitter disappointment the project was abandoned just as I had reached home to pick up some clothes. I stayed to have tea with Mother, Father and Peggy Crewe. The latter was delighted to hear that Weygand,* whom she knows well and respects greatly, is to succeed Gamelin.

The P.M. started writing his speech at 6.00 to broadcast at 9.00. I heard it from home, where I dined. It was good and it brought out the full seriousness of the hour, but it was not Winston at his best, nor quite the clarion-call I had expected.

At Admiralty House there was the usual "evening party", the Chiefs of Staff, Beaverbrook, Eden, etc. The P.M. sent a telegram to Roosevelt asking for fighter aircraft and implying that without them we should be in a parlous state, even though this country would never give up the struggle. Considering the soothing words he always uses to America, and in particular to the President, I was somewhat taken aback when he said to me, "Here's a telegram for those bloody Yankees. Send it off tonight." I duly sent it to Herschel Johnson at the American Embassy and was somewhat annoyed to be woken up at 2.30 a.m. and told that the P.M. wanted it back to review what he had said – particularly as he made no alteration after all. In telegraphing to the President he always calls himself "A former Naval Person".

Winston also dictated a telegram to Reynaud, expressing his distress at the plight of the French army and insinuating that we had been rather let down. I gather the French Government are in a deplorable state of pessimism and depression.

Monday, May 20th

Every morning now at No. 10 there is a time of feverish activity when the P.M.'s box returns. It contains all the work he has done overnight, in fact everything that it has not been possible to thrust under his nose during the previous days – telegrams, letters,

Cabinet papers, C.O.S. reports, etc. Many of them come back untouched and have to be placed in the next night's box; others have illegible instructions scrawled on them in red ink and have to be dealt with immediately.

The B.E.F.'s march to the Arras–Amiens Line begins today. I said to Seal: "It looks like the retreat from Mons beginning all over again. It is awful the way history repeats itself." He replied: "I wish history would repeat itself, but I am afraid it is not going to. There seems to be no proper liaison or co-operation between the French, British and Belgian Staffs and the whole thing is dropping to pieces through sheer ineptitude." We need another Charles Martel,[1] but let us hope the decisive battle will be fought and won before the invaders reach Poitiers.

David[2] came to dinner. He is proposing to join the R.N.V.R.

Tuesday, May 21st

The situation in France is extraordinary. Owing to the rapid advance of armoured troops, the Germans are in many places behind the Allied lines. Enemy columns have reached Amiens and are thought to be on the way to Abbeville; it is clear that the main thrust is north-westwards towards the Channel ports.

To the House with the P.M. for Questions. He intends to take them once a week.

News that German tanks are approaching Boulogne. Listened in, rather unscrupulously but with the approval of Tony and Peck, to a green-line telephone conversation between the P.M. and C.I.G.S. They expect to be able to hold Boulogne, but it is a shock that the Germans should have penetrated so far and obviously the B.E.F.'s communications are in danger. The German advance is now really dangerous, and it is staggering that France should have so far put up less resistance to invasion than did Poland, Norway or Holland. Preparations are being made for the evacuation of the B.E.F. in case of necessity.

Dined at Betty Montagu's flat with her and Zara Mainwaring. We cooked our own dinner consisting of an omelette (which I made), peas, asparagus and stewed raspberries, and tried unsuccessfully not to talk about the war. From what Betts and Zara said it is clear that the full horror of the situation is dawning on people, and perhaps they think it even worse than it is. But I think Betts

---

[1] King of the Franks who stemmed the tide of the Moorish invasion of Europe by his great victory at Poitiers in A.D. 732.
[2] My eldest brother.*

was typical of the whole country when she said, "We shall not be beaten; even if Paris and London fall we shall win."

At Admiralty House there was chaos, owing to the lack of information being received, because communications have broken down. I have not seen Winston so depressed, and while I stood by him, trying to get M. Reynaud on the telephone, he said: "In all the history of war, I have never seen such mismanagement." Against the advice of the Chiefs of Staff and all present, he decided to go to Paris early tomorrow morning to see Weygand* and Reynaud and to impress upon them that it is no use concentrating on the destruction of German motorised columns which have penetrated far into France, but that we must withstand the main German advance and ourselves attack. Sir C. Newall,[1] the Chief of Air Staff, told me he thought the B.E.F. was in grave danger; but at least they seem to be fighting well, unlike their French allies.

At about 1.30 a.m., just after the P.M. had gone upstairs, the Air Ministry rang up to say that General Billotte,[2] whose weakness and vacillation are thought to have contributed to much of our discomfiture, had been seriously injured in a motor smash. They thought the P.M. would be relieved. I found him in his bedroom, a comic sight clad in nothing but a vest. All he said was "Poor man, poor man" – but without much sign of grief in his tones!

Wednesday, May 22nd

Pouring rain for the first time for months. A quiet day owing to the P.M.'s absence in Paris.

About 7.00 p.m. the party returned. Pug Ismay said that at least they now knew the French had a real man to command them. Weygand was magnificent, youthful despite his years and capable of realising what sort of war this is. We had asked him point-blank whether he could get the French army to fight and he had replied, "I will try"; but reports of their fighting spirit were bad. Pug said he was really worried. He was afraid the Germans would offer the French generous terms, the latter would then ask us for forty divisions and fifteen more fighter squadrons, and when we replied with a *non possumus* would say they were very sorry, they could not continue the struggle. So we have got to think of a first-rate C. in C. for our forces in this country and to prepare for the worst. I think Pug is unduly alarmist, because I cannot see the French shaming themselves quite to that extent.

[1] Later succeeded by Sir Charles Portal. Given a peerage and appointed Governor General of New Zealand.

[2] Commanded the first French group of armies. Lord Gort's immediate superior. Unhinged by the speed of the German advance.

Thursday, May 23rd

Yesterday the Government obtained permission from the House to take over fuller powers than any British Government has ever possessed. The purpose is largely that if we are invaded, or otherwise *in extremis*, the rights of individuals and institutions must not be allowed to stand in the way of the country's safety. Houses must be demolished to stop advancing tanks, labour must if necessary be coerced, industrial plant requisitioned. Now if ever *salus populi suprema lex*, and in a totalitarian war even a democracy must surrender its liberties. But what a precedent for future peacetime Governments; and will state control, once instituted, ever be abandoned?

The situation this morning is still blacker. The B.E.F.'s communications have been cut and their food supplies are in danger. Moreover enemy infantry columns have nearly reached Amiens, and strong armoured columns are very close to Dunkirk, Calais and Boulogne.

A dramatic afternoon, mostly spent in the Upper War Room at the Admiralty. It began with the news that the Germans were in Boulogne, that the B.E.F. could not break through southwards to join up with the French, and that they only had two days' food left. It seemed all but certain that our army would have to retire precipitously and try to embark, under Herculean difficulties, for England. Then the P.M. spoke on the telephone to Reynaud and Weygand. The latter claimed that the French had recaptured Amiens and Peronne. If true the news is stupendous, although the position of the B.E.F. still remains critical and they will have to fight their way southwards against heavy odds.

After dinner the Admiralty became normally hectic. Brendan Bracken insulted Philip Broad[1] on the telephone. Most immediate telegrams were despatched to most of the existing Generals, Prime Ministers and Presidents. Lord Beaverbrook was sent for and plied with whisky. Pug Ismay was dismal and depressing. And I got to bed, at No. 10, about 1.45.

Friday, May 24th

Went early to Admiralty House and met the P.M., dressed in the most brilliant of flowery dressing-gowns and puffing a long cigar as he ascended from the Upper War Room to his bedroom. He had one or two telephone conversations with the C.I.G.S. and Sir Roger Keyes (from Belgium), emerging from his bath in a towel in order to do so.

---

[1] Resident Clerk in the Foreign Office.

We have two new faces at No. 10, a private secretary called Martin* from the C.O. and a clerk from the Ministry of Pensions. We are thus ridiculously overstaffed, but at least we shall have somewhat shorter hours. At the moment we are not overworked, but overtired by the length of time we remain on duty.

Sunday, May 26th [At Oxford]
Gay[1] and I had a tremendous discussion on socialism, she just having become affiliated to the Party. I understand and sympathise with her point of view, which is founded on a sense of pity for the poor and disgust at their lack of opportunity. But I do not feel socialism is the proper remedy: private enterprise is valuable because it is efficient, while state control makes for petty tyranny by Government officials and for lack of drive or imagination. Local government is now in socialist hands and the result has been overspending of public money and the spread of corruption in local government. The Conservatives, on the other hand, have failed to take sufficiently strong measures: as was said of Erasmus, they have "sought to heal by incantations a wound which required the surgeon's knife". They and we may have to pay dearly for it in the social unrest which must inevitably follow this war.

Before dinner the sun came out and we were able to walk placidly in Christchurch Meadows. We dined once again at The Trout, but in glorious conditions this time: a blue sky, a setting sun and enough clouds to make the sun still more effective. We ate on a seat by the river, and then walked along the tow path, watching children at play and listening to plovers calling. There has never been a more beautiful setting in which to be happy and I have never felt greater serenity or contentment. Gay did too and said that she believed happiness could only be attained if one lived for the moment.

Monday, May 27th
At Downing Street I was distressed to find the situation much blacker than when I left on Friday. It appears that a grave deterioration has taken place in the last forty-eight hours: the B.E.F., unable to force their way southwards, have got to retreat to the coast as best they can and re-embark for England from whatever Channel ports remain open to them. The French seem to be demoralised and there is now a serious fear that they may collapse. The Cabinet are feverishly considering our ability to carry on the war alone in such circumstances, and there are signs that Hali-

---

[1] Gay Margesson, younger daughter of Captain David Margesson. Married the Hon. Martin Charteris, later Lord Charteris of Amisfield.

fax is being defeatist. He says that our aim can no longer be to crush Germany but rather to preserve our own integrity and independence.

Fortunately Ironside has gone and Dill, who inspires great confidence, has taken his place; but I do not envy him, confronted as he is with the problem of salving the wreckage of the B.E.F.

I still feel convinced that we shall win, even if the French collapse; but we have reached all but the last ditch and a timely miracle would be acceptable.

In the afternoon came a telegram from Lothian describing a conversation with Roosevelt, who seems to think that if we really are *in extremis* the U.S. will come in. R. suggests that with the resources of the Allied empires, and provided the navy remains intact, we could carry on the war from Canada; but he makes the curious suggestion that the seat of Government should be Bermuda and not Ottawa, as the American republics would dislike the idea of a monarchy functioning on the American Continent!

There was a Cabinet at 10.00 p.m. to discuss the situation caused by King Leopold's determination, despite the opposition of his Government on English soil, to ask for an armistice. This defection of the Belgians leaves the B.E.F. in an exposed and extremely dangerous position. Duff Cooper told me he was afraid "a lot of them will be scuppered".

After the Cabinet I went over to Admiralty House with the P.M. He said he did not think the French would give in and that at any rate they ought not to do so. At midnight, after reading a few papers and saying "Pour me out a whisky and soda, very weak, there's a good boy", he went to bed.

Tuesday, May 28th

Sir R. Keyes, who arrived from Belgium this morning, says that Lord Gort, whom he saw recently, does not rate the chances of saving the B.E.F. very high. Winston, in his statement to the House this afternoon, spoke of "hard and heavy tidings to come", and Duff Cooper made a sensible but intentionally depressing broadcast in the evening. We have lost the first great battle of the war, but it is by no means the last.

Sir R. Campbell, from Paris, says that Reynaud is firm, but Daladier cannot be counted on. The best of the French Ministers is Mandel,[1] at Home Security, who is both efficient and determined.

---

[1] Clemenceau's *Chef de Cabinet* in the First World War. Churchill hoped to lure him to England to lead a Free French movement, but he declined to leave, though strongly opposed to surrender. He was murdered by the Vichy *milices*.

As it was my early night I got away at 6.00. We have arranged that John Peck and I shall take alternate late nights, so that every other day will be an easy one. I went to see Betts and Rosemary Hinchingbrooke,[1] the latter very relieved that Hinch. has returned safely from France. I then took Betts home to dinner with Father and Mother, both of whom were interesting about their reminiscences of London as it used to be. Father said he remembered how on the 1st of May men used to walk through the streets with Maypoles, surrounded by a throng of dancing people. He remembered Northumberland House and Princes' Cricket ground which was where Cadogan Square, etc., now stands.

I have decided that if the war continues I must make a determined effort to go and fight; but I gather there will be opposition from the Foreign Office authorities. However, in present circumstances what is reasonable has to take second place to what one's conscience dictates. I shall wait a month and then move heaven and earth to go.

Wednesday, May 29th

Ciano has told Loraine that Italy's entry into the war is now certain and will be a matter of days. The fault is Mussolini's alone and on him the entire blame must rest. He is presumably convinced that Germany is going to win and he considers the moment for a diversion to the southwards to be opportune. There are signs that the attack will be made through Switzerland.

Lunched with Tony Bevir at the Travellers. Sir Kenneth Clark,[2] who came and talked to us during lunch, is trying to arrange for the pictures in the National Gallery and Royal collections to be sent to Canada. He also spoke of the pacifism in Wales, which he says is largely due to the attitude of the clergy. Tony sensibly suggested calling in Tom Jones to assist. After lunch Tony and I talked about socialism, and I made the point, which I believe to be justified, that socialists almost always create their Utopia in theory and then attempt to work backwards from it. It is wiser to struggle forwards, with a definite objective in view, but prepared to adapt that objective as obstacles on the way and the conditions prevailing at the end may necessitate. *Idées fixes* are always dangerous when they relate to the future, because it is past human

[1] Rosemary Peto, married to Betty Montagu's brother, Viscount Hinchingbrooke, M.P.
[2] Director of the National Gallery, 1934–45; Chairman of the Arts Council, 1953–60; at one time Chairman of the Independent Television Authority and a widely praised demonstrator of the finest works of art on television. Made a peer in 1969.

ingenuity to guide the course of events. It is for this reason that cut-and-dried peace plans are so futile, since it is impossible to assess the conditions of peace. We may win outright or we may be obliged to compromise: that we shall lose I do not for a moment believe.

News received that we have taken Narvik. We sorely need some restorative just now.

Dined with Zara at Luigi's. She is so attractive and her vivacity is a tonic in these depressing days. We used to dislike each other so profoundly and now we get on admirably.

At Admiralty House after dinner. The evacuation of the B.E.F. is proceeding more satisfactorily than had been expected and 70,000 have been saved already. While the P.M. was in the Upper War Room with the Chiefs of Staff I heard that we had shot down seventy-seven German aeroplanes today for the loss of sixteen. When I told Sir Cyril Newall, the Chief of Air Staff, he refused to believe it possible. I saw a letter from Lloyd George to the P.M. refusing to accept office except on the most unqualified terms. L.G. said he was "genuinely anxious to help to extricate my country from the most terrible disaster into which it has ever been plunged by the ineptitude of its rulers. Several of the architects of this catastrophe are still leading members of your Government and two of them are in the Cabinet that directs the war" (i.e. Chamberlain and Halifax). The P.M. replied by saying that he would not abandon the loyalty he felt for Chamberlain, who had stood by him and was giving him all the support in his power.

Winston's ceaseless industry is impressive. He is always having ideas which he puts down on paper in the form of questions and despatches to Ismay or the C.I.G.S. for examination. Sometimes they relate to matters of major importance, such as the measures to be taken against invasion, or the provision of more aeroplanes, and sometimes they relate to quite trivial questions. This is the sort of thing: "General Ismay. Inquire into the number of German guns now trophies in this country and whether any can be reconditioned for blocking exits from beaches against tanks conceivably landed thereon." Another today asked whether wax could be supplied to troops to put in their ears in order to deaden the noise of warfare.

Thursday, May 30th

Back to No. 10 by four o'clock and heard that half the B.E.F. were now away but that Dunkirk, the port of embarkation, was scarcely usable any more.

Returned to No. 10 to sleep. I am glad to see the Cabinet are already thinking about building up a new expeditionary force, based on St Nazaire, and Winston has already telegraphed in this sense to Reynaud and Weygand.

Friday, May 31st

Everybody elated by the progress of the evacuation. One of the world's greatest defeats is being redeemed by an outstanding achievement of organisation and gallantry. The B.E.F. rearguards, though decimated, are standing firm against fearful odds; the R.A.F. activity over Dunkirk is ceaseless; the navy has attempted and achieved the incredible. Two hundred and twenty-two men of war have been used in the evacuation and 665 other vessels. The sailors are so tired that they are working automatically, but they are apparently quite undaunted.

Meanwhile the Secret Service reports from Germany show that the difficulties there are increasing and that the Nazis are terrified of failing to win the war this summer. There is general apathy at home in Germany, the casualties have been heavy, the shortages of food and raw materials are making themselves felt, and the production of tanks and aircraft is falling off by forty per cent. If these reports are true, the war may well be over by Christmas, despite the German people's and army's famous staying power.

The P.M. flew to Paris this morning with Attlee and the C.I.G.S., but, alas, without taking a Private Secretary. As a result I had very little to do but gossip with Brendan Bracken, the Chief Whip, etc.

Indirect attempts are being made, through the Dominions' High Commissioners, etc., to bring the U.S. into the war by painting to members of the Administration the most sombre portrait of what we expect from Germany and by harping on the possibility of France giving up the struggle.

Although Italy is making every preparation for immediate war, I think there is still a chance it is all stupendous bluff. If Musso were serious he would scarcely be so blatant about it all.

Had a long talk with Eden from whom I gathered enough information to make me almost sure that Philip is south-west of the Somme and thus comparatively safe. Eden is amazed by the success of the evacuation. As Brendan Bracken put it "we should have sold out for 40,000 a few days ago", and now 170,000 are already home. Edward Bridges said cynically: "Evacuation is becoming our greatest national industry."

6

Collapse of France

June 1940

Saturday, June 1st

Very busy all the morning, especially when the P.M. returned from Paris with a box full of straggling papers. His minute on the paper in which Tony had asked about sending the National Gallery pictures to Canada was: "No, bury them in caves and cellars. None must go. We are going to beat them."

Brendan Bracken is always complaining about "yes-men". It was therefore amusing to see somebody not behaving as a "yes-man" as far as he personally is concerned. The P.M. wants to make him a Privy Councillor. The King has caused Alec Hardinge[1] to write and expostulate. Winston, however, who is nothing if not loyal to his friends, has taken up the cudgels vigorously and, in his reply, complains that it is indeed hard if his most loyal supporter, who has stood alone with him in the wilderness prophesying the wrath to come, is to be refused this honour. I suppose Winston will get his way, but it is clear that the King has a mind of his own.

I had a somewhat stormy passage this afternoon with the P.M., because the Chiefs of Staff were not at Admiralty House when he wanted them. He rated me soundly, but I did not mind as my conscience was, in this case, clear and as he always pitches upon the first available person to display his wrath, irrespective of who is to blame. But he bears no grudge. Spoke to Lord Gort who returned from Dunkirk this morning.

Had tea with Mrs Churchill in the drawing-room of the flat on the top floor of Admiralty House. She was full of conversation and

---

[1] Assistant Private Secretary to George V. Private Secretary to Edward VIII, with whom he got on badly, and to George VI. Succeeded his father, who had been Permanent Under Secretary at the Foreign Office, Ambassador in Paris and Viceroy of India, as Lord Hardinge of Penshurst.

pleasurably excited at the prospect of going to Chequers for the first time. She and Winston went down there in the evening, but there was enough happening to prevent my going down to Cambridge to stay the night as I had intended.

Seal agreed that, as far as he was concerned, I could go and fight and he promised to arrange to get me a Commission in the R.N.V.R. But Mallet, of the F.O., whom I immediately went to see, said that there were many similar aspirants in the F.O., but that for the moment Alec Cadogan had refused to release anyone. I could not be released unless others were also. He said he thought there might be a change soon, if operations continued at this intense pressure, and he promised to let me know as soon as possible.

Sunday, June 2nd
Lunched with Grandfather and Peggy. Talking about Italy, Grandfather said that the Italians had a certain grievance against us. We made lavish promises in the secret Treaty of London of 1915 and we could not fulfil them. In the last war we had been prepared to do almost anything to win new Allies and the results had often been disastrous – viz. the Balfour Declaration.

After lunch I walked through Chelsea with Peggy who is much exercised about Fifth Columnists and the lack of deep air-raid shelters.

I returned to No. 10 just before the P.M. got back from Chequers. The Chiefs of Staff arrived and I gathered that the evacuation was proceeding smoothly. Now all attention centres on two matters: the expected drive against the French towards Paris and the provision of equipment for a new B.E.F. Reynaud has telegraphed for more fighters, more bombers and more troops in order to withstand the great attack expected shortly on the Somme and on the Aisne. This annoys Winston who considers the French grasping and whose main energies are now turned to consolidating our home defences, conserving our air strength, and building up a new army from the remnants of the old and from the troops now in India and Palestine. However, it is vital to sustain French morale and give no excuse for a collapse.

I went back to Admiralty House after dinner, but little happened and I was able to get home early. Eden made an admirable speech before the 9.00 news about the success of the evacuation from Dunkirk: a first rate performance.

Monday, June 3rd
Winston is tired of our always being on the defensive and is contemplating raids on the enemy's territory. "How wonderful it

would be," he writes to Ismay, "if the Germans could be made to wonder where they were going to be struck next instead of forcing us to try to wall in the Island and roof it over. An effort must be made to shake off the mental and moral prostration to the will and initiative of the enemy from which we suffer."

Found Horace Wilson at lunch in the Travellers and sat down beside him. I thought he was a little depressed, as indeed the loss of his powers behind the throne is likely to make him, and especially as there is inevitably a great deal of criticism now aimed at those thought to be responsible for the deficiencies in our armament and aeroplane production. I broached the question of being allowed, as a civil servant, to go and fight, because he is still Head of the Civil Service and might be able to help me. He showed himself sympathetic and promised to see what could be done.

Tuesday, June 4th
Our evacuation of Narvik, which I am sure is a mistake, is being delayed to allow the discussion of a Swedish plan for a settlement with Germany which would leave the King of Norway the northern half of the country.

The problem of the day is the French Government's demand for fresh divisions and more fighters. Apparently our aircraft losses in the last fortnight have seriously weakened our air defences, and Newall says that unless we have a respite he cannot guarantee the safety of this country against concentrated air attack for more than forty-eight hours. So we cannot afford to send fighter reinforcements to the French. We are sending two more divisions but our ability to provide more is dependent upon the speed with which we can replace the equipment we have lost.

Went to the House to hear the P.M.'s statement on the evacuation from Dunkirk. It was a magnificent oration which obviously moved the House. Speaking of the awful possibilities in store for us, and the chances of invasion, he made the following impressive peroration:

Even though large tracts of Europe have fallen into the grip of the Gestapo, and all the odious apparatus of Nazi rule, we shall not flag or fail. We shall go on to the end. We shall fight in France. We shall fight on the seas and oceans. We shall fight with growing confidence and growing strength in the air. We shall defend our Island, whatever the cost may be. We shall fight on the beaches. We shall fight on the landing grounds. We shall fight in the fields and streets. We shall fight in the hills. We shall never surrender. And even if, which I do not for a moment believe, this Island or a large part of it were subjugated and starving, then our Empire beyond the oceans, armed and guarded by the British fleet, will carry on the struggle until in God's good time the New World with all its power and might sets forth to the rescue and liberation of the old.

He did not finally mention in his speech (although he had originally intended to do so) that King Leopold, whom he castigated soundly, had given Lord Gort a pledge of continued resistance.

At Admiralty House after dinner Winston was a little on edge. He kept on ringing the bell and complaining that we were making too much noise. The last time he did so, he said, "What is all this bloody jaw? Who is it?" I said, "It's the First Lord, sir," and he smiled, saying, "Well, you've got me this time."

The First Lord, Alexander, was full of talk. He told me that he had tried three times to oppose the evacuation of Narvik, but it had been decided upon and he could do no more. He did not think much of the French navy. We talked about Maxton and I said I admired him for being an idealist and for having the courage to admit in Parliament that he did not see how his ideals could be put into effect. Alexander said Maxton was muddle-headed and that it was people like me, who listened to people like Maxton, that were responsible for the country being where it is today. Tony, who came in just then, hinted that this responsibility rested with the Labour Party as much as with anyone, and Alexander had the grace to agree. A. showed me an extraordinary telegram from Lord Cork at Narvik saying that the Norwegians were frightened of the Russians taking over the country, were therefore thinking of capitulating to the Germans, and would like us to leave our equipment behind so that the Germans could use it against the Russians!!

An encouraging report on aircraft production which shows that the number of new planes has exceeded those destroyed in the past few weeks. Lord Beaverbrook is producing the goods in an astonishing way.

Wednesday, June 5th

Winston is still full of offensive zeal and thinks that the Australians should be used for small forays on the coasts of occupied countries such as Denmark, Holland and Belgium. "Enterprises must be prepared," he minutes to Ismay, "with specially trained troops of the hunter class who can develop a reign of terror down these coasts, first of all on the 'butcher and bolt' policy, but later on, or perhaps as soon as we are organised, we should surprise Calais or Boulogne, kill and capture the Hun garrisons and hold the place until all the preparations to reduce it by siege or heavy storm have been made, and then away." Light armoured units must, he says, "crawl ashore, do a deep raid inland cutting a vital communication, and then back leaving a trail of German corpses behind them. It is probable that when the best troops go on to the attack on Paris, only the ordinary German troops of the line will be left. The lives of these must be made an intense torment."

Turning to more trivial subjects, the P.M. wrote this morning to Eden suggesting the restoration to officers of the leather shoulder-strap, abolished by "your foolish predecessor, Belisha".

Lunched with Cecil Syers at the Travellers. He agreed with me that history would probably judge King Leopold's action very differently from people today, and that he had proved a most useful scapegoat to the Allies.

The Germans have today begun another great offensive towards Paris, being anxious, no doubt, to allow our routed armies no respite. The French are demanding immense fighter support from us. Winston would like to send more than the air experts will agree. The latter say that we must have time for reorganisation and that we cannot leave this country exposed.

Thursday, June 6th

In the early hours I was disturbed by a Yellow warning, but fortunately the raid did not reach London.

Interesting censorship report on public opinion, as shown in letters. There is no frenzied fury against the Germans but much cold and reasoned hatred. The war has now for the first time become the question of paramount importance to the average Englishman. There is no sign of bad morale, and little wish for peace at any price, but it is noteworthy that discouraged and defeatist women outnumber men by two to one.

Lunched with Janet Margesson at Luigi's (incidentally the Home Secretary reports that the waiters at a lot of restaurants, including Quaglino's, the Café Royal and the Dorchester, are thought to be dangerous). Afterwards Jan and I sat in the shade in St James's Park and thought what a lovely town London was.

Dined with Lady Wolverton.[1] The Dutch Minister and his wife

[1] Daughter of the famous beauty, Georgiana, Countess of Dudley. Lived in St James's Place till her house was destroyed by a bomb. She had a forceful personality and her contemporaries found her alarming, but she was kind to young people. She told me to marry Audrey Paget, but as far as I know did not consult Audrey. And I had a matrimonial obsession elsewhere.

were there, also Sir George Clerk.[1] The latter said that in order to
wage war Democracies had to convert themselves into Dicta-
torships. We had our Dictator; in France there was only one
potential one, M. Mandel, and he, as a Jew, would find it difficult
to establish himself, particularly when M. Blum[2] and the Front
Populaire were still so vividly impressed on the minds of the French
bourgeoisie.

The P.M. went to a cinema, to see the Dunkirk film, and
returned to Admiralty House in rather a bad temper. He bade me
light the fire, although it was the hottest of hot nights, and then
proceeded to work till 1.30. He was cross with the French, who are
being persistent in their demands for further air support. Pétain*
and Weygand are saying that if we do not send fighters, the present
battle will be lost and France will have to capitulate. Pétain told
Reynaud that if he had not the courage to do so, he, Pétain, would
undertake the task. I think the French are trying to frighten us,
for bargaining purposes, but Winston is justifiably angry with
Vuillemin[3] who referred to our tremendous air efforts in the first
battle as "tardy, inadequate but nevertheless of value". Pug Ismay
says the French are nothing short of outrageous: we have thrown
no bricks at them despite the fact that they let down our Expeditionary Force; and they, without one word of gratitude for the help
we gave them in evacuation and in air fighting, do nothing but sling
mud at us. All this talk on their part of Allied solidarity is shown in
effect to refer only to the necessity of preserving the sacred soil of
France. We should be insane to send them all our fighters, because
if they were lost this country would be beaten in two days, whereas
even if France surrenders we shall still win the war – provided our
air defences are intact.

The P.M. was in an impatient frame of mind. He was angry with
the First Sea Lord, who is being excessively cautious about Winston's cherished OPERATION PAUL (which is to interrupt by mine-
laying the Lulea iron-ore traffic), and with the Secretary of State
for War (Anthony Eden) who is making difficulties about bringing
battalions of trained troops back from Palestine. "We are indeed
the victims of a feeble and weary departmentalism," he wrote; and
after comparing the success of our efforts in providing divisions in
the last war with our inability to do so in this, he wrote, "Our

---

[1] Ambassador in Paris in the 1930s.
[2] Leader of the *Front Populaire* and twice socialist Prime Minister of France in
the 1930s. A patriot and idealist.
[3] Commander in Chief of the ill-equipped and largely ineffective French air
force.

weakness, slowness, lack of grip and drive are very apparent on the background of what was done twenty-five years ago."

Friday, June 7th
As Winston went down to Chartwell at lunch-time there was very little to do and I sat in the shade most of the afternoon in the garden at No. 10, reading a book of war stories called *The Green Curve*.

After tea I motored down to Uppark for the night. Herbert Meade, who represents I suppose, a large section of opinion in the country, said he hoped that when we had won the war we should bomb German towns and show the German people it did not pay to make war. Perhaps there is much to be said for firmness, but I think sheer vindictiveness is neither a right nor a paying policy.

There is great excitement in Sussex over the organisation of the new Local Defence Volunteers.

Sunday, June 9th
At Stansted.

Lord Bessborough is wholly occupied with the Fifth Column, which he avows is very powerful in Sussex and will not be squashed until the Fascist party is declared illegal. I shall arrange for him to come to No. 10 and see Morton.* Meanwhile the most decisive battle in history is at its climax.

Monday, June 10th
Left Stansted at 7.30 and drove up to London, dropping Eric at Petersfield *en route*. The roads are now barricaded and guarded by soldiers.

In the afternoon there was chaos at Admiralty House. Winston made one of his lightning decisions to go to Paris, and just as he was about to leave for Hendon, a telegram was thrust into my hand to say that the French Government were going to leave Paris. "What the Hell?" was all the P.M. said, but subsequently as there was no aerodrome available at which he could land he reluctantly concluded that "there was no perch on which he could alight" and gave up the plan. After much telephoning and shilly-shallying, Mary Churchill turned Winston out of "the flat", because she had Mark Howard coming to tea, and we all moved downstairs to the state rooms.

The news from France is distressing. The Germans have taken Rouen and the French are making more and more extravagant demands for air support. Winston thinks it good that the French Government is leaving Paris because it shows that they intend to go on fighting; but he is afraid that Flandin[1] and other "Quislings"[2] may stay behind and make terms with the invader.

Mussolini decided to come into the war, and we had to wake up Winston from his afternoon slumber and tell him of this added complication. At least it was not unexpected – though I personally thought it might not happen. There has never been such a flourish of trumpets to announce a grand entry; but the Italians have a sense of the melodramatic. In any case they have given us time to make our dispositions and move heavy bombers to the south of France. We are to make a grand attack by air tomorrow night.

At Admiralty House the possibility of the French giving in, or being defeated, was of greater interest to all present than the approaching entry of Italy into the war. All Winston said about the latter event was, "People who go to Italy to look at ruins won't have to go as far as Naples and Pompeii in future." He was in a very bad temper, snapped almost everybody's head off, wrote angry minutes to the First Sea Lord, and refused to pay any attention to messages given him orally. We all listened to Roosevelt's speech from America: it mentioned Italy's "stab in the back" and was about as useful as it could have been in the circumstances.

Tuesday, June 11th
The P.M. went to France to bolster up the fainting French morale.

Wednesday, June 12th
The news today is darker than it has yet been. General Haining[3] says Paris will almost certainly fall within the next forty-eight hours. The French, although fighting with grim determination, are at the end of their tether, and although Reynaud wishes to fight to the end Pétain is willing to make peace. He is worse than Bazaine[4] in 1870. Meanwhile our 51st Division is cornered at St Valéry and has been ordered to surrender by the French. Its commander has refused, but as evacuation of the remaining men is now all but impossible submission may be inevitable. The French troops at St

---

[1] Had been French Minister of Commerce, of Finance and of Foreign Affairs and, briefly, Prime Minister. Arrested by the Free French in Algiers in 1943, but acquitted of collaboration when brought to trial after the war. Abetted by Randolph, Churchill did his best to help him and his support possibly swayed the verdict.

[2] The word, taken from the name of a Norwegian traitor, was already coming into general use.

[3] Vice Chief of the Imperial General Staff, 1940–41.

[4] Marshal François Bazaine. In the Franco-Prussian War of 1870, having lost the battle of Gravelotte, he surrendered the fortress of Metz with 173,000 men and without putting up a fight.

Valéry are already hanging out white flags. Pray God Philip is with those of our troops who are at Havre and whose embarkation at Cherbourg for home seems to be progressing favourably. Some of his luggage arrived today, labelled Havre, and so there is every hope; but the journey home by ship will be very dangerous.

Last night the French tried to prevent our bombers setting out to attack Italy. They even placed lorries on the aerodromes to prevent the Wellingtons taking off. Such is their spirit of co-operation. They are afraid of Italian retaliation; but, poor things, they are naturally in a state of desperation.

After dinner I read the account of Winston's conversations with the French yesterday (he returned at lunch-time today). Apparently the Generals have no reserves left. Their divisions are decimated and every man and weapon has been thrown into the line; but nothing can stop the German steamroller. Weygand and Georges talk about the impossibility of carrying on the struggle, at any rate on co-ordinated lines, but Reynaud is as indomitable as Pétain is defeatist. There is the usual cry for the use of our whole air force, and we are now going to send far more than we can afford. But we must save enough to carry on the war victoriously in the event of France surrendering. There is apparently a young French General called de Gaulle,* of whom Winston thinks a great deal, and perhaps he might organise further resistance in Brittany or on the Atlantic seaboard, to which our divisions could be sent. Soon we shall have another army, but as Weygand says it is no longer a matter of weeks or days, but of hours.

Winston has sent a graphic telegram to Roosevelt, describing the impending catastrophe, and he seems to hope that America will come in now, at any rate as a non-belligerent ally. But can American support, in materials, be made effective in time?

At Admiralty House there was great activity. Beaverbrook made a lot of noise, presumably hoping to cheer people up thereby, and all the Air Ministry heads were there concocting a telegram to France about the number of bombers and fighters we can send tomorrow. Unfortunately the effective range of our fighters will not enable them to go far up the Seine, but it would be suicidal to send them to aerodromes in France where they would be destroyed on the ground.

After midnight Reynaud rang up. Winston could not hear him, because the line was so bad and eventually de Margerie[1] and I had

[1] Roland de Margerie, Minister at the French Embassy in London under Monsieur Corbin, was now *Chef de Cabinet* to Reynaud. His son was a popular and effective Ambassador in London in the 1980s and was then posted to Washington.

to carry on a conversation through the intermediary of telephone operators. Reynaud asked that Winston should go back to France tomorrow, arriving at the Prefecture at Tours by 2.45. This looks as if the French mean to give in, because Reynaud promised to consult Winston again before any fundamental decision was taken, and this sudden summons is ominous. Perhaps W. will be able to persuade them to carry on the war, west of Paris, on a guerilla basis. The Germans must be exhausted and their lines of communication are immense, so if only the French could hold yet a few days the skies might clear.

Winston was furious because Reynaud would talk of the hour of arrival and destination over an open line: he thought it very dangerous and spent a long time considering how to deceive the Germans who had, he felt sure, listened to the conversation. Finally he decided to go very early in the morning with a strong escort of fighters; but at one moment he was ordering me to ring up de Margerie and say, untruthfully, that it was impossible for him to go. This would have caused chaos at the other end and, at the risk of having my head bitten off, I dissuaded him.

Speaking of the surrender of the 51st Division, W. said it was the most "brutal disaster" we had yet suffered.

Thursday, June 13th
Winston came back from France about dinner-time; but as it was my early night I gave Moore Crosthwaite[1] dinner at the Apéritif, in payment of an ill-advised bet that Chamberlain's Government would not fall. He tells me there is great rancour against Chamberlain and his colleagues because of the lack of equipment, and that much of the credit for the recent rapid improvement is being given to Morrison and Bevin as having called in the Trade Unions to redress the mistakes and omissions of the manufacturers and ruling classes. This is unfair, because although the Trade Unions have certainly co-operated handsomely, it is Winston and Beaverbrook who have really galvanised the country and the Government departments. I think that Moore is probably right in saying that the Prime Minister's personality has a great effect on the speed with which Government departments work and the energy they display. Chamberlain had drive, but he had not Winston's probing and restless mind: he expected his subordinates to work with the same tirelessness and efficiency that he showed himself, but never

---

[1] An intelligent Fabian intellectual, with an acerbic wit, who had been a colleague of mine in the Eastern Department and was in due course Ambassador to the Lebanon and to Sweden.

questioned their ability to do so. Winston, on the other hand, is always looking for shortcomings and inspires others to be as zealous ferrets as himself. But, of course, Chamberlain never had the "complete powers" or the universal support which events have given Winston.

When I got back to No. 10, to sleep, I found that Winston had returned from Tours and was recounting his experiences to the Cabinet. Apparently Weygand was suggesting an Armistice in order that he might still retain the vestige of an army to deal with disaffection. "They were very nearly gone," Winston said, and they asked to be released from their pledge not to make a separate peace. This W. refused on behalf of the British Government.

At an opportune moment came a message from Roosevelt to Reynaud, promising support. This raised in Winston's mind hopes of approaching American intervention as an active Ally, but I fear these hopes may be doomed to disappointment because it is for Congress and not for the President to decide. However the message cheered up the French, who are desperately anxious to see "some gleam of light at the far end of the tunnel". Winston therefore telegraphed to Roosevelt asking leave to publish the telegram to Reynaud: such action would revitalise the French and prevent Hitler from dictating peace in Paris. "All the far-reaching plans, strategic, economic, political and moral which your message expounds may be still-born if the French cut out now," Winston continued: "We fully realise that the moment Hitler finds he cannot dictate a Nazi peace in Paris he will turn his fury on us", and he explained that we much regretted our inability through force of circumstances, to take our full share of the present battle on land.

Friday, June 14th

Mr Kennedy rang up to refuse permission to publish Roosevelt's message to Reynaud. It seems that the P.M.'s expectations last night of immediate American help were exaggerated. Roosevelt has got to proceed cautiously, but the plain truth is that America has been caught napping, militarily and industrially. She may be really useful to us in a year; but we are living from hour to hour.

News that Paris has fallen. I am still reading *War and Peace*, which I never have had time to finish, and have reached the point where the French are entering Moscow. The position is in some respects analogous, except that the winter with its cold and ice is further off today than it was in September 1812. If the French will go on fighting, we must now fall back on the Atlantic, creating new lines of Torres Vedras[1] behind which British divisions and American supplies can be concentrated. Paris is not France, and provided defeatism in the French High Command can be thwarted there is no reason to suppose the Germans will be able to subdue the whole country. Guerilla warfare on long lines of communications should be most effective.

In the afternoon came a telegram from our Military Mission in France to Dill, who brought it over to show the P.M. It said that organised resistance in France was at an end, that the French army was disintegrating into disorganised groups, and that Weygand, Georges and Brooke were agreed as to the impossibility of holding Brittany. Obviously a French collapse can now only be averted by a miracle or by the heroism of France's leaders. The former seems the more probable of the two, although Reynaud, de Gaulle, etc., are full of zeal. America's attitude is of vital importance to French morale; but America is the slowest to act of all the democracies, and that is saying much.

The Churchills are moving into No. 10 today, but the P.M. thought it best to spend the night with Lord Beaverbrook. He came to No. 10 after dinner and had a long conference with David Margesson, Desmond Morton, Brendan Bracken and Duncan Sandys[2] (who shows no *gêne* about sitting here and drinking in all the most secret information) regarding the suggestion that 250,000 French troops should be brought here with their equipment in order to make this Island stiff with soldiers and lessen the likelihood of a successful invasion. It is now almost certain that the French will ask for an armistice as their powers of resistance are at an end and Reynaud can scarcely stand up alone to the pressure from his Cabinet and his Generals. It is thus a question of salvage: the 120,000 British troops in France and as much French material and manpower as we can evacuate.

About 2.00 a.m. Herschel Johnson brought round from the American Embassy Roosevelt's reply to the "Former Naval Person's" last telegram. It promised all support possible, but was careful to define what that possibility was. Active and open support does not seem as near as the P.M. thought and encouraged Reynaud to believe. W. told Eden he thought France would crack internally in a day or two.

The general opinion now is that nothing can save France, whatever may be the fate of her Colonies and fleet, but that

---

[1] The three concentric lines of defence, built by Wellington to cover Lisbon, which halted the advance of Marshal Masséna in 1810.
[2] Later Lord Duncan-Sandys.*

nevertheless if we can hold on until November we shall have won the war. The holding-on is going to be a grim business, a chance for the whale to prove his superiority to the elephant.

Saturday, June 15th

Had intended to go to West Wycombe for the night to stay with the Dashwoods, but it was decided that I should go to Chequers with the P.M.

After tea Winston dictated long telegrams to Roosevelt and to the Dominions (whose premiers had all sent the most touching and encouraging messages) pointing out that we had now got to face the most trying ordeal of heavy bombing and saying to all that he personally was convinced that the carnage and destruction in this country would bring the U.S. into the war. He said that the French condition for carrying on had been a promise of active U.S. support: the promise of redoubled supplies which had been received was not sufficient, and though France might fight on from her Colonies her resistance at home would now almost certainly come to an end. "If words counted, we should win this war," he said, as a comment on his own telegraphic efforts.

We arrived at Chequers in time to dine at 9.30. The party consisted of Winston, Duncan and Diana Sandys, Lindemann and myself. It was at once the most dramatic and the most fantastic evening I have ever spent. Before going into the dining-room Tony Bevir told me on the telephone that telegrams had been received from Bordeaux to the effect that the position was deteriorating fast and the request to be allowed to make a separate peace was being put in a more brutal form. I imparted this to Winston who was immediately very depressed. Dinner began lugubriously, W. eating fast and greedily, his face almost in his plate, and every now and then firing some technical question at Lindemann, who was quietly consuming his vegetarian diet. The Sandyses and I sat silent, because our spasmodic efforts at conversation were not well received. However champagne and brandy and cigars did their work and we soon became talkative, even garrulous. Winston, in order to cheer himself and us up, read aloud the messages he had received from the Dominions and the replies he had sent to them and to Roosevelt. "The war is bound to become a bloody one for us now," he said, "but I hope our people will stand up to bombing and the Huns aren't liking what we are giving them. But what a tragedy that our victory in the last war should have been snatched from us by a lot of softies."

Winston and Duncan Sandys paced up and down the rose garden in the moonlight while Diana, Lindemann and I walked on the other side of the house. It was light and deliciously warm, but the sentries, with tin helmets and fixed bayonets, who were placed all round the house, kept us fully alive to the horrors of reality. I spent most of the time telephoning, searching for Winston among the roses and listening to his comments on the war. I told him that fuller information had now been received about the French attitude, which appeared to be slipping. "Tell them," he said, "that if they let us have their fleet we shall never forget, but that if they surrender without consulting us we shall never forgive. We shall blacken their name for a thousand years!" Then, half afraid that I might take him seriously, he added: "Don't, of course, do that just yet." He was in high spirits, repeating poetry, dilating on the drama of the present situation, maintaining that he and Hitler only had one thing in common – a horror of whistling – offering everybody cigars, and spasmodically murmuring, "Bang, Bang, Bang, goes the farmer's gun, run rabbit, run rabbit, run, run, run."

Kennedy telephoned and Winston, becoming serious for a minute, poured into his ears a flood of eloquence about the part that America could and should play in saving civilisation. Referring to promises of industrial and financial support, he said such an offer "would be a laughing-stock on the stage of history", and he begged that "we should not let our friend's (President R.) efforts peter out in grimaces and futility".

About 1.00 a.m. Winston came in from the garden and we all stood in the central hall while the Great Man lay on the sofa, puffed his cigar, discoursed on the building up of our fighter strength, and told one or two dirty stories. Finally, saying "Goodnight, my children", he went to bed at 1.30.

Sunday, June 16th

Woken at 6.30 by the telephone and shortly afterwards by a despatch rider who brought the full facts about the French from London. When I heard that the P.M. was awake, about 7.30, I took them to his room and found him lying in bed, looking just like a rather nice pig, clad in a silk vest. He ruminated for some time and then decided to call the Cabinet in London at 10.15, abandoning his project of having the French General de Gaulle, together with Eden and the C.I.G.S., to lunch at Chequers. So I hurried back to my room, ate a hasty breakfast, and was ready to leave by 8.30. I had to wait till after 9.00 before we started, being called from time to time to W.'s bedroom, where he was wasting time with Duncan Sandys, to receive orders. Finally we drove back to London in pouring rain, disregarding traffic lights and speeding down the Mall, to arrive just as the Cabinet assembled.

On the way to London the P.M. dictated a number of minutes to Mrs Hill[1] and did enough work to keep us all busy during the morning. It is one of the great differences between Chamberlain and Churchill that whereas the former, in reading Cabinet papers, seldom made any comments and only on questions of the highest policy, Churchill scrutinises every document which has anything to do with the war and does not disdain to enquire into the most trivial point.

The Cabinet met again at 3.00 and I ushered Corbin and de Gaulle into Desmond Morton's room to wait until they were summoned. Shortly afterwards I saw Morton who told me what the meeting was for and why the stern telegrams sent off this morning, refusing to release France from her "No separate peace" pledge, but in reality agreeing to an armistice, were being held up. Apparently there is a stupendous idea of declaring the political unity of England and France, and Reynaud has said that in these circumstances France would fight on, having seen "the ray of light at the end of the tunnel". I am not clear about the details of this epoch-making idea; but apparently Chamberlain is "in on it" with Salter,[2] Amery, Lloyd and Vansittart, and de Gaulle is one of its most ardent supporters. "De Gaulle is a magnificent crook," said Morton, "another Max Beaverbrook, just what we want!"

Bridges came out of the Cabinet and dictated the Declaration of Union to Mrs Hill in my room. It sounded inspiring, something which will revive the flagging energies of the French and invigorate our own people. It is a historic document and its effects will be more far-reaching than anything that has occurred this century – and more permanent?

Morton tells me that Horace Wilson has been working like a black on this proposal, that Van, one of its principal sponsors, has suddenly returned into the limelight, and that Monnet[3] is the man to whom the chief credit for the idea should be given. Apparently most of the day has been spent telephoning to Reynaud and Mandel, persuading them to hold fast and not give in to the defeatist pressure of their colleagues. De Gaulle has been strutting

[1] Kathleen Hill, the senior of Churchill's personal secretaries, who looked after his personal and constituency affairs and took his dictation (often straight on to the typewriter). She was patient, long-suffering, good-natured and a skilled violinist. Churchill was devoted to her.

[2] Distinguished academic and expert on shipping. Fellow of All Souls. M.P. for Oxford University from 1937. Chairman of the World Bank Advisory Council after the war and Minister of Materials in Churchill's 1951 Government. Ennobled in 1953.

[3] A founding father of the Common Market.

about in the Cabinet, with Corbin too; the Cabinet meeting turned into a sort of promenade, Winston beginning a speech in the Cabinet room and finishing it in Morton's room; and everybody has been slapping de Gaulle on the back and telling him he shall be Commander in Chief (Winston muttering *"je l'arrangerai"*). Is he to be a new Napoleon? From what I hear, it seems that a lot of people think so. He treats Reynaud (whom he called *"ce poisson gelé"*) like dirt and discourses familiarly on what he will do in France; yet he is only a Major General just recently discovered.

Meanwhile the King does not know what is being done to his Empire. The Lord President is going to see him at 7.00 and will break the news. Who knows, we may yet see the "fleurs de lys" restored to the Royal Standard!

7.00 p.m. Since writing the above I have obtained a clearer idea of the events of this astonishing day. On Friday night one of the Whips put David Margesson in touch with a Frenchman, called Pleven, who produced this idea of union together with that of evacuating French troops to the U.K. David got in touch with Desmond Morton, who welcomed the idea which was similar to that on which Monnet had been working, and David went up to No. 11, where the Halifaxes were dining with the Chamberlains, to propound the scheme. He became eloquent (he says) but was not enthusiastically received. Finally, after discovering that Horace Wilson knew about the matter, David and Desmond persuaded Brendan Bracken to let them take Pleven to see Winston. W. was bored and critical, but eventually went upstairs to discuss the matter with Chamberlain. Nothing more occurred here and certainly, last night, the whole idea was far from Winston's mind and he was preoccupied with the necessity of saving the French fleet if France capitulated. At this morning's Cabinet a telegram was drafted and actually despatched to Reynaud which said, in effect, "ask for an armistice and let us have the fleet" (though it did not release the French from their pledge not to make a separate peace). Winston lunched at the Carlton Club with Corbin, de Gaulle, Eden, C.I.G.S., and presumably de Gaulle persuaded him to consider seriously this revolutionary project – on which, of course, Monnet, Amery, Salter, etc., had busily been working behind the scenes. The Cabinet met hurriedly at 3.00; the declaration was re-drafted several times; and it was agreed that Winston, Attlee, Sinclair, Ismay and the Chiefs of Staff should tonight go to Brittany and meet Reynaud.

I went back to No. 10 at 9.00 and found that a telegram had been received from Bordeaux cancelling the meeting with Reynaud. Why?

Monday, June 17th

Reynaud has resigned, unable to withstand the pressure, despite the fact that the proposed Declaration was telegraphed to him yesterday afternoon. Pétain has formed a Government of Quislings, including Laval, and France will now certainly ask for an armistice in spite of her pledge to us. However a telegram from Baudouin, the new Minister of Foreign Affairs,[1] makes it appear that the surrender of the fleet will be refused. The Spanish are to be used as intermediaries and not the Americans as was expected. I gather that French demoralisation is complete and that Weygand is afraid that the troops may turn on their officers. In any case the internal explosion, which Winston prophesied the other day, is now quite probable. Perhaps the new Government will, in the end, accept the Declaration, if they consider Germany's terms cannot honourably be accepted, but it is all too likely now that yesterday's "cloud-capped towers, the gorgeous palaces . . . shall dissolve and . . . leave not a rack behind", and that the visions of a golden future which the Declaration held out are doomed to vanish. I feel like a deflated soufflé.

The Cabinet met at 11.00 and shortly afterwards we heard that Pétain had ordered the French army to lay down its arms. Lord Lloyd told me that he had seen Weygand a few days ago and that he was shrivelled up physically and mentally by the ordeal he had been through. If only the Declaration had been approved twenty-four hours earlier, Reynaud, supported by Mandel, de Gaulle – and, who knows, "by a whiff of grapeshot" – might have saved the situation, and the terms of the Declaration "against subjection to a system which reduces mankind to a life of robots and slaves" would have assuredly found response in France and the U.S. There would have been great difficulties to surmount, but we had before us the bridge to a new world, the first elements of European or even World Federation.

After the Cabinet the P.M. paced backwards and forwards in the garden, alone, his head bowed, his hands behind his back. He was doubtless considering how best the French fleet, the air force and the Colonies could be saved. He, I am sure, will remain undaunted.

4.00: Went over to the F.O. to see if I could discover any news. I met Van, who said that he thought the Declaration was by no means dead, that the German terms would very probably be such that the French could not accept them, and that he had just drafted

---

[1] A banker by profession. Strongly supported Pétain, Laval and the "Peace Party" against Reynaud.

a telegram in French from the P.M. to Pétain appealing to the latter's sense of honour, which was very real, talking about the "*vainqueur de Verdun*", etc., and stressing the things we could do to help France. It was important to get at Pétain's feelings of honour before it was too late, and if telegrams were impossible the message must be taken by Lord Lloyd in an aeroplane immediately. General Spears was no good; he was too implicated with Reynaud. Van looked well and full of energy; he has come into his own, like so many black sheep and discarded statesmen.

Sir Robert Vansittart, made a peer by Churchill in 1941, was a man of striking intellectual ability, profound literary knowledge and poor judgment. He was Permanent Under Secretary when I joined the Foreign Office in 1937 and had established a high reputation at home and abroad. Indeed it was too high for his comfort, Anthony Eden much disliking the general belief that Van (as he was always called) was the power behind his throne and the real originator of all diplomatic initiatives. With the support of Chamberlain who, like most Prime Ministers, resented the Foreign Office, Eden arranged for Sir Alexander Cadogan to succeed Van. He was given the high-sounding but empty title of Chief Diplomatic Adviser to the Government, was left in the Permanent Under Secretary's corner office on the ground floor and was deprived of all active work in the department.

When Churchill came to power, Van doubtless hoped for renewed influence since he had constantly warned of the German danger in the years before the war. However, though Churchill felt the usual Prime Ministerial distaste for the Foreign Office, he did not seek to interfere in that department's internal arrangements. He was always ready to read the memoranda Van addressed to him, but he was well aware of his tendency to box the compass every twenty-four hours if some fresh intellectual concept obsessed him.

Lady Vansittart, whose sister was married to Sir Eric Phipps, Ambassador both in Paris and in Berlin, had beautiful green eyes and was an entrancing companion. Her son by her first marriage, Sir Colville Barclay, was an exact contemporary of mine in the Foreign Office, agreeable and serious minded, but keener to be a painter than a diplomat. He was, at this time, deeply enamoured of Winston Churchill's niece, the beautiful Clarissa; but his passion was unrequited and she soon had many other dedicated admirers, one of whom, Anthony Eden, she eventually married.

I have a feeling that today may have been rather wasted. We ought surely to have been spreading sedition among French Colonial Governors and instructing our agents to commit sabotage in France. Perhaps we have not been inactive, but the necessary orders do not seem to have come from the top.

The P.M. telegraphed to Pétain expressing his disbelief that "the illustrious Marshal Pétain and the famous General Weygand will injure their ally by delivering over to the enemy the fine French fleet. Such an act would scarify their names for a thousand years of history." Van's telegram in French does not seem to have been approved.

Tuesday, June 18th
The day of Waterloo – a poignant anniversary.

The French are apparently continuing to fight on the Loire and there are indications that Darlan does not intend to let the fleet fall into German hands. I spoke to Hartington[1] on the telephone and he told me that Philip was with the Beauman force, which seems to have borne the brunt of the fighting. The Central War Room informed me that the headquarters of this force were at Avranches, on the sea; so if Philip has survived he should be home at any moment now.

On a minute about the proposal to take away the King of Italy's Garter, the P.M. has scribbled: "I think there should be the utmost ignominy and publicity in the case of this miserable puppet." So much for the House of Savoy! Mother thinks that the Pope should have protested powerfully against Italy entering the war, and that in omitting to do so he has sacrificed great kudos which the R.C. Church might have won.

I see from the Cabinet conclusions that many of our Territorial officers have shown themselves inadequate and Storm Troopers are to be formed. In order to win this war we have to approximate closely and still more closely to the Nazis: complete governmental powers, internment camps and now Storm Troopers.

Mother rang up in the morning to say Philip was back – the last Guardsman to leave France. An indescribable relief.

This morning the Cabinet is discussing a declaration which de Gaulle wishes to make in French on the wireless in this country. Though not *apparently* disloyal to Pétain's Government, it is so in effect, and is intended to rally Frenchmen in this country and elsewhere to de Gaulle himself. He had better not go back to

---

[1] The Marquess of Hartington, elder son of the Duke of Devonshire. Married Kathleen, daughter of Joseph P. Kennedy. Killed in action in 1944.

France just yet or else, as David suggested yesterday, all Gaul may be divided into three parts once again.

The Declaration of Union has been published in today's press not, Desmond Morton tells me, because it is a dead letter but in order that it may have its effect on U.S. opinion. It may still be practicable if Herriot[1] and a Government of die-hards succeed Pétain and fight on from outside France.

Went to the House and heard the P.M. speak on the collapse of France and the question of invasion and air bombardment here. He spoke less well than on the last occasion, and referred more often to his notes; but he ended magnificently. I was amused that he brought in Marvell's lines,

> He nothing common did or mean,
> Upon that memorable scene,

because he has been repeating it consistently and often for the last fortnight. Last Saturday he came out with it several times in the course of the evening and could not resist quoting it to the American Ambassador on the telephone while demanding assistance from the U.S.

After the speech I told him Attlee wanted to see him. He was performing his toilet (!) and said: "So does Amery; he is very tiresome, always wanting to air his views about how to win the war, on behalf of the Junior Ministers, instead of getting on with his work at the India Office."

General Spears came in, asking to see Winston. He said that the Cabinet had turned down de Gaulle's broadcast, because they were anxious not to offend the present French Government yet; now, however, he had evidence to show why it was essential that de Gaulle should speak. It was a question of saving in time a large number of aeroplanes at Bordeaux. Winston told Spears he would agree provided the rest of the War Cabinet concurred, and Spears, looking miserable and hot, set forth on his tour of conversion. Later in the afternoon Vansittart and Morton insisted on my going up to wake Winston, who had just taken to his bed: they wanted to urge on him a new scheme of Van's which entailed Lord Lloyd flying out to Bordeaux to put H.M.G.'s views fairly and squarely to the French Government. Van thought that this would be preferable to, and would exclude, de Gaulle broadcasting.

I went up to the P.M.'s bedroom. The blinds were drawn and Winston himself was right under the bedclothes. When he emerged he had a bandage over his eyes to keep out the light. Finally it was

[1] French elder statesman. President of the Chamber of Deputies and at one time a Prime Minister and Foreign Minister of European renown.

agreed that Van's project, which Halifax and Morton think a forlorn hope, should be put into effect *and* that de Gaulle should broadcast. Halifax thought that we should pull all strings at once: they might get crossed, e.g. Lord Lloyd might get a cool reception if de Gaulle spoke; but there was already such chaos in France that a little more would scarcely do any harm.

Just before dinner a telegram came in from Campbell[1], saying that the French thought it would be dishonourable to negotiate an armistice unless their armed forces were still intact, but it seemed likely that the fleet would be denied to the Germans. I took this telegram up to the P.M., who was dressing. When he saw me coming with a telegram he said: "Another bloody country gone west, I'll bet."

As I went out to dinner I met Morton and Lindemann and together we gossiped, at the top of the steps leading down to the F.O., about the extraordinary de Gaulle intrigues, etc. Lindemann said cynically that the only thing in which production was going ahead really fast was theories.

Dined with Sylvia Henley. Her brother Oliver Stanley[2], Juliet Henley and Judy Montagu[3] were there. At 9.00 the P.M. spoke on the wireless, almost word for word what he had said in the House. It was too long and he sounded tired. Juliet said it was like listening to a bishop. He smoked a cigar the whole time he was broadcasting.

Back at No. 10 after dinner. The usual evening party assembled, i.e. Beaverbrook, also Van, Morton and Cadogan. Beaverbrook told me that the Air Ministry was a rotten Ministry and Sinclair a thoroughly bad Minister who was hoodwinked by his subordinates. Pug Ismay says the Chiefs of Staff are too old and slow. There ought to be a chairman who could preside over them and enforce decisions. He thought the P.M. would end by being appointed C. in C. of all three forces.

Winston was furious because the morning papers, which he likes to see before going to bed, had not arrived. In his emotion he upset his whisky and soda over all his papers. I asked him if he would see General Sikorski[4] tomorrow. "I will see him," he said, "at noon,"

[1] Sir Ronald Hugh Campbell, British Ambassador in Paris.
[2] Brother of Lord Stanley of Alderley, not to be confused with the well-known politician.
[3] Only child of Edwin Montagu, member of Mr Asquith's Government and author of the Montagu–Chelmsford constitutional reforms in India, and Venetia Stanley, for whom Mr Asquith, when Prime Minister, conceived an irrepressible passion.
[4] A hero of the Polish campaign against the Red Army in 1920. Prime Minister and Commander in Chief of the Poles in exile in Britain. Killed in an air crash at Gibraltar in 1942.

and then went on to quote some entirely bogus quotation about that time of day, which he pretended was spoken by the nurse in *Romeo and Juliet.*

I had a long conversation with General Spears outside the door of No. 10. He told me: (i) That he had been with Reynaud when de Gaulle telephoned to him the text of the Declaration of Union. R. had been immensely impressed, but his colleagues had said that the British were trying to make France a Dominion. (ii) That the importance of de Gaulle's speech lay in the fact that Germany was bound to inundate France with propaganda and that it was, therefore, vital to be sure of a focus for Frenchmen on foreign soil, around which all the men and material that escaped could be grouped. Inside France itself a Government of Traitors would soon be established and it would be said that France had been uselessly sacrificed on England's behalf. (iii) That Weygand's strategy in the late battle had been unbelievably bad. The French troops could have no confidence in their High Command which had made mistakes that any intelligent boy-scout could have avoided.

Wednesday, June 19th
Full moon last night: the air-raids will now begin. They were bigger last night than hitherto, and Cambridge was hit, a row of houses being destroyed. David has been called up and will join his unit at Hove on Friday. Philip is to return to the Holding Battalion at Wellington Barracks.

A comparatively uneventful morning, though there are now signs that the French navy is not going to allow itself to be taken. The French Colonial Governors are wobbling but their military commanders are almost all threatening to arrest them if they give in. I told Morton that I did not think enough capital had been made out of the Declaration of Union, especially in the French Empire. He agreed, and the B.B.C. are, I hope, going to remedy the matter in their broadcast tonight.

President R. has turned down our demand for forty destroyers, but at Van's instigation the matter is not to be allowed to drop. We need them badly.

Saw a letter from Bob Boothby who claims that there is now a revolutionary spirit in the country which ought to be turned to advantage. He is for drastic measures: the conversion of the War Cabinet into a Committee of Public Safety, the adoption of really dictatorial powers, the proclamation of Martial Law. He says: "This is essentially a young man's war. . . . It is this incredible conception of a movement (in Germany), young, virile, dynamic and violent, which is advancing irresistibly to overthrow a decaying old world, that we must continue to bear in mind; for it is the main source of the Nazi strength and power." Boothby claims that our leaders (as Pug Ismay said last night), are too old for this kind of war and that there is growing discontent with the fact among the younger officers. He thinks, however, that Lloyd George is an exception and should be brought back to office.

Boothby also claims to have information, gained in Switzerland, that the German invasion of this country will have three elements: by sea from ports stretching from Petsamo to Havre, and including amphibious tanks; by parachute landings in the West Country; by violent bombardment of the ports.

He is certainly a man with drive and, as Tony Bevir remarked, will probably obtain a seat in the most revolutionary post-war Government.

There is evidence to show that Spain is likely to enter the war against us at an early date, and that the military in Japan are bringing great weight to bear in favour of not letting the present opportunity slip.

Went with Mother and Aunt Nancy to see *The Tempest* at the Old Vic. Prospero is not the part for John Gielgud, but Marius Goring as Ariel and Jack Hawkins as Caliban were excellent, and Peggy Ashcroft made an enchanting Miranda, even though she is beginning to look rather too mature for these maidenly parts. The stalls were practically empty, owing presumably to the general preoccupation with other things, but the gallery was full and enthusiastic.

Thursday, June 20th

Miriam Pease[1] came to breakfast. She is a factory inspector and told me that the conditions in armament factories are now appalling. Even boys of fourteen are working a seventy-hour week, and as it is impossible to work in shifts owing to the lack of skilled labour, efficiency is bound to suffer. Ventilation of factories is bad, she says. The Ministry of Labour cause confusion by setting up innumerable committees to deal with matters which had better be dealt with by experienced and trained experts in industrial conditions.

Heavy air-raids last night in which Southampton, Yorkshire and South Wales seem to have suffered. I suppose the real air armada will come soon, troop carriers and all. Spears thinks we are not by any means sure of being able to deal with it or with tank landings.

---

[1] Daughter of Lord Gainford and an old friend of my mother. A professional factory inspector of long experience.

Winston is goading the C. in C. Home Forces (Ironside), who seems to lack imagination, and he is busy forming special anti-tank forces of mobile troops. He is also taking the question of supply very seriously and has meetings almost every morning now. Lindemann is his right-hand man in this.

The real trouble about air-raids is that night-bombing is unexpectedly accurate and anti-aircraft fire extraordinarily ineffective. To intercept aircraft at night is apparently impossible so far, but we have a new very secret device called A.I. which is expected to help. So far there are only six sets with properly experienced handlers and these are in the Thames estuary.

Secret Session at the House on Home Defence. There was apparently some trouble when Hore-Belisha, replying to Bellenger,[1] implied that one of the reasons for his resignation in January was a difference with the Generals about fortifications from the Maginot Line to the sea. This was quite untrue and Chamberlain got up and rebutted the accusation. Winston spoke later, with great success I hear.

At about 11.30 p.m. Winston went back to No. 10 taking Alexander and Duff Cooper with him: "two dreadnoughts and a battleship", as he described the party on getting into the car. I had great difficulty in returning in my car owing to the formidable defences of Whitehall, and I found the Grenadiers on duty most unhelpful. Eventually I more or less forced my way through barriers on to the Horse Guards Parade and had quite an acrimonious *"passage d'armes"* with the officer in charge.

Lord Lloyd was at No. 10, just back from Bordeaux. He said things were much better and that continued resistance in North Africa, and the departure of the Government from France were now almost certain. Pétain was hopeless, as was Weygand; but Admiral Darlan was full of spirit.

Friday, June 21st
Winston sent the following note to the Foreign Secretary: "Do you think there is much use in promising to discuss the cession of Gibraltar to Spain after the war? The Spanish know that if we lose they will get it anyhow, and they would be great fools to believe that if we win we shall mark our admiration for their conduct by giving it to them. The news that we were willing to entertain the idea of giving up Gibraltar would do no end of harm."

We were all awaiting the German peace terms to France. I fear

[1] Captain Frederick Bellenger. Subsequently a member of Attlee's 1945 Labour Government.

that they may be sufficiently generous to tempt the French Government, but the general opinion is that they will be crushing. The chief excitement of the day is the possibility of six cruisers intercepting the *Scharnhorst*, escorted by destroyers, off the Norwegian coast. She was torpedoed last night by one of our submarines, the *Clyde*. As I write, 8.30 p.m., the two forces ought just to have become engaged; but of course the *Scharnhorst* may turn into Stavanger fjord. Winston, with whom I drove back from the Upper War Room at the Admiralty, remarked that a few weeks ago we should have thought this news thrilling, but now it seems like a minor incident.

Saturday, June 22nd
The expected naval encounter has not come off, the enemy having fled into Stavanger where he is to be bombed today.

The news from France is not good, and there are signs that the determination of the French Government to continue their resistance is weakening. Laval is said to be busy with members of the Chamber and that is a bad sign.

During the Cabinet a telegram came in to say that the German armistice terms were being telegraphed from Bordeaux, and that the part concerning the fleet was following fast. I telephoned this down to Chequers, and everybody is waiting anxiously to know what the terms will be. Can the Germans be so foolish as to make them unacceptable and so drive the French Government overseas to continue the battle? I fear not, even though a day or two ago all preparations for the President and Government to go had been made.

Sunday, June 23rd [at Ardley – my sister-in-law, Joan Colville's house near Bicester]
In the afternoon we played a little bridge, and after dinner listened, between hands of "Slippery Jane", to the crushing terms which Marshal Pétain has thought it honourable to accept. De Gaulle broadcast at 10.00, preaching sedition – an action which I later heard was resented by many Frenchmen. H.M.G. published a message supporting de Gaulle, and this, I gather, was done by the F.O. on Lord Halifax's authority; but again the reactions from many French quarters were bad. Very tired.

Tuesday, June 25th
When I reached No. 10 I found that things had not been going well. Noguès,[1] in Algeria, is half-hearted; there is every reason to think

---

[1] Commander in Chief of the French troops there.

that Darlan is behaving badly; the French fleet does not seem disposed to fight on under British orders, or even as an Ally, against the Germans and Italians; and, incredible though it may sound, the Bordeaux Government seem disposed to accept Hitler's assurances about the fleet and to trust his word. The name of France will assuredly be blackened, as Winston said, for years to come. And, of course, they, the French, will maintain it is all our fault for not providing more support on land.

De Gaulle does not appear to have enough prestige to rally the more determined Frenchmen to himself, and it is a thousand pities that nothing is being done – so far as I can discover – to form a really strong Imperial French Government which could disavow Bordeaux and win the allegiance of military, naval and civil authorities in the French Empire. At present only Syria, the Cameroons, the French West Indies and Indo-China are steadfast.

Ismay has produced a first-rate note (which was, I understand, written by Colonel Jacob*) about the offensive action which we can take. When we have the equipment and the aeroplanes we must invade the continent, because Germany will not be defeated until her armies are defeated on the field of battle, a result for which the blockade will contribute much but will not alone suffice. We have got to plan this offensive now and discover an excellent young general to whom its preparation can be entrusted under the direction of the Chiefs of Staff and of Winston himself.

Dined with Seal at the Travellers wisely and well. He was interesting about Winston, explaining how much he had changed since becoming P.M. He had sobered down, become less violent, less wild, less impetuous. Seal thinks that W. believes in his mission, to extricate this country from its present troubles, and he will certainly kill himself, if necessary, in order to achieve his object. He is superstitious: Seal cited the case of the *Royal Oak*, which sank at the end of a day, Friday, November 13th, on which Winston had mistakenly put on a black tie instead of his usual spotted one – facts to which he attached great importance.

Everything now seems to point to my being released for active service soon. Seal says that the Treasury agree, and I have more or less persuaded the F.O. But I am afraid eyesight will bar me for the navy and I shall try the Guards.

Returning to Downing Street we had great trouble with the barricades, which infuriated the somewhat easily provoked Seal.

General Sikorski (Polish P.M.) came to see Winston. His A.D.C. said that the way in which the French ran away was indescribable: they showed no fighting spirit. I hear from all sides that the Poles have been fighting magnificently in France: they seem to be our most formidable allies.

Slept at No. 10 on a bed which has been set up in the room in which I work – a rather sordid arrangement.

Wednesday, June 26th

Slept well in spite of the surroundings and various Yellow air-raid warnings, alarums and excursions. First thing in the morning Captain Pim[1] came round from the war room to report the news: 150 planes over England, eight brought down, practically no damage. The Germans seem to have no training in night bombing, and in this we have a great advantage.

Yesterday the P.M. received the following letter:

Dear Prime Minister

Why not declare war on France and capture her fleet (which would gladly strike its colors to us) before A.H. recovers his breath?

Surely that is the logic of the situation?

Tactically,

G. Bernard Shaw.

Belgrade and Bucharest, which are always prolific with their reports from Berlin, foreshadow a peace offensive or the summoning by Hitler of a European Economic Congress, excluding Great Britain and Turkey. From Berne comes a report that the plan of invasion has been postponed, if not abandoned, and that the Germans were surprised by the intelligent heroism of our troops in France. Personally I think a peace offensive is almost certain, unless it has dawned on Hitler that we shall not stop fighting until we have won. When his terms are rejected, very heavy bombing is, I suppose, inevitable.

Smuts has telegraphed to Winston saying that arms and men should be poured into South Africa. The British Isles will withstand the threat of invasion, providing no vital mistakes are made, but the Near East, India and Africa are in deadly peril, and from them Hitler could obtain enough resources to maintain himself and his régime. In his reply Winston says that, as far as Germany is concerned, he does not think that winter's strain will prove decisive, but next year, or even this, he hopes that we shall take the offensive and begin "large-scale amphibious operations" on the

---

[1] In charge of the Prime Minister's private and personal map room. Afterwards head of the Royal Ulster Constabulary.

continent. This will keep Hitler occupied because he "has vast hungry areas to defend and we have the command of the sea".

At tea George Steward told us of a conversation he had had during lunch with French journalists. These said that although de Gaulle was an honest straightforward man, he was not the person to establish a new French Government and they mistrusted the judgment of Spears, who had launched de Gaulle. (Actually it was never intended that de Gaulle should be any more than a rallying point for expatriated Frenchmen: it was the fault of the Ministry of Information that a false impression on this point has been given.) The new French Government must be established on French Colonial soil, in liaison with the British Government, and they thought Peyrouton[1] was the man to lead it. But much depended on the decision which Noguès finally adopted.

Orders have been given to our ships to capture the new French battleship *Richelieu* and, if she puts to sea from Casablanca, the *Jean Bart* as well. Unless things go much more satisfactorily in North Africa than we now expect, we shall end by seizing by force as much of the French fleet as we can intercept.

Thursday, June 27th

Went up to the P.M.'s bedroom at about 10.00. He was lying in bed, in a red dressing-gown, smoking a cigar and dictating to Mrs Hill, who sat with a typewriter at the foot of the bed. His box, half full of papers, stood open on his bed and by his side was a vast chromium-plated cuspidor. His black cat Nelson, which has quite replaced our old No. 10 black cat, sprawled at the foot of the bed and every now and then Winston would gaze at it affectionately and say "Cat, darling".

Among this morning's minutes was one he wrote to the Secretary of State for Air about the shortcomings of the Air Ministry and the flaws in its organisation (criticisms based on a memorandum sent from the F.O.). He described the Air Ministry as "a most cumbrous and ill-working administrative machine".

During the Cabinet news came out that both Noguès and Mittelhauser,[2] in Syria, had abandoned all idea of resistance and were going to be loyal to the Bordeaux Government. This is tragic news as it virtually delivers North Africa, with its vast supplies, into the hands of the enemy. In France itself the Germans will procure large stocks of petroleum, steel, fats and an immense sum in gold.

---

[1] Marcel Peyrouton, Vichy Minister of the Interior. Rallied to the Western Allies in 1942 and was appointed, on American initiative, Governor General of Algeria. Removed by de Gaulle.

[2] French General with a command in Syria.

Now, with North Africa gone, the position is more serious still and our lifeline in the Near East is threatened. It is doubtful whether the French, even those that are loyal to their Allies, will do much effective sabotage: the way in which they delayed handing over to us captured German pilots, when they might still have done so, until it was too late, is not encouraging.

It seems years since we had even a gleam of good news!

There is a good deal of Anglophobia in France and Algeria, partly on account of Winston's hard remarks about the Pétain Government and partly because it is said that we did not provide France with enough support. There is a good deal more Francophobia in England. Such is the fate of the Entente Cordiale.

America is disheartened, inclined to blame us for the defeat of France, and less ready than before to counter Japanese designs in the Far East.

Friday, June 28th

The Russian ultimatum to Roumania about Bessarabia may be good news. It is possible that the Soviet will impede the supply of oil from Roumania to Germany. They can scarcely be overjoyed by the prospect of German hegemony over Europe; but unfortunately events have shown that it is impossible to put much faith in Russia.

The P.M. is, as ever, actively interested in every small question relating to the war. This morning: "Home Secretary: Let me see a list of prominent persons you have arrested."

In a minute to the P.M. Amery examines the possibility of developing India's resources in men and armaments. We must, he says, visualise the possibility of being driven out of Egypt and Palestine during the next few months, back on to Iraq and Aden. "After that, if not next year then in 1942, a great Army of Liberation from the south-east, carrying forward with it the armies of Turkey and the Balkan States, may march into the heart of Europe to meet our Army of Liberation from the west."

Went to Chequers, driving down with Mrs Churchill in her car. We talked a good deal of politics, about which her views are as ill-judged as they are decisive. She spoke much of the time wasted in the last nine months and I tried to convince her laboriously that Chamberlain's Government could not achieve great results without full powers and that full powers could only be obtained by a National Government. Until the Norwegian affair this was impossible, because Labour and the Liberals refused all invitations to co-operate, maintaining that an Opposition and criticism were essential in war-time. "Then Chamberlain ought to have resigned," said Mrs C.; and I could not make the proper retort that there was nobody to take his place and that the country would never have accepted Winston.

Lindemann was at Chequers, also Mary Churchill, Judy Montagu and Ismay, who came to dine and sleep. We arrived just after 9.00 p.m., at the same time as the guests for dinner, Sir Robert and Lady Vansittart and M. Léger.[1] During dinner the P.M. said to Lady Van, who was on his right, while I was next to her: "He wants to go and fight, but I won't let him." I asked him if he would let me go eventually, and he promised he would if the country really needed me but said that at present my duty was to stay in the job for which I was trained.

When the ladies had left the dining-room, Winston, Léger and Van discussed the collapse of France. Winston told Léger he was speaking to a "*cercle sacré*" and must express himself frankly. He foresaw the possibility of France declaring war on us and he wanted to know how we could maintain the goodwill of the French people, for whose salvation we were the last hope, while we were obliged to starve them by blockade and destroy their towns by bombs. How could we convince them that we were being cruel in order to be kind? It was essential to keep the French well disposed to us, even if their Government went to war with Great Britain. Léger replied that it was important to maintain contact with the Bordeaux Government, to send a chargé d'affaires to France and not to leave this country unrepresented there.

Apart from that he saw three ways in which we might influence the French people:

(i) By clever use of the press and wireless. English broadcasting was more heard in France than was French broadcasting, and now it alone could be expected to provide news from untainted sources. Similarly English newspapers would find their way into France. They must be sympathetic and avoid recrimination.

(ii) By not doing anything unnecessarily provocative to French sentiment. It might be necessary to oppose the Government, e.g. by bombing French ports in occupied territory and by tightening the blockade, but French national sentiment must not be antagonised. As regards the fleet, which was, he agreed, the major problem of the moment, he suggested that the French might be asked to invite a third power to act as an intermediary in keeping it immobilised in French ports. This the Axis powers would refuse to

---

[1] For many years permanent head of the Quai d'Orsay (French Foreign Ministry). Much more involved with internal politics than his British equivalents, Vansittart and Cadogan.

allow, and then we should have a good pretext for seizing as much of the fleet as we could with the probable compliance of the French navy and approval of the people. Winston was not impressed by this suggestion: he is contemplating violent action against French ships in African ports.

(iii) By doing all possible in the U.S. from the point of view of propaganda. The U.S. had always been sympathetic to France and they might easily be led to believe that France had only collapsed because we had given her inadequate support. If the British were blamed in America, the French would increase their own propaganda on these lines (which in their heart of hearts they must know to be untrue) and the effect of American opinion on France was immense.

Winston would have none of this (although Van backed Léger up): he has received such reports from Lothian, whom he and Van think little of; he has been pressed on all sides to pander to American opinion; and he maintains it is entirely a waste of time. "Propaganda is all very well," he said to Léger, "but it is events that move the world. If we smash the Huns here we shall need no propaganda in the United States." It was, he said, "the night before the battle. It may be long: now we must live; next year we shall be winning; the year after we shall triumph". But if we could hold the Germans in this coming critical month of July, and deny this country to them, then our position would be quite different from today and "a very different wind will be blowing on the world".

Léger said that Reynaud had been less devoted to the Allied cause than we had supposed. He was under the thumb of a mistress who was in the pocket of the pro-Axis party in France, and on the advice of "cette femme" Léger himself had been dismissed, de Gaulle had been sent off to the front, and Baudouin, etc., had gained Reynaud's ear. R. had long been thinking on the lines of a German–Italian–French entente and only the P.M.'s visits had served to keep him to the straight and narrow path. "I wish now that I had stayed there ten days," said Winston, "and had left Neville to carry on at home." I felt sure (and I think Winston did too) that Léger's remarks about Reynaud were coloured by the fact that it was from Reynaud he had received his dismissal.

The Vansittarts and Léger left about 1.00 a.m. and afterwards the P.M. discussed with Ismay the organisation of the War Office and Air Ministry. The latter, in particular, disturbs him and it is the cause of serious differences between Sinclair and Beaverbrook. He told Ismay there was too much "top hamper" in both departments: they would have to be simplified and useless officials must be ruthlessly eliminated. Speaking of the Chiefs of Staff, W. said he thought a lot of Pound, although he was slow; Newall had many good points (but Beaverbrook says "he was an observer in the last war, and he has remained an observer ever since"); Dill had, unfortunately, aged a great deal in every way (c.f. Weygand's sudden senility in the course of a few weeks).

Saturday, June 29th

Prof. (Lindemann) says that the French collapse has helped Germany a lot economically, even though, as far as fats are concerned, the effect may not be visible until next spring. But I am afraid it is very likely to lengthen the war by saving Germany the necessity of tightening her belt still further. Winston is perturbed. He writes this morning: "It seems to me the blockade is largely ruined, in which case the sole decisive weapon in our hands would be overwhelming air attack upon Germany."

I awoke at 8.00 and made telephonic enquiries about the results of last night's air-raids and the naval situation. But the P.M. did not send for me till 9.30 and he lay in bed all the morning working. I was able to give him the news about H.M.S. *Dainty* which, in the Mediterranean, reported that she had sunk three Italian submarines and was pursuing six more. I also told him that Balbo had been killed flying and suggested that this had been engineered by Mussolini. He said he thought it very probable.

Beaverbrook and Brendan Bracken came down to lunch. The conversation began with a discussion on the evacuation of the Channel Islands and the food which had been left behind. Turning to me Winston said: "Tell the Ministry of Food to evaluate it, and the Admiralty to evacuate it." I carried out this peremptory order which, of course, led to much trouble – the cattle in Jersey had foot-and-mouth disease, etc., etc. Winston was obviously pleased with his epigram and did not look beyond. After lunch Beaverbrook raised the question of whether we should continue to increase our aircraft production or should improve the engines and armaments. There is an important decision to make: should we aim at quantity or quality? B. says he can maintain our present level of output in any case and that should give a certain measure of safety.

I sat in the garden much of the afternoon with Mrs C., Mary (whom I find very much nicer on closer acquaintance) and Judy Montagu. The P.M. talked with Beaverbrook, and later with Alec Hardinge, who came after tea. They discussed the position of the Duke of Windsor who is in Madrid trying to impose conditions, financial and otherwise, about his return to this country. It is incredible to haggle in such a way at this time, and Winston proposes to send him a very stiff telegram pointing out that he is a soldier under orders and must obey. The King approves and says he will hear of no conditions, about the Duchess or otherwise.

We had tea in the morning-room upstairs and while we were there the Sandyses arrived. Shortly afterwards came Randolph Churchill* and his wife.[1] I thought Randolph one of the most objectionable people I had ever met: noisy, self-assertive, whining and frankly unpleasant. He did not strike me as intelligent. At dinner he was anything but kind to Winston, who adores him, and he made a scene in front of General Paget about complacency in high places, inefficiency of the Generals, lack of equipment, etc., etc. Duncan Sandys appeared charming by contrast, although I daresay he is an opportunist. Diana Sandys I liked.

In reply to a request from the P.M., the Home Secretary sent a list of 150 "prominent people" whom he had arrested. Of the first three on the list two, Lady Mosley[2] and Geo Pitt-Rivers,[3] were cousins of the Churchills – a fact which piqued Winston and caused much merriment among his children!

General Paget,[4] who did so well in South Norway against tremendous odds, came to dine and sleep. When the ladies had gone, Winston got going and gave an interesting résumé of the French campaign as it appeared to him. He said that there had been a rot in France which had affected every class and stratum of the community: it was not merely the Generals and the politicians but the whole country. There had, said Winston, been "nothing like it, ever", and its feeble reaction was now apparent in the outbreak of Anglophobia. Winston described how Gamelin had said to him, after the breakthrough at Sedan, "They are superior in numbers, they are superior in armaments, they are superior in method." When W. asked him what he was going to do about it, G. just shrugged his shoulders, and Winston remarked to us bitterly: "Gamelin was occupied in saving not France but his own position." He still believed, however, that Georges had been a good commander.

Winston went on to expatiate on the incredible success of the German armoured divisions and the curious inability of the French to evolve any method of dealing with them. He said it was

[1] Pamela, daughter of Lord Digby. Later wife of Leland Hayward and, after his death, of Averell Harriman.*
[2] Diana Mitford, daughter of Lord Redesdale, wife of Sir Oswald Mosley.
[3] Mosley's second in command in the British Union of Fascists. Married at one time to Rosalind, Mrs Henley's scientist daughter.
[4] Chief of the Home Forces General Staff. Later Commander in Chief, Home Forces.

something new in warfare which he did not fully understand. It was astounding that 4,000 excellent troops in Calais should so easily have been driven out and he thought Gort had missed an opportunity in not making a lightning move to the relief of Calais with one of his divisions. Such action would almost certainly have been successful and would have given the B.E.F. a far larger area from which to evacuate.

After dinner I went for a short walk with Mary and Judy, and we were challenged in the most alarming way by ferocious sentries. I had thought the P.M. was walking with Paget, but unfortunately he had changed his mind and I had to run precipitately back, at the risk of my life, and screaming the password "Tofrek", in order to be ready for his commands. Later in the evening the Air Ministry, in giving me details of the raids then taking place said that enemy planes were passing south of Aylesbury. I told Winston who said, "I'll bet you a monkey to a mouse-trap they don't hit the house", and hurried excitedly out of the house to see if he could see anything, shouting at a sentry: "Friend – Tofrek – Prime Minister" (a formula which entirely nonplussed the unfortunate soldier). General Paget and I followed behind in a leisurely way, the former saying to me "what a wonderful tonic he is".

I see from intelligence reports that the German long-range bomber *Geschwäder*[1] will be refitted and ready by July 8th. Their fighters are already prepared for action, and it is considered that a major offensive is likely about July 8th and is possible any time after June 30th. The nightly raids we now endure are presumably just intended to test our defences.

Winston went to bed shortly after 1.00 a.m. and I resisted the now drunken Randolph's attempt to make me sit up with him and discuss the Fifth Column (which, incidentally, Winston thinks a much less serious menace than had been supposed). Randolph was in a horrible state, gross, coarse and aggressive. I felt ashamed of him for Winston's sake and yet W. said, when he asked to be allowed some more active part in the war, that if R. were killed he would not be able to carry on his work.

Sunday, June 30th
Winston asked for me at 7.30 a.m., which was inconsiderate, to find out if there was any news. As he lay in bed all the morning, dictating to Mrs Hill, I was at a loose end, but did not dare to go more than a few yards from the house in case Winston or the telephone should ring. So I sat in a chair in the sun outside the window of my sitting-room, reading descriptions of the Pavilion at

[1] Approximate equivalent of an R.A.F. "Wing".

Brighton and a small German Court before the war by Mary McCarthy. The ladies of the party (except Mrs Randolph) went to church.

It is a curious feeling to stay for the week-end in a country house, not as a guest and yet, for a number of reasons, on fairly close terms with the family. It was much like any week-end party except for the conversation which, of course, was brilliant. It is a pleasure to hear really well-informed talk, unpunctuated by foolish and ignorant remarks (except occasionally from Randolph), and it is a relief to be in the background with occasional commissions to execute, but few views to express, instead of being expected to be interesting because one is the P.M.'s Private Secretary.

Chequers itself, though not arranged with perfect taste, has an air of calm and happiness about it. The surrounding country is exquisite. Looking through the Visitors' Book I saw that Marshal Foch had written in it: *Les affaires de l'Angleterre iront encore mieux quand son premier ministre pourra se reposer à Chequers.* Let us hope he will not be as wrong about that as he was about Weygand. ("When France is in danger send for Weygand.")

Mr Amery and General Thorne[1] (commanding XIIth Corps, south of the Thames) came to lunch. Randolph said something unpleasant about the former Government and claimed that its leaders ought to be punished. "We don't want to punish anyone now – except the enemy," replied Winston. W. is, however, less cautious about his criticism of Baldwin, etc., even though he never countenances a word against Chamberlain, and when I told him that the Germans had bombed the works of "Guest, Keen and Baldwin", in South Wales, all he said was: "Very ungrateful of them."

I told Amery at lunch the dictum about the Harrow and Eton opening batsmen (Harrow: W.S.C. and Lord Gort; Eton: King Leopold and Captain Ramsay[2]) and was amused to hear Amery include his own name in the Harrovian list, and exclude Lord Gort, when he repeated the story to Winston.

After lunch Winston and Thorne examined the whole question of invasion and all the possibilities. Thorne thinks 80,000 men will be landed on the beaches between Thanet and Pevensey (which is Thorne's area); Winston is less pessimistic and thinks the navy will have much to say to this. W. is not sanguine about our ability to

[1] A gallant Grenadier with three D.S.Os. Had commanded a division in the Dunkirk campaign and now commanded a corps in the threatened invasion area.

[2] M.P. of genuine patriotism, however misguided, who made no effort to conceal his admiration for Hitler and fascism.

hold the whole expanse of beaches and points out that a river line has never proved a real obstacle to an enemy. He thinks it will not be difficult for the enemy to find soft patches into which he can probe. Thorne, who was Military Attaché in Berlin, is convinced that the Germans, acting according to their rule, will concentrate all their forces against one place, even if they make feints elsewhere.

Winston is inclined to think that Hitler's plans have had to be changed: H. cannot have foreseen the collapse of France and must have planned his strategy of invasion on the assumption that the French armies would be holding out on the Somme, or at least on the Seine, and that the B.E.F. would either be assisting them or else have been wiped out. The situation is now very different: on the one hand many more ways of invasion are open (although if the invading troops are to be escorted, it will still be difficult for the escorting ships to penetrate the Straits of Dover): on the other the whole of the B.E.F. is now back in this country to defend it. Thorne agreed, but said that the Divisions in his area were scarcely equipped at all and only partly trained. He thought the German left wing could be held in Ashdown Forest, but he did not see what could prevent the right wing advancing through Canterbury to London, especially if his only trained and equipped Division (the 3rd) was to be moved away to Northern Ireland. The P.M. promised that this should not be done.

We left Chequers about 4.00 p.m., I driving up to London with Mr Amery and General Thorne (both of whose sons were with me at West Downs).[1] We had a very pleasant conversation on every kind of subject. Amery said he thought Winston ought to be Minister of Defence and P.M. only in name: I said that this was in fact the case – he spent most of the day with the Chiefs of Staff. General Thorne said that that was as it should be: it was most desirable that one of the greatest students of military history and of war should himself play the leading part in the direction of this war's strategy. Winston was more vital to this country than Hitler to Germany, because the former was unique and irreplaceable and the latter had established a school of leaders. The obvious comment is that Hitler may be a self-educated corporal and Winston may be an experienced student of tactics; but unfortunately Germany is organised as a war machine and England has only just realised the meaning of modern warfare.

It was interesting to hear from Brendan Bracken, when I got back to No. 10, that Mr Alexander[2] had told him he and the other

[1] A preparatory school near Winchester.
[2] Afterwards Earl Alexander of Hillsborough.*

Labour Ministers were beginning to realise what Chamberlain was and to admit that their condemnation of him had been to a great extent unjustified.

I have among my papers a note which I gave to the Prime Minister in June, 1940, which shows the bitterness of our feelings over the French collapse. For the first and only time in my life I became, for a brief period, a Francophobe; and I was certainly not alone in that. It is a quotation I found in Shakespeare's Henry VI, Part 3:

HASTINGS: *Why, knows not Montague that of itself*
            England is safe, if true within itself?
MONTAGUE: *But the safer when 'tis back'd with France.*
HASTINGS: *'Tis better using France than trusting France.*
            Let us be back'd with God, and with the seas,
            Which He hath giv'n for fence impregnable,
            And with their helps only defend ourselves.
            In them and in ourselves our safety lies.

7

Alone

July 1940

Monday, July 1st
On a secret F.O. paper Roger Makins[1] has written: "What happened at Bordeaux was a coup d'état engineered by the most corrupt elements in France making use of famous names." It is accepted here that the anti-Bolshevik feelings of Pétain, Weygand, etc., were exploited by Laval and Baudouin; and the general Anglophobia, spreading over the country, is a natural reaction to events. It has an element of justification, in that we did not provide many divisions, but it really springs from the unwillingness of the French to admit their own shame. It was thus that Leopold was the scapegoat for the incredible French blunder on the Meuse at Sedan (of which neither Winston nor Paget could find any explanation last Saturday at Chequers), and now inadequate British assistance is the thin excuse used to explain the total collapse of France.

The Prime Minister has instructed Ismay to investigate the question of "drenching" beaches with mustard gas if the Germans land. He considers that gas warfare would be justified in such an event. The other day he said to General Thorne: "I have no scruples, except not to do anything dishonourable," and I suppose he does not consider gassing Germans dishonourable.

Tuesday, July 2nd
Tomorrow at dawn we put into operation a plan called CATAPULT which entails the seizure of all French ships in British ports and, later in the day, an ultimatum to the big French capital ships at Oran.

The P.M. says that in the event of invasion London should be

---

[1] Later Lord Sherfield.*

defended. To take it would cost the Germans many lives. Secret Service reports from Norway make it clear that invasion is being prepared from there as well as from other quarters. It is suggested that Iceland and the Shetlands may be among the first objectives, that a feint will be made against the East Coast, but that the real attack will be from the West.

Beaverbrook wants to resign because of his difficulties with the Air Ministry and, in particular, with the Air Marshals. Winston won't hear of any such thing at the present moment and, of course, it does rather look as if B. wanted to leave now, at the peak of success in aircraft production, before new difficulties arise. It is like trying to stop playing cards immediately after a run of luck.

Brendan Bracken is apparently to be allowed to supervise the appointment of bishops – which I find a little hard to stomach. Brendan is all very well – intelligent, forceful and often sensible – but he is not the man to deal with bishops.[1]

Winston returned about 10.45 p.m. from a tour of defences in the South and life became both hot and hectic.

Wednesday, July 3rd
At No. 10 chief interest centres on the Operation CATAPULT. First we heard of the operations at Portsmouth and Plymouth, then that the attack on Oran was to take place at 1.30. During the afternoon came news of various postponements in the hope that the French resolve to fight was weakening.

At about 7.00 p.m. signals began to come through that we were heavily engaged with the French. I was alone most of the time with Lord Lloyd and Sir John Dill. The former had been summoned to consider a project for making the Duke of Windsor Governor of the Bahamas. The latter, who had been sent for presumably to discuss some question of defence, told me that Winston confined himself to telling him the story of the situation and to walking up and down saying "Terrible, terrible". Dill said that he had never seen anything comparable: the two nations who were fighting for civilisation had turned and rent each other while the barbarians sat back and laughed. It is indeed the most tragic irony in history and an event that could not have been entertained as possible a fortnight ago.

There was the greatest excitement about the operations taking place and an 11.30 p.m. meeting of the Chiefs of Staff. Winston said to the First Lord that the French were now fighting with all

---

[1] I did not appreciate Brendan's genuine and conscientious interest in things ecclesiastical, hidden behind a mask of agnosticism.

their vigour for the first time since war broke out. He did not see how we could avoid being at war with France tomorrow.

Apparently Brendan Bracken had been indiscreet and given the whole situation away at a dinner party, so it will have to be published quickly. The shock to public opinion will be greater than any to date. War is said to be always full of surprises – but this is a fantasy.

While we were standing about outside the Cabinet Room Edward Bridges declaimed on the danger of "looking over our shoulder". We have got to withstand the new technique of war, an offensive against our morale, and nothing is more helpful to Hitler than to say we must start thinking about preparing skeleton Government departments in Canada, etc. Already incalculable harm is being done by attacks on the Civil Service, Mr Chamberlain, the Chiefs of Staff and the C. in C. Home Forces (Ironside). If enough people say that these people and institutions are rotten (which they are not), it will be believed and the Germans will have cause to rub their hands. We should burn our boats, stand firm and refuse to contemplate anything but victory. Being on the defensive brings many disadvantages and dangers.

Before going to bed the P.M. rang for me and asked me to take down a telegram to the Duke of Windsor, offering him the Governorship of the Bahamas. Before dictating a sentence he always muttered it wheezingly under his breath and he seemed to gain intellectual stimulus from pushing in with his stomach the chairs standing round the Cabinet table! "I think it is a very good suggestion of mine, Max," he said to Beaverbrook, who was there. "Do you think he will take it?" "Sure he will," said B., "and he'll find it a great relief." "Not half as much as his brother will," replied W. When I gave him the dictated telegram he said: "What a beautiful handwriting(!!), but, my dear boy, when I say stop you must write stop and not just put a blob." (He is always pedantic about small things.)

Thursday, July 4th
The action against the French fleet at Oran was very successful, although it was unfortunate the *Strasbourg* escaped. At Alexandria we heard, early in the morning, that trouble was brewing and it looked as if the French would scuttle their ships and block the harbour.

The P.M. made a statement in the House, to which I listened. He told the whole story of Oran and the House listened enthralled and amazed. Gasps of surprise were audible but it was clear that the action taken was unanimously approved. When the speech was over all the Members rose to their feet, waved their order papers and cheered loudly. Winston left the House visibly affected. I heard him say to Hore-Belisha: "This is heartbreaking for me."

Jarrett[1] (Alexander's Private Secretary) and I sat in my room at the House and received news from the Admiralty. Part was good and unexpected: a satisfactory agreement had been reached about the French ships at Alexandria. Part was bad: a serious air-raid had taken place at Portland and much damage was done. Twenty dive-bombers took part and were not intercepted – a bad look-out for the future if this can be done with impunity in broad daylight.

Dined with Grandfather and Peggy at Argyll House and felt very much better for his remarkable old brandy and her witty conversation.

Friday, July 5th

The world's reactions to the Battle of Oran are favourable, it seems. As Mother says, there is a strange admiration for force everywhere today, even among those who suffer from it. It is a curious disease: even exiled German Jews have been known to speak with awe and respect of the Nazi power which is responsible for their distress. Thus it may be that even in France our action will be approved.

The P.M. has telegraphed again to Roosevelt explaining our dire need for an immediate supply of destroyers and motor-torpedo boats. With the whole French coast in enemy hands the importance of our naval strength is double as great, and America's responsibility will be heavy (or "grievous" as the P.M. puts it) if she fails us now.

[*He has not sent this off owing to objections from Halifax on certain points. (JRC – 13.7.40).*]

From German sources it is reported that the French Government has broken off diplomatic relations with us. But we have heard nothing!

Saturday, July 6 [at Cambridge]

In this halcyon summer the only rain we get invariably falls during my week-ends off. This is no exception.

After dinner I called upon the Vice Master of Trinity, Winstanley,[2] and drank beer with him as I used so often to do. He told me that the Master was failing and it might soon fall to my lot to consider the appointment of a new Master of Trinity. We

---

[1] Sir Clifford Jarrett, Permanent Secretary to the Admiralty, 1962–64.
[2] Historian of Whig politics in the eighteenth century and of Cambridge University.

discussed the matter and he said that Adrian[1] would be the appointment most congenial to the Fellows.

In speaking of the war I expressed the opinion that the two most disappointing and discredited men of recent months were King Victor Emmanuel and the Pope. The House of Savoy, though opposed to war, had not had the courage of its convictions; the Pope, who must realise that as never before this war was one between right and wrong, Christianity and barbarism, should have boldly laid the Fascist Government under an Interdict. In so doing he would have martyrised the Italian Church and himself, but he would have raised the prestige and power of Catholicism to great heights throughout the world and the Church would ultimately have benefited. Winstanley, though agreeing about the House of Savoy, was less sure as regards the Pope. But I am convinced that a spiritual power should never compromise between justice and injustice and in standing aloof Pius XII has betrayed the memory of Hildebrand,[2] whose dying words were: "*Dilexi justitiam et odivi iniquitatem: ergo morior in exilio*" [I have loved justice and hated iniquity: therefore I die in exile].

Monday, July 8th
Today is supposed to be the day on which the German bomber force should be ready and refitted. I have the impression that Germany is collecting herself for a great spring; and it is an uncomfortable impression.

I went up to see the P.M. in bed and he gave me a note, for instant despatch to Lord Beaverbrook, of which the following is an extract:

> When I look round to see how we can win the war I see that there is only one sure path. We have no continental army which can defeat the German military power. The blockade is broken and Hitler has Asia and probably Africa to draw from. Should he be repulsed here or not try invasion he will recoil eastward and we have nothing to stop him. But there is one thing that will bring him back and bring him down, and that is an absolutely devastating, exterminating attack by very heavy bombers from this country upon the Nazi homeland. We must be able to over-

[1] World-famous physiologist, Nobel Prize winner and holder of the Order of Merit. Succeeded Professor George Trevelyan as Master of Trinity.
[2] Hildebrand, Pope Gregory VII, died in exile at Salerno in 1085 after a long struggle with the Holy Roman Emperor, Henry IV, over the rival claims of the spiritual and temporal powers.

whelm them by this means without which I do not see a way through.

This is a curious war. Early today we think we inflicted serious damage on the *Richelieu* at Dakar. Now we are suggesting that our Consul General there might be able to discover how serious that damage in fact is! Meanwhile the French are becoming very ferocious and one of our submarines has inadvertently sunk a French cruiser at a time and place when it should not have done so. Result: an apology by H.M.G. to the French Government at the same time as we are tentatively suggesting the appointment of a Chargé d'Affaires in unoccupied France.

Tuesday, July 9th
The invasion and great attack is now said to be due on Thursday. Meanwhile Russia seems disposed to try bullying Turkey about the Straits.

Spent part of today reading Sir R. Campbell's account of the last days of France. From the time that the Somme could no longer be held the politicians and Generals apparently gave up hope: "a lamentable influence was General Weygand's mystic mood which led him to believe that France, having made mistakes, deserved to suffer." Campbell does not think the seed of France's decay lay in her constitution, even though the multiplicity of small parties made it impossible for a real leader to emerge. It was the inconceivable collapse of the army which destroyed all further will to resistance and made France "like a man who, stunned by an unexpected blow, was unable to rise to his feet before his opponent delivered the *coup de grâce*".

Lunched with Pat Hancock. He is private secretary to Dalton at the Ministry of Economic Warfare, and thinks him good. He says that there is a good deal of attempted jobbery by the Labour Party, which still thinks very much on party lines.

Winston went off to see some new aeroplanes, an improved Hurricane, a machine called the Tornado, etc., and I took the opportunity to go and have an hour's sleep at the Travellers. Just as I was leaving I heard from the Admiralty that the C. in C., Mediterranean, was engaging a superior Italian fleet, consisting of three battleships, thirteen cruisers and fifteen destroyers. Unfortunately the Italians quickly scuttled for home. But we are now proposing to take offensive action in the Mediterranean, to raid the Channel Isles and (Operation SUSAN) to establish a force at Casablanca. On duty late. Spent most of the time trying to instil some semblance of order into the P.M.'s box and listening to

Beaverbrook's philippics against the Air Ministry, Lord Halifax, the employment of old men, etc., etc.

Wednesday, July 10th

Winston is displeased with the War Office. In a letter to Eden[1] complaining of a number of things, he says: "I do not think we are having the help from General Dill which we hoped for at the time of his appointment, and he strikes me as being very tired, disheartened and over-impressed with the might of Germany." It is a pity, because no man has greater charm or was expected to give greater confidence.

There is some indication that Hitler will propose an economic conference of European powers (excluding this country) in order to air his grandiose views about the organisation of the future. Such a plan could be attractively worded and might win favour in a war-weary world, although of course it would imply German economic, and thus political, domination. Accordingly we are consulting with the U.S. about the best method of countering such a move in advance and an admirable telegram has been sent to Lothian. It is suggested that the principle to be followed is that "a plan much discussed and exposed beforehand can often be made to fall flat when it is launched". We might try to anticipate Hitler by public discussion of the likelihood of his dressing up German and Nazi–Fascist domination in the guise of an economic paradise. We could show that it is merely a device to harness all European wealth and production to the Nazi chariot wheels – an extended German "autarky" – for the military aggrandisement of the "superior" German race and for the suppression of freedom everywhere.

At the same time it is proposed that we ourselves should make some more positive suggestions defining "the advantages of the international economic structure which we and the U.S. wish to see emerge as part of the peace settlement". "Our two nations firmly believe that undue interference by the State frustrates the real economic aims and functions of mankind as well as involving the negation of liberty. We prefer to do things because reason tells us they are worth doing, not because we fear the sanctions attaching to failure to do them." (What do Messrs Attlee, Greenwood, etc., say to this?)

In general our aim is "to break down the artificial barriers to trade which impede any general rise in the standard of living"; but I personally think that our positive proposals, if they are to carry any

---

[1] Secretary of State for War.

weight, must descend from the Olympian height of principle and deal with practical details.

On the way home to lunch I met Horace Wilson in a bus. He said he was sorry Winston had thwarted my wish to join up, but that he always, in every question, took the short view rather than the long view. It was the latter that was really important in the end. Is this a fair criticism? I think it is; but the short view is forced on us at present and there is no greater master in dealing with that than W.

Thursday, July 11th
Went to see the Dean of Westminster about Brendan's sugges-
tion that Bishop Hensley Henson[1] should be offered the vacant canonry of Westminster. The Dean seemed to jump at the idea.

Left at 2.30 to visit the defences of the South-East Coast with Winston. We travelled in a special – and very comfortable – train to Dover, the other members of the party being Ismay, Duncan Sandys, Colonel Jacob and Commander Thompson.[2] At Dover we were met by the Admiral in Command and General Thorne and proceeded to the castle, into which we penetrated by subterranean passages through the chalk. We hoped for an air-raid (yesterday 150 machines were dog-fighting off Dover) but although we saw the A.A. gun men show sudden signs of activity, no enemy planes came. From the Admiral's room, in the face of the cliff, we looked across the sunlit Channel to France and could scarcely bring ourselves to realise it was enemy territory. From Dover we drove to inspect the emplacement for a 14-inch gun which, owing to a caprice of Winston's, is being prepared at considerable risk, and with immense labour, for the purpose of bombarding the coast of France. It will require three valuable and vulnerable cranes to put it in position and will only last for 100 rounds: the military authorities call it "a pure stunt".

We looked at defences, pill-boxes and troops the whole way along the coast, from Dover to Whitstable. The countryside was strangely deserted, most of the population having been evacuated, but it was encouraging to see the fields of waving corn and

---

[1] A controversial and contentious cleric who had been Bishop of Durham.

[2] Commander C. R. Thompson, Flag Lieutenant at the Admiralty, brought to No. 10 by Churchill. He arranged the Prime Minister's journeys at home and abroad and was near to the foreground in most photographs. More esteemed by Churchill than by his staff. At the end of the war he unscrupulously purloined the official diary of the Prime Minister's activities which had been meticulously maintained by the private secretaries. 10 Downing Street, Chartwell and the Cabinet offices were vainly searched for them when Churchill required them for the writing of his History of the Second World War.

cultivated land – an unaccustomed sight in England. There were road blocks and guns and soldiers everywhere, and from Deal we looked at the masts of a large number of wrecks, sunk by mine or by collision since the outbreak of war. We also saw a German hospital plane beached quite intact after having been forced down the previous day. It was painted white with a Red Cross in front and a Swastika on the tail.

It was a glorious evening with excellent visibility, and we could see Cap Gris-Nez thirty miles away over an expanse of rolling Kentish downs. But it was too clear and cloudless for enemy planes and for an aerial spectacle we had to be content with patrols of Spitfires glinting in the sun 10,000 feet above us. Winston was disappointed; the whole object of his journey had really been to see an air-raid!

We boarded the train at Canterbury and dined on the way back to London. I sat at a table with Colonel Jacob and tried to listen to what he had to say when his words were not drowned by the adjacent Winston. Jacob is in a good position to see the events of the last few years in their proper perspective; he is a soldier, and thus practical in his outlook; and he has been working in the Committee of Imperial Defence and Cabinet Offices, where the best information is available. His view of Chamberlain was that he had a heavy load of responsibility for our present state of un-preparedness, although his work for peace could not be over-estimated. As Chancellor of the Exchequer, and afterwards Prime Minister, he had starved the fighting forces and refused seriously to consider their expansion, because he believed in – and staked all on – the maintenance of peace. Had war never broken out, as it appeared to many good judges that it might not, Chamberlain would have rightly been thought a superman; but as events have turned out he cannot escape a large measure of blame for what we now call short-sightedness.

Jacob said he thought Winston was the only man who could hold the country united, but if he had a fault it was his inclination to go too much into detail. All these tours of defence areas, and his ceaseless output of minutes to Ministers and to Ismay, are the very antithesis of Chamberlain's practice; but they are not really the function of a Prime Minister. Jacob bewailed the fact that there were no politicians of outstanding merit. I ascribed this fact to three causes: (i) that the flower of a whole generation was de-stroyed between 1914–1918, (ii) that entrance into politics, as a Conservative, postulates considerable private means and, as a Labour member, influence with the Trade Unions, (iii) that modern education turns out mass-produced material which is essentially inferior to the "handwoven" product of a hundred years ago, when the syllabus was simple and unvarying but the inducement to think for oneself great.

We were back by 10.00 p.m. I suggested to Brendan Bracken that the remedy for inefficiency in the Civil Service is the grant of pensions at an earlier age than sixty, so that men who lack drive and imagination can, without undue cruelty, be shelved. The younger men would thus be given a chance to prove their worth. I suggested that now was the time for such a measure, when opinion in the country was influenced against the Civil Service. Brendan was taken with the idea and promised to put it to Winston.[1]

I see that we now have definite evidence that the Germans are assembling a force in Norway which could be used for a descent on Scotland, the Orkneys, the Shetlands or the Faroes. The reports of our bombing in North and North-West Germany are extremely encouraging and come from too many different sources to be untrue. So I think we must expect retaliation soon.

Friday, July 12th
At 6.00 p.m. I left with the P.M., Ismay, Sandys, Seal and Elliot[2] (from the Cabinet Offices) for Kenley, to inspect the Hurricane squadron of which Winston is Honorary Air Commodore. Winston was arrayed in R.A.F. uniform which, curiously enough, suited him well. We inspected the men and machines in pouring rain, watched twelve Hurricanes take off for patrol and went to see the operations room from which the activities of all aircraft in the area are directed. Then we got into a large machine, called a Flamingo, and flew very low, some 400 feet off the ground, to Northolt. The visibility was too bad for us to fly nearer Chequers. Ismay and I drove on together and he discoursed to me about polo!

Mrs Churchill and Horatia Seymour[3] were at Chequers. Generals Paget and Auchinleck[4] (who are two of the best younger generals and very much finer soldiers than Dill, Haining, Ironside, etc.) came to dine and sleep, as did Ismay and Sandys.

At dinner I sat between Ismay and Paget. The latter is charming and particularly easy to talk to. Winston began describing yesterday's tour of the South-East area and said that he had enjoyed a

---

[1] This proposal, which was subsequently adopted, had not, at least to my knowledge, been mooted in 1940.

[2] Subsequently Air Chief Marshal Sir William Elliot.

[3] Beautiful and cultivated member of the pre-First World War Asquithian set. Lived in one of the Churchill cottages at Chartwell.

[4] Field Marshal Sir Claude Auchinleck,* Wavell's successor as C. in C. in North Africa.

real "Hun-hate" with one of the Generals there. "I never hated the Germans in the last war, but now I hate them like . . . well, like an earwig."

After the ladies had left the conversation became more serious and Paget and Auchinleck were put through their paces. They gave a good account of themselves. Winston then gave a brief account of what he thought might be the course of the war. He could not see much hope of a decision before 1942. For the next three months we must fight for the negative purpose of preventing invasion and defeating it if it comes. The winter will be terrible for Europe, but "Hitler will take the other children's candy" and W. does not think it will put an end to German resistance. Next year we shall be building up a great offensive army and we hope to have fifty-five divisions. We shall plan large-scale "butcher and bolt" raids on the continent and Hitler will find himself hard put to it to hold 2,000 miles of coast line. Moreover we shall be approaching numerical equality in the air. By 1942 we shall have achieved air superiority and shall be ready for great offensive operations on land against Germany. But, said Winston, it is impossible to be precise: in the last war we kept on saying "How are we going to win", and then while we were still unable to answer the question, we quite suddenly and unexpectedly found ourselves in a winning position.

The discussion turned to invasion. Winston does not think this is feasible in fishing boats from Norway, as is now said to be likely. Paget and Auchinleck thought that advance troops might arrive in this way in quite insignificant numbers. Simultaneously troop carriers, gliders and parachutists would be utilised to seize a port from which the main body could land. W. does not believe in dispersing our troops along the beaches, but in concentrating effective and mobile divisions behind so that they may quickly be moved to any area where a serious threat materialises. He emphasised that the great invasion scare (which we only ceased to deride six weeks ago) is serving a most useful purpose: it is well on the way to providing us with the finest offensive army we have ever possessed and it is keeping every man and woman tuned to a high pitch of readiness. He does not wish the scare to abate therefore, and although personally he doubts whether invasion is a serious menace he intends to give that impression, and to talk about long and dangerous vigils, etc., when he broadcasts on Sunday.

There followed an argument about encouraging the populace to fight. If they meet the invader with scythes and brickbats they will be massacred. Paget thinks they had better stay at home; Winston says they will not and Auchinleck says they ought not. W. is sufficiently ruthless to point out that in war quarter is given, not on grounds of compassion but in order to discourage the enemy from fighting to the bitter end. But here we want every citizen to fight desperately and they will do so the more if they know that the alternative is massacre. The L.D.V. (Local Defence Volunteers) must be armed and prepared (but not, insists Paget, at the expense of the regular army) and even women must, if they wish, be enrolled as combatants. Sandys here pointed out that in Spain the fact of women fighting made the men fight still more keenly. Today large quantities of arms and ammunition have arrived from the U.S. and are being distributed to the L.D.V. (or Home Guard as Winston wants to call them). The outlook is not gloomy.

After dinner Winston, Sandys and the three Generals retired with a number of maps to discuss the details of invasion and I thought it discreet to leave them to themselves. To bed by 1.30.

Saturday, July 13th

I was up by 8.30 procuring the latest news from the Admiralty and taking it to Winston in my dressing-gown. I told him that the French Cameroons had renounced their allegiance to the Pétain Government and were to continue fighting. Of course the French dependencies are more bellicose in proportion as they are further away from Europe, but possibly the defection of the Cameroons may start a very satisfactory Colonial rot.

At lunch I sat between Horatia Seymour and Duncan Sandys. I shocked Miss S. and Ismay deeply last night by saying that I couldn't help liking the Germans; however she seemed to have recovered and we got on admirably. Winston showed greater animation and exuberance than I have seen before. He began by maintaining the arguable thesis that "Human beings don't require rest; what they require is change or else they become bloody-minded". He then went on to praise brass bands, to curse Hore-Belisha for abolishing them, to say they should return to every regiment and to ask what that large instrument was that he liked so much. I tentatively suggested a saxophone, whereupon he beamed philanthropically and said: "You haven't been brought up in the army; you have been brought up in night-clubs", proceeding to tell the general company that I wanted to go and fight and desert him and he jolly well wasn't going to let me until the killing really began, etc., etc.

He reiterated his now familiar scheme of our future strategy and said it gave him confidence to be able to see clearly how this war could and should be won instead of groping forwards uncertainly. This week-end he felt more cheerful than at any time since he took office. He spoke of the "armoured panther springs" which our mechanised divisions would make on the continent next year and of the bombing supremacy we should attain. Even if "that man" (as he always calls Hitler) were at the Caspian – and there was nothing to stop him from going there – we should bring him back "to find a fire in his own backyard and we will make Germany a desert, yes a desert". Hitler could do anything he liked where there was no salt water to cross, but it would avail him nothing if he reached the Great Wall of China and this Island remained undefeated. He could not survive if we devastated his homeland and if our excursions on the continent, made whenever we chose to land, were continually taxing his strength outside Germany. Therefore in the end he must probably be driven to attempt invasion, even if he decided against it now and went eastwards; and he would not succeed. Thus our vigil might be long and trying, and we shall have to be on our guard against surprise attack at any time of year and in any conditions. We should be put to the greatest test.

After lunch Auchinleck departed and Ismay too. Paget had left after breakfast. I walked up to Beacon Hill, when Winston was safely asleep, and sprawled on the grass, gazing for miles and miles across country. The air is most invigorating, the Chilterns green and the woods sublime. As I lay on the hilltop, thinking that England was the most beautiful country in the world and I could never bear to leave it, Mrs Churchill and Miss Seymour appeared and I walked back with them, gossiping.

Sir Henry Strakosch* arrived at tea-time and during that meal we looked at the ring which was taken from Queen Elizabeth's dying finger and carried to James VI to prove to him that he was King of England. It is a lovely jewel with an E that opens and shows two tiny jewelled miniatures of Elizabeth herself and of Anne Boleyn.

Air Marshal Sir Hugh Dowding* (C. in C., Fighter Command) and another R.A.F. officer came to dinner. He began by telling the P.M. that the only thing that worried him in life was the ridiculous dreams he had every night: last night he dreamt that there was only one man in England who could use a Bofors gun and his name was William Shakespeare. It was, he said, most disturbing.

During dinner we talked of air matters. Winston said the last four days had been the most glorious in the history of the R.A.F. Those days had been the test: the enemy had come and had lost 5 to 1. We could now be confident of our superiority. The discussion turned to technical questions of the superiority of the Hurricane, the defects of the Defiant,[1] and the curious fact that the Germans

---

[1] A newly-developed fighter aircraft intended primarily for night interception.

had not yet put armour behind their engines. If they should do so, said Dowding, our tactics would become much more difficult. They also spoke of the new German beam, called Headache, which guides the enemy machines to their targets. The Germans do not know that we have discovered this, and Lindemann, who arrived this evening with all his albums of statistics, was horrified that Winston should mention it before Strakosch, who is a chatterbox.

We have reports, from Maisky amongst others, that the Germans will use gas if they invade us. So perhaps Winston is wise to contemplate "drenching" the beaches with mustard gas.

W. started dictating his speech at midnight and I got leave to go to bed.

Sunday, July 14th

One of the amenities of Chequers is being called with one's breakfast, and I confess it is a form of laziness I begin to appreciate, even though it makes me feel still more emphatically that I am not suffering my full share of hardship in this war.

There is an ominous calm. For the first time in a month there were no air-raids last night, all the German submarines except two have gone home, and it looks as if *der Tag* may be imminent. The P.M. thinks it highly probable and keeps on repeating that "Hitler must invade or fail. If he fails he is bound to go East, and fail he will."

I went to church with Miss Seymour, having obtained permission from the P.M. who said, "Go and pray for me: *ora pro nobis.*" It is a lovely church on a hill and there was an immense congregation. Returning from church I played backgammon with Mrs Churchill whose skill is slight, but who talks so much that she wins by *force majeure.* She said that she had been intended to marry Lord Bessborough and had been left with him in a maze all one afternoon.

The Jimmy Rothschilds[1] came to lunch and Winston walked about with him afterwards expatiating on the beauty of the pictures. There is, in particular, a little Rubens in the dining-room about which Winston went into ecstasies. I thought he was a little tactless to Dolly Rothschild in talking about the disgrace of France.

At about 4.00 we left Chequers and went to look at the R.A.F. establishment at Halton, by which the P.M. was obviously bored. I

---

[1] Son of the French Baron Edmond de Rothschild, Liberal M.P. for the Isle of Ely and owner of Waddesdon in Buckinghamshire. His wife gave it with its superb contents to the National Trust. He married Dorothy (Dolly) Pinto, a knowledgeable and most agreeable French lady.

nearly got into hot water for leaving tonight's speech behind but, by undeserved good fortune, Mrs Hill had a spare copy and I was saved! It is fun driving in the P.M.'s cortège: no attention is paid to traffic lights or speed limits.

The P.M. has strong views on food rationing. He thinks it absurd to make it excessive when our supplies are as good as at present. In a letter to his Minister of Food, Lord Woolton, he says: "Almost all the food faddists I have ever known, nut eaters and the like, have died young after a long period of senile decay. The British soldier is far more likely to be right than the scientists. All he cares about is beef . . . The way to lose the war is to try to force the British public into a diet of milk, oatmeal, potatoes, etc., washed down on gala occasions with a little limejuice." The ideas are, I think, taken from Nat Gubbins in the *Sunday Express*, whom Winston and all his family read with avidity.

Monday, July 15th

St Swithin's Day and pouring rain, a fact to cheer the farmers in this year of drought.

Very little work apart from the normal drudgery of answering letters sent by the well-meaning or self-seeking public. The latter predominate.

Lunched with Tony Bevir and Seal at the United Universities Club, which is the haunt of respectable Civil Servants. We talked, deprecatingly, of a scurrilous unsigned attack on Horace Wilson handed to the P.M. by Attlee. The influence of Ismay will be used to smooth matters out. We also spoke of Winston who, think Seal and Bevir, will one day bring about his downfall by excessive loyalty to his friends and a natural disinclination to hurt anybody's feelings. This vice – or virtue – has already cost him much in leading him to support King Edward VIII: by so doing he forfeited the confidence of the House of Commons and of the country.

Tuesday, July 16th

Lunched with George Steward at the Travellers. He seems to have conceived the strongest dislike for Kingsley Wood and he says that Arthur Rucker is not advising Chamberlain well. Neither Horace nor David Margesson nor Arthur were really helpful to the old man because the first could never tell a dishonest man and the other two had no judgment of men's capacity. Beaverbrook he described as twenty-five per cent thug, fifteen per cent crook and the remainder a combination of genius and real goodness of heart.

On late duty. Nothing much happened except the usual nocturnal visits, which included Dr Dalton, whom I thought agreeable.

Speaking to Beaverbrook on the telephone the P.M. said: "I feel better. The air boys have done it. We live on their wings." I was, however, rather depressed to read a note by Dowding on our inability to prevent indiscriminate night bombing (once Hitler has got over his fear of retaliation) and on the increased dangers as the nights grow longer. Apparently we are almost certain to evolve an effective technique for intercepting bombers by night ("the smeller", Winston calls our device), but we have no night fighter capable of making real use of this invention and even if we had the effect would be limited. Dowding thinks each side must sooner or later begin a race for the destruction of the other's aircraft industry, and this, of course, will imply bombing the civilian population. Then the real test will begin: have we or the Germans the sterner civilian morale?

Wednesday, July 17th
The P.M. went off with Seal at 8.45 to inspect defences at Portsmouth.

I see M. Corbin has written to the P.M. on leaving the Embassy: "*Je souhaite que malgré les évènements des dernières semaines nos deux nations ne perdent jamais de vue les intérêts permanents qui les unissent et que leur amitié renaisse un jour plus forte que par le passé.*" Actually I can see little hope of the French forgiving us, especially if we win and restore their freedom. Halifax thinks that the plans of permanent Anglo-French co-operation, which reached their climax in the proposed union of the two countries, will have to be abandoned in favour of more intimate relations with the United States. I think this is logical and it is surely natural that the beginnings of world co-operation should come through closer co-operation between the two great English-speaking Empires. Spain and the Latin Americas might then follow suit.

Brendan tells me that the Germans have a 2-ton bomb – which would certainly create havoc. The big aerial onslaught is expected daily now, followed perhaps by a peace offensive rather than by an invasion. But since St Swithin's Day it has rained and blown ceaselessly, so we may expect a respite until the sun shines again.

There is a great deal of feeling in the country against Chamberlain and the "Men of Munich" and a demand for their removal from office. This W. would never countenance unless he considered them incompetent; and he does not.

Friday, July 19th
Apart from the fact that the Duke of Windsor is being cantankerous and maddening there is no news, only waiting.

Lunched with Lord and Lady Lloyd to meet Madame Tabouis.[1] Sir Harry and Lady Joan Verney[2] were there and also Sir John and Lady Shuckburgh (he is Permanent Under Secretary to Lord Lloyd at the Colonial Office). I sat next to Madame Tabouis who was a bit *effarée*, understandably as she has been proscribed by the Germans and has had to leave her family in France. I said that I had heard (from Sir Orme Sargent at the F.O.) that the Bordeaux Government were thinking of restoring the monarchy and that the Comte de Paris was in France. Madame T. said: "The Pétain Government will make every mistake except that one."

Monday, July 22nd
The Germans in Washington are telling our Embassy that they can produce the terms of peace which Germany would accept. Now, I think, is the psychological moment to define our own war aims and state our terms. They would be such that Hitler must refuse them, but in so doing he would lose credit in the eyes of the outside world and also in those of his own people. Mr Kurt Hahn,[3] former headmaster of Salem, has produced an interesting note on this subject which Tony Bevir has obtained and passed on to the P.M. But I fear the Government lacks the imagination to make such a move, even though I think they have been right to keep their war aims vague up till now (and in any case agreement with the French on the subject was unattainable).

Hore-Belisha has written to suggest that we should support the Duc de Guise,[4] in an effort to rally the royalist French fleet and the Colonies to our side. He thinks that such a move would attract both the Left (which wants to carry on the war) and the Right (which would like a monarchy) in France. He forgets the Centre which is numerically and politically the most important element in France.

Late at No. 10, where I slept. I talked to the Prof. about his secret weapons, the U.P., the P.F. (proximity fuse), G.L. and P.E. He thinks these may be really effective next year and if they are, there is a distinct possibility that aircraft will be ruled out as a weapon of war, because anti-aircraft fire will become not merely effective but deadly.

[1] A widely-read, left-of-Centre French journalist.
[2] Formerly Private Secretary to Queen Mary. Lady Joan was a lady-in-waiting.
[3] A liberal German educationalist who was a profound thinker. He left Germany, and came to Britain, when Hitler came to power and founded Gordonstoun School near Elgin.
[4] Orleanist Pretender to the French throne. Father of the Comte de Paris.

Professor Lindemann believed that since the enemy had military supremacy, the way to defeat them was by scientific ingenuity. The U.P. weapon was an aerial minefield which might have been a valuable deterrent to dive-bombers, but was not put to much effective use. The proximity fuse, which caused a shell to explode when close to a metal object such as an aeroplane, was eventually perfected and mass-produced in America, though it was a British invention. The G.L. was a radar-controlled searchlight and the photo-electric fuse (P.E.) was the parent of many successful later developments.

There were others, including the A.I., which would lead night fighters to enemy bombers, the Sticky Bomb for dealing with tanks, and the Blacker Bombard. The Prof. with the Prime Minister's support, was tireless in promoting these devices, but few of them were far enough advanced to play a significant part in the achievement of victory.

The Prof. was also, with Sir John Anderson, Churchill's liaison with the most important of all Anglo-American scientific activities, the development of the Atomic Bomb, given the code-name Tube Alloys. *This ranked with the breaking of the ciphers of the German armed forces as the most jealously guarded secret of the war.*

The P.M. was in a cantankerous frame of mind, demanding papers which were not available.

At about 1.00 a.m. Brendan, Prof., Tony and I had a discussion about Kurt Hahn's proposals, which are generally thought to be intelligent. It is important that the odium of saying "No" to peace terms should be laid on Hitler and not on ourselves. Hahn thinks that Hitler, who must realise that the aid to be expected from Quislings in this country is small, might hope to discover a Lansdowne, who would advocate a compromise peace.[1]

Wednesday, July 24th
The P.M.'s comment on a long telegram of July 22nd from the Viceroy (Linlithgow)[2] about the proposals for new Indian constitutional measures is "long-winded as ever and a piece of hypocrisy from beginning to end".

[1] In November 1917, Lord Lansdowne, a former Foreign Secretary, wrote a letter to the *Daily Telegraph* calling for peace terms. Despite the devastating losses on the Western Front and at Gallipoli, he was bitterly attacked as an unpatriotic defeatist.

[2] "Hopey", 2nd Marquess of Linlithgow, Viceroy of India, 1936–43, Chancellor of Edinburgh University and, after the war, Chairman of the Midland Bank.

On a note from Vansittart about a possible answer to the speech Hitler made last Sunday, Winston has written: "I do not propose to say anything in reply to Herr Hitler's speech, not being on speaking terms with him."

Thursday, July 25th
David, having returned from Liverpool where he has been coping with French sailors, told me horrifying stories of the casual and tactless way in which they have been handled. The climax of idiocy was to repatriate these highly susceptible Latins on a mule ship from which the mules' manure had not been removed. I repeated the story to Desmond Morton who told it to Winston with a view to having this question of the French in England co-ordinated under Lord Hankey. Winston passed it to the Chiefs of Staff for a report.

The Archbishop of York[1] has written to the P.M. complaining (i) of the recent Burma Road Agreement[2] with the Japanese, whereby we have betrayed China, (ii) the wholesale internment of enemy aliens and the accompanying hardship to many well-disposed and technically useful Germans, Austrians, etc. Both of these questions are causing a stir in the public mind, and the Government are wisely temporising over the second. As regards the first, the argument is that when we are fighting for our life we cannot afford to risk Japanese hostility. But it is a moral defeat to sacrifice in one part of the world the principles we are defending in another, and I feel sure we shall in the long run suffer for yielding to Japanese pressure. The Archbishop says that at least we should boldly admit the reason for our action: "nothing 'saves face' so completely as the honesty which has no interest in face-saving".

Dined with Mrs Churchill and Mary and went with them to see Sarah[3] act in a play of Ivor Novello's, *Murder in Mayfair*, at the "Q" Theatre. Sarah has the reputation of being a thoroughly bad actress, and so I was agreeably surprised to find that she gave a

---

[1] William Temple, whose influence on the Church of England was profound and who became Archbishop of Canterbury in 1942.
[2] The Burma Road was the main route by which China, having lost most of her sea ports, was supplied in her struggle against Japan.
[3] She had long tresses of beautiful dark red hair and was perhaps Winston Churchill's favourite child. I had known her since we were both eighteen (and even took her twice to see the Grand National). She had an obsession with the stage, but in the war joined the W.A.A.F. and was a competent analyst of the R.A.F. photographic surveys. She wrote good poetry and had great depth of feeling. None of her three matrimonial experiments ended happily.

good performance and looked much lovelier than she in fact is. Her mass of red hair was very effective on the stage. I sat beside Mary who was in raptures; she has a naive and rather charming adoration for everything connected with her family (except Randolph). After the play we went on, with the Sandyses, to have supper with Sarah and Vic [Oliver] in their extremely luxurious flat. The Churchills *en famille* were delightful and very amusing. They made a certain amount of fun of the Chamberlains and Mary described how Mrs Chamberlain had taken her for the wife of one of the officers on the *Exeter*. Sarah seems much older (she is only my age), but apparently thrives on the life of movement, instability and restlessness which she and Vic have chosen. Vic, munching a sandwich while the rest of us swilled champagne, talked of the broadcast to the U.S. which he was due to make in half an hour. I devoured cherries, gossiped with Diana, and aroused Mary's indignation to a high pitch by telling her that when Chamberlain was P.M. I had refused to wake him up to see the papers which Winston sent over sporadically from the Admiralty at 2.00 a.m. "You dared to do that to Papa!" she said. Mrs Churchill told me of her disapproval of Sir John Anderson[1] (a feeling which is widely shared).

Friday, July 26th
There is some agitation for an authoritative reply to Hitler's speech, and I think Winston should make one, stating our terms and our aims subtly but clearly. However W. remains adamant and Vansittart encourages him to maintain "a forbidding silence".

Halifax's speech on the wireless, in which he spoke of God more than of Hitler, has aroused a certain amount of criticism in the *New Statesman*, etc.; but generally speaking it has been well received here and apparently appreciated in the country. Though his delivery is bad, Halifax's speeches are invariably beautiful to read.

Amery, whose policy with regard to India has been almost universally opposed in the Cabinet, came to see Winston after tea and from all appearances they had a "blood row". It looks as if Amery will resign. Later Winston produced a telegram which he wanted sent to the Viceroy without Amery or the India Office knowing; so I had to go over to the India Office, suborn one of the men in the telegram despatch room, and cypher the telegram with him. It was a sharp rebuke to Linlithgow for carrying on a secret correspondence with Amery behind the backs of the War Cabinet and demanded permission to show this correspondence to the Cabinet.

[1] Later Viscount Waverley.*

Back at No. 10 I talked to Arthur Rucker.[1] He defended Sir J. Anderson over the refugee question, saying that he had been averse to locking them up indiscriminately in the first place and had pleaded for a reasonable policy. He had given in, or rather had been forced by the Government to give in, owing to popular clamour and fear of Fifth Columnists. Now Sir John was anxious to avoid swinging the balance too far the other way just because people were beginning to feel sorry for the refugees. Left to himself he would have preserved a sane policy of discrimination. Arthur also defended the Government's Burma Road policy on the ground that without this concession we should have had to fight Japan. He claimed that our great fault in recent years had been to let our diplomacy outrun our strength, to threaten what we could not fulfil. It was essential to return to a system of *realpolitik*.

Saturday, July 27th
Alone at No. 10 with John Martin who is a most agreeable companion. We had a reasonably quiet and undisturbed day, except that I had to go over to the India Office and decypher the Viceroy's humble reply to Winston, suborning another cypherer in the process.

The press have made fools of themselves by harping on our wonderful supply of destroyers – just when we are crying poverty to the U.S. in the hope of procuring fifty from them. Winston is now appealing eloquently to the President, both directly and through Lothian.

From Berne the Minister reports that Paravicini[2] – who cannot be suspected of anything but benevolence – has reliable information that the majority of the German General Staff, formerly opposed to an attack on this country, have swung round in favour of it. Dowding, C. in C. Fighter Command, estimates that one mass raid of 3,000 machines could be launched against us, but that over a period of days a maximum of 500 a day and 200 a night could be maintained. It is significant that yesterday and today German raiders turned away when they saw our fighters approaching. They have been "grievously mauled", as Winston would say, on their recent daylight visits.

---

[1] He had remained Private Secretary to Neville Chamberlain, who was now Lord President of the Council and living at 11 Downing Street.
[2] Swiss Minister in London for many years before the war and, with his American wife, popular in social and political circles. Madame Paravicini was of invaluable assistance to British prisoners of war in Germany and to their families at home.

Sunday, July 28th

Spent the morning at No. 10, where I was in constant touch with Chequers about India. The story, in brief, is that Amery has been telegraphing to Linlithgow about a public declaration which it is proposed the Viceroy should make concerning the attitude of H.M.G. to India's status and Constitution after the war. Amery has tried to push his ideas (which would give a blank cheque to an Indian Constituent Assembly of the future) through without really consulting the Cabinet, and his telegrams, which Winston demanded to see on Friday and which may now be circulated as a Cabinet paper, contain a number of ill-advised references to Winston himself and complaints that he is driving the Cabinet to adopt his own views about the form this declaration should take. The Viceroy has been placed in an embarrassing position by Amery's impetuosity and now, as far as Amery is concerned, the fat is in the fire. Winston, after consultation with Lord Simon,[1] has redrafted the last paragraph of the declaration.

Went back to No. 10 at 6.30 to meet Winston on his return. Talked to Edward Bridges about Sir John Anderson. He says that the latter is really a very sound administrator, the best we have. He supports Arthur Rucker's view of Anderson and the refugee problem and says that he has been much maligned and made a scapegoat for actions that were taken too quickly owing to the caprices of public opinion which were reflected in the Government.

After dinner I had a conversation with Attlee about Public Schools and Universities. He was much more agreeable and forthcoming than I had thought.

Chamberlain has been taken ill and may have to have an abdominal operation, poor old man. Brendan tells me that Lord Beaverbrook is to be brought into the Cabinet as Minister of Production if Herbert Morrison (who may object to playing second fiddle as Minister of Supply) can be squared. Brendan also wants to bring in Lloyd George and thinks that with the temporary disappearance of Chamberlain the opportunity has come. I said I thought that with the examples of Hindenburg and Pétain before us, we should be careful of enlisting the support of hoary survivors from the last war.

Brendan and I also talked about the Ecclesiastical patronage. Although an agnostic he feels very strongly the importance of good appointments being made and of deeply spiritual and saintly men being encouraged to enter the Church. We need Saints, he says,

[1] Lord Chancellor. Formerly Sir John Simon.*

not good administrators, and the P.M. should rely on the advice of men in the Government, such as Halifax and Caldecote[1] (as representatives of the two extremes of churchmanship) who take their Ecclesiastical responsibilities seriously.

Monday, July 29th
It is being put about, Attlee has discovered, that Amery's liberal and statesmanlike proposals with regard to India are being sabotaged by Churchill. This is not true because Amery had merely wanted to make a woolly promise that H.M.G., after the war, would assent to whatever constitutional proposals a representative body in India should propose. It would be impossible to collect a really representative body and, secondly, such a wide and general promise would arouse expectations which might, and almost certainly would, be unfulfilled in the event. However, there is a real danger that if Amery goes, as I think he must, his resignation will be misinterpreted and the Government branded as reactionary.

My final visit to my masseuse.[2] She talks a lot of nonsense and insists on my living on tomatoes, but curiously enough I do feel much better and less sluggish for her ministrations.

Tuesday, July 30th
Rode at Richmond before breakfast, despite the tank traps. The P.M. and the First Lord are having a bit of a tiff, owing to the former's comments on the sinking of five ships and the damaging of six others in a raid on a Channel convoy last Friday. The P.M. complained that the Admiralty's precautions were "utterly ineffectual", and said: "I must consider this one of the most lamentable episodes of the naval war so far as it has yet developed." A. V. Alexander flared up and wrote asking that this minute might be withdrawn. In his reply, refusing to do so, Winston said: "I was naturally wounded to read of the massacre of all these poor little ships and I do not think I was wrong in describing the episode as 'lamentable'. The word lamentable expresses grief and not necessarily judgment."

---

[1] As Sir Thomas Inskip responsible for rearmament before the war. He approached this task with excessive caution. A devout low churchman in contrast to the high-church Halifax. Created Viscount Caldecote by Chamberlain. Briefly Lord Chancellor in 1939–40, he was appointed Lord Chief Justice in October 1940.

[2] As the antidote to long nights, insufficient exercise and a general feeling of unhealthiness I had placed myself in the hands of an energetic but ugly masseuse.

Wednesday, July 31st

Rode again at Richmond, where a searchlight was attacked by machine-gun fire last night. The ford which I usually cross from Wimbledon has been blocked with pits and barriers and in the park itself, near Louis Greig's* house, a village of unsightly grey huts with blue windows has sprung up. Fortunately the sun and the early morning air are proof against warlike preparations.

Winston has gone off on one of his tours of inspection, this time to the North. Desmond Morton tells me that "C", the head of the Secret Service, has now received news of imminent invasion from over 260 sources. The main attack will be against the South, with diversions against Hull, Scotland and Ireland, which will be exploited if successful. Parachutists will be used only in the South. It is clear that all preparations have been made; whether they will be used depends on Hitler's caprice. It is significant that German troops are concentrating in the East and it is on the cards that Hitler has immediate designs against the Ukraine.

One of the items on the Chiefs of Staffs' agenda is the situation caused by the insistence of innumerable spectators on crowding the pier at Dover to watch the aerial battles. It is encouraging that the passion for sightseeing should still be greater than that for self-preservation.

Winston has finally sent an appeal to Roosevelt for destroyers, flying boats and motor-torpedo boats. He says: "We are hitting that man hard both in repelling attacks and in bombing Germany; but we have lost a lot of destroyers lately and we cannot get a substantial reinforcement. The whole fate of the war may be decided by this minor and easily remediable factor . . . I am beginning to feel very hopeful about this war if we can get round the next three or four months."

After dinner I talked to Desmond Morton about the Foreign Office proposal that a number of American foodships should be allowed to sail, under safeguards, to ports in unoccupied France. Desmond, and the Ministry of Economic Warfare, feel violently that the Foreign Office is trying to "appease" the Vichy Government in the same way that, throughout the winter, they tried to prevent Italy coming into the war by relaxing the blockade in her favour. Halifax, Ronnie Campbell and Van maintain that to allow enough food into unoccupied France would not affect Germany's position but would suffice to keep the French people, as opposed to their Government, well-disposed to us, to counter German propaganda about our brutality in starving women and children, and to allay misplaced humanitarian feelings in America. I should feel more open to conviction by the Foreign Office arguments if they could produce one example of successful appeasement. I am afraid that as far as France is concerned we shall have to harden our hearts and block our ears.

Japan has arrested a number of British subjects on charges of espionage and feeling is running high. New Zealand and Australia are naturally anxious that we should avoid war.

The Italians are said to have bombed one of their own battle cruisers in mistake for the *Hood*.

8

Battle of Britain

August 1940

Thursday, August 1st

David's story of the treatment of French sailors at Aintree, re-
peated by Desmond Morton and sent by the P.M. to the Chiefs of
Staff, has returned with the comments of the First Sea Lord and
C.I.G.S. They deny most of the allegations and say that the trouble
was largely due to the sulky and unco-operative attitude of the
French themselves.

Priestley[1] has sent the P.M. an article he has written pleading for
Government benevolence towards the people's recreation. We
will give up our Bank Holidays, but let us have laughter and fun
and untaxed books (the Chancellor in his much-criticised budget
proposes to tax books and has aroused a justifiable storm of
protest). Priestley declaims against the drift towards dreariness.
What is far more dangerous, as Mother points out, is the film-fed
public's insatiate longing for sensation. It has often been said that
the Dictators could only survive if they took some dramatic action
every six months, and now the British public, drugged by Holly-
wood and by the stirring events of recent months, seems to need
incessant change and excitement. It is already being said in the
provinces that Churchill is "played out" and must go. There is no
such murmur in London, but London does not represent England
any more than Paris does France.

At tea we talked of the Civil Service and I complained of the slow
promotion in the F.O. "You'll never get beyond the rank of
Second Secretary," said Seal. "Oh yes, he will," said Desmond
Morton, "he has got such a capacity for intrigue!"

The Archbishop of Canterbury came to see the P.M. about the

---

[1] J. B. Priestley, the novelist.

appointment of a new Bishop of St Edmundsbury and Ipswich, a matter which has been occupying me for some months. After a good deal of discussion I recommended Archdeacon Brook of Coventry, a safe but not spectacular appointment for this rural diocese. The P.M. and the Archbishop agreed to make the offer.

Friday, August 2nd

During the night the Germans dropped pamphlets in England, containing part of the text of Hitler's speech.

The German press is busy educating its readers not to expect an immediate success against England. It looks as if the military authorities are becoming doubtful of their ability to invade us rapidly and successfully. Meanwhile German dive-bombers have arrived in South Italy and I feel sure that the Axis powers contemplate forceful action in the Mediterranean.

Lothian has telegraphed the American reaction to Winston's demand for destroyers. The President would like to send them, but does not think he can obtain the consent of Congress unless one of two conditions is accepted: (i) that Canada is given a lien on some of our fast cruisers which could be used in the defence of North America if this country were defeated; (ii) we should agree, without transfer of sovereignty, to give the U.S.A. military facilities in Trinidad and the West Indies. Although the Americans are not showing signs of appreciating the full seriousness of the situation, and are themselves showing the lack of realism for which they so freely criticised us before the war, this is evidently not a time to haggle, and Lothian points out that there is much to be said for constructing an Anglo-American battle front in the West Indies and Western Atlantic.

In an interview with Lord Halifax, the Duke of Alba[1] asserted that the French have always laid the blame for their national disasters on the treachery of other Frenchmen. Thus the death of Roland was ascribed to the treachery of Ganelon, the defeat of Francis I at Pavia to the betrayal of the Constable of Bourbon, and the loss of the Franco-Prussian War to the treason of Bazaine. No doubt the blame for the present disaster would be laid at the door of the whole republican system. Alba said that Pétain undoubtedly intended to restore the monarchy, and he thought this would conduce to the improvement of Franco-Spanish relations and might well be acceptable to the French peasantry.

Mr Duff Cooper is in trouble with the press, whom he has criticised, and has himself been criticised on all sides for trying to

---

[1] Spanish Ambassador in London.

send people into the homes of the citizens of this country to investigate their owners' morale. The campaign against "Cooper's Snoopers" has thrown Duff Cooper himself into discredit. Certainly he has not produced many results as Minister of Information, and I think there are signs that Chamberlain was justified in refusing to give him a job.

Monday, August 5th

At 1.30 a military agreement was signed in the Cabinet Room by the P.M., Halifax and representatives of the Polish Government, including General Sikorski. A photographer, for the first time in history, took a photograph of the signatories in the Cabinet Room. Afterwards we went out into the garden and drank champagne. Winston prowling round and proposing toasts to the common cause, etc.

In a minute on the production of the U.P. weapon (which gave satisfactory results the other day at Dover), the P.E. fuse, etc., the P.M. urges that the greatest facilities be given by the Ministry of Supply to the scientist in charge, Dr Crowe. He says: "The whole character of the war both by sea and land in 1941 may be affected by the development of these weapons."

Interest centres on Operation SCIPIO, by which it is hoped that General de Gaulle may be enabled to land in French West Africa and seize power. The forces employed are to be French troops, but the main difficulty is the decision about the escorting British men-of-war. Are they to engage ships of the Vichy Government if the latter attempt to intercept General de Gaulle's forces? H.M.G. are anxious to avoid this. This afternoon the P.M. signed a letter to the General agreeing to recognise a French "Council of Defence" in the French Colonies to which all anti-Vichy elements can rally. De Gaulle's agents will leave by air tomorrow for Nigeria with copies of this document.

Operation RAZZLE, for burning the German crops, is also under discussion, but only a fraction of these are within range of our aircraft.

Tuesday, August 6th

The day was an uneventful one except for the news that the Italians are advancing into British Somaliland and have proceeded a considerable distance towards Berbera. Materially the loss of this territory would be slight, but psychologically, in Italy and the Near East, the effects would be lamentable. We are moving the Black Watch from Aden to Berbera.

Winston was in a nervous and irritable frame of mind in the evening, occupied with the question of obtaining from the U.S. the fifty destroyers we so badly need. He refuses to contemplate a promise to give Canada, and thus the U.S., a lien on our warships if these islands are conquered and brands any such proposal as defeatism. We could only give such an undertaking in return for an Anglo-U.S. Alliance. Thus Winston declares that the only *quid pro quo* we could give the U.S. would be the lease of air and naval bases in the West Indies. This would be justifiable because it is in our interest to encourage a strong Anglo-American defence line in the Western Atlantic.

W. protested strongly at the noise being made in the Private Secretaries' room and finally threatened to sack the next offender. This next offender was the Chief of the Air Staff, but the real culprit is Desmond Morton whose voice would penetrate the ramparts of a mediaeval castle.

Wednesday, August 7th

Winston has gone off to East Anglia to inspect defences, taking with him Randolph and Major Jack Churchill.[1] I am afraid his naturally affectionate nature disposes him towards nepotism. He has given Duncan Sandys an important job at the Cabinet Offices, under Ismay, and a staff job is being arranged for Randolph.[2]

I had a very busy day, alone most of the afternoon and immersed in a jungle of unimportant but harassing detail. The piles of desperately boring letters awaiting my signature became increasingly unmanageable.

Desmond Morton tells me the Secret Service have absconded with £13,000,000 in francs which they discovered in the courtyard of a French bank in occupied France. This money will be used to finance de Gaulle. So the Secret Service are not entirely useless.

The King of Sweden [Gustav V] has telegraphed to the King and to Hitler offering his services as a mediator. It is apparently the King's personal initiative. The F.O. draft declining King Gustav's offer, which will be considered by the Cabinet tomorrow, is a masterpiece of dignified language.

Dined with Lady Wolverton, Marion Hyde and Esmé Glyn.[3]

[1] Winston Churchill's younger brother, to whom he was devoted. He lived at No. 10 and was a member of the staff mess. He married the lovely Lady Gwendeline Bertie by whom Winston had also been captivated in his youth. Their children were John, Peregrine and Clarissa.

[2] This is a libel. He was given a job in the Commandos but had a staff job later, before being parachuted into Yugoslavia.

[3] The elder of Lady Wolverton's two daughters was a lady-in-waiting to Queen Elizabeth. The younger, Esmé, worked hard in the Women's Voluntary Service as adjutant to Lady Reading. She later married Nigel Birch, M.P., who held high political office and was created Lord Rhyl.

Marion tells me that though the King and Queen appreciate Winston's qualities, and see that he is the man for the occasion, they are a little ruffled by the off-hand way in which he treats them. They much preferred Chamberlain's habit of going to the Palace regularly once a week and explaining the situation in a careful unhurried way. Winston says he will come at 6.00, puts it off by telephone till 6.30 and is inclined to turn up for ten hectic minutes at 7.00. Unfortunately the King, doubtless on the advice of Alec Hardinge, has chosen to oppose Winston on a number of questions, about which it would have been more tactful to remain silent, namely the appointment of Beaverbrook as Minister of Aircraft Production, the gift of a Privy Councillorship to Brendan, and the offer of a peerage to Ironside. But Winston, however cavalierly he may treat his sovereign, is at heart a most vehement Royalist.

Relations between the King and the Prime Minister soon became excellent and even Queen Mary developed an immense admiration for Winston. The Prime Minister was, in fact, always scrupulous in consulting as well as informing the King on all matters of major importance and never missed his weekly audience if he could possibly avoid it. Suspicions which the King and Queen may have had about Winston's support of the Duke of Windsor rapidly evaporated when the Duke made difficulties in connection with his appointment as Governor of the Bahamas and the Prime Minister himself sought the King's permission to reply to the Duke's complaints with considerable severity. As the war proceeded the King and Queen became as devoted to Winston Churchill as he consistently was to them.

Having dropped Esmé in a taxi at Tothill Street (headquarters of the Women's Voluntary Service), where she is spending the night on duty, I went back to No. 10 and found Winston rending the Chiefs of Staff who are being unenthusiastic about the projected Operation SCIPIO in West Africa. De Gaulle came to sign an agreement; Newall, Dill and the Vice Chief of the Naval Staff (Admiral Philipps, minute but brilliant) talked with Ismay about the situation in Somaliland and the possibilities of invasion here; Desmond Morton and General Spears waited dutifully in my room for three hours in case they should be needed.

The First Lord told me on the telephone about 1.00 a.m. that a troopship had been torpedoed off Ireland. This depressed Winston greatly; however he recovered when he heard that nearly all the men had been saved and that there were no valuable stores on board, merely remarking that the navy were not being as successful against U-boats as in the past. (We have lost much shipping lately.)

Thursday, August 8th
Another busy day. After an early lunch I heard from the Air Ministry that violent fighting had taken place over a convoy off St Catherine's Point.[1] We appear to have destroyed a large number of German aircraft, but several ships in the convoy were sunk, two by E-boats. I told the P.M. this while he was lunching with Mrs Churchill and Dr Beneš[2] and he said: "And the British navy let them (the E-boats) sink those poor little ships in broad daylight!"

According to the Joint Intelligence Committee's weekly summary, which is a document well worth perusing, the result of Germany's delay in attacking this country is that "a small cloud of doubt as to Germany's invincibility has arisen on the European horizon". There are reports that Italy is pressing Germany to take the offensive in the North Sea and that Germany is urging an Italian offensive in the Mediterranean. Personally I think that the German attack on this country, whether by air or by invasion, will not be delayed much longer: Germany is probably gathering herself for a formidable blow. But it is comforting that an eminent German recently confided to a neutral that Germany's position was "splendid but hopeless".

As regards Russia, where Molotov recently made a speech attacking this country and the U.S., and reaffirming Russia's friendship with Germany, the F.O. comment:

M. Molotov's speech need not be taken altogether at its face value. The Soviet Government have no friends in the world and no spiritual affinities with other Governments. They merely enter into temporary diplomatic associations with countries for purely opportunist purposes. They distrust and are distrusted by those with whom they associate, but take care not to let their distrust be exploited by others. (i.e. by us). Hence the anxiety they display to re-emphasise on every suitable occasion the friendly character of their relations with Germany.

Friday, August 9th
The bag in yesterday's attack on a convoy off the Isle of Wight seems to have been about sixty German aircraft for the loss of

---

[1] Southern point of the Isle of Wight.
[2] Prime Minister of Czechoslovakia, forced into exile when the Nazis occupied his country.

sixteen. Five ships in the convoy were sunk and a number damaged.

Went to Chequers, motoring down with Mrs Churchill and Mary. Mr Eden, Sir John Dill, Sir Archibald Wavell* (C. in C., Middle East) and Ismay came to dine and sleep. About two minutes before dinner it transpired that the P.M. had invited the First Sea Lord but had omitted to tell anybody! This occasioned some hectic rearranging of the dinner table. I sat between Ismay and the First Sea Lord (Pound). Towards the end of dinner we had a triangular discussion, Eden, Ismay and I, about the fall of France. Both Eden and Ismay seemed to think that her shame had been so great that she could never rise again. W. disagrees.

After the ladies had gone, a variety of subjects were discussed, beginning with the attack on the convoy yesterday. Winston seemed to think we must go on using these coastal vessels as bait, although he admitted that "the surviving bait are getting a bit fed up". In drawing the German attack thus we stood to lose little (Pound pointed out that we even had a surplus of coasting vessels) while in the ensuing aerial battles we definitely proved to ourselves and to the world that we were superior to the Germans. Winston said the enemy must be "less all-powerful" in the air than we had supposed. If their strength were as great as we had believed, they would have come again today; they would have been bombing our ports incessantly. Eden could not understand why the Germans expended so great an effort against comparatively unimportant objects. It was suggested that they still thought they could starve us out and did not realise the unimportance of these coastal convoys. In that case it hardly looks as if the Germans are conserving everything for an invasion and mass-attack.

Pound suggested that the Germans had made a great mistake in going on, after they had proved the weakness of the French army, to strike a knock-out blow: they should have stopped after crossing the Somme and turned on us. Eden pointed out that the Germans probably thought, as did we, that the French would rally. The P.M. said that this mistake, if it was one, merely made the Germans slightly less admirable, but one could not detract from the brilliance of their strategy and of their unhesitating advance through Abbeville and Boulogne to Calais – and nearly to Dunkirk. The men of Calais were the bit of grit that saved us by stopping them as Sidney Smith stopped Napoleon at Acre.

The conversation turned to home defence, and Winston and Eden both said that the only real worry was the acute shortage of small-arms ammunition. But think where we should have been if the fighting had begun in March and had still been going on in

France! Dill said that might be true, but in actual fact people never ran out of small arms ammunition. Their real requirements always fell below what they estimated. Eden said the new "Molotov Cocktail" was a vast improvement on the old and the anti-tank mine on the beaches had been shown to be most devastating. In fact the latter had already accounted for too many of our own people: Winston instanced the golfer who recently drove his ball on to the beach; he took his niblick down to the beach, played the ball, and all that remained visible afterwards was the ball which returned safely to the green.

The P.M. said: "Fancy, next year we shall have ten armoured divisions!" Eden and Dill dissented, saying that we should not have the equipment. "Well," said Winston, "if you'll produce the men (cries of "oh, we can do that") I'll see you get the weapons." Then we should be able to undertake formidable raids on the continent. This autumn we should land small forces of 5,000 men (and all the Generals seemed enthusiastic about this idea of taking the offensive), thus giving valuable experience and training to individual brigades or battalions which would form a core for future operations. We had much open to us: a landing in Holland followed by a destructive raid into the Ruhr; the seizure of the Cherbourg peninsula; and invasion of Italy. Wavell suggested Norway: "We shall need skis for that," said Winston, "and we don't want to go and get Namsosed again. We've had enough of that." Eden said that Sicily would be the soft spot in Italy's armour, because the Sicilians had always been anti-fascists.

The P.M., turning to Wavell, said that he promised he would not ask him to effect a landing in enemy territory until we could clear the air over the place of disembarkation. There was every hope that with the P.E. (photo-electric) rocket, the "Spaniel" (a rocket which pursues aircraft and is not dependent on accurate aiming), and a similar radio-rocket for use at night, we should be able to make it difficult for enemy aircraft to operate – and then the possibilities of offensive action would be great indeed.

After dinner Winston, the Generals and Pound retired to the Hawtrey room for a conference, and I arranged papers in the box and read various memoranda until nearly 3.00 a.m. At one moment a German raider came over the house and we all stumbled out into the garden to look. The First Sea Lord fell down first one flight of steps and then, having picked himself up disconsolately, he tumbled down another, ending in a heap on the ground where a sentry threatened him with a bayonet. He came back saying, "This is not the place for a First Sea Lord." Winston's comment was,

"Try and remember you are an Admiral of the Fleet and not a Midshipman!"

Saturday, August 10th
In a telegram to the Prime Ministers of Australia and New Zealand, promising that we will abandon the Mediterranean and send our fleet eastwards in the event of Japan attacking Australia or N.Z., Winston has written: "If Hitler fails to invade and conquer Britain before the weather breaks, he has received his first and probably fatal check."

Sir Stafford Cripps has sent an interesting letter from Moscow to Lord Halifax about the future of the British Empire. He speaks of the new international groupings, of which there will be four:
  (a) An Asiatic, probably under Japanese but possibly under Sino-Japanese hegemony.
  (b) A Euro-Asiatic, including the Baltic states and part of the Balkans, under Russia.
  (c) A European, including Scandinavia, part of the Balkans and the Middle East, under one European power.
  (d) An American under the U.S.A.

Into these groups the British Empire does not naturally fall as a unit. Cripps' solution is for us to be associated closely in an Anglo-Saxon group with the U.S., G.B. being the European outpost of this group. Such an idea would, in addition, make it easier for the British Government to move to Canada in case of necessity. Winston wrote on this paper a note for circulation, which he afterwards tore up. It ran as follows:

It seems to me that the ideas set forth by Sir S. Cripps upon the post-war position of the British Empire are far too airy and speculative to be useful at the present moment, when we have to win the war in order to survive. In these circumstances, unless any of my colleagues desire it, it seems hardly necessary to bring this excursion of our Ambassador to the U.S.S.R. formally before the Cabinet.

Later on, at lunch, Winston gave me his own views about war aims and the future. He said there was only one aim, to destroy Hitler. Let those who say they do not know what they are fighting for stop fighting and they will see. France is now discovering what she was fighting for. After the last war people had done much constructive thinking and the League of Nations had been a magnificent idea. Something of the kind would have to be built up again: there would be a United States of Europe, and this Island would be the link connecting this Federation with the new world and able to hold the balance between the two. "A new conception of the balance of power?" I said. "No," he replied, "the balance of virtue."

I lunched *en famille* with the P.M., Mrs C. and Mary, and it could not have been more enjoyable. Winston was in the best of humours. He talked brilliantly on every topic from Ruskin to Lord Baldwin, from the future of Europe to the strength of the Tory Party. When he spoke of our lamentable lack of equipment, of that "boob" Inskip, etc., he said: "We shall win, but we don't deserve it; at least, we do deserve it because of our virtues, but not because of our intelligence." He said that the Tory Party was the strength of the country: few things need to be changed quickly and drastically; what conservatism, as envisaged by Disraeli, stood for was the gradual increase of amenities for an ever larger number of people, who should enjoy the benefits previously reserved for a very few (i.e. a levelling upwards, not a levelling downwards). The future depended not on the political system, but, once every man had sufficient, on the inner heart and soul of the individual. He was in a very friendly and garrulous mood and extremely pleased by some of the examples of bad verse (such as that by Edmund Gosse's housemaid) which I quoted to him:

> Oh, Moon, lovely Moon, with thy beautiful face
> Careering throughout the boundaries of space
> Whenever I see thee, I think in my mind,
> Shall I ever, oh ever, behold thy behind.[1]

Lord Beaverbrook rang up to say that the Germans had bombed an important factory at Rochester heavily but had contrived to miss with all their bombs. The Almighty is not always against us, he said, "In fact God is the Minister of Aircraft Production and I am his deputy."

After lunch I went for a long walk with Mrs Churchill and Mary to the summit of a neighbouring hill. Inadvisedly I raced Mary to the top, and though I won I reached my objective feeling iller than I have ever felt and was quite unable to see or think. Having recovered sufficiently, I walked home with Mrs C. discussing what could be done to make Lord Bessborough acceptable to Peggy, and others, as Chairman of the French Welfare Committees, etc., to which office Winston has appointed him.

Arrived back in time to receive de Gaulle and Spears who came

---

[1] Had she lived a hundred years later she would have.

to discuss the former's proposed action at Dakar and in West Africa. I spent a very busy evening with papers and innumerable telephone conversations with Lord Lloyd about a propaganda matter.

Sir R. Gordon Finlayson, C. in C. Western Command, and Sir H. Pownall,[1] who commands the Home Guard, came to dine and sleep. Colonel Jacob and Prof. Lindemann also arrived. At dinner I sat between Mary and Jacob and, when not discussing blood-sports with the former, listened to Winston. He mentioned the numerous projects, inventions, etc., which he had in view and compared himself to a farmer driving pigs along a road, who always had to be prodding them on and preventing them from straying. He praised the splendid *sang-froid* and morale of the people, and said he could not quite see why he appeared to be so popular. After all since he came into power, everything had gone wrong and he had had nothing but disasters to announce. His platform was only "blood, sweat and tears".

He sent Prof. and me for some of his cherished graphs and diagrams and began to expound the supply position. Beaverbrook, he said, had genius and, what was more, brutal ruthlessness. He had never in his life, at the Ministry of Munitions or anywhere else, seen such startling results as Beaverbrook had produced; and Pownall, looking at the Aircraft Production charts, agreed that there had never been such an achievement. W. regretted that the Ministry of Supply had shown themselves incapable of producing similar results for the army.

He proceeded to examine the statistics, calling on Prof. for frequent explanations, and declaring that we were already over-hauling the Germans in numbers (our production already exceeds theirs by one third). It was generally agreed that Hitler's aircraft position *must* be less good than we had supposed; otherwise why the delay, why the sparsity of attack?

After dinner (i.e. about 11.15!) we walked up and down beneath the stars, a habit which Winston has formed. When he came in I showed him a letter from Nelson to Lord Spencer (First Lord of the Admiralty), written a week after the Battle of the Nile, which I had found in one of the rooms. It began: "My Lord, was I to die at this moment want of frigates would be found stamped on my heart. No words of mine can express what I have and am suffering for want of them . . ." I suggested to W. that he might so begin a "Former Naval Person" telegram to Roosevelt, substituting "destroyers" for "frigates". He answered that we were certainly going to get the

---

[1] Chief of Staff to Lord Gort in the British Expeditionary Force, 1939–40.

destroyers from America. But it is curious how history repeats itself even in small details.

The Generals retired to the Hawtrey room to discuss the Home Guard until 2.00 a.m. when we went to bed.

Sunday, August 11th

Walked in the garden with Jacob. He says that Beaverbrook is a pirate; he steals the things which his colleagues, such as the Minister of Supply, want and there is a real danger that he will cause trouble with his Labour colleagues, especially as the P.M. supports all his demands and backs him against Sinclair and Morrison.[1] I think that Beaverbrook should be made Minister of Munitions, with a Tory as Minister of Supply under him, and Morrison should be sent to the Ministry of Information. Jacob comments that Beaverbrook as Minister of Aircraft Production is still Beaverbrook the Press King: he attaches supreme importance to the numbers of aircraft he can produce, as he formerly did to the numbers of the *Daily Express* he could sell. "Circulation" is his paramount interest.

Jacob thinks the P.M. should invite people from the War Office and Admiralty, as well as the Generals, down here so that they might realise how forceful and competent a person he is. At present the departments are driven to exasperation by the flow of enquiries, demands and comments which reach them every morning from No. 10 and from Ismay's staff (now to be known as the Office of the Minister of Defence).

Speaking of Chamberlain Jacob described him aptly as "a perfect Chairman of the Board of Directors, but not a good Managing Director".

Air Marshal Bowhill (C. in C., Coastal Command) came to lunch, also the Randolph Churchills. The chief excitement was another big aerial engagement and I kept on having to ring up Fighter Command to discover "the latest score". W. was very excited and kept on saying that "the swine had needed three days in which to lick their wounds" before they came again and that their air superiority was clearly less than we had feared.

The P.M. spoke on the telephone to Beaverbrook, who is coming tonight. B. (whose comment scrawled on a bit of paper to explain why this week's totals of aircraft deliveries are smaller than last week's, is: "Bevin's holiday and more holidays to come – and the Germans too perhaps") talked of his troubles with Herbert Morrison. He said that Morrison is never in his office and has no

---

[1] Herbert Morrison.

idea how to run a business: he tries to work it on the same lines as the L.C.C. They discussed the possibility of Morrison being replaced and agreed that tonight, when Ernest Bevin is coming, would be a good opportunity to approach the subject. The best way of influencing Morrison is through Bevin.[1]

After lunch I was soundly beaten by Mrs C. at croquet and then walked to the top of Beacon Hill with Mary. We sat on the top in the sunshine and prattled gaily, looking at the magnificent view of the plain below. Even though she takes herself a little seriously – as she confesses – she is a charming girl and very pleasant to look upon.

After tea I accompanied the P.M. to a rifle range nearby, where he fired with his Mannlicher rifle at targets 100, 200 and 300 yards away. He also fired his revolver, still smoking a cigar, with commendable accuracy. Despite his age, size and lack of practice, he acquitted himself well. The whole time he talked of the best method of killing Huns. Soft-nose bullets were the thing to use and he must get some. But, said Randolph, they are illegal in war; to which the P.M. replied that the Germans would make very short work of him if they caught him, and so he didn't see why he should have any mercy on them. He always seems to visualise the possibility of having to defend himself against German troops!

Beaverbrook and Bevin arrived, and I dined alone with them and Winston. Grouse has been specially ordered, it having become legal to shoot them on August 5th this year. Winston politely hinted before dinner that it was a good thing to leave politicians to talk alone (they want to work on Bevin about the Morrison question) and so I retired discreetly as soon as I had procured myself a cigar. During dinner it was amusing to hear Beaverbrook flatter Bevin, calling him a natural House of Commons man and saying that he was the only orator in the Labour Party. Bevin said the war would be won in the Middle East and it was essential, for the sake of morale in this country, to deal the Italians a resounding blow. One was enough; after that they would collapse. Beaverbrook said he thought the morale in this country was all right, and when we received set-backs we braced ourselves the more. Bevin was doubtful and considered that success was sorely needed. I wondered who knew best, the newspaper magnate or the Labour leader. I am inclined to think the latter.

[1] As events showed, it was the worst. Ernest Bevin* detested Morrison. In any case, though Churchill always listened to Beaverbrook, he had no intention of taking part in his political intrigues (without which life had no zest for Beaverbrook).

There were a number of sly allusions to capitalism and socialism and, I thought, a certain atmosphere of *gêne*, but this wore off by degrees. Agriculture was discussed, both Beaverbrook and Bevin considering themselves experts on the subject, and the former tried to persuade the P.M. that it was advisable to plough up 2,000,000 acres. "1,500,000," said Winston, "you are looking at what you think will be useful after the war. We have got to use all the labour we have to win the war and after that we'll make this country a fit place to live in." Talking on the same subject he said he did not think much of "that young man", by whom I understood him to mean Rob Hudson, the Minister of Agriculture.

Bevin asked for two things: (i) a Ministry of Buildings, to be responsible for all government construction and to co-ordinate this with the needs of the building trade; (ii) to be allowed to be in charge of amusements, from philharmonic concerts to horse-racing, in order that the public's entertainment might not be neglected in war-time. We have not got to be gloomy in order to be worthy of winning the war. The P.M. assented heartily. "There's nothing like singing to keep your spirits up," said Bevin finally. "As you know I have organised more strikes than anybody in the country, and when we ran out of money I always got the men to sing."

After dinner there were the usual starlight walks, Beaverbrook coming in after a few minutes and protesting it was a loathsome habit of the P.M. Then politics were discussed and, from what I heard, a ministerial reshuffle. Beaverbrook wants Greenwood to go; the other night he even announced to his guests at dinner that there were three ministers who were rotten – Greenwood, Sinclair and Duff Cooper (a nice thing for a Minister of the Crown to say publicly). I gather that it was being suggested Bevin should go to some other post and that he was asserting he must stay at the Ministry of Labour.

The P.M. asked me to come and talk to him while he was undressing and was most genial. He said Bevin was a good old thing and had "the right stuff in him" – no defeatist tendencies. He expatiated on the debt we owed to our airmen and claimed that the life of the country depended on their intrepid spirit. What a slender thread, he exclaimed, his voice tremulous with emotion, the greatest of things can hang by! He has cause to be elated: today our fighters accounted for about seventy German planes over the Channel.

Monday, August 12th

At the P.M.'s request I had breakfast with Bevin at 8.15. He was a little on his guard in these unaccustomed surroundings, but soon became more at ease and even ate honey off his knife. We talked about the press. He said that he thought the great fault of the newspapers had been, and was, to pander to such a low level of intelligence. The Berrys[1] had done a great disservice by trying to monopolise the provincial press: it was worse to have the newspapers controlled by one private interest than by the State, though both alternatives were undesirable. The present lack of competition had killed the profession of journalism and there was no longer a school of experience which could produce men like Spender and Garvin for the future.

Left for London at 11.15, speeding to London most dangerously in order to be back for the Cabinet at 12.30. I drove in the police-car with Sawyers,[2] the butler, who said that he had been with Lord Wigram and remembered me as a page, coming in a carriage to pick up Neville and insisting on keeping my feathered hat on (I remember thinking it a cruel waste to carry such a beautiful thing under one's arm).

Lunched with Grandfather and Peggy. The party included the Cranbornes,[3] Mrs Ronnie Greville,[4] Mrs Simon Elwes[5] and some others. I sat between Lady Cranborne and Mrs Elwes, and found the former particularly agreeable.

Tuesday, August 13th

Telegram from Sweden to the effect that the Germans are embarking on the Norwegian coast for the purpose of invasion.

The P.M. is very much on edge, concerned with the quickest method of sending reinforcements to the Near East before the expected attack on Egypt. The War Office and the Admiralty want to send these via the Cape; Winston is intent on a dash through the Mediterranean (Operation HATS).

The other problem is the provision of R.A.F. pilots, W. being

---

[1] Lords Camrose* and Kemsley and their estimable partner, Lord Iliffe.
[2] Sawyers went everywhere with Churchill, of whom he took the utmost care. He was a considerable character and would have made a fortune on the stage. His memory of me dated from the 1920s, when Neville Wigram and I were pages of honour to George V.
[3] Robert Cecil, later 5th Marquess of Salisbury.* His wife Betty was the daughter of Lord Richard and Lady Moyra Cavendish.
[4] Affluent owner of Polesden Lacey near Reigate, where she entertained lavishly. King George VI and Queen Elizabeth spent their honeymoon there.
[5] Daughter of Lord Rennell, former Ambassador in Rome.

convinced that the shortage is partly due to the Air Ministry's policy of keeping too many pilots for training and ground jobs. Beaverbrook and Archie Sinclair are, as ever, at it hammer and tongs.

Had tea with Mary and Clarissa Churchill in Mary's sitting-room. It is difficult to make conversation to two entirely different types of person. Whatever I might say to interest one would, whether it succeeded or not, be certain to bore the other.

At No. 10 I heard the astonishing result of today's air battle: seventy-eight German planes destroyed for certain and we only lost three pilots. This is indeed a victory and will do much for the public morale. The Germans can hardly sustain their present losses with equanimity and it looks as if the tide may be turning. Prof., unlike most prophets, hopes for a crack in the German front this winter.

The long discussions on how to reinforce the Middle East continued after dinner, Winston (who did not have his sleep this afternoon) being in the worst of tempers. He has written today to Eden:

> I am favourably impressed with General Wavell in many ways, but I do not feel in him that sense of mental vigour and resolve to overcome obstacles, which is indispensable to successful war. I find, instead, tame acceptance of a variety of local circumstances in different theatres, which is leading to a lamentable lack of concentration upon the decisive point . . . Pray do not forget that the loss of Alexandria means the end of British sea power in the Eastern Mediterranean, with all its consequences.

In his reply Eden said that the main trouble in the Near East was the absence of sufficient equipment for those troops who were already there. Referring to the C. in C., he wrote: "Dill and I were much perturbed at your judgment of Wavell. Neither of us knows of any General Officer in the army better qualified to fill this very difficult post at this critical time."

The question everyone is asking today is, what is the motive of these gigantic daylight raids, which cost so much and effect so little? Are they reconnaissance in force, or a diversion, or just the cavalry attack before the main offensive? Presumably the next few days will show.

Wednesday, August 14th
In the afternoon I accompanied the P.M. to a meeting at the Admiralty Upper War Room. I walked back with him across the

Horse Guards Parade and he confided to me that it was very difficult to make "those fellows" (the First Lord and the First Sea Lord) be sensible about sending troops through the Mediterranean. They were so confoundedly cautious.

Dined at the Mirabelle with Zara Mainwaring, whose charm and good looks were emphasised by the fact that she was beautifully dressed. We went on to see an amusing, gripping but impossible spy story called *Night Train to Munich*.

Thursday, August 15th
The President has sent a message to the effect that he can persuade Congress to let us have our fifty destroyers if we give him an assurance, not necessarily for publication, that we will not allow the British Fleet to be scuttled or surrendered, and if we sell or lease to the U.S. naval and air bases in all British possessions from Newfoundland southwards (this rather smacks of Russia's demands on Finland). In his reply Winston says he is cheered by this information and continues: "You will, I am sure, send us everything you can, for you know well that the worth of every destroyer you can spare to us is measured in rubies."

In Somaliland we have met with disaster, our strong fortified position at Tug Argan having been overwhelmed by vastly superior Italian forces. The blow against Egypt can hardly be long delayed, but there we shall be in a position to make a stiffer resistance.

When the P.M. makes his own arrangements he is inclined to forget to tell any of us and then to forget himself. Thus today at 4.00 the room was full of military dignitaries, Eden, Dill, Wavell and Ismay, and the P.M. was quietly enjoying a whisky and soda in the smoking-room at the House. While we waited I reminded Wavell about Mary Roxburghe (who was stranded in Palestine) and he said that he would attend to the matter personally when he got back to Cairo.

Today there took place the greatest and most successful air battle of all. The figures of enemy planes destroyed kept on mounting and mounting until finally Winston, consumed with excitement, got into his car and drove off to Fighter Command at Stanmore. When he came back he told me the total was well over a hundred and asked me to ring up the Lord President, who is in the country recovering from an operation. I did so and found Mr Chamberlain somewhat cold at being disturbed in the middle of dinner. However he was overcome with joy when he heard the news and very touched at Winston thinking of him. It is typical of W. to do a small thing like this which could give such great pleasure. "The Lord President was very grateful to you," I said to

Winston. "So he ought to be," replied W., "this is one of the greatest days in history."

Everybody is very elated and Somaliland falls into the background: the German confirmed losses have risen to 161, with a good many "probables" in addition and we have lost but thirty-four machines and eighteen pilots.

After dinner the P.M. sat down and dictated straight off a "directive" about operations in the Middle East. I thought it a masterly document, long but clear and to the point. First of all he considered how we could best assemble the maximum number of troops in the Delta area, then what our tactics should be. This is the first time I have seen his long experience as a strategist and student of war put into effect with such rapidity and confidence. He will discuss the matter tomorrow with Eden and Dill; but, of course, time presses and the Italians may not give us an opportunity to make all the dispositions we could wish. Somaliland is to be evacuated, and although this sounds like "sour grapes", the necessity is in itself a virtue since we need the Somaliland troops elsewhere.

To bed just before 2 a.m.

Friday, August 16th

12.30 p.m. Another air-raid warning has sounded and the Central War Room tell me Chatham is being heavily bombed, as well as Kenley where the P.M.'s squadron is stationed.[1] The P.M. has decided to hold the Cabinet as usual, but there has been difficulty in extricating some of its members who have gone to ground. Beaverbrook looks a little blue because he says the Germans are concentrating on his aircraft factories (yesterday they destroyed Short's, an important bomber factory at Rochester).

Lunched with Grandfather and Peggy. Lady Ward, the Reggie Felloweses, Lady Victor Paget and an American called Bertram Cruger were there. I sat between the notorious Daisy Fellowes, friend of the Duke of Windsor and leader of the most decadent cosmopolitan set in Paris, and Lady Victor Paget. I talked to Cruger afterwards and said I hoped we won this war without American help (he having said he felt sure America would come in). He said he sympathised with that feeling, but that our complacency, if we won single-handed, would be unbearable. He has been urging Duff Cooper, who is a friend of his, to send documentary newsreels to America, on the grounds that they are the most effective propaganda; but he has met with scant success.

---

[1] No. 615 Squadron of which he was Honorary Air Commodore.

At about 5.00 p.m., while I was with the P.M. in his bedroom, the sirens sounded once again, for the third time in twenty-four hours. I ran downstairs to find out from the Central War Room what we were to expect and, tripping up at the bottom, arrived with such a noise that the C.I.G.S thought a bomb had fallen. I spent the "warning" having tea on the lawn with Mrs Churchill, Mary and Seal, and left for Stansted just before the all-clear sounded. A bomb had fallen in the middle of the Kingston by-pass and necessitated a traffic diversion.

Lord Bessborough's train being two hours late – owing to a bomb on the railway line – I dined alone with Lady Bessborough and Moyra and afterwards went for a moonlight walk with Moyra.

Saturday, August 17th

A hot and sunny day devoid of aerial activity. In the morning Moyra and I, having visited the garden for the sake of the peaches, walked to look at the wreck of a JU.88 which had crashed nearby.

Sunday, August 18th

I said, half seriously, that my motive for coming to stay was to see one of these great air battles. I got my wish: after several warnings in the morning, we eventually had a grandstand view of a fight from the terrace of the house. It was after lunch and we were sitting on the terrace looking towards Thorney Island with the Portsmouth balloons just visible over the trees to our right. Suddenly we heard the sound of A.A. fire and saw puffs of white smoke as the shells burst over Portsmouth. Then to our left, from the direction of Chichester and Tangmere, came the roar of engines and the noise of machine-gun fire. "There they are," exclaimed Moyra, and shading our eyes to escape the glare of this August day we saw not far in front of us about twenty machines engaged in a fight. Soon a German bomber came hurtling down with smoke pouring from its tail and we lost sight of it behind the trees. A parachute opened and sank gracefully down through the whirling fighters and bombers. Out of the mêlée came a dive-bomber, hovered like a bird of prey and then sped steeply down on Thorney Island. There were vast explosions as another and then another followed, and my attention was diverted from the fight as clouds of smoke rose from the burning hangars of Thorney aerodrome. In all, the battle only lasted about two minutes and then moved away seawards, with at least two German aircraft left smouldering on the ground.

There seemed to be more machines about because the A.A. guns kept on firing, and presently, standing on the terrace balustrade, I saw four of the barrage balloons at Portsmouth collapse in flames. A number of bombs fell and one seemed to be of the "screaming" variety.

When peace was restored Moyra, Jean Meade (who had come over to lunch and was in ecstasies about the *"pain perdu"*) and I sat on the terrace in high spirits, elated by what we had seen.

After tea Moyra and I again played tennis until she was summoned away to deal with casualties at Chichester Hospital.

Today's bag was 141 certainly destroyed for ten pilots lost.

Monday, August 19th
Drove up to London without adventure, though the Kingston by-pass was still impassable. Found Miss Watson in a deplorable state of nerves, German aircraft having passed close to her window during the week-end.

The P.M. seems to have made an exception of Horace Wilson in the general forgiveness he has bestowed on the Men of Munich. Today H.J.[1] sent a note attached to a letter: "Mr Seal. The P.M. may be interested to see." Winston put a red circle round the word "interested" and wrote at the bottom "Why?".

I dined with Grandfather and Mother at Argyll House.

Back at No. 10 I read the first edition of the speech which the P.M. is to make in the House tomorrow and on which he has spent many hours this afternoon. It is curious to see how, as it were, he fertilises a phrase or a line of poetry for weeks and then gives birth to it in a speech. On many occasions recently I have heard him speak of our bombing attacks on Germany and say that even if Hitler is at the Caspian these attacks will bring him back to defend his home. Now I see that the Caspian is featuring in the speech! The sentence I like most is that referring to the German air claims (which included a statement that we lost 150 machines yesterday); if these claims continue Hitler's "reputation for veracity will be seriously impugned".

The P.M. went to bed shortly after midnight expressing delight that the Germans had refrained from raiding on a big scale today and saying they were making a big mistake in giving us a respite.

Tuesday, August 20th
At 9.00 I was commanded to stop the hammering on the Horse Guards Parade. This is an almost daily complaint and must cause considerable delay in the measures being taken to defend Whitehall.

---

[1] Sir Horace John Wilson was often referred to as H.J.

Lunched with Mother and Miss Bondfield,[1] the first (and only) woman ever to be a Cabinet Minister. Her experience as a Trade Unionist and in other fields is very wide and her conversation proportionately interesting. Speaking of the future she said that peace must depend on the success of economic federation. Each nation should be left to develop its own culture and genius within its traditional frontiers, but the economic basis must be far wider. She would like to hear this emphasised every week by some responsible statesman. She told of the reactions to Munich of the United States, where she was at the time, and traced back the mistakes of recent years to the raising of American tariffs in the first place, then to Ottawa (which arose from America's action),[2] to the rejection of the Lytton report on Manchuria and so to the failure of collective security over Abyssinia.

Although the gallery was crowded I made my way down to the House to hear the P.M. speak.[3] It was less oratory than usual and the point of chief interest to the House was the account of the bargain with America about the lease of air-bases in the West Indies (he did not divulge what we hoped to get as a *quid pro quo*). On the whole, except for bright patches – like that about "the Führer's reputation for veracity", which had a great success – the speech seemed to drag and the House, which is not used to sitting in August, was languid. The P.M. ended by comparing Anglo-American co-operation (will it one day be unity?) to the Missouri river and saying, "Let it roll on!" I drove back with him in the car and he sang "Ole Man River" (out of tune) the whole way back to Downing Street.

Dined with Audrey Paget at the Mirabelle (where Lord Kemsley, quite out of the blue, presented me with an enormous cigar), took her to see a satisfactory thriller called *Cottage to Let* and went on to an empty, dull and sordid nightclub called "Slippin". We flirted more brazenly than ever and at one moment it looked like becoming more than a flirtation; but I feel a little conscience-stricken about committing the crime for which Socrates was condemned.[4]

---

[1] Member of Ramsay MacDonald's administration. The first female Privy Councillor.

[2] The Ottawa Agreement of 1931 initiated the policy of Imperial Preference for trade between Britain and the Dominions.

[3] This speech contained the sentence "Never in the field of human conflict has so much been owed by so many to so few", but it did not strike me very forcibly at the time. I saved the first draft from the waste-paper basket. It is now on loan to Chequers.

[4] Corrupting the youth.

Wednesday, August 21st

A busy morning composing gushing letters for the P.M.'s signature.

There is a hitch about Operation MENACE (ex-SCIPIO) since it seems unlikely that de Gaulle could effect an unopposed landing at Dakar.

The Americans are trying to make the provision of destroyers into the other half of a bargain involving the lease of bases in Bermuda, etc. This is obnoxious to the Cabinet who wish the two questions kept entirely separate and both based on the goodwill the two countries feel towards each other. As Winston proposes to say, in a telegram to the Canadian P.M., "it would be better to do without the destroyers, sorely as we need them, than to get drawn into a haggling match between the experts as to what we ought to give in return for the munitions. Immediately people would say, 'How much are they worth in money?' and 'Is not advantage being taken of our being hard pressed?' Any discussion of this kind would be injurious to the great movement of events. Each should give all he can without any invidious comparison."

The P.M. also makes this clear to Roosevelt, but ends his telegram from "A Former Naval Person" by saying: "Although the air attack has slackened in the last few days and our strength is growing in many ways, I do not think that bad man has yet struck his full blow. We are having considerable losses in merchant ships in the North-Western Approaches, now our only channel of regular communication with the Oceans, and your fifty destroyers, if they came along at once, would be a precious help."

After dinner, while the P.M. sat upstairs with Eden discussing the Middle East and Operation MENACE, I read an interesting paper about the future by Duff Cooper which will be before the Cabinet tomorrow. He proposes the establishment of a committee, representing all parties and including Chamberlain, Attlee and Sinclair, to present to the Government and to the public some idea of the post-war world. He maintains that for Europe a federal plan should be drawn up as a democratic answer to Hitler's "New European Order". For this country proposals should be put forward to deal with unemployment, to give equal educational opportunities to all, to sweep away privilege and to bring men nearer to equality. No country would be better qualified to lead the way than Great Britain since no country has done more in the last fifty years in the way of social reform. It is noteworthy that this paper has been written by a Conservative and that the proposed committee will be largely Conservative in composition: as in Disraeli's time perhaps the Tory party may prove to be the initiators of social revolution. Lord Halifax has produced slightly improved terms of reference for the committee.

Graeco-Italian relations are at breaking point, but Greece declares that rather than submit she "will set the Balkans on fire". It is thought that Mussolini will not actually attack for the time being – and while he delays Turkey increases daily in strength. The Germans, having temporarily abandoned their mass raids, today machine-gunned the residents of Bournemouth and the Scilly Isles.

Thursday, August 22nd

The P.M. is not unnaturally indignant because the gun – his gun – so laboriously installed at Dover was not ready to fire in reply to some shore batteries from the other side which bombarded first a convoy and then Dover today.

The Cabinet discussed the financial situation. Our reserves of gold and foreign securities are desperately low and we can only carry on a few months longer. Nevertheless the Cabinet decided to go on placing orders for armaments in the U.S., in the belief that after the Presidential election the American Government might show itself more generous and helpful. The Lord President in a letter to Winston says that we must gamble on the chance of obtaining American support; and Winston, in the Cabinet, said it would be better to give the Americans a lien on British industry rather than run short of supplies. In the last resort we may requisition wedding rings, gold ornaments, etc., in order to shame the U.S.; but the amount so raised would be only about £20 million.

I was just peacefully asleep when the sirens went. I refused to be disturbed, but was of course subsequently aroused by the all-clear. There is a double sting about air-raids at night. I gather that at No. 10 the P.M. strode about the house, having been aroused by gunfire in North London, wearing his flowery dressing-gown and a tin hat.

Monday, August 26th

At No. 10 I found the P.M. not yet returned from Chequers. The news is not too good: our shipping losses by submarine are becoming serious. London has been bombed – by a single aircraft on Saturday night – and in retaliation we sent eighty-nine bombers over Berlin last night. We may therefore expect a big raid on London tonight, I fear. However perhaps Goering will exhaust his air force: an R.A.F. officer (Group Captain Cochrane), whom I met at Hinchingbrooke on Saturday, told me that in the last war Goering drove the Richthofen Squadron to death when he took over the command.

The first air-raid warning – which came to nothing – sounded just after lunch. The P.M., who thought it would be serious owing to last night's adventures, ordered everybody to the shelter and then telephoned to the C.A.S. to express disgust that tonight we were going to bomb Leipzig rather than Berlin. "Now that they have begun to molest the capital," he said, "I want you to hit them hard – and Berlin is the place to hit them."

I dined with Sidney Cuthbert, who is on the King's Guard at St James's Palace. We fed out of the way well and afterwards a piper of the Scots Guards marched round the table playing to us. He had just started a second performance, and was well launched into "Speed Bonny Boat", when we were told that the sirens were sounding. So, relinquishing our cigars, we made for the Palace shelter, the officers changing from their immaculate blue mess-kit into battledress and steel helmets.

It is now 12.30 and the all-clear has not yet sounded. This distraction is merely due to a few single aircraft, and because of them production has stopped and even the newspapers have given up printing. The searchlights, concentrated through the warm haze on first one spot then another, have been magnificent to see and from time to time (as at this moment) we have heard the drone of enemy aircraft overhead and heard the noise of anti-aircraft fire. The P.M. has driven everybody to the shelter except myself, John Peck, Herbert Morrison (who has been hiccuping loudly over a whisky and soda), Archie Sinclair and Air Marshal Courtenay.

I stood in the garden, heard midnight strike on Big Ben, watched the searchlight display and wondered at the unaccustomed stillness of London. Not a sound, and scarcely a breath of air. Then suddenly the noise of an engine and the flash of a distant gun.

The P.M., undressed at midnight, came down in his particularly magnificent golden dragon dressing-gown and, tin hat in hand, retired to sleep in the shelter. I sat a long time gossiping with Brendan and Prof. and supposing that this is the first of many such disturbed nights.

After pacing the lawn for some time the P.M. finally retired to bed in the air-raid shelter where, unaroused by the all-clear at 3.45 a.m., he spent the night. I sat up till after 2.00 and then, convinced that my vigil was useless, went to bed – but was not allowed to sleep peacefully or long.

Tuesday, August 27th

One of the most immediate questions is the extension of training for R.A.F. pilots and its transfer abroad where it may take place unhampered. Beaverbrook says he does not see the point in this transfer, and W.'s reaction to that is: "I attach the greatest importance to your opinion, but you must either face the facts and answer them effectively and with a positive plan or allow the opinion of those who are responsible to prevail."

The P.M.'s system of working includes the enlistment of outside authorities to vet and supplement the labours of the officially responsible department. Thus today he sends over to P. J. Grigg at the War Office a batch of telegrams from India with the following mandate: "I will from time to time send you other Indian telegrams in order that you may warn me if amid all their wordage there is anything being done counter to the policy now agreed."

When I returned to No. 10 after an early dinner, there was a good deal to do and I was deeply involved in arranging papers when, at about 9.30, the sirens began. I went up to tell the P.M. that it was all due to one aeroplane and stayed to drink some coffee and smoke a cigar. Winston, to his obvious regret, refused brandy and demanded iced soda-water, saying that he was ashamed of the easy life he led and had never before lived in such luxury. Desmond Morton said that the P.M.'s staff had different views on this question of an easy life! W. went on to declare that his object was to preserve "the maximum initiative-energy". "Every night," he said, "I try myself by court martial to see if I have done anything effective during the day. I don't mean just pawing the ground; anyone can go through the motions; but something really effective."

Got away shortly after midnight, in between two air-raid warnings, having heard from Desmond Morton that the Cameroons had just announced their secession to de Gaulle.

Wednesday, August 28th

The P.M. set forth on a journey to inspect the South-East defences and so we had a quiet day. I was even able to go to sleep in the afternoon, having been infected by Winstonian habits.

I dined with Seal at the R.A.C. The inevitable air-raid came at 9.00 while our bombers were setting off to bomb Berlin. The P.M. came back at about 11.00, having seen numerous air battles and been much affected by the plight of those whose houses have been destroyed or badly damaged by raids. He was, he said, determined that they should receive full compensation up to £1,000 and made a note to the effect that he would browbeat the Chancellor of the Exchequer on the subject next day.

The air-raid lasted till 4.00 a.m.; the searchlight displays were magnificent but ineffective; and we heard bombs falling not far away, in Chelsea and on the south side of the river.

Morton tells me that the French Congo has now declared for de Gaulle.

Thursday, August 29th
Kingsley Wood came about compensation and proved himself the perfect yes-man. Afterwards I enjoyed listening to him pandering to Beaverbrook and Brendan, both of whom flattered him and treated him as an inferior being.[1]

Lunched with Seal at Wyndham's and had a most interesting discussion about Munich and wisdom-after-the-event. He pointed out that it was only the events after Munich which united the country and made it ready for war. In September 1938 there would have been a strong anti-war party.

Friday, August 30th
Motored to Chequers with Mrs Churchill and Pamela. I found at the last moment that the P.M. was going to stop at Fighter Command, but though disappointed at missing this I thought it would be rude to tell Mrs C. I did not want to go with her.

General Ismay came and also the Joint Planners, representing the three services, whose duty it is to plan our military operations. They are Air Commodore Slessor who seems to be the most forceful of the three, Brigadier Playfair and Captain Daniel, R.N. I showed them the house and garden before the P.M. arrived and when telling Captain Daniel of Nelson's letter about "want of frigates" was surprised to find he knew it almost by heart and the approximate date on which it was written.

At dinner, fortified by 1911 champagne, the P.M. talked brilliantly, though less epigramatically than usual. He said there were only three things that worried him: when, as yesterday, the proportion of our air losses was too high; the startling shipping losses in the North-Western Approaches, where lay the seeds of something that "might be mortal" if allowed to get out of hand; and the gun

---

[1] He suggested on one occasion that as we were providing the Dutch Government with vast financial support the present unequal division of Shell and Royal Dutch, with forty per cent owned by Shell and sixty per cent by Royal Dutch, should be remedied. We should demand a fifty-fifty re-organisation. Churchill, who objected to taking advantage of another country's misfortunes, said that he never again wished to hear such a suggestion.

batteries at Gris Nez which would make the passage of our convoys through the Straits almost impossible and would mean that Dover might be "laid in ashes". He proposed to destroy those batteries – from the sea. (Captain Daniel wants to do it by landing troops.)

The reason why he had brought the Joint Planners down was to give them his general idea, which they could elaborate, of the campaign of 1941. He would not look as far as 1942, which must "be the child of 1941", but would like to discuss the offensive action we should be able to take next year in order to turn the tables on the Germans and make them wonder, for a change, where they were going to be struck next. The essential pre-requisite was the command of the air over the beaches where we should disembark our troops and armoured divisions. We had a large number of weapons, well on the road to development, which could help us in this: the A.I., which would for the first time be used in a Beaufighter plane tomorrow night and would soon be available in sufficiently large numbers to discomfort the enemy "night prowlers", unescorted as they were by fighters; the "Yagi" (now called "Elsie") or wireless-controlled searchlights; and above all the P.E. fuse which was cheap, and easy to produce, and would shortly be given its trial in the clear atmosphere of Malta. Once these weapons were available, and the likelihood of being "Namsosed" again had passed away, we could land on the continent.

He then outlined a number of possibilities which he wished the Joint Planners to study in the months to come: the capture of Oslo and the consequent undoing of Hitler's first great achievement; the invasion of Italy by sea; the cutting off of the Cherbourg peninsula (this might be used as a feint, because he did not wish to fight in France); and, most attractive of all, a landing in the Low Countries followed by the seizure of the Ruhr, or at any rate North German territory, so that the enemy might be made to experience war in his own land. Forces of 100–120,000 men could be used, and if these operations were successful, who could tell to what they might lead?

Brigadier Playfair suggested it might be dangerous to use the P.E. fuse at Malta, in case its existence should become known and steps taken to parry it. But the P.M. said that there was no reason why it should be distinguished from accurate A.A. fire, and, moreover, if it were successful at Malta not only should we be able to plan our other operations with confidence, but also the fleet would once again have a secure base which would be fatal to Italy's communications with Libya and would alter the whole situation in the Mediterranean.

After dinner I did a certain amount of work, interrupted by

periodic excursions into the garden to watch the searchlights fruitlessly attempt to pick up German aircraft as they passed overhead. To bed by 2.00.

Saturday, August 31st
I had to break to the P.M. at 8.30 that three more big ships had been torpedoed off the Bloody Foreland (one of them 15,000 tons, carrying children to New York). This distressed him particularly, because the North-Western Approaches are a very sore spot which shows no immediate sign of healing. On the other hand the news of our raids on Berlin last night is excellent: we seem to have found our objectives and damaged them severely.

Beaverbrook rang up and, speaking of the heavy attacks which are developing this morning (in good weather conditions for our fighters, I think), said that he felt sure the enemy was now trying to reach a conclusion over here. He is satisfied with our fighter production figures.

There are more signs of German shipping concentrations at Emden (which we bombed last night) and off the Norwegian coast. Possibly a raid is contemplated, but I think serious invasion must depend on the ability of the German air force to obtain the mastery – and that seems more than doubtful.

Sir Roger Keyes came to lunch and the Joint Planners stayed. The P.M. talked a lot. Pouring out another glass of brandy, and eyeing us all benevolently, he said that these Planners, on whose deliberation so much depended, could not afford to have more than one glass of brandy; but it was different for him who had only to take the responsibility. It was curious but in this war he had had no success but had received nothing but praise, whereas in the last war he had done several things which he thought were good and had got nothing but abuse for them.

Speaking of the Americans, who favoured many of the measures, such as violating Swiss neutrality in the air, which we are now taking, he said that their morale was very good – in applauding the valiant deeds done by others!

Sir R. Keyes then became the centre of conversation, the P.M. beginning by saying: "I make myself detestable to everybody (i.e. by his refusal to let sleeping dogs lie or acquiesce in inactivity) except Roger whose dupe I am." This is true because he has given Keyes a job out of loyalty and affection and in so doing has much angered the younger men in the navy. He told Keyes how he hoped that he would be able to undertake a raid on the Channel Islands soon, and Sir R. said that would be easy. The provision of air protection would however be difficult, insisted Slessor.

Keyes said he hoped we should seize Casablanca when we took Dakar, but the P.M. replied that de Gaulle, who would have to be consulted, was now on the high seas. Apparently de Gaulle's movements will be disguised by the fact that he will speak twice weekly on the wireless from London – from records already made. Similarly a bogus notice appeared in the press the other day to the effect that Larminat,[1] now in Equatorial Africa, had lunched with the P.M. On the whole I formed the impression that one of Sir R. Keyes' major characteristics was a well-developed tendency to self-glorification.

The P.M. went to see the fighter pilots at Uxbridge, and watched a great battle in progress, while I went for a series of walks, alone, with Mrs Churchill and with Pamela. Unfortunately while I was on one of these, enjoying the magnificent evening, the P.M. returned, decided to work, demanded his box, found it in complete disorder and was most displeased. I felt a worm that had neglected its duties.

Sir H. Dowding, C. in C. Fighter Command, and Sir C. Portal,[2] C. in C. Bomber Command, came to dinner. Dowding is splendid: he stands up to the P.M., refuses to be particularly unpleasant about the Germans, and is the very antithesis of the complacency with which so many Englishmen are afflicted. He told me that he could not understand why the Germans kept on coming in waves instead of concentrating on one mass raid a day which could not be effectively parried. Ismay suggested that they might be short of planes and have to use bombers twice daily. There was a great discussion about the ethics of shooting down enemy pilots landing by parachute: Dowding maintaining it should be done and the P.M. saying that an escaping pilot was like a drowning sailor. Otherwise he was in a very ruthless frame of mind.

Portal told me it was not true that the captured German airmen were, as is commonly reported, exceptionally young. On the contrary their average age was twenty-five or twenty-six.

A pressing question is how often air-raid sirens should be sounded in order to attain the maximum security and the minimum disturbance. Lord Beaverbrook is for none; the Air Marshals are for lots. The Cabinet must decide.

After dinner the First Lord rang up from Brighton to say that enemy ships were steering westwards from Terschelling. The invasion may be pending (though I'll lay 10–1 against!) and all

---

[1] General de Larminat. Rallied to de Gaulle in 1940. Captured Brazzaville for the Free French. Committed suicide in 1961 when appointed by de Gaulle to try the French generals who had rebelled in Algiers.

[2] Later Lord Portal of Hungerford. *

H.M. Forces are taking up their positions. If these German ships came on they would reach the coast of Norfolk tomorrow morning.

The P.M. and the Air Marshals, with Lindemann, looked at diagrams showing the working of the German Headache beam which, directed from Germany, guides the bombers to their objectives whatever the weather conditions or the visibility. We, having learnt of this, are in process of discovering how to jam and how to divert it. Diversion is more fun: it sends the enemy to wrong destinations.

The final figures for today's fighting are eighty-five certain, thirty-four probable, thirty-three damaged. We lost thirty-seven aircraft, twelve pilots being killed and fourteen wounded. Our increased losses are due to the fact that the Germans have now thought of armouring their planes behind – a precaution we took long ago – and the fighting is therefore much harder. The P.M. was deeply moved by what he saw this afternoon at Uxbridge: he said that what he saw there brought the war home to him.

9

London Bombarded

September 1940

Sunday, September 1st
The supposed invasion proved to be nothing, but three of our destroyers, which were investigating matters, ran into a minefield and one was sunk.

I walked with Ismay round the camp of the soldiers (Coldstream now) who guard Chequers. He quoted to me by heart passages from the P.M.'s *World Crisis* (particularly the tribute to the British army after the Somme) which he considers some of the finest prose in English literature. His admiration for the P.M., as a man who has himself experienced the warfare which he now directs, knows no bounds.

At lunch the P.M., talking of *Why England Slept*,[1] turned to me and said, "You slept too, didn't you!" – a good-natured jibe at my professed "Munichois" views!

In the afternoon I went with the P.M., Lindemann and Ismay to Uxbridge, headquarters of No. 11 Group which controls all the Fighter Squadrons in the South-East. We talked to Air Marshal Park[2] who confirmed the P.M.'s view that the Germans must already have developed their maximum attack and could not stand the strain much longer as far as an air offensive was concerned. The P.M. expressed delight at the success of our pilots, but said, "It is terrible – terrible – that the British Empire should have been gambled on this." He had already remarked at lunch, talking of Poland and the failure of France to maintain its position in Eastern

---

[1] A book written by John F. Kennedy, later President of the United States.
[2] Air Chief Marshal Sir Keith Park. Commanded 11 Group, the main fighter force in the Battle of Britain, was later A.O.C. in C., Egypt for a year and then in command of the R.A.F. during the siege of Malta when Lord Gort was Governor.

Europe, "This is one of the most unnecessary wars, and it will probably be one of the most terrible." The Poles, he pointed out, had fought much better than the French and had shown infinitely greater spirit.

After talking to the Air Marshal, we went to the operations room, with its maps, its men and W.A.A.F.s in shirt-sleeves acting as croupiers, its coloured lights and intricate apparatus. There were no raids of importance in progress – the enemy having been smitten harder than he liked both yesterday and this morning – but it was interesting to see how the reports of the R.D.F. (Radar), and observation corps were shown on the map. This room is in the bowels of the earth, fifty feet or more underground.

When we returned to Chequers I heard that a brand-new cruiser, the *Fiji*, escorting de Gaulle and his party to their objective, had been torpedoed. "The Admiralty," said Winston, "is now the weak spot; the air is all right."

Air Marshal Park and his wife came to dinner as did two Coldstream officers from the soldiers guarding Chequers. Their names were John Sparrow (a barrister – Fellow of All Souls)[1] and Rickards, an Eton Master. It amused me mildly that Mrs C., who does nothing but profess democratic and radical sentiments, should put off inviting any of the officers to dine until the guard consisted of the Coldstream. The Oxford and Bucks Light Infantry were never invited inside. At dinner the P.M., thinking of our new weapons, said that we could not hope to pile up sufficient men and munitions to outmatch the Germans. This was a war of science, a war that would be won with new weapons.

Monday, September 2nd
Drove up from Chequers with Lindemann who described to me the new weapons and their prospects of success.

Sir Stafford Cripps telegraphs from Moscow that the Russo-German alliance is very close, closer indeed than before since Russia is afraid of Germany and friendship is a means of defence. We must not rely on any breach between them or look for divergence of policy. This is the opinion I have held all along and it is interesting that such an ardent supporter of the extreme Left as Cripps should support it.

Movements of German bomber squadrons to advanced bases in France are thought to indicate an intensification of air attack towards the end of this week. It is already on a sufficiently large scale!

---

[1] Later Warden of All Souls.

Postal censorship reports show that the morale of the country is extremely high. There is much hatred of Hitler but little of Germany. France is spoken of with supreme contempt and little sympathy. It is widely realised that the support we are getting from America is paid for in hard cash.

I dined rapidly with Zara and Betts at Pruniers, where we sat on high stools against the counter and fed most expensively. I then went back to No. 10 in time for an air-raid. Winston returned with Beaverbrook, having dined well at the American Embassy, and was most importunate, demanding papers, information, etc. He dictated to me a telegram for Lothian, apparently oblivious of the fact that I can't write shorthand. I managed somehow to scrawl down what he said and to get it off to America: it was an instruction about the exchange of aide-memoires on the destroyer question which were due for signature in Washington within an hour.

Tuesday, September 3rd

Went to a service at Westminster Abbey to commemorate the first anniversary of the war. The King and Queen were to have gone, but an air-raid warning sounded just before the service began. However the P.M. and a good many Ministers attended. I rescued Eden and Dill from a garden where they had been isolated by an over-zealous verger and where they would otherwise have been left and forgotten.

Bishop Hensley Henson, the new Canon, preached an eloquent fighting sermon, containing much alliteration, many fiery denunciations, a good deal of politics and no Christianity – which was what Winston had come to hear.

Wednesday, September 4th

Attended the funeral of Sir J. J. Thomson[1] in Westminster Abbey, as representative of the P.M. It was moving in itself: the procession of clergy in their black vestments, the sunlight blazing diagonally on the coffin and altar, the almost garish effect of the many candles. It was also moving because it seemed to me that in him the Trinity which I knew so well had passed away: though only a figurehead in the college, he was representative of a period in its history.

Returning to No. 10 I busied myself with the question of appointing a new Master, my last job before handing over patron-

---

[1] Master of Trinity College, Cambridge. Nobel Prize winning physicist who, with Lord Rutherford, first split the atom and was thus one of the originators of nuclear fission.

age questions to Tony Bevir. The College want to leave the Mastership in abeyance till after the war, but Brendan thinks this would be a mistake, as the office is one of more than academic importance, and I agree with him. So it has been decided to try and persuade George Trevelyan[1] to accept.

September 5th–15th
Stayed at Helperby and greatly profited from the rest and quiet. We walked partridges most days, played tennis and gambled. Mother and Philip left on the 11th. Aunt Celia[2] was very cheerful and exceedingly hospitable, and Uncle Clive did his best to provide us with partridges to shoot and was lavish with his remarkable '63 and '70 port.

While I was away, the great raids on London started and much damage was done, Buckingham Palace being singled out for attack.

Sunday, September 15th
Motored back to London after lunch, stopping at Hinchingbrooke for tea. I have caught Betty Harris's[3] cold and as she has come out with chicken-pox this morning I am in quarantine for that miserable disease.

I reached London in time for the air-raids, and the noise of guns and bombs was deafening all night. The house shook and the reports were so loud that it seemed as if the guns were firing from the garden outside. But we brought down 186 German planes today, for the loss of thirteen pilots, and it looks as if Hitler cannot keep up this pressure for long.

Monday, September 16th
Mother, who leaves for Badminton today, thank God, said at breakfast that if one looked on all this as ordinary civilian life it was indeed hellish, but if one thought of it as a siege then it was certainly one of the most comfortable in history.

At No. 10 there is a certain chaos caused by the fact that the building is thought to be unsafe. The basement is being fitted up for the P.M. to live and to work in, and meanwhile much of the time, both by day and by night, is being spent in the disagreeable

---

1 Eminent historian and successor to J. J. Thomson as Master of Trinity.
2 My mother's greatly loved twin sister, Lady Celia Coates, married to Sir Clive Coates of Helperby Hall, Yorkshire. She celebrated her hundredth birthday in 1984, being the last surviving person to have known Mr Gladstone.
3 Lady Celia Coates' younger daughter. My first cousin and close friend, she married William Harris, Q.C., who was serving in the Coldstream Guards.

atmosphere of the Central War Room. We may move altogether: possibly to the newly-constructed Church House, Westminster. Brendan suggests Bridgewater House as a solid stone building.

I am disappointed to hear from Desmond Morton that Operation MENACE (ex SCIPIO) has been abandoned because the Admiralty allowed French ships to get to Dakar first. I wonder if Vichy got wind of the proposed coup?[1]

Tuesday, September 17th

After another night of loud explosions, apparent earthquakes and general discomfort, I went early to No. 10, where I found the P.M. up and about early, having spent the night in the C.W.R. Brendan and Prof. and Tony had slept with the staff in bunks in the air-raid shelter (at No. 10).

We lunched off beer and bottled tongue and then I went down to the House to hear the P.M. make a statement on the air-raids, etc. Just as he was about to speak, the spotters on the roof (who now supplement air-raid warnings by blowing whistles when the enemy are really near) became active and the House of Commons repaired to its dug-outs. I remained in my room having so far preserved a healthy contempt for these alarums and excursions – except after dark when the shell splinters fly. The P.M. subsequently spoke very eloquently.

Some telegrams from de Gaulle arrived, expressing his disappointment at the abandonment of MENACE and declaring his intention to proceed against Dakar by land.

I walked back to No. 10 and just as I was about to enter there was a vast explosion. I met the P.M. who swore he had seen, from his bedroom window, a bomb hit Buckingham Palace. Everybody was packed off to the shelter, but it transpired that the noise was due to a time-bomb in the Palace garden which had been purposely exploded.

8.00 p.m. is about zero-hour for the night raid and the accompanying gun fire. The Private Secretaries now have a car at their disposal, with a soldier as driver, and so I went home in that about 8.30 with my tin helmet firmly pressed down over my ears and my eyes fixed on the gun flashes. The early advent of the equinoctial gales has made raiding less easy today, the westerly wind reaching great strength.

---

[1] It was said that Free French officers dining at l'Ecu de France shortly before they sailed rose to their feet in the restaurant and drank "à Dakar". This may have got back to Vichy through a member of a foreign embassy who was also dining in the restaurant.

Wednesday, September 18th

Lunched with Father at the Travellers after going down to the House, where the Cabinet met, and returning during an air-raid while the exhaust of our fighters streaked the blue sky with white lines and circles.

After lunch I showed No. 10 to a Japanese journalist, who is to write an article on the P.M. for the paper *Asaki*, and extolled Winston's merits to him in the most lavish terms. With typical Japanese contempt for the truth he explained to me how he proposed to say that he had shaken hands with the P.M., noted the eagle look in his eye, etc., etc. I said I must draw the line at his producing a fictitious conversation.

Miss Violet Markham[1] came to see me to talk about the effect of air-raids on the people. It is, she pointed out, a question of *"pourvu que les civiles tiennent"*. At the moment nothing was being done to ensure their safe transport home – the buses stopped running in raids – and no steps were being taken to feed them when they came out of shelters after long, cold and weary vigils. I rang up Sir John Reith (Minister of Transport) and arranged that she should go and see him and promised to see that further steps were taken from here if satisfactory results were not achieved. It is clearly most important that everything possible should be done to lighten the cross which the people of London have got to bear – particularly as their lot will become increasingly unpleasant as the winter draws on.

Back to No. 10 to sleep. The P.M. went over to the C.W.R. for the night with Seal. Brendan, Prof. and Jack Churchill slept in the shelter at No. 10, in quarters resembling third-class accommodation on a Channel steamer. The typists and servants sleep on mattresses in the bigger room in the shelter. Enemy aircraft boomed overhead and once or twice I looked out into the garden to watch the shells and the bombs, until the falling shell splinters – one of which came unpleasantly near – drove me in. One splinter is embedded firmly in the inside wall of our room as a result of last night's activities.

After Brendan, Jack Churchill and I had gossiped for a little I went over to the C.W.R. and had a whisky-and-soda with Seal, Ismay, Hollis* and the rest. Pug Ismay was giving his usual description of the French collapse and the helplessness of the statesmen and Generals. So I hurried away to No. 10, a bomb falling close as

---

[1] Mrs James Carruthers, who retained her maiden name. She was one of the best-known and respected social workers in the country and was an associate of my mother, at whose suggestion she came to see me at Downing Street.

I entered the Foreign Office arch. Then Brendan and I did some sightseeing, watching the A.A. barrage at work on planes directly over our heads. There was an orange glow as a balloon above us collapsed in flames and then, in the direction of the river, we saw a parachute descending through the moonbeams. "A parachutist," said one policeman. "A pilot escaping; that orange glow was an enemy plane down," said another (the big fat one who guards the door); but a third said, "No, it is coming down too fast, it's something worse than that." A few seconds later he was proved to be right: a landmine exploded on the County Hall and even the windows in Downing Street and the F.O. were shattered. Slept uncomfortably in the shelter.

Thursday, September 19th

The P.M. is sufficiently undismayed by the air-raids to take note of trivialities. Yesterday he sent the following note: "First Lord. Surely you can run to a new Admiralty flag. It grieves me to see the present dingy object every morning. W.S.C."

MENACE is on again, de Gaulle and our commanders with him having made the strongest representations.

The Bomber Command have been instructed to make the heaviest possible bombing attack on Berlin as soon as the weather is suitable. This morning Winston said that as the Germans were dropping these parachute mines indiscriminately, we must say that we would drop two for every one of theirs.

The Germans are making more tentative peace-feelers through Stockholm. Needless to say these are not even considered. Despite their successes, and our present discomfiture, the Germans cannot be too happy:

i.   They have another cold and hungry winter before them.
ii. The destroyer agreement with America has made a deep impression in Rome and Berlin.
iii. There appears to be some estrangement with Russia over the settlement of the Roumanian question.
iv. It is obvious that France is becoming increasingly Anglophile and that the R.A.F. victories have had a tonic effect on Europe.

America is sitting on the fence as usual and Mr Hull[1] declares that the likelihood of the U.S. giving us assistance in the event of trouble with Japan – if we reopen the Burma Road next month – must depend on the progress of the Battle of Britain in the next few weeks. The Americans still do not realise that their own fate, as

---

[1] American Secretary of State.

well as that of Civilisation, hangs on the result of that battle and it is no use just oozing goodwill and saying, as one of their journalists did the other day, that the attacks on London made Americans quite "ill with anger".

I had a talk with Sir Walford Selby, Ambassador in Lisbon, who came to see the P.M. He said that the Anglo-Portuguese Alliance had greatly helped to keep Spain out of the war and Salazar's influence had been very useful to us at Madrid. Salazar was the hardest of bargainers and suspicious, but entirely honest. Selby said he considered the Germans had been laying the foundations of their present military power in 1926 and 1927. By giving way to Brüning and Stresemann[1] we had weakened them and strengthened German militarism.

Friday, September 20th
General Catroux,[2] who may be used to head a revolt against Vichy in Syria, came to see the P.M. He looks forceful and is, I am told, much the greatest "name" that de Gaulle has to dispose of.

I motored down to Chequers with Randolph Churchill, who was pleasant but as usual talked a lot of vituperative nonsense about Horace Wilson, etc. We followed the P.M. and Mrs Churchill to Dollis Hill where the Cabinet's emergency headquarters are. We inspected the flats where we should live and the deep underground rooms, safe from the biggest bomb, where the Cabinet and its satellites (e.g. me) would work and, if necessary, sleep. They are impressive but rather forbidding; I suppose if the present intensive bombing continues we must get used to being troglodytes ("trogs" as the P.M. puts it). I begin to understand what the early Christians must have felt about living in the Catacombs.

At Chequers were the P.M. and Mrs C., Randolph and Pamela (whose baby is expected hourly), Mary and General Ismay. We dined well and not too seriously. I repeated to Mrs C. what Violet Markham had told me and she wants to start a mobile canteen to feed the dreary and depressed citizens as they emerge from public shelters in the early hours. Violet Markham, having failed to move the Ministry of Food, is starting one herself. I also told the P.M. what Violet M. had told me about transport difficulties and he asked me to prepare a note on which he could take action.

---

[1] German Chancellor in 1923 and a prime mover in the negotiations for the Locarno Treaty of 1925, an attempt to make a future war between France and Germany impossible.

[2] The only senior French General to rally to de Gaulle (who was inclined to be jealous and therefore to denigrate him).

We talked about the possibility of the Germans using poison gas, but the P.M. and Ismay are confident that nothing new, or more devilish than mustard gas, is available. He is doubtful whether invasion will be tried in the near future, but says that there is no doubt every preparation has been made. He is becoming less and less benevolent towards the Germans (having been much moved by the examples of their frightfulness in Wandsworth which he has been to see: a landmine caused very great devastation there) and talks about castrating the lot. He says there will be no nonsense about a "just peace". I feel sure this is the wrong attitude – not only immoral but unwise. We should aim at crushing them and then being firm but magnanimous victors.

Towards bedtime the P.M., very animated, reminisced about the South African War (the last enjoyable war, he called it) and the beauties of the Veld. His thirst for talking military strategy is unquenchable.

Saturday, September 21st
Summer has returned and the weather is glorious, but that did not console me for being summoned to the presence before 8.00 a.m. It is quite difficult to sleep in this perfect quiet after five nights of incessant bombardment.

I was kept pretty busy all day. Part of the morning was spent planning an adequate air-raid shelter with office-of-works architects and the P.M., who was clad in his air-force blue, zip-fastened cloth overall which he straps tightly round his stomach and in which he looks like an Eskimo.

The Sandyses came to lunch and afterwards, while the P.M. slept, we played croquet on the lawn. I subsequently snatched three-quarters of an hour to go for a walk up Beacon Hill with the charming, if somewhat tense, Mary.

Lord Gort and Sir Hugh Dowding came to dinner. Conversation turned at first to the German use of landmines in their air-raids. As these cannot be aimed, and mean indiscriminate slaughter, the P.M., though averse to such action on principle, is bent on retaliation. He proposes that one should be dropped on an open German town for each dropped in this country. "It is the only language they understand," said Lord Gort.

Sir H. Dowding said the Poles in our Fighter Squadrons were very dashing but totally undisciplined. It was generally agreed they were magnificent fighters. "When we have abolished Germany," said the P.M., "we will certainly establish Poland – and make them a permanent thing in Europe." He suggested that one

Pole was worth three Frenchmen; Gort and Dowding said nearer ten!

It becomes daily more apparent how well prepared the enemy is for invasion. The P.M. thinks that from the North Foreland to Dungeness is the real danger point and that the most dangerous condition will be fog. Ismay is sceptical about the Germans being able to keep contact in thick fog. Gort says he would guarantee to land on that coast in a fog and he points out that once landed the Germans will push straight ahead. He is afraid of the mentality of the British army which, based on Lady Butler's picture of "The Thin Red Line", is always to fall back in order to keep the line intact. This was what ruined the French: against rapid penetration by small forces the only thing to do is to stand firm and let isolated detachments get through. The P.M., Dowding and Gort think that the first wave of invaders would be storm troops – all picked men – lightly armed and conveyed in fast motor boats. The second would be tanks, landed from craft with specially constructed bows. The third would be heavy artillery and the mass of the infantry. The first two should be able to effect a landing before darkness or the fog lifted. But, of course, meanwhile our bombers would be throwing their full weight against the ports of embarkation. The P.M. seems rather more apprehensive than I had realised about the possibility of invasion in the immediate future and he keeps on ringing up the Admiralty and asking about the weather in the Channel.

Dowding produced a paper ("masterly" the P.M. described it to Beaverbrook) about the prospects of night-interception in the near future: a skilful blending of the A.I. (which was tried for the first time last night in a Beaufighter, albeit without results) and the G.L. (wireless-controlled A.A. and searchlight).

I gather that it is presumed the Germans would use this "beam", by which they guide their aircraft, to guide an invading force also; and this would give them great advantage in a fog.

It is interesting that on the German side no new weapons have so far been produced. Their "beam" has long been used in America for guiding aircraft at night; the magnetic mine is only an improvement on an old weapon; there is nothing new, in the scientific sense, in the parachute mines they let fall on London. This is all in striking contrast to their military strategy which, in France, was daringly and successfully new. Scientifically we have high hopes of being the side to produce the new weapons.

Sunday, September 22nd

Barker[1] awoke me on the telephone to dictate a telegram from Roosevelt who has heard from a "most reliable source" in Berlin that the invasion will be put in train at 3.00 a.m. today.

The P.M., though slightly sceptical (as who would not be after so many false alarms throughout the summer), kept himself busy telephoning to people about it all morning. I aroused Lord Gort (whose flat was bombed last night for the second time in succession) and he said that frankly he did not think invasion very likely. I then went and told Mrs C. and Mary who were sitting side by side in the same bed, with trays on their laps, and who treated the whole matter as a most entertaining joke. What is not entertaining is the fact that we lost another large number of ships off the Bloody Foreland last night, as well as the night before. These losses are assuming serious proportions and the P.M. is very displeased with the Admiralty.

The P.M. gave vent to a most horrific display of abusive epithets when he saw a telegram about Sir S. Syme, Governor General of the Sudan, who is said to be "bored with the war". So strongly did he feel that he had to call me back and say, "Don't put it to Cadogan in quite those terms." (The report had come from Lampson[2] at Cairo.)

12.50 p.m.: The prospects do not look good for invasion. Pouring rain and a gale blowing up. It is significant, particularly in view of what the P.M. said last night, that the Germans are reported to be practising disembarkation under cover of a yellow vapour intended to represent fog.

Sir F. Pile, C. in C. Anti-Aircraft, and General Lock of the War Office came to lunch, when there was a good deal of talk about the P.E. fuse, etc. We talked of France, the P.M. expressing surprise at the speed with which we had been able to re-orientate ourselves to the collapse of an ally upon whose support so much seemed to be staked. He said that a fortnight before the débacle, when the possibility first began to dawn on him, he had thought to himself that the position would be little worse than if Germany had right at the beginning masked France and thrown the full weight of her air force against us. Mary, who seldom speaks when her father is

---

[1] Charles Barker, Chief Clerk at No. 10. Efficient and entertaining, he was popular with the Private Secretaries. An expert on old silver. He had two intelligent men, Pat Kinna and Donald MacKay, working under him and jointly they kept the office in apple-pie order.

[2] Sir Miles Lampson, British Ambassador to Egypt, created Lord Killearn. Large and imposing, he was wont to treat the wayward King Farouk as an incorrigibly naughty schoolboy.

present, thought of a *bon mot*, confided it to me and then interposed nervously, "Never before has so much been betrayed for so many by so few."[1]

After lunch the troop of Generals, the P.M. and Prof. (who says, *sotto voce*, that Dowding's "masterly" paper is his first admission of a number of facts which have been impressed on him for ages) retired to the Hawtrey room to discuss the Egyptian battle which now seems to be opening. The P.M. is full of confidence and says that we have enough good troops out there to do what is necessary "unless, of course, our men fight like skunks and the Italians like heroes". But he feels the opposite is more likely to be the case.

I have made a note about London transport difficulties and have shown it to the P.M. who has sent it to Sir J. Reith with the following minute: "Action this Day. Minister of Transport. This matter certainly requires your attention and I shall be glad to receive your report on the subject."

Motored up from Chequers after tea. The P.M. drove with Gort whom he seems to like. I shall not be surprised to find him back in high military office before long. On the way up we stopped at Lord Gort's twice bombed flat, which is a mess of charred wood and water. The P.M. was most compassionate, but Lord G. seemed unmoved by the havoc.

As we drove to No. 10 I noticed how many houses, in Berkeley Square and Bruton Street, are crumbled to dust. It almost makes me think I had better give up sleeping on the third floor at Eccleston Square.

The report about invasion today came from Kirke, the American Chargé d'Affaires in Berlin, who was right about the invasion of Holland and Belgium – though a change in the weather made him twenty-four hours too soon on that occasion.

I went home to dine with Father. Before we sat down there were loud explosions and the sky became red with the glow of a large fire south of the river. We climbed to the top of the house to look at it and as we watched we heard the whistle of a falling bomb close at hand. It struck a building about a quarter of a mile away, in the direction of the Abbey, and in the flash of the explosion I saw the house topple over sideways. It was nightmarish, and with our tails between our legs we crept downstairs to the dining-room.

Before going to my uneasy couch I went into Philip's room and knelt by the window. The night was cloudless and starry, with the moon rising over Westminster. Nothing could have been more

---

[1] At that time variations on this theme had not become as fashionable as they did subsequently.

beautiful and the searchlights interlaced at certain points on the horizon, the star-like flashes in the sky where shells were bursting, the light of distant fires, all added to the scene. It was magnificent and terrible: the spasmodic drone of enemy aircraft overhead, the thunder of gunfire, sometimes close sometimes in the distance, the illumination, like that of electric trains in peace-time, as the guns fired, and the myriad stars, real and artificial, in the firmament. Never was there such a contrast of natural splendour and human vileness. Later thick palls of smoke rose from the Embankment where bombs had fallen on Dolphin Square – and it went on all night long.

Monday, September 23rd

Today at dawn MENACE takes place. During the morning the Admiralty telephoned the messages from Dakar as they came in. So far (12.30 p.m.) all seems to be going according to plan.

Lunched with Betty Montagu in Hyde Park. A few shells burst over our heads, but otherwise it was warm and peaceful.

When I got back I found that MENACE was proceeding less favourably. The French had opened fire and all prospects of a peaceful landing had had to be abandoned. I told the P.M. who said, cheerfully, "Let 'em have it. Remember this: never maltreat your enemy by halves. Once the battle is joined, let 'em have it."

Dined with Philip at Wellington barracks and sat between the Commanding Officer and Peter Carrington.[1] Afterwards, despite the fact that all the lights went out owing to enemy action, Philip, Lionel Berry,[2] Captain Lindsay and I played bridge.

Tonight we bomb Berlin with 120 heavy bombers.

Tuesday, September 24th

Father, I am glad to say, goes off to Badminton today to stay with Queen Mary. He is badly in need of sleep and quiet, but has borne up wonderfully under all the strain of the bombardment.

David is now in the French ship *Chevreuil*, the officers and crew of which are apparently quite unskilled in nautical matters – a fact which alarms him considerably. Today I learn from secret sources that she is to be used to capture the French Island of St Pierre and to bring the fishing fleet home. Poor David will be most alarmed when he knows he is to put to sea with the French.

[1] Many years later, Minister of Defence and Foreign Secretary. By a remarkable feat of in-breeding he is at once my first cousin once removed and my second cousin.

[2] Eldest son of Lord Kemsley.

MENACE is not proceeding according to plan. The Vichy French are resisting fiercely and the P.M. tells me he is afraid this may have a bad effect. A rapid and bloodless *fait accompli*, for which we all hoped, would have been accepted in France; this hard fighting may have different results. We are unlucky in having bad visibility in which to operate.

Mr Chamberlain has offered to resign, since his operation is giving him trouble and he is not well enough to stay in London and stand the noise. The P.M. has asked him to remain and to return when he is well, saying: "Let us go on together through the storm. These are great days."

Dined with Betts and Janet Margesson at the former's flat. I had a cantankerous political argument with Jan, which was silly because she obviously does not understand what she is talking about and has swallowed a large number of catchwords which she has ill-digested. But at this moment, when our lives and liberties are at stake, it is annoying to hear such travesties of the facts as that this country financed Nazi Germany and made Hitler's rise to power possible by subsidies.

I travelled home in an armoured car but was hardly in bed when I was aroused by the fall nearby of incendiary bombs. These started a number of glaring fires, uncomfortably close, and the thick pall of smoke in the night, together with a catch in the throat due to smoking too many cigarettes, gave me the unpleasant feeling that the Germans were using gas (a not unlikely eventuality).

Wednesday, September 25th

MENACE has proved a miserable fiasco, with what results it is only too easy to prophesy. I sat most of the morning in the Central War Room, where Winston holds most of his meetings now, and after the position had been fully examined, first by the Chiefs of Staff and service Ministers and then by the Cabinet, Winston came out and dictated to Mrs Hill a telegram calling off the expedition and ordering the fleet back to Gibraltar (which Rock the French bombed yesterday in retaliation for MENACE). This may be the end of de Gaulle; it will at any rate give his cause a serious set-back.

Sir John Reith has answered Miss Markham's criticisms very unsatisfactorily. He rang me up to ask if I agreed with his reply and I told him I did not think it met her main point, which is to provide transport to get people off the streets, even if they then have to wait in traffic jams. He promised to look into this and I attached a note to that effect to his reply for the P.M. to see.

The P.M. has today signed a letter which I drafted to George Trevelyan expressing the hope that he will accept the Mastership of

Trinity. After consulting Jim Butler,[1] who works at the C.W.R. now, I wrote to Winstanley and asked him to drop the hint to Trevelyan that if he refused, the Mastership would *not* be left in abeyance but would be offered to some other person, probably less acceptable to the Fellows.[2]

Dined at home and then went to call on Zara and Betts. Zara told me she was engaged to Ronald Strutt,[3] after knowing him for only ten days. Betts said all people in love were intolerable, but Zara had a dreamy, blissful unwarconscious look on her face which it did me good to see. Betts talked much nonsense about religion and the ineffectiveness of our propaganda in America, her remarks on the latter being based entirely on hearsay. It is a waste of time, and exasperating, to talk to most women on serious subjects. Sex, the Arts and the Abstract seem to me the only topics to discuss with women.

Thursday, September 26th

Everybody is perturbed about Dakar and people seem to think that once started we should have gone through with it. In fact we were not strong enough to do so after the *Resolution* was torpedoed.

In an interview with General Sikorski Lord Halifax said that he sometimes wondered whether the threat of invasion to this country was not designed to prevent us from reinforcing Egypt. It is more than possible that the whole Axis effort will be thrown in that direction: we have enough to meet the Italians there, but if the Germans join in we shall be hard pressed. Sikorski thinks Rome should be bombed. Halifax said it had a very special position in the world. Sikorski replied that London had also.

That part of Africa which has already declared for de Gaulle seems to be holding firm in spite of Dakar. The Cameroons sent an encouraging telegram to Winston and I sent an immediate reply in which, trying to copy the Churchillian style, I said that H.M.G. knew that the French in the Cameroons would "continue to struggle side by side with the peoples of the British Empire until France is freed and restored and the shadow of German tyranny has been driven from the face of the earth for ever". By a Gargantuan effort I got this approved and through to the Ministry

---

[1] Professor Sir James Butler, notable classicist and historian, had been one of my Directors of Studies at Trinity. Subsequently Chief Editor of the Official War Histories. A shy but lovable scholar of profound erudition.

[2] I deliberately let it be thought that the choice might fall on Lindemann when I paid a visit to Trinity, a stratagem of which Lindemann himself knew nothing.

[3] An officer in the Coldstream Guards, afterwards Lord Belper.

of Information in time for tonight's broadcasts and tomorrow's papers.

Friday, September 27th
During breakfast the bombers came and were most disturbingly close. Apparently eighteen, out of a big raid of 250, had managed to break through our fighter defences. They were over again later in the morning and I stood on the terrace at No. 10 with the Chief Whip trying to see them.

The papers in New York and this country are now stigmatising Dakar as a major blunder. It will be difficult for Winston to escape criticism.

At 12.15 p.m., while I was over at the C.W.R. where the Cabinet was meeting, Sammy Hood rang me up to say that Germany, Italy and Japan were to sign a Three-Power pact. I took this information into the Cabinet and gave it to Winston who looked pensive. Of course we have known for some time that Germany and Japan were negotiating something and presumably the recent Ciano–Ribbentrop conversations at Rome were on the same subject. This brings into the open anything that still remained obscure and the U.S. must surely now define her position. Unfortunately this accursed presidential election does not take place till November and until that issue is decided America is paralysed. Later, on going in to the Cabinet Room, I heard the P.M. proclaim that one of the clauses of the Agreement was "aimed plum at the United States".

Overheard in the Cabinet: the P.M. – "Personally I should like to wage war on a great scale in the Middle East. By next spring I hope we shall have sufficient forces there." He has been taking tremendous pains lately about the despatch of reinforcements to Egypt and the position of the Australian and New Zealand contingents in that part of the world.

Herschel Johnson lunched with me at the Travellers. He tells me that he thinks Roosevelt will get in and that America will almost certainly give us credits when it is made clear to the Government and people that there is no alternative if we are to be saved from bankruptcy.

Monday, September 30th
At No. 10 I found Cabinet changes in the air. Chamberlain is now clearly too ill to continue and I gather that Halifax has advised Winston to accept his resignation, already proffered but at first refused. Probably Halifax will become Lord President, Eden S. of S. for Foreign Affairs, Oliver Lyttelton[1] (hitherto politically un-

[1] Later Viscount Chandos.*

known) S. of S. for War, Morrison Home Secretary and Beaverbrook Minister for all branches of supply. John Anderson may go to the Dominions Office and then become Viceroy (this will break Sam Hoare's heart).[1] Such a reshuffle would solve the supply problem, to the solution of which Herbert Morrison was an obstacle, but I expect Beaverbrook will favour aircraft at the expense of tanks and other army equipment.

There was an air-raid in the lunch-hour. Admiral Tovey,[2] who was lunching with the P.M., was in the shelter. I gather the P.M. has him in mind for a high naval appointment, possibly C. in C., Home Fleet.

George Trevelyan has accepted the Mastership of Trinity. In his letter to the P.M. he says: "I am touched by your kindness and fortified by your good opinion. In your great way, and in my small way, we have been called to unexpected destinies, since the time when as your junior at Harrow I admired from a distance the driving force of your character, which is now our nation's great support."

David Margesson tells me he is opposed to Eden going to the F.O. or being Lord President. He wants Anderson, our best administrator, to be in the War Cabinet (the P.M. wants Eden) and he thinks that if Oliver Lyttelton is to come into the Government he should go to the Ministry of Supply (the idea occurred to him while we talked). He is a business man and he works for the Ministry now. Beaverbrook is being tiresome. He doesn't want to be responsible for all supply questions and has refused to dine with the P.M. tonight to discuss the problem with Winston and David, on the grounds of a temperature – a very last minute and political temperature!

[1] Hoare believed he had been promised the reversion of the Viceroyalty of India when Lord Linlithgow retired. Churchill knew nothing of any such undertaking and felt no obligation to consider it.

[2] Commanded the Home Fleet, 1940–43, and was thereafter C. in C., The Nore.

10

Britain Besieged

October 1940

Tuesday, October 1st
Beaverbrook has written to the P.M. as follows:

> My Dear Winston. I gathered from our conversation tonight that you expect me to undertake more responsibilities. But my asthma drives me to the unhappy conclusion that the cold weather and sharp winds bring my labours to nothing. I have tried many devices but nights pass in procession without any sleep for me. If I live through the war I shall give you thanks for winning it, even though you may die now. For the example you gave the nation in the last four months and the leadership of the dark days of the flight from France decided the battle in our favour. Your devoted Max. Sept. 30. 1940.

In another letter he says he is going to resign. Of course, he is a crafty man and what he says is not necessarily the truth, but Brendan tells me that he really is suffering a great deal.

Halifax has been given the choice of becoming Lord President, and Number Two in the Government, or remaining where he is. He has chosen to remain and has written to propose that John Anderson should be Lord President and a member of the War Cabinet. He writes that he is "doubtful whether Anthony" (whom Winston wishes to make Lord President if Halifax prefers the F.O.), "would in fact do your tying-up jobs in the Cabinet as well as J.A. J.A. has got that sort of orderly mind which Neville had – and which I don't think Anthony has . . . I have reached these conclusions independently of David Margesson."

Eden, for his part, says he will do anything asked of him. His personal predilection is to remain at the War Office.

David Margesson told me last night that the P.M. would not make up his mind. He is always taking decisions and then repenting of them. David says life would be much easier if people would take a clear line. I have sometimes felt that about his own daughter.

Sir Stafford Cripps' comments on Soviet reactions to the Germano-Japanese-Italian pact are that while the pact will make Russia less well-disposed to the Axis, it will make her more afraid and therefore more subservient. Thus our only policy is to aim at convincing Russia that her hope of self-preservation lies in a victory for this country. I think that there are signs of the thieves falling out among themselves: M. Kiosseivanoff, former Bulgarian Prime Minister, says that Germany and Italy have quarrelled over Italy's wish to invade Greece; and the U.S.S.R. must know that Italy hates her and that Germany uses but despises her.

Lunched with Pat Hancock most exquisitely at the Jardin des Gourmets. He is P.S. to Dalton whom he thinks brilliant but unlovable.

Went home to bed and found Mother, just returned from Badminton, with the news from Lord Claud Hamilton[1] that Chamberlain has cancer.

Wednesday, October 2nd

Busy Cabinet making. Herbert Morrison was recalcitrant about accepting the Home Office, probably because he thinks the offer a reflection on his success at the Ministry of Supply – which it is. He is an unpleasant-looking man and not much good as a Minister. John Anderson is to be Lord President, Andrew Duncan Minister of Supply, Oliver Lyttelton President of the Board of Trade, Lord Cranborne Secretary of State for the Dominions, Caldecote Lord Chief Justice, Reith Office of Works, Moore-Brabazon[2] Minister of Transport. Bevin is to come in to the War Cabinet and Kingsley Wood also. Brendan says the latter has "oiled his way in" by flattery; he and Eden, whom Brendan calls "the film star at the War Office", lay it on very thick – and most successfully. I think all these appointments will be well received in the country, except for Kingsley Wood's entry into the War Cabinet.

The matter which chiefly interests the Cabinet at the moment is

[1] Brother of the Duke of Abercorn and Comptroller to Queen Mary.
[2] Holder of Pilot's Licence No. 1. M.P. since 1918 and Churchill's Parliamentary Private Secretary at the Air Ministry in 1919. Succeeded Beaverbrook as Minister of Aircraft Production in 1941. Quoted at a nominally private gathering as saying he hoped Germany and the Soviet Union would destroy each other. This effectively ended his political career, but Churchill made him a peer in 1942.

our attitude to the Vichy Government. Halifax comes perilously near advocating appeasement, saying that all we require is an assurance that the French Colonies are "healthily anti-German and anti-Italian". If they are, it does not matter whether they are nominally under Vichy or de Gaulle. We must be careful not to let de Gaulle down, I feel very strongly; but perhaps there is no harm in our flirting with M. Baudouin, through the Embassy at Madrid, about questions of interest to both countries.

The French, of course, want us to let food into France through the blockade; but it will be difficult to devise a means of guaranteeing it from falling into German hands. Should the Germans decide to take over the whole of France, it looks as if the Vichy Government – presumably minus Laval – might fly to North Africa; and then of course the whole of the French Empire would rejoin us in active resistance to the enemy. Meanwhile the Monarchists, under the Comte de Paris, are active and have the support of Weygand and his friends.

At the same time as the Government is being reconstituted, the Chiefs of Staff, who are sound, but old and slow, are being purged. Newall goes to New Zealand as Governor General and will be succeeded as Chief of the Air Staff by Portal. Pound will, I suppose, cease to be First Sea Lord and in any case there is to be a drastic change in the higher naval command. This is certainly called for: the continued loss of merchant shipping is serious and the navy has not shown up well of late.

David Margesson went down to see Mr Chamberlain because the latter's letter of resignation was not considered suitable and he had to be persuaded to write another. This he did, accompanying it with a private one from which the following is an extract: "It is kind of you to think of putting me forward for so great an honour as the Garter, but you will, I think, not misunderstand me when I say that I prefer to die plain 'Mr Chamberlain' like my father before me, unadorned by any title. This applies to the Garter just as much as to a peerage which you once before suggested to me."

David tells me he is wonderfully brave. He fought hard for peace and his hardest for victory. He has been greatly maligned; but I believe historians, if they try to throw themselves back into the conditions in which decisions were taken, and refrain from judging solely by what happened afterwards, will mix their censure with much praise for his honest efforts.

Thursday, October 3rd
The P.M., Cabinet, Chiefs of Staff, etc., all went off for a trial day at Dollis Hill and John Martin and I remained alone at No. 10

dealing placidly with our business, unhampered by bells, visitors and the general atmosphere of rush which surrounds the P.M.

It is terrible how our new weapons are being talked about. Philip tells me that he has several times heard descriptions in general terms of what is obviously the A.I.

Sumner Welles has told Lothian that the new Japanese pact with the Axis has knocked Isolationism on the head once and for all in the U.S.

Friday, October 4th

Went with Mrs Churchill to Chingford to see the damage in the P.M.'s constituency. We toured the place with the Mayor and some of the councillors and inspected the havoc wrought by bombs and parachute mines. The saddest sight was the homeless refugees in a school. One woman, wheeling a baby in a pram, told me she had twice been bombed out of her house and kept on saying disconsolately: "A load of trouble, a load of trouble." One woman said: "It is all very well for them," (looking at us!) "who have all they want; but we have lost everything." We lunched with the Mayor and civic dignitaries in a pub called "The Cock" at Epping. Civic dignitaries are strangely boring people.

Monday, October 7th

Dined at home where I found that Father and Mother have accepted an invitation from Grandfather and Peggy to go to Madeley, which is being opened up. This will mean the removal of furniture from Eccleston Square and I shall live as a troglodyte at No. 10. Mother is much disgruntled at leaving London – she is afraid of nothing – but Father is desperately anxious to go. He will also be able to effect great economies by living at Madeley and that becomes increasingly necessary. The move is a big and weary undertaking which must be put in hand quickly – as the sight of so many gutted and crumbled houses, increasing in number every day, makes clear.

Madeley Manor in Staffordshire was a regency house at the southern end of my grandfather's once extensive property in Cheshire and Staffordshire. He had sold Crewe Hall and most of the Cheshire estates in the 1930s. When the raids on London became heavy he opened Madeley, in which the family had not lived for a century, and invited his eldest daughter, Lady Annabel Dodds (formerly O'Neill), and my mother, neither of whom had houses in the country, to move there with their husbands. His two other daughters, Lady Celia Coates and the Duchess of

Roxburghe, had their own houses in the country, the one at Helper-by in the North Riding of Yorkshire, the other at Floors Castle, Kelso, where they were both most hospitable to me when I was able to escape from duty.

Today German and Italian troops entered Roumania. Eden says this is obviously part of a pincer movement aimed at the Middle East – but the Germans will have no easy task in advancing through Anatolia in the face of Turkish opposition. The threat to the Bosphorus and the Aegean is now immediate and Eden wants to fly out to Egypt this week-end.

Tuesday, October 8th
When I reached No. 10 I found everybody crouching in the shelter because bombs had fallen in the Horse Guards Parade and on the War Office.

The P.M. made a long speech in the House to which I listened. He discussed the bombing of London, our attitude to Japan and the position of Spain (a fine passage which the F.O. did their best to make him omit). I heard the P.M. tell Halifax on the telephone that he set great store on speaking of Spain as "a leading and famous member of the family of Europe and of Christendom".

He was skilful in dealing with Dakar and insisted that "this series of accidents and some errors" should be regarded in its true perspective. His peroration with its reminder that "long dark months of trial and tribulation lie before us", with misfortunes, shortcomings, mistakes and disappointments, was eloquently spoken and enthusiastically received. "Death and sorrow," he said, "will be the companions of our journey, hardship our garment; constancy and valour are our only shield. We must be united; we must be undaunted; we must be inflexible. Our qualities and our deeds must burn and glow through the gloom of Europe till they become the veritable beacon of its salvation." I followed the speech from a flimsy of the P.M.'s notes, which are typed in a way which Halifax says is like the printing of the psalms. Afterwards John Peck and I corrected the official report and altered the text in many places to improve the style and the grammar; for the P.M.'s speeches are essentially oratorical masterpieces and in speaking he inserts much that sounds well and reads badly.

Before the speech Randolph, recently elected M.P. for Preston was introduced, amidst applause, by Winston and David Marges-son (a fact which, said R., made him shiver). The applause, needless to say, was for Winston whose popularity in the House, as in the country, remains untarnished.

The P.M., dressed in his blue "siren-suit", dined with Eden in his new dining-room at No. 10 – formerly the typists' room in the basement and now redecorated and reinforced. He was in great form – as always after a speech has been successfully achieved – and amused Eden and me very much by his conversation with Nelson, the black cat, whom he chided for being afraid of the guns and unworthy of the name he bore. "Try and remember," he said to Nelson reprovingly, "what those boys in the R.A.F. are doing."

Prof., whom I talked to after dinner, is rather gloomy about the initial lack of success won by the A.I., G.L., etc., and he also says he thinks the Germans, who started the war behind us in this respect, have produced new aircraft types while we have been left standing. He alternates between startling optimism and querulous pessimism.

The air in the shelter went wrong in the middle of the night and I almost stifled. That coupled with the fact that John Martin tossed about ceaselessly in his bed above mine made the night most uncomfortable.

Wednesday, October 9th

A scandal is brewing owing to the action of Bob Boothby, Parliamentary Under Secretary to the Ministry of Food, in pushing the case of a Czech called Weininger – whom in addition M.I.5 suspect of being a spy – alleged to be in return for ten per cent of the proceeds. This is rare in English politics, but, if true, extremely serious in the case of a member of the Government.[1]

The P.M. went to a meeting of the Conservative Party to accept the Leadership. I read the typescript of his speech and saw that in giving the reasons for his acceptance he intended to say: "I have always faithfully served two supreme public causes – the maintenance of the enduring greatness of Britain and her Empire and the historic certainty of our Island life. Alone among the peoples we have reconciled democracy and tradition . . . The Conservative Party will not allow any party to excel it in the sacrifice of party interests and party feelings." This is his apologia for Conservatism.

The F.O. Weekly Summary gives an unpleasant picture of life in Poland. The Russians are taking whole families and dividing them up, sending the men to Siberia, the women to South Russia, the children elsewhere. So, many Poles are trying to escape to the German-

---

[1] Boothby forcefully asserted his innocence. That this was generally accepted is shown by the fact that Churchill made him a K.B.E. in 1953 and in 1958, presumably after full consideration by the Political Honours Scrutiny Committee, Macmillan recommended him for a peerage.

occupied area where last week twenty men were shot in one place, and the remaining male members of the town subjected to a mass flogging, because one Polish bandit shot one German gendarme. There is much to be said for the theory that civilisation stops at the Rhine and the Danube, the frontiers of the Roman Empire.

Sir S. Cripps advocates our reaching a rapid compromise with the U.S.S.R. on the present vexed issue of the assets of the Baltic States – recently occupied by Russia – which we have frozen. Cripps feels that now is the moment to "cash in" on the malaise caused in Russia by the recent Japanese pact with the Axis.

Betty Montagu and Mrs Crosthwaite[1] came to dinner and Mother and I went with them to inspect one of the Rest Centres – in Kentish Town – provided for those whose homes have been destroyed. These were in a lamentable state a few days ago, owing to the lack of co-ordination between the various central and local authorities responsible for them; but there has been a great improvement and the one we saw was much better than I had expected. The inmates, who stay for anything from two to ten days, sleep on rough mattresses on the floor and have army blankets. The sanitary arrangements consist of unscreened buckets; the only lighting is from hurricane lamps, though electricity is to be installed shortly; the atmosphere is hot and stuffy; the building, an L.C.C. elementary school, is solid but not underground or safe from a direct hit; there is not really enough space and many of the mattresses are laid in the passage. On the other hand the food is good and well-prepared, there was a piano playing and the people were dancing, the atmosphere is one of willingness to be helpful and of sympathy, there are few complaints and the cheerfulness of the homeless, as of the staff, is remarkable. I suggested they should procure electric fans which would make a great difference to the air in the building.

We motored back through the clear night, leaving Mrs Crosthwaite at the shelter, and saw parachute flares at which tracer bullets, which seemed to be red, were being fired. A number of bombs fell on and near Victoria Station and shook the house most unpleasantly.

Thursday, October 10th
In the early hours a bomb hit St Paul's Cathedral. Today I have been one year at No. 10 and I have seen many changes in the interval.

---

[1] Indefatigable social worker and mother of my Foreign Office friend, Moore Crosthwaite.

Lunched with Philip at Wellington barracks and played billiards. The Commanding Officer showed me a subversive pamphlet handed to Grenadier Guardsmen outside a cinema and I subsequently gave this to the P.M. for whatever action he might think appropriate.

I talked to the P.M. while he was changing into his siren-suit for dinner and described what we had seen at the rest centre at Kentish Town. He told me to procure for him a full report on the subject of both rest centres and shelters, showing who was responsible for what. I asked Bridges to supply this. The P.M. went off after dinner to see A.A. and Searchlights at Richmond and Kenley.

Friday, October 11th

There are two unexploded bombs on the Horse Guards Parade. "Will they do us any damage when they explode?" asked the P.M. lying in bed. "I shouldn't think so, Sir," I said. "Is that just your opinion," he replied, "because if so it's worth nothing. You have never seen an unexploded bomb go off. Go and ask for an official report." Such is the result of hazarding opinions to the P.M. if one has nothing with which to back them. But I was vindicated by the experts.

To Chequers for the week-end. I drove down with a slightly affected, opinionated and supercilious youth called Alastair Forbes,[1] a friend of Mary. He was in the Dakar expedition. Venetia Montagu was at Chequers; and the C. in C., Home Forces, Sir Alan Brooke, the C. in C., Anti-Aircraft Defences, Sir F. Pile, and Ismay came to dine and sleep.

At dinner I sat between Mary and Diana. The P.M was cheerful, despite the facts that our air results today and yesterday have been bad. He proclaimed that "the man's effort is flagging". He talked with Brooke about the French campaign, called Gamelin a "barber's block" who knew about nothing but artillery, repeated the oft-told story about *supériorité de nombres, supériorité d'armes, supériorité de méthodes* – and a shrug.[2]

He said that Georges, the only French General with intellect and ability, had been worn out by a two-year struggle for his rights with Gamelin. He wanted to send him a message: *"en penser souvent, en*

---

[1] Enlisted as a marine and was attached to the Free French, on whose sometimes vicious activities at their Duke Street headquarters he reported indignantly. Became a favourite of Ann O'Neill and after she married Lord Rothermere he wrote regularly for the *Daily Mail*.

[2] General Gamelin's reply to Churchill, when in May 1940 he asked what accounted for the German breakthrough. When Churchill asked him what he proposed to do about it, he merely shrugged his shoulders.

parler jamais" – that was all. The French "Maginot Line complex" was discussed. Winston said that a fortified line was useless without a field army to manoeuvre within it. Brooke and Ismay declared that the French had refused us the information we required about the disposition of their troops because they despised our army and thought of themselves as the invincible, experienced soldiers. Brooke described how the winter had been wasted and no progress had been made with the extension of the Maginot Line north of Luxembourg. All agreed in praising the tank and lamenting the fact that we neglected the evolution of our own discovery. Randolph said that the Germans had taken twenty years to learn what it had taken us twenty years to forget about tanks. They had obtained the information they wanted from the "Purple Primer" sold to them by Lieutenant Baillie Stewart;[1] but in England that Primer had remained unread and unappreciated.

The conversation turned to General Hobart, an erratic genius on tanks whose services are not being used. Brooke said he was too wild, but Winston reminded him of Wolfe standing on a chair in front of Chatham and brandishing his sword. "You cannot expect," he said, "to have the genius type with a conventional copy-book style."

Some apprehension was expressed about the vulnerability of Chequers, which would make an easy target for bombs. "Probably," said Winston, "they don't think I am so foolish as to come here; but I stand to lose a lot, three generations at a swoop." (Randolph's and Pamela's son was born two days ago.) Certainly there is a danger: in Norway, Poland and Holland the Germans showed it was their policy to go all out for the Government, and Winston is worth more to them than the whole Cabinets of those three countries rolled into one. To bed at 2.15 a.m.

Saturday, October 12th

A glorious day, the beginning of St Luke's Summer I hope. I was kept busy all day, with brief interludes. At lunch we talked chiefly of the air-raids and their effects. The P.M., sitting in his siren-suit and smoking an immense cigar, said he thought this was the sort of war which would suit the English people once they were used to it. They would prefer all to be in the front line, taking part in the Battle of London, than to look on helplessly at mass slaughters like Passchendaele.

After lunch we all walked to look at the craters caused by some bombs which fell all too near the house a few nights ago. I think it

---

[1] Imprisoned in the Tower of London before the war for treason.

was chance that they fell so close, but the P.M. and Ismay incline to the view that it was a trial shot and may well have been done on purpose.

Two of the Coldstream officers came to tea. The P.M., talking of the official policy of restricting consumption and expenditure, said, "Personally I prefer to make my number by increased effort rather than by self-denial." We also spoke of Fifth Column dangers and the P.M. said he much disliked locking people up and the suspension of Habeas Corpus. In any case he thought "those filthy Communists" were really more dangerous than the fascists.

I have persuaded the P.M. to take up the question of heating, etc., in private shelters during the winter and he says he will try and put a stop to the proposal to impose the purchase-tax on oil stoves, thermoses, etc.

Cripps and several of our Balkan Ministers now telegraph that Russia is likely to become more amenable, presumably because of the German domination of Roumania. The Soviet are making up their differences with Iran and with Turkey, and though bashful as far as we are concerned they may be open to discreet blandishments. The press is complicating matters, to the fury of Cripps, by publishing reports of Anglo-Soviet-Turkish-Greek-Yugoslav collaboration in the face of Axis threats to South-Eastern Europe. This has already had the effect of making the Russians draw in their horns.

That most charming of men, Sir John Dill, arrived to dine and sleep, as did the Lord Privy Seal and Mrs Attlee. I sat next to Diana and Venetia Montagu (whom Ruby Linsday[1] unjustly accuses of halitosis) and had a vehement conversation about ambition with Diana.

The P.M. is obviously worried about the possibility of an attack on Chequers and says that he does not object to chance "but feels it a mistake to be the victim of design". With the evolution of the German "beam" methods, he fears that accurate blind bombing may become a reality.

After dinner, politics and the House of Commons were discussed. Attlee said that David Margesson, in all his dealings with the Labour Party since 1931, had always been absolutely straight. Even Randolph agreed about his remarkable ability as Chief Whip. The P.M. considered that Ramsay MacDonald had made a great and unnecessary mistake in 1931: the National Government had been a sham and its effect had been to destroy party politics

---

[1] Rosemary Hinchingbrooke's mother.

and thus to remove the opportunity for back-benchers to attain ability through experience. This was the reason for the dearth of talent in the back benches on both sides of the House. Ramsay MacDonald had in 1931 lost the place which, by his raising of the Labour Party to a power in the land, he had formerly won for himself in history. Attlee and the P.M. then fell to swapping stories of their electioneering experiences and the P.M. said that he had learned one great lesson from his father: never to be afraid of British democracy.

Randolph thought that Baldwin had destroyed the fire in politics by adopting the technique of humble frankness which was intended to, and did, count on the generosity of his opponents and remove the sting from their attack. Attlee answered that this was a true estimate.

I heard that the War Office had this evening received two direct hits, that the National Gallery had been hit and that a bomb had fallen near King Charles' statue and had gone through to the underground, where in spite of the Government's disapproval thousands congregate every night, causing a hundred casualties. This report later proved to be exaggerated. The accurate bombing much disturbed the P.M., Attlee and Dill who all feel that Whitehall – and particularly No. 10 – is extremely dangerous. The P.M. is thinking on authoritarian lines about shelters and talks of forcibly preventing people from going into the underground and allotting to each a place of safety so that the optimum dispersal may be achieved.

Sunday, October 13th

In a note to Lord Halifax the P.M. writes: "Bombing of military objectives seems at present our main road home."

The Attlees stayed to lunch and Lady Digby[1] and Major General Hobart came. Winston's only noteworthy remark during lunch was, "A Hun alive is a war in prospect." Afterwards the Home Guard was discussed at length.

Master Winston Churchill, Randolph's four-day-old son, lay crying in his pram before the front door, open to inspection.

I walked up Beacon Hill and admired the autumn colouring of the beech trees. It is a glorious and exhilarating place. Then Diana Sandys and I walked to the Happy Valley where we sat and talked politics. I defended David Margesson and Halifax; we both expressed our loathing of Hore-Belisha.

Lady Digby tells me her nephew Ronald Strutt, who has de-

---

[1] Pamela Churchill's mother.

serted his post as Captain of the Guard to spend the week-end with Zara Mainwaring, is a bore, heavy in hand and only interested in horses, though certainly possessed of a nice character. I think Zara deserves to marry somebody more sparkling, but if she will insist on getting engaged after ten days' acquaintanceship she may have to pay the penalty.

Sir H. Dowding, Sir Dudley Pound and the new C.A.S., Sir Charles Portal, dined and, with the exception of Dowding, slept. After dinner there was air conversation: the bombing of London, the smallness of the bombs we have been using, the difficulties in the way of using the A.I. and our other inventions, which are still in their teething stage. There was much speculation why the Germans have not yet made a mass night raid on London (I fear it is to come) concentrating on one small area with first incendiaries and then high explosive. Portal says we intend to do this on Germany when we have the necessary strength. Dowding says that the German attack has been almost exclusively lacking in purpose: they show no signs of concentrating on detailed objectives or concentrating their striking force for one purpose. Presumably the advantages of so doing will one day dawn upon them as has, at last, the idiocy of letting their valuable bombers be destroyed in scores by daylight, when they can be much more alarming by night and when their fighters can maintain a nuisance value by day. For the last week the German day raids have taken place with impunity: large forces of fighters have come at great height, dropping their bombs at random and departing before they can be intercepted. We have accounted for few.

After dinner I conversed with Randolph whose fantastic arguments make one shudder. He talks of world domination as the greatest ideal and says he admires the Germans for desiring it. He wants it to be our aim and decries our ineptitude in the last century for not including South America and the Dutch East Indies in the British Empire. My thesis that Hitler's mistake was not to realise just how far he could go, and not to consolidate the gains he had made without war, he denounced as wishy-washy and, becoming at once arrogant and insolent, said it was people like me and Ramsay MacDonald and Baldwin that deprived this country of its greatness. Randolph is a most unattractive combination of the bombastic, the cantankerous and the unwise; and yet at times he makes shrewd and penetrating comments and at times he can be pleasant. He has none of Winston's reasonableness.

Today, in the Children's Hour, Princess Elizabeth spoke for the first time on the wireless. Diana Sandys and I, who listened, were embarrassed by the sloppy sentiment she was made to express, but her voice was most impressive and, if the monarchy survives, Queen Elizabeth II should be a most successful radio Queen.

The P.M. has today written, for the consideration of the Chiefs of Staff, a masterly paper on our strategy in the Mediterranean and elsewhere. The salient point is the re-occupation of Malta by the Mediterranean Fleet which can only be accomplished when the island has been reinforced with men, guns and U.P. weapon, etc. The strength of the Mediterranean Fleet is to be increased, more divisions are to be sent to the Middle East, with bombers and fighters too, so that by January we shall have a large army there and unquestionable naval control of the Eastern Mediterranean. These plans are to be pursued without pandering to the Vichy Government: we should continue to put pressure on the French in the belief that this will not fundamentally change the increasingly Anglophile sentiments of most Frenchmen. The P.M. believes it is becoming more and more difficult for the Vichy Government to drive the country into war against us however stringently we may impose the blockade, however strongly we support de Gaulle, however many unfortunate naval incidents occur. We must also maintain our strength at home and must prepare mobile divisions for amphibious operations on the continent. For the Bomber Command the great German battleships *Bismark* and *Tirpitz* must be primary objectives so that the *King George V* may be released for the Mediterranean.

I told the P.M. how much I admired this review, and he replied that it was by no means in a finished state: he had just written down what he had in his head. It shows great breadth of vision.

As the P.M. said goodnight to the Air Marshals, he told them he was sure we were going to win the war, but he confessed he did not see clearly how it was to be achieved. Prof. and I, discussing the matter afterwards, thought that if the U.S.A. came in, Russia "turned ugly" – as she has every reason to do – and Italy received a setback in North Africa, the end might well be sooner than was expected. Such a sequence of events would break their hearts, said Prof.

Prof. now attaches great hopes to the aerial mine-barrage which is being developed. (The U.P. weapon.) It works on the same principle as the naval wire barrage and should be very effective against night raiders. To bed at 2.00 a.m.

Monday, October 14th
Motored up to London with Prof. Almost every street is now scarred by bombs and the piles of debris and shattered houses are tragic to see.

Wednesday, October 16th
I returned from Cambridge to London, which has been very heavily raided and has suffered severely during the last two nights. Leicester Square is a desert, Pall Mall is badly damaged (the Carlton has collapsed and the Travellers was hit) and a bomb just missed No. 10, doing great damage to the Treasury and wrecking some of the rooms in No. 10 itself. Coming into Liverpool Street by train I saw such devastation by the railway line as is impossible to describe. Poor London.

Thursday, October 17th
A very busy day for me, but I had time to go with Brendan and others to inspect the basement and refuges at No. 11, where we may have to live in future after the raiding hours have begun.

The Spanish Minister of Foreign Affairs tells Sam Hoare that Hitler is going to meet Franco on the Pyrenees. He may try to bully F. into letting German troops attack Gibraltar through Spain.

I received an alarming letter from Miss Markham about the fall in morale among the citizens of London and the still unsolved transport problem. I showed this to the P.M. who dealt with it at a "shelter meeting" he held during the afternoon. A committee has been set up to enquire into the question of heating private shelters and providing oil-stoves, etc., which I brought to the P.M.'s notice last week-end.

Dined at the C.W.R. with Seal, Bridges, Wilkinson and Ismay. The food comes out of tins but the company is sufficiently entertaining to compensate for that.

Slept at No. 10 after talking to Jack Churchill in the P.M.'s dining-room till bed time. I had not fallen asleep before the crash of a falling bomb dragged us all from our beds. The air was thick with smoke and the choking smell of sulphur and gunpowder. Once outside the house I walked in my dressing-gown towards the Treasury which was hidden in a dense cloud of smoke. In Whitehall a bomb had made a huge crater just outside the Home Office, but when the smoke had cleared I could see the real havoc, the complete destruction of a large part of the Treasury. Our shelter at No. 10 – on the site of the old seventeenth-century Cockpit – is only about forty yards away from where the bomb fell. Four members of the Home Guard were trapped – and I fear killed – beneath the debris. I followed the demolition squad and A.R.P. men along an underground passage beneath the ruins, but we could get no reply to knocks and calls from the room in which the men had been caught.

This is the second hit within four days in almost the same place. Brendan and I said we thought it could only be a question of days before No. 10 fell a victim. Jack Churchill and Prof. were shivering with alarm.

Friday, October 18th
The great advantage of being young is that one can sleep after such events without opening an eyelid. But it is disconcerting to be woken up with the news that there is a mine in St James's Park which may blow to pieces everything within four hundred yards. The P.M. refused to leave No. 10 when I reported this unwelcome prospect and was chiefly worried about the fate of "those poor little birds" in St James's Park lake. By the time I returned from breakfast the mine had been rendered innocuous by the gallant Unexploded Bomb squad and the danger was over.

Miss Nettlefold[1] and Mrs Crosthwaite confirm Violet Markham's statement that the morale of Londoners has deteriorated. There is less of "We can take it" and an inclination to say "This must stop at all costs". It appears that transport muddles have much to do with it. The shelter situation is improving and will improve.

Travelling by underground is revolting now. Trains are sparse and travellers are legion.

The P.M. went off to Chequers. Tony and I remain in London. The whole establishment at No. 10 is to be moved over to the more solid Office of Works and C.W.R. during the week-end.[2]

Owing to a mistake about the cars I had to walk a mile through the "blitz" to dine with Sidney Cuthbert on Guard at St James's Palace. It is alarming to walk that distance when the guns are firing and enemy planes are overhead; moreover Whitehall and Trafalgar Square are full of craters and pitfalls. Dinner, which the King provides on a lavish scale, was excellent and I liked Sidney's two brother officers, Anthony Balfour and Eddie Hope. The latter, who seems to be a sensible Tory – my favourite brand of Conservative Radical – is nursing a constituency in Islington. We had an

---

[1] A social worker whose family had been well-known iron and steel masters.

[2] The Churchills had a flat over the C.W.R., above ground level, where the offices of the staff were also installed. It was thenceforward known as No. 10 Annexe. On the floor above that, Professor Lindemann and Desmond Morton had their offices, and there was also a "Mess" in which the No. 10 staff dined, established with an admirable Swedish cook supplied by Brendan Bracken.

involved argument about whether Duff Cooper was justified in throwing Caporetto[1] in the teeth of the Italians during a broadcast: Sidney and Hope thought he was: Balfour and I said it was (a) cheap, (b) impolitic (when so many Italians are opposed to the war).

A night at No. 10 which, owing to a downpour of rain, would have been quiet had it not been for an unimportant telegram, marked Most Immediate, that arrived at 3.00 a.m. Eden, who is now in Egypt, in order to gratify his self-esteem has arranged for a private cypher which does not go through the War Office. We are supposed to decypher these telegrams ourselves but, not having the time, we suborn a military cypherer. However, it was no easy task to get hold of him at 3.00 a.m. Eden is worried about the weakness of our air force in the Middle East – a fact which has worried our people out there, and the F.O. in London, for many weeks.

Saturday, October 19th

The Minister without Portfolio, Arthur Greenwood, has shocked the Treasury by suggesting that his economic experts should consider a number of problems of the present and future and the methods of dealing with them. Measures which he thinks should be visualised are, amongst others: (i) lower limit for income-tax exemption, (ii) extension of the scope of the purchase tax, (iii) forced saving. He also discusses an upper limit of spendable income and the possibility of a capital levy now or after the war. Sir Kingsley Wood objects to Greenwood trying to steal the Treasury's thunder and points out that he has got some of the ablest economists in the country, such as Keynes and Denis Robertson,[2] to advise him. Nevertheless I think the title of Greenwood's paper, "The Urgent Need for an Enquiry into the Economic and Financial Outlook", is one that contains much truth in itself.

I have been reading a telegram from Smuts, dated October 12th, in which he as usual makes some shrewd observations.

The neutral report that the Brenner meeting decided on a big offensive upon Egypt via Constantinople and Syria confirms the fears I have repeatedly expressed in previous messages. Such a move would be the greatest danger facing the British Empire

---

[1] Caporetto was the humiliating defeat by the Austrians which the Italians suffered in the First World War.

[2] Fellow of Trinity College, Cambridge, and University Professor of Political Economy.

now that the blitzkrieg against Great Britain has been partially checked . . . The reported plan is likely because it is grandiose enough to appeal to a mind like Hitler's. It promises vast results if successful, as it would open the way to Baghdad and Persia and the oil, and it would cut vital Empire communications and give Mussolini hope . . . The great counter-attack on land which the P.M. has foreshadowed may take place not in Western Europe, where conditions favour Germany, but in the Middle East where they are against her.

Smuts emphatically underlines the necessity of building up a strong force in Egypt and of co-operating with potential allies *before* they are overrun: "We should be there in time to co-operate fully with Greece and Turkey . . . I am myself suspicious of Russia. Is she not going to betray us again and has Germany not already bribed her with promises of Constantinople?"

After dining at home I was driven back to Downing Street in one of the army cars which are now at our disposal. Seeing an immense glow ahead I told the driver to go along the Embankment and we saw a big warehouse east of the County Hall entirely enveloped in flames. The fire obviously made the surrounding district an easy target and so we made for Downing Street with all speed. As we entered Whitehall a high explosive bomb seemed to hit the Admiralty on the Horse Guards Parade. I jumped out of the car at the entrance to the Treasury passage. I had not walked five yards before a parcel of incendiaries fell all round me. I threw myself flat on the ground in the mud and none fell nearer than ten yards from me. One set the F.O. roof on fire; two more fell among the ruins of the Treasury; several fell in the open. Somewhat shaken, I clambered into No. 10, through the shelter emergency exit, and spent the evening in the P.M.'s strengthened basement dining-room.

The night was peaceful except for periodic telephone calls which said "Purple" or "White" or something equally useless to people in a shelter and for the sound of the electric fan which resembles an enemy aeroplane.

Sunday, October 20th
Today began the move from No. 10 to the Office of Works. Only the Cabinet Room and that next door are to remain furnished. It is sad to leave the old building, especially as I fear it will not survive the Battle of London.

As I was sitting at the C.W.R., drinking lager with Tony Bevir, I said what a remarkable man Smuts was and how shrewd in the comments he sends from thousands of miles away. Tony suggested he might be Prime Minister if anything happened to Winston (which God forbid). This seemed to me a great Imperial idea: to have a Dominion politician as Prime Minister of England would be a living proof of the solidarity of the Commonwealth; and Smuts, a member of the Imperial War Cabinet in the last war, the man whose tact broke the Welsh coal strike at a critical moment, has the experience, the wisdom, the drive and the reputation to prove himself a worthy successor to Winston. There would, of course, be difficulties: the jealousy of the other Dominions, the strength of opposition and division of opinion in South Africa; but the idea seems to me so grandiose that I wrote to Mother and proposed that she should put it to Queen Mary with the idea of its filtering through to the King. The King chooses the Prime Minister and can send for whomsoever he wishes. It is thus wise to let the thought reach H.M. and I shall also suggest it to David Margesson and others.

General Smuts' reputation stood high, not only with Churchill, but with all parties in the Cabinet, with the leaders of the armed forces and with informed opinion throughout the Commonwealth and Empire. The South African policy of apartheid, *to which Smuts would have subscribed (though with less emphasis and conviction than the Nationalist Party) did not at this period occupy anybody's thoughts. It was as a wise elder statesman, with military knowledge and governmental experience in the First World War, that Smuts was respected and admired. Careful attention was always given to his suggestions, and not only in the wide field of strategy. Thus when Sir Stafford Cripps was appointed Minister of Aircraft Production in 1942, it was done at the suggestion of Smuts.*

The P.M. has taken up the transport problem with vigour and has sent drastic proposals to Moore-Brabazon for the use of private cars, lorries, etc., to get the people off the streets.

Monday, October 21st
Rode on Wimbledon Common in fine rain; my first exercise for weeks. Eccleston Square is in chaos, most of the furniture departing for Madeley; No. 10 is in chaos, most of the furniture going over to the Office of Works. I spent much of the day looking through one of Pitt's speeches, of the 3rd of February 1800, to find certain passages applicable to the present day for the P.M. to see. The sentence which struck me as most appropriate was: "It is only from the alliance of the most horrid principles with the most horrid

means, that such miseries could have been brought upon Europe." I was also interested by his conservative declaration that "whatever may be the defects of any particular constitution, those who live under it will prefer its continuance to the experiment of changes which may plunge them in the unfathomable abyss of revolution, or extricate them from it only to expose them to the terrors of military despotism."

Philip rang me up and said that two bombs had burst on the Officers' Mess at Wanstead, where he was, the night before. Fortunately he was not even scratched, though the room in which he was had been destroyed.

In the last few days two convoys have suffered badly, one losing seventeen ships and the other fourteen (it is due to the Germans using R.D.F. [radar] captured in France). This naturally preys on the P.M.'s mind greatly; but the position should be better when the American destroyers are in commission and when our new anti-U Boat craft are ready.

The P.M. made a gaffe. He is speaking on the wireless in French tonight, and just before dinner he came into the room, where the French B.B.C. expert and translator, M. Duchesne, was standing, and exclaimed: "Where is my frog speech?" M. Duchesne looked pained.

Dined with Father and slept at Eccleston Square for the last time for many a long day. Most of the furniture has now gone.

Tuesday, October 22nd
Rode on a splendid chestnut of Louis Greig's in Richmond Park, where a thick mist made riding hazardous owing to the large number of bomb-craters and unexploded bombs.

During a Cabinet Meeting at the House I talked to Colonel Moore-Brabazon, the new Minister of Transport, who has seen Violet Markham and told me she was most helpful. He sounds as if he is at last going to get things moving, unlike Reith (whom M.-B. described as "sticky").

Mrs Churchill was abusive. She seemed to expect me to make the arrangements for a visit to Glasgow she is making on Thursday and as I was extremely busy owing to the move, and also object to acting as Mrs C.'s private secretary, I gave most of the instructions to Miss Hamblin,[1] Mrs C.'s secretary. She was furious and said I gave myself airs, etc., etc., much to the amusement of Brendan

---

[1] Grace Hamblin. Churchill's secretary before the war, his wife's during and after it. A tower of strength to the Churchill family, all of whom were fond of her. Wise and competent, she became the National Trust's curator of Chartwell after Churchill's death.

The Prime Minister with his Private Office taken on the author's departure to join the R.A.F., September 29, 1941. FRONT ROW: the author, the Prime Minister, John Martin, Anthony Bevir. BEHIND (L. TO R.): Leslie Rowan, John Peck, Miss Watson, Commander Thompson, Charles Barker.

Mrs. Churchill and the author. Chequers, 1941.

Three influential advisers. TOP: Churchill, with Lord Beaverbrook at Marrakech. ABOVE: Brendan Bracken. RIGHT: Professor Lindemann (later Lord Cherwell).

Laying the Prime Minister's wreath at the Cenotaph, November 11, 1940.

Lord Halifax and Lord Cranborne (subsequently Marquess of Salisbury).

Meeting of the Governments exiled in London, held at St. James's Palace on June 12, 1941. On the right of King George VI, Mr. Gerbrandy (Dutch Prime Minister), on his left General Sikorski (Poland). At extreme right, Edward Bridges, Brendan Bracken, Desmond Morton. At extreme left: R. A. Butler, the author, Sir Archibald Sinclair.

who was sitting in the car with her while all this transpired. Mrs C. considers it one of her missions in life to put people in their place and prides herself on being outspoken.

Left by train for Scotland to accompany the P.M. on one of his tours. The party included Mrs Churchill (calmed and assuaged by this time), the C.I.G.S., Ismay, Commander Thompson and Victor Cazalet[1] who was told three times that he was not wanted but appeared on the platform and brazenly asked Winston to take him.

I dined at the same table as Ismay and Victor Cazalet. Ismay said that at the time of Munich there was no thought in the Government of waiting until we were better prepared. To avert war, not to postpone it, was the sole object.

Later in the evening the P.M. said a lot of people talked a lot of nonsense when they said wars never settled anything; nothing in history was ever settled except by wars. He said that what we are now going through is of importance only on the stage of history, by which I suppose he meant that we are achieving nothing constructive but are definitely influencing the future course of events and are laying up a stock of experience from which other generations may learn.

There was much talk about the British army and its lack of good officers. The P.M. said that every prospective officer should follow General Gordon's recommendation and read Plutarch's *Lives*; Dill said a study of Stonewall Jackson was the best possible course. The present trouble was that officers were admirably versed in weapon training but had little stimulus to use their imagination and look at military problems with a broad view.

Wednesday, October 23rd

We had breakfast in a siding and steamed in to Coupar Angus at 9.00 a.m. General Sikorski and his entourage boarded the train, the P.M. put on his strange hat, expressed indignation at the failure to produce his iced soda-water, and finally sallied forth in pouring rain to inspect a Polish battalion. We drove to a place called Tentsmuir where more Poles were drawn up and then stood by the roadside while first a mobile column and then the infantry, performing a kind of goose-step (which knocked all their steel helmets awry), marched past. Later we looked at a camp and at some beach defences north of the Forth. At St Andrews we walked in a procession along the coast for the same purpose, Mrs Churchill

---

[1] Owner of Fairlawne near Tonbridge. Conservative M.P., outstanding racquets and tennis player and supporter of Churchill in the pre-war struggle for re-armament.

being draped in the overcoat of a Polish General. The Poles seemed hardy and fit and gave the impression of being anxious to tear every living German in shreds.

Sikorski and his suite came to lunch on the train, after we had waited for some time on St Andrews platform while the P.M. signed autograph books and formed an object of great excitement to the crowd. I sat with two distinguished and gallant Poles, General Paskiewicz who commanded a division and won the equivalent of three V.C.s and Colonel Klimecki. The former looked grim, expressed his contempt for the French and disgust with the Russians, but spoke little. The latter, with steely blue eyes and a courteous manner, talked of methods for extracting from Poland intelligence about Germany.

After lunch the Poles, accompanied by a charming M.P., bearleader, Colonel Mitchell,[1] departed and Lord Rosebery[2] joined us. We made an extensive tour of Rosyth dockyard and spent much time on the great new battleship, *King George V*, completing in dry dock before doing her trials. We saw the luxurious ward-room and sick-bay, officers' compartment, kitchens and turrets. In descending through the tiny hole into one of the 14-inch turrets both the P.M. and Lord Rosebery all but got stuck. The P.M. had a long talk with the C. in C., Home Fleet, Sir Charles Forbes,[3] and then, dressed in his yachting cap and navy-blue brass-buttoned suit, addressed the ship's company about their ship and the necessity of having her in good trim before the *Bismarck* was out and at sea.

Mrs Churchill left with Lord Lamington, and the rest of the party saw many parts of the dockyard and a huge coastal command aerodrome. Then we left by train for Dalmeny and found the Duchess of Kent[4] and Mary Herbert[5] at the station. We crossed the Forth Bridge, the P.M. obviously delighted by the stirring reception given him by all the people, civilians and others, who had seen him that day.

Ismay and I drove to Edinburgh and dined in the train while the

---

[1] Sir Harold Mitchell, M.P. In 1953 he lent Churchill his Jamaican house at Ocho Rios for a holiday after a busy visit to Washington.

[2] Harry, 6th Earl of Rosebery, son of the Liberal Prime Minister and brother of Peggy Crewe. Regional commissioner for Scotland till 1945 and then Secretary of State. Leading racehorse owner, keen cricketer (at one time, as Lord Dalmeny, Captain of Surrey) and Master of Foxhounds.

[3] C. in C., Home Fleet, 1938–40, and then C. in C., Plymouth.

[4] Princess Marina of Greece, married to Prince George, Duke of Kent, King George V's youngest son.

[5] Lady Mary Hope, sister of the Marquess of Linlithgow, Viceroy of India, and married to Sidney Herbert, afterwards Earl of Pembroke. She was a great friend of both my parents.

P.M., C.I.G.S., and Thompson dined with Lord R. at Dalmeny. I played backgammon most successfully with Ismay while the P.M. talked to Dill and worked until 2.00 a.m. I heard the tail-end of a discussion in which Dill was being lectured on the desirability of employing General Hobart (who is disliked by the army – and by Dill): "Remember," said the P.M. with a meaning look at Dill, "it isn't only the good boys who help to win wars; it is the sneaks and the stinkers as well."

Thursday, October 24th
The train was very late and we had breakfast in comfort before reaching King's Cross. The P.M. passed the time in abusing the Foreign Office with Dill, who complained that the middle ranks in the Diplomatic Service were so poor. The P.M. said a large number should be pensioned off: "What is wanted in that department is a substantial application of the boot."

I drove back with him to No. 10. He said as the passers-by cheered, "I represent to them something which they wholeheartedly support: the determination to win. For a year or two they will cheer me." He pointed out that we were not yet a nation in arms: it took four years for a nation to reach its peak in war production; Germany had reached that maximum state, while we were only at the end of the second year of our effort. I asked him what he thought of the *King George V*. He replied that she was "a monument to Chatfield's folly". A four-gun turret had been taken out of her to allow for aeroplane hangars and she had been armed with 14-inch guns instead of the 16-inch he would have liked to see. Chatfield had been able to overrule some weak and ignorant First Lord, because, the P.M. said, "You see, Neville never seemed to think it mattered who he appointed to the Admiralty."

I found our new apartment at the Office of Works in a state of chaos. As Brendan said, to call it a mad-house would be an insult to lunatics. So I spent most of the day at No. 10 ministering to the wants of the P.M. who elected to work in the Cabinet Room.

John Martin and I dined at the C.W.R. and then repaired to Downing Street when, after drafting a message from the P.M. to the Polish nation, I sat in the underground dining-room with Jack Churchill and Brendan and listened to the latter's most amusing account of electioneering with the P.M. and in particular the Westminster Election of 1923.

Friday, October 25th
At 4.00 a.m. a box was brought to me containing two Most Immediate telegrams from Hoare in Madrid. The French Ambas-

sador had told him that the Vichy Government would, at a meeting today at noon, decide whether to hand over Toulon, their ports and their fleet to Germany. Pétain and Weygand were against it; Darlan and Laval in favour. It was suggested that a telegram from the King or the P.M. to Pétain might turn the scales. I got back into bed determined to leave the telegram till the P.M., who was sleeping the night in the tube at Down Street,[1] should awake at 7.00. But when I thought of the short interval allowed us I got up, seized the telephone, rang up Alec Cadogan, arranged that the American Embassy should send a message through their Chargé d'Affaires at Vichy, spoke to Lord Halifax and was generally cold and hectic until about 7.30.

The P.M. came back and got into bed at No. 10 to draft a message from the King. He told me that he "had an instinct" this was going to happen and that was why he had sent a telegram to Sam Hoare for communication to the French Ambassador last week. Brendan confirmed that the P.M. had been very uneasy about the whole question for the last few days – and particularly last night. An air-raid alarm drove us all into the shelter and an influx of many people from the half-ruined Treasury caused such a disturbance that the P.M. could hardly concentrate on his drafting. Moreover I was dressing in the inner shelter and he had to sit in the outer. The alarm passed and he went back to bed in his room, but a few minutes later the "Jim Crow"[1] sounded once more and we all went scurrying for safety. Such were the conditions in which this vitally important document, in a race against time, had to be composed. Meanwhile, on the P.M.'s instructions, I had arranged for the telegrams to be cabled to Washington for transmission to the President who, it is hoped, may encourage Pétain and Weygand to resist. But the wretched old Marshal has had to have an interview with Hitler – who has also been seeing Franco – and it is doubtful whether there is much he can do, especially as Darlan and the navy are fanatically Anglophobe.

In three days' time we were to have backed de Gaulle in an assault on Libreville. This will now have to be postponed or cancelled.

Sunday, October 27th
Lord Bessborough tells me that the de Gaulle headquarters in London are appalling and he thinks that unless something is done

---

[1] Until the early 1930s there had been a station at Down Street, off Piccadilly. The London Transport Executive converted it into a comfortable, indeed luxurious, air-raid shelter.
[2] Early warning signal of an air-raid.

about them Winston, whose personal prestige is involved, may suffer. He also thinks that the influence of Spears is pernicious and says that Winston has always had bad judgment. Certainly it is true that Spears' emphatic telegrams persuaded the Cabinet to revert to the Dakar scheme after it had, on the advice of the Chiefs of Staff, been abandoned.

Monday, October 28th
Arrived back at Downing Street Annexe (as we call the Office of Works flat) to find everybody completely befogged about what has been happening in France. The F.O. have no information but are trying to obtain some through the Americans.

I found the P.M. in his bedroom at the C.W.R. with Beaverbrook and told him that Athens had been bombed this morning. "Then we must bomb Rome," he said without hesitation and asked me to summon the Chiefs of Staff at once.

Wednesday, October 30th
Having breakfasted scrappily I went to No. 10 and spent most of the morning there dictating. I had an interesting talk with one of the P.M.'s visitors, an American newspaper magnate called Ingersoll, who is amazed by the spirit of the people of London but, quite justifiably, not impressed by the welfare arrangements. He wanted to know all about the P.M.'s habits, whether he drank tea or coffee for breakfast and a score of other journalese Americanisms.

Violet Markham came to see me. Yesterday afternoon Mrs C. and I went to look at her canteen in Southwark, where her initiative has been well repaid, and also saw the miles of underground shelter, in a converted tube, where thousands spend the night. Mrs C., who was ridiculously overdressed in a leopard-skin coat, was loudly acclaimed and both she and I were impressed by the universal cheerfulness in squalid conditions.

Violet Markham gave me the advice I wanted about Mrs Crosthwaite's plea that the services of the trained professional social workers are not being used. She also shed an interesting light on the inefficiency and lack of sympathy shown by the L.C.C. in dealing with the shelter and other kindred problems. This has given rise to a feeling among the poor that "they" – the authorities – are being callous. She confirmed what I had heard, that the trouble at rest centres and elsewhere was very largely due to local jealousies and the obtuseness of Borough Councils; but she says that in particular during the last few weeks all her illusions about the L.C.C. have vanished. The transport problem is much improved and Colonel Moore-Brabazon has shown great vigour and determination.

The P.M. lunched with Herbert Morrison and I was bidden to drink brandy with them. The P.M. began by saying that he had never doubted the ability of London to stand up to bombardment, though Herbert Morrison said he had not been sure how they would take it. The P.M. cited the wonderful courage of the Cockney regiments in the last war and pointed out that a large portion of the navy was recruited from London[1] (it appears that nearly the whole navy is drawn from Chatham, Portsmouth and Plymouth). He told us that Beaverbrook had produced figures to prove that only about thirty per cent of the R.A.F. pilots came from Public Schools, the remainder being products of the Elementary Schools and professional classes. It was striking that none of the aristocracy chose the R.A.F. – they left it to the lower middle class. The P.M. then waxed eloquent on the disappearance of the aristocracy from the stage and their replacement by these excellent sons of the lower middle classes. He paid a tribute to what they had done for England. Morrison, to my surprise, said it would be a pity if they vanished altogether. The P.M. commented on the difference between this country and France: there the aristocracy had been separated from the people by a gulf of blood; here they were sinking noiselessly and unresisting into the background. I had a feeling that the P.M. was flattering Morrison by his praise of the lower orders, and Morrison the P.M. by his admiration for many of the qualities of the upper classes. It made me feel rather uncomfortable.

The P.M. then proceeded to slang Baldwin, Ramsay Mac-Donald and the unnatural National Government. He stigmatised Baldwin as "the greatest of non-statesmen", said that this was the most unnecessary war in history and proclaimed that it was a war far harder to win than to avoid.

After dinner at the C.W.R. Ismay and I went to Down Street tube station where the P.M. was dining with Bevin. With General Crossman, commanding the London A.A. defences, we penetrated into the bowels of the earth and extricated the diners. Bevin, who had been well plied with brandy, was extremely loquacious. He and I got into a lift together and had great difficulty in getting out owing to his insistence on trying to open the gates before the lift had stopped. Then a policeman tried to arrest the P.M. for having too bright side-lights and was finally dismissed with a loud "Go to Hell, man".

[1] In which Churchill included Chatham.

Finally we reached Raynes Park and stumped across a wet field to see a battery of A.A. guns and the G.L. set which controls their fire. It was raining, no enemy aircraft entered our sector, and the guns remained silent; so after looking at the G.L., a clumsy contrivance like a caravan, and walking round the guns, we repaired to the Officers' Mess and the P.M., dressed in his R.A.F. overcoat, sat in a chair looking strangely like Napoleon while Bevin chattered and the officers gave us whisky. The P.M. said that when the G.L. and the other apparatus were perfected the war would take a different aspect: the air would cease to be formidable and the land and sea would come back to their own. It was a long way off, but it would come. Bevin said this was the dawn of a new era – whether he meant in war or in the application of these wireless miracles to other spheres I do not know. The officers seemed very pleased with the G.L. and confident of its ultimate success when the present teething troubles had been overcome.

Thursday, October 31st

Rose at 7.00, dressed in the P.M.'s empty bedroom and went off to Richmond to ride Louis Greig's horse. After a refreshing gallop I had breakfast with the Greig family and Victor Cazalet. On the way up to London Louis Greig and Cazalet told me of Weizmann's[1] new discovery of 120 per cent octane oil which may revolutionise flying. It is apparently being strongly opposed by the oil interests and has met with great obstruction in high circles. It is deplorable that vested interests in this country should be able to act in such a way.

Lunched with Jasper Rootham[2] at White's. Determined to join the army and forbidden to do so by Civil Service rules, he has resigned from the Treasury and will join up next month. Presumably he will be taken back after the war, but he is still badly off, his pay stops and generally speaking I think he is most gallant. He complains that the Government makes provision for conscientious objectors, but none for those who are forbidden to fight and conscientiously object to not doing so.

We talked about Neville Chamberlain and Horace Wilson and he had formed a more definite opinion than I had of the former's dependence on the latter. We agreed that Horace, though a good

[1] Chaim Weizmann, first President of Israel, whom Churchill admired and respected.

[2] My predecessor as junior Private Secretary to Neville Chamberlain. The Treasury, quite disgracefully, declined to re-instate him after the war, in which he served as a liaison officer with the Yugoslav guerillas. He joined the Bank of England and on retirement wrote elegant verses.

and genuinely public-spirited man, was fatally addicted to the policy of cautious advance and excessive circumspection in every task he undertook.

The P.M. felt ill, was sick and went off to Down Street where he had no dinner ("which I much resented – but it was very good for me"). I dined with John Martin and John Peck at the C.W.R. The latter, who has a gift for the ridiculous, amused himself by typing the following minute:

Action this Day
Pray let six new offices be fitted for my use, in Selfridge's, Lambeth Palace, Stanmore, Tooting Bec, the Palladium and Mile End Road. I will inform you at 6 each evening at which office I shall dine, work and sleep. Accommodation will be required for Mrs Churchill, two shorthand typists, three secretaries and Nelson.[1] There should be shelter for all and a place for me to watch air-raids from the roof. This should be completed by Monday. There is to be no hammering during office hours, that is between 7 a.m. and 3 a.m.

W.S.C.
31.10.40.

The above, very realistically produced, entirely convinced Morton, Jacob, Seal, Ismay and others of its authenticity – which only goes to show the state of attrition to which all these moves and constantly changing plans have reduced the P.M.'s entourage.

At the end of a year at war during which he had been at the forefront in the Norwegian disaster, the Dunkirk episode, the invasion threat and the battle of Britain – not to mention the battle of the Atlantic which was now threatening survival – it would have been surprising if Churchill had not been tense with emotion and turbulent in mood.

He did not shout, as actors in films and television productions imagine; nor did I ever see him drunk, as the media and the less well-informed writers sometimes suggest that he frequently was. But never notably considerate, except to those in pain or in trouble, he was more than normally inconsiderate and demanding during the last months of 1940. He complained of delays when there were none; he changed carefully prepared plans at the last minute; he cancelled meetings and appointments without caring for anybody's convenience but his own; and he was continually

---

[1] The black cat.

insisting on personal amenities which gave much trouble to overworked people and were, in a small way, diversions from the war effort. The sound of hammering, often on account of building activities he himself had set in train, caused outbursts of fury, and his staff spent much time searching Whitehall for the source of the irritant in the hope of appeasing their sometimes unreasonable master.

Mrs Churchill, at one stage in the summer of 1940, wrote him a letter on the subject. Long experience had convinced her that when she really wanted him to pay attention written representations were more effective than oral. He may have accepted the rebuke, but it was some months before he reformed. If, however, he had been unjustly angry, he seldom failed to make amends, not indeed by saying he was sorry but by praising the injured party generously for some entirely dissociated virtue.

So if John Peck's spoof minute was an imaginative parody, it was not altogether wide of the mark.

Churchill's ill-tempered phase was a passing one, nor was it constant. What was constant was the respect, admiration and affection that almost all those with whom he was in touch felt for him despite his engaging but sometimes infuriating idiosyncrasies.

11

Mediterranean Dilemma

November 1940

Friday, November 1st

After the P.M. had had his afternoon sleep we left for Chequers. I travelled with him in his car and after a sticky beginning found him most affable. He was dressed in his R.A.F. uniform and we stopped at Northolt to inspect the Hurricane Squadron, No. 615, of which he is Honorary Air Commodore. They had been up four times today and told us of their experiences in the Mess while we drank whisky and soda. When we continued our journey the P.M. talked about the Italians, whose impertinence in sending bombers to attack this country has much annoyed him. He said he intended to attack Rome before long, as soon as we had enough Wellingtons at Malta. Last night our bombers successfully attacked Naples from there and today the press, ignorant of the truth, is chortling about the magnificent 3,000 mile flight from England to Naples and back. I said to the P.M. that I hoped if we bombed Rome we should be careful to spare the Coliseum. The P.M. answered that it wouldn't hurt the Coliseum to have a few more bricks knocked off it and then, becoming pensive, quoted:

> While stands the Coliseum Rome shall stand
> When falls the Coliseum Rome shall fall . . .[1]

We talked about the Public Schools and he said he wished he had learned Greek. He said he would go down to Harrow to hear School Songs if I would arrange it, and then he reverted to his lament about the almost entire failure of Eton, Harrow and Winchester to contribute pilots to the R.A.F. I repeated Lord

[1] From Byron's *Childe Harold's Pilgrimage*.

Bessborough's condemnation of the de Gaulle headquarters and the P.M. said that de Gaulle was definitely an embarrassment to us now in our dealings with Vichy and the French people. I also told him what Louis Greig had said about Weizmann's discovery of 120 per cent octane oil and he said that if I could show him that the oil interests really were opposing this for their own ends he would soon put a stop to their machinations.

He gave it as his view, emphatically, that Roosevelt would win the election by a far greater majority than was supposed and he said he thought America would come into the war. He praised the instinctive intelligence of the British press in showing no sign of the eagerness with which we desired a Roosevelt victory. He said he quite understood the exasperation which so many English people feel with the American attitude of criticism combined with ineffective assistance; but we must be patient and we must conceal our irritation. (All this was punctuated with bursts of "Under the spreading Chestnut Tree").

"I should now like," said the P.M. as we neared Chequers, "to have dinner – at Monte Carlo – and then to go and gamble!" He proceeded to expound the pleasures of chemin de fer and the exultation he found in gambling on the Riviera.

Despite his excellent humour, the P.M. was still suffering slightly from the effects of yesterday's sickness and he went straight to bed. I dined with Mrs Churchill, Mary, Judy Montagu and Ismay. I spent most of the evening bickering with Mary who was feeling cantankerous and is in any case a shade too prim. Ismay and I then talked about the megalomania of Sir Roger Keyes who has had the effrontery to suggest that the P.M. should appoint him his deputy to preside over the Chiefs of Staff.

Saturday, November 2nd
I spent the whole day indoors at my writing table, coping with a stream of incoming pouches and outgoing orders.

The First Lord, the First Sea Lord and the C.I.G.S. came to lunch. Speaking of Vichy, and their recent negotiations with the Germans, the P.M. said, "Owing to our unexpected resistance they have been able to market their treachery at a slightly higher rate than would otherwise have been possible." He referred to them with loathing and said that while he could understand people being wicked he could not understand their being so contemptible. He now thinks the invasion is off, but that can only be because of our constant vigilance. If we relaxed that, invasion would be an imminent danger. But of course this meant our keeping great forces immobilised at home, and similarly the North African threat meant our concentrating all the rest we possessed in Egypt. Thus the Axis powers could keep our forces concentrated in one or two spots while they amused themselves elsewhere.

Nevertheless the P.M. is determined that all possible, by land, sea and air, shall be done for Greece and when, after a long post-prandial discussion, Dill drove away at tea-time the P.M.'s last words were, "Don't forget – the maximum possible for Greece." Similarly in a minute this morning to the C.A.S. about sending air support to the Greeks, the P.M. wrote: "Perhaps you will say that all I propose is impossible. If so, I shall be very sorry, because a great opportunity will have been missed, and we shall have to pay heavily hereafter for it. Please try your best."

It was one of those days when almost everything went wrong: the electric light spasmodically failed; the Green Line telephone was out of order; a telegram to Eden in Cairo, bidding him stay there, was unduly delayed in despatch; I incurred the P.M.'s displeasure by sending up to London the flimsies of some minutes he had dictated and wanted again. I was rushed off my feet by an overwhelming volume of papers; Peggy Crewe rang up about some trifling Air Raid Precaution troubles in Chelsea which she wanted me to put right; I spent ages with Mrs Churchill poring over some notes of Violet Markham's about lack of compensation for Civil Defence Workers and the unsympathetic attitude of the L.C.C. as regards welfare work.

The new C. in C., Bomber Command, Sir Richard Peirse,[1] two pilots from No. 615 Squadron, and the Coldstream Company Commander, Sir George Forestier-Walker, came to dinner, when the conversation was mostly on fighter tactics and bombing prospects. The German fighters can outfly ours, but their pilots are very timid. We have some new bombers on the way, Halifaxes, Manchesters and Stirlings which will be most destructive, and by the end of next year the P.M. hopes to be bombing "every Hun corner" every night. Peirse tells me that the much-vaunted American "Flying Fortresses" are obsolete and we have refused to take them. As regards bombing Rome, the P.M. said to Peirse, as he said to me yesterday, "We must be careful not to bomb the Pope; he has a lot of influential friends!" After dinner the P.M. with great pride showed the young air-force officers some of his albums of aircraft production; he is never happier than when displaying the

---

[1] C. in C., Bomber Command, until replaced by Sir Arthur Harris in 1942, when he went to India as A.O.C. in C. Caused a scandal by running off with General Auchinleck's wife.

spectacular strides that have been made since Beaverbrook and the new government came into power.

The P.M., closeted with Peirse and Ismay, produced another telegram to Eden which Ismay is to submit to the Chiefs of Staff tomorrow.

> However unjust it may be, the collapse of Greece without any effort by us will have deadly effect on Turkey and on future of war . . . Quite understand how everyone with you fixed on idea of set-piece battle at Mersa Matruh. For that very reason unlikely it will occur . . . No one will thank us for sitting tight in Egypt with ever growing forces while Greek situation and all that hangs on it is cast away . . . New emergencies must be met in war as they come and local views must not subjugate main issue . . . Trust you will grasp situation firmly (abandoning negative and passive policies)[1] and seizing opportunity which has come into our hands. Safety First is the road to ruin in war even if you had the safety which you have not.

All this was interspersed in a longer and much more detailed telegram.

Sunday, November 3rd

The P.M. was upset by a broadcast made by the First Lord (A. V. Alexander) giving an extravagant picture of what we were doing, and would do, for Greece. "Such a nice fellow – but, really . . ." he said. Of course the press have blazoned his remarks across their front pages and false hopes will be raised.

Then a telegram came from Eden saying he must return in order to discuss the position with the P.M. I took it up to his bedroom, written in pencil, and waited while he drafted a reply telling Eden to wait till he had seen the P.M.'s latest telegram – which the Chiefs of Staff are sending off this morning. He lay there in his four-post bed with its flowery chintz hangings, his bed-table by his side. Mrs Hill sat patiently opposite while he chewed his cigar, drank frequent sips of iced soda-water, fidgeted his toes beneath the bed-clothes and muttered stertorously under his breath what he contemplated saying. To watch him compose some telegram or minute for dictation is to make one feel that one is present at the birth of a child, so tense is his expression, so restless his turnings from side to side, so curious the noises he emits under his breath. Then comes out some masterly sentence and finally with a "Gimme" he takes

---

[1] The sentence in brackets was subsequently omitted.

the sheet of typewritten paper and initials it or alters it with his fountain-pen, which he holds most awkwardly halfway up the holder.

A note arrived from Lord Beaverbrook, announcing his resignation because of asthma (actually he is cross with the Air Ministry and piqued because the P.M. has thrown some cold water on his grandiose scheme for making Faraday House the seat and centre of Government – thus upsetting all the Post Office arrangements). The P.M. smiled wryly when I gave him the note, knowing that Lord Beaverbrook resigns every few days; and then he rang him up and said if he did so there would be a public outcry, it would be called desertion, and anyhow why couldn't he just take a fortnight's or a month's holiday.

Lunch was a quiet meal: the family, myself and a Coldstream officer called Waddilove. We listened to a Winstonian dissertation on Sadowa[1] and Austria and Bismarck. Waddilove said that Bismarck was the last German who knew where to stop; the P.M. said he would show these present Germans where they were to stop – in the grave.

After lunch I played backgammon with Mrs Churchill while the P.M. thought out the speech he is to make in the House on Tuesday to the accompaniment of Strauss waltzes on Mary's gramophone. Having received sufficient inspiration he went into the Hawtrey room to dictate the speech to Mrs Hill, and I walked in the pouring rain with Mary and Judy.

After tea the three Chiefs of Staff and Lady Portal (wife of the C.A.S.) arrived to dine and sleep, as did Prof. The purpose is to discuss the plan, which they have been working on all day, for assistance to Greece. Ismay says there is nothing we can do on a sufficiently large scale to save the Greeks and the C.O.S. seem rather unenthusiastic about the P.M.'s determination to throw considerable forces into the fray even at the expense of weakening Egypt. Ismay thinks that concentrated air-attack, with little opposition, will break Greece as it broke Poland and France.

The P.M. is highly delighted by the Italian admission of their casualties in Africa which are more than ten times as great as ours. He says that "the Italians are easier to kill than to catch".

After dinner, before leaving the dining-room, projects for capturing Pantellaria ("by 300 determined men, with blackened faces, knives between their teeth and revolvers under their tails", as the P.M. envisaged the operation) and Rhodes were discussed. The Pantellaria scheme could be left to Sir R. Keyes and his comman-

---

[1] The decisive victory of the Prussians in the Austro-Prussian War of 1866.

dos; he has been pressing to be allowed to do it. Rhodes would be a harder job, but the P.M. thinks it would be agreeable to seize it and give it to Turkey: the Turks would not be able to resist the offer and then they would be embroiled with Italy.

For long hours I sat up while assistance for Greece was discussed, the numbers of aircraft we could send was ascertained, telegrams were received from Eden saying that if troops were sent from Egypt Wavell would be prevented from carrying out a prospective hard blow at the Italians and Eden was told not to be faint-hearted, parochially minded, over-cautious, etc., etc. During an interlude I took Dill to look at some despatch riders, who had just arrived, in order to prove to him that the military mackintosh was not waterproof.

Prof. thinks it fantastic that no plan should have been ready for instant use in the event of an Italian attack on Greece. Ismay's reply is that no ready-made plan is applicable to the special circumstances existing when the attack is made and that as far as Greece was concerned our previously worked out plans depended on French co-operation. We had intended to occupy Crete in such an event and we had already done so. My impression is that we are now going beyond what is intended because the P.M. realises the moral and strategic value of preventing a Greek collapse. He thinks the Greeks will fight well (and cites the wars of 1911 and 1921 to show they are not despicable). They may well prove a match for the aggressors on land – and it is up to us to provide air support.

From 9.00 p.m. till 2.00 a.m. telegrams to Eden were drafted and redrafted and finally in a state of complete exhaustion we all went to bed after 2.00. London had its first night free of air-raids for many a long day.

Monday, November 4th
The P.M. has ordered enquiries to be made into Violet Markham's two points about compensation for Civil Defence workers in case of death and about the unsympathetic attitude of the L.C.C. as regards welfare work. I am to take these points up with the departments concerned.

The P.M. is much impressed by the slackening of air attacks and says it is not all due to the weather. The Germans have to continue them in order to try and hide their defeat, but evidently they do not like the reception they get or the retaliation on Berlin.

Depressing news from the sea: two big armed merchant cruisers, the *Laurentic* and the *Patroclus*, have been torpedoed together with a merchant ship off Ireland.

When I got up to find out the news the P.M. was already down, in his siren-suit, bidding farewell to the departing Chiefs of Staff. Shortly afterwards we ourselves left for London.

I lunched with Father at White's and then, after spending enough time in the office to put some semblance of order into my overflowing trays, I motored down to Ardley in the pouring rain and arrived there as darkness fell. Mother was there staying with Joan and Ann. She told me that my suggestion about General Smuts as a successor, if need should ever arise, to the P.M. much affected Queen Mary, who said that it was an idea which had greatly appealed to King George V. She therefore passed it on to the King who reacted favourably.

Tuesday, November 5th
Polling day in the U.S. A close contest is generally expected.

Wednesday, November 6th
After an idle morning, during which it poured for the fifth day in succession, I drove Mother up to London and went to No. 10. The Greeks are holding out well; the presidential election has gone the right way; and the Admiralty are much exercised by the apparent presence of another pocket battleship in the Atlantic.

After dinner at the Central War Room (endless tinned soup and sausages) John Peck and I went over to No. 10 and, sitting in the P.M.'s dining-room, drank brandy and gossiped with Brendan (who tells me he wants to buy the *Observer*) and Jack Churchill.

Thursday, November 7th
I was on duty from 8.00 a.m. till 9.30 and then had breakfast at Wyndham's. (The Travellers is bombed and in disuse.)

The House of Commons met for the first time at Church House, which is thought to be safer than the Palace of Westminster. The Cabinet was also held there and as I was in attendance on the P.M. part of the time I had time to steal into the Assembly Room where the House meets and watch that sparse gathering of M.P.s in their small and unwonted surroundings. The official gallery is on a kind of rostrum behind the Speaker's Chair. I noticed that Rab Butler, on the Front Bench, so far followed the traditions of the House as to put his feet up on the Table.

The amount of papers in the P.M.'s box is becoming unwieldy. In order to keep a full and comprehensive diary of events I ought to give a summary of the matters dealt with; but it would be a whole-time job to summarise this farrago of operational, civil, political and scientific matter.

The P.M. was much displeased by a minute in a War Office file which referred to one of "his scribbles" as being unintelligible. He sent a furious minute to P. J. Grigg demanding an apology and deploring that the officer in question (General McCready, A.C.I.G.S.) should have made more use of his critical faculties than of his intelligence.

Seven bombs in succession shook our equanimity at the C.W.R.

Friday, November 8th
At night I dined at the C.W.R. and then, leaving Seal and Bevir to cope with the P.M. at the C.W.R. (where he fed not wisely and all too well with Eden, who today returned from Cairo), I went over to No. 10 and read *Madame Bovary* before going to bed.

We bombed Munich in force.

Saturday, November 9th
Rode early at Richmond on Louis Greig's horse and had breakfast with him and his family afterwards. He is the soul of hospitality and affability.

I am amused to see the following minute by the P.M., attached to an earlier one he had written about assistance for Greece: "Although I bowed before the difficulties so industriously assembled by the Joint Planners in their report of August 31st, and the general attitude of negation, I should be very much obliged to the C.O.S. Committee if they would kindly read my minute and see if there was not something in it after all."

The P.M. spent most of the morning dictating a speech he is to make at a Mansion House lunch today and with the composition of which he was so behindhand that he asked to be allowed to be half an hour late for lunch.

Tony Bevir gave Desmond Morton, John Peck and me an excellent lunch at the United Universities Club. We talked of the incapacity of Archie Sinclair and the fact that "the Prof." shows signs of breaking up under the strain. Desmond also retailed two of the P.M.'s latest remarks, one to General Sikorski who wanted foreign exchange: "*Mon Général, devant la vieille dame de Threadneedle Street je suis impotent*"; the other a 2.00 a.m. Parthian shot at the Chiefs of Staff: "I am obliged to wage modern warfare with ancient weapons."

Horace Wilson rang me up to say that Mr Chamberlain died this evening. He had cancer but his death was painless. I rang up Seal who has gone with the P.M. to Ditchley, fearing an attack on Chequers by the light of the waxing moon.

One can be quite comfortable these days in spite of the bombs. I had a bath in the P.M.'s bath at No. 10, and then sat in his downstairs room in my dressing-gown, reading *Madame Bovary* and drinking some delicious brown ale provided by Barker.

Sunday, November 10th

Went to the early service in Westminster Abbey. The altar is now set up in the nave before the gates of the choir. The Dean asked our prayers for Mr Neville Chamberlain as if he were still alive – the news will not be published till this afternoon.

I breakfasted at No. 10 and then went over to the Annexe for the morning, after wrestling with the Duke of Westminster's[1] secretary about His Grace's lady-friend who has been seized by M.I.5 on her arrival in this country. The Duke wants Winston to intervene – a monstrous suggestion which I trust the P.M. will resist.

The Free French forces seem to be making a successful attack on Libreville in Gabon, but their activities are now rather an embarrassment in our relations with Vichy. De Gaulle has been asked to come back to London, and Spears too; but the P.M. doubts whether they are on sufficiently good terms to come back on the same ship.

There are rumours from the Balkans that Russia might join in an Axis advance south-eastwards so as to ensure her control of the Black Sea ports and the Straits. She is pursuing a policy of the most abject "appeasement" towards Germany.

Our Balkan Missions are pouring in telegrams which stress the psychological necessity of supporting Greece; but the problem is best summed up in the F.O. weekly political summary:

We are still paying for our failure to re-arm in good time. Our military resources in the Eastern Mediterranean do not permit us to disperse our strength and the air help which Greece so sorely needs can be given only at the expense of other interests. The problem of aid for Greece is a military one which has been gravely complicated by the collapse of France. But, from the political point of view, the advantages of swift and effective help are pre-eminent.

The raids, which began early, were very intense and drove me and *Madame Bovary* out of the P.M.'s sitting-room into the shelter

---

[1] Bendor, 2nd Duke of Westminster. Old friend of Churchill with whom he made several military expeditions by armoured car in the First World War. Churchill hunted wild boars on his Normandy estate and painted many pictures when staying at his other French property near Bordeaux.

after a very short attempt at concentration. The sky and the balloons were reddened by two fierce fires, but the nights are becoming cold for street-prowling in dressing-gowns and bedroom slippers, however remarkable the sights.

Monday, November 11th

Rose at 7.00 and while it was yet dark (summer time is to continue throughout the winter) set out to ride at Wimbledon. The ground was white with the first frost of the winter, but the sky was blue, streaked with pink clouds, and the leaves, though now a dull brown, were still on the oak trees. The bomb craters are filling with pools of water.

At 10.15 I laid a wreath on the Cenotaph, as representative of the Prime Minister. There was no ceremony: the traffic was just stopped, I placed the wreath and a large number of press photographers clicked their cameras.

The P.M. came back from Ditchley at lunch-time. Afterwards he went to sleep but had to be disturbed owing to the shriek of bombs nearby. He soon got tired of the shelter and returned to his bedroom, where he gave me a lecture on the excellence of his teeth-cleaning apparatus, an electrical appliance which spurts water at a high velocity into his mouth and removes the taste of cigars. He said that if young men like me were sensible enough to use them they would never have bad teeth.

He is very cross with Archie Sinclair who (after the attack in the Beer Cellar at Munich) gave an interview to the *Daily Express* saying that dictators were military objectives. The P.M. thinks this may cause unpleasant reactions on himself and says such a statement almost amounts to incitement to assassination. But, if you are allowed to bomb Heads of States, surely you may shoot them?

Today we have shot down more raiders than usual and, for the first time over England, at least eight Italian planes amongst them. The P.M. gave a whoop of joy when I told him.

After dinner I sat in the dining-room and talked at length to Brendan. He thought it a tragedy that Philip Sassoon didn't leave Trent to the P.M. (Brendan cannot bear Chequers.) He also spoke of the beauties of a certain Stene Chapel, near Banbury, built by Nathaniel Crewe, Bishop of Durham and Oxford. We also discussed the shipping situation which is very serious.

Tuesday, November 12th

Lord Lothian has drafted a telegram for the P.M. to send to Roosevelt. It stresses very frankly our need for American support in obtaining the Irish naval bases, in guarding Singapore, in getting more ships and above all in buying munitions and aircraft on credit. It is intended to make R. feel that if we go down, the responsibility will be America's. Brendan tells me the P.M. thinks it so admirably written that he could not improve a word of it; but it will go before the Cabinet for consideration.

At 12.00 noon the P.M. rose in the unfamiliar surroundings of Church House and paid before the House of Commons his moving and eloquent tribute to Mr Chamberlain. The noise of Seal and Miss Watson coming on to the dais (which takes the place of the official gallery), the coughs and creaks from members, were very disturbing in the small chamber used for debate, and I did not think the P.M.'s delivery was equal to the magnificence of his language and the balance of his phrases. I was struck by his words when, in speaking of the verdict of the future, he said:

> History with its flickering lamp stumbles along the trail of the past, trying to reconstruct its scenes, to revive its echoes, and kindle with pale gleams the passion of former days. What is the worth of all this? The only guide to a man is his conscience. The only shield to his memory is the rectitude and sincerity of his actions. It is very imprudent to walk through life without this shield, because we are so often mocked by the failure of our hopes and the upsetting of our calculations; but with this shield, however the fates may play, we march always in the ranks of honour.

Tommy Lascelles,[1] with whom I talked after lunch at Wyndham's, said that only the P.M., of living orators, could make one realise what it must have been like to hear Burke or Chatham.

Our depression at the huge shipping losses in the North Western Approaches, which if continued at their present rate would bring us to our knees, has been relieved by the success of the Fleet Air Arm in destroying the Italian fleet in Taranto harbour and setting fire to Durazzo and Valona, the only supply ports for the Italian army in Greece.

---

[1] Sir Alan Lascelles (only Churchill called him Alan rather than Tommy) was Hardinge's successor as the King's Private Secretary. He was a wise counsellor, well-read, a good historian and a lover of Wagner. He wrote the best of letters and when, one day, his diaries are published they will doubtless be a document of unusual importance. Married the younger daughter of a Viceroy, Lord Chelmsford.

Wednesday, November 13th

The First Lord is a queer fish. I congratulated him on the Taranto affair and he said the praise was due to Cunningham,[1] C. in C., Mediterranean. "But," he continued, "in fairness to Pound I must say that I suggested it to him the other day and he telegraphed it out to Cunningham." This unself-conscious egotism is probably due to Mr A.'s disappointment that the P.M. is going to steal the Admiralty's laurels by himself announcing the victory in the House.

The P.M. frantically composed his speech and I drove down to Church House with him while he discoursed upon the difference this event makes to the whole of our naval disposition and the panic which the Italians, in their inner harbour, must have felt at the unexpected attack. His description of "this glorious episode" to the House was greeted with enthusiastic cheers from an assembly hungry for something cheerful.

A vile, hot and hectic afternoon, starting with a tour of the new building operations[2] – where the P.M. leapt deftly over girders and crawled through holes – and ending with great pressure of work.

The Molotov visit to Berlin may presage any of three things:

i.   A Peace offensive (no one but me subscribes to this view!).
ii.   Pressure on Turkey for the control of the Straits. Russia would be anxious to be sure of the Black Sea ports. This is the most likely interpretation of the meeting.
iii. A division of power in the Far East and Asia, Russia taking, in some form or another, Iran and Afghanistan.

This rumour comes from Craigie[3] in Tokyo.

At dinner in the C.W.R. I had a talk with Sir Reginald Dorman Smith (Minister of Agriculture in Chamberlain's government), who says that the P.M.'s recent letter to the farmers (saying "stick it and don't grumble") has had a deplorable effect. It was written by Beaverbrook, who in many respects is a mischievous person. Dorman Smith spoke enthusiastically of Chamberlain and agreed wholeheartedly with a letter I received this morning from Arthur Rucker saying: "Neville's last months were a bitter tragedy, but I believe that he will some day be regarded as the greatest Englishman of his times."

---

[1] Sir Andrew Cunningham, known as A.B.C., First Sea Lord after Sir Dudley Pound's death in 1943.

[2] These excursions, of which I always seemed to be the victim, were made because Churchill, as a keen amateur builder, was fascinated by the work in progress to make the Central War Room more bomb-proof. He examined the plans and suggested alterations, including the construction of brick traverses.

[3] Sir Robert Craigie, British Ambassador.

Thursday, November 14th

Rode in Richmond Park on Jean Greig's large brown horse and gratefully drank in the cold clear morning air after nights of air-conditioning. At breakfast I listened to a discourse by Louis Greig on the iniquitous behaviour of Beaverbrook, who is, of course, at daggers drawn with Louis' chief, Archie Sinclair, and is stealing all the materials required by the Ministry of Supply.

Neville Chamberlain's funeral took place in Westminster Abbey at noon. Tony and I were among the ushers. A huge congregation assembled, and froze as they sat beneath the shattered windows. All the Ministers were there in the choir stalls; the P.M., David, and most of the War Cabinet were pall-bearers. The Duke of Gloucester represented the King, and the Chiefs of Staff represented the three services. The time and place had been a well-kept secret, announced to both Houses in secret session; for a judiciously placed bomb would have had spectacular results.

I noticed the look of blank indifference, almost of disdain, on Duff Cooper's face, the boredom of Bevin. Only Anderson and Hankey sang the hymns. Lady Oxford marched out at the end of the service, side by side with Lord Horder,[1] and among the family mourners. Publicity is her God.

In the afternoon the P.M. set out for Ditchley; but having heard, just before he started, that a German operation entitled MOONLIGHT SONATA was likely to take place tonight, he changed his mind before he had gone far and returned to London. This operation is known from the contents of these mysterious buff boxes, which the P.M. alone opens, sent every day by Brigadier Menzies.[2] It is obviously some major air operation – possibly stimulated by our success at Taranto – but its exact destination the Air Ministry find it difficult to determine. In any case we all decided to take the necessary precautions and to sleep in the safest place.

One of the two best kept secrets of the war (the other was nuclear research) was our possession of the Enigma machine, provided with immense courage by the Poles, that enabled us to decipher at Bletchley first the signals of the German Luftwaffe and later those of the German navy and army as well. These deciphered signals were known in central Government circles by the code-word Boniface *and their circulation was so closely restricted that not even the Prime Minister's secretaries were supposed to see them,*

---

[1] Prominent and fashionable general practitioner. Neville Chamberlain's doctor.
[2] Brigadier Stewart Menzies, head of M.I.6 and referred to as "C".

although we soon became aware of their origin. Brigadier Menzies used to deliver them personally to No. 10, in ancient buff-coloured boxes marked V.R.I. and the Prime Minister himself kept the only key. Sometimes he would forget and show one of us a particularly interesting intercept; but that was later in the war.

Immense credit is due to the French cryptologists who worked on Enigma alongside the British until the collapse of France and never spoke a word to the Vichy Government. The Free French, who were notoriously liable to leak, were not told the secret; nor, until shortly before they came into the war, were the Americans who were thought to be only marginally better at keeping secrets. The Russians were provided with information but not informed of its source.

Although the first successful "decrypts" were produced early in 1940, it was not until the end of May – the time of Dunkirk – that it became possible to decipher the Luftwaffe signals within a short period of their interception. The German naval signals were mastered in the early summer of 1941 and those of the army in 1942.

A typical incident happened just before lunch today. The P.M. had invited Cross, the Minister of Shipping, to lunch and was showing him great affability. Suddenly he charged back into the room at No. 10, where I was telephoning, and whispered hoarsely in my ear, "What is the name of the Minister of Shipping?" "Cross," I whispered back furtively, because the Minister was standing in the doorway. "Oh," said the P.M. "Well, what's his Christian name?" Cross must have heard the whole conversation.

John Peck and I dined at Down Street Station ("the burrow", Winston calls it) where we fed excellently, and slept there in great comfort. The P.M. spent the night at the C.W.R. to await the MOONLIGHT SONATA, and became so impatient that he spent much of the time on the Air Ministry roof.

Friday, November 15th
London had a quiet night but Coventry was subjected to violent bombardment – possibly the First Movement of the Sonata, which may continue throughout the moon period.

The P.M. has sent a real snorter to Lampson, in Egypt, who in a private telegram to Eden stigmatised one of the decisions of the Cabinet as "crazy".

P. J. Grigg, whom I saw this morning, was loud in his condemnation of his master, Eden. "Complete junk," he called him.

Moyra Ponsonby lunched with me at Pruniers, and after eating oysters on high stools against the counter, we went together to Zara Mainwaring's wedding at the small and exceedingly attractive Chelsea Old Church.[1] There were few people in the church, as the service was at 1.45, but the bride looked radiantly lovely compared with her somewhat morose-looking bridegroom. With astonishing inappropriateness the last hymn chosen was "Through the Night of Doubt and Sorrow" – which before the wedding night seemed a strange choice.

Flushed with champagne I motored down to Camfield to stay the week-end with Audrey Paget.

Saturday, November 16th

Audrey and I rode for an hour and then I took her, lovely in her new M.T.C. uniform,[2] to Cambridge where I lunched in Hall at Trinity with the Master and Fellows on the occasion of the installation of George Trevelyan as Master. I sat between the Dean, Hollond, and the distinguished and charming Dr Adrian, a Nobel Prize winner and probably future Master of Trinity. The Vice Master, Winstanley, made a beautifully turned speech welcoming Trevelyan and the latter replied with a review of the history of the College and a sombre lament on the war and the future.

Monday, November 18th

When I got back to No. 10 Annexe the P.M. was downstairs looking at Intelligence Reports, putting red ink circles round the names of Greek towns and chortling as he thought of the discomfiture of the Italians. Then, after expressing to me his disgust with Admiral Somerville[3] who let twelve Hurricanes bound for Malta take off from an aircraft carrier too soon, so that eight came down in the sea and were lost, he went to bed and slept until the Cabinet was due.

Towards dinner-time, while I was desperately coping with mountainous papers on my desk, the P.M. appeared and, bidding me bring a torch, led me away to look at girders in the basement, intended to support the building. With astonishing agility he climbed over girders, balanced himself on their upturned edges, some five feet above ground, and leapt from one to another

---

[1] Entirely destroyed by a land-mine the following April.

[2] She was driving for the Polish officers as a member of the Military Transport Corps. "What is it like?" I asked her one day. "Well," she replied, "I have to say Yes, Sir, all day and No, Sir, all night."

[3] Admiral of the Fleet Sir James Somerville, commanding Force H in the Mediterranean. Later C. in C. of the British Fleet in the Far East.

without any sign of undue effort. Extraordinary in a man of almost sixty-six who never takes exercise of any sort.

Tuesday, November 19th
A morning of extreme gravity at Church House where the P.M.'s "Cuspidor" had vanished! The real gravity of the situation at present lies (i) in the submarine menace, which without the use of bases in Eire is a pressing problem; (ii) the continued failure to deal with the night raiders, which reduced Coventry to ashes despite its quantity of A.A. guns and the 100 Hurricanes which were sent up to defend it. It is vitally important to make the A.I. and the Beaufighters function efficiently or the Germans may be sensible enough to concentrate their attack on town after town and Sheffield, Birmingham, Bristol, Southampton may share Coventry's fate. The P.M. and the Air Ministry are cudgelling their brains.

The Greeks continue their astonishing successes and are now well established on Albanian soil. They are demanding fighter support and in a minor degree we are confronted with the same problem as during the Battle of France. However it looks as if the Greeks of today may avenge the submission of their ancestors to the military supremacy of Rome, and Byron did not die in vain.

I went with the P.M. to Down Street for the night and dined excellently, far beneath the level of the street, with Sir Ralph Wedgwood (brother of the egregious Colonel Jos.[1] and Chairman of the Railway Executive), Cole Deacon (the Secretary) and his wife. The L.P.T.B. do themselves well: caviar (almost unobtainable in these days of restricted imports), Perrier Jouet 1928, 1865 brandy and excellent cigars.

After dinner the Defence Committee, consisting of the Chiefs of Staff, the service Ministers and Pug Ismay, met to discuss the unending topic of air-reinforcements for the Middle East and the difficulty of supplying Greece without dangerously weakening Egypt. That megalomaniac Sir R. Keyes was sent for in the armoured car to attend part of the meeting, presumably connected with "special combined operations".

After midnight I took in a long list of places bombed in London tonight and news of a heavy attack on Birmingham with streams of bombers passing over the country on their way there. "Complete failure of all our methods," commented the P.M. grimly. "Four days have passed since Coventry and no remedy has been found."

---

[1] Colonel Josiah Wedgwood, outspoken Labour M.P. and friend of Churchill.

Wednesday, November 20th

I breakfasted very well at Down Street and then went to No. 10 where the P.M. worked in the Cabinet Room, demanding many things which were difficult to find and showing great reluctance to be photographed by Cecil Beaton who was waiting patiently outside.

The P.M. feels that as we can hardly give any other sort of help to Greece we should do all we can financially. In a minute to the Chancellor of the Exchequer: "I do hope that this will not be an occasion for the Treasury to do one of their regular departmental grimaces, which no doubt are very necessary in ordinary circumstances, but would be very much out of place now." Another acrobatic tour of the girders.

Thursday, November 21st

At about 6.00 p.m., Winston having left for Chequers with Seal, I went over to No. 10 to make up a little lost sleep. But David Margesson walked in to gossip and disturbed my slumbers. In common with most Tories – and with Brendan – he is cross with Bevin who made a speech yesterday condemning the private profit motive. Whether Bevin is right or wrong, he should not in a time of supposed national unity raise party issues. There would be terrible trouble if Conservative Ministers went about denouncing socialism and proclaimed their panaceas for the future. David is also annoyed by the continued attacks on him and points out that the critics of his rigid control of the party in the House forget that the British Constitution is run on a two-party system and eschews a multiplicity of political cliques. In actual fact since 1931 there had been many occasions when backbenchers had opposed the Government's policy – e.g. the India Bill and the National Defence Contribution – and David had often had to warn the Government to modify its intentions because of feeling in the House. David also said that people who blamed him for his appointments, always forgot the successful ones such as Andrew Duncan. The P.M. has taken up the cudgels on his behalf (as has Attlee!) and wrote a strong letter to Vyvian Adams[1] recently when the latter attacked David on the adjournment.

Friday, November 22nd

The Greek successes make us all feel better. Rosy prospects of Italy being driven out of Albania and suing for peace begin to

---

[1] Conservative M.P. for Leeds and Director of Home Intelligence at the Ministry of Information.

unfold, although still based on a good deal of wishful thinking. But the continued shipping losses (more today) are a canker which urgently needs the surgeon's knife. The night raiders are ravaging Birmingham tonight, but the threat they present is as nothing to that of the submarines.

Saturday, November 23rd

The economic position in Spain is so bad, largely owing to the incompetence and corruption of the Government and their mishandling of an American offer to supply a limited amount of food under guarantees, that Sam Hoare foresees a total collapse entailing the fall of Spain into Axis clutches. Being a born appeaser, Sam H. recommends large credits to Spain and the turning of a blind eye to some supplies from the U.S. percolating through to Germany and Italy.

The censorship reports on letters from France bear witness to the growing volume of support for this country, the rapacity of the Germans, and the striking contrast between the two zones. In unoccupied France there is dazed and listless acquiescence combined with veneration for Pétain. In occupied France there is a spirit of revolt and defiance, longing for an English victory, and a refusal to be either appeased or abashed by the Germans.

After dinner – as usual at the C.W.R., where I am becoming tired of tinned soup and sausages – I took over to the F.O. a Former Naval Person telegram urging Roosevelt to allow controlled amounts of food into Spain in order to avert a collapse. So Sam Hoare *has* been listened to! I drank a glass of rum with Bill Bentinck,[1] Fitzroy Maclean* and Edward Warner and listened to Bill B.'s comments on the P.M.'s "rococo style".

Sunday, November 24th

Yugoslavia seems to be on the brink of the abyss and Sir Ronald Campbell[2] has sent a request for permission to assure the Prince Regent that if he resists Axis pressure we will "supply him with all the help in our power". This of course is small, but we can at least guarantee to restore the country when victory has been won. Ronnie Campbell's proposed communication to the Yugoslavs was typical of the F.O. at its worst: long-winded, reserved and unilluminating.

[1] Victor Frederick William, last Duke of Portland. During the war he was Chairman of the Joint Intelligence Committee to the great satisfaction of the three service departments and of the Intelligence Services.

[2] Sir Ronald Ian Campbell, easily confused with Sir Ronald Hugh Campbell, Ambassador in Paris and in Lisbon.

The P.M. and Halifax both think that the prospects held out by the Greek triumph are great, but the P.M. in a minute to Halifax says: "I greatly fear a German attack through Bulgaria. Every effort should be made to firm up Turkey and Yugoslavia against this. The impending fortnight is momentous."

Lunched at White's where I met and conversed with Lord Lloyd, whose life as Colonial Secretary is much burdened by Jews and Arabs. He is a strong man and yet a curiously uncertain one – and a little bit inclined to whine. He expressed great hopes that the P.M. would be careful in his dealings with de Gaulle and Spears, who returned from Africa this week-end, and would at all costs not re-employ Spears.

Went to the American Embassy to get a telegram which had just arrived from the President (about the French fleet) and found Herschel Johnson, now Head of the U.S. Mission to the Court of St James, sitting alone sadly typing the telegram with one finger. Such is the effect of Sunday afternoon even in war-time. Pétain has promised to let the President know before the *Richelieu* or the *Jean Bart* are moved from Dakar and Casablanca into the Mediterranean.

A quiet night. London has been very little bombed for the last week in spite of clear weather. The Germans have apparently learned that they cannot break our spirits by fear and they are wisely concentrating their night efforts on industry. Bristol suffered tonight; Southampton last night.

Monday, November 25th
Rode in a fog at Richmond on an excellent old hunter of Louis Greig's.

The P.M. returned at lunch-time and busied himself with picking holes in a F.O. telegram giving the pros and cons of pushing Turkey into war. He demanded a report on the subject while he was having lunch – an unreasonable request which caused much perturbation to me and the F.O. Having settled the matter to everybody's satisfaction but the P.M.'s, Jim Bowker and I went off to lunch harmoniously at the Wyndham Club. Jim points out that the reasons for keeping Turkey out of the war are stronger than those for driving her in; but the whole question depends on whether we shall be able to bring her in at the psychological moment.

Spent much time running between No. 10 and the Annexe (the Marines, who act as messengers at the Annexe, move so slowly and with such dignity) in order to procure papers which the P.M. demanded.

Thursday, November 28th

I got back to No. 10 by 9.30 and was disgusted to find that in my absence (on forty-eight hours' leave) the *Daily Express* had published an article by Mr Ingersoll of the American paper *P.M.* who described his interview with Winston and added a large and inaccurate account of what I had told him. He described me as a "dark, slim man in the middle thirties"! and proceeded to put into my mouth the cheapest account of a largely fictitious conversation. Winston was, I believe, furious and I feel both ashamed and angry.

Lady Londonderry[1] has written a deplorable letter asking the P.M. to relax the restrictions in force in order to let relations and guests go over to Northern Ireland for the wedding of Derek Keppel[2] and Mairi Stewart. I wanted to send a damping reply to this outrageous request, but Mrs C., who can never resist an opportunity of taking the opposite view, insists on being polite and would get Winston to intervene with the Home Secretary if she could.[3]

Dined at the C.W.R., worked a little and then John Martin and I sat gossiping with Brendan at No. 10 until after midnight. Brendan was feeling in an iconoclastic mood and spent most of the time attacking Chamberlain for his failure to rearm the country. It seems to me that the blame must be sought in the theory of Government upheld by the Baldwin régime: namely that it is the function of democratic government to act in accordance with public opinion rather than to form public opinion. From 1931–38 the people of this country were against rearmament and pacifist in sentiment. The Government did not attempt to oppose the people's wishes; perhaps their fault lay in pandering to those wishes by statements tending to over-estimate our strength and readiness. We were lulled by Baldwinian assurances into a sleep from which it took more than the mere outbreak of war to disturb us.

Today John Peck, who lunched with me at the Wyndham, aptly described Randolph Churchill as "carrying on a perpetual preventive war".

Friday, November 29th

The P.M. having gone to Chequers yesterday to celebrate his sixty-sixth birthday and the christening of his grandson, life in

---

[1] Edith, Marchioness of Londonderry, wife of Churchill's cousin who had been Secretary of State for Air in Ramsay MacDonald's National Government. Travel to Northern Ireland was strictly limited to those on military or civilian business.

[2] Elder brother of my friend Cynthia Keppel.

[3] This would undoubtedly have led to a hostile parliamentary question.

London was quiet and there was time to dispose of much accumulated correspondence.

I had breakfast at No. 10, went for a walk in the cold sunlight, visited Coutts and broke my resolution to give up smoking Chesterfields.

Jim Bowker took me down to dine and spend the night in a charming Regency house he has taken on the Green at Kew (No. 71). Its rooms are beautifully proportioned, its view on both sides is of grass and trees, its external appearance is as pleasant as the interior. After dinner we settled down comfortably, Jim to finish some work, I to browse in a coarse but attractive book of Defoe's called *Moll Flanders*. But it was a noisy night, the worst since MOONLIGHT SONATA, and the sky was red with fires and flares. Periodically we slipped off our chairs and lay prone on the floor as a bomb came whistling down in the vicinity. Just as I had got into bed three fell together and shook the house to its foundations.

Saturday, November 30th

We got up in the dark, breakfasted and returned to London. The F.O. now begin work at 9.00 a.m. – two hours earlier than normal.

It is the P.M.'s birthday and the atmosphere is thick with messages and telegrams of congratulation.

The P.M. has at last completed his long letter to Roosevelt, on the lines suggested to him by Lothian. I was put to great exertions having the letter printed for the Cabinet, having it telegraphed to Washington and besieging the Treasury, Foreign Office and Admiralty with demands for comments.

The main focus of the letter is the serious shipping position. "The decision for 1941 lies upon the seas", is the predominant note.

The danger of Great Britain being destroyed by a swift overwhelming blow, has for the time being very greatly receded. In its place there is a long gradually maturing danger, less sudden and less spectacular, but equally deadly . . . It is in shipping, and the power to transport across the oceans, particularly the Atlantic Ocean, that in 1941 the crunch of the whole war will be found. If, on the other hand, we are able to move the necessary tonnage to and fro across salt water indefinitely, it may well be that the application of superior air power to the German homeland and the rising anger of the German and other Nazi-gripped populations, will bring the agony of civilisation to a merciful and glorious end. But let us not underrate the task . . .

He ends by a reference to the financial question which both sides know must soon be broached (Lothian has already said so indiscreetly to pressmen on his return to the U.S.). One extract, which the Chancellor of the Exchequer has now recommended should be altered, runs as follows:

While we will do our utmost, and shrink from no proper sacrifice to make payments across the Exchange, I should not myself be willing, even in the height of this struggle, to divest Great Britain of every conceivable saleable asset, so that after the victory was won with our blood and sweat, and civilisation saved and the time gained for the United States to be fully armed against all eventualities, we should stand stripped to the bone. Such a course would not be in the moral or economic interests of either of our countries.

He gives details of the assistance we need: merchant shipping, destroyers, American help in obtaining the Eire bases, use of American men-of-war to convoy American merchant vessels; and he ends a fifteen-page letter by saying: "If, as I take it, you are satisfied, Mr President, that the defeat of the Nazi and Fascist tyranny is a matter of high consequence to the people of the United States and to the Western Hemisphere, you will regard this letter not as an appeal for aid, but as a statement of the minimum action necessary to achieve our common purpose."

Lunched at the Wyndham with Charles Peake and Sammy Hood, who tell me Duff Cooper is very lazy. They are anxious that we should be rid of George Steward from No. 10 as being indolent and ineffective. I stood up for him then and afterwards with Brendan.

I dined at White's with Pat Hancock. We drank excellent burgundy, smoked huge cigars and became very mellow. Pat describes Dalton as capable but unlovable.

Note on an Intelligence Summary in which Leros was called by its Greek name: "General Ismay. Leros only is to be used in these reports. Also Constantinople instead of Istanbul."

12

Marking time

December 1940

Monday, December 2nd

I have never spent a more exacting day. Although the P.M. did not return from Chequers till after lunch (and was greeted with yet another letter of resignation from Lord Beaverbrook), I was confronted with the necessity of dealing with birthday greetings, the ordinary post, Parliamentary Questions (Miss Watson being ill) and the usual medley of current operational matters.

The P.M., Mrs C. and Eden dined at the Annexe, which is now coming into full use, and I acted as watchdog.

Am re-reading *Pride and Prejudice* at the behest of Pat Hancock who says my character has many of Mr Darcy's traits. Curiously enough Gay always used to say he was her ideal character in fiction, but I don't think Pat meant it in an altogether complimentary sense.

Tuesday, December 3rd

The P.M. began by saying he would work at the Annexe, where he had breakfast, and then, maddened by hammering, transferred the seat of Government to No. 10. As always when these last-minute changes of mind take place, there was much confusion and a good deal of ill-temper.

At 12.00 noon the Chiefs of Staff arrived to discuss operation WORKSHOP, by Sir Roger Keyes and his Commandos, in the Mediterranean. [The proposed seizure of the Italian island of Pantellaria.] While this was happening I read a curious document by Liddell-Hart who advocates peace with Germany since he believes we can only overthrow the Nazis by propaganda and cannot, in the military field, expect more than a stalemate, with exhaustion, disease and devastation on both sides, if indeed we are not defeated. This document, which has been privately circulated, is thought by the Admiralty to show traces of enemy propaganda and to be not spontaneous. The First Lord has written on it: "Probably no technical correspondent has more responsibility than Liddell-Hart for the accepted military theories propagated before the war and which were so disproved in the Battle of France. I should have thought he would have preferred to hide his head rather than produce still yet another theory as pregnant with defeat as his former theories, which are now proved heresies."

Personally, although preferring anything to the triumph of Nazi principles, which I believe a compromise peace would imply, I cannot help shuddering at the picture which Liddell-Hart presents to the imagination and which may not be far from the truth: Western Europe racked by warfare and economic hardship; the legacy of centuries, in art and culture, swept away; the health of the nation dangerously impaired by malnutrition, nervous strain and epidemics; Russia and possibly the U.S. profiting from our exhaustion; and at the end of it all compromise or a Pyrrhic victory. A terrible glimpse of the future; and yet I know we should be wrong to hesitate, because so great a moral question is at issue. In one thing I believe Liddell-Hart may be right: he says that the fear of sharing Napoleon's fate must embolden Hitler himself, and the belief, based on much that we say over here, in a worse-than-Versailles if they are defeated must encourage the Germans to resist desperately. I am convinced, despite all that Winston says, that a firm but just declaration of peace aims would have a powerful psychological effect in our favour.

Before lunch I listened to a little monologue by the P.M., addressed to the Chiefs of Staff, on the means of helping Greece, by preparing advanced air bases, and on the desirability of putting severe economic pressure on Ireland in order to make her lend us the bases we so badly need. As regards Greece, Sir John Dill said: "What is Germany doing?" "They are preparing something terrible," said the P.M. He pointed out how carefully the attack on Poland had been planned, how Mussolini had been drawn into war by the sight of the overwhelming strength deployed against France, and how doubtful Pétain now is, having presumably been told something of Germany's might, about our ability to withstand the attack that is to come.

Back at No. 10 I worked the epidiascope in the Cabinet Room and showed the P.M. and Sir R. Keyes large-scale photographs of the objective of OPERATION WORKSHOP.

The P.M.'s comment on the First Lord's note about Liddell-

Hart is: "It is out of date and he seems more a candidate for a mental home than for more serious action."

The P.M. changed his mind at least eight times as to whether he would sleep and dine at No. 10 or at the Annexe and three times as to what time he would see Dr Dalton (whom he dislikes).

At dinner he conspired with Cranborne, Rob Hudson, Kingsley Wood and Oliver Lyttelton about the means of bringing pressure to bear on Ireland. Refusal to buy her food, to lend her our shipping or to pay her our present subsidies seem calculated to bring De Valera to his knees in a very short time. On the other hand the Irish are an explosive race and economic coercion might mean trouble. But the issues at stake justify risks.

Wednesday, December 4th

In speaking to the C.A.S. the P.M. demanded that in view of the Germans' systematic attack on each of our towns in turn, we should reconsider a real mass-scale attack on one German town followed by the publication of a list of German towns which we shall duly devastate if the Germans continue their present policy against us.

My time has been much occupied with the vexed question whether the church bells should be rung on Christmas Day.[1] The P.M. was disposed to say yes in reply to a Parliamentary Question, but after much discussion the C. in C., Home Forces, has produced such overwhelming arguments against it that the P.M. has agreed to refuse. I was in a position to get the Question answered affirmatively before the contrary arguments could be marshalled, and I all but did so; but then the thought of the responsibility that would be mine if any disaster occurred on Christmas Day made me pause.

After lunch David Margesson asked me whether Beaverbrook had withdrawn his resignation. We both agreed it was time he went; he has done his job. "Who would you suggest putting in his place? Moore-Brabazon?" I asked. "Stafford Cripps", was the astonishing reply from the Tory Chief Whip. David pointed out that Stafford Cripps' outstanding ability was being wasted in Moscow, where little can be done as is now lamentably clear, whereas at home Cripps would not only be a great asset as a Minister but also a counter-weight to Bevin in the Labour Party. Bevin is inclined to throw his weight about too much.

I remarked to David on the excellence of Winston's latest long

[1] In the preceding summer it had been decreed that church bells were only to be rung as a signal of invasion.

letter to the President. David answered that he wished W. were as great an administrator as he is leader, orator and writer. The criticism is a fair one.

"This place," said the Prime Minister, as he entered the Annexe after the evening Cabinet, "is too hot. Tell them to turn off the central heating." And the same man complained, on the hottest of June nights at Admiralty House, because his fire had not been lit!

Thursday, December 5th
At 8.30, as soon as it was light, I mounted one of Louis Greig's horses and galloped round Richmond Park, relieving my lungs of nights of air-conditioning and glorying in the cold sunrise.

Cripps, whose telegrams are always to the point and never long-winded like some Ambassadors, says in speaking of Anglo-Soviet relations: "While I do not advocate impatience or irritation I disagree that we should at present appear helpful or forthcoming. Having received no encouragement whatever as regards either our political or our commercial proposals, we should at all costs avoid the appearance of running after the Soviet Government (which would only be interpreted as weakness) and should await advances from them." Seldom do left-wing ideologists take so realistic a view. Cripps, I feel sure, will go far, whether Right or Left are in control. He is much the ablest man in the Labour Party.

After dinner John Peck and I sat down to the three-hour task of sticking Lord Lothian's comments on the P.M.'s letter to Roosevelt on pieces of paper next to the P.M.'s original text. It was a complicated and laborious job but we thought we did it rather skilfully.

Friday, December 6th
The P.M. was not at all gracious about our handiwork and complained that we had had parts of the text retyped instead of sticking in every unamended word of the print. However his irritability was due to the fact that he did not care for many of Lothian's alterations and he described the whole thing as a "bloody business".

Lunched with Arthur Rucker. We talked of old times at No. 10 and the great differences that have taken place. Arthur said he chiefly remembered the unimportant incidents such as when he stole my umbrella; I said that keeping a diary helped one to remember the more important events. "A very dangerous document," commented Arthur. And I suppose this one is.

As we walked back we met P. J. Grigg, who after running down his Secretary of State as usual, said that the only time he had any real power was when he was Private Secretary (to Winston as Chancellor of the Exchequer).

Monday, December 9th
Motored from Hinchingbrooke back to London, where the great excitement is the beginning of our offensive against the Italian army in Egypt. The P.M., who returned from Chequers after lunch with a cold in the head, said to the C.I.G.S. on the telephone: "So we shan't have to make use of General Papagos[1] after all!" implying that at last our generals are living up to the Greek example of boldness and initiative.

Tuesday, December 10th
The news from North Africa is increasingly good. Though the operation is a small one, it shows the inability of the Italians to stand up to attack – if indeed any proof were required.

Wednesday, December 11th
The P.M. had been going down to Harrow today, with all the Old Harrovian members of the Government, to hear School Songs. However his cold is heavier and the trip had to be postponed.

In the Censorship Report (which incidentally shows a certain lower-class opinion, apparently worked on by propaganda, that the war is being engineered for financial and upper-class interests), I marked a number of passages which I thought particularly interesting and I noticed that the P.M. marked in red ink one phrase quoted from a letter: "It's difficult to think politically, or socially, in classes any more . . . *there's a kind of warmth pervading England.*" An extract that amused me was from a letter written by an East End Jew:

> It is terrible here at night – every night. Lord God, what have we done to deserve it? Death rains from the Clouds . . . Now, there is abundance of food which, though dear, we could well pay for; (never was the shop so profitable; people pay what you ask without question) but the raids, the machine-gunning, it is murder. The English are not so highly strung as we. They do not seem to mind until they actually see some of their own family killed in front of their noses. Then, instead of being frightened or praying, they say: 'Damn those bloody bastards'.

---

[1] Commander in Chief of the Greek army in its outstanding success against the Italian aggressors.

Just before dinner the P.M. rang up the King to tell him the glad news that Sidi Barrani had fallen. "My humble congratulations to you, Sir, on a great British victory – a great Imperial victory."

It is the first time since war began that we have really been able to make use of the word victory.

One of the P.M.'s first reactions – a curious one – was to ask to see and peruse the two books General Wavell has written.

Thursday, December 12th

At Church House the P.M. made a subdued but very welcome statement on the North African operations.

Drove myself down to Chequers in my own car and arrived there an hour before the P.M. I had tea in the White Parlour with Mary, who has an adorable sheepdog puppy and who was full of charm and gossip. She was also very anxious to read my diary but was with difficulty restrained.

Lord Lothian died suddenly in Washington; a tragic blow to our relations with the United States where his ability was so marked and his drive so fruitful.

Mrs Churchill having a migraine, Mary and I dined alone with the P.M. He began by saying he was going to read his book (Boswell's *Tour to the Hebrides*) – "you children can talk" – but the tastelessness of the soup so excited his frenzy that he rushed out of the room to harangue the cook and returned to give a disquisition on the inadequacy of the food at Chequers and the fact that ability to make good soup is the test of a cook. Having mastered his indignation he began to lament the death of Lothian and to demand who he should put in his place. He would like to try L.G. if he could trust him. I suggested Cranborne or Vansittart. He had thought of both and considered Cranborne particularly suitable. But as the evening wore on he "sweetened to the idea of L.G.", as he put it, saying that his knowledge of munitions problems and his fiery personality marked him out. He thought L.G. would be willing to serve and in order to sweeten the pill of serving under Halifax (which I suggested would be an obstacle from L.G.'s point of view) he would make him a member of the War Cabinet. He believed L.G. would be loyal to him; if not he could always sack him. The suitability of Cranborne, on which he had waxed eloquent, slowly receded into the background, and when I suggested that Cripps was being wasted in Russia, he replied that he was a lunatic in a country of lunatics and it would be a pity to move him.

Mary left us and I had a long tête-à-tête with Winston over the brandy. He grew very expansive, elated by the thought of our successes, continually growing in size, in North Africa. He spoke of the dignity of the Italians, who possessed every requisite for Empire except courage, and of the terrible miscalculation they had made about us. We had had a wonderful escape in these last months and it was now difficult to remember what we had been through.

Talking of the future he sketched the European Confederations that would have to be formed ("with their Diets of Worms") and shuddered as he thought of the intricate currency problems, etc. He did not understand such things and he would be out of it. He did not wish to lead a party struggle or a class struggle against the Labour leaders who were now serving him so well. He would retire to Chartwell and write a book on the war, which he already had mapped out in his mind chapter by chapter. This was the moment for him; he was determined not to prolong his career into the period of reconstruction. I said I thought he would be demanded by the people; there was no other leader. (This was not just Boswellian; there is not at present any man of the right calibre, nor any sign of one on the horizon.)

After a few slashes at Baldwin for not making better use of the sanctions period against Italy, he moved from the dining-room, with his multi-coloured dressing-gown over his siren-suit, rang up Gwylym Lloyd George to sound him about his father, and then stood beaming in front of the fire in the Great Hall. He asked if I had heard L.G. during the debate in which the Chamberlain Government fell. I said I had, and deplored Chamberlain's mistake in saying "I have my friends" to the hostile minority in the House. The P.M. said it had been a wonderful opportunity for him: the stars in their courses had fought on his side. He had been able to defend his chief to the utmost and only to win esteem and support in so doing. No one could say he had been disloyal or had intrigued against Chamberlain – "and I never have done that sort of thing".

Remarking that tomorrow was Friday, 13th, I said that last year, on Friday, November 13th, the B.B.C. had gloated over the date as having been a bad one for German submarines. Four hours later the *Royal Oak* was sunk. "I wrote that communiqué," replied Winston laconically. I subsided.

After some observations on the utility of his system of personal minutes to Ministers, and some praise by me of the effectiveness of "Action this Day", the P.M. retired into the Hawtrey room and dictated telegrams to the Dominions and the U.S. To bed at 1.20 a.m.

Friday, December 13th

When the P.M. spoke to Halifax about the Washington appointment, H. suggested Eden (who would not take it) and then Lord Dudley, but seemed quite to approve of L.G.

The Chief of the Air Staff spoke about ABIGAIL, an operation whereby we shall single out a German town, as they singled out Coventry, and destroy it, at the same time allowing a list of German towns destined for a similar fate to become known. The moral scruples of the Cabinet on this subject have been overcome.

There was a question, much discussed on the telephone, whether the Duke of Devonshire[1] was to be given the Garter. The P.M. kept on repeating that he was not bad as Dukes go and that anyway there was "no damned merit about it".

General de Gaulle and Major Morton came to lunch. The P.M. held forth in his execrable but expressive French. There was a good deal of purring over Sidi Barrani, which de G. said would make an excellent name for the battle. "No," said the P.M., "it should be called the Battle of Libya." There was an interlude while we talked about eating octopuses, as the Italians do, and as I have done in Sicily; then we got on to the serious topic of war. What were the Germans going to do? De Gaulle said, as Winston said last night, that Spain seemed the obvious objective, and through Spain Africa. But the Spanish people, *"fier et misérable"*, might well resist.

De Gaulle said he thought we should make more of the fact that we stood alone, *"le champion du monde"* against Hitler, and if we were accepted as such all our actions would be excused; Oran would seem natural, merely because the world was at stake. Winston said he was inclined to lay stress on the fact that we were fighting the Nazis rather than Germany, even though many an Englishman now had murderous thoughts towards the whole German race. "But," objected de Gaulle, "we fought the last war against the Hohenzollerns and German militarism; we crushed them both; and then came Hitler – *et toujours le militarisme allemand*. So there was something to be said for those who blamed the Germans as a whole."

De Gaulle said that Laval hated this country, but would try and keep out of war. Darlan, on the other hand, might well take an opportunity to bring in the French fleet against us: *"La France ne marchera pas, mais la flotte – peut-être."*

[1] Edward, 10th Duke of Devonshire, successively Under Secretary for the Dominions, India and the Colonies under Chamberlain and Churchill. At this time the Garter and the Thistle were still bestowed on the recommendation of the Prime Minister, a practice Mr Attlee renounced in 1945.

The conversation then turned to the relationship of de Gaulle and Spears, which is correct though not cordial (de G. finds S. intelligent but egotistic and hampering because of his unpopularity in the War Office, etc.). After lunch Ismay arrived and a future operation of the Free French forces was discussed. I went for a long solitary walk through the woods and up the hills, almost killing myself by going too fast up a steep hill (it is shattering to be in such a bad state of training – and I have visions of joining one of the Commandos!).

I had tea with Mary and some Coldstream officers and then the P.M. worked till dinner-time. We wanted news from the War Office ("that House of Shame", Pug calls it): the C.I.G.S. had gone off for ten days' leave and the V.C.I.G.S., in charge of the W.O., was found to know less up-to-date news than anyone else in the building. People condemn the Civil Servants; but what of the serving officers!

The V.C.N.S. (Tom Phillips) and Prof. came to dinner. We began with talk of the Sidi Barrani operation, COMPASS as it was called, the best-kept secret of the war. The P.M. said he had been living on hopes of it for five weeks and had been terrified some sandstorm would give the men on the spot a chance to back out. It had been well planned and brilliantly executed, unlike Narvik which of all the fiascos for which he had had any responsibility had been the worst – except for Dakar.

What a monstrous thing, exclaimed the P.M., that Lothian should not have allowed a doctor to be called ("I had at last come to like Philip, after years of prejudice"). "Is anyone here a Christian Scientist?" "Well," said Prof., "I am if you divide the two words – a Christian and a Scientist." "I am willing to admit you may have some claim to be the latter." "Which is the only one of the two on which you have any qualifications to judge."

The P.M. reverted, in some detail, to his ideas for the future. We had got to admit that Germany was going to remain in the European family. "Germany existed before the Gestapo." When we had won he visualised five great European nations: England, France, Italy, Spain and Prussia. In addition there would be four confederations: the Northern, with its capital at The Hague; the Mitteleuropa, with its capital at Warsaw or Prague; the Danubian, consisting of Bavaria, Württemberg, Austria, Hungary, etc., with its capital at Vienna; and the Balkan with Turkey at its head and Constantinople as its capital. These nine powers would meet in a Council of Europe, which would have a supreme judiciary and a Supreme Economic Council to settle currency questions, etc. Each power would contribute an air cohort – Prussia included – and boys of sixteen would be selected for it. Once enrolled they would be under no national jurisdiction, but they would never be obliged to co-operate in an attack on their own country. All air forces, military and civil, would be internationalised. As regards armies, every power would be allowed its own militia, because Democracy must be based on a people's army and not left to oligarchs or Secret Police. Prussia alone would, for a hundred years, be denied all armaments beyond her air contingent. The Council would be unrestricted in its methods of dealing with a Power condemned by the remainder in Council.

The English speaking world would be apart from this, but closely connected with it, and it alone would control the seas, as the reward of victory. It would be bound by covenant to respect the trading and colonial rights of all peoples, and England and America would have exactly equal navies. Russia would fit into an Eastern re-organisation, and the whole problem of Asia would have to be faced. But as far as Europe was concerned, only by such a system of Confederations could the small powers continue to exist and we must at all costs avoid the old mistake of "Balkanising" Europe.

There would be no war debts, no reparations and no demands on Prussia. Certain territories might have to be ceded and certain exchanges of population, on the lines of that so successfully effected by Greece and Turkey, would have to take place. But there should be no pariahs and Prussia, though unarmed, would be secured by the guarantee of the Council of Europe. Only the Nazis, the murderers of June 30th, 1934,[1] and the Gestapo would be made to suffer for their misdeeds.

But all this was a thing of the still distant future: we might have to give it one hundred years to work. At present he could utter no such ideals when every cottage in Europe was calling for German blood and when the English themselves were demanding that all Germans should be massacred or castrated.

We all liked this "Grand Design", powerfully expounded as it was and I very much hope that Winston may live to lay its foundations. My only comments, unvoiced, were, "Supposing the members of the European Council divided themselves into axes or armed camps? War would still be possible, even with national militias, and the international air contingents could easily fly their machines home – even though they had become *dépaysé* at sixteen.

---

[1] The Night of the Long Knives when Hitler had the S.A. (brown-shirt) leaders and his predecessor as Chancellor, General Schleicher, murdered by black-uniformed S.S.

Moreover, would the mere disarmament of Prussia render impotent the traditions of force and ruthlessness in which generations have been reared or eradicate the evil teaching impregnated by Nazism in the minds of young Germans?" Whatever Winston would have replied, his scheme is a noble and lofty one, worthy of his fine imagination and his sensitiveness to the lessons history has taught. His reverence for tradition (which he would never allow to warp his judgment of what is expedient) is shown in his statement that Spain should remain a separate unit because of the individuality with which her past, as well as her geographical position, invests her.

We ended dinner by discussing a projected German operation, which seems aimed either at Ireland or Spain. The P.M. thinks Spain; he would go that way if he were Hitler. We discussed our strategy either in the event of Spain resisting or allowing German troops to pass.

The P.M. was much incensed by a request of Seal's that all the staff at No. 10 should be allowed a week's Christmas leave. He said that we should all go on working as usual with the exception of one and a half hours off for divine service! Continuity of work never harmed anyone.

A late despatch rider brought telegrams from Tangier announcing the intention of the Spanish Government to take over the International Zone. This together with their allowing two damaged Italian submarines to escape from Tangier has infuriated H.M.G. and the F.O. have drafted a – for them – severe telegram threatening not to allow the Spaniards the cargoes of wheat they want and without which Spain, "*fier et misérable*", will starve.

The P.M. thinks this a sign of big things to come and believes the projected German operation (called FELIX), about which we know, will be in Spain. This may entail a drastic re-organisation of four or five of our own operations (BRISK, SHRAPNEL, EXCESS, CHALLENGE, etc.) which are pending, as he considers it would be undesirable to have our forces and our transports "sprawled" about the world at such a moment.

The F.O. had foolishly kept no copy of their telegram and I had laboriously to dictate it back to the Resident Clerk (who failed to produce a shorthand typist) a task which took me until nearly 3.00 a.m.

Saturday, December 14th
At about 6.00 a.m. Nelson woke me by climbing on to my bed and preparing to go to sleep on my feet. I am a little suspicious of black cats: they always seem to frequent me on the eve of great events.

The Treasury Cat (or "Munich Mouser" as the Churchills call him) very seldom paid me any attention, but on two or three occasions I found him curled up on my blotting pad at No. 10: once at the time of the Norwegian crisis and once at the worst moment of the Battle of France. But perhaps Nelson, on the eve of a Spanish crisis, may portend another Trafalgar.

The P.M. was amusing last night about the North African campaign. He said we had taken the right course: we had risked sending troops and material to Egypt when still under the threat of invasion at home, and we had sent substantial air assistance to Greece in spite of the fact that we were preparing for a "Spring of the Lion" in North Africa. But if events had taken a different course, as they might have, what would history have said? He quoted dramatically from a mythical history book of the future, denouncing the criminal gambler who sent overseas the divisions which might have turned the scale against the German invasion at home, or the vacillators who sent to Greece the aeroplanes which could have turned the North African fiasco into a success. It was a good commentary on my favourite, and boring, thesis about the ease of being wise after the event.

Pound, Portal and Haining (the V.C.I.G.S.) arrived at 11.00 and went into conference with the P.M., Ismay and Phillips until lunch-time. Sir Roger Keyes arrived late and Lord Halifax, who thought we were at Ditchley and went there by mistake (the fault being the P.M.'s) only reached Chequers at the end of lunch. There was the usual chortling over our North African exploits and the effect they would have on our prestige in the world. "We have now reached the stage," said Phillips, "where we shall suddenly find we have got many more friends than we thought." The P.M. enjoys mocking the Italians, whose civilisation and achievements he greatly admires but of whom he finds it easy and irresistible to make fun.

I found Haining very agreeable and informative on the methods of obtaining information from enemy prisoners and occupied territories. Apparently as far as the latter is concerned we worked on a system with the French, and their defection left a gap in our organisation.

After lunch the conference about Tangier and Spain continued in the Hawtrey room. I drove off through the blizzard to Ditchley, taking with me one of the telephone girls, a nice creature whose attitude to life was largely summed up in the fact that the thing she chiefly admired in Chester was the new café. Her husband was in the balloon barrage and she said military discipline had taken something away from his character which could never be replaced.

Ditchley is a lovely house and still kept up in pre-war style. On arrival, about an hour before the P.M., I found Ronnie Tree and his very attractive wife, Mrs Churchill, Lady Cranborne and Brendan. General Alexander,[1] the new C. in C., Southern Command, an unusually delightful person, arrived to dine and sleep. The P.M. spent most of the time before dinner showing him the Prof.'s albums, while I sat in my Louis Quinze office and drank an Old Fashioned cocktail.

The Trees, who are very hospitable, put the house entirely at the P.M.'s disposal. They are of course delighted to have him, but it must be something of a trial when he arrives with such a vast following.

There was a large dinner party, at which I sat between the Duchess of Marlborough and Ronnie Tree, with both of whom I had very pleasant conversations. After dinner there was a film: Charlie Chaplin's *The Great Dictator* which has not yet been released in this country and which everyone has been eagerly awaiting. Mary Rose Fitzroy[2] and Dinah Brand,[3] who are living here but have been turned out for the week-end, came over for the film and stayed to talk and eat afterwards. That affected marine, Alastair Forbes, and a young Australian called Booth, handsome but rough, to whom I gathered Dinah Brand is engaged, were also of the party.

The film, at which we all laughed a great deal – Mary Rose moaning pitifully with excessive mirth – being over, Winston dictated to me a short telegram to Roosevelt, asking whether L.G. would be acceptable as Ambassador, and went to bed early. He twice complimented me on my "beautiful handwriting", which he esteems far beyond its real merits. Roger Keyes, who has been scheming to come to Ditchley for the last two days, rang up and asked point blank. Winston, who is at long last becoming bored with his importunity, refused to speak to him and sent a snubbing answer through me.

Sunday, December 15th
I arose in a leisurely way in my luxurious bedroom, had breakfast and settled down to work with the December sun streaming in through the windows.

General Wavell's comments on past and future operations in

---

[1] Later Field Marshal Earl Alexander of Tunis.*
[2] Sister of John, Duke of Grafton, my contemporary at Harrow and Cambridge. She married Francis Williams.
[3] Delightful daughter of the Hon. Robert Brand, the Treasury adviser. Afterwards Mrs Christopher Bridge.

North Africa are now beginning to arrive. He says: "Rome will not be unbuilt in a day, but hope recent and future events will shake foundations." Meanwhile we heard last night that Laval has been dismissed and Flandin, who is a little better, put in his place. Also communications with Switzerland have been cut; the last message to reach New York was: "Something big is coming." The P.M. inclines to think this means, not an invasion of Switzerland (which would be pointless) but the preliminaries of an operation against Spain.

Comes a telegram from South Africa saying that Smuts, impressed by the German military potential, thinks our propaganda in the U.S. must be more aggressive and that we must make a supreme effort to bring in America as a belligerent. The military and air power of the British Commonwealth, together with the economic blockade, will be insufficient to bring about Germany's fall even in 1942.

The interminable wrangle between the M.A.P. and the Air Ministry goes on, like The Brook, for ever. But Winston, in a minute this morning to Beaverbrook, says: "I am definitely of the opinion that it is more in the public interest that there should be sharp criticism and counter-criticism between the two departments than that they should be handing each other out ceremonious bouquets."

Beaverbrook is also in trouble from some quarters about the activities of his newspapers which have attacked certain Ministers. He replies: "I do not agree with Low.[1] I have rarely done so. I do not interfere with Low. I have never done so." He goes on to say that he would be much more useful outside the Government and earnestly wishes to resign, and at the end: "The aircraft industry is in good shape. The best work I have done so far is dispersal. That is a policy I adopted in the face of opposition and amidst turmoil and abuse. The little bit of credit I will get on your day of victory will be due to the same policy of dispersal." Result: the usual soothing and appreciative reply from the P.M. who says: "Anyhow, let us keep plodding on together and see how things look in another year. I think they will look much better. Yours ever, W."

At lunch I sat between Richard Law,[2] who is staying here, and the officer commanding the guard. Towards the end Winston and Lord Cranborne, who arrived this morning, had a discussion about the sanctions period and agreed in denouncing Baldwin's thesis

---

[1] The *Evening Standard* cartoonist.
[2] Parliamentary Under Secretary, and later Minister of State, in the Foreign Office. A son of the former Prime Minister, Bonar Law. He was briefly Minister of Education in 1945.

that we could exert pressure no further than it might be done with safety.

It was suggested that the Duke of Aosta,[1] now Viceroy of Abyssinia, might be used to head a movement against Mussolini. "Yes," said Winston, "he would desert his tired and about-to-be-emasculated army, enter a sumptuous aeroplane and return to restore the soul of Italy to Democracy!" Mr Justice Singleton,[2] who was lunching, thought that Mussolini might save his position by changing his régime. Winston said that he gave the blighter the credit for being a brave man who would go down with his ship, and, as far as changing his policy was concerned, "I believe it is not in his character; I am sure it is not in his reach."

After lunch the P.M. went off to Blenheim with Lady Cranborne, and I went for a walk with Ronnie Tree, his wife and Richard Law. I changed my mind about Ronnie Tree, whom I had always looked upon as the epitome of an idle rich Tory M.P. I found him interesting and sensible in his views of the Conservative future: there must be a new Tory Democracy, prepared to sacrifice wealth and vested interest, radical but sensible. In Ronnie Tree's view, the indispensable pre-requisites were to reform the central office, pay candidates' expenses – and get rid of the Chief Whip. I agreed in all but the last. He thought Lloyd George too old for Washington, and I agree. We have the examples of Pétain and Hindenburg to warn us. Cranborne, he considered, would be ideal: a man who was already looking ahead to the 1950s, he would be able to make the speeches which American opinion would appreciate.

We reached the front door just as the P.M. and Lady Cranborne returned from Blenheim. The P.M. went straight to bed, to sleep and to work, while I had tea and talked with the charming and modest Lady Cranborne.

Sir R. Keyes, in spite of all injunctions, arrived! He was greeted by an indignant P.M. who, however, agreed to talk to him. His whole aim is to undo the decisions reached at yesterday's conferences, namely that operations WORKSHOP and EXCESS, in which he was to have taken part, should be postponed in view of the threat of developments in Spain or elsewhere. We were all thunderstruck by his audacity: he carries the Zeebrugge spirit too far into private life.

Eden arrived for the night and made himself extremely affable.

---

[1] Cousin of the King of Italy and Commander of the Italian army in Abyssinia.
[2] Judge of the High Court and previously an M.P. Commissioned by Churchill to examine all the evidence available about the strength of the German air forces.

Ronnie Tree thinks him a future P.M., but I feel that many as are his qualities, they are not very solid.

At dinner Richard Law said to me that the secret of Hitler's power was his demand for sacrifice. The P.M. understood this and his own speeches were brilliant in this respect, but Bevin thought that he could buoy people up by promising them higher wages and better times. He was wrong.

We saw *Gone with the Wind* which lasted till 2.00 a.m. I thought the photography superb. Scarlett reminded me a little bit of Audrey. The P.M. said he was "pulverised by the strength of their feelings and emotions".

After some conversation between the P.M. and Eden about N. Africa I got to bed at 3.00 a.m.; but the P.M., throwing himself on a chair in his bedroom, collapsed between the chair and the stool, ending in a most absurd position on the floor with his feet in the air. Having no false dignity, he treated it as a complete joke and repeated several times, "A real Charlie Chaplin!"

Monday, December 16th

When the P.M.'s party had left Ditchley for London, I said goodbye to Mrs Tree and drove to Ardley. David was just home, after an agonising ordeal on the *Chevreuil* off the coast of Scotland where it seemed at one time as if they were done for. He feels very bitter about the French.

Tuesday, December 17th

In the morning the sun shone brilliantly and while Ann, who is lazy, stayed behind, David, Joan and I walked over to Middleton, visited Lady Jersey and went on to have a drink with Diane Maxwell.[1]

In the afternoon we motored over to Stene to see the Chapel built by Nathaniel, Lord Crewe, Bishop of Oxford and of Durham. The chapel contains the only marble altar in the Church of England, but its real glory are the tombs of the Crewe family, exquisitely sculptured in marble and retaining their original colouring. The inscriptions are most pleasing. Thus of Temperance Crewe, wife of the Speaker, Sir Thomas, it is written:

Coniunx Casta, Parens felix, Matrona pudica;
Sara viro, mundo Martha, Maria Deo.

---

[1] Only daughter of Sir Austen Chamberlain, married to Colonel Terence Maxwell, soldier, banker and industrialist.

And in the English inscription she is described as a woman

> who with her lott was well contented,
> who lived desyred and dyed lamented.

Little of the episcopal palace remains, but what does forms a very charming country house which David much covets.

Wednesday, December 18th
Motored to London in ice and fog.

After lunch the visit to Harrow, which I had done much to make possible, came off. The P.M. drove down with Mrs Churchill; I with David Margesson; and Amery, Moore Brabazon, Geoffrey Lloyd[1] and Jack Churchill also came. If Sir Donald Somervell, the Attorney General, had not been prevented from coming, all the Old Harrovian members of the administration would have been present.

The school sang well in spite of its depleted numbers, and Winston thoroughly enjoyed himself. An extra verse had been inserted into "Stet Fortuna Domus" in his honour and he asked for two extra songs, "Giants" and "Boy". He sang lustily, as did we all, and seemed to remember most of the words without referring to the book. Before "Forty Years On" he made a brilliant impromptu speech to the school, saying how much Harrow Songs had meant to him, what an inspiration they had been at certain stages of his life, and pointing out that although Hitler claimed the Adolf Hitler Schools had shown their superiority to Eton, he had forgotten Harrow! He then said that after the war the advantages of the Public Schools must be extended to the whole country, on a broader and better basis. He was wildly applauded.

When we got back to No. 10 the P.M. saw Halifax and offered him the Ambassadorship to Washington, L.G. having refused on grounds of age. David Margesson told me in the car on the way to Harrow that Eden would go to the Foreign Office and perhaps Amery to the War Office. David thinks Rab Butler should be given his chance and sent to the India Office.

Friday, December 20th
Over to the Annexe at 8.30. The P.M. gave me a manuscript letter he wished sent to Halifax. It appears that Halifax left the decision about Washington in the P.M.'s hands and the P.M. has decided he shall go. Probably Sir Gerald Campbell will be made Minister and thus H. will be able to return frequently to this country where he will still be a member of the War Cabinet.

[1] Later Lord Geoffrey-Lloyd.*

Before lunch the P.M. discoursed to me on the difficulty of his interview with Halifax, who told him yesterday that both his judgment and his inclination were against going to Washington. But, said the P.M., he would never live down the reputation for appeasement which he and the F.O. had won themselves here. He had no future in this country. On the other hand he had a glorious opportunity in America; because unless the U.S. came into the war we could not win, or at least we could not win a really satisfactory peace. If Halifax succeeded in his mission over there, he would come home on the crest of the wave. The P.M.'s judgment has, I think, been considerably influenced by the monthly Censorship Reports which show Halifax to be unpopular over here and to have inherited the criticism that was Chamberlain's.

The P.M. lunched with Beaverbrook and L.G. and upset everybody very much by appearing to listen to the former's wild remarks about the proposed Cabinet reshuffle (consequent on Halifax's appointment) and to a suggestion that L.G. should enter the Government in some agricultural capacity, in which he would certainly quarrel with Rob Hudson.

Everyone waited for the departure to Chequers, but when all was ready the P.M. suddenly went off to his bedroom and slept – keeping us all hanging about for hours. I talked to David Margesson who told me that if he had "carried bigger guns" he would so much have liked to go to Washington. He had been pressed to go to the War Office, but had refused because he did not think himself suitable for the job. The P.M.'s present intention was that he should go to the Dominions Office, where his lack of departmental experience – he had been in the Whip's office since 1924 – would not matter so much. Actually I think his great organising capacity, about which Gay and Jan wax eloquent to the disparagement of all his other qualities, might be very advantageous in the proverbially incompetent War Office.

Saturday, December 21st
Quiet reigned.

Among the papers returning from Chequers was a letter offering a peerage to Lord Hugh Cecil[1] "to repel the onset of the Adolf

---

[1] Son of the 3rd Marquess of Salisbury, Prime Minister at the turn of the century. Best man at Churchill's wedding and leader of the rebel "Hughligans" in the Commons, a group which had included Churchill. Devout Churchman and prominent member of the Church Assembly. Became Provost of Eton in 1936 though he had hated his own schooldays there and disliked schoolboys.

The "Hughligans" were a group of four young Tory M.P.s who frequently attacked their own Government, of which A. J. Balfour was Prime Minister, shortly after the turn of the century.

Hitler Schools, to sustain the aristocratic morale, and to chide the bishops when they err; and now that I read in the newspapers that the Eton flogging block is destroyed by enemy action, you may have more leisure and strength. Anyhow I should like to see a brother Hughligan in the legislature . . ."

In a note to Lord Halifax: "We have not had anything from the U.S. that we have not paid for and what we have had has not played an essential part in our resistance."

David Margesson rang up Chequers and afterwards told me on the telephone that he had been pressed into accepting the War Office. I congratulated him warmly and sincerely. He said he was pleased in that it was a great honour, but he was very diffident about his capacity to undertake it. I said I should have to treat him with greater respect in future. "No you won't, old boy," he replied.

He will have to speak in the House which will give his former subjects a chance of getting their own back. He thought they would enjoy that, and I have little doubt they will make the best of their opportunities.

Sunday, December 22nd
Went to the early service in St Faith's chapel, lit with candles and crowded.

Lunched with Sammy Hood, and then after an afternoon's work drove down to Farnham to stay with the Kemsleys. The last thing I did before leaving was to release the information about the Cabinet changes; the first thing I heard on arrival was Lord Kemsley receiving the news from his office. He gave instructions that Halifax's and Eden's appointments were to be applauded but David Margesson was not to be greeted with open arms.

During dinner, at which Lord and Lady K., Pam and Lionel Berry, and an atrociously affected young man called Sir John Phillips were present, we had a hot discussion about the War Office appointment. I upheld David's appointment very strongly and emphasised his organising ability. Lord Kemsley said a good businessman would have been better. I pointed out that the Government of the country is based on the House of Commons: we already have four outsiders in the administration, Duncan, Woolton, Reith and Oliver Lyttelton; to appoint another would be to make a mockery of Parliamentary institutions – and anyhow David ought to be given a chance, by the public and the press.

Tuesday, December 24th
Came up from Farnham early and found a great accumulation of work. After lunch the P.M. signed a number of books, which he is

giving us all as Christmas presents, and sent off presents to the King and Queen: a siren-suit for the King and Fowler's *English Usage* for the Queen! As he left the room he said, remembering our plea for a Christmas holiday, "A busy Christmas and a frantic New Year."

Dined at the C.W.R. gaily festooned with Christmas decorations. We are not going to bomb Germany tonight, but should they attack us we shall return in great force tomorrow. However with the aid of bad weather, it looks as if the Luftwaffe will get the credit for respecting this *Stille Nacht, heilige Nacht.*

In a letter to the P.M., General Catroux, discussing the prospects of winning over Syria and French North Africa, holds out little hope of securing Weygand (which is an expectation generally entertained). He says: "*Weygand, sous ses apparences de modéstie est un orgueilleux qui hésitera a avouer qu'il s'est trompé en signant un déplorable armistice.*" ["Weygand, with his apparent modesty, is a conceited man who will hesitate to admit that he erred in signing a deplorable Armistice."]

Wednesday, December 25th
The first Christmas Day that I can remember spending in London. I went to the Abbey for the early service, where hundreds of people came, through the gloom and the blackout, and knelt in the candle-lit nave.

I had breakfast at the Wyndham and read a little of a book called *The Importance of Living*, by a Chinese philosopher called Lin Yutang, given me by Gay for Christmas. It is amusingly written, but not very profound.

I cat-burgled 66 Eccleston Square in an attempt to get a bottle of champagne for the typists; but after hazardous descents down drainpipes I found the inner doors barred against me.

Nicholas Lawford[1] dined with me at White's and as Lord Gort was the only other person present he joined us. We had a very long conversation during and after dinner, ranging from the megalomania of Sir Roger Keyes to the weakness of the French, but centring on the Battle of France and Dunkirk. Lord G. was critical of the information he had received from home and confirmed that he had received no warning of the Belgian collapse; but the subject on which he chiefly dwelt was the order sent to him, after the Amiens gap had been made, to march south and join the French. He said that the reports of the French having crossed the Somme, and

[1] V. G. Lawford, amusing and erudite second private secretary at the Foreign Office.

being in a position to march northwards and close the gap had no truth in them. But the Cabinet and Chiefs of Staff seemed to think that he could march his nine infantry divisions southwards, against eight armoured German divisions in the gap and a reserve of motorised divisions behind. The order which he received took no account of the reality of the situation, scouted the tactical impossibility of facing an army about while it was engaged with the enemy on the other side, and did not consider the position of the Belgian army on Gort's left flank. History would have much to say on this order. Had he tried to obey it, he would have lost the whole B.E.F. and the war.

He said that it was only by good fortune, and by some sort of premonition, that he had made arrangements for the protection of his left flank. If he had not done so, the position would have been desperate when the Belgians collapsed.

He talked very modestly throughout, never vaunting himself or complaining of his treatment; but he obviously has a certain grievance against those in authority and feels the injustice of holding up the publication of his despatches. He spoke with the utmost contempt of Hore-Belisha.

The unofficial Christmas truce has been kept by both sides. We have not bombed Germany, nor they us.

Saturday, December 28th [At Helperby, in the North Riding of Yorkshire]
Hunted with the York and Ainsty (North), which met at Helperby. We drew all the small coverts, which I know so well from shooting, and spent much of the morning cantering indecisively about Brafferton Springs. In the warmth and the sunshine even the poorness of the scent could not spoil our pleasure. Finally a fox from Thibet[1] broke well away and we had an exhilarating run, through Pilmoor and across country, jumping a dozen good fences. My hireling was the best of jumpers, but during a second run in the afternoon it landed in a ditch and fell. We were both unhurt and continued an enjoyable hunt until dusk.

Sunday, December 29th
The Germans added to their growing list of atrocities by showering thousands of incendiaries on the City and destroying the Guildhall and eight Wren churches (thank Heavens that Mother and I took the trouble to make a tour of them and admire their beauties one summer's evening two years ago).

[1] One of the coverts on the Helperby estate amicably shared by pheasants and foxes.

Tuesday, December 31st

Having reached Downing Street at 7.45 a.m., set to work to cope with arrears and spent much of the day in attendance on the P.M., who was in mellow mood especially when inspecting two of Herbert Morrison's new domestic shelters (intended, I suspect, as rivals to Anderson's successful creation) upon the stresses and strains of which he could demonstrate his technical knowledge as a builder.

Eric Seal is going to try to wangle me into the army, by support of the P.M., over the head of the recalcitrant Foreign Office, but says I must wait till the spring.

Dined at the C.W.R., where General Ismay plied Tommy Thompson and me with brandy and regaled us with stories of the field of battle, and then proceeded upstairs to drink to the New Year in champagne.

13

Reconnaissance by the U.S.A.

January 1941

Wednesday, January 1st

The P.M. has circulated a minute about preserving the secrecy of documents which suddenly makes me feel rather conscious-stricken about this diary. I haven't the heart to destroy it and shall compromise by keeping it locked up here, even more strictly than hitherto.

This evening the P.M. met his Waterloo when inspecting the girders and constructions above the C.W.R. He would not wait for me to return with an effective light and, using only the torch in the handle of his walking-stick, sank up to his ankles in thick liquid cement.[1]

Desmond told us of M.I.5's discovery that Muselier[2] and several of his staff were traitors, agents of the Vichy Government who had betrayed our intentions at Dakar (we have documents to prove it). When he told the P.M., the latter gave orders that they should be arrested tonight and de Gaulle informed by special messenger.

I stayed on duty late, until the P.M. in the early hours ascended to the roof to look at the stars and the new moon. Eden and Kingsley Wood spent much of the evening here discussing the question of financial assistance from America. I sat in the room while the P.M. drafted a forceful telegram to Roosevelt, not hiding from him the dangerous drain on our resources. Sombre though the telegram was, with its warning that only by American financial help could Hitlerism be "extirpated from Europe, Africa and Asia", the P.M. seemed to enjoy drafting it and his *obiter dicta* to

---

[1] When I said he had met his Waterloo, he replied, "How dare you! Anyhow, Blenheim, not Waterloo."

[2] The sole French naval officer of flag rank to rally to de Gaulle. He therefore commanded the French navy. De Gaulle disliked him.

Kingsley Wood who sat perched on the edge of his armchair, were not particularly depressing. But he obviously fears that the Americans' love of doing good business may lead them to denude us of all our realisable resources before they show any inclination to be the Good Samaritan.

M.I.5 went off to arrest Muselier, another Frenchman and two French ladies. One of the ladies was found in bed with a doctor attached to the Free French forces. In the house of the other was found the Second Secretary of the Brazilian Embassy, stark naked. It was through the Brazilian Embassy that information was passed to Vichy. The Admiral himself was found to be in possession of dangerous drugs.

Thursday, January 2nd
The P.M. told Brendan, whose help I had solicited, that I could not join up. So that is that until the spring, when I shall try again.

Friday, January 3rd
Nothing worth recording in the war, except that the defences of Bardia[1] have at last been pierced.

The Germans remain ominously quiet. Many people think the invasion is really being prepared. In any case it seems clear that we have got to expect havoc from air-raids on an increasing scale. Big fire-raids are the order of the day. The devastation of the City was followed by a concentrated attack on Bremen.

Saturday, January 4th
Ordinary routine duties and not very onerous. Biting wind and intense cold made it unpleasant to venture out. Sir Walter Layton has sent the P.M. an interesting poem by an American woman, called "The White Cliffs". Very good propaganda for us.

Dorothy Sayers[2] has sent a poem which represents what a great many people in this country are feeling:

THE BURDEN OF IRELAND

O never trouble Ireland; her lamps are shining bright,
While the wicked cities of England are plunged in fear and night,
For Ireland may go lightly and draw her easy breath,
With the hard heart of England set between her and death.

---

[1] Italian held town in Libya.
[2] Writer of excellent detective stories and creator of the amateur sleuth, Lord Peter Wimsey. A dedicated Anglican.

O never trouble Ireland, for she may sleep sound
While the reek of blood and burning goes up from English ground.
She lies down lightly with a smile upon her lips,
Her bulwarks built of English bones and the wreck of the English
    ships.

O never trouble Ireland; her fields are green with mirth,
While the sharp share of battle ploughs the cursed English earth;
She may wrap her from the winter in a warm English cloak,
For the naked breast of England is wrapped in fire and smoke.

O never trouble Ireland, for Ireland is free –
It is only the men of other lands that groan for liberty.
It is only cruel England thinks such men worth a stir;
But do not trouble Ireland – it does not trouble her.

Say only of Catholic Ireland that she remained at home
When the Pagan and the apostate set heel on the neck of Rome,
When the Cross lay under the fylfot, bowed down to the axe and
    rod,
And the dirty English Protestant went out to die for God.

And say of gallant Ireland, she does not stand alone;
She sits in the shield of England's arm and bites her to the bone.
She has shortened the sword of England without shewing fight –
God rest you merry, Irish men, let nothing you affright.

And say of conquered Ireland that she has won her war;
She has taken the bounty of England to settle the English score,
She has spilt the blood of England without drawing blade –
And England may go lightly now, for all her debts are paid.

But do not trouble England with a tale of Irish wrongs,
Or wring the heart of England with the old heroic songs,
Or bend the Irish blarney to woo the English ear –
For the laughter of England will not be good to hear.

And trouble not for Ireland; though St Patrick lies asleep,
St Andrew and St David and St George are on the deep,
St Michael of the Angels shall guard our Western wall,
Our Lady of Victories pray for us all.[1]

---

[1] Dorothy Sayers did not take account of the large number of Southern Irishmen
who came to England to volunteer for service in the British armed forces
despite their Government's craven neutrality.

Sunday, January 5th
Bardia has fallen and the P.M., in a peculiarly charming letter to the King, refers to today as "Bardia Day". In a great tribute to the King, he says, "Your Majesties are more beloved by all classes and conditions than any of the princes of the past."

Monday, January 6th
Lunched at the Wyndham where I sat with Horace Wilson and Peter Loxley.[1] The former talked of the method of governing by committees. He says the P.M. does not understand the use of them, but both he and Peter considered they served a purpose in providing for decisions without the passage of long and innumerable letters. Beaverbrook – who has just sent another letter of resignation – looks at the same question from another angle. He refused the chairmanship of the new Production Executive because, like a businessman, he believes that committees complicate and slow up decisions which ought to be taken by one man. Beaverbrook and Horace illustrate very clearly the difference between the civil servant's and the businessman's approach. The new plan, which is being published today, for eliminating many committees and establishing two new ones, the Production Executive and the Imports Executive, looks as if it may simplify a machinery which was becoming too intricate.

Vansittart has written a violent paper about Germany, denouncing any attempt to distinguish Germans from Nazis or to hold out hopes of gentle treatment when we have won, and saying that if we look for a revolution from that placid and disciplined people we shall, in the words of Nietzsche, "starve upon expectations". The P.M. disagrees with this outburst and writes in reply: "I contemplate a reunited European family in which Germany will have a great place. We must not let our vision be darkened by hatred or obscured by sentiment. A much more fruitful line is to try to separate the Prussians from the South Germans . . . The expressions to which I attach importance and intend to give emphasis are 'Nazi tyranny' and 'Prussian militarism'." What a contrast between the erratic, feverish genius and the wisdom of a statesman!

We are now making overtures to Vichy because we have hopes that the French may continue the war in North Africa and we realise that Pétain is so widely venerated in France that to attack him is both useless and impolitic.

I was at No. 10 from 2.00 p.m. till 8.15 and had an exhausting

---

[1] Highly regarded member of the Diplomatic Service, killed in an air crash on the way to the Yalta Conference in February 1945.

time what with the issue of press communiqués about the new Production Executive, etc., and wrangles with Lord Beaverbrook. The P.M. had his sleep and while he was dressing treated me to a discourse on the siege of Ladysmith and why he always remembered January 6th. On the way over to the Annexe for dinner, he said, "I think Anthony is putting his hand on the Foreign Office. I see a different touch in the telegrams."

I was on duty after dinner when an encouraging telegram came which makes it look as if Tobruk may fall close after Bardia. Then we shall have to make a decision: whether to press on to Benghazi or whether to stop and divert our striking force elsewhere. The threat of a German advance into the Balkans, and the slowing up of the Greek offensive in Albania in the face of more determined resistance, give cause to think. It would be disastrous to let the Greek triumph end in defeat, as did the victories of the Finnish army last winter.

The P.M. worked intensively till 2.00 a.m. and sent yet another eloquent note to Lord Beaverbrook, ending "Danton, no weakness". Then he went to bed and, as he snuggled beneath the bed clothes, smiling at the thought of Bardia and, he hopes soon, Tobruk, he had the grace for once to apologise for keeping me up so late.

Tuesday, January 7th
Brendan tells me that he argued ceaselessly last night with Lord B. about his resignation, but all to no avail. He is determined to go. No bad thing in itself, but it will upset the P.M. terribly.

Thursday, January 9th
I was at No. 10 from 4.00 p.m. till dinner-time, the main preoccupation being with General de Gaulle, since it has now been discovered that the documents incriminating Admiral Muselier were false and had been forged by two disgruntled officers of the Free French forces. The P.M. was greatly pleased because de Gaulle "behaved like a Gentleman", was not at all cantankerous about the episode, and said that his only interest was to see that honour and justice were satisfied.

James Stuart[1] came to No. 10 and was offered, and accepted, the post of Chief Whip. He had been deputy to David Margesson, now promoted to the War Office.

---

[1] Afterwards Viscount Stuart of Findhorn.*

Friday, January 10th
The President's envoy, Mr Hopkins,* was lunching with the P.M.
and they were so impressed with each other that their tête-à-tête
did not break up till nearly 4.00. Then we left for Ditchley, I
travelling down with Brendan. Brendan said that Hopkins, the
confidant of Roosevelt, was the most important American visitor
to this country we had ever had. He had come to tell the President
what we needed and to form an opinion of the country's morale.
He could influence the President more than any living man. At
Lisbon Ronnie Campbell had made a bad impression by saying
that "the morale of the lower classes was wonderful" – a remark
which offended the liberal and democratic Hopkins. But apparently Hopkins had been much impressed by Halifax, whose religious
views and variety of interests would, he said, appeal to Roosevelt.
While we were thus discoursing, an icy mist descended and we
collided with a fish-and-chips wagon which burst into flames.
Nobody was hurt and we arrived safely at Ditchley.

Besides the Trees, Venetia Montagu was there, Dinah Brand
(with her Australian beau) and the Captain of the Guard, a former
schoolmaster, who seemed very intelligent. Before dinner we
drank and thawed while Winston pointed out, in reply to Mrs Tree,
that Wavell had done very well but that the Italians were the sort of
enemy against whom any General should be only too happy to be
matched.

Dinner was an exquisite meal at which I sat next to Mrs Tree.
Afterwards Winston smoked the biggest cigar in history and
became very mellow. There was an interlude in which I talked to
the exceptionally pleasant Dinah, after which Winston retired to
bed with a very full box and in an excellent temper while I whiled
away the time arranging the box in my beautiful working room
below.

After the drafting of a long and intricate telegram to Wavell, for
consideration by the Chiefs of Staff, we went to bed at about 1.30.
The point of the telegram was that in view of the imminence of a
German attack in the Balkans we must relax our effort in Libya,
once Tobruk has fallen, and divert a part of our forces to the aid of
Greece. The army authorities in the Middle East are in despair at
this; they believe the Balkan threat is only a bluff.

Tobruk is proving a tougher nut to crack than we had supposed.
It may take a week, the P.M. says.

Saturday, January 11th
Very annoyed at being disturbed early by the P.M.

He is delighted by the new American bill which allows British warships the use of American ports and contains wide powers for the President in every sphere of assistance to us. He says this is tantamount to a declaration of war by the United States. At any rate it is an open challenge to Germany to declare war if she dares. In view of this bill it will be more difficult for us to resist the American tendency – which Kingsley Wood lamented to me yesterday – to strip us of everything we possess in payment for what we are about to receive.

Ronnie Tree went off to his constituency and his wife, at 4.00 a.m. this morning, had to rush off with her squadron of mobile canteens to Portsmouth which received the full force of the blitz last night. So at lunch we had no host or hostess, although the son of the house[1] – a trooper in the Life Guards – came in towards the end. But Mr Hopkins arrived and his quiet charm and dignity held the table. He said that the new Presidential bill would arouse loud controversy, but he felt sure it would succeed. He told us of the Duke of Windsor's recent visit to the President on his yacht when the former spoke very charmingly of the King (a fact which touched Winston), and he said that the Duke's entourage was very bad. Moreover H.R.H.'s recent yachting trip with a violently pro-Nazi Swede did not create a good impression. It was the astounding success of the King and Queen's visit to the U.S. which had made America give up its partisanship of the Windsors.

Winston expressed the opinion, forcibly, that socialism was bad, that jingoism was worse, and that the two combined, in a kind of debased Italian fascism, was the worst creed ever designed by man.

The Marquesa de Casa Maury[2] (formerly Mrs Dudley Ward) came at tea-time and also Oliver Lyttelton and the Prof. Brendan, who had taken Hopkins over to Blenheim, said that Hopkins had told him his mission was to see what we needed so that we might get it – even if it meant transferring to us armaments belonging to the U.S. forces. The President was resolved that we should have the means of survival and of victory.

Dinner at Ditchley takes place in a magnificent setting. The dining-room is lit only by candles, in a large chandelier and on the walls. The table is not over-decorated: four gilt candle sticks with tall yellow tapers and a single gilt cup in the centre. The food is in keeping with the surroundings, though I notice some attempt to be less lavish since Lord Woolton's recent strictures on over-feeding.

The P.M. has been troubled by *The Times'* attack on his new Production Executive, etc., and indeed the criticisms voiced there

[1] Michael Tree, married Lady Anne Cavendish.
[2] A woman of exceptional charm, for many years friend, confidante and mistress of the Prince of Wales (Edward VIII).

reflect a widely-felt complaint. So he has taken the trouble to write a full explanation to Geoffrey Dawson,[1] and at dinner he expounded his views, emphasising that he had no use for committees in a purely advisory capacity but that there was no one man today who could be an economic dictator or maintain a position similar to his, on the military side, as Minister of Defence. His exercise of this office was only made possible by the power which he possessed as Prime Minister.

When the ladies had gone, Mr Hopkins paid a graceful tribute to the P.M.'s speeches which had, he said, produced the most stirring and revolutionary effect on all classes and districts in America. At an American Cabinet meeting the President had had a wireless-set brought in so that all might listen to the Prime Minister. The P.M. was touched and gratified. He said that he hardly knew what he said in his speeches last summer; he had just been imbued with the feeling that "it would be better for us to be destroyed than to see the triumph of such an imposter". When, at the time of Dunkirk, he had addressed a meeting of Ministers "below the line" he had realised that there was only one thing they wanted to hear him say: that whatever happened to our army we should still go on. He had said it.

After the war he could never lead a party Government against the Opposition leaders who had co-operated so loyally. He hoped a national Government would continue for two or three years after the war so that the country might be undivided in its efforts to put into effect certain principles – or rather measures – of reconstruction. He then proceeded to give – after saying that the text of the American bill that morning had made him feel that a new world had come into being – a graphic description of the future, as he visualised it, from an international point of view. He began by saying that there must be a United States of Europe and he believed it should be built by the English; if the Russians built it, there would be communism and squalor; if the Germans built it, there would be tyranny and brute force. He then outlined his ideas, which I have related before, in the quick unhesitating manner which means he has really warmed to his subject.

He asked Hopkins what he thought, and the reply, slow, deliberate, halting was a remarkable contrast to the ceaseless flow of eloquence to which we had listened. Hopkins said that there were two kinds of men: those who talked and those who acted. The President, like the Prime Minister, was one of the latter. Although

[1] Editor of *The Times*. Strong supporter of Munich and of appeasement. Friend of Lady Astor and Lord Lothian and member of the so-called "Cliveden Set". About to hand over his editorship to Robin Barrington-Ward.

Hopkins had heard him sketch out an idea very similar to the P.M.'s, Roosevelt refused to listen to those who talked so much of war aims and was intent only upon one end: the destruction of Hitler. Winston hastily explained that he had been speaking very freely and was just anxious to let Hopkins realise that we were not all devoid of thoughts of the future: he would be the first to agree that the destruction of "those foul swine" was the primary and over-riding objective.

At this point Mrs Tree evicted us forcibly from the dining-room to see a film of the Mormons called *Brigham Young*. I sat next to Mrs Dudley Ward and thought I understood why the Prince of Wales felt the way he did. The film, though it had its *longueurs*, was a moving one and stimulating to one's thought. It showed the great quality of simple faith (which, as Tennyson pointed out, is more than Norman blood) and the nobility of refusing to compromise with the principles one has deliberately adopted as right. After this film was over we saw some German news films which included a scene at the Brenner meeting, which with its salutes and its absurdity was funnier than anything Charlie Chaplin produced in *The Great Dictator*. To bed by 2.00 a.m.

Sunday, January 12th

The P.M.'s respect for General Smuts' wise and comprehensive telegrams is shown in the final sentence of a telegram he has just sent to the General: "Most grateful for all your help and above all for your sure-footed judgment which marches with our laboriously reached conclusions."

Lunch lasted a long time, but eventually, while the P.M. conferred with Prof. and Mr Justice Singleton about the strength of the German air force, I managed to go out for a walk with my host and hostess, whom I like more and more. They live ostentatiously but are the opposite themselves.

The discussion after dinner was largely about America, and in particular the American principle of coping with unemployment by providing work instead of a dole – a plan which costs four times as much or would, at any rate, in England. The P.M. asked what the Americans would do when they had accumulated all the gold in the world and the other countries then decided that gold was of no value except for filling teeth. "Well," said Mr Hopkins, "we shall be able to make use of our unemployed in guarding it!"

We saw several films including *Night Train to Munich*, which I had seen before. In the middle the telephone rang and I was told that H.M.S. *Southampton* had been destroyed by dive-bombers in the Mediterranean. When I took the P.M. aside afterwards and broke the news to him, he was less upset than I expected, though he bitterly regretted that he had been dissuaded from allowing Operation WORKSHOP[1] to go through. "I flinched," he said, "and now I have cause to regret it." I asked Prof. why the U.P. weapon had not come into play and he replied that the service experts had decided dive-bombing was no longer a danger and that the U.P. should be adapted for use against high-altitude flying.

From midnight till 2.00 a.m. the P.M., smoking a phenomenally large cigar, paced about in front of the fire at the far end of the library and gave, for Hopkins' benefit, an appreciation of the war up to date. Ronnie Tree, Oliver Lyttelton, Prof., Tommy Thompson and I sat and goggled, while Hopkins occasionally made some short comment. He began by discussing the future. The question of populations was important. Germany had sixty millions on whom she could count; the remainder were at least a drag and potentially a danger. The British Empire had more white inhabitants than that, and if the U.S. were with us – as he seemed in this discourse to assume they actively would be – there would be another 120 millions. So we were not outmatched in numbers any more than we were in courage and resolution. He did not believe that Japan would come in against the threat of Anglo-American armed resistance and he thought it more than probable that the Germans would be obliged to occupy the whole of France, thus driving the French to take up arms again in North Africa. (He later said he believed that if he had gone to Bordeaux in those last fateful days he would have been able to tip the balance in favour of further resistance overseas.)

Turning to the past, he sketched the whole history of the war, Norway, the trap when we marched our men right up into Belgium, his visits to France, the air battles, Libya, and, above all, the threat of invasion. He believed that Oran had been the turning-point in our fortunes: it made the world realise that we were in earnest in our intentions to carry on. He sketched the possibilities of invasion, of "lodgements", of the use of gas, but he said he now felt quite confident, even though it was wrong to say that we should actually welcome invasion as so many people were now feeling. I think Hopkins must have been impressed.

With Oliver Lyttelton, who radiates charm, I had what he called "a little whisky-and-soda treason before going to bed". We discussed the Government and he told me he had no opinion of Bevin's capacity, though he thought Morrison was doing his job well.

[1] The seizure of Pantellaria.

Monday, January 13th

Having breakfasted with Mrs Churchill, Venetia Montagu and Mrs Dudley Ward, I cleared up the remnants of a week-end's input and output from boxes, and the P.M. was ready to leave for London by 10.45.

I travelled with the Prof. There was an unreasonable outburst of anger from the P.M. en route because a box (with a few quite unimportant papers) had not reached us when we left for Ditchley and we could not induce the car containing it to stop when we met. The P.M. stopped his car by the side of the road, just outside Oxford, and threatened to wait an hour till the box was retrieved. Fortunately we only waited three minutes.

I invited Jan Margesson and Betty Montagu to lunch at the Mirabelle and we sat talking, most pleasurably, till past 3.00. Jan had been attending, as a delegate, a meeting of a Communist-organised "People's Convention" which the P.M. recently instructed the Home Secretary to watch carefully. The present Communist policy is apparently to support the war (which they denounced a very short time ago) but in so doing to sow every possible dissension and disrupt the national effort. They don't look as if they are making much headway, but the Cabinet is today considering the possibility of suspending the *Daily Worker*, a difficult decision owing to deep-rooted feelings about the freedom of the press. I led Jan to believe that the Government's policy was to ignore all such movements and organisations because of their insignificance.

That Janet Margesson, daughter of the ultra-Tory Chief Whip, should be a member of the Communist Party seemed less surprising then that it would now. After all Mrs Churchill was a dedicated Liberal, much disliking the Conservative Party except in her husband's constituency; and Mrs Attlee told me that she had voted Conservative until 1945. Stanley Baldwin's elder son was a Labour M.P. and neither Asquith's nor Lloyd George's sons were ostentatiously Liberal in their political sympathies.

In my own family my father was a Conservative, but my mother, a staunch Liberal, would vote Labour rather than Conservative if no Liberal were standing. In 1945 she voted Conservative, saying shame-facedly to me, "I have never done such a thing before, but as you are with Winston I just felt I had to support him."

In the mid 1980s the public would be surprised if Mr Thatcher was a socialist or if Mrs Kinnock or Mrs Wedgwood Benn were Tories. In the 1930s and 1940s such a state of affairs would not

have seemed remarkable, and it may well be that family divergen-
cies in politics were wholesome.

Tuesday, January 14th

The P.M. went north to Scapa Flow to see Lord Halifax off to the United States and to visit the Fleet.

Prince Paul of Yugoslavia[1] is terrified at the prospect of our sending great assistance to Greece. He feels sure it will bring the Germans down. The P.M.'s reaction to his panicky telegrams from Belgrade is that the Germans will not be either hurried or deflected from their carefully laid plans by any minor troop movements on our part. Prince Paul is like a man in a cage with a tiger, "hoping not to provoke him while steadily dinner-time approaches".

Wednesday, January 15th

The terrible problem of the strength of the German air force, into which Singleton has been enquiring, has produced many complications which kept me busy for much of the day. The conclusion reached seems to be that the Germans are very little superior to us except in long-range bombers. Their main advantage lies in the short distance they have to come.

Having dined frugally at the C.W.R. I joined a party at the Ecu de France consisting of the Hinchingbrookes, Martin Charteris,* Mrs Simon Whitbread, Colonel Clark, Faith and Betty Montagu. Everybody was in a delightful frame of mind and we went on to the Four Hundred where we enjoyed ourselves greatly until after 2.00 a.m.

Thursday, January 16th

Sir Stafford Cripps reports that Russia looks like standing aside and letting Germany have her way in the Balkans. He considers a German offensive through Bulgaria is assured within the next few months and thinks it will be synchronised with other offensives elsewhere. He says: "If events go badly for Turkey then she (Russia) may attack that country and Iran or make very large demands on them. It is likely that she will make demands on Iran as soon as Turkey is thoroughly engaged with Germany." So one leader of the extreme Left has no illusions left about Russian intentions.

It seems clear that Germany must make a determined effort to reach a decision, at whatever cost, before American help becomes

[1] Cousin of the murdered King Alexander and regent for the young King Peter. Married to the dazzlingly beautiful Princess Olga, sister of the Duchess of Kent.

effective. The spring is going to be critical, and it makes one shudder to see the reports from many and different sources of the manufacture and storage of German gas bombs.

Friday, January 17th

Helen Dashwood gave a dance at West Wycombe, in aid of the Red Cross, and I went there for the weekend. It seemed to be a children's party, at which Fitzroy Maclean and I were the only adults, but later in the evening, as more people arrived, things livened up considerably. In any case it was lovely to hear a band and to see people dancing.

Monday, January 20th

Thick snow gave way to thicker slush and I goaded my car through miles of it from West Wycombe to London, accompanied by two sodden journalists to whom I gave a lift.

The P.M. did not return to London till after lunch, so John Martin and I fed unhurriedly and well at Boodles and I listened to his description of the Scottish trip which seems to have been almost farcical at times, especially when the U.P. weapon was fired in the P.M.'s honour and all but ended in exploding on top of the whole party.

The Cabinet was at 5.00 at the C.W.R., as always on Mondays, and afterwards the P.M. was feeling very polite. He even went so far as to say (after I had fetched him his red ink pen and much else besides): "Will you add yet another to all the kindnesses you have been heaping on my head by turning out the electric fire?" which is not the way he usually asks for things.

Heavy air attacks have taken place on Malta, and it is thought possible that the next German move will be either an attack on Malta or an invasion, by German and Italian forces, of Tunis with the idea of destroying any chance of renewed French activity and of reinforcing the sorely beleaguered Graziani[1] in Libya. But we are not letting the grass grow under our feet.

After dinner I was on duty while the P.M. held a Defence Committee Meeting. Having finished my work, I read M. Dupuy's (the Canadian Minister) enlightening report on his visit to Vichy, where he found Pétain much more alert than we had supposed and anxious for a British victory. The one fear that many Frenchmen had was that a British victory would mean the return of the old politicians who had brought about France's downfall. It had been

---

[1] Marshal Graziani, commander of the Italian armies in North Africa. Soundly defeated by General Wavell.

impressed upon Dupuy that the appearance of Anglo-French tension must be preserved in order to hoodwink the Germans and Laval; but secret discussions could take place behind this veil. The French have two great levers against Germany: their fleet and their Colonies. We have one great bargaining counter with them: the relaxation, under guarantees, of the blockade in certain articles. Dupuy ends his report with the words: "The problem of Franco-British relations depends on two things – goodwill and psychology. The goodwill already exists on both sides – there remains the question of psychology."

The Foreign Office weekly summary describes how in Poland the Germans, having failed to terrorise the Poles, are now trying to demoralise them by the encouragement of gambling, erotic litera-ture and improper displays and the banning of more serious forms of entertainment. An interesting foretaste of Hitler's New Order.

The P.M. went to bed, very benevolently, about 2.00 a.m. and spent a rotten night.

Tuesday, January 21st
The House of Commons met, in the old House. David Margesson made his first appearance as a Minister and had forty Questions to answer, a heavy task which he achieved with great credit. Then, after Questions, the House debated Manpower, Production and Supply. The P.M. sat on the Front Bench, and I in the box, while Bevin read out a long oration. Everybody yawned, and the incor-rigible Mr Austin Hopkinson[1] even suggested rudely that to save Mr Bevin trouble the Clerk of the Table should read the speech for him; but the House sat up with a start and gaped when Industrial Registration, to make possible conscription in industries of nation-al importance, was announced. After Bevin had spoken for over an hour, Lord Winterton[2] rose and made an eloquent attack on the Government. He said, with some truth, that there was danger of our forming a kind of "Maginot Line Complex" about American help. We must not rely on any but our own efforts.

Gave Barker a late but extensive lunch at Boodles and was surprised to find what bloodthirsty and merciless sentiments he nurtured towards Germany. I find less and less support for my belief that when we have won, mercy should season justice.

[1] Independent M.P. for the Mossley division of Lancashire who asked endless irritating Parliamentary Questions.

[2] 6th Earl Winterton. Irish peer who was M.P. for Horsham and sat in the House of Commons for forty-five years, rising from being Baby of the House in 1904 to Father of the House. Amiable but eccentric, and very outspoken, he held Cabinet office briefly in 1938–39 and then, as a backbench Privy Councillor, became a gadfly stinging all administrations impartially.

Wednesday, January 22nd

The debate in the House continued and I spent most of the day there until the Police shouted "Who goes home?" at 4.00 p.m.

At the end of questions Morrison made a statement on the suppression of the *Daily Worker*, and although the House was clearly in favour of this Aneurin Bevan[1] pressed the P.M. for a debate and carried his point.

I lunched with Eric Seal at the House, and then we both went into the box to hear the P.M. wind up the debate. He did so extremely well, explaining his reasons for the new committee machinery (which has been much criticised) with the utmost clearness and cogency. The House was entertained by his quips and his mastery of the art of anti-climax. He expounded the little understood facts about the slowness of changing from peace to war production and the increased need of manpower, in industry rather than the forces, as that transfer takes place. He answered the demand for a dictator on the Home Front, to correspond with the Minister of Defence on the military side, by disparaging dictators in general and by pointing out that he could only maintain his ascendancy as Minister of Defence because he was also Prime Minister. In general he welcomed criticism even when, for the sake of emphasis, it parted company with reality.

Tobruk fell.

I am continually impressed by the P.M.'s genuine love of democracy; viz. a recent minute to the Foreign Secretary about Egypt:

I trust the time will come when the interests of the Fellaheen will be cherished by H.M.G., even if some of the rich pashas and landowners and other pretended nationalists have to pay the same kind of taxes as are paid by wealthy people in Britain. A little of the radical democratic sledge-hammer is needed in the Delta, where so many fat, insolent class and party interests have grown up under our tolerant protection.

Friday, January 24th

The P.M. took Mr Hopkins off to see the batteries at Dover. I could have gone, but preferred to drive myself down to Chequers

---

[1] Labour M.P. for Ebbw Vale. Made himself leader of an unofficial opposition and was thought by Churchill, rightly or wrongly, to subordinate national interest to political advantage. Churchill usually outwitted him, brilliant debater though he was. A thorn in Attlee's flesh in the post-war Labour Government, but a major contributor to the establishment of the Welfare State.

independently and to clear up the considerable amount of work which confronted me.

In the late afternoon I drove Jack Churchill to Chequers. Mrs Churchill, Lady Gwendeline Churchill, Judy Montagu and Mary were there, and the P.M. and Harry Hopkins arrived about 7.00.

At dinner Hopkins said how impressed he had been to see when dining with Bevin, Morrison and Sir Andrew Duncan, on what friendly and familiar terms a great industrialist could be with Labour leaders. Such a thing could not happen in America.

Hopkins told the P.M. that during the afternoon at Dover he had heard one workman say to another, as Winston passed, "There goes the bloody British Empire." Winston's face wreathed itself in smiles and, turning to me, he lisped, "*Very* nice." I don't think anything has given him such pleasure for a long time.

The P.M. said he did not now see how invasion could be successful and he now woke up in the mornings, as he nearly always had, feeling as if he had a bottle of champagne inside him and glad that another day had come. In May and June, however, he had been sorry when the nights were over and he had often thought about death, not, he said, "that I much believe in personal survival after death, at least not of the memory". He was not, he said, much worried by the chance of being bombed – in this connection he is fond of quoting M. Poincaré's[1] statement, "I take refuge beneath the impenetrable arch of probability".

Jack Churchill asked when we were going to recapture British Somaliland. The P.M. replied that we must concentrate on the major operation. As Napoleon said, "*Frappez la masse et le reste vient par surcrôit.*"

Hopkins thought that a statement to the effect that any move by Japan against American interests in the East would be considered an unfriendly act by Great Britain, would have a most important effect in the U.S. The P.M. was delighted and promised to say this as soon as the President let him know the time was ripe.

After dinner I read to the C.I.G.S.[2] on the "Scrambler" (our new telephonic secrecy device) a long telegram from the P.M. to Wavell protesting against the latter's enormous demand for rearward services. Wavell had well over 300,000 men in North Africa but could only put 45,000 into the field. The C.I.G.S. didn't like this telegram and subsequently I had to ring him up again so that he and the P.M. might wrangle about it. Eventually the P.M. agreed

---

[1] President of the French Republic in the First World War and subsequently for two years Prime Minister. In the Third Republic Prime Ministers normally lasted only a few months and sometimes only weeks.

[2] Sir John Dill.

to tone down the wording, but said that plain-speaking was necessary in war and he didn't see why Wavell should want still more Y.M.C.A.s etc. behind the lines.

At midnight the P.M. and Harry Hopkins came into my office and talked. The P.M. was much impressed by the fact that there are 200,000 white civilians in Abyssinia and he is a little worried about their fate when "those savage warriors, who have been burned with poison gas" get among them. If the Duke of Aosta will surrender in time, the P.M. thinks we might be able to hold the Abyssinians back.

"Never give in," said the P.M., "and you will never regret it." A negotiated peace would be a German victory and would leave open the way for another and final "spring of the tiger" in a few years' time. Hopkins agreed and said that Lindbergh,[1] and others in America who favoured a negotiated peace, really desired a German victory. The P.M. wound up by saying that after the last war he had been asked to provide an inscription for a French war memorial. His suggestion, which was rejected, had been: "In war fury, in defeat defiance, in victory magnanimity, in peace goodwill."

The P.M. summoned me into his bedroom and, as he undressed, said very nicely that he didn't think there was much point in his letting me join up in the Guards, though there was every point in my wanting to do so. This was not like the last war when every man was needed, and there were too many able men who had gone into the army and were doing jobs which did not make full use of their capacities. If things really started to move, he promised to let me go and to see that I was well placed. He would take care of my interests and he would not forget. He thought a commission in the Marines, which he could procure for me, was the thing. I should not need much preliminary training. I said, "What about a Commando?" "You mightn't get a commission in that," he replied. I said I wouldn't mind going in the ranks, but he said that was silly (which I don't think it is).

I put in a plea, rather feebly, for permission to go soon on the grounds that members of the Diplomatic Service were too inclined to see life from the drawing-room sofa angle and that it would be an excellent thing to have a wider experience. But I was told that this war was not being waged in order that I might complete my education.

---

[1] Famous American aviator who became a standard-bearer for the Isolationists.

Saturday, January 25th

The Duke and Duchess of Marlborough came to lunch and conversation was much more general than usual. Harry Hopkins talked about Lisbon and the undesirable Americans there.

The P.M., alarmed by the number of papers in his box, worked all the afternoon in bed. I arranged for Mrs C. and Mr Hopkins to go and see West Wycombe, but Mr Hopkins fell asleep and Mrs C. decided not to go – which distressed Helen Dashwood very much. From her voice on the telephone she sounded like one who has returned from a Safari and seen no trace of the lions she has been promised.

A considerable amount of work was done, including a letter to the editor of the *Daily Mirror*, protesting against that newspaper's Fifth Column attitude, and an enormous memorandum to David Margesson about manpower, the army's excessive dependence on rearward services and the distribution of the thirty-seven divisions we now have available.

Sir John Dill came after tea and contributed his unaffected charm and urbanity.

I sat between Judy Montagu and Mary at dinner, the former very agreeable and forthcoming (and apparently smitten by the graces of Bruce Grimston[1]), the latter, although in reality intelligent and sensible, inclined this evening to be captious and tiresome.

Over the brandy Hopkins showed the P.M. and Dill the details of the American rearmament programme, which I had already perused. It is clear that gigantic efforts are being made, but the P.M. warned Hopkins that the results could not be expected for about eighteen months. Our own war factories were only just beginning their full production (e.g. last week our ammunition output doubled).

Then the C.I.G.S. produced the papers about Operation VICTOR, a military exercise which has been taking place during the last few days as practice against invasion. The papers include an able appreciation of the advantages and tactics of invasion written, as if by the German Staff, by General Weeks[2] of the War Office. It is very comprehensive and sensible, much impressed the P.M., and would certainly do great credit to the Germans if genuine. I was asked to read this out aloud, and afterwards an account of the first stages of the exercise. This account contained, as an appendix, a

---

[1] Younger son of the Earl of Verulam. Good-looking, amusing and a gallant R.A.F. pilot. Killed in action in Bomber Command as was his brother Brian.

[2] Sir Ronald Weeks, subsequently Chairman of Vickers Ltd and of the English Steel Corporation.

broadcast by the P.M. on the beginning of invasion. I read this out aloud and its language caused much amusement, though the P.M. promised he would produce a far better one in the event and said that the sham one was a good example of the mistake of using conventional adjectives, attached to conventional nouns, merely for the sake of effect. If he did have to make such a speech he would end it: "The hour has come; kill the Hun."

There was some discussion about Eire, Dill putting forward the theory that the Germans would invade Ireland as a diversion, like they did Norway, before the main attack materialised.

The rest of the evening was spent in the Great Hall, where the gramophone played and the P.M., in the intervals of discoursing to Hopkins or Dill, tripped a little measure. Hopkins seems doubtful whether we shall have any warning of invasion, but the P.M. and Dill are confident that complete surprise is impossible.

I drank five different sorts of alcohol, in an effort to stifle a cold, but remained quite sober.

Sunday, January 26th

I arranged for Mr Hopkins to go to West Wycombe and then on to see the Fred Crippses (Mrs C. and Lady Gwendeline Churchill both suspect he is attracted by Mrs Cripps[1]). The lady proved so attractive that he stayed to lunch. Mrs C. made a great fuss about Mr Hopkins going to West Wycombe as she felt she ought to have gone too. But I managed to pacify her. In fact Mr H. did not want her to go with him.

In thanking the P.M. for his tribute to him in the House the other day, Beaverbrook writes: "You have given me a certificate of character which will carry me through my days. And that is good for me. Because there is a difference between us. You will be talked of even more widely after you are dead than during your lifetime. But I am talked of while I live, and save for my association with you, I will be forgotten thereafter." Lord B. knows how to lay it on – and also how to forward his own cause in his unceasing struggles with the Air Ministry, of which the P.M. said to me on Friday that he was heartily sick.

Hamish St Clair Erskine (of the Guard) came to lunch and was entertaining. Dill had gone and Hopkins was not back, so we had a rest from war and politics and talked about food and people.

Sir Charles and Lady Portal arrived at tea-time and, as Mrs C. was still out, the P.M. escorted them up to the Long Gallery for

---

[1] Violet, previously one of the Duke of Westminster's four wives. Married to Fred Cripps, brother of Sir Stafford but far from sharing his political and dietary views.

tea, together with Hopkins and Prof., who came today. We started talking about the Classics, Portal being a Wykehamist and thus presumably learned, and the P.M. said that the use of the new pronunciation in Latin was one of the few things he felt passionate about. Latin spoken in the old way was beautiful to hear; the new way was not only ugly but by hiding the resemblance between English and Latin words removed one of the first utilitarian arguments in favour of the Classics.

We got on to the House of Lords and the P.M. said that in England our architecture produced our manner of living and not vice versa. Thus the two-party system owed its supremacy here partly to the shape of the Houses of Parliament. You had to be on one side or the other and it was difficult to cross the floor. He had done it and he knew. Indeed he had re-done it, which everybody said was impossible. They had said you could rat but you couldn't re-rat.

During dinner the P.M. was very hilarious and in the same amiable frame of mind as he has been the whole week-end. He mentioned Generis Mainwaring[1] (pronouncing the G as a J) and I told him she had been bitten by a rat and nearly died. He asked if she had grown a tail and couldn't keep off the subject for at least five minutes. Afterwards he reminisced about the Cuban campaign and South African War.

When the women had gone to bed, I listened in the Great Hall to as interesting a discussion as I ever hope to hear. We sat in a circle, Portal, Hopkins, Jack Churchill, myself and Prof., while the P.M. stood with his back against the mantelpiece, a cigar between his teeth, his hands in the armpits of his waistcoat. Every few seconds he would start forward, trip over the marble grate, walk four or five paces, turn abruptly and resume his position against the mantelpiece. All the while a torrent of eloquence flowed from his lips, and he would fix one or another of us with his eye as he drove home some point. He talked of the past, the present and the future, and the subject matter of his talk was roughly as follows:

In recent history two men had been the most harmful influence in English politics, Joseph Chamberlain and Baldwin. The first had pushed us into the Boer War and, by setting Europe against us, had stimulated the Germans to build a fleet. The second had dominated the scene for fifteen years. He had pushed out of public life the men with the greatest experience, L.G., Birkenhead, etc.; and he had made possible the resurgence of Germany and the decay of our

[1] Daughter of Sir Richard and Lady Magdalen Williams-Bulkeley and mother of Zara Mainwaring.

own strength. He was just sufficiently good to be suffering now acutely for what he had done. This led to a digression about the "Carthaginian peace" of Versailles: we had exacted 1,000 millions in reparations; we and the U.S. had contributed 2,000 millions in loans to set Germany on her feet again and rebuild her power. It was possible that in some twenty months we and the U.S. would again have to make a peace settlement and there would once more be those who wished to help Germany on to her feet. "Only one thing in history is certain: that mankind is unteachable."

There was some discussion of currency problems, the P.M. coming out strongly in favour of "the commodity dollar", the rate of which would be fixed by the prices of a number of selected commodities. He compared the currency problem to that of daylight saving; by a little tampering with the clock great benefits could be reaped; but by overdoing it in either direction all advantage must be lost. Hopkins agreed that the present financial system was unsatisfactory, and said that the President was in favour of some such scheme as the P.M. had outlined; but the opposition of Wall Street had been intense. However in favour of the financiers, the P.M. pointed out that today everybody wanted credit but nobody had any patience with creditors.

The P.M. said that when the war was over there would be a short lull during which we had the opportunity to establish a few basic principles, of justice, of respect for the rights and property of other nations, and indeed of respect for private property so long as its owner was honest and its scope moderate. We could find nothing better than Christian ethics on which to build and the more closely we followed the Sermon on the Mount, the more likely we were to succeed in our endeavours. But all this talk about war aims was absurd at the present time: the Cabinet Committee to examine the question had produced a vague paper, four-fifths of which was from the Sermon on the Mount and the remainder an election address.

Japan and the U.S. was the next topic, and Hopkins expressed the belief that if America came into the war the incident would be with Japan. The P.M. said that the advantage of America as an ally to the disadvantage of Japan as an enemy was as 10 to 1. Why, look at their respective power of steel production – and "modern war is waged with steel". Besides Japan must have been greatly affected by the fate of the Italian navy, which on paper had been so strong. "Fate holds terrible forfeits for those who gamble on certainties."

The P.M. sat down heavily on the sofa, said he had talked too much, and asked Hopkins for his views. Speaking slowly but emphatically. Hopkins stated that the President was not much concerned with the future. His preoccupation was with the next few months. As far as war aims were concerned, there were only very few people in America, liberal intellectuals, who cared about the matter; and they were nearly all on our side. He believed the same to be true of people in this country. All he would say of the future was that he believed the Anglo-Saxon peoples would have to do the rearrangement: the other nations would not be ripe for co-operation for a long time. He thought the problems of reconstruction would be very great, greater than the P.M. had implied, and we should have to send men to the conference table who were tough and not sentimental.

As far as the present was concerned, there were four divisions of public opinion in America: a small group of Nazis and Communists, sheltering behind Lindbergh, who declared for a negotiated peace and wanted a German victory; a group, represented by Joe Kennedy, which said "Help Britain, but make damn sure you don't get into any danger of war"; a majority group which supported the President's determination to send the maximum assistance at whatever risk; and about ten per cent or fifteen per cent of the country, including Knox,[1] Stimson[2] and most of the armed forces, who were in favour of immediate war.

The important element in the situation was the boldness of the President, who would lead opinion and not follow it, who was convinced that if England lost, America, too, would be encircled and beaten. He would use his powers if necessary; he would not scruple to interpret existing laws for the furtherance of his aim; he would make people gape with surprise, as the British Foreign Office must have gaped when it saw the terms of the Lease and Lend Bill. The boldness of the President was a striking factor in the situation. He did not want war, indeed he looked upon America as an arsenal which should provide the weapons for the conflict and not count the cost; but he would not shrink from war.

I talked to the P.M. as he went to bed and found him most communicative and benign. Nobody is more lovable than he when he is in this frame of mind. He recounted to me the difficulties in the way of an invader whose lines of communications would be cut and who could not dominate the air during the daytime. But, I said, the Germans must know this as well as we do and surely the implication is that they will not invade. "To tell you the truth," he said, "that is what I think, and so does Portal. But the others don't think so." He said he would not feel so confident, remembering as

[1] Frank Knox, U.S. Secretary of the Navy.
[2] Henry L. Stimson, U.S. Secretary of the Army.

he did Neville Chamberlain's conviction a year ago that Germany would not invade Holland and Belgium, were it not for the fact that we had air superiority in the day and that we were not pinning our faith in the Maginot Line, "a great China Wall", but in our troops *behind* the beaches who would attack any lodgment and make each separate one into a Sidi Barrani, a Bardia or a Tobruk.

He snuggled down beneath the bedclothes, I gave him his Boswell's *Tour of the Hebrides*, and smiling sweetly he wished me goodnight.

Monday, January 27th
Hopkins, who has smoked most of my Chesterfields, departed with the Prof. who is giving him an album of statistics showing our possessions and our requirements. The P.M. worked in bed till eleven and then went up to London, while I got into my car and drove to Ardley. It has been a particularly agreeable week-end, interesting and not too hectic, and the P.M. has throughout been at his most entertaining and shown the sunniest side of his disposition. He said last night at dinner that he hated nobody and didn't feel he had any enemies – except the Huns, and that was professional! Few men are as good-natured, and it is an interesting spotlight on No. 10 last winter that he should have been regarded with such dislike and mistrust.

Thursday, January 30th
As a result of last night's meeting, the P.M. drafted at No. 10 a telegram to the Turkish President asking that in view of the certainty of a German move through Bulgaria we should be allowed to base a number of squadrons on Turkey. From every source news comes that Germany's intentions in the Balkans are serious, and from whatever angle the Chiefs of Staff regard the matter it remains evident that Turkey is the key to the situation. Hence the P.M.'s telegram.

I went to see David Margesson at the War Office about the pay of army nurses, a matter which Queen Mary wished me to raise with the P.M. David was quite prepared to be helpful, and very friendly, although his first suggestion, true to form, was that the nurses should increase their earnings by trading their charms to the troops! I thought the War Office a horrid crowded place, but the Secretary of State's room is by contrast rather distinguished and its occupant gains in dignity by the fact that one has to walk the whole length of the room before one reaches his desk (a technique, as I pointed out to him, much utilised by foreign dictators).

Friday, January 31st

Spent most of the morning coping with the affairs of our new Mess at No. 10 Annexe, which is to open on Monday, Tommy Thompson, whose job it is, having shirked part of the responsibility.

Today and yesterday, for the first time in weeks, there have been numerous daylight raids and bombs have been dropped. This period of quiet has been partly due to the weather, but is doubtless also on account of the great German preparations which are taking place. There can now be little hesitation in predicting a German move through Bulgaria, which has finally succumbed to German influence and infiltration and where heavy German concentrations are taking place. The point at issue is whether Turkey will resist and will concert measures with Yugoslavia in time.

Meanwhile Derna has fallen and the C.I.G.S. is disappointed because, contrary to expectation, Wavell says he cannot hope to take Benghazi before the end of February. The P.M. has decided that our main effort must now be diverted to the Balkans where Germans, and not Italians, will have to be faced.

14

Brighter News
February–March 1941

Sunday, February 2nd
The Roumanians, in the course of their civil upheaval, are committing sadistic atrocities unsurpassed in horror. For instance they have been taking hundreds of Jews to cattle slaughter-houses and killing them according to the Jews' own ritual practices in slaughtering animals. The P.M. has sent a minute to the Foreign Secretary: "Would it not be well to tell General Antonescu that we will hold him and his immediate circle personally responsible in life and limb if such a vile act is committed. (Some specific atrocity forecast in an F.O. telegram.) Perhaps you may think of something more diplomatic than this." It seems that we are back in the time of Mr Gladstone and the Bashi-Bazouks.

Monday, February 3rd
Everything is marking time in the military sphere, except in Italian East Africa where the prospects become brighter daily. Meanwhile the P.M. is busy with appointments of new Under Secretaries and High Commissioners. He wants to get rid of Malcolm MacDonald by sending him as High Commissioner to Canada and Winterton is to be offered the High Commissionership in South Africa.

Lunched at the Wyndham Club, where I sat with Clifford Norton who was interesting about Vansittart, whose P.S. he was. Our meeting Horace Wilson in the passage started us on the old, old topic of responsibility for the war. Norton said that Van had been uttering warnings about Germany since 1932, and that he and Eden had really seen eye to eye on the matter; but Eden could not stand it being thought that any opinion he uttered in the Cabinet was really the voice of Van.

After spending some of the afternoon at No. 10, I went to have a drink with the S. of S. for Air and Lady Sinclair in their flat above the Air Ministry. Catherine and Elizabeth Sinclair were there, as well as Hugh Seely,[1] a number of airmen – and Frances Day.[2] Conversation was general and entertaining and Archie Sinclair laid himself out to be pleasant. I like Lady Sinclair despite her austerity.

On late duty, but the P.M. obligingly thought of going to bed at 11.30.

Tuesday, February 4th

Represented the P.M. at General Metaxas's[3] memorial service in the Greek Church, Moscow Road. The Kents were there, and I sat in the row behind them with the Secretaries of State for Air, War, and Foreign Affairs. Lady Oxford slithered into a stall at the side and afterwards managed to pose with all the celebrities in turn as they left the church in front of a battery of photographers. I agree with Winston in thinking the Duchess of Kent the most beautiful woman I have ever seen. She is excellently dressed, her hair is as well done as it can be, and her natural beauty is only increased by the taste with which she paints and clothes herself.

The service was quite short. Some Orthodox priests emerged from behind the painted screen, accompanied by a man with an Imperial and a deep bass voice, and chanted, unintelligibly to most of the congregation, for half an hour in front of the draped catafalque, on which candles burnt and a chalice of incense stood. It was much less impressive than Mount Athos,[4] but there was the same air of languid indifference strangely combined with devotional attention on the part of the Greeks present. Sheik Hafiz Wahba[5] and General de Gaulle lent an incongruous touch to the scene.

Today I talked to Malcolm MacDonald, who is reluctant to accept Canada. The P.M. admits that he has not done badly at the Ministry of Health, but obviously does not much care for him and repeated both to James Stuart and to me that he would have great

---

[1] Sir Hugh Seely, 3rd Bt., was a Liberal M.P. appointed to be Sir Archibald Sinclair's Joint Parliamentary Under Secretary. Created Lord Sherwood at Sinclair's request, he expressed republican sentiments in the Smoking Room of the House of Commons and Churchill thereupon ordered the submission for the peerage to be retrieved. It was too late; the King had signed it.

[2] Well-known, good-looking and popular actress, born in the U.S.A. but anglicised.

[3] Greek Prime Minister who had restored King George II to the throne, put an end to the anarchic Greek Parliamentary situation, and thereafter ruled firmly but well.

[4] In 1934 I had spent ten days in the monastic republic of Mount Athos.

[5] Saudi Arabian Minister.

opportunities in Canada. He adopted the same attitude when Halifax was reluctant to go to America.

I also saw Tom Johnston,[1] whom the P.M. thinks one of the best of the Labour Party. He is to be offered the Scottish Office.

Strange negotiations are going on between Germany and France. Pétain seems to be obstinately refusing to take back Laval or to modify the terms of the Armistice and he has, as his great bargaining counters, the threat to continue the war with the fleet and in the Colonies. The Germans are clearly furious with Vichy and even Darlan seems to have incurred their wrath.

The Mess had its opening night and looks like being a success. The cook is evidently first-rate and the company is stimulating. Desmond and Brendan expressed a good many anti-Chamberlain and anti-Baldwin sentiments and it was unanimously agreed that Kingsley Wood ("Little Joe" as Brendan and Beaverbrook call him) was the arch time-server. There was no dissent from Eric Seal's judgment that appeasement backed by strength may be good policy; appeasement through weakness is fatal. We had a long discussion on the reform of the Civil Service, begun by my begging Brendan to get the P.M. to make use of the present opportunity to initiate retirement in the Civil Service from forty-five onwards with a proportionate pension. Eric and Desmond put forward the view that each new entrant to the Civil Service should do a year's training to discover his bent and that some time after the age of thirty he should, if suitable, go to something equivalent to the Staff College before receiving higher promotion.

Wednesday, February 5th

Being on duty at 8.30 a.m. I read Keynes's interesting counter-blast to Hitler's new order, which states our war aims – and the hollowness of Germany's – in the economic sphere, promises drastic measures to deal with unemployment and proclaims a currency based on the exchange of goods. The Treasury have hacked it about a little and Sir Orme Sargent[2] has redrafted it

---

[1] Scottish journalist M.P., originally with extreme left-wing views. Among the first to warn of the Nazi danger, he was appointed Regional Commissioner for Scotland by Chamberlain in 1939, with Lords Rosebery and Airlie as his deputies. On accepting the Scottish Office he made the unusual proviso that he should be assisted by a council containing all the previous Secretaries of State for Scotland.

[2] Witty and cynical Under Secretary at the Foreign Office who was loved and respected by all his colleagues and universally known as Moley, though far from being a mole. Succeeded Sir Alexander Cadogan as Permanent Under Secretary after the war. Churchill set great store by his judgment.

entirely; but I prefer Keynes's original, which is pungent and comprehensible to the inexpert.

The Censorship Report on Home Opinion, which I am summarising for the P.M., makes it clear that there is a general expectation that this war must bring the end of class distinction and the abolition of great inequalities of wealth. There is no anti-democratic feeling. Obviously – and rightly – the fact that rationing and shortages affect the rich very little, since they can pay the extra price and feed in well-stocked restaurants, is causing some bitterness. A demand for war aims comes only from the intelligentsia and the main feeling seems to be hatred of the Germans and a demand for their annihilation – this particularly from the working classes. Employers and Labour both claim that the other is profiting from the war.

Edward Bridges and Prof. both dined in the Mess which promises to be a great success.

Thursday, February 6th

At the House the P.M. paid a tribute to Lord Lloyd, who died on Sunday. He spoke of him simply and well and said that, though an imperialist and in some ways an authoritarian, he had been among the first to see the danger of Nazism and had worked in complete harmony with his Labour colleagues. His knowledge of the Moslems was great and since the King–Emperor had under his rule more Moslems than any other Prince, Lloyd's loss was especially heavy.

In the evening the P.M. got busy with the appointment of large numbers of Under Secretaries and Ministers. Lord Moyne* succeeds Lloyd, Ernest Brown[1] becomes Minister of Health instead of Malcolm MacDonald, and Tom Johnston S. of S. for Scotland. The P.M. told me he was delighted with the "lay-out" which includes the Editor of *Forward* (Tom Johnston) and the Premier Duke[2] (Under-Secretary for Agriculture) and thus shows the breadth of the administration.

Tommy Dugdale, who has just come back from Palestine, is to be Deputy Chief Whip.

---

[1] Eloquent Baptist Liberal-National, renowned for his loud voice. A man of high quality, he was successively Minister of Labour, Secretary of State for Scotland (though as English as could be), Chancellor of the Duchy of Lancaster and briefly, in 1945, Minister of Aircraft Production. He lost his seat at Leith in the 1945 election.

[2] Bernard, 16th Duke of Norfolk and Earl Marshal. Brilliant organiser of state functions, including two coronations and Churchill's State Funeral.

Friday, February 7th

The P.M. went off on a tour to Colchester. At about 10.30 I was able to ring up and give the good news that Benghazi had surrendered. Wavell had doubted his ability to take it before the end of the month.

I met Philip at Euston and travelled with him to Crewe, dining on the train and proceeding from Crewe to Madeley in a taxi. The first impression of Madeley is pleasing, in spite of the overcrowding with furniture and pictures from Crewe, Crewe House, Horsley and Eccleston Square. The rooms are well proportioned and spacious and large fires burn in every grate.

Saturday, February 8th

Mother, Philip and I walked far in the morning, through the park and round by the village. The surrounding country is undulating and pretty, quite unspoilt by the sight of an occasional colliery and the nearness of the Potteries and the Five Towns. The house outside is much less attractive than within, in fact distinctly disappointing as it was built in a good period (c. 1800).

Peggy arrived at lunch-time and made herself very agreeable. She particularly wanted to hear "all the low-down" about Muselier's mistaken arrest, of which she had already heard. Secrets do not last long.

After tea I went to see Grandfather in his room upstairs. He has had a touch of pleurisy, which at eighty-three is serious. However he looks astonishingly well and youthful; his cheeks have sunk a little but his appearance is still distinguished; he is growing deaf, and he sometimes stutters a little, but his eye and brain are clear and he expresses himself well if sometimes haltingly. His memory is remarkable, both for what he has seen and what he has read. We talked of politics. He said the Prime Minister had greatly mellowed of recent years and had, he thought, lost the sudden fits of unreasonable temper to which he had once been subject. He agreed that Baldwin would receive the roughest treatment at the hands of posterity, rougher than Chamberlain, but he did not believe this would be entirely justified although Baldwin's understanding of foreign affairs had been very slight. In other circumstances he might well have been a great Prime Minister. He had the capacity as his handling of the Abdication had shown.

Sunday, February 9th

Constant rain. We went to Mattins in the old red sandstone church which was almost filled by a large congregation.

After dinner we listened to Winston's first-rate broadcast, triumphant and yet not over-optimistic, addressed very largely to American ears. He mentioned the gallantry of the police which I had suggested that he should do.

At this stage of the proceedings I decided to leave the three fat volumes of my diary locked up at Madeley because its indiscretions were considerable. I also felt it would be a pity if it were burnt in some conflagration during the blitz. On leaving Madeley on February 10th I wrote as follows:

I am confident that we have won. We shall see much serious damage and undergo many trials and dangers; but with the certainty of American material help and the determination of the people, the ultimate issue cannot be in doubt. The aftermath is unforeseeable, but there is reason to hope that we have learnt enough from the experiences of the recent past to see the folly of allowing the ideal to part company from the practical.

As soon as I got back to London I could not resist keeping a small pocket diary and the entries grew fuller as the days went by. I soon added to this much longer notes written after occasions which seemed to me particularly interesting, especially travels with the Prime Minister and week-ends at Chequers. In the entries that follow I have inserted these in their proper place. They account, however, for occasional repetitions in the narrative.

Tuesday, February 11th
Went to the Sinclairs' flat on top of the Air Ministry to have a drink with Lady S. and Catherine. Air Marshal Sir Philip Joubert de la Ferté was there, and I thought him most entertaining, if a shade specious.

Douglas, one of the nicest people in the Treasury, dined in the Mess. Brendan says we must not have so many Civil Servants to dine: they are dreary.

Wednesday, February 12th
Frantic arguments at dinner between Desmond and Brendan about theology and in particular the Church of Rome. Very late with the P.M.: read Pepys.

Beaverbrook told the P.M. on the telephone that in three things he had shown great vision: in his treatment of Hopkins; in his treatment of Wendell Willkie;[1] in the timing of his broadcast last Sunday, which had just caught the American public on the right reaction.

Desmond Morton told me that there was great opposition to the P.M.'s decision not to press on to Tripoli but to divert our effort to Greece and Turkey. In continuing our African campaign we had the practical certainty of winning all North Africa and holding an impregnable position. In forming a bridgehead in Greece we ran the risk of another Dunkirk. The C.I.G.S. felt so strongly about it that he was almost thinking of resigning, and the military were making a determined effort to get Wavell to intervene. There was no constitutional means of forcing Wavell to obey; c.f. the old controversy between Haig and Lloyd George. Desmond pointed out that this was the vital decision of the first stage of the war.

To Sir John Anderson, who has shown himself unsympathetic to a complaint of Burgin[2] about the Government's indifference to certain cases of suffering, the P.M. has minuted: "When one is in office one has no idea how damnable things can feel to the ordinary rank and file of the public."

Saturday, February 15th
Nose to the grindstone all day in the absence of everybody but Seal, Barker and myself (the first taking no part in routine work). The noise of workmen strengthening our block of buildings is enough to induce lunacy.

Monday, February 17th
Philip and I both went on leave. Drove P. up to Helperby, stopping to lunch with the Sandwiches at Hinchingbrooke.

Mother, Aunt Celia and Colin[3] at Helperby. Am reading Baudelaire's *Fleurs du Mal*.

Wednesday, February 19th
We had been going to hunt, but snow made it impossible to our great disappointment. So I read Dostoevsky's *The Idiot* (which is a wonderful book), slept and, in the afternoon, walked with Philip

---

[1] Wendell Willkie, wholly dedicated to the cause of the Allies, was Republican candidate in the 1940 presidential election. He brought to England a message from Roosevelt and the verse, in the President's handwriting, "Sail on, O Ship of State" by Longfellow. Churchill received Willkie with courtesy and took much trouble to inform him about the current state of affairs.

[2] Leslie Burgin, M.P., had been Minister of Supply in Chamberlain's administration, but was dropped from the Government in May 1940.

[3] Colin Dodds (later Crewe), elder son of Lady Annabel Dodds by her second husband.

through the driving snowflakes. During the afternoon an enemy raider surprisingly descended from the clouds and dropped eight bombs nearby – one hitting a train full of chocolate. Aunt Celia upset a silver kettle of scalding water over Lady Graham, but this was not cause and effect. Father arrived from Madeley.

Thursday, February 20th
Snow still falling and no signs of its force diminishing. Emerged once or twice from the house, but for health not pleasure. Passed the day with bridge, sleep and Dostoevsky.

Friday, February 21st
Brilliant sunshine and warmth, but the snow is deep and takes a lot of melting. Philip, Mother and I walked to Myton in the morning to look at an exceedingly beautiful Charles II farmhouse.

Saturday, February 22nd
Lady Chesterfield[1] came over to lunch from Beningbrough. The same party as yesterday, with the addition of Uncle Clive, waited in the kale field, this time ineffectively, but had a very good pigeon shoot in the evening. In Carr's plantation I got twelve, shooting with accuracy.

Wednesday, February 26th
Lunched late at the Wyndham and then went to Hatchards to buy myself some books as a birthday present from David. There I met and conversed with Nancy Tree, Sir Godfrey Thomas, Catherine Sinclair and Juliet Henley. Hatchards is a twentieth-century coffee-house.

Chips Channon (just back from Yugoslavia) and Norman Brook dined. I was on late duty, the P.M. spending the evening composing his speech for the debate in the House tomorrow on the Disqualification of Members (or Malcolm MacDonald) Bill. This afternoon I heard the Chief Whip and Brendan pitch into Attlee because the Labour Party have decided not to put on the Whips for tomorrow's debate. To bed at 3.15 a.m.

After dinner the P.M. dictated his speech, which was full of historical allusions and legal intricacies, on the Disqualification of Members Bill, which has been occasioned by the appointment of Malcolm MacDonald as High Commissioner for Canada. The

---

[1] Enid, last Countess of Chesterfield, owned Beningbrough Hall in the North Riding and bred racehorses. "Who was the architect?" I once asked her when shooting woodcock in the bracken near the house. "Gainsborough," she replied. "*Gainsborough?*" I asked incredulously. "Oh, well, perhaps it was Vanburgh. I have a yearling by one and a house by the other. It is so confusing."

P.M. will get away with it of course, but I think he is unwise to use his personal influence with the House in an instance which is of little immediate importance. By so doing he may weaken his power on an occasion when it is really necessary. He is a great House of Commons man and loves to make use of his Parliamentary art; but I believe his prestige in the House would be even greater if he only appeared there on rare and solemn occasions.

In the early hours news came from the Admiralty of another serious disaster to a convoy. Brendan and I commented gloomily on the great threat to our lifeline which is developing and will continue to develop. He suggested I should not tell the P.M. tonight as it would prevent him sleeping. But at 3.00 a.m. he asked me point-blank if there was any news from the Admiralty and I had to tell him. He became very pensive. "It is very distressing," I said weakly. "Distressing!" he replied. "It is terrifying. If it goes on it will be the end of us."

Thursday, February 27th

The P.M. spent all day at the House where he delivered his speech in the afternoon. I was at the F.O. most of the morning checking certain historical allusions with the help of Gaselee.[1]

Heard the P.M.'s speech which was amusing and well-received in spite of its length. The issue at stake – the holding of "offices of profit" under the Crown by M.P.s – seemed of greater academic than immediate interest; but it was a good lesson in the intricacies and obscurities of British Constitutional practice. I took a long time checking the speech with the Official Reporter.

Friday, February 28th

The P.M. spent the morning at No. 10, presiding over a meeting of the Import Executive about the means of relieving our shipping difficulties. I was in attendance most of the time, working in the congenial atmosphere of No. 10 which is so preferable to the gaunt and dusty Annexe.

Heard that Sandy Vereker[2] had committed suicide. A tragic waste of charm, good looks and talent.

---

[1] Sir Stephen Gaselee was the immensely erudite Foreign Office Librarian, always dressed as if King Edward VII were still on the throne.

[2] Only son of Lord Gort. A contemporary of mine at Harrow and Cambridge. A gifted painter, a keen Wagnerian (his room at Harrow was adorned by his own excellent paintings of scenes from *The Ring*) and the best-looking young man of my generation. He hated military life, as a reaction from his father, but acquitted himself well on the Dunkirk beaches. He shot himself when seriously concussed after a crash on a motor-cycle.

Monday, March 3rd

Rode at Richmond and saw a perfect sunrise. A soft blue sky and a watery sun and the birds singing as if spring were already here. Drove Louis Greig to London and said on a sudden impulse that I should like to be in a bomber crew. He promised to arrange a medical interview for me and I think that if I can tell Winston the R.A.F. have a place for me he may let me go (however obstructive he is about the army or navy).

Spent much time trying to get somebody to write an obituary for Sandy Vereker.

Lunched and laughed with Betty [Montagu] at the Civil Service Canteen in the National Gallery. The P.M. has a cold and is staying at Chequers.

I may here pay a tribute to Louis Greig. He rose from nothing to considerable wealth and quite a lot of influence, partly by marrying a rich woman but more particularly by a genuine and constantly pursued ambition to pull strings on behalf of other people. He seldom if ever pulled them for himself but he thoroughly enjoyed helping others.

During the war he lent me a horse to ride in Richmond Park and I often used to stay the night at Thatched House Lodge, the Greigs' house in the Park. He died after the war, loved by a great many people to whom he had given pleasure without ever seeking any return. His two singularly pleasant daughters (one of whom, Jean, was happily married to Joe Cooper, the pianist) died, far too young, not long after their father.

Tuesday, March 4th

The P.M. returned from Chequers at noon and saw Colonel Donovan,[1] just back from the Balkans, where the stage is set and the curtain about to rise.

The P.M. had Herschel Johnson and Winant* to dine and discussed with them the American bases problem. I had to rush away from the dinner-table three times in order to procure various telegrams. It is very difficult to find what the P.M. wants because his descriptions are so elliptical. To bed 12.30 a.m.

---

[1] "Big Bill" Donovan. Won the Congressional Medal of Honour in France in 1918. He was a successful lawyer of humble Irish immigrant origin. With much help from the British, he created from nothing the American Intelligence system in the Second World War, founded the Office of Strategic Services (O.S.S.) and was thus indirectly an originator of the C.I.A.

Wednesday, March 5th

Busy and interesting day, during which vital and far-reaching issues were under discussion.

I only managed to snatch a quarter of an hour for lunch and went to the National Gallery where I found Miss Campbell, formerly Mr Chamberlain's personal private secretary. We talked of former days at No. 10 when the atmosphere was quieter – and much less gay. Winston's régime is certainly entertaining.

Today has been one of great activity and varied interest. At 11.30 the P.M. met Lord Moyne and Cranborne, Herschel Johnson and Winant, the new U.S. Ambassador, in the Cabinet Room at No. 10, to discuss the vexed problem of the American bases in the West Indies, which we have given on lease for ninety-nine years in return for fifty obsolete destroyers. The West Indian Colonies themselves, the oldest of the Crown, are resentful and their feelings are shared by many people here in view of the conditions which the Americans have demanded and which amount to capitulations. Both sides are haggling and ill-feeling has arisen. Bridges thinks that if the Government accepted all the American desiderata they would be defeated in the House of Commons. The Colonial Office are frightened that in the heat of conflict we shall cede much that will afterwards be most regrettable. Lord Cranborne sees in the American attitude a dangerous emphasis on hemisphere defence: an inclination to make special concessions to Canada because she is an American nation; a tendency which might well lead to Western hemisphere isolationism after the war.

But the P.M. is ill-satisfied with the point of view expressed by his colleagues. He believes that the safety of the state is at stake, that America in providing us with credits will enable us to win the war which we could not otherwise do, and that we cannot afford to risk the major issue in order to maintain our pride and to preserve the dignity of a few small islands.

I think his view is statesmanlike, but America, if she persists, is going to arouse a lot of bitterness in England and set back the cause of Anglo-American unity.

While the P.M. was trying to reach a *modus vivendi* on this question, an alarming telegram arrived from Eden. It showed the Greek situation in a sombre light. Eden, Dill and Wavell have found General Papagos discouraged and obviously weakened by the loss of Metaxas. They have accepted a strategic position which will mean that our troops will find themselves in a dangerous plight. Yugoslavia is weak and vacillating; Turkey is in no position to do anything but remain on the defensive. Eden says: "This is as tough a proposition as ever I have known."

Last night David Margesson told me how much he disliked the whole venture upon which we are about to embark. Many others feel the same. It was thrust upon us partly because, in the first place, the P.M. felt that our prestige in France, in Spain and in the U.S., could not stand our desertion of Greece; partly because Eden, Dill, Wavell and Cunningham (who has now telegraphed to point out the extreme length to which his resources are stretched) recommended it so strongly.[1] But the danger of another Norway, Dunkirk and Dakar rolled into one, looms threateningly before us.

More telegrams came. The P.M. went very late to lunch with Oliver Lyttelton, and I snatched a quarter of an hour for a quick mouthful. After his afternoon sleep, the P.M., emerging from beneath the bedclothes and yawning, said, voicing his waking thought: "The poor Chiefs of the Staff will get very much out of breath in their desire to run away." I showed him a telegram from Eden urging that a high decoration for General Papagos would help matters. "Too cheap," he commented with a disgusted gesture.

The Cabinet met at 5.00 and afterwards the P.M. drafted a telegram to Eden urging that we should not be justified in preventing the Greeks from accepting German terms if they felt themselves unable to resist. If they wished to fight, well and good; we should have to do our utmost.

This telegram was discussed at a 10.00 p.m. Defence Meeting.

Thursday, March 6th
Rush continued. Very short handed. The P.M. harangued the Chiefs of Staff at No. 10 continuously from 11.30 to 1.30.

Lunched with Father at the Turf, which was full. I am glad to see the sideboard is less groaning with cold meat than when last I was there; but certainly the rich can still feed sumptuously.

Rab Butler dined with me in the Mess, where Brendan's flow of eloquence was ceaseless and very funny. The P.M. was cross because he could not find any of us during dinner, but was laughed out of his ill-temper by Brendan who compared him to Mr Sparrow[2] (from Nathaniel Gubbins in the *Sunday Express*).

Slept upstairs, out of the shelter, for the first time.

---

[1] Wavell, having been opposed to the whole scheme of intervention on behalf of Greece, veered round and became its warm exponent.
[2] Mr Sparrow was the curmudgeonly husband in the Sparrows' nest which was a feature of Nat Gubbins' column.

Friday, March 7th

Very anxious decisions have been in the air, making the P.M. impatient, the atmosphere electric and the pace tremendous.

In the morning I went over to see Vansittart in the F.O. to let him know what the P.M. is thinking about the American bases question. He was emphatic about the importance of reaching agreement before the American press becomes vociferous.

Travelled down late to Chequers. Pug and Edward Bridges came, also Oliver Stanley. There was a good deal of reminiscing about the early stages of the war and, later, a number of important telegrams telephoned down from London.

The P.M. was much happier. His mind is relieved now that a great decision has been irrevocably taken. He was witty and entertaining.

Saturday, March 8th

Sir Arthur Salter and Sir William Beveridge[1] came to lunch and talked of shipping and manpower. The P.M. pulled their legs a good deal and kept on winking at Tommy Thompson and me, the others present. He said that socialism was folly, that the profit motive was essential to efficiency, and many other things that must have shocked Salter. Beveridge said he thought there would be a Conservative reaction after the war.

A short but much needed walk, followed by tea with Pamela Churchill in the Great Hall. Mr Menzies,[2] the Australian Prime Minister, came to stay; so did General de Gaulle, General Spears, and Duncan and Diana Sandys. An interesting evening, punctuated with rumours of an impending naval battle and news of a blitz on London, the first for weeks. The Café de Paris was hit and a hundred people trapped. Mr Hopkins rang me up from New York at 3.00 a.m. to say the Lease and Lend Bill had passed.

At dinner this evening there were present, besides the Prime Minister, General de Gaulle, General Spears, Mr Menzies, Duncan and Diana Sandys, Tommy Thompson and myself.

---

[1] Author of the Beveridge Plan and thus of the Welfare State. A Liberal who was a gifted economist and social scientist. Originally a civil servant, he became Vice Chancellor of London University and Master of University College, Oxford. Created a peer in 1946.

[2] Sir Robert Menzies, Prime Minister of Australia until the Labour Party won a General Election in 1941. He spent several months in England and was invited to attend the War Cabinet meetings. A staunch imperialist, he returned to power in 1949 and won a reputation for wisdom and statesmanship. On his retirement the Queen appointed him Lord Warden of the Cinque Ports. She had already made him a Knight of the Thistle.

We talked of Germany and the Germans.

De Gaulle said that the important thing for people living in an occupied territory was to remain aloof and superior. The Germans knew that they were inferior beings and were susceptible on the point. Moreover, this being so, it was important to stress that the war was a world war. The Germans could see themselves as lords of Europe, but the idea of the world gave them vertigo. As for Hitler, he said: *"Vous ne le prendrez pas, et cette fois il n'y aura pas un Doorn."*[1]

Duncan Sandys was bloodthirsty. He wanted to destroy Germany by laying the country waste and burning towns and factories, so that for years the German people might be occupied in reconstruction. He wanted to destroy their books and libraries so that an illiterate generation might grow up.

Louis Spears replied that this would make the Germans more hardy and virile, while their Western conquerors would be growing effete on the fruits of victory. In his view Richelieu was the greatest of modern European statesmen. He had understood the Germans and at the Diet of Ratisbon he had so divided them that they took centuries to unite. The P.M. replied that this was not applicable to modern conditions, though Prussia must be separated from South Germany.

The P.M. said he was in no way moved by Duncan's words. He did not believe in pariah nations, and he saw no alternative to the acceptance of Germany as part of the family of Europe. In the event of invasion he would not even approve of the civil population murdering the Germans quartered on them. Still less would he condone atrocities against the German civil population if we were in a position to commit them. He cited an incident in Ancient Greece when the Athenians spared a city which had massacred some of their citizens, not because its inhabitants were men, but "because of the nature of man". This impressed Mr Menzies.

Mr Menzies contributed to the discussion by a slightly irrelevant, though amusing, account of the way in which an insect called the Cactoblastus, imported from California, destroyed the dense growth of Prickly Pear jungle in Australia. Duncan hoped for a similar *deus ex machina* to deal with the Germans.

The conversation turned to Rome and Carthage. The P.M. drew a comparison between this country and Carthage, but pointed out that the Carthaginians were vanquished because they lost com-

---

[1] "You will not capture him, and this time there will not be a Doorn." Doorn was the country house in Holland where Kaiser Wilhelm II found asylum when the British and French Governments wanted to put him on trial after 1918.

mand of the sea. Mr Menzies said that moreover they had not had a Winston Churchill (forgetting Hannibal!). Anyhow, said the P.M., the Almighty had given Carthage a raw deal last time and might alter the outcome on this occasion.

Sunday, March 9th
Saw de Gaulle off and talked with Colonel Donovan who came to see the P.M. and told me about his Balkan and Peninsular tour.

Sir Alan Brooke, C. in C., Home Forces, came to dine and sleep. Prof. L. and Alastair Forbes dined also and there was a lot of flippant conversation about metaphysics, solipsists and higher mathematics. Afterwards the gramophone played marches and old-fashioned songs of a martial kind (such as the P.M. loves) while W.S.C. gave us a display of arms drill with his big game rifle. To bed at the record hour of 11.30 p.m.

Monday, March 10th
The P.M. has been suffering from bronchitis and is not going back to London. His capacity for work is totally unimpaired and his temper is scarcely ruffled. He came down to lunch with Mary, Tommy Thompson and me. Afterwards he told us about Robert Graves's book on the American War of Independence (*Sergeant Lamb*), which he is reading with particular enjoyment, and lamented the difficulties caused by the bases agreement.

Lord Moyne (S. of S. for the Colonies) and Sir Richard Peirse (C. in C., Bomber Command) came for the night. Big bombs (the new 4,000-pounders) alternated with West Indian bases as the main topic and I sat up late arranging the P.M.'s complex papers about the latter.

Tuesday, March 11th
Early bedside conference with Lord Moyne. The P.M. decided to tackle the bases problem with the American Ambassador this afternoon.

His bronchitis is still bad, but in spite of everybody's wishes he insisted on returning to London in time for the usual Tuesday lunch with the King. I dined with Eileen[1] and Tommy Davies at the Dorchester. The others in the party included Fitzroy Maclean (who has resigned from the F.O. to become a private in the Camerons).

---

[1] A childhood friend married to Colonel Thomas Davies, Grenadier Guards.

Wednesday, March 12th

Went to the House with the P.M. and heard him sing a paean of praise to the U.S. for having passed the Lease and Lend Bill. He described it as a second Magna Carta (using words suggested by Professor Whitehead of the F.O.).[1]

He then saw the Bermudan delegates and spoke to them so charmingly about their losses over the bases question that they told me they thought he felt it as keenly as they themselves. I quoted *The Tempest* to them: "the still-vexed Bermoothes".

Brendan invited his financier-collector friend, Chester Beatty,[2] to dine and Cole Deacon of the Railway Executive also came. I made an allusion to Roumania being the Botany Bay of the Roman Empire, which incensed Brendan – though I believe he is Irish and not Australian at all.

Tuesday, March 18th

The P.M. made a speech at the Pilgrim's luncheon. Lunch was at 1.15: he was still dictating his speech at 1.30!

Left at 6.30 to stay the night with Lilly[3] and Tom Motion at Serge Hill for a day's hunting. Cousin Nelly[4] was there – a very delightful personality, aristocratic in the true sense, intelligent, dignified and of great simplicity. We talked of the three Sheridan sisters[5] and particularly Caroline Norton.

Wednesday, March 19th

Hunted with the Hertfordshire, accompanied by my host and hostess. We met at Putteridge and a thick mist gave way to radiant heat and sunshine. We did not find till late, but there could have

---

[1] This was the only occasion I remember during the war when Winston Churchill used somebody else's draft, or at any rate a portion of it, in making a speech to the House of Commons. In all other cases the text was entirely his own.

[2] A successful mining engineer, born an American but naturalised a British subject. Chairman of Selection Trust and other large mining enterprises.

[3] Best looking of the six daughters of the 3rd Earl of Verulam. My mother's first cousin. My father fell briefly in love with her before he met my mother and when, at my mother's suggestion, she became a lady-in-waiting, King George V found her so attractive that Queen Mary thought it prudent to dispense with her services.

[4] Lady Helen Graham.*

[5] Sheridan's three beautiful and talented grand-daughters were Lady Dufferin, Mrs Norton and the Duchess of Somerset. Caroline Norton wrote verses and novels, was a pioneer of the Married Women's Property Act and had an intimate, though probably platonic, relationship with Lord Melbourne. She was a well-known figure in Victorian intellectual circles and George Meredith portrayed her as "Diana of the Crossways".

been no better day for riding about the countryside which is exquisite in this part of the country. We finally found in a ploughed field to which we were led by two Miss Harrisons (of the famous eight sisters)[1] and had a short but fast run before the fox went to ground. He got up from a furrow twenty-five yards in front of hounds and the chase was spectacular.

Back to London after tea. The P.M. had the Americans Biddle[2] (Ambassador to all our fugitive allies over here) and Harriman* (President R.'s personal representative on shipping and supply questions) to dinner and as there was a heavy raid he took his guests and his whole private office up to the roof of the Air Ministry to watch the fun. He quoted to us Tennyson's prescient lines about aerial warfare.

Thursday, March 20th
At the House for Questions and the Cabinet. There was a scene over Boothby who is committing breaches of privilege. On the way home in the car the P.M., speaking of this, said he would have no part in the matter; if there was one thing in the world he found odious, it was a man-hunt.

Our master having gone to dine at the Other Club,[3] we took the opportunity of playing noisy and childish games in the Mess, and were much excited by the news that the *Scharnhorst* and *Gneisenau* had been located in the Atlantic and might well be intercepted.

Saturday, March 22nd
Very busy. Tony Bevir has many qualities but he is apt to vanish for hours at a stretch and leave a solitary colleague to bear the heat and burden of the day.

Jack Churchill was quite entertaining in the Mess (he is often very boring) and gave vivid descriptions of F.E. (Lord Birkenhead).

The diplomatic battle for the soul of Yugoslavia is reaching its height and sways either way with vertiginous speed.

Sunday, March 23rd
During the course of the morning I strolled out for a few minutes and walked into the Abbey where, even in this sceptical age, hundreds of people were attending a service in the nave in observance of the National Day of Prayer.

[1] The eight daughters of Major J. F. Harrison of King's Waldenbury, Hitchin, were ardent riders to hounds.
[2] U.S. Ambassador to all the exiled foreign Governments in London.
[3] Dining Club founded by Churchill and F. E. Smith (Lord Birkenhead) in 1911 when they were both blackballed from The Club.

Edward Bridges and Bill Cavendish Bentinck dined. The latter is witty and talks well; also has good judgment, I think. He is *au courant* with what is going on and full of ideas on the subject.

Tuesday, March 25th
The message which I drafted for the P.M. to send to the 'Greeks on their Independence Day was published in this evening's paper:

> Mr Churchill, the Prime Minister, has sent the following message to the Greek people, who yesterday celebrated Greek Independence Day:
> "On this day of proud memories, I would add one brief tribute to those which the whole civilised world is paying to the valour of the Greek nation.
> One hundred and twenty years ago, all that was noblest in England strove in the cause of Greek independence and rejoiced in its achievement. Today that epic struggle is being repeated against greater odds, but with equal courage and with no less certainty of success. We in England know that the cause for which Byron died is a sacred cause: we are resolved to sustain it."

While the Prime Minister always wrote his own speeches I became, at this period and again when I returned to No. 10 at the end of 1943, the principal drafter of messages, prefaces, etc. Although Mr Churchill at his best was beyond plagiarism, it was possible to imitate his style fairly closely on matters which were not of supreme importance and I reached the stage where I could draft most of his shorter compositions without his correcting them. Having thus acquired a certain ability to imitate his style I did, after 1951, write quite a number of his speeches although very few of those, and then only on ceremonial occasions, which he delivered to Parliament.

Thursday, March 27th
Walked round St James's Park lake with Rab Butler who has, somewhat reluctantly, come to admire the P.M. though he still clearly does not think much of his own Secretary of State [Anthony Eden].

A great day. Revolution in Belgrade, which puts an entirely different complexion on events in the Balkans and turns darkness into dawn. The P.M. is overjoyed and I should be too, if I had not got a liver attack. He announced the glad tidings in two speeches, at a Conservative Association meeting and at a T.U.C. meeting. The whole country is in ecstasies.[1]

News of Keren's[2] fall was the final cause of rejoicing. P.M. thrilled, but says we must now expect bad news.

Friday, March 28th

To Chequers, arriving just in time for dinner. Party consisted of P.M., Sir John Anderson, Pug, Tommy, Mary and Pamela. Chief excitement was report of naval engagement with Italians off Crete – this time a true one. Talk ranged from foreign policy to the home front. P.M. said people were very much happier in the war than might have been expected. Anderson went further and thought the war might prove to have been a real blessing to the country. He is a pompous ass, but clever.

The P.M., in praising Chamberlain's courage during his illness, said that he knew not the first thing about war, Europe or foreign politics. Discourse on the Admiralty: Pound the best brain in the navy, though the most cautious. Alexander would have had to face much hostile criticism if he had not been a Labour man.

Saturday, March 29th

A family luncheon party after which the P.M. gave me a short lecture on the various invaders of Russia, especially Charles XII. Later Sarah took Mrs C., Tommy and me over to see her new and luxurious (but very filmstar) house at Waddesdon.

Mr Winant, Averell Harriman, Mr Menzies and the Cranbornes came for the week-end. I sat next to Menzies at dinner and had a lively conversation with him about Ireland, the English and the Diplomatic Service.

Sunday, March 30th

The Duke and Duchess of Kent came to lunch. I sat between Lord Cranborne, who is exceptionally agreeable, and Averell Harri-

---

[1] The Regent of Yugoslavia, Prince Paul, was summoned by Hitler in March 1941 and reluctantly obliged to sign a pact with the Axis. This caused a revolution in Belgrade. On March 26th General Simovic deposed the Regent, declared King Peter ruler of the country and formed an anti-German government. The Germans thereupon diverted troops southwards, bombed Belgrade and occupied the country. The King had to escape to London and the former Regent was placed in custody by the British. This Yugoslav diversion, followed in April by the British landing in Greece, may have caused Hitler to postpone his invasion of Russia, originally planned for May 1st.

[2] Keren, in Eritrea, had been tenaciously defended by the Duke of Aosta's Italian army.

man. Afterwards the Duke inspected the Guard while I struggled with his chauffeur-less car and the Duchess. Mr Menzies photographed the proceedings assiduously.

The news of the great naval victory off Cape Matapan, for which we have been waiting, came through just after the Kents had left and was greeted with yells of delight. "How lucky the Italians came in," said the P.M.

Sarah came to tea and there was more photography by Mr Menzies. Prof. arrived.

"The tearing up of the paper fleet of Italy," was Winston's comment on today's news.

Monday, March 31st
This has been a wonderful week-end, the culmination of a week of victories. Our visitors are Winant, Harriman, Menzies, the Cranbornes.

The P.M. has been elated by the naval victory following so close on the Yugoslav revolution, the fall of Keren and the capture of Harar.[1] He emphasises the effect it will have on Japan and he has written a letter to Matsuoka,[2] now on his way to Vichy, in a similar vein, though somewhat more threatening, to that he sent last June to Mussolini. He begins by asking: "Will Germany, without the command of the sea or the command of the British daylight air, be able to invade and conquer Great Britain in the spring, summer or autumn of 1941? Will Germany try to do so? Would it not be in the interests of Japan to wait until these questions have answered themselves?" He asks seven other equally pertinent questions and concludes: "From the answers to these questions may spring the avoidance by Japan of a serious catastrophe, and a marked improvement in the relations between Japan and the two great sea powers of the West."

The P.M. told me he was now sure Germany would attack Yugoslavia before Greece or Turkey and he is very hopeful on that front.

The naval news has stirred him to compose several brilliant telegrams, to Roosevelt, etc., and he has spent much of the week-end pacing – or rather tripping – up and down the Great Hall

---

[1] Town in Ethiopia defended by the Italians.
[2] Japanese Foreign Minister and moving spirit behind Japan's decision to join the Berlin–Rome Axis. He also wanted to make friends with the Soviet Union and isolate the U.S.A. In April 1941 he went to Moscow, via Rome and Berlin, but Hitler told him nothing of his plan to invade Russia. Thus he looked foolish when, on reaching Moscow, he signed a treaty with the Soviet Union just before it was attacked by his Axis allies. He had to resign.

to the sound of the gramophone (playing martial airs, waltzes and the most vulgar kind of brass-band songs) deep in thought all the while.

In the evening Diana Quilter took me, with Middy Gascoigne, Brigadier Gibbs and a guardsman called Arnold Vivian, to see the Stepney Shelters. We drank sherry and ate smoked-salmon sandwiches at Diana's First Aid Post and were then escorted to the crypt of Christchurch, Spitalfields; the Kent and Essex Hay-yard (which was deserted); the Tilbury shelter; the Arches, Watney Street; and Gooche's. They have greatly improved; some are even cheerful, though it is terrible to see human beings living in such cramped conditions. But many were well dressed and few looked miserable. Two personalities impressed me: Father Groser who has organised a social centre at the Arches, with a canteen and lectures or debates every night; and the nurse, young but downright and completely self-possessed, at Gooche's.

15

African Reverse: Greek Fiasco

April 1941

Wednesday, April 2nd
Glamorous pay-party at Claridges, organised by Ann O'Neill.[1]
There has been nothing like it since the war. Our party was Middy,
Terence, Rosemary Hinchingbrooke, Betty Montagu, Martin
Charteris, Diana Quilter and others. It was wonderful to see a
display of real evening dresses again and to meet people I had not
seen since 1939. All London was there and the gaiety was great.

In the early hours I went on to the Four Hundred with Martin,
Rosemary, Betty and Peter and Diana Tiarks. War is a great cure
for blasé-ness as far as these sort of entertainments go. It would all
have seemed commonplace and dull two years ago.

Thursday, April 3rd
We have been compelled to evacuate Benghazi in face of the
German advance from Tripoli. The P.M. is greatly worried, but
Pug refuses to take it too tragically. However the proposed visit to
Liverpool and Manchester this evening is cancelled.

Sunday, April 6th
We heard on the wireless that Germany had invaded both Greece
and Yugoslavia.

---

[1] Born Ann Charteris, she married my cousin Shane, Lord O'Neill, who was
killed in action in 1944. She then married Esmond, Viscount Rothermere, and
finally Ian Fleming, the creator of James Bond. Vivacious and quick-witted, she
sought the company of men of power. Lord Beaverbrook unkindly dubbed her
"Idiots' Delight", but she delighted many men and some women who were by
no means idiots.

Monday, April 7th

There is no news from the Balkan front but that from Libya is bad. The German attack has taken us by surprise and an armoured brigade has been cut up.

Budget: income tax ten shillings in the pound. Nobody seems to mind. Brendan says the House and the Country take a masochistic pleasure in it, like flagellating friars.

After dinner (to which Brendan invited Sir Walter Layton) there was a short Chiefs of Staff meeting. The P.M. confided to me that he thought Wavell, etc., had been very silly in North Africa and should have been prepared to meet an attack there.

There was a film display in the Air Council room at the Air Ministry. I went with the P.M. We saw a new propaganda film, and the latest *March of Time*.

Tuesday, April 8th

The P.M. spent all the afternoon composing his speech for tomorrow. After dinner I took part of it round to the American Embassy to show Winant. He made four pertinent observations in respect of the effect on U.S. opinion and I was deeply impressed by his unassertive shrewdness and wisdom. I afterwards explained these points to the P.M. who accepted them.

While I was with the Ambassador a blitz started. He did not even raise his head. Massawa has fallen into our hands; but the news from Yugoslavia is disturbing and the Germans have already entered Salonica.

Wednesday, April 9th

I listened to the P.M.'s speech on the war situation in the House of Commons. It was well received. He painted a picture dark and yet encouraging, and he stressed that the Battle of the Atlantic was the real issue of the war. He did not attempt to minimise the hazards with which we are faced in Greece and North Africa. He explained how unity in the Balkans had been a possibility. If Yugoslavia, Greece and Turkey had stood firm together, they could have presented to Germany a strong front defended by seventy divisions.

Thursday, April 10th

The P.M. was terribly upset by a serious motor smash involving Duncan Sandys.

Left for a tour of the South-West with the P.M., Winant, Harriman, Mrs Churchill, Mary, Ismay, Tommy and a batch of officers connected with the new technical inventions. We all slept on the train.

Friday, April 11th
Good Friday. Reached Swansea at 8.00 a.m. and spent the morning among the City's battered ruins and inspecting detachments of Civil Defence Workers. The centre of the town has not a house standing. I was amazed by the eagerness and cheerfulness of the population. W. had a great reception.

We went on by train to Cardigan and motored from there to Aberporth on Cardigan Bay, where we saw a noisy but interesting display of rockets, U.P. projectors, etc., such as would have delighted the Prof.'s heart if he had not been laid up with a chill at Marlow. The firing of the rockets was bad and at the first display a childishly easy target was repeatedly missed; but the multiple projectors seemed promising; so did the aerial mines descending with parachutes.

During the morning at Swansea I walked much of the time with Mr David Grenfell, local M.P. and also Minister of Mines, who began life as a miner. He talked in Welsh to most of his constituents.

We slept on the train at a wayside station called Whitland.

Saturday, April 12th
Arrived early at Bristol. Bathed and breakfasted with the P.M. and Harriman at the Grand Hotel. The rest of the party joined us from the train and led by the Lord Mayor we walked and motored through devastation such as I had never thought possible. Swansea is mild in comparison. There had been a bad raid during the night and many of the ruins were still smoking. The people looked bewildered but, as at Swansea, were brave and were thrilled by the sight of Winston who drove about sitting on the hood of an open car and waving his hat.

At the university the P.M., as Chancellor, conferred honorary degrees on Winant and Menzies and made an excellent impromptu speech in which he likened the fortitude of Bristol to that which we are accustomed "to associate with Ancient Rome and modern Greece". The gowns and pageantry were a strange contrast to the smoking ruins just outside.[1]

Reached Chequers for dinner. Mr and Mrs Eden and Sir J. Dill

---

[1] Menzies, who spoke poorly on this occasion, told me afterwards that he never spoke with notes. He always found it was politically more impressive, and seldom risky, to speak impromptu. In this discovery he was luckier than most politicians.

came. A hectic night starting in gloom and ending in glad momentous news from the U.S.A. – Winant received a telegram for the P.M. from Roosevelt announcing America's intention to extend her patrol area as far west as the 25th meridian.

Sunday, April 13th

Easter Day. The C.I.G.S. took Mary and me to the early service in his car. The Chiefs of Staff, Eden, Amery, Horace Seymour[1] and Pug met all the morning to discuss Iraq, where a pro-axis coup d'état has taken place under Rashid Ali, and Yugoslavia, where resistance to the Germans by the semi-mobilised army seems to be stiffening a little. In Libya we heard that the Germans had taken Bardia and attacked Tobruk.

I asked Harriman if he did not think last night's news from the U.S. might mean war with Germany. "That's what I hope," he said.

At lunch I sat between Brendan (who shuns Chequers except on rare occasions) and Seymour. Afterwards the conclave continued till tea-time, Amery, who had been summoned about Iraq, pushing himself into the Yugoslav discussions. When the P.M. went to sleep Mary and I went for an invigorating walk in the fresh wind, she overbrimming with life and gaiety.

Menzies arrived for dinner, at which only the P.M., Mary, Harriman and Tommy were present in addition. Afterwards we talked, pulled Mary's leg and played the gramophone. The P.M. worked till 2.15 a.m.

Wednesday, April 16th

Organised resistance in Yugoslavia has ceased. In Greece the Germans are entering Volo and there is much talk of a stand in the pass of Thermopylae. We are holding our own at Tobruk.

Gladwyn Jebb came to dinner. A raid started in the middle and grew, in the course of the night, to be the worst London has yet had. During it I went to the American Embassy in the armoured car to discuss a telegram with Winant and also met his wife. Later, as 450 planes droned over London, bombs came down like hailstones and on my way to No. 10, at 1.45 a.m., I had quite a disagreeable walk.

During this period of the war Jack Churchill and I slept on the top floor of 10 Downing Street itself, in the Prime Minister's and Mrs

---

[1] A diplomat since before the First World War. Minister at Teheran in the 1930s, an Under Secretary in the Foreign Office for the first half of the war and then Ambassador to China.

Churchill's former bedrooms, which were still furnished. This was comfortable, but also noisy and vulnerable. In the autumn of 1944, when I returned to Downing Street during the "V" weapon bombardment, I slept for a time in the underground quarters beneath the Central War Room where all the rest of the Secretaries slept, as well as the Chiefs of Staff and members of the Cabinet Offices. This was certainly safe, but it looked and smelt like a battleship and one emerged in the morning gasping for fresh air.

Thursday, April 17th

London looks bleary-eyed and disfigured. There is a great gash in the Admiralty. St Peter's, Eaton Square, has been hit (and Mr Austin Thompson[1] killed), Chelsea Old Church is demolished, Jermyn Street is wrecked. Mayfair has suffered badly.

After breakfast Eric Seal and I walked in the sun on the Horse Guards Parade and found Pamela Churchill and Averell Harriman also examining the devastation. The streets were soon full of people intent on sightseeing. The roads everywhere were covered with glass.

In the evening Brendan regaled us with his electioneering experiences, which are remarkably funny, and Pug told for the twelfth time the story of Gamelin and the defeat of France.

Our planes set out to bomb Berlin and thus showed we are not afraid of reprisal threats.

Friday, April 18th

Got up and rode early on the Thatched House Lodge chestnut, afterwards breakfasting with Louis.

Lunched with Esmé Glyn at the Carlton Grill. She took me to see her mother's house in St James's Place gutted by fire and by a landmine yesterday morning. Only the shell remains and there was still a fire burning inside. The butler was stalwartly saving what he could from the ruins. Except for No. 23, Jimmy Rothschild's house, the whole street of charming houses is laid waste. Rain added to the desolation of the scene.

The P.M. saw the press editors to prepare their minds for grave possibilities in Greece. At 6.00 he left for Ditchley.

A statement was issued to the press that we would bomb Rome if Athens or Cairo were bombed and that we should continue to raid Berlin, not as reprisals but as policy, whenever convenient.

---

[1] Much loved vicar of St Peter's, Eaton Square. He went out on to the steps of the church to call people into the comparative safety of the solidly-built edifice and was struck by a bomb.

Saturday, April 19th

After dinner another raid started and rapidly increased in intensity. As I write a bomb has exploded close by and there seem to be many aircraft overhead.

Tony says that London is now beginning to look a little like what he expected it to be thirty-six hours after the outbreak of war. Certainly as I walk through the streets I look at London's landmarks more carefully now, with a feeling that it may be the last time I shall see them.

Sunday, April 20th

Early service at Westminster Abbey and then walked down the Embankment in the sun. London from Westminster Bridge on a spring morning is very different from the day when Wordsworth saw it, but it now has a modern splendour. Boadicea's[1] statue is a monument to successful imperialism (*aet.* 1902):

> Realms that Caesar never knew
> Thy posterity shall sway.

Monday, April 21st

The P.M. returned from Ditchley at 11.30 and immediately had a Defence Committee. Today is a critical day in the history of the war as far as Greece is concerned. Final decision to evacuate was taken.

Lunched with Father at the Turf, one of the few surviving clubs. Sammy Hood dined in the Mess. I was on late duty and very late it was, the P.M. almost finishing his box.

A momentous decision was taken today, not only in Greece. Operation TIGER[2] was adopted.

Tuesday, April 22nd

To the new House (the old has been damaged) for Questions and a short statement as to why there should be no statement! Tripoli has been bombarded by the fleet, though it is not yet clear with how much success. The P.M. had Hore-Belisha to lunch and it was a strange coincidence that for the first time a press photographer was

---

[1] Now called Boudicca, with the same pedantry that turns Jehovah into Yahweh, thus demonstrating an academic ambition to be thought clever by dethroning names that have been in general use for centuries. Adam and Eve have miraculously escaped so far.

[2] The despatch at great risk through the Mediterranean of tanks required to enable Wavell to take the offensive.

seen to be waiting outside the Annexe. I asked David Margesson, who was also lunching, whether he thought the P.M. had anything in mind for Belisha. He said he thought the P.M. had, at the back of his mind, because he saw incipient opposition in that quarter and Winston is inclined to defeat opposition by means of favour rather than by fear. David has the lowest opinion of Belisha; so has Duff Cooper with whom I also talked of him this afternoon.

Wednesday, April 23rd
The surrender of the Western Greek armies and departure of the Government were made public.

The Home Censorship Report (on letters sent abroad from this country) is for the first time a little bit alarming. It shows a certain amount of discontent. People seem to think that "the ruling classes" are doing well out of the war – which they certainly are not. There is a good deal of criticism of the Government and a lot of the B.B.C. In particular people seem to be getting sick of the hearty propaganda of the "Are we downhearted?" kind, sponsored by the Government. Brendan points out that there is bound to be criticism of the Government: its "honeymoon period" is over and "the grim realities of marriage" have to be faced.

Tommy Dugdale dined with me. We had a long talk, largely about the tendency to discontent visible in the House and in the country.

Thursday, April 24th
With the P.M. in the Upper War Room, Admiralty, most of the afternoon. We walked back down Whitehall and he expatiated on the beauty of the Banqueting Hall, saying he could not think why it had not been copied for Government offices. He told me that today New Zealand troops were fully engaged at Thermopylae – an historic event which he had been certain would happen. I remember how blood red the pass looked when I went by it at sunrise, seven years ago, on the way to Athens from Salonika.

The P.M. left for a tour of Liverpool and Manchester.

Dined with Clarissa Churchill at the Coq d'Or. She is singularly beautiful and talks well, but is cold and, I think, callous. However I found her sympathetic this evening and we had quite interesting conversations, punctuated with awkward silences, at the Four Hundred to which we repaired after dinner.

Friday, April 25th
A medical interview for the R.A.F. Passed A.1. in everything but eyesight in which I was border-line. Was told I might be able to fly –

as a pilot – if I had contact lenses. If I chose to get them at my own expense I could be reconsidered, but without any guarantee that I should be taken. The various medical tests lasted over two hours and were very thorough.

Sunday, April 27th [at Hinchingbrooke]
Faith and I did some firing practice after tea with a heavy revolver of hers.

Winston spoke on the wireless, less vividly than usual, but painting a sombre picture of the position in the east and bidding us to turn our eyes westwards.

Monday, April 28th
Back at No. 10 there is a tense feeling as the evacuation of our troops from Greece is now taking place.

The P.M.'s speech has been well received though there is inevitably some disillusionment after the brilliant successes of the last few months. Many people think too much emphasis has been laid on the part played by Anzacs and New Zealanders. From the papers one would hardly suppose British troops had been fighting in Greece or Africa at all. It was, of course, the same at Gallipoli in the last war.

There is some consolation in the fact that our successes in Abyssinia and East Africa proceed undiminished.

On late duty. Most of the time the P.M. spent at a Defence Committee considering urgent problems arising out of the Mediterranean situation and in particular Operations TIGER and JAGUAR. To these Defence Meetings come the Lord Privy Seal (Attlee), the Foreign Secretary, the three service Ministers, the Chiefs of Staff, and Ismay, Hollis and Jacob.

Tuesday, April 29th
To the House for Questions. The P.M. had three tiresome ones (about War Aims, small War Cabinet, etc.) and gave the same answer to all three in succession: "No, Sir."

An afternoon of busy operational discussions: we must save Egypt and Suez at all costs. The evacuation of Greece seems to have been fairly successful and we have got over 40,000 away out of 55,000 all told. The Germans are crowing, but are furious about Winston's speech yesterday.

Wednesday, April 30th
To the House with the P.M. who made a brief statement on the result of the evacuation from Greece. Lunched at the Trafalgar

Square canteen with Christopher Eastwood,[1] who says Moyne is a surprisingly effective Colonial Secretary though he tends to trust the Colonial Office too much.

Dined with Mrs Churchill at 7.30 and took her to Stepney where Father Groser showed us the Arches shelter, his social centres and various other shelters. Mrs C., who looked beautiful, was followed by an admiring crowd of women and made quite a good speech standing on a chair in the shelter. The doctor who went round with us (Cronin by name) said the people were very brave in spite of the havoc and devastation around them, but that they were annoyed (a) by the constant claims that we could defeat the night bomber (b) by the insincere attitude of the press towards our defeats in Africa.

---

[1] Pleasant Colonial Office official who was a friend of John Martin.

16

Hess, Crete and the Bismarck

May 1941

Thursday, May 1st
The day was spent breathlessly arranging Government changes, whereby Lord Spitfire (i.e. Beaverbrook) becomes Minister of State, Moore-Brabazon goes to the Ministry of Aircraft Production, Mr Leathers* Minister of Shipping and Transport.

Lunched with Mother at the Spanish restaurant in Swallow Street. She is a really remarkable woman, disinterested without being priggish, good and yet not smug, intelligent but always humble and, finally, never afraid to say and do what she believes. I could not have chosen a more desirable parent, had I been given the choice.

Left for a tour of Plymouth after dinner with the P.M., Mrs Churchill, First Sea Lord, his Secretary (Brockman),[1] Averell Harriman, Pug and Tommy. Plymouth has been cruelly laid waste in the last fortnight.

On the way to Paddington in the car, the P.M. told me that Leathers was entirely his own choice and that he hoped great things of his experience and tried ability.

Friday, May 2nd
We awoke in the train which was stationary on the line somewhere in Devonshire between banks of primroses and violets. At 9.30 we drew into Plymouth where we were greeted by the two M.P.s Lady Astor (also Lady Mayoress) and Mrs Rathbone,[2] who squabbled

---

[1] Ronald Brockman, Naval Secretary to two First Sea Lords and then, for sixteen years, Mountbatten's devoted and efficient Secretary in all his various offices, including the Viceroyalty of India. Rose to be Vice Admiral. Knighted 1965.

[2] Intelligent and vivacious American constrained by her husband's constituents to take on his Plymouth seat after his death in an air crash. Thus the second American woman (after Lady Astor) to be a British M.P. Later married Sir Paul Wright and was Ambassadress in the Congo and the Lebanon.

like two she-cats until the P.M., who was still shaving when we arrived, emerged on to the platform.

The whole party went to Admiralty House, Devonport, to meet the new C. in C., Sir Charles Forbes. Then began the morning's tour of the dockyard. Brockman and I did not go to Mount Batten, but waited to get the news and then proceeded to the North Yard where we looked at the melancholy ruins of a terrace of lovely houses in which Brockman's had been. The P.M. arrived in a launch and we then walked for miles, along quays, through workshops, over ships. We saw *Centurion*, now a decoy ship made to look like one of the *K.G.V.* class. Just before lunch we reached the R.N. barracks, where bombs had killed a number of sailors. There was a gruesome sight in the gymnasium: beds in which some forty slightly injured men lay, separated only by a low curtain from some coffins which were being nailed down. The hammering must have been horrible to the injured men, but such has been the damage that there was nowhere else it could be done.

The men lunched in the barracks, in a room decorated with a frieze of wooden ships representing the Armada, designed by Wylie.[1] We had a revolting lunch (tepid Brown Windsor soup, etc.) and then returned to Admiralty House so that the P.M. might sleep.

At 3.30 we drove round Plymouth. It has suffered five heavy raids in nine nights and scarcely a house seems to be habitable. It is far worse than Bristol: the whole city is wrecked except, characteristically, the important parts of the naval establishment. Mount Edgecumbe, where we used to land from the sea, is burnt out as well. In Plymouth itself I saw a bus which had been carried bodily, by the force of an explosion, on to the roof of a building some 150 yards from where it had been standing.

We had tea at Lady Astor's house. At 6.30 we left the scene of horror and desolation on the return journey to Chequers, where we arrived at midnight.

There was news to make the P.M. gravely depressed. A long telegram from Roosevelt explaining that the U.S. could not co-operate with us in preventing Germany from seizing the Azores and Cape Verde Islands; news that one of the ships containing many tanks for the reinforcement of Wavell (Operation TIGER) had developed serious engine trouble; a signal that H.M.S. *Jersey*, one of Lord Louis Mountbatten's destroyers, had sunk at Malta blocking the Grand Harbour; and finally the fact that the Iraqis, who

[1] Well-known painter of naval scenes and actions.

opened fire on our troops this morning (two hours before we had intended firing on them!) were fighting well and were not proving to be the rabble we expected.

So the P.M., in worse gloom than I have ever seen him, dictated a telegram to the President drawing a sombre picture of what a collapse in the Middle East would entail. Then he sketched to Harriman, Pug and me a world in which Hitler dominated all Europe, Asia and Africa and left the U.S. and ourselves no option but an unwilling peace.

It is clear that Spain, Vichy and Turkey are waiting on the result of the issue in North Africa, where Tobruk still resists valiantly. If Suez were to fall the Middle East would be lost, and Hitler's robot new order would receive the inspiration which might give it real life.

In a less dark mood the P.M. said that this moment is decisive: it is being established not whether we shall win or lose, but whether the duration of the war will be long or short. With Hitler in control of Iraq oil and Ukrainian wheat, not all the staunchness of "our Plymouth brethren" will shorten the ordeal.

I think it is largely Plymouth that has caused him such melancholy – he keeps on repeating: "I've never seen the like."

Mrs C. said to me suddenly in the train this morning: "Jock, do you think we are going to win?" I said truthfully and unhesitatingly: "Yes."

Saturday, May 3rd
Too little sleep made the P.M. irritable all the morning and morose at lunch when he discovered that Mrs C. had used some of his favourite honey, sent from Queensland, to sweeten the rhubarb.

A lovely spring day. Everything is very late, but the trees are at last beginning to come out.

Eric Duncannon and Moyra Ponsonby came to stay. Eric is making up to Mary and Mrs C. thinks he is going to propose, which worries her. Eric was really only invited for lunch tomorrow, but pretended he was invited for the week-end. Mary is disconcerted by Mrs C.'s cold view of the idea and by Sarah's frank ridicule.

The P.M. broadcast to the Poles and did it superbly, though there was a terrible rush to have it ready in time. We dined at 9.30. The P.M., some of whose worries have been relieved and who is inspired by the fact that a real fight is taking place at Tobruk, was very mellow and stayed up till 3.30 laughing, chaffing and alternating business with conversation. Eden, who came to dine, was made to stay the night in spite of his lacking even a toothbrush; but the C. in C., Fighter Command got away at 3.00.

The P.M. said to Eric Duncannon and me that Tobruk was playing the same part as Acre did against Napoleon. It was a speck of sand in the desert which might ruin all Hitler's calculations.

Sunday, May 4th

The clocks put forward an hour, making double summer-time. It was obvious that Eric was expected to make advances to Mary and that the prospect was viewed with nervous pleasure by Mary, with approbation by Moyra, with dislike by Mrs C. and with amusement by Clarissa – who arrived for lunch, looking quite beautiful, with Captain Hillgarth, Naval Attaché at Madrid and a fervent disciple of Sam Hoare.

At lunch I sat next to Clarissa while Eric was on her other side. We had a three-cornered conversation on a rather tiresome intellectual plane.

We all went into the rose-garden to bask in the sun and while I lingered behind to show the P.M. some service telegrams about Iraq, Eric and Clarissa went off for a long walk, leaving Mary. His motives were either Clarissa's attraction, which she did not attempt to keep in the background, or else the belief that it was good policy to arouse Mary's jealousy. Having returned from his walk, and Clarissa having gone, Eric proceeded to go to sleep until such time as he could make a dramatic entry into the Long Gallery at tea-time when we were all assembled together with Sarah Oliver and the Dashwoods, who had come over from West Wycombe. I think all this is a flutter, which pleases Eric's theatrical feelings and stirs Mary's youthful emotions, but will have no serious consequence.

Meanwhile the P.M., tempted by the warmth, sat in the garden working and glancing at me with suspicion from time to time in the belief that I was trying to read the contents of his special buff boxes.

The C. in C., Bomber Command (Peirse) came to dine and sleep. Lady Goonie[1] and I had a talk about calling people by their Christian names[2] ("Dear Bracken called me Goonie the first time I ever saw him").

The P.M. worked till after 2.00 a.m. in bed, almost emptying a

[1] Lady Gwendeline Churchill, wife of Major Jack Churchill.
[2] This familiarity has now become almost universal, but it used to be reserved for relations, contemporaries and close friends. Churchill asked me to call him Winston shortly after the war, but intimately as both my wife and I knew Lady Churchill, we never called her Clemmie to her dying day.

very full box while the Prof. sat in his bedroom acting as a wastepaper basket and I stood at the foot of the bed collecting those papers with which he had dealt.

Monday, May 5th

Reached London in a state of exhaustion. Lunched at the Travellers which reopened today. The Library is being used as a dining-room and I sat there with Sammy Hood, Peter Loxley and Roger Makins.

Rode at Richmond for an hour, then slept at No. 10, and finally took my car to pick up Betty Montagu and go to Chobham to spend a night with Rosemary and Hinch. Dropped Betty at Jacqueline Dyer's[1] house and had a drink there with Jacqueline, Zara and Ronnie Strutt.

We had a party in the evening at a very nice country club nearby. Zara and Ronnie came, Peter Cazalet,[2] Diana Tiarks and Martin Charteris. Dinner was excellent but the evening was less successful afterwards. We danced to the gramophone, but Ronnie Strutt stood glumly in front of the fire and for some reason the party just did not go.

Wednesday, May 7th

Lunched at the Travellers, sitting next to the C.A.S. with whom I broached the subject of entering the R.A.F. After discussing the matter with Mother last night I am prepared to resign from the F.O. if necessary.

The P.M. wound up a debate on the war in the House, scoring a great Parliamentary success and utterly confounding Lloyd George and Hore-Belisha.

He went early to bed elated by his forensic success. I pointed out to him that it was just a year since the debate in which Chamberlain fell.

Tonight we shot down more night raiders than ever before: at least twenty-three fell to guns and fighters.

Thursday, May 8th

The Cabinet met at the House and I had a conversation with the dynamic and excellent Tom Johnston, S. of S. for Scotland, who told me of the incredible tactlessness shown by many employers in Lanarkshire. He said the morale of the workers on Clydeside was

[1] Later Mrs Vincent Paravicini.
[2] Celebrated trainer of steeplechasers. Succeeded to Fairlawne after his brother, Victor, was killed with General Sikorski. After the death of his first wife he married Zara (née Mainwaring), at the time of this diary entry Mrs Ronnie Strutt.

much better since they had been bombed and he could not help wishing Lanarkshire would be bombed too.

Eric Seal is going on a special mission to the U.S. and we are to have a new Principal Private Secretary. Meanwhile Brendan, to whom I entrusted the task, has failed to persuade the P.M. to release me for the R.A.F. and before taking further steps I shall have now to wait till Seal's successor is installed.

Our biggest raid on Germany: 380 aircraft.

Friday, May 9th
The Bessboroughs and Eric lunched at the Annexe and afterwards Mary came to tell me she was engaged to Eric. I was relieved to be able simply to wish her happiness: I had feared she might be going to ask my opinion.

The P.M. went off to Ditchley very excited about Operation TIGER. The convoy has passed through the narrows between Sicily and N. Africa and only one ship out of five, carrying a huge consignment of tanks for Wavell, has gone down. The P.M. thinks this will have far-reaching consequences on the war. He said to me: "The poor Tiger has already lost one claw and another is damaged; but still I would close on what is left."

Saturday, May 10th
Things are going better again – in Iraq, in Spain (where the Falange[1] and Suñer[2] have been worsted), and there are bright prospects in N. Africa now that TIGER is through.

The full moon. Just as I was going to bed one of London's worst raids started and I descended to the shelter where my bed was periodically shaken by the explosion of bombs on the Horse Guards Parade. It was strange that on every occasion I awoke about five seconds before the bomb actually exploded.

Sunday, May 11th
Awoke thinking unaccountably of Peter Fleming's book *Flying Visit*[3] and day-dreaming of what would happen if we captured Goering during one of his alleged flights over London.

I walked out into Downing Street at 8.00 a.m. on my way to the early service at Westminster Abbey. It was really a sunny day with blue skies, but the smoke from many fires lay thick over London

[1] Spanish fascist party founded by Miguel Primo de Rivera.
[2] Spanish Foreign Minister. Brother-in-law of General Franco and considered strongly pro-German.
[3] An amusing fantasy, published in the early months of the war, about the embarrassment caused by Hitler's unheralded arrival in England by parachute.

and obscured the sun. Burnt paper, from some demolished paper mill, was falling like leaves on a windy autumn day.

Whitehall was thronged with people, mostly sightseers but some of them Civil Defence workers with blackened faces and haggard looks. One of them, a boy of eighteen or nineteen, pointed towards the Houses of Parliament and said, "Is that the sun?" But the great orange glow at which we were looking was the light of many fires south of the river. At Westminster Abbey there were fire-engines and the policeman at the door said to me, "There will not be any services in the Abbey today, Sir", exactly as if it were closed for spring cleaning. I turned towards Westminster Hall, on the roof of which I could see flames still leaping. Smoke rose from some invisible point in the pile of Parliament buildings beyond. I talked to a fireman. He showed me Big Ben, the face of which was pocked and scarred, and told me a bomb had gone right through the Tower. The one thing that had given him great pleasure during the night was that Big Ben had struck two o'clock a few minutes after being hit. It was still giving the proper time.

I stood on Westminster Bridge and thought ironically of Wordsworth and 1802. St Thomas's Hospital was ablaze, the livid colour of the sky extended from Lambeth to St Paul's, flames were visible all along the Embankment, there was smoke rising thickly as far as the eye could see. After no previous raid has London looked so wounded next day.

After breakfast I rang up the P.M. at Ditchley and described what I had seen. He was very grieved that William Rufus's roof at Westminster Hall should have gone. He told me we had shot down forty-five which, out of 380 operating, is a good result.[1]

Great excitement over an E. Phillips Oppenheim story concerning the Duke of Hamilton[2] and a crashed Nazi plane. The Duke flew to London and I had been going to Northolt to meet him; but he was switched straight through to Ditchley.

I had walked over to the Foreign Office during the morning in order to gossip with Nicolas Lawford, a clever and amusing diplomat, who was Anthony Eden's Second Private Secretary and

---

[1] An exaggerated estimate given by Fighter Command. Thirty-three was the true number.

[2] Douglas, 14th Duke of Hamilton and Brandon. Skilful pilot and pugnacious amateur boxer. The first man to look down on Mount Everest, having organised an expedition to fly over it. A Conservative M.P. for ten years before succeeding his father. When Hess, whom he had only seen once, at the Berlin Olympic Games, arrived in Scotland, Hamilton was serving as Group Captain in the R.A.F.

was on duty over the week-end. As I entered the room he was on the telephone. He turned round and said to the person to whom he was speaking, "Hold on a minute. I think this is your man." Lawford, holding his hand over the receiver, explained that it was the Duke of Hamilton who had got some fantastic story, which he refused to reveal in detail, and that he wanted the Prime Minister's Secretary to meet him at Northolt aerodrome, to which he intended to fly. He also wanted Sir Alexander Cadogan to go. Lawford handed me the telephone. It might, of course, be a lunatic pretending to be a Duke. The caller declined to be more specific but said he could only compare what had happened to an E. Phillips Oppenheim novel and that it had to do with a crashed Nazi plane. At that moment I vividly remembered my early waking thoughts on Peter Fleming's book and I felt sure that either Hitler or Goering had arrived. In the event I was only one wrong in the Nazi hierarchy. I telephoned to Ditchley and the Prime Minister instructed me to have the Duke driven directly there, but I was to ensure it really was the Duke and not a lunatic.

Monday, May 12th

The P.M. returned from Ditchley bringing the Duke of Hamilton with him. I managed to have a few words with the Duke, while the P.M. was excitedly talking to Eden, and to elicit that the occupant of the crashed Nazi plane was Rudolph Hess. There has never been such a fantastic occurrence.

Lunched with John Martin whom the P.M. has definitely appointed Principal Private Secretary, at the Travellers.

Dined with Philip in the Mess of the 4th Battalion, Grenadiers, at Wanstead. We had a delicious dinner, with champagne, etc., and afterwards played bridge. The 9.00 news was turned on and I heard an announcement of a German communiqué about Hess's disappearance. Nobody paid any attention or seemed to grasp what it meant. I said nothing. Back at No. 10 in time to hear of a statement on the subject which the P.M. has drafted for publication.

During the afternoon Mary told me that her engagement to Eric was off – and that she felt at the bottom of her heart it would never be on again.

Tuesday, May 13th

The Hess story has, of course, made everyone gape. This morning, after returning from the House with the P.M., I saw an account of Hess's interview with Kirkpatrick, which is only being shown to Eden, Attlee and Beaverbrook. It is clear that Hess is no traitor but genuinely believes he can persuade us that we cannot win and that a compromise peace is obtainable. His essential prerequisite is the fall of the Churchill Government. The poor Duke of Hamilton feels acutely the slur of being taken for a potential Quisling – which he certainly is not.

In the Travellers at lunch-time there was no other topic. The rumours and theories are diverse and amusing.

Wednesday, May 14th

During the later afternoon "C", Alec Cadogan, Duff Cooper and Brendan assembled in my room at No. 10 and I listened to many intelligent theories and suggestions about Hess. Cadogan says that if only the parachute had failed to open, he would be a happier and more efficient man. The handling of the whole business is difficult but very important psychologically.

Thursday, May 15th

The day started badly. I summoned the D.N.I.[1] for the P.M. instead of the D.M.I.[1] The P.M. answered Questions (inadvertently letting fall in answer to a supplementary that the Ministry of Economic Warfare was connected with propaganda) and then proposed a resolution thanking the House of Peers for their message of condolence on the loss of the Chamber of the House of Commons.

Gladwyn Jebb dined and made a great fuss about this morning's Question, maintaining that the P.M. had jeopardised the secrecy of Dr Dalton's organisation. Desmond and I thought him very silly about it all and concluded that his motive was to be able to go back to Dalton and say that he had given us a piece of his mind. Incidentally the P.M. had refused to see Dalton about it as he cannot bear the sight of him.

Monday, May 19th

Reached London at lunch-time and burst in on a farewell luncheon party which Brendan was giving for Seal in the Annexe. It ended with short, embarrassed speeches punctuated by witticisms from Brendan.

Brendan had Commander Fletcher (A. V. Alexander's P.P.S.) to dine. While the P.M. and the Defence Committee were deciding how to react to Vichy's latest treason in Syria (where German planes have been allowed to use aerodromes), I gossiped with

---

[1] Directors of Naval and of Military Intelligence.

Antony Head* and the C.I.G.S.'s two A.D.C.s (Nutting and MacDonald Buchanan) in the C.W.R.

Before going to bed the P.M. told me he expected the German attack on Crete to begin tomorrow.

Tuesday, May 20th

The Germans are attacking Crete. At the House the P.M. made an impromptu statement covering Aosta's surrender, our recapture of Sollum and the Cretan adventure. On the way back in the car I showed him two urgent telegrams about Syria. He said, "We must go in" and immediately summoned a Defence Committee.

Lunched with Tommy Lascelles and discussed whether very great men usually had a touch of charlatanism in them.

At 5.00 the P.M. sped down to the House again and interrupted their business to give them the latest "hot news" from Crete, clasping a tattered postcard on which I had scrawled the last signal.

Wednesday, May 21st

Another brief statement in the House of Commons on Crete where the fight is hard but so far successful. There is a general demand for the execution of German parachutists who are alleged to have landed in New Zealand uniforms.

Thursday, May 22nd

The navy are having a heavy task off Crete and have lost a lot of ships, including *Gloucester* and *Fiji*. I expressed grief to the P.M. who replied, "What do you think we build the ships for?" He deprecates the navy's way of treating ships as if they were too precious ever to risk.

Tom Troubridge dined in the Mess. An interesting discussion on Germany, especially propaganda. Troubridge said the Germans loved jazz which is prohibited by the Nazis: instead of broadcasting that, the B.B.C. produce programmes of German music! He said the obtuseness of the Ministry of Information was largely due to the warring cliques within it.

The *Bismarck* and another German ship are out, probably on a substantial raid in the Atlantic. Now is the time to test the efficacy of American naval help.

Friday, Mary 23rd

Lunched with Herschel Johnson at Claridges to meet members of the American Embassy.

Drove my own car to Chequers. P.M. arrived later from a tank inspection, bringing with him David Margesson, Pownall (the new

Vice Chief of the Imperial General Staff), Macready (Assistant C.I.G.S.), Averell Harriman, Jack Churchill and Ismay.

An entirely male party. The P.M. laments very strongly that the tanks which he asked Wavell to send to Crete were not sent. They might have made the whole difference to the battle.

The *Bismarck* is near Iceland, hotly pursued by the *Prince of Wales* and the *Hood*. There is an excellent chance of catching her at dawn in the Denmark Straits.

Saturday, May 24th
Awoken at 6.00 a.m. by the Duty Captain, Admiralty, who said *Prince of Wales* and *Hood* were engaging *Bismarck*. At 9.00 when I emerged from my bedroom Mrs Hill told me the *Hood* was lost.

In the morning there was a conference on conscription in Northern Ireland, an issue which is impassioning Eire and causing unfavourable repercussions in the U.S. and Canada. The P.M. is very insistent on conscription. The Prime Minister of Northern Ireland (Andrews)[1] arrived, accompanied by two of his Ministers, and others present were Herbert Morrison, Bevin, Cranborne, John Anderson, Bridges and Pownall (who has just given up the post of G.O.C. Northern Ireland). At lunch I sat next to Pownall. He is optimistic about Crete and thinks the odds slightly in favour of our victory: yesterday he would have laid 6–4 on; today he thought it about evens. He pointed out that we had had three great victories in this war which counted for much more than our various military catastrophes. These victories were the success of the R.A.F. in defeating the daylight bomber, of the navy in keeping the seas open, and, above all, of the civilian population in holding firm against air bombardment.

Crete is now serious, as became clear during the afternoon and evening. The Germans are fighting with blind courage and have complete control of the air. The crux of the matter is how long the navy can carry out its dangerous task of preventing seaborne landings.

First night of the Chequers cinema, which the P.M. has had installed. The guests of the day had all gone. Andrew Cavendish,[2] who is one of the officers at the camp, dined and afterwards we saw a film in the Great Parlour: Marlene Dietrich in *Seven Sinners* – very alluring.

All ships are converging on the *Bismarck* and the C. in C. proposes to attack at 9.00 a.m. tomorrow.

---

[1] Rt. Hon. J. M. Andrews, Prime Minister of Northern Ireland, 1940–43.
[2] Subsequently 11th Duke of Devonshire. Minister of State for Commonwealth Relations in Harold Macmillan's Government.

Sunday, May 25th

Bismarck has been lost during the hours of darkness. A day of fearful gloom ensued. The P.M. cannot understand why the *Prince of Wales* did not press home her attack yesterday and keeps on saying it is the worst thing since Troubridge turned away from the *Goeben* in 1914. He rated the First Lord and the First Sea Lord continuously, both on this account and because in the Mediterranean the navy shows, he thinks, a tendency to shirk its task of preventing a seaborne landing in Crete since Cunningham fears severe losses from bombing. The P.M.'s line is that Cunningham must be made to take every risk: the loss of half the Mediterranean fleet would be worthwhile in order to save Crete.

The Fred Crippses came to lunch, and Beaverbrook afterwards in a new (and very vulgar) suit to celebrate his birthday. The P.M. treated us to a discourse on the heroism of China and Chiang Kai-shek, for whom he longed to be able to do something.

Winant came at tea-time and stayed till after 8.00, putting very forcibly Roosevelt's objections to conscription in Northern Ireland.

The P.M. cheered up at dinner, which was a family affair (by which I mean Ismay, Tommy, Jack Churchill, self and the Prof., who is soon to be a peer). He criticised Wavell very heavily about tanks for Crete and expressed amazement that W. should have thought he could get reinforcements ashore after the fight had begun. He considered the Middle East had been very badly managed. If he could be put in command there he would gladly lay down his present office – yes, and even renounce cigars and alcohol!

After dinner we had a film: *Western Union* (with Red Indians and all the Wild West trappings) and the P.M.'s favourite *March of Time*.

With a final comment that these three days had been the worst yet, he went to bed at 2.15 a.m. There is, however, still a chance that the *Ark Royal* and the *Rodney* may catch the *Bismarck* before she reaches the French port for which she seems to be making.

Monday, May 26th

Left Chequers at 12.30, following the P.M.'s cortège in my car at breakneck speed. The Cretan situation seems slightly better and at the P.M.'s instigation the Chiefs of Staff have sent a signal to the C. in C. that no risk can be considered too heavy to win the battle.

Rowan,* our new Private Secretary from the Treasury, arrived.

Brendan and Desmond both think President R.'s speech tomorrow might be very important to the outcome of the war. It looks as if Vichy, Japan, Spain are all lined up waiting to fall on the British Empire if it shows any further signs of disintegration.

Tuesday, May 27th

To the House, where the P.M. made a statement on Crete and the *Bismarck* and announced the Government's decision not to introduce conscription into Northern Ireland. This culminated in a dramatic scene when we rushed to the P.M., just after he had sat down, a slip of paper saying the *Bismarck* had been sunk.

The Crete situation is deplorable. It seems that we are finished there owing to lack of air support.

Went to have first fitting for contact lenses as I am now resolved to get into the R.A.F. as a fighter pilot if humanly possible, even at the cost of resignation from the Diplomatic Service.

Wednesday, May 28th

My head is full of plans for a new life in the R.A.F. and, of course, of improbable day-dreams on the subject.

Decision to withdraw from Crete was taken.

Thursday, May 29th

Rode at Richmond. Melville[1] rode the horse I usually ride and it ran away, throwing him into a sandpit.

P.M. much upset by telegram from Wavell who shows some sign of defeatism. "He sounds a tired and disheartened man," said the P.M.

Attended conference in Desmond's room with Prof. and Victor Rothschild[2] about security as regards cigars, etc., sent to the P.M.

---

[1] Ronnie Melville, Principal Private Secretary to the Secretary of State for Air. A first-class classicist with a fine sense of humour. Afterwards held a number of senior posts in Whitehall, including two Permanent Under Secretaryships. He does not list riding among his hobbies in *Who's Who*.

[2] Victor, 3rd Lord Rothschild. A notable scientist, whose research tended to concentrate on intimate biological matters, he was a Fellow of Trinity College, Cambridge, Chairman of Shell Research, Chairman of the Royal Commission on gambling, first head of the Central Policy Review Staff (the "Think Tank") and a winner of the George Medal for unravelling fiendish enemy booby-traps. His incisive comments brought terror to some, but admiration to all.

17

Thieves Fall Out

June 1941

Monday, June 2nd

Late in the afternoon I accompanied the P.M. and Mrs Churchill to Chartwell where they plan to have a few days' rest. I am sleeping in the cottage which the P.M. built with his own hands and have his very comfortable bedroom.

We dined in the cottage; the P.M., Mrs C., Tommy, Miss White[1] and I. Mrs C. and I played backgammon; the P.M. professed extreme tiredness and at one moment even lay prostrate on the dining-room floor while Mrs C. and I continued to rattle the dice and Tommy sipped his brandy pensively.

After dinner the P.M. went up to the big house and worked till 1.30, dictating to Miss Layton[2] while I sat in his study, looked at his books, and plied him with papers when supplies ran short.

He is much perturbed by the fact that the rearguard, consisting of Royal Marines, was left behind in Crete. He blamed the navy and went so far as to describe it as a shameful episode.

Tuesday, June 3rd

It was cold and raining, so that the P.M., lying dismally in bed, decided to go back to London after lunch and curtail his holiday.

He said to David Margesson on the telephone that he had no doubts of the wisdom of what we had done in Crete though

---

[1] A cousin of Clementine Churchill who was Mary's guide, philosopher and friend, known as Moppet and much loved by the whole family.

[2] One of Churchill's personal secretaries, pleasant to look at and good-natured. At a stop on a return flight from Moscow, the Russians erroneously judged her to be Churchill's mistress and toasted her effusively. She married, went to live in South Africa and as Elizabeth Nel wrote a book, *Mr Churchill's Secretary*, of which Lady Churchill highly approved.

sometimes he had doubts about the Greek campaign. However we had at least done what was honourable.

I started reading *My Early Life*,[1] of which I found an annotated copy in the office, with the object of using some of the facts in it when I come to make my bid for release.

I had lunch alone with the P.M. and the Yellow Cat, which sat in a chair on his right-hand side and attracted most of his attention. He was meditating deeply on the Middle East, where he is intent on reorganising the rearward services, and on Lord Beaverbrook who is proving particularly troublesome. The P.M. said that Lord B. just did not begin to understand how to get on with the military. While he brooded on these matters, he kept up a running conversation with the cat, cleaning its eyes with his napkin, offering it mutton and expressing regret that it could not have cream in war-time. Finally he said some very harsh things about Wavell, whose excessive caution and inclination to pessimism he finds very antipathetic.

After dinner in the Mess I went to see first Desmond and then Archie Sinclair about Louis Greig who has, as I heard by chance, become involved with a company of financial crooks. In view of his great and continuous hospitality to me I should like to give him a hint, but thought it better to do so through Archie Sinclair.

Wednesday, June 4th
Lunched at the Travellers between Moley Sargent and Horace Wilson. The former thinks Sir M. Robertson's[2] plans to reform the Diplomatic Service (which have now been adopted by the Cabinet) good though he doubts the wisdom of amalgamating the Diplomatic and Consular Service as the duds are bound to be pushed into the consular posts and our Consular Service will suffer. We talked of Horace after he had left and Sargent thought he had suffered greatly from Chamberlain pushing him into something for which he had no qualifications and by which his reputation and his future were bound to be compromised. Both Sargent and Horace said No. 10 was partly to blame for the inadequacy of our news and propaganda to the U.S.: the spokesmen of the service departments were terrified of saying anything that might incur the Prime Minister's displeasure and so took refuge in silence.

The Kaiser died, in obscurity and contempt. *The Times* said:

[1] Winston Churchill's account of his childhood and youth.
[2] Joined the Foreign Office in Queen Victoria's reign and was at various times Ambassador in Buenos Aires, Chairman of Spillers Ltd, Chairman of the British Council and a Member of Parliament. He regularly interviewed aspirants for the Diplomatic Service (including me) and asked searching questions.

"History will some day have to assess the respective responsibilities of the crowned and uncrowned demagogue in bringing ruin upon the head of the German people and calamity on the peaceful civilisation of Europe."

Thursday, June 5th
Rode in Richmond Park, jumping several hurdles and having two long breakneck gallops.

New appointments are under consideration, connected with the establishment of a ministry of light, fuel, heat, etc. Beaverbrook has refused an offer of Agriculture *and* Food. Brendan says that he takes up more of the P.M.'s time than Hitler.

Criticism of the Crete episode is rife; the press are being cantankerous; and the Government will have to face an important debate in the House next week. Our propaganda is very much at fault, at home and abroad.

Friday, June 6th
Lunched with Jim Bowker at the Travellers. He spoke of the determination of the Turks not to commit themselves. He was critical of our fighting in Crete, believing that we had still failed to understand the lessons that complete domination of the air is a decisive factor and that when the Germans attack they do so ruthlessly and without reserve.

The P.M. returned, instead of going straight on to Ditchley, on account of telegrams from Washington which show that Pétain and Weygand have both agreed to military co-operation with Germany, and of difficulties connected with the Free French, General Spears, Syria and innumerable complications related to matters of prestige and *amour propre.*

On late duty. The P.M. dictated his speech for next Tuesday, rather cantankerous in tone and likely, unless substantially toned down, to cause a good deal of unfavourable comment. Pug says he thinks it is impossible to run a war efficiently if so much time has to be devoted to justifying one's actions in the House of Commons. At the risk of seeming smug he maintains that no error or misconception was made in the direction of the campaign from this end. General Freyberg[1] specifically said he was not afraid of the air.

Went to bed exhausted at 2.30 a.m.

[1] Soldier of heroic fame who won a V.C. and three D.S.O.s, was wounded countless times, almost swum the Channel, was G.O.C. of the New Zealand forces from 1939 to 1945, was Governor General of New Zealand after the war and ended as Governor of Windsor Castle. His wife, Barbara Jekyll, was a childhood friend of my mother at the Viceregal Lodge in Dublin.

Saturday, June 7th
The Prime Minister saw the editors of the newspapers this morning with a view to damping down their criticism and explaining the position.

De Gaulle is showing himself highly-strung and quarrelsome. Desmond Morton actually thinks he might go over to Vichy. Much will depend on events in the very near future.

The P.M. went off to Ditchley at tea-time and I spent a peaceful evening reading *My Early Life* (with a view to proving to the P.M. that he would have left no stone unturned to take an active part in the war if he had been me) and listening to a fiery denunciation of Horace Wilson's pettiness by Anthony Bevir.

Sunday, June 8th
Went to church early at Westminster Abbey. Anthony and Brendan are occupying their minds in a search for a successor to Cosmo Cantuar in case anything should befall that prelate. I have put forward the suggestion of Robert Moberley, Bishop of Stepney.

Today our forces, together with those of de Gaulle, advance into Syria for the implementation of Operation EXPORTER. It may mean war with Vichy; but the P.M. is convinced that this would not imply war with France.

Meanwhile negotiations between Germany and Russia are proceeding and look like ending, in the very near future, with a complete alignment of the two countries or an invasion of Russia if she proves recalcitrant. Having so wholeheartedly taken over the mantle of appeasement, I think Russia is more likely to collaborate than to fight.

Barclay, an interpreter attached to the Ministry of Defence, dined in the Mess. He says that he has been following the deliberations of Mr Arthur Greenwood's committee on reconstruction after the war and that they give him no confidence. Lord Reith's contribution on material reconstruction, e.g. town-planning, is the only one that is at all practical and businesslike. The rest talk airily of freedom, equality, justice – and all the other things which J. S. Mill wrote about much more competently and which, I think, seem a mockery to the subdued nations of Europe.

Tuesday, June 10th
Rode in a torrential downpour. Spent most of the day at Church House listening to the debate on Crete. Hore-Belisha spoke well, if acrimoniously, but he has not got the sympathy of the House. Lord Winterton, who is both fluent and amusing, attacked his own party and Labour, employers and workmen, with equal versatility and

expressed the hope that the P.M. would not take refuge from criticism in rhetoric. He also objected strongly to the P.M. comparing Lloyd George to Marshal Pétain.

The Prime Minister wound up the debate with a forceful speech lasting one and a half hours, in which he denied the House's right to have information on tactical matters and objected to being called to account for every phase of the war. Did Hitler call the Reichstag to explain the loss of the *Bismarck* or Mussolini feel constrained to give an apologia for Italian disasters in Africa? He also said some harsh things to Hore-Belisha, though not as harsh as he had originally intended.

I corrected the speech for Hansard, which took a long time, and then went to have a drink with the Sinclairs. There was a young man there called Michael Young,[1] a friend of Rosemary Hinchingbrooke, who extolled to me the virtues of Communism and asked me if the Communists at Cambridge in my time had not been "the élite of the students". I offended him deeply by referring to their personal uncleanliness.

For the first time since war broke out I feel discontented and unsettled, bored by most people I meet and destitute of ideas. I certainly need a change and think an active, practical life in the R.A.F. is the real solution. I am not anxious to immolate myself on the altar of Mars, but have reached the stage of thinking that nothing matters.

Lunched today with Colly Barclay[2] at the St James's Club. He is rather dismal, but like me he feels the intolerable position of living a life of pampered ease and comparative safety in the midst of all this suffering and danger.

Wednesday, June 11th
Lord Simon, the Lord Chancellor, has seen Hess and it becomes increasingly clear that the latter came here of his own volition, that he utterly misconceived politics and opinion in this country, that there is very little valuable information to be got out of him. Although Hitler's personal friend and right-hand man, I doubt if he knew as much of plans and production even as Brendan; certainly no more.

Shigemitsu, the lame Japanese Ambassador, came to say goodbye to the P.M. at No. 10. I suppose he is being recalled on account of his known Anglophile views.

[1] After a diverse and distinguished academic career, he was created Lord Young of Dartington, the *avant-garde* and occasionally notorious progressive school which was the object of his and Rosemary Hinchingbrooke's adulation.

[2] Step-son of Sir Robert Vansittart. Entered the Foreign Office in the same year as I did.

Dined with Clarissa Churchill in a good Soho restaurant. I enjoyed my evening greatly and see how right Gay is in her praises of Clarissa: she is extremely agreeable and one of the most intelligent of women, more balanced than most. She tells me that after a few weeks in the Communications Department of the F.O. she is being paid £6 a week free of tax – almost as much as I get – with short hours and no skill attached to the job. After dinner we walked in Regent's Park till 11.00 p.m. when it began to be dark, and then adjourned to the Four Hundred till 1.15 a.m.

Thursday, June 12th
The Honours List. Prof. L. gets a barony which will cause anger in many quarters and especially at Oxford, but not as much as when it is learned that he proposes to call himself Lord Cherwell of Oxford.

The President of the Royal Society, Sir Henry Dale, accompanied by Professors A. V. Hill and A. C. Egerton and by Sir Henry Tizard, came to No. 10 to admit the P.M. a Fellow. He kept them waiting forty minutes, during which time I conversed with them pleasantly, and then signed his name in their historic book which starts with "Charles R. Founder" and contains every great name since, people so diverse as Sir Winston Churchill (father of the first Duke of Marlborough), Sir Isaac Newton, Queen Victoria and Freud!

At 12.00 began the Meeting of Allied Representatives in the picture gallery at St James's Palace. I attended and sat at a table with Edward Bridges, Nicholas Lawford and Roger Makins. The P.M. made a powerful speech of invective against the enemy, which he enjoys and at which he excels. The representatives of ten nations sat round the long table and listened appreciatively, but the dignity of the scene was marred by such modern appliances as microphones, cinema apparatus and innumerable photographers. This did not disturb the P.M. who shook his finger at the microphone as if it had been the Führer himself that he was addressing. When he came to a passage in which he spoke of the stain on the German name which nothing would eradicate for hundreds of years, Van (who today becomes Lord Van) became wreathed in appreciative smiles. Hatred and harsh words are the methods which he prescribes.

The meeting adjourned for lunch and Brendan took me to White's to have a gin and lime. Later in the day one of the Free French representatives made this mystifying statement to Desmond Morton: "Ah, that is Bracken. I have heard of him. He has the vocabulary of Mr Churchill but of the left."

In the afternoon representatives of our nine Allies spoke: Sikorski, Pierlot (the Belgian P.M. who is most eloquent), Gerbrandy (the Dutchman), the speakers on behalf of Free France, Czechoslovakia, Norway, Greece, Yugoslavia and Luxembourg. Only Ethiopia was left out: there is no Ethiopian, of sufficient standing, in England. At 4.00 came the King, in naval uniform, and walked round the room talking to all in turn. Evidently the meeting was a success and Eden, in his winding-up speech, expressed the hope that it would be the first of those which, on a basis of international collaboration, should settle the peace and reorganise Europe.

Chief interest now centres on: (1) the prospect of a Soviet–German clash which, according to many and diverse sources, seems imminent. I can't see the sense of it from Hitler's point of view unless, as Bridges suggests, the intention is to dissuade the U.S. from war; (2) the now declared intention of the U.S. Government to take over the occupation of Iceland from us very shortly; (3) Syria, where progress is slow but where General Spears and the War Office believe all opposition will crumble after an initial display of resistance.

The P.M. was much impressed by a photograph of today's conference, brought by a young man from the *Daily Sketch*, and said it was the most artistic grouping he had ever seen, better than any of the groups painted by Sargent, etc., on similar occasions and yet quite haphazard.[1]

Friday, June 13th
Attlee tells me he had to converse with the Czech representative, Sramek, in Latin yesterday.

Sunday, June 15th
Today our offensive in North Africa began. Great hopes are placed on this Operation BATTLEAXE (formerly TIGERCUBS and afterwards BRUISER). For the first time British armoured forces meet the Germans on equal terms and without marked air inferiority.

Monday, June 16th
Summer, hot and sunny, at last.
Lunched with George Rendel[2] at the Travellers. He has been

---

[1] See photograph opposite p. 273.
[2] A man of great goodness and a devout Roman Catholic who was head of the Foreign Office Eastern Department when I joined it in 1937. He was, however, incorrigibly long-winded in the minutes and memoranda he wrote, to the grave dissatisfaction of the Under Secretaries and the Secretary of State.

given the job of working out the reform of the Foreign Office. He says that amalgamating the Diplomatic and Consular services is like amalgamating the House of Commons and the L.C.C. Their functions are different; their scope is different.

In the afternoon the P.M. broadcast to Rochester University from which he receives an honorary degree. A very-well-phrased speech, the burden of which was "United we stand; divided we fall".

After dinner I went for a walk round Westminster with Brendan. His knowledge of houses and architects is remarkable and he told me much that was interesting about the precincts of Westminster Abbey and School and the neighbouring streets.

The fighting round Sollum[1] is very fierce. At dinner in the Mess we all, except Brendan and Tommy, thought that Russia would give way to Germany without a fight. That Germany is prepared to fight there can be no question. Sir Stafford Cripps, just back from Moscow, whom I saw today, says that the issue of war rests entirely with Hitler: Stalin will have no choice one way or the other.

Tuesday, June 17th
The P.M. went to Chartwell for the afternoon after hearing that Vichy troops had captured Kynteira in Syria, forcing a British battalion to surrender. This looks bad and I fear the prospect in the Western Desert is none too bright either. Later the prospect seemed still gloomier.

Wednesday, June 18th
Operation BATTLEAXE has obviously failed and we have to face the bitter fact of being beaten by the Germans on equal terms. Indeed we should have had superiority were not Wavell so lavish with his rearward services and so cautious about using his full strength. The P.M. is gravely disappointed as he had placed great hopes on this operation for which Operation TIGER had been staged. Fortunately it will not appear as a major defeat as we merely return to our positions after a sharp and costly battle; but neither the general public nor the Germans know what hopes were set by the Cabinet (though not by Wavell or Dill) on a successful offensive.

In the afternoon, as the P.M. had gone off to see a rocket demonstration, I went riding and dallied pleasantly in a large wood at Richmond where bank after bank of rhododendrons in full flower surrounded me on every side. I have never seen such profusion. At Exbury the quality may be greater, but not the

---

[1] On the Egypt–Cyrenaica frontier.

quantity. The heat was tropical and the air heavy with the scent of flowers. I rode in this wood for half an hour, forcing my way along the overgrown footpaths, and then galloped full tilt down the avenue to White Lodge, jumping a series of hurdles and a stream on the way.

Brendan had Walter Elliot[1] to dinner and also an American, Glancey by name, who is head of General Motors and is working with Harriman. He gave us impressive forecasts of what American industry can produce. He was enthusiastic about the prospects next spring if we can hang on till then. For example America will be producing small arms ammunition at the rate of 1,000,000 rounds an hour. Walter Elliot said that to win this war soldiers should give up studying any military history since the Plantagenets and Angevins: we had returned to the feudal military conception of knights and peasants, only now the knights rode in tanks and the peasants were infantry. Armour has come back to its own.

While waiting for the P.M. to return I played backgammon with Mrs C. and enlisted her support for my R.A.F. project. She advises me to put my application to the P.M. in writing. Mrs C. spoke in no unmeasured terms of her relief that Mary had broken off her engagement with Eric.

When the P.M. came back he was in good spirits, less perturbed than I had expected by the fiasco of BATTLEAXE, and told me that he was now busy considering where next we could take the offensive.

Thursday, June 19th
French advances for an armistice in Syria reached us through Washington.

At the House of Commons Tommy Dugdale lamented to me the first signs of a new class feeling between the two sides of the House. The Tories, conscious of the great sacrifices they are making financially and of the exceedingly high wages being paid to war workers, are cantankerous about the many reports of slackness, absenteeism, etc., in the factories. The Labour Party resent this criticism and blame the managers and employers for any short-comings. A Conservative M.P., Henderson Stewart, discussed the matter with me in very strong terms: he wants the P.M. to have stringent investigations made in all factories.

[1] Erudite Scottish M.P., highly acclaimed as Minister of Agriculture and of Health, and as Secretary of State for Scotland. At one time regarded as a future Prime Minister. His wife, daughter of Sir Charles Tennant and half-sister of Lady Oxford and Asquith, was made a peeress in her own right and worked assiduously in the House of Lords.

Lunched with Peggy Crewe at the Ritz. She says that criticism of the Government is increasing, though not of Winston personally. I certainly have the impression that discontent is growing, and it is inevitable with so many setbacks.

John Peck and I agreed that the P.M. does not help the Government machine to run smoothly and his inconsiderate treatment of the service departments would cause trouble were it not for the great personal loyalty of the service Ministers to himself. He supplies drive and initiative, but he often meddles where he would better leave things alone and the operational side of the war might profit if he gave it a respite and turned to grapple with labour and production.

Audrey Stanley,[1] Diana Quilter, John Martin and I went to see *Patience* well produced at the Savoy Theatre. After dining at absurd expense in the Savoy Grill we proceeded to the Four Hundred to drink gin and discourse. Audrey Stanley said that the P.M. would go down in history not as a great Prime Minister but as a great poet.

Friday, June 20th
Departed at 9.15 for Dover with the P.M. and a large party including Archie Sinclair, Mr Glancey, Sir R. Keyes and Dill, besides several generals and Desmond Morton. We saw an 18-inch gun on a railway mounting, a formidable object with a brass plate "H.M.G. Boche-Buster". I could not bear the prospect of seeing more guns and so went to Dover Castle with the Vice Admiral, Dover's Flag Lieutenant (a charming youth called Gibb), and after telephoning to Ismay about the P.M.'s latest project – the replacement of Wavell by Auchinleck – awaited the arrival of the party. The haze and heat made it impossible to see the coast of France, so the P.M. consoled himself by ordering the firing of rounds by the U.P. batteries.

At lunch on the train I sat with General Loch, head of the A.A. Section in the War Office. He is an erudite man but much of his learning was lost owing to the softness of his voice and the frequency of the tunnels. We talked of Hore-Belisha, and Loch, though disagreeing with him as a politician and administrator, defended him as a man.

Left the train with the P.M. at a small station and spent the afternoon at Chartwell. The garden was glorious. After a long

---

[1] Lady Audrey Talbot, first wife of the ebullient, clever and frequently offensive Edward, Lord Stanley of Alderley, who was a bosom friend of Randolph Churchill and Evelyn Waugh.

sleep the P.M. in a purple dressing-gown and grey felt hat took me to see his goldfish. He was ruminating deeply about the fate of Tobruk since the failure of BATTLEAXE and contemplating means of resuming the offensive. He continued this train of thought in the cottage, conversing the while with the Yellow Cat and with Desmond about his garden.

Back in London an emissary from Marshal Pétain came to see the P.M., sponsored by "C".

The P.M. received a letter from H. G. Wells suggesting measures to relieve German pressure on Russia. "Russia is his only religion," the P.M. said to me with contempt.

Saturday, June 21st
The *Daily Mail* is full of schemes for reorganising the War Cabinet. The P.M. is nettled and fretful about the attitude of the press (just as I remember his predecessor being) and said to Beaverbrook that he must have more control of the whole war machine or else go. These murmured threats of resignation to Lord B. are indeed a turn of the tables.

The *Daily Mirror* has a front-page headline about "War Minister's daughter going to Washington as delegate to Red conference". Jan, of course. In an interview she said it was Munich that turned her socialist. I well remember that at Hinchingbrooke in October 1938 she was the only person who supported me in defence of Munich!

Returning from lunch, limp with the heat, I found Lord Louis Mountbatten* who recently played a heroic part in the naval action off Crete. He described how he sank several "Caiques" and foolishly, being old-fashioned, didn't shoot the men in the water; subsequently when his own ship was sunk the Germans machine-gunned him and his crew as they swam. He said that Crete emphasised the lesson which ought to have been learned long ago: that no naval or military operation should be undertaken without strong air cover. The navy felt a little aggrieved at their inclusion in the Cretan defeat: they had performed the task allotted to them, namely the prevention of a German seaborne landing.

During the morning I went to Waterloo to greet, on the P.M.'s behalf, Mr Fraser,[1] P.M. of New Zealand.

After lunch I took to the War Office telegrams from the P.M. appointing Auchinleck C. in C., Middle East, and transferring

---

[1] Emigrated from Glasgow to New Zealand in his youth. Once his shyness was penetrated, gold shone and he was seen to be a sincere, unassuming and deep-thinking statesman.

Wavell (in whom the P.M. has never really had much confidence) to India. David Margesson greeted me with: "Well, what do you think of that little bitch Jan?" and then went on to say that he approved of the Wavell change. The C.I.G.S., whom I also saw, obviously disapproves but thinks that it is no use keeping Wavell as he has not got the P.M.'s confidence. Wavell, he says, has got twice Auchinleck's brain. In any case he thinks it a mistake to send Wavell to India where he will arrive with the reputation of "failed B.A.".

To Chequers in time for dinner. Party consisted of P.M. and Mrs C., Mary, Judy Montagu, Tommy, Mr and Mrs Winant, Mr and Mrs Eden, Edward Bridges.

During dinner the talk turned to the demand for an Imperial War Cabinet. "Well," said the P.M., "you can easily turn the War Cabinet into a museum of Imperial celebrities, but then you have to have another body to manage the war."

The P.M. says a German attack on Russia is certain and Russia will assuredly be defeated. He thinks that Hitler is counting on enlisting capitalist and right-wing sympathies in this country and the U.S. The P.M. says he is wrong: he will go all out to help Russia. Winant asserts that the same will be true in the U.S. After dinner, when I was walking on the lawn with the P.M., he elaborated this and I said that for him, the arch anti-Communist, this was bowing down in the House of Rimmon. He replied that he had only one single purpose – the destruction of Hitler – and his life was much simplified thereby. If Hitler invaded Hell he would at least make a favourable reference to the Devil!

During dinner there was much talk on the U.S. coming into the war and also on Pétain's emissary, who has made it clear that what was holding Frenchmen back from us was their uncertainty about our victory and about the U.S. coming in. Eden said this was a contemptible attitude and compared very unfavourably with that of the Yugoslavs. "I hate *all* Frenchmen," he said to me, half-laughing, half-serious, when after dinner I showed him a telegram about de Gaulle's hurt feelings over something connected with peace negotiations in Syria.

When I was alone in the garden with the P.M. he said to me, "You will live through many wars, but you will never have such an interesting time as you are having now – and you may get some fighting later on." He then spoke of Wavell and Auchinleck and said it had been very difficult. I wondered if Wavell might not sulk and refuse India, but the P.M. said he had been afraid of just putting him on the shelf as that would excite much comment and attention. I suggested (as the C.I.G.S. had) that Wavell would use his pen after the war; the P.M. replied that he could use his too and would bet he sold more copies.

There were various nocturnal prowls before we went to bed. During one of them Eden, while holding forth on some topic, took a step backwards and disappeared head over heels into the deep ha-ha and barbed-wire fence at the edge of the lawn.

Sunday, June 22nd
Awoken by the telephone with the news that Germany had attacked Russia. I went a round of the bedrooms breaking the news and produced a smile of satisfaction on the faces of the P.M., Eden and Winant. Winant, however, suspects it may all be a put-up job between Hitler and Stalin (later the P.M. and Cripps laughed this to scorn).

Eden rushed off to the F.O. for the day; the P.M. decided to broadcast and actually came down to the Hawtrey room at 11.0 a.m. to prepare it; Sir Stafford and Lady Cripps motored over to discuss the situation and ended by staying to lunch and dine. Mr Fraser, the dull Labour Prime Minister of New Zealand, came to lunch and to stay the night, as did Cranborne and Beaverbrook.

At lunch the P.M. trailed his coat for Cripps, castigating Communism and saying that Russians were barbarians. Finally he declared that not even the slenderest thread connected Communists to the very basest type of humanity. Cripps took it all in good part and was amused.

During the afternoon I braved the heat and walked with Lady Cripps up to Beacon Hill. She is intelligent and sensitive and obviously very observant.

The P.M.'s broadcast was not ready till twenty minutes before he was due to deliver it and it gave me great anxiety, but even more so to Eden who wanted to vet the text and couldn't. But when it was made it impressed us all: it was dramatic and it gave a clear decision of policy-support for Russia.

After the ladies had left the dining-room there ensued a vivacious and witty debate between the P.M., supported in spirit but not much in words by Sir S. Cripps, on the one hand and Cranborne and Eden on the other. Fraser tried to make a few commonplace observations but could scarcely get a word in. Edward Bridges and I sat, fascinated and yet convulsed with laughter. The question at issue was: "Should there be a debate in the House on Tuesday about Russia?" Eden and Cranborne took the Tory standpoint that if there was it should be confined to the purely military aspect, as politically Russia was as bad as Germany and half the country would object to being associated with her too closely. The P.M.'s view was that Russia was now at war; innocent peasants were being slaughtered; and we should forget about Soviet systems or the Comintern and extend our hand to fellow human beings in distress. The argument was extremely vehement. I have never spent a more enjoyable evening.

Later, the night being very warm, we all walked in the garden and I gossiped with Edward Bridges while the P.M. continued an onslaught, begun at dinner, on the people who had let us in for this most unnecessary of all wars. He was harsh about Chamberlain whom he called "the narrowest, most ignorant, most ungenerous of men". At dinner it had been Chatfield whom he belaboured and the people at the Admiralty and elsewhere whose desire for "absurd self-abasement had brought us to the verge of annihilation".

On going to bed the P.M. kept on repeating how wonderful it was that Russia had come in against Germany when she might so easily have been with her. He is also very pleased with our daylight sorties by fighters which, today and yesterday, accounted for fifty-eight enemy planes over France for the loss of three pilots. We seem to command the daylight air over enemy territory as well as our own.

Monday, June 23rd
The P.M. is now toying with the idea of an armed raid on the French coast while the Germans are busy in Russia. Now, he says, is the time "to make hell while the sun shines".

Went down to Ardley for the night to see David who is on leave. He is violently opposed to my joining the R.A.F. His reasons were many of them offensive (such as my practical incapacity in which he and Philip firmly, but wrongly, believe) but I did not mind as I knew they were in reality based on nothing but affection and the fear that I should be killed. Joan supports my intention.

Tuesday, June 24th
There is something to be said for "influence" – at least so I thought this morning when stopped in Birdcage Walk for speeding and then let off because the policeman recognised me as Private Secretary to the P.M.

The House of Commons met for the first time in the Chamber of the House of Lords, their Lordships having removed to the Royal Gallery. It is an inconveniently long way from the new Chamber to the P.M.'s room and as I had to run from one to the other three times in this tropical heat I all but succumbed.

Brendan invited Vincent Sheean[1] and Duncan Sandys to dinner and there ensued a violent religious argument, Sheean being an atheist and Brendan and Duncan, rather surprisingly, both being stalwart partisans of Christianity, as of course were Desmond, John Martin, Anthony and myself. Brendan is very sensitive to any anti-religious opinion and has, I think, a religious temperament beneath his blasphemous exterior. The level of argument was not very high, but there was a compensating intensity of feeling.

Wednesday, June 25th
The troubles of the Ministry of Information have reached a climax and it is now essential to define what powers Mr Duff Cooper has and what his relations with the service departments are to be. Sammy Hood, with whom I lunched at the Travellers, says it is impossible to carry on as at present.

In Secret Session the P.M. told the House of Commons the facts about the shipping position and the Battle of the Atlantic, which show real signs of improvement. Last week-end Winant told me America hoped next year to build 2,000,000 tons of shipping more than was scheduled.

Finished *My Early Life* while the P.M. discussed his new proposal for sending a Cabinet Minister to take up permanent residence in the Middle East. This has been stimulated by a telegram from Randolph. Oliver Lyttelton has been selected.

Thursday, June 26th
Lunched with the George Rendels, one of their daughters and Sir W. Malkin (Legal Adviser to the F.O.) at the Ladies' Carlton. George told me some more about the F.O. reform which he is working out and said he hoped to increase efficiency by making people's positions less secure. He also talked of the Balkans, and of the chances we missed in Bulgaria. But Balkan solidarity proved illusory owing to the general antagonism to Bulgaria, the fact that none of the Balkan States had air forces, and the determination of H.M.G. to believe everything Prince Paul said and suspect everything King Boris said.

Saturday, June 28th (at Madeley)
Grandfather told me some interesting things about Lord Randolph Churchill, whom he had known well, and who, he said, could be more offensive than any man though he could also be more charming. He had an encyclopaedic memory only surpassed by Mr Gladstone.

[1] A somewhat brash Irish author and playwright of not very high quality.

Sunday, June 29th

In the afternoon I lay on a chaise longue in the sun reading Shelley's *Alastor*, Keats' *Endymion* and excerpts from Lord Chesterfield's *Letters to his Son*.

Mother had gone up to London to broadcast and during dinner we listened to her admirably conceived and delivered appeal on behalf of the various girls' societies. She is a most accomplished speaker. The postscript to the news was by an American journalist, Quentin Reynolds, who addressed himself to Dr Goebbels personally. I agreed with Grandfather in thinking it one of the most effective broadcasts I had ever heard. England and America had, he said, only one point of difference: the English drove on the left of the road and the Americans on the right; we were both going to drive down the same road, each keeping our own side, until together we reached its end – Berlin.

Monday, June 30th

The Russians, who are being driven back by the Germans, are showing unbelievable reticence to our military mission in Moscow. Molotov will tell us nothing beyond what is in the official communiqués. Now, in their hour of need, the Soviet Government – or at any rate Molotov – is as suspicious and unco-operative as when we were negotiating a treaty in the summer of 1939. I suppose our own left wing will say it is all the fault of H.M.G.

The announcement was made today of Beaverbrook's appointment as Minister of Supply (where, with more specific duties, he may become less importunate). Andrew Duncan goes to the Board of Trade and Oliver Lyttelton becomes Minister of State with special duties in the Middle East.

Finding the Annexe stuffy on these hot summer evenings the P.M. now proposes to dine and work at No. 10. I was on duty there until 1.30 while the terms of the communiqués about the new Middle East appointments, and the methods of announcing them, were thrashed out. Eden, whom Brendan now calls Robert Taylor,[1] came over and complained vociferously about Stafford Cripps who, he says, changes his opinion every few minutes and wants to teach him (Eden) how to manage Foreign Affairs.

---

[1] A good looking, if "flashy" American film actor, whose most recent films had been *Escape* and *Flight Command*.

18

Lull in the Storms

July 1941

Tuesday, July 1st
The P.M. gave different instructions to me, Rowan and Ismay about the Middle East announcements. He is petrified of a leakage through some foreign Embassy which would enable Lord Haw Haw[1] to be first with the news.

Lunched at the Reform with Charles Fletcher Cooke,[2] whom I used to know at Cambridge as a socialist President of the Union. I found that his views of the desirability of state control had been shaken by working as a civil servant in the Admiralty. It was not the Administrative Grades which he criticised but "the people who walk about all day with tea-pots". He was beginning to think there was something to be said for private enterprise. His suggestion about recruiting civil servants is that they should serve a five-year apprenticeship and then be given a lump sum down and sent out into the world for ten years to make their way. Those that did so would afterwards be taken back and given key jobs.

Wednesday, July 2nd
The changes in the Middle Eastern Command and the appointment of Oliver Lyttelton have a good press, though the removal of Wavell has caused surprise.

The Bishop of Birmingham, the notorious Dr Barnes,[3] came to

---

[1] William Joyce. His affected voice earned him his nickname and his daily broadcasts from Berlin caused more amusement than alarm. Tried at the Old Bailey after the war and hanged for treason.

[2] A Cambridge contemporary and ardent socialist debater in the Union. Later became a barrister of merit, a Conservative M.P. and Parliamentary Under Secretary at the Home Office.

[3] Right Revd E. W. Barnes, a Cambridge don of high intellect, but outspokenly iconoclastic and much criticised by most Anglicans.

see me, in Anthony Bevir's absence, about a crown living in his diocese. He described how the church of St Jude was next door to a pork butcher and all the pigs had been driven into the church during a bad raid. "Quite right too, I thought," added this Prince of the Church.

Thursday, July 3rd
The Russians are being driven back on all fronts but seem to be fighting hard and not disheartened.

Brendan had an M.P., Archie James, and the London Editor of the *New York Times* to dinner. We talked about the Ministry of Information and the general consensus of opinion seems to be that the Government's new compromise scheme for improving it is worthless. It should either be expanded and given great powers or contracted and the control of publicity vested in the individual departments concerned.

Friday, July 4th
I foresee an outcry: the I.L.P. maintain that Beaverbrook, before the formation of the present Government, offered to finance Peace candidates. The P.M. denied this in the House the other day. McGovern[1] now produces a circumstantial account for which Maxton will vouch – and most people will believe Maxton before Beaverbrook.

Saturday, July 5th
Alone with Barker at No. 10, the P.M. having gone to Chartwell in search of peace. So I was kept more pleasantly busy than is usually the case now with this large staff.

Gave Jasper Rootham lunch at the Travellers. He rejoices in exchanging the Civil Service for a tank. He told me that the one member of Chamberlain's Government who opposed the return of the Irish bases to De Valera in 1938 was Lord Hailsham.[2]

In the late afternoon I sat beneath the tree in the garden at No. 10 and read and re-read T. S. Eliot's poem *Burnt Norton*. His sense of rhythm and his use of words are beyond praise. His meaning is less easy to assess.

Sunday, July 6th
Went to church early at Westminster Abbey. A quiet day of blazing heat and sunshine. Part of it I spent trying on my contact

[1] Independent Labour Party M.P. for the Shettleston division of Glasgow.
[2] Quintin Hogg, 1st Viscount Hailsham, Lord Chancellor twice and also Secretary of State for War. Had the distinction of producing a son who was also Lord Chancellor twice, for even longer than himself, and First Lord of the Admiralty.

lenses, which are not comfortable, and part in reading A. J. A. Symons' astonishing, highly readable book, *The Quest for Corvo*.

Dined at Claridges with Herschel Johnson and talked most agreeably till 11.00. I elaborated my thesis that Hitler has been so impressed by the skill of his own staff-work, and by the speed and regularity with which his objects have been achieved, that he has ceased to believe anything impossible. Whereas our authorities are apt to take a gloomy view of an operation, and in any case to prepare a very slow timetable, German operations have invariably succeeded – at any rate on land – and German squadrons and divisions are moved from east to west or north to south in as many days as our forces require weeks. Thus I believe that Hitler did not contemplate the possibility of a check in Russia: everything would work out with the same clockwork precision as before. Perhaps it will; many of our experts think so; but I do not.

Herschel said that an American resents the indifference of an Englishman; he would not mind mere rudeness. An American is often offensive, but he does not understand silent contempt.

As I left Herschel told me that Monty Sherman had once said to him, "I never feel able to criticise anyone's motives." Monty, though very tolerant, was a man who often condemned people's actions.

Tuesday, July 8th

After lunching with Father at the Turf, I got back to No. 10 and went down to talk to the P.M. while he was preparing to go to sleep. "I hear you are plotting to abandon me," he said. "You know I can stop you. I can't make you stay with me against your will but I can put you somewhere else." I said yes, but I hoped he wouldn't; and after I had taken out one of my unfinished contact lenses to show him, he said I might go and agreed that the short, sharp battle of the fighter pilot was far better than the long wait of a bomber crew before they reached their objective. He made a few remarks about how wrong I was to go when I knew the routine of the office (though he clearly thought I was right) and said he would not have let me if the bombing in London had been heavy, but as there was a lull he couldn't say no.

The tropical heatwave, which started more than three weeks ago, continues – at well over 90° in the shade.

Wednesday, July 9th

Philip, to whom I told the P.M.'s decision on the telephone, was not at all elated. He takes the same view as David of my practical incapacity – and I think for the same affectionate reasons.

The P.M. and most of his family went down to Chequers for the night, for Lady Goonie's funeral tomorrow. Being in attendance I drove Diana Sandys there in my car. The sentries refused to let us in, but we forced an entrance by the back door. The Sinclairs also came.

At dinner I sat between Lady Sinclair and Mrs Churchill. The P.M. talked afterwards of the political future, the conversation arising from his congratulations to Archie Sinclair on his K.T. [Order of the Thistle] and Archie saying that a K.G. for Anthony Eden would ruin his chances of being P.M. Winston said that Eden now had a serious competitor: Oliver Lyttelton, who was *persona grata* to the Conservative Party and who had an opportunity of establishing his reputation in Egypt. Anthony Eden was not supported in the House or in the party though personally he, Winston, admired his great moral and physical courage. "He would equally well charge a battery or go to the stake for his principles – even though the principles might be wrongly conceived and he might charge the battery from the wrong angle." Oliver Lyttelton was "tough and stuffy" – and ready to take responsibility.

After dinner the P.M. and Archie talked till 2.00 a.m. while I played the gramophone for them. The P.M. showed Archie with great glee the parody of "To be or not to be" written at the time of Napoleon's invasion threat and now hung in the passage at Chequers. They talked of what should be done with the enemy leaders after the war. The P.M. thought that when the war was over there should be an end to all bloodshed, though he would like to see Mussolini, the bogus mimic of Ancient Rome, strangled like Vercingetorix in old Roman fashion. Hitler and the Nazis he would segregate on some island, though he would not so desecrate St Helena. But we still had a long way to go.

The P.M. inveighed against defeatism and said it would be better to make this island a sea of blood than to surrender if invasion came. He had been impressed by a letter from Reynaud to Pétain, sent some weeks ago, in which the former recalled how the Generals had said to him that after the Franco-German Armistice England would have "her neck wrung like a chicken" in three weeks. Reynaud had sent copies of this letter through the American Ambassador at Vichy to the P.M. and to the President. It is impressive reading.

Finally the P.M. and the S. of S. agreed that the French had acted shamefully in demanding more fighter squadrons from us after they knew the battle was lost.

The P.M. seems reconciled to my joining the R.A.F. and, as he went to bed, said that a fighter pilot had greater excitement than a polo-player, big game shot and hunting-man rolled into one. I owe my release largely to Mrs C.'s spirited intervention on my behalf.

Thursday, July 10th

The whole party went off to Lady Goonie's funeral in the morning and returned to lunch bringing with them Clarissa and Peregrine.[1]

After lunch I drove Clarissa up to London. She had been shy and silent at lunch (realising no doubt that she is not at present held in high esteem by her relations) but was more cheerful in the car.

Friday, July 11th

Rode and bathed at Richmond. Each succeeding day is if possible hotter than the last.

Went to Cowes to stay with Father at the Squadron, almost succumbing to the unbearable heat in the train to Portsmouth. Cowes itself was cool and fresh, and I delighted in its narrow streets and familiar smells after an absence of almost two years.

Colonel Charteris,[2] deafer than ever but still gay and debonair, was staying at the club; also Major Saville, a charming old man who told me of his life as a cowboy in Colorado in the year 1880.

I broke to Father my intention of joining the air force. He said: "I'm sorry", but was less obviously disturbed than I had feared and seemed to forget all about it.

Monday, July 14th

Returned from Cowes with Father. At Winchester Clarissa got into the train, with all her mother's effects in a number of trunks, and I travelled with her to Waterloo where she unloaded her trunks on me for deposit at No. 10.

There are to be changes in the Administration, with a view to disposing of Duff Cooper and Lord Hankey. It is proposed that Brendan – very much against his will, he says – should be Minister of Information, a job in which every holder of the office has failed but for which he has great qualifications. Rab will be President of the Board of Education. The P.M. wants to make Duncan Sandys Financial Secretary to the War Office (Dick Law succeeding Rab at the F.O.). This will cause accusations of nepotism.

---

[1] Younger son of Major Jack and Lady Gwendeline Churchill.

[2] Owner of Cahir, Co. Tipperary. A friendly, generous man, well known in both racing and yachting circles and loved by Irishmen of all persuasions. During "the troubles" his castle was occupied forcibly by De Valera and the Sinn Fein leaders and on regaining his property he was surprised to find they had all signed their names in the Visitors' Book. He married a lady from the music-hall stage known as "The Copper Queen".

Very hot and trying searches for a telegram which Eden, Desmond and I thought did not exist and which the P.M. swore did. It did; and the P.M. suggested I should perform hari-kiri.

Feel strongly that I am achieving nothing here but living very comfortably on false pretences and growing lazy through the lack of incentive to effort.

Tuesday, July 15th

Went to the House with the P.M. who made a statement on Production (criticisms in the recent debate have galled him), Syria and the Russian alliance.

Desmond says there are signs that Vichy is playing a double game and that the emissary from Pétain and Huntziger,[1] who came the other day, was not all that he appeared to be. The aim may be to cause a breach between ourselves and de Gaulle.

Brendan tells me that the letters and requests he gets from people wanting honours and jobs defy belief.

Wednesday, July 16th

The Russians, though still retiring, are evidently taking severe toll of the Germans who, for the first time, are short of fighter support. Thus our daily raids on Northern France are serving their purpose, even though they are not a sufficiently formidable diversion and we ought to do something more. But as usual the attitude of the Chiefs of Staff is as negative as it can be.

I talked to Dr Wellington Koo, the new Chinese Ambassador, who told me how effective the "scorched earth" tactics, now being used by the Russians against the German invader, can be. They were widely adopted in China against the Japanese. H.E. was full of optimism; he did not see how the immense anti-Axis front could fail. Like the P.M. he is impressed by the numbers now opposed to Germany: 1,200 million, or three-quarters of the world's population.

Lunched with Milo Talbot at the Junior Carlton and discussed the situation which would arise if the Nazis were overthrown and the German Generals offered peace, with their armed strength unbroken. I believe that then will be the moment to declare peace aims – and specifically at that. German resistance would be sustained by the fear of a Carthaginian peace. A generous offer, demanding in return the disarmament of Germany under strict guarantees, might well tempt a war-weary people to coerce even

---

[1] Commanded the French 2nd Army in May 1940. Subsequently rallied to Pétain, though he had been more in favour of continued resistance than most of the French Generals and de Gaulle thought well of him.

the army leaders. We also discussed Russia. I now think that Russia's action in 1939 and subsequently was due to fear and a wish to appease rather than the Machiavellian hope of seeing Europe so devastated that the seeds of Communism could be planted successfully in the shell holes. So they paid Danegeld.

The P.M. apparently wanted to make Duncan Sandys Under Secretary for Foreign Affairs – the most important and responsible of the Under Secretaryships. Eden has tactfully expressed a preference for Richard Law on grounds of experience. So Duncan will go to the War Office. Stirred by this example of nepotism John Peck offers me £5 to suggest that the best choice for Minister of Information would be Vic Oliver.

Thursday, July 17th

A report of Brendan's appointment as Minister of Information has appeared in the newspapers – leaked from Heaven knows where – and at lunch-time in the Travellers I was bombarded with questions.

At 5.30 Harry Hopkins appeared, having suddenly arrived from America in a bomber, laden with ham, cheese, cigars, etc., for the P.M. and American cigarettes which, to my envy, he gave to Tommy.

Friday, July 18th

Went to Chequers, where there is a large party: Harry Hopkins, Averell Harriman and his daughter Kathleen,[1] Pamela Churchill, Pug, Brendan. The latter is filled with gloom at his new appointment and says he hates the very idea of it.

Harry Hopkins is full of optimism about American production, especially with regard to tanks for the Middle East and an American maintenance staff there.

I sat next to Kathleen Harriman at dinner. She is pretty but convinced of the superiority of the United States in all things.

Saturday, July 19th

General Alexander, C. in C., Southern Command, came to lunch.

At tea-time the Soviet Ambassador[2] arrived, bringing a tele-

---

[1] Competent hostess and constant companion of her father when he was Ambassador in Moscow, 1943–46.

[2] Ivan Maisky, Soviet Ambassador in London for eleven years. Churchill had known and liked him since the 1930s. He was evidently more popular in London than in Moscow; Stalin incarcerated him for four years.

gram for the P.M. from Stalin who asks for diversions in various places by English forces. It is hard for the Russians to understand how unprepared we still are to take the offensive. I was present while the P.M. explained the whole situation very clearly to poor, uninformed Maisky.

Sir Alan Brooke (C. in C., Home Forces), Colonel Bob Laycock[1] (who commanded the S.A.S. battalion in Crete) and Peregrine Churchill came to dine and sleep. Sir Dudley Pound also.

Sunday, July 20th

Better weather, though since St Swithin's day there has been no whole day without rain.

Raymond Gram Swing, the American wireless commentator, came to lunch. So did Professor Lord Cherwell.

Sat on the lawn a great part of the afternoon, dozing, conversing spasmodically and playing backgammon with Mrs C.

The P.M. dictated a clever reply to Stalin which made me very late for dinner and caused me considerable inconvenience afterwards (long conversations with Eden, Pound, Sargent, etc., on the channel by which it should be sent – a matter which the P.M. had already decided).

The Attlees came to dine and sleep and Sir Richard and Lady Peirse to dine. We listened to Raymond Gram Swing's masterly commentary after the news. It almost seemed to be addressed to those in the room: the remarks about the P.M. and Harry Hopkins were surely made in the light of the lunch-time conversation and in the knowledge they were listening.

After dinner we had a deplorable American film, *Citizen Kane*,[2] based on the personality of William Randolph Hearst. The P.M. was so bored that he walked out before the end. Kathleen Harriman thought it wonderful and said that all Americans did. The fact that we did not, revealed to her much about English people. I replied that the fact Americans did, revealed to me nothing about Americans.

After the film we sat up till 3.00 while the P.M. talked about food supplies and imports. Hopkins said that the export of finished steel

---

[1] Formerly an officer in the Blues and intimate friend of Antony Head. He led the Commandos in Crete and in 1943 succeeded Lord Louis Mountbatten as Chief of Combined Operations and a member of the Chiefs of Staff Committee. After the war he was Governor of Malta. He combined charm with driving energy. He married a daughter of the Marquesa de Casa Maury (Mrs Dudley Ward).

[2] Not thought deplorable by most people. It brought fame and celebrity to Orson Welles.

goods such as knives and aluminium fishing rods to the U.S., while of no economic importance, was playing into the hands of the Isolationists, who declared that America was sending us products she could ill afford in order that we might support our exports. Nonsense, of course; but the political issue was quite considerable when vast Lease-Lend appropriations were before Congress. Hopkins also said that the U.S. could and should send us more food.

Finally Attlee and Harriman were yawning so much that Hopkins insisted that the P.M., in irrepressible spirits, should go to bed. When Winston started on what he was going to do to the Nazi leaders after the war – and the Nazi cities during it – Hopkins said that he, Winston, only read the bits of the Bible that suited him and that they were drawn from the Old Testament. "I'm not surprised they all leave you, the way you go on: there's Tommy lost at least two stone, there's Jock going into the Air Corps (beware of the coloured gals in Alabama if you go to be trained there), there's Seal gone to the United States, and you have to give that girl (Mrs Hill) of yours a medal to have her stay." At that moment everybody started looking at their watches and the P.M. was forcibly taken to bed.

Monday, July 21st

On the way back to London we all, in a great cortège of cars, stopped at Northolt to see the new big bombers. A Stirling, a Halifax, a Lancaster, a B.17 (Flying Fortress) and a B.24 (Liberator) were all drawn up for inspection. With the Attlees, Pamela, and Kathleen Harriman, I climbed inside most of them and was astounded by the intricacy of the mechanism as well as thrilled by the expanse of the wings and the sense of power. Then the five planes took off and flew past, very low, while we stood in a vast group which included Archie Sinclair, the C.A.S., Peirse, Moore-Brabazon and numbers of American officers and experts. The Lancaster was the most impressive of all, though the Flying Fortress, designed for civilian use, is the most beautiful.

Lady Malcolm[1] (daughter of Lillie Langtry, "The Jersey Lily") took me to the first night of the Vic-Wells Ballet at the New Theatre. I had expected to be bored but was entranced. We saw *Giselle* and *The Prospect Before Us*. Robert Helpmann may not be Massine nor Margot Fonteyn Danilova, but their performance was as good as any I have seen in the Ballet Russe before the war. The

---

[1] Her father was not Mr Langtry but Prince Louis of Battenberg. She was thus a half-sister of Lord Louis Mountbatten.

other members of the party were Americans, Mrs Johnny Dodge, and Drexel Biddle's right-hand man, Rudolph Schön, whom I found very conversible at dinner at La Coquille. He refuses to agree that the war may now be a short one, though he admits the potential effect of heavy bombing on German towns. But he thinks we have got to beat them militarily.

Tuesday, July 22nd
The more I see of the Chiefs of Staff's conclusions, the more depressed I am by the negative attitude they adopt. They seem convinced that their function is to find reasons against every offensive proposal put forward and to suggest some anodyne, ineffective alternative. Their excuse may be shortage of equipment, shipping and manpower; but they show no disposition to improvise or to take risks.

The P.M. held a meeting on American aircraft, since Harry Hopkins and Averell Harriman think we are not making full use of the B.17s and B.24s we have received.

Brendan, very scathing after his first day at the Ministry of Information ("Bloomersbury" he calls it), invited Lord Moore[1] to dine and our new P.P.S., Colonel Harvie-Watt[2] was also there. We talked of price stabilisation and wages. Brendan says that no Chancellor of the Exchequer has had the courage to say that if you are to have any chance of successfully stabilising prices, you must prevent an all-round rise in wages.

Wednesday, July 23rd
Another meeting with the Americans, this time about tanks.

My contact lenses are at last finished and today, for the first time, I wore them with the lenses fitted.

Bob Coates,[3] just back from Iceland, dined with me in the Mess and afterwards I took him, by invitation of Brendan, to see a number of films at the Ministry of Information. There were newsreels of the Russian war, arrived via Sweden this morning, and an admirable English propaganda film, called *Target for Tonight*, about an R.A.F. bomber squadron.

---

[1] Garrett, afterwards 11th Earl of Drogheda, Managing Director and Chairman of the *Financial Times* and an outstanding Chairman of Covent Garden. A man of wide knowledge and great sensitivity, married to a pianist of high quality.

[2] M.P. for Richmond, Surrey. He wrote for Churchill excellent weekly summaries of proceedings in the House of Commons. Chairman of Consolidated Goldfields after the war.

[3] Elder son of Sir Clive and Lady Celia Coates. Commanded a battalion of the Coldstream Guards, won a D.S.O. and was the best of good company.

Thursday, July 24th

Lunched with the P.M. and Mrs Churchill at the Annexe. The other guests were Sir William[1] and Lady Jowitt, Lady Ridley, Lady Wimborne (Alice), Sir Henry Strakosch, Venetia Montagu and Mr Chuter Ede.[2] I sat between Lady Jowitt, gushing and talkative, and Lady Wimborne, who looks very young and has lots to say.

The P.M. said that one of the most striking things about this age was "the lamentable lack of Charlotte Cordays".

Sir Henry Strakosch is optimistic about German oil. He thinks they only have five million tons' reserve and that if the Russians hold out another two months Germany will be exhausted for lack of it. Sir W. Jowitt, an intellectual and distinguished-looking man, was eloquent in his denunciation of Vichy – the most contemptible thing in history.

If Brendan is to be believed, he has already tackled the Admiralty and persuaded them to be more generous with their supply of straw for the Ministry of Information bricks.

De Gaulle is behaving abominably in Cairo: quarrelsome and neurotic. Oliver Lyttelton seems to be treating him tactfully in order to avoid a breach.

On late duty at No. 10 where future strategy in the Middle East was being discussed. First Harry Hopkins and then the P.M. spoke to President Roosevelt on the telephone, and the P.M., forgetting he was not on the "scrambler", said some things about a certain rendez-vous which he afterwards bitterly regretted.

Friday, July 25th

Rode and bathed at Richmond. Louis Greig says he can make arrangements to prevent my call-up being delayed so that, if I pass the medical, I can start my training soon. Accounts reaching the P.M. show that the training schools in the U.S. are hard and spartan and the standard very high. Meanwhile one of my contact lenses is being troublesome – letting in bubbles.

Spent the night at Horsley with Grandfather and Peggy, who are most agreeable hosts.

Saturday, July 26th

Returned to London, giving a lift to a vivacious Frenchwoman, whose conversation was so enjoyable that I exceeded the speed limit and was apprehended.

---

[1] A Liberal M.P., of strikingly handsome appearance, converted to Labour. Minister of National Insurance in Churchill's Government and Lord Chancellor when Attlee took office in 1945.

[2] Prominent Labour M.P. Home Secretary in Attlee's post-war government.

Went to Badminton with Philip. It is a large, beautiful grey house. Mother and Jack Coke[1] were there when we arrived and also Lord and Lady Coke, who had come over to tea. Queen Mary who had invited us because of her great affection for Mother, although she never has guests to stay, came in to tea and later I walked with her in the garden, telling her many things which, in view of her great discretion, I thought I might safely say. She was grateful and said how sadly she missed the information which in the last war the King had always confided to her.

The Duchess of Beaufort,[2] who had been working in a canteen, was back in time for dinner and I thought her downright, frank manner very attractive. She loathes Jack Coke with a deep and unalterable conviction.

Sunday, July 27th
The Duke of Beaufort arrived from Windsor for a late breakfast. At 11.00 we went to church in the church attached to the house, a fine building with good marble tombstones of various Dukes of Beaufort, executed by Italian sculptors. We sat in a large gallery at the back of the church, in huge armchairs and confronted with immense prayer books dating from the eighteenth century, looking down on the congregation below.

Before lunch Mother and I walked with the tedious Louise, Dowager Duchess of Beaufort, to look at her house in the village and resplendent garden. The village of Badminton is unspoilt and beautiful.

In the afternoon Queen Mary motored Mother and me into Bath, and we gave a lift in the car to a hot and embarrassed private soldier from the Badminton guard. I had not been to Bath for some five years. Under the auspices of Lady Noble we went over several houses in Lansdowne Crescent – including Moley Sargent's flat – and in the famous Royal Crescent. Their interiors were exquisite and redolent of Jane Austen and Fanny Burney. We had tea with Lady Noble, whose dining-room in Park Crescent is embellished with large paintings by Sert. We also saw the mayor's house, in itself fine but tastelessly decorated.

Back at Badminton I had another long conversation with Queen Mary in her private sitting-room, which, in the best royal tradition, is crammed with family photographs. H.M. was very pleasant and talkative. I can see why Mother has formed so great an affection for

---

[1] Uncle of Lord Leicester and equerry to Queen Mary from 1937. Friendly, entertaining, but alarmingly indiscreet.
[2] Mary, daughter of Queen Mary's eldest brother, Prince Adolphus of Teck, who was created Marquess of Cambridge in 1917, and of Lady Margaret Grosvenor.

her. She has dignity which is natural and knowledge which is unaccompanied by arrogance or affectation.

Philip had returned to Sandhurst, where he is taking a tank course, by the time we returned from Bath. We dined, as last night, in the small oak-panelled dining-room, with the family device of a portcullis engraved on the panels. The Queen wore a mass of jewels, diamond collar and bracelets, brooches and necklaces, which she carries without any appearance of ostentation or over-dressing. In obedience to Lord Woolton we only had two courses but four pages and footmen to serve them. Altogether the Queen's household is a strange mixture of simplicity and royal state.

When we had listened to Harry Hopkins broadcasting (rather poorly, I thought), and the Queen had gone upstairs, Jack Coke and I had a somewhat acrimonious argument about the war.

Monday, July 28th
Back in London, where there had been a small raid last night in retaliation for some bombs we dropped on Berlin. After lunch I sat with the P.M. and Mrs Churchill in the garden while they told me about a book of Cecil Beaton's – *My Royal Past* – with which they are both delighted. The P.M. also talked about the long speech on production which he is to make tomorrow and which is eagerly awaited by his growing body of critics. Apparently he has been working on it all the week-end – until 10 to 5 one morning. It is very important from the point of view of informed opinion in the country.

Today I kept my contact lenses in for two hours without the appearance of a bubble.

Tuesday, July 29th
The Production debate, in which the P.M. made a very long speech that failed wholly to satisfy the critics and the newspapers, who demand the appointment of a Minister of Production.

Leslie and I spent the whole afternoon correcting the Hansard proof, so shocking are the acoustics of the House of Lords.

Drank sherry with Lady Sinclair and Sylvia Henley. We discussed leakages. Lady S. said that the surest way of making people repeat things was to say "Don't quote me". This prefix always convinced people that the statement was important and true. Sir Archibald Sinclair never told her anything: he was what Lady Violet Bonham-Carter called "in a Trappist mood".

Wednesday, July 30th

Was present at the signing of the Russo-Polish treaty in the Secretary of State's room at the F.O. It was signed against a background of spotlights and a foreground of cameramen by the P.M., Eden, Sikorski and Maisky, while a bust of the Younger Pitt looked down, rather disapprovingly I thought. Although this treaty abrogates the Soviet–German treaty of 1939, and leaves the frontier question unsettled, it has caused a lot of Polish heart-burning, including, I believe, the resignation of the President. To a Pole, a Russian has no advantages over a German – and history makes this very understandable.

Auchinleck, the new C. in C., Middle East, dined with the P.M. and I had a conversation with him beforehand. He thought the situation in the Western Desert had been mishandled – "not by the High Command, but tactically I mean". He entirely discounted the possibility of the Germans moving an armoured division from Libya to the Russian front. He thinks de Gaulle is mad and consumed with personal ambition, which makes him care little for our fortunes in the war. But, says A., Oliver Lyttelton has handled him very well. Auchinleck is an impressive man, but – as one sometimes finds on a racecourse – looks do not always bear great relation to form.

Thursday, July 31st

The P.M. walked back from the House after the Cabinet, a thing he has never done before, and though he was talking to me at the top of his voice about war memorials (a train of thought engendered by the Cenotaph) hardly anybody in the street recognised him.

On late duty at No. 10. The P.M. returned from the Other Club, somewhat cantankerous, and dictated voluminous notes about the war until 2.15 a.m.

Meanwhile Desmond has made the horrifying discovery that the press, or at any rate Lord Camrose and his staff, have found out about the most closely guarded secret of the war: namely the contents of those buff boxes which "C" sends to the P.M.[1] Leakages increase in number and seriousness.

---

[1] If Desmond Morton's information was correct, Lord Camrose and his staff showed commendable discretion; for no word of what was subsequently called the Ultra Secret was printed till several decades after the war.

19

Special Relationship Confirmed

August 1941

Friday, August 1st

I went to the Air Ministry for my "medical", with my contact lenses in place, and – oh rapture! – was passed entirely fit. On my return I visited Horace Wilson, who was sympathetic and prepared to be helpful, and then bearded Harvey and Mallet at the F.O., who were the very opposite but were reluctantly persuaded to acquiesce.

The P.M. disappeared to Chequers and I shall not see him for a fortnight as he is very shortly off on a historic journey (Operation RIVIERA). He is as excited as a schoolboy on the last day of the term. Brendan has persuaded him, against his will, to take two newspaper reporters.

Dined with Hugh Dodds;[1] among much that was boring he gave me some interesting news about France and said that southern France could only be restored to its honour and life by a German occupation. He thinks we should work for this. Desmond Morton thinks so too.

Saturday, August 2nd

The Russians seem to be holding their position and the situation at Smolensk is satisfactory. If they can but hold another three months the war is as good as won and Napoleon's precedent will have been followed with almost uncanny exactitude.

---

[1] Second husband of my Aunt Nancy (Annabel). He had been Consul in Addis Ababa and Tripoli, and ended his career as Consul General in Nice. He got into trouble, unfairly, with the Foreign Office for transporting the Duke and Duchess of Windsor over the Pyrenees in June 1940 while leaving his subordinates to deal with the flood of other refugees and escaped prisoners of war who swarmed into Nice.

In the evening I went to see Clarissa who is in hospital with lumbago and looks radiantly attractive in bed.

St Swithin who, since July 15th, has been very jealous of his reputation, showed signs of relenting today and the sun shone with the brilliance of a month ago.

Sunday, August 3rd
We raided Berlin heavily last night.

The P.M. left for the north with a retinue which Cardinal Wolsey might have envied.

Monday, August 4th
Received a moving letter from Mother: "Well, Darling, I am glad (I think), absolutely thrilled anyhow, and *very* proud to hear of my new Air Force son. I hope the *ardua* won't be too tedious or exacting and that the *astra* will fulfil all your hopes concerning them . . . Father has said very little, and is reluctantly resigned."

Sat next to John Addis[1] at lunch. He tells me he is the twelfth child of a twelfth child!

The P.M.'s absence makes an astonishing difference: there is practically nothing to do, though Attlee – who is deputising in the P.M.'s absence – keeps on ringing up to know whether there are any papers for him to sign, like a child with a new toy it is longing to use.

Went to see Diana Quilter, who is working in the prisoners-of-war depot at Trent. Apparently all the prisoners think Hitler made a big mistake in going into Russia; and apparently they all have a real loathing of us. Diana says she is convinced our fate would be worse than that of the Poles if the Germans ever got here.

From Diana's house I went to comfort Clarissa in her nursing home, but finding Colly Barclay there, and knowing him to be an ardent suitor, I did not stay long.

Tuesday, August 5th
The P.M. being away, an unnatural calm reigns. I represented him at the memorial service for Sir Emsley Carr (proprietor of the *News of the World*) at St Dunstan's in the West, Fleet Street and, giving Sammy Hood a lift back in my staff car, learned that the German Trans-ocean Wireless had already broadcast that the P.M. and Roosevelt were to meet.

Motored to Stratford on Avon after lunch to stay with the

---

[1] Entered the Foreign Office in 1938 and succeeded me at No. 10 in 1945. Eventually Ambassador in Peking.

Sandwiches in a very ancient house once inhabited by Shakespeare's daughter and, for a time, by Shakespeare himself.

We went to see an extremely enjoyable performance of *The Merchant of Venice*, and the two principal actors, Baliol Holloway (Shylock) and Margaretta Scott (Portia), came back to dine afterwards and to talk about the stage.

Monday, August 11th

Back in London I found everything quiet and even "the military" admitting that the Russian army was technically better equipped and trained than had been expected. Apparently part of Russia's successful stand has been due to her using her whole bomber force for army co-operation. Stalin is confident he can hold out till winter without losing Moscow, Kiev, or Leningrad.

There seemed to be little doing and so I went to bed early, thus missing the arrival of a telegram from the P.M. about the joint declaration – in effect a statement of war aims – which President R. wishes published. The Cabinet met at 1.00 a.m. and substantially accepted the P.M.'s view on the subject.

Tuesday, August 12th

The Cabinet met at 10.00 to resume last night's discussions. The P.M. appears to have cajoled the President into accepting the terms of the joint declaration which he desires. Moreover the President and the P.M. have concerted measures against Japan.

Wednesday, August 13th

The P.M. sent another batch of telegrams which were very entertaining and showed great satisfaction with his conversations. In parts they were flippant: e.g. "See also Roosevelt–Churchill message to dear, old Joe" – who is being promised a great deal of material help.

The "Home Opinion" Censorship Report displays a great upward surge of public morale as a result of Russia's continued resistance. Indeed a great many people seem to hope for victory by Christmas. There is little reservation in the enthusiasm shown for Russia and practically no defeatism, but some bitterness against vested interests, Mr Bevin, and in particular able-bodied men and women who live in comfort at such places as Harrogate, disregarding the war as far as they can and concentrating on food and amusement.

A Pole, Count Zamoyski,[1] and Ronnie Melville dined with me.

---

[1] A.D.C. to General Sikorski. Married a rich lady and settled in England, spending much of his time playing bridge (rather badly) at White's Club.

Zamoyski, who strikes me as sensible and realistic, is nevertheless very resolute in his hatred of Germany and wants as much destruction as possible done now, since he does not believe that we could destroy Germany's strength in cold blood after the war. A nice Christian frame of mind we are all reaching! Z. also confirmed what I have been told previously, that the Russian occupation of Poland was on the whole more terrible than the German.

Thursday, August 14th
At 3.00 p.m. Attlee announced on the wireless the meeting of the P.M. and Roosevelt and read the Declaration of War Aims which they had agreed. It sounded tame, though the significance of America agreeing to collaborate in keeping the aggressor states disarmed is considerable.

Friday, August 15th
Went to Euston House at 8.45 a.m. for the formalities connected with joining the air force and left at 12.00 with 2/6d pay, an Aircraftsman 2nd Class in the R.A.F.V.R.

I was given three written tests in Mathematics, Intelligence and General Knowledge. They were very searching, to my surprise. To be confronted with even elementary algebra and geometry is disconcerting after eleven years – and I felt rather foolish when I remembered recording, on another form, that I had won "credits" in the School Certificate in Elementary and Advanced Mathematics. Fortunately I remembered about Pythagoras. The Air Vice Marshal on the Selection Board seemed to think some technical knowledge of engineering desirable; which was a blow. He discounted my theory that ability to ride a horse was useful for a pilot but said that sailing a boat was. By dint of heavy wire-pulling it looks as if I shall be able to be called up when I wish: namely about September 30th. In company with six other men clasping Bibles I swore allegiance in very solemn terms to the King, his Heirs and Successors.

Went down to West Horsley for the night with Mother. We had a delightful evening. I trotted out my thesis that our contribution to the Peace Settlement must be the acceptance of Washington instead of London as the centre of gravity of the Anglo-Saxon World, the British Isles becoming the English Speaking outpost in Europe. Why, said Mother, should we make this sacrifice in order to establish a lower basis of political and commercial morality – which would in effect be the result? There is force in this.

Saturday, August 16th

Peacefully denuded the loganberry bushes in the garden for half an hour (what occupation can be more agreeable?) and then drove M. to London.

The reactions to the Churchill–Roosevelt meeting are now crystallising, and the significance of the declaration is more appreciated as the initial disappointment that something more startling did not emerge wears off.

At the Ministry of Information Brendan provided a display of the films of the Prime Minister's voyage which have just been flown back to London. They were not yet cut or edited and some of the effects produced – in particular the singing of "Onward Christian Soldiers" at the service on H.M.S. *Prince of Wales* – were almost unbearably funny. Lord Cherwell and Inspector Thompson[1] in yachting caps were also mirth giving, not to mention the gestures and twitchings of Tommy Thompson who always contrives to be in the forefront of the photographic battle. Nevertheless the films, which lasted over an hour, when suitably bowdlerised should provide a good record of an historic occasion.

Monday, August 18th

I lunched with Mrs Churchill and Mary at No. 10. Mary is shortly going away to join the A.T.S.

Afterwards, the cat being away, it seemed reasonable that the mice should play tennis, and Leslie Rowan and I played two energetic sets in Eccleston Square.

Brendan asked us all to the Ministry of Information to see the finished version of the Churchill–Roosevelt film. I could never have believed so good a result could be achieved from so uninspiring and amorphous a farrago of material. It was typical of Brendan to think of asking all the P.M.'s servants and to meet them himself at the entrance to the Ministry, not allowing the films to begin without them. The comment of Moley Sargent, whom I took in my car, was that the P.M. looked more like Mr Pickwick every day.

Had a conversation with Sir Frederick Leith Ross[2] who was Mr Asquith's private secretary in 1910. He considered that Cabinet business was much more easily and efficiently conducted when no papers were circulated and Ministers conveyed decisions to their departments by word of mouth. There had never in his experience

---

[1] Churchill's senior detective who had been with him, in good times and bad, for a great many years.

[2] One of the most revered civil servants of his generation. Chief economic adviser to the Government from 1938 to 1946.

been any subsequent argument about the nature or scope of a decision.

Jack Churchill, Desmond and I discussed the rising annoyance in the House of Commons at the P.M.'s personal resentment of criticism – which is meant to be helpful – and the offence which has been given to many people, including Ministers, by his treatment of them. Desmond goes so far as to say that the P.M. is losing many people's friendship. The P.M. himself does not expect to retain his popularity if he wins the war for us: he has before him the examples of Wellington and Disraeli amongst others. But that he should lose his personal friends owing to the impatience of his manner is unfortunate – and unfair to one so innately lovable and generous.

Tuesday, August 19th

The P.M. arrived back in London. The Cabinet met him at King's Cross; Leslie Rowan, John Peck and I greeted him on the steps of the Annexe as he emerged from his car, smiling broadly, still dressed in his nautical clothes. Ralph Assheton[1] had brought his wife and child to see the return; nobody else was there.

John Martin told me he had heard Roosevelt say that he did not intend to declare war: he intended to wage it.

Wednesday, August 20th

Just before going down to dress for dinner the P.M., nodding his head gloomily, said that the situation was very grim. I suppose he was referring to the German progress in the Ukraine and towards Leningrad; or perhaps to certain failures and disappointments in our production. It is an attitude very dissimilar from that of the general public, whose optimism is almost too buoyant at present.

After dinner the P.M. asked me about the tests I had undergone at Euston House. I described the questions in the Intelligence test (which would appeal to a crossword puzzle enthusiast who was also fond of tricky mathematical problems, e.g. Philip) and the P.M. said that if that was the standard, Nelson and Napoleon would have been considered unsuitable. What, he wanted to know, was the use of catering for a lot of "chess-players who would die young of epilepsy"?

He was incensed by a letter from the cranky, pacifist Duke of Bedford and ended his scathing remarks on the subject by saying he was so glad that when this war was over he would be old enough "to leave it all: the scorn that I have for them." By them I think he

---

[1] Financial Secretary to the Treasury in 1942 and Chairman of the Conservative Party from 1944 to 1946. Created Lord Clitheroe.

meant politics. Whatever may in fact happen, he certainly now has the intention of washing his hands of politics after the war and retiring to Chartwell to write a book. But he thinks it will be a long war yet; and can he retain his position until the end of it? There are no signs of his popularity diminishing or authority weakening, and this American journey, coupled with his speech on Russia,[1] has regained any prestige he had lost. But public opinion is fickle.

Thursday, August 21st

Mr Fraser, Prime Minister of New Zealand, who improves very much on acquaintance, came to say goodbye to the P.M. I showed him Dorothy Sayers' bitter poem about Ireland, which greatly took his fancy and so, although it is unpublished, I sent him a copy.

Hardly had he left when another Dominion Prime Minister, Mackenzie King[2] of Canada, arrived, and after being greeted by the P.M., went straight into a meeting of the Cabinet.

Dined at the Ritz with Zamoyski and Lipski, who was Polish Ambassador in Berlin when war broke out and subsequently joined up as a private in the Polish army in France. They were both very scathing about the French. Lipski told me that opposite the Saar, where he had been posted, there was a complete gap in the Maginot Line: the French, uncertain which way the Saar plebiscite would go, had thought it proper to economise when the Line was originally built. Lipski also described to me the German schools for Leaders, which he had visited. These were vast establishments, with every possible sporting amenity and great forests for shooting, where the chosen *Jugend* were subjected to much physical culture (though decadent games like golf and tennis were excluded) and a good deal of Nazi political theory.

Lipski's description of his escape from France was fascinating. He is going to write a book about it. He told me he had learned more during one year as an army private than in twenty as a diplomat.

Zamoyski devoted half an hour to asking that the P.M. should include encouraging words about Poland in his broadcast next Sunday. The Polish Government is facing great difficulties with its own people who hate the idea of an alliance with Russia. Only the P.M.'s prestige can persuade them to accept the situation. Mr

[1] His speech broadcast on the day Russia was invaded.

[2] Liberal Prime Minister of Canada for long periods. A son of the Manse, an astute politician, but disliked and distrusted by many who worked for him. The King gave him the Order of Merit, though his achievements were not those for which the Order was created by Edward VII.

Eden is not sufficient – but it is difficult to insinuate this fact tactfully.

Friday, August 22nd
Negotiated with the F.O. on the Polish question and reached agreement with Eden and Strang[1] on a note which I am to submit to the P.M.

Went to Madeley for the week-end. Grandfather and Peggy, Father and Mother were there.

Saturday, August 23rd
Pouring rain all day; but today is the last of St Swithin's forty.

Grandfather produced some of his magnificent 1902 Hock and 1858 brandy.

Sunday, August 24th
After dinner we heard Winston's splendid speech on the wireless, describing his American journey, and containing a spirited message to each of the enslaved countries.

Monday, August 25th
Travelled to London with Peggy, whose company made the train journey seem short. She told me two things I had never suspected: that Grandfather was highly-strung; that Mother, had she wished, could have married Lord Halifax. She had, said Peggy, more admirers than Aunt Celia or Aunt Nancy – which I can believe, as her intrinsic worth is great and her unworldliness so endearing.

Today our long-planned invasion of Persia began. I am afraid it is an aggressive and not really warranted act, which is difficult to justify except on the, in this case dubious, principle of *Salus populi surprema lex*.

Tuesday, August 26th
The Persian adventure has started successfully, though we do not seem to have a very large force employed.

Saw a Czech Jew, Dr Rabinovicz, who wants to publish a book of extracts from the P.M.'s speeches and writings on the Jewish problem. Discouraged him.

Miss Rees, of the Gt Marlborough St Labour Exchange, brought

---

[1] A man of ability and tireless energy chosen in the summer of 1939 as head of the mission to Russia, which vainly sought to reach an understanding with the Soviet Government. An outstanding bureaucrat, he was Sir Orme Sargent's successor as Permanent Under Secretary at the Foreign Office and was given a peerage.

to see me a Miss Hewitt, nominally though not effectively in charge of woman labour at the Royal Ordnance Factories. She painted a lamentable picture of disorganisation, lack of training facilities and petty departmental jealousies. I am taking the matter up with Lord Cherwell with a view to approaching the P.M., because production is seriously hampered. It is difficult because Lord Beaverbrook, as Minister of Supply, is jealous of outside interference. Miss Hewitt told me that her experience had thrown her, a professed socialist, into the arms of private enterprise. She had seen what state control and a salaried administration could produce.

The P.M. is angry to find that Haining, lately V.C.I.G.S., and now Intendant General in the Middle East, is no good. So Oliver Lyttelton says. The P.M. suspects, very possibly with justice, that the War Office, and in particular Dill, strongly recommended him to send out Haining because they wanted to get rid of him.

Churchill himself was inclined to offer posts abroad to those of whom he found it convenient to be rid. There was quite a bit of "my language fails, go out and govern New South Wales" in the despatch of Hoare to Madrid, Cross to Canberra, Malcolm MacDonald to Canada, Dorman-Smith to Burma and even Lord Halifax to Washington. He failed to persuade Lord Winterton to be High Commissioner in South Africa, but prevailed on Lord Harlech, who had been Secretary of State for the Colonies, to go instead.

Wednesday, August 27th

In the morning the P.M. had a conference with Halifax, who is just back from Washington, Beaverbrook, Sinclair and Eden about supplies from America and to Russia. Meanwhile Maisky complains that we are in effect doing nothing for Russia: we say we cannot form a "second front" and we only supply inadequate armaments. Thus the U.S., in spite of all the fanfares, has only delivered five bombers to the U.S.S.R. It is difficult to see what we can do: geography, and shortage of trained, equipped men, make a military diversion out of the question. We are sending a lot of fighters and are helping economically. It is no use recriminating, but after all when we were fighting alone and for our lives the Russians were actually supplying Germany with the material means of attacking us.

The military situation is not good today. The Germans are driving south-eastwards, behind Kiev, and threaten to cut off the southern armies of the U.S.S.R. and turn all their positions on the Dnieper.

Spent an hour at the dentist owing to an air force decision that two of my teeth, which my dentist said need not be filled, should be filled.

I was on late duty and most of the time was occupied with de Gaulle, whose attitude is deplorable and whose pronouncements, private and public, are intolerable. The P.M. is sick to death of him.

Laval was shot to the dissatisfaction of nobody here. At last a Charlotte Corday! [He was only wounded.]

Thursday, August 28th
At lunch-time we heard the news that the Persians had ceased to resist.

Friday, August 29th
The P.M. has telegraphed to Stalin offering further help in aeroplanes. He has also telegraphed to Hopkins about the disquiet which the Cabinet are feeling at the slowing-down of the tempo in America and the apparent check to the growing open assistance we were receiving.

To Chequers, driving down with Tommy and Mary. Brigadier Shearer, who was formerly managing director of Fortnum and Mason and is now on the Staff of the C. in C., Middle East, was the only guest. Points from the conversation at dinner were:

Jubilation over our success in Persia, which had been very well received all over the world. The P.M. said that last Sunday morning he had had qualms. We had been doing something for which we had justification but no right. The man in the street, on the other hand, seemed elated that we had at last taken a leaf from Hitler's notebook. In support of this Shearer quoted the liftman at his hotel, a figure who played in his conversation the same recurring role as the schoolboy in Macaulay's essays.

Referring to a certain operation, the P.M. said he mistrusted set pieces which were rehearsed, like a play, so fully that nothing could go wrong – and then just before the performance the theatre caught fire or the Lord Chamberlain withdrew his licence.

Mr Churchill showed considerable optimism. He compared the situation in the Middle East a year ago, when we had but 80,000 ill-equipped troops, with that today, when apart from a tremendous army, we are in possession of Syria, Iraq, Abyssinia, Eritrea, both Somalilands and Persia, and are confident in the Western Desert.

The Yugoslav revolution when Prince Paul fled, might well have played a vital part in the war: it caused Hitler to bring back his

Panzer divisions from the north and postponed for six weeks the attack on Russia.

Shearer thought Hitler had made two bad miscalculations: (i) in attacking Russia (about which his Intelligence was bad); (ii) in failing to go into Syria when he could still have done so and could have made our hold on Suez precarious.

Saturday, August 30th

The P.M. stayed in bed for lunch, working at his box. He had spent most of the morning composing a long letter to Auchinleck about the future and I all but died of heart failure trying to get hold of it in time to catch Brigadier Shearer at Paddington on his return to the Middle East.

The Halifaxes arrived at tea-time. Lord Halifax, whose reputation in this country and the U.S. makes him out a reactionary and an obscurantist, seemed very Liberal in his conversation with the P.M. over the tea-table in the Long Gallery. He was emphatic that we must "cough up supplies for Russia", and he said, in discussing the future of the Conservative Party, that Secondary Schoolboys were on the whole better educated than Public Schoolboys. To this Winston said, "They have saved this country; they have the right to rule it." He was referring to the R.A.F. pilots, the majority of whom had come from the Secondary Schools.

The P.M. considered that the only hope for the Tory Party at the next election was to choose young candidates who had won their spurs in the war. To succeed in politics a man should enter the H. of C. if possible in the twenties.

They discussed the fourth point of the Atlantic Charter, which declares for freedom of trade and access to raw materials. The P.M. thought that this would in fact be achieved and foresaw a great increase in wealth as a result. Halifax said the Tories would not object, except perhaps Amery.

When he went to bed, after tea, the P.M. who is always talking about my joining up – with approval – said, as he unlocked one of his "buff boxes": "You will have to forget a great many things. Be wise rather than well-informed. Give your opinion but not the reasons for it. Then you will have a valuable contribution to make."

The Edens arrived and also the American Ambassador. At dinner I sat next to Mrs Eden,[1] whom I found easy to get on with. Over the brandy, the P.M., periodically supported by Halifax and

[1] Beatrice, first wife of Anthony Eden, was the daughter of Sir Gervase Beckett. The Edens were divorced in 1950 and in 1952 he married Clarissa Churchill.

Eden, made an impassioned appeal to Winant to realise the importance of the issues hanging on America entering the war. (Winant, of course, like Roosevelt, is no sufferer from illusions about this.) The P.M. said that after the joint declaration, America could not honourably stay out. She could not fight with mercenaries. Better she should come in now and give us no supplies for six months than stay out and double her supplies. If she came in, the conviction of an Allied victory would be founded in a dozen countries. This was "a war of science and psychology". America could not produce men, or the ships to transport them, for years: we did not ask for that, but we must have an American declaration of war, or else, though we cannot now be defeated, the war might drag on for another four or five years, and civilisation and culture would be wiped out. If America came in, she could stop this. She alone could bring the war to an end – her belligerency might mean victory in 1943. (Eden thought 1942.)

Winant said that on the day he was killed, Purvis[1] had told him he thought the U.S. might be in the war next March. This prospect seemed to give Winston little satisfaction. He thought the delay too long. He asked whether he should not commit a calculated indiscretion on the subject. Winant said it was better to leave that to his Government.

Eden said that we had now won the war for existence; we had not yet started the war for victory.

As a less serious epilogue, the P.M. discoursed on egalitarianism and the White Ant. He recommended Lord Halifax to read Maeterlinck. Socialism would make our society comparable to that of the White Ant. He also gave an interesting account of the love life of the duck-billed platypus.

After dinner we saw films of the Russian campaign. Coward, the wounded R.A.F. officer in charge of the roof-spotters, murmured to me as an alleged German plane was coming down in flames: "That's a Spitfire!" But Russian propaganda is effective even if it parts company with strict veracity.

Sunday, August 31st
As it was hot and sunny, the P.M. got up before lunch and sat in the garden with Halifax, Winant and, when they arrived, Prof. and Lord Melchett.[2]

---

[1] Dynamic head of the British Purchasing Commission in the U.S.A. where he had great influence. Killed in a flying accident.

[2] Henry, 2nd Lord Melchett, son of Sir Alfred Mond, creator of I.C.I. and of Mond Nickel.

The P.M. went off to see a "bombard" display, the Halifaxes left, and Mrs Churchill and I played croquet at which she, being an expert, beat me hopelessly.

Lord Gort and Admiral Somerville (Commanding Force "H") dined. As the conversation, about the defence of Gibraltar, seemed likely to be tedious, I slipped away at the end of dinner and, with Mary, saw a sentimental film about a circus.

The P.M. would not stop talking and we did not go to bed until 3.00 a.m. Lord G. seems to be enjoying himself as Governor and C. in C. of Gibraltar.

20

First Good-bye to Downing Street

September 1941

Monday, September 1st
While waiting for the P.M. to start for London, I read the Home
Censorship Report. The increasing support for, and admiration of,
Russia is striking. So is the high proportion of facile optimists who
think the war will be over by Christmas. There is a certain dread of
the approaching winter and a renewal of raids.

We are forgetting about sirens. None sounded in London during
August and only one in July. There has been no proper air-raid
since May.

Wednesday, September 3rd
Moore-Brabazon has raised a storm by saying in a recent extem-
pore speech that he hoped the Russians and Germans would
exterminate each other (a sentiment widely felt). Tanner, of the
A.E.U., maliciously announced this at a meeting of the T.U.C.
The P.M. spoke to Moore-Brabazon on the telephone and was
quite particularly nice about it, although the matter may well cause
him trouble when the House meets. He told M.-B. not to worry
about anything but producing more aeroplanes, the production of
which is giving great anxiety.

On late duty. The P.M., after holding a C.O.S. meeting, expressed himself forcibly about the pusillanimity and negative
attitude shown by our military advisers. "And you are one of the
worst," he said to the indignant Pug Ismay.

Thursday, September 4th
Acute indigestion. Barker says I eat too fast.

The following typical example of Lord Beaverbrook's style is the
beginning of a paper he has circulated to the Cabinet: "The Royal

Air Force bombs asked for by the Air Ministry under its expansion programme cannot be made, cannot be filled and cannot be thrown . . ."

As Mary and Judy Montagu are tomorrow joining the A.T.S., Mrs Churchill and Venetia Montagu gave a large farewell dinner party at the Dorchester. When the P.M. arrived he was clapped right through the hotel. I sat between Diana Sandys, who talked interminably about her children and evacuation, and an attractive girl with large deep-set blue eyes, a fringe and great intelligence. Her name is Fiona Forbes – a sister of Mary's friend Alastair, who improves on acquaintance – and I thought her fascinating. Having lived in France and passed her Baccalaureat, she is really well educated and sensitive too.

The older members of the party – Brendan, Barbara Rothschild, Pug, the Trees, Rupert Belville, etc. – melted away and the younger ones went a round of the night clubs. Mary, Judy, Fiona Forbes, Rosemary Scott Ellis, Bruce Grimston, Anthony Coates, Tommy Buckhurst, Alastair Forbes, Juliet Henley and I went first to the Four Hundred, then to the Nut House to see the Cabaret, and finally to the Coconut Grove to eat bacon and eggs.[1] Home by 4.30 a.m.

The P.M. had retired at 10.00 to see Eden and Maisky who brought him telegrams of grave significance from Stalin.

Friday, September 5th

In view of these telegrams the Prime Minister cancelled his projected trip to Dover. The Russians are hard pressed, both in the fighting and in supply questions, and Stalin, going directly to the point, raises a number of fundamental issues. We look like being faced with a decision of the same kind as that in the closing stages of the Battle of France: throw in everything to save our Allies or reserve our strength in case the worst happens. Fortunately in this case our cupboard is not so bare.

The P.M. and Mrs Churchill have given me a lovely silver cigarette case from Cartier with the inscription: "To Jock from Winston and Clementine Churchill. May 10th, 1940–October 1st, 1941." It is particularly generous of them and I am both touched and gratified.

Saturday, September 6th (At Stansted)

Spent the day shooting. It was dull and misty and admirable for duck. I stood in a cluster of bullrushes, behind a large bush, and

---

[1] All the young men, apart from Alastair Forbes and myself, were later killed in action.

shot twenty-three (twenty-one mallard and two teal) at the first stand. Later I accounted for three more.

Having shot brilliantly I subsequently failed entirely to cope with the partridges, only destroying four, although there were several probables and, I regret, a number damaged. Colonel Eben Pike[1] was with us for the duck and Robin Baring[2] arrived at lunch-time to pursue the partridges.

Eric, who was at his simplest and most charming, told me he can still think of nothing but Mary Churchill.

Monday, September 8th
The P.M. arrived back from Ditchley, his attention divided between his speech in the House tomorrow and supplies for Russia.

Tuesday, September 9th
The House has reassembled for one week and I went down to hear the P.M. make a statement on the situation. His speech, which dealt with the U.S., Persia and Russia, was quite well received although, for the first time, a number of members left while he was still speaking. He himself thought it a very good speech, "well-designed" as he said to me on the way back in the car.

The Chiefs of Staff only kept their tempers with the utmost difficulty when they attended a meeting at No. 10 to hear the views and complaints of Sir Roger Keyes on combined operations.

Tommy Dugdale dined with me in the Mess. We talked about the formation of a "second front" in Europe and he said, with great truth, that the general public have no conception of the meaning in war of time and space. They cannot visualise the practical difficulties in the way of landing an army on the continent and of bringing armed assistance to Russia. Tommy told me that the Labour Party is now terrified of the Communists and is devoting all its energy and power to combating them.

Personally I think that the trend is towards the employment of our maximum effort in the Middle East, where our forces would form a southward extension of the Russian line, using Basra and Suez for purposes of supply. At present it looks as if Western Europe will be out of the picture for some time, though Desmond and Tommy Dugdale both think the German air attacks on England will start again when winter stabilises the Russian front.

---

[1] A First World War Grenadier married to Olive Snell, the portrait painter, and father of two beautiful daughters.

[2] Lord Bessborough's nephew. Afterwards senior partner of Panmure, Gordon, Stockbrokers.

Thursday, September 11th

Desmond Morton tells me that we know from secret sources that the Third International has given orders to its followers in this country to keep alive discontent with the alleged inadequacy of support for Russia in order to use this to overthrow the Churchill Government when the time is ripe. Further he says that Stalin is lukewarm in his determination to go on fighting and Molotov is definitely opposed to so doing; but there are others, representing Russian youth organisations, who are resolute.

There is much speculation on the interview which the P.M. is to have with de Gaulle tomorrow. Sparks will fly, but de Gaulle apparently thinks he can appease the P.M. by playing the "Soldier of France", etc. Meanwhile he continues to use very anti-British language in his conversations with others.

The P.M. was dining with Beaverbrook at No. 12. I took them in a large file of papers on gas warfare, about which the P.M. has sent many instructions and minutes in the last year. I sat with them while they talked about it and reviewed our present much-improved position in this respect. Beaverbrook is convinced the Germans will use gas. He says he is certain of it. Winston thinks Hitler's followers may prevent him *if* they consider they are fighting a losing battle.

The P.M. worked till 2.00. I sat beside him most of the time and tried to answer his questions. The King has offered him the Lord Wardenship of the Cinque Ports (in succession to Lord Willingdon). The idea was Anthony Bevir's, who suggested it *sub rosa* to Alec Hardinge. The P.M. is much attracted by the historic splendour of the appointment, which was held by Pitt, Wellington and Palmerston, but daunted by the rates, taxes and cost of upkeep of Walmer Castle.

Monday, September 22nd

I find the P.M. has been busy with the missions to Russia and that it has been decided to give large numbers of fighters and supplies of munitions to the Soviet Government at great expense to ourselves. But, as the P.M. says, it is worthwhile in order to keep Russia in the war.

The Minister of State (Oliver Lyttelton) returned from Cairo and dined with the P.M., who has much to discuss with him.

Tuesday, September 23rd

Rode at Richmond. Louis Greig, just back from Canada where he has been accompanying the Duke of Kent, tells me the Air Training Schools are excellent and advises me to go there.

Francis Brown,[1] my successor at No. 10, arrived. It seems odd to recall a Brigade Intelligence Officer of the Coldstream Guards to become an untrained Private Secretary and to let me go off to become an untrained aircraftsman. Being responsible I feel rather guilty, but nevertheless not repentant.

After drinking a few gins and lime with Herschel Johnson at White's I went to dine with Sylvia Henley and Juliet. Back to No. 10 on late duty. The P.M. spent the time till 2.00 a.m. in discussing the dissensions in the Free French movement. A breach between de Gaulle and Muselier threatens to cause a public rift in the movement. De Gaulle is autocratic and right wing; Muselier is a Liberal (and a very loose-living one) who wants de Gaulle's powers to be delegated to a Council. The P.M., who is heartily sick of the Free French, ended by handing the whole matter over to the reluctant Eden.

Thursday, September 25th

The new Lord Warden left Victoria at 12.45 to visit his Cinque Ports, travelling in the new railway coach which has been prepared for him and taking with him Mrs C., Jack Churchill, Tommy, John Martin (for today only) and me. Walmer Castle disappointed its new owner and Mrs C. in particular thought it gloomy and un-wieldy. Having a liking for feudal relics I admired the deep moat and the bastions, and was also interested to see the chairs in which Mr Pitt read and the Duke of Wellington died.

We proceeded by car to Manston, saw and had tea with the P.M.'s Fighter Squadron (No. 615) and looked at the Hurricanes. I had a long talk with the Squadron Leader who showed me the cases of maps, food, matches, money, etc., carried by all fighter pilots in case they should come down in France. We also saw a short film of the Squadron's latest attack on an enemy convoy. I met Air Vice Marshal Leigh-Mallory who succeeded Park in command of No. 11 Group.

We spent the night in a quiet siding, half a mile from a stone marking the centre of England and a few miles short of Coventry.

The P.M. dictated half of his speech for the House of Commons next Tuesday. It promises to be one of his best.

---

[1] Passed first into the Foreign Office in 1938. Being under twenty-five when the war broke out (as, indeed, was I) he joined the Coldstream Guards, rejoined them when I returned from the R.A.F. in December 1943, was wounded in Normandy and died at an early age after the war.

Friday, September 26th

We arrived at Coventry platform and the P.M. was not dressed. He always assumes he can get up, shave and have a bath in fifteen minutes whereas in reality it takes him twenty minutes. Consequently he is late for everything. Mrs C. seethed with anger.

Lord Dudley (the Regional Commissioner) and the mayor met us. We went to the centre of the town, where the P.M. inspected a parade of the Civil Defence Services, and then to the Cathedral. The German bombers assuredly did their worst at Coventry.

The P.M. *will* give the V sign with two fingers in spite of the representations repeatedly made to him that this gesture has quite another significance.

We toured very thoroughly the Armstrong Siddeley factory, where aircraft parts and torpedos are made, and the P.M. had a rousing reception. As we entered each workshop all the men clanged their hammers in a deafening welcome.

I drove with Jack Churchill whom some of the crowd took for Maisky.

The Whitley bomber factory is a hotbed of Communism and there was some doubt of the reception the P.M. would get. But his appearance with cigar and semi-top-hat quite captivated the workers who gave him vociferous applause. We saw the lines of finished bombers and amongst them a rickety biplane built in the same factory during the last war. A new Whitley took off and flew past, a Hurricane pilot did stunts, and No. 605 squadron of Hurricanes flew over in astonishingly tight formation. When we drove away the men and women of the factory quite forgot their Communism and rushed forward in serried ranks to say goodbye. But I was disgusted to hear that their production-tempo had not really grown until Russia came into the war.

We lunched on the train, after visiting the cemetery where Coventry's air-raid dead are buried in one common grave. Lord Dudley lunched with us.

At 2.30 we reached Birmingham and there visited a tank factory, where the enthusiasm was even greater than at Coventry, and the Spitfire works at Castle Bromwich. Last of all we saw a display of aerobatics by two test pilots, one in a Hurricane and the other in a Spitfire. Their performance was so daring as to be positively frightening and we all shuddered as Henshaw, the Spitfire pilot, flew over us upside down, some forty feet from the ground.

The drive back to the station was a triumphant procession. The crowds stood on the pavements, as thick as for the opening of Parliament in London, for miles and miles along the route. They waved, they cheered, they shouted: every face seemed happy and excited. I have seen the P.M. have many enthusiastic receptions, but never one to equal this. It is clear that his name and fame are as great today as they have ever been. He was deeply moved.

We spent the night in a siding. There was a storm cloud owing to the non-arrival of a pouch but after much lightning and many claps of thunder (some of which were telephoned to John Peck at No. 10), the sky cleared with the advent of dinner and lots of champagne.

The P.M. finished his speech and I tried laboriously to teach myself mathematics. To bed at 2.00.

Saturday, September 27th
We reached Liverpool. The P.M., in his curious semi-naval garb, toured the new aircraft-carrier *Indomitable*. After we had climbed up and down endless companions and seen the aircraft on deck, he made a speech to the assembled ship's company. I am always impressed by his skill in suiting his words to his audience. On this occasion he spoke of the man-of-war and his wife, or sweetheart, the aircraft carrier who goes out to find his dinner for him and sometimes cooks it or has it done to a turn so that the man-of-war may eat it. It was thus with the *Bismarck*, it might well be the same with the *Tirpitz*.

The docks at Liverpool are a scene of great devastation. Many acres have been entirely cleared of buildings by the bombs.

The P.M. visited C. in C., Western Approaches, at his headquarters, where Lord Derby,[1] also awaited him, and then the party returned to the train for lunch.

In the afternoon we slept and I played some backgammon with Mrs Churchill. It was a stiflingly hot day for so late in the year. We reached Chequers before 6.00. Clarissa was there and Venetia Montagu. We all sat in the garden and the P.M. played with Mary's dog, Suki, which is a very engaging poodle.

Oliver Lyttelton (the Minister of State) came for the week-end with his son Anthony, a precocious youth who is a private in the Marines.

The P.M. was in a happy frame of mind at dinner. Having described Mr Granville, M.P., as "the son of a bitch", he remarked that there must have been a great many bitches in the last generation.

---

[1] Edward, 17th Earl of Derby. Secretary of State for War in the First World War and then Ambassador in Paris. Both his sons, Edward and Oliver, held ministerial office. He had great influence in Lancashire of which he was Lord Lieutenant.

After dinner we saw a bad English film, *Cottage to Let*, produced by Anthony Asquith. Later a pouch arrived containing the following telegram: "*Général Catroux à Ld. Warden des Cinque Ports. Reçevez je vous prie mes chaleureuses félicitations pour votre élévation a la pairie qui réjouit tous mes camarades Français Libres. Général Catroux.*" The P.M. was highly entertained and sent the following reply: "*Mille remerciements mais ce n'est pas si grave que ça. Vive La France Libre.* (signed) Mister Churchill."

Sunday, September 28th

Mr Winant came to lunch, bringing with him Mr Myron Taylor, U.S. representative at the Vatican. Mr Hanson, leader of the Opposition in the Canadian Parliament, also came and brought with him four of his colleagues with whom he is touring England.

So we were fourteen men to lunch and Clarissa. The latter, who is recovering from her illness, was obviously bored with poor Anthony Lyttelton and showed it. She has very bad manners.

I had a talk with Winant about the Vatican. He said that he was sure the late Pope would have taken a much more forcible line against the Axis, but the present Pope was a very skilful diplomat and was, Winant believed, playing his hand with the utmost intelligence. I think, and said, that there are times when it may be more right, and more paying in the long run, to kick over the traces.

The P.M. talked to me while he was dressing for dinner. He said that so far the Government had only made one error of judgment: Greece. He had instinctively had doubts. We could and should have defended Crete and advised the Greek Government to make the best terms it could. But the campaign, and the Yugoslav volte-face which it entailed, had delayed Germany and might after all prove to have been an advantage. (I was surprised at the P.M.'s assertion that he had doubted the wisdom of going to Greece. I seem to remember his influencing the decision in favour of an expedition and Dill being against it. Incidentally he has now got his knife right into Dill and frequently disparages him. He says he has an alternative C.I.G.S. in mind: Sir Alan Brooke, C. in C., Home Forces.) He went on to say that we cannot afford military failures. As regards all this talk of a diversion on the Western Front, a landing on the continent could only have one outcome. The War Office would not do the job properly; indeed it was unfair to ask them to pit themselves against German organisation, experience and resources. They had neither the means nor the intelligence. But critics would ask how we were going to win the war and that was difficult to answer. On one or two occasions lately I have heard him say he thinks it will last for several years more in all probability.

Finally he said that he ought really to have procured me a commission in the R.A.F. straight away. There was no advantage in going through the ranks. I disagree and said so, but was squashed.

While the P.M. was in his bath I was able to persuade him to delete a passage in his speech referring to Persia in which he spoke of the Foreign Office "in all its long and chequered career".

At dinner there was much good-natured but scathing comment on Hore-Belisha, Winterton, Jack Seely[1] and Oliver Stanley (who, said the P.M., was really suited to be Dean of a Cathedral, walking round the monastic fish-ponds and contemplating some academic "mot" which he could bring out next time he was invited to dine with the Fellows of his old College). The P.M. admitted that he had been responsible for the appointment of Jack Seely as S. of S. for War: he had suggested it to Asquith during a cruise on the *Enchantress* on the only occasion on which Asquith had mentioned politics, and at the time it had seemed to him to have distinct possibilities. Oliver Lyttelton recalled how just after Munich Crinks Johnstone[2] had told Duff Cooper he had been the worst S. of S. for War of the century and Duff Cooper had replied: "How dare you say such a thing in the presence of Jack Seely."

The P.M. launched an attack on Shinwell who had refused office in May 1940, because he thought the post offered him was inadequate to his deserts, and now took refuge in talking of the Government as a lot of "pinchbeck Napoleons". Then he reminisced about Harrow, where he said he had spent the unhappiest days of his life, and told how he and F. E. Smith had been booed when they went there in 1912. However he was going down again to hear the songs (he repeated several word-perfect by heart) and would recall me from wherever I then might be so that I could accompany him.

---

[1] Major General J. E. B. Seely, later Lord Mottistone. At Harrow with Churchill who was always fond of him. Secretary of State for War (at Churchill's suggestion) in Mr Asquith's Government. He was not highly regarded at the War Office and his tenure of office unfortunately coincided with the Curragh mutiny, when the British officers at the Curragh declared they would disobey if ordered to march against Ulster. He was a man of great good nature and unflinching courage but, unlike most brave men, he was boastful. It was alleged that there was a delay in publishing his book, *Fear and Be Slain*, because the printer ran out of capital "I"'s. People laughed at him, but they loved him.

[2] Liberal Whip, *bon viveur* and friend of Sir Archibald Sinclair (who was not a *bon viveur*).

After dinner we saw an American film called *John Doe*, which I enjoyed, and the P.M. then closeted himself with Oliver Lyttelton in the Hawtrey room and talked so long, as well as dictating telegrams, that I did not get into bed till 3.35. The P.M. said he supposed I was looking forward to the R.A.F. and lights out at 10.00 p.m.

Between the hours of 2.00 a.m. and 3.00 a.m. the Prof., who arrived at lunch-time today, gave me a brief and very clear exposition of certain navigational questions. He was a little pained to find reposing on top of his charts, papers and boxes a work entitled *Teach Yourself Mathematics*.

Monday, September 29th

I am rather sad to say goodbye to Chequers. Though gloomy, it is comfortable and the surrounding country is glorious. I have had much fun there and it has been the scene of very many interesting conversations to which I have listened.

Reached London at 1.00 p.m. Leslie Rowan gave John Martin and me lunch at the Union Club. I shall miss them.

At 3.00 p.m. the Private Secretaries, Barker and Tommy assembled at No. 10 and were photographed with the P.M. in the garden. "Well," said the P.M., "let me have three copies and put them down to Mr Colville; they are being done in his honour. And, by the way, we had better have a photograph of the Cabinet. They are an ugly lot, but still."

John Martin gave a sherry party to say goodbye to me. Brendan's cook, Mrs Norgren, did her very best, with notable results, and she made me a cake with a little aeroplane on it. The whole of Whitehall seemed to be there, from the P.M. and Mrs Churchill downwards. The P.M. told me he would not for the world miss an opportunity of seeing me off the premises! Mother also came and obviously enjoyed herself. So did I, immensely, but I found it a little tedious to be asked by a hundred people when I was off and where I was going.

I dined in the Mess for the last time as a member of the P.M.'s staff.

Tuesday, September 30th

I galloped round Richmond Park, where autumn tints are just beginning to appear and where the sun shone on a million cobwebs wet with dew among the long grass. Louis and Lady Greig, with their usual kindness, begged me to come and stay whenever it was convenient.

I packed frantically all the morning. At lunch-time, when the

P.M. had returned from the House of Commons after making a highly successful speech, I went into the Cabinet Room to say goodbye to him. He said it must only be "au revoir" as he hoped I should often come back and see him. He ought not to be letting me go, and Eden had been "very sour" about it and about recalling a trained officer from the army to take my place; but I had so much wanted to go and he thought I was doing a very gallant thing. He said, "I have the greatest affection for you; we all have, Clemmy and I especially. Goodbye and God bless you." I went out of the room with a lump in my throat such as I have not had for many years.

Part Two

October 1941–August 1945

21

Contrasts

October 1941–December 1943

"How old are you?" asked Winston Churchill when I was about to leave 10 Downing Street.

"Twenty-six," I replied.

"At twenty-six Napoleon commanded the armies of Italy."

"Pitt was Prime Minister at twenty-four."

"On that round you win," admitted the sixty-six-year-old Prime Minister.

It was a rare triumph to score against him by repartee.

The shock I experienced in change of life-style was volcanic. At one moment I was living in luxury, at least by war-time standards, and basking in the Prime Minister's favour. A few days later I was sleeping on the floor of an unfurnished flat off Regent's Park, an Aircraftsman 2nd Class at the Aircrew Receiving Centre known in the R.A.F., not at all affectionately, as Arsy-Tarsy. We were fed, by no means lavishly, in the Zoo. The pay was two shillings a day,[1] but the Treasury, with surprising generosity, decided to make up the balance of the £400 a year I had been earning at 10 Downing Street.

After a fortnight of injections, kitting out in uniform and total boredom I was drafted with a group of fellow-aspirants for flying duties to an Initial Training Wing at Cambridge. On arrival in those familiar surroundings, I was sitting patiently in one of the courts at Magdalene College, with my heavy white kit-bag beside me, when I saw approaching two ancient Fellows wearing long gowns, top-hats and high starched collars. One I recognised as that paladin of good English, Sir Arthur Quiller-Couch. The other, sporting an Old Etonian bow-tie, was the erudite Foreign Office

[1] Raised to 2/6d when I was promoted to Leading Aircraftsman.

Librarian, Sir Stephen Gaselee. I rose and greeted him. He looked at me in my aircraftsman's uniform and shuddered. "What," he exclaimed, "has the Diplomatic Service come to?" Quiller-Couch nodded mournfully and they passed on.

Eight weeks of drill, gymnastics and rugger on "the Backs", coupled with elementary lessons in navigation and signals, passed without great tribulation, even though we slept on palliasses, four in a room, in the neo-Gothic extension of St John's College and spent tedious hours during the night as sentries on the Bridge of Sighs. I never discovered what we were protecting and against whom. I passed one or two guard-duties learning, by moonlight, several of Shakespeare's sonnets from a small volume given to me by Gay Margesson and easily pushed into a tunic pocket on the approach of an officer or N.C.O. When not on guard I could escape to dine with friendly dons at Trinity and other colleges, though there were those who looked askance at anything so common as an A.C.2 at the High Table.

I set that right on discovering that Bachelors of Arts in the armed forces could be admitted to the degree of Master of Arts for a fee of £1. When I duly presented myself in the Senate House, the Vice Chancellor announced in Latin (using the old pronunciation) that I was the first man ever to be admitted to that degree in the uniform of the Other Ranks of His Majesty's forces. So I acquired the right to dine at the Trinity High Table free of charge four times a year and presumably still can.

After a short Christmas leave with my family, regaled with my Uncle Clive Coates' 1870 and even 1848 pre-phylloxera port, I spent the first ten freezing days of an exceptionally cold January in a bleak embarkation camp at Padgate near Warrington. There were tiers of doubtfully clean bunks in a corrugated-iron Nissen hut in which a small coke-consuming stove smelt vile and failed to supply the heat needed to raise the temperature far above freezing-point. I did not know a soul in the camp and there was nothing whatever to do. So in the evening I used to take a bus to Manchester and read a novel in a comparatively warm hotel. One day, by way of a pleasant contrast, Lord Derby sent his Rolls-Royce to take me to dine at Knowsley. Another evening, as I sat in a blacked-out Warrington café awaiting a bus to Padgate, I was embroiled in a rough-house when two disgruntled soldiers assaulted the café-owner on the grounds that they had been "twisted". They had ordered Welsh Rarebit and received toasted cheese instead of the rabbit pie they expected. The inmates of the café took sides: I fought for the café-owner and received a bloody nose. It was a change from the previous evening at Knowsley.

On January 10th, 1942, a band led a contingent from Padgate, including me, to the railway station where we entrained for Liverpool. Our ultimate destination was South Africa, though I alone among the airmen knew it. That band was the last cheerful thing I saw or heard for nearly six weeks. At Liverpool the Orient liner S.S. *Otranto*, painted grey and converted into a troop-ship, awaited us.

Our quarters in the mess-decks were daunting. There were long narrow tables to each of which eighteen of us were allocated. They would have been just large enough for twelve. Over them we were supposed to swing our hammocks; but there were only enough hammocks for half of us and there were nightly fights to secure one. The unsuccessful slept, fully dressed and using a life-belt as a pillow, either on the tables or on the filthy floor.

On board were three hundred aircrew under training, over two thousand soldiers bound for Singapore (where, in the event, they went almost straight into Japanese prison camps) and a number of unruly merchant-seamen bound for Durban to pick up crewless merchantmen. There was a fearsome body of marines charged to keep order and several attractive nurses and W.A.A.F.s who shared the comforts of A- and B-decks with the officers. The rest of us, some three thousand in all, were herded like cattle into the totally inadequate space of C-, D- and E-decks. The water was turned on for an hour twice in twenty-four hours, so that scrimmages rather than queues were the order of the day, and as we were not allowed to undress, in case the ship should be torpedoed, unhygienic is too mild a word to describe what we became, at least until we were ordered, as we approached the Equator, to change into the tropical dress of khaki shirt and shorts, black tie, woollen khaki stockings and a topi.

The convoy in which we sailed contained over fifty ships, guarded by a battleship and six destroyers. We had not been at sea long when a German Focke-Wulf Condor flew over us and was missed by several hundred anti-aircraft guns. Knowing that it would signal our position to the U-boat packs, the Commodore of the convoy changed course to due west, so that before stopping for a day or two in the steaming heat of Freetown, we had sailed almost to the coast of Brazil. We were not allowed ashore at Freetown, and it was over five weeks before, with shattered morale and fed on such delicacies as tinned tripe, we finally anchored off Durban. Meanwhile one young airman had died of meningitis and we had all been ordered to parade at 5.00 a.m. for the macabre ceremony of committing his body to the deep. After that we had to sleep as best we could on the crowded, hard, teak decks in case the infection should spread in the stuffy atmosphere below.

So lamentable had been the effect of the voyage on those in the troop-decks that, although I had firmly decided to seek no help or sympathy from 10 Downing Street during my R.A.F. career, one of the first things I did on arriving in South Africa was to write a descriptive letter to Mrs Churchill and prevail upon the High Commissioner, Lord Harlech (who gave me welcome and entertaining week-end hospitality during most of my time in the Transvaal), to send it home by bag.

In the letter I explained that while the over-crowding on the lower decks was so intense that it was only sometimes possible to lie flat on deck, or avoid bodily contact with others, the officers and nurses had the two spacious top decks to themselves. In the evenings, as we stood or sat disconsolately below, we watched the dancing on A-deck and listened to the music from a string orchestra. The menus of the five-course dinners for the commissioned ranks were handed round on the mess-decks while we fed on our unsavoury rations. At our cramped meals, the orderly officer would appear and say with monotonous regularity: "Any complaints, other than the food?"

It is not surprising that strong and bitter political feeling was rampant on the lower decks long before we reached Durban. All this I emphasised in my letter to Mrs Churchill. She at once showed it to the Prime Minister, as I knew she would. As I afterwards heard, he had the relevant parts sent to the Secretary of State for Air and threatened condign sanctions if anybody tried to discover who was the author of the letter, not that (as Sir Archibald Sinclair subsequently told me) there was the slightest doubt of its origin. Churchill insisted that conditions in troop-ships be examined urgently. This had a rapid effect; but I was hoist with my own petard, for when I finally returned to England, as a sergeant-pilot proudly adorned with my pilot's wings, we all shared the same food and even the officers were six in a cabin.

That happened twelve months later, the training period being long-drawn-out because of the shortage of spare parts for our Miles Master aircraft. I sailed for home on my twenty-eighth birthday, January 28th, 1943, on another Orient liner, S.S. *Orion*, in convoy with three large merchant-men. We were accompanied by H.M.S. *Valiant*, repaired after a limpet-mine attack in Alexandria harbour, and she was guarded by four destroyers. This was fortunate for us because several ships sailing unescorted had recently been torpedoed off the coast of South-West Africa. Strangely for February, perhaps uniquely, there was not a wave between Cape Town and the Clyde, and so as we steamed northwards in a veritable mill-pond I sat on deck and tried with only moderate success to teach fifty French *matelots*, bound for Britain to rally to de Gaulle, how to speak English. Teaching was an unexpected addition to my experience.

Back in England I was commissioned as a Pilot Officer. This enabled me to join an army co-operation squadron which for some inexplicable reason would not accept sergeant-pilots. At the end of September 1943, a few days after my father died, I joined No. 268 Squadron of the Second Tactical Air Force, equipped with single-seater, four-cannon, Mustangs. We lived in tents at Funtington, almost at the gates of Stansted where I had spent so many hospitable week-ends earlier in the war. By the mere chance of standing in for an experienced pilot while he went to have tea, I had my first operational flight, involving an air-sea rescue off the coast of Cherbourg, within two days of joining the Squadron. I then developed the disgusting disease of impetigo as the result of sleeping in infected blankets. The hospitable Lady Bessborough, undeterred by my hideous sores, insisted on my moving into Stansted.

A few weeks later, out of the blue, my commanding officer, greatly puzzled (for he knew nothing of my previous career) informed me that I was to report to 10 Downing Street on the following morning at 11.00 a.m. sharp.

"It is time," said the Prime Minister, "that you came back here."

"But I have only done one operational flight."

"Well, you may do six. Then back to work."

I was posted to 168 Squadron and completed the six from Sawbridgeworth, without mishap, flying across the Channel at five feet above the waves to escape the enemy radar. One non-operational incident made a deep impression on me. I was on a practice cross-country flight over the eastern counties when my single Pratt and Witney engine suddenly cut out. Looking anxiously down I saw an aerodrome with a long tarmac runway on which I contrived to make a glide approach and landing.

It was only a few miles from Cambridge and I asked if I might have transport to the railway station. The duty officers said yes, but I must await the take-off of that night's raid; for it was a bomber airfield, lined with Lancasters and Halifaxes due for inclusion in a gigantic assault on Berlin. So I stood outside a hangar and watched one three-ton lorry after another debouch a hundred or more young men, who walked silently and unsmiling to their allotted aircraft. Accustomed as I had already become to the gaiety and laughter of fighter pilots, I was distressed by the tense bearing and drawn faces of the bomber crews. At that time, late in November 1943, some eighty per cent were failing to complete unscathed their tours of thirty operations. Of courage they had plenty, but there was nothing but lip-biting gloom registered on those faces.

I returned to Sawbridgeworth much more thoughtful and disturbed than when I set out that morning. Yet when I flew the following day on an operational sortie over Northern France, hoping to find some trains to riddle with cannon-shot, it was with contrasting enthusiasm and excitement that four of us taxied to the take-off. I had reason to be thankful that since I wore contact lenses and could only keep them in for some two hours, I had been allocated to a Fighter rather than to a Bomber or Coastal Command Squadron.

I said goodbye sadly, sure that I was going to miss the spirit of adventure, the friendliness of my brother officers and the exhilaration. I assumed that I should fly no more and felt that I had wasted time and effort in order to make six uneventful operational flights. Just as on several occasions when I thought I was leaving No. 10 for the last time, I was proved wrong.

On December 15th, 1943, while I was enjoying a few days' respite at Madeley, the Prime Minister having left for the Cairo and Teheran Conferences with Roosevelt and Stalin, I received an urgent summons to return to No. 10 in uniform. Though surprised by the latter requirement, I did so. I discovered that Churchill was seriously, perhaps mortally, ill with pneumonia at Carthage and that I was to escort Mrs Churchill to his bedside.

I had kept a diary in the R.A.F., which is of scant interest, and I continued to do so on returning to the Prime Minister's staff. Except for the week-ends I was at Chequers, the entries were shorter than those for 1940 and 1941 and more concerned with personal, family and social affairs. When abroad I either made notes which I amplified on returning to Downing Street or wrote fuller descriptions and later pasted them into my diary, but I have excluded those which I judge to be trivial. The following selected extracts begin when I was summoned back to London from Madeley in December 1943.

Thursday, December 16th
Went to the House of Commons to hear Attlee announce the P.M.'s illness which he did in very lugubrious tones. A "clamp" looked like preventing our departure, but finally we heard that we could take off in a Liberator from Lyneham. Mary accompanied Mrs Churchill, and I drove with Miss Hamblin – a seemingly endless journey in the mist and blackout. We dined at Lyneham, a

rather sticky dinner in a special Mess, but Mrs C. was calm and managed to seem cheerful. We took off at 11.30, Mrs C., Miss Hamblin and I on mattresses stretched on the floor of the Liberator, and spent most of the night sitting up, talking and drinking coffee as Mrs Churchill could not sleep and was rather alarmed. The weather, except for the take-off, was perfect and we had a calm flight at 5,000 feet.

Friday, December 17th

It was still dark when we landed at Gibraltar. We had breakfast at Government House, where we found General Ismay on his way home, and took off again for Tunis at 9.30. We flew over Algeria and the Kasserine Gap. I took over the controls for a short time. We landed at 3.00 p.m., being met by a large party including Sarah, Tommy Thompson, John Martin and Air Chief Marshal Tedder[1]* We drove to the White House at Carthage, where the P.M. was lying. He sent for me and I found instead of a recumbent invalid a cheerful figure with a large cigar and a whisky and soda in his hand.

I was billeted in a magnificent villa, with gaudy mosaic decoration, in the Arab village of Sidi Bou Said. It belongs to the d'Erlangers.

Saturday, December 18th

A fleet of American cars stood waiting before the doors of the White House, ready to take anyone anywhere. With John Martin I went into Tunis, stopping to look at a German cemetery at Carthage – very well kept in contrast with ours. Tunis is a dull town. It is quite unscathed by the bombing except for the docks which are flat.

The Coldstream are guarding us. Bill Harris[2] is Second in Command. Visited them in their Mess.

Sunday, December 19th

Began to take an active part in the work of the Private Office. Strange after more than two years' absence; but though the P.M. was much better, there was little doing.

Bill Harris and I walked up to the Cathedral at Carthage where Louis IX died and is buried.

---

[1] Air officer commanding the Desert Air Force.
[2] Married to my cousin Betty Coates. He and I were at the same preparatory school, in the same House at Harrow and in the same college at Cambridge. After the war he became a Q.C.

The party at the White House included Mrs Churchill, Sarah, Tommy, Joe Hollis, John Martin, Francis Brown, Lord Moran* and three other doctors; also Randolph. The Tedders were in and out all day.

Monday, December 20th
Bill Harris lunched and escorted some of us to Longstop Hill and Medjes el Bab. The signs of battle are few and the scene is a notable contrast to the French battlefields after the 1918 war.

Tuesday, December 21st
Accompanied Bedford and Pulvertaft (two of the doctors) on a tour of the native quarter of "Kasbah" of Tunis. Prices exorbitant.

Randolph was very silly with the P.M., producing exaggerated accounts of the French arrests of Flandin, Boisson, etc. Winston almost had apoplexy and Lord Moran was seriously perturbed.

At tea-time the P.M. suddenly got up and walked into the large white hall in his dressing-gown.

Generals Neame and O'Connor and Air Vice Marshal Boyd, all in army battle dress, came to dinner. They have just escaped from prisoners' camps in Italy. I sat next to Tedder who was flippant but agreeable.

Wednesday, December 22nd
An expedition to Dougga. We found it with difficulty but it was well worth the long drive. The Roman remains, especially the theatre, are first class and the site of the whole ruin is superb.

Randolph is causing considerable strife in the family and entourage. But the P.M. likes playing bezique with him.

Friday, December 24th
Walked slowly down from Sidi Bou Said (where nearly all of us sleep) with General Alexander, whom I did not find an easy conversationalist, though he is pleasant.

There was a great influx of Generals and others to discuss Operation SHINGLE[1] and, in particular, the question of providing landing craft. Maitland Wilson (C. in C. elect),[2] Tedder, Air

---

[1] The projected landing in Anzio, north of Naples.
[2] Field Marshal Lord Wilson. Commanded the British forces in Greece in 1941 and held numerous commands in the Middle East, becoming Supreme Allied Commander in the Mediterranean (excluding Italy) in 1944.

Vice Marshal Park (from Sicily), General Gale (Quartermaster General) and others were there. The P.M. rose from his sick bed to hold a conference in the dining-room.

After dinner I made a strange sortie with Randolph to call on some French people, whom we surprised in the middle of a large dinner party. We sat embarrassed on the sofa until they rose from the table. I was a bit ashamed of these shock tactics.

Christmas Day

General Alexander, Mrs C., Sarah, Lord Moran and I went to an early service arranged by the Coldstream in an ammunition shed. There was a dramatic culmination when, as the Padre said the *Gloria in Excelsis*, the bells of Carthage Cathedral pealed loudly from the hill above and a white dove, which had been roosting on a beam in the shed, fluttered down in front of the congregation.

There was a great conference, which included five Commanders in Chief: Eisenhower,* Maitland Wilson, Alexander, Tedder and Admiral Sir John Cunningham.[1]

At luncheon the P.M. proposed everybody's health in turn. Harold Macmillan[2] and Desmond Morton arrived just before it.

In the evening there was a cocktail party to which many were bidden. The party, through the midst of which the P.M. walked as if in perfect health, merged into a cold stand-up dinner and everybody finished the day feeling the merrier for Christmas.

I thought Harold Macmillan, with whom I had a long talk, rather finicky and probably a little insincere.

Sunday, December 26th

The Generals and Randolph left.

I walked with Mrs C., Sarah and Lord Moran to look at the remains of Carthage docks. The old Punic town stretched along by the sea, just where we are living, but so thoroughly was *Carthago deleta* that the only remains date from a later Roman epoch.

The P.M. dined in the dining-room for the first time. After dinner I took a paper of Lord Cherwell's, about the new German reprisal weapon (the V.1), to show Tedder and found him, his wife and staff finishing dinner at his headquarters. I sat long talking to him, with brandy, champagne and cigars (Christmas celebrations presumably), and found him particularly agreeable, thoughtful and interesting.

[1] Commander in Chief, Mediterranean.
[2] British Resident Minister in North Africa. Later Earl of Stockton.*

Monday, December 27th

We flew to Marrakech. The P.M. went in his York. Joe Hollis and I went in a Liberator with all the W.A.A.F. cypherers and had a very bumpy journey. One of the engines cut dead and a side panel blew in. The air was icy, the W.A.A.F.s shrieked and Joe and I had to hold the panel in place with all the strength we had until the flight engineer contrived to make temporary repairs.

On arrival we drove to the spacious and luxurious, if slightly vulgar, Villa Taylor where the P.M. had already arrived. Excellent food cooked by a French chef, formerly of the French Embassy in Moscow. I was sleeping at the villa; most of the rest of the staff were at the Hotel Mamounia.

The villa was lent by the Americans and Americans were both guarding us and organising our entertainment, a task they performed without counting the cost.

Tuesday, December 28th

Lord Beaverbrook arrived unannounced though expected. He was in high spirits. Max Aitken[1] came with him en route for Cairo.

John Martin and I penetrated into the back streets of the Medina, the genuine unspoilt and very beautiful native town, which is fortunately out of bounds to the American troops.

After dinner the P.M. decorated Max Aitken with the ribbon of the 1939–43[2] Star (hastily cut off my second tunic). "Little Max" has an imposing array of decorations. Then we played poker, unruly but amusing. I made the mistake of trying to call Lord Beaverbrook's bluff but ended by losing only £2.10.0. The P.M. was wildly rash but successful. He divided the gains and losses by 1,000, with Lord Beaverbrook's agreement, to suit my economic position. Otherwise I should have lost £2,500, which I certainly do not possess.

Wednesday, December 29th

After lunching at the villa we all motored into the foothills of the Atlas mountains and admired the glorious scenery. We returned in time to entertain some of the W.A.A.F. cypherers to tea (they came in batches throughout the visit until all had been). The P.M. took them up the tower to look at the walled Medina and to watch the sunset.

---

[1] Group Captain Max Aitken, D.S.O., D.F.C., a hero of the Battle of Britain. Succeeded his father as Chairman of Beaverbrook Newspapers until the company was sold to Trafalgar House. Renounced the Beaverbrook peerage because he thought people should know of only one Lord Beaverbrook.

[2] Later the 1939–45 Star War medal.

At dinner the P.M. made the first apologia I have ever heard him make for the Baldwin Government: "The climate of public opinion on people is overpowering."

But he says this war will be known in history as the Unnecessary War.

Thursday, December 30th
We picnicked near a river in the Atlas foothills against a background of prickly pear. All of us except the P.M. and Lord B. walked up the valley, through a ramshackle Jewish village, and Mrs C. and I forded a stream on a donkey while the others, led by Lord Moran, preferred wading to the risk of verminous contact. But neither Mrs C. nor I suffered for our rashness.

The Beaver was greatly impressed by the antagonism of the Moorish and Jewish children who refused to play with one another. The Jews looked much less happy and self-confident than the Moors. We fed them with biscuits, cakes and oranges and gave a larger share to the Jews. Went to the great square in the Medina with Lord B., Mrs C. and Sarah.

Friday, December 31st
General Eisenhower came to dinner and General Montgomery* with his A.D.C., Noel Chavasse, came for the night. We saw the New Year in early so that General M. could go to bed. Punch was brewed, the P.M. made a little speech, the clerks, typists and some of the servants appeared, and we formed a circle to sing "Auld Lang Syne". I was linked arm in arm with General Montgomery and the American barman.

Mrs Churchill was the only person I knew who always succeeded in subduing General Montgomery, though she became fond of him. On this occasion when it was time to have a bath before dinner, she turned to the A.D.C., Noel Chavasse, and said she looked forward to seeing him in half an hour.

"My A.D.C.s don't dine with the Prime Minister," said Monty tartly.

Mrs Churchill gave him a withering look. "In my house, General Montgomery, I invite who I wish and I don't require your advice."

Noel Chavasse dined.

On another occasion, some years later, Monty announced on the croquet lawn at Chartwell that all politicians were dishonest. Mrs Churchill, with flashing eyes, said that if that was his view he should leave Chartwell at once. She would arrange to have his bags packed. He apologised profusely, and stayed.

She was equally forthright, though less withering, with General de Gaulle who, whatever his periodical differences with her husband, never ceased to respect and admire her.

22

Marrakech

January 1944

Saturday, January 1st [Marrakech]
The whole party, including Montgomery, picnicked in an olive grove. Monty was talkative but not bombastic. He made two notable remarks in the presence of Lords Moran and Beaverbrook, though not in mine. They were that his chaplains were more important to him than his artillery, and that he thought the 8th Army would vote in an election as he told them to vote.

Monty left by air after dinner to take up his new Command in England.[1]

Sunday, January 2nd
Lord B. was going to take Sarah and me to Fez in the Liberator, but he changed his mind just as we were setting off.

I rode a white horse with a mouth of iron in company with Nairn,[2] the British Consul at Marrakech. We cantered through the orange groves and olive trees of the gardens belonging to the Sultan of Morocco's palace.

At dinner the P.M. and the Beaver went over the whole course of the last war and of this. At one moment the P.M. turned and said to Commander Thompson, "But, Tommy, you will bear witness that I do not repeat my stories so often as my dear friend, the President of the United States."

Speaking of the Chiefs of Staff, he said, "They may say I lead them up the garden path, but at every stage of the garden they have found delectable fruit and wholesome vegetables."

---

[1] The operational command of the Allied land forces for the re-entry into Northern Europe, Operation OVERLORD.
[2] Subsequently Consul at Bordeaux where the Churchills again made friends with him and his wife, an accomplished artist who accompanied Churchill on his painting expeditions during a holiday at Hendaye after the defeat of Germany.

Monday, January 3rd
There was a picnic followed by a beautiful but long drive above the snowline of the Atlas. We stopped many times to admire the scenery, in particular at a forester's house built in a sublime position. The forester's wife recognised the P.M. and was overcome.

The local French General and his wife (de Villate) dined and offered to arrange a wild boar hunt for us. It could and should have easily been arranged, had Tommy subsequently shown a little more initiative.

Tuesday, January 4th
President Beneš came to lunch. He is agreeable but specious and, perhaps, unduly optimistic. He told us (1) that Russian aid for Czechoslovakia would certainly have been forthcoming at the time of Munich; (2) that the famous Russian treason trials had been fully justified. Tuchachevsky, Kamenev, etc., had been plotting with Germany because, as sincere Trotskyists, they thought that German help in the overthrow of Stalin was morally justifiable and that they were acting in the true interests of Russia. The plot had been discovered by the Czechs; Beneš had thought that the Soviet Government were intriguing with Germany; he had protested to the Russian Minister at Prague who had been amazed at his unfounded accusations and had reported them to Moscow in complete bewilderment; these accusations had put the Soviet Government on the scent; (3) that he had discussed the Polish and Czech frontiers with Stalin (he was on his way back from Moscow), and had agreed to a common Russo-Czech frontier in the east. He discussed the new Russo-Polish frontier at length with the P.M. on the basis of the Curzon line.[1] Stalin is determined to have Lvov.

Beneš, Smutmy (one of B.'s ministers) and Lebedev, Soviet Ambassador to the Czechs – who spoke no word of English, French or German and had hair like a virtuoso – came to dine.

The P.M. talked of flying to Malta to discuss Operation SHINGLE further, but strong pressure was brought against his so doing. The Operation, scheduled for January 22nd (I am writing this on January 22nd, having decided to write no word of future operations in this diary, however securely I may keep it at No. 10) was showing signs of flagging owing to landing craft problems.

---

[1] The frontier proposed after the First World War but extended eastwards after Poland's defeat of the Red Army in 1920.

Wednesday, January 5th

Generals Bedell Smith (Eisenhower's Chief of Staff), Gale (Quartermaster General at Algiers), Gammell and Devers arrived for an hour or two on their way back from London. I went to meet them at the Mamounia (Tommy, the Flag Commander, was still in bed) and brought them up to the villa.

I did not go with the others on a picnic but had an agreeable lunch in the garden with Lord Beaverbrook, Lord Moran and Joe Hollis.

Beneš, whose aircraft went u/s last night, again came to dine. Talk was of when the war would end. The P.M. was cautious: "I wouldn't guarantee it won't end in 1944." Beneš was confident: "We must be ready for a German collapse any day after May 1st." The P.M. put it to the vote round the table whether Hitler would still be in power on September 3rd, 1944: There voted:

Yes – the P.M., Lord Beaverbrook, Captain Sanderson (Grenadier Guards) and I.

No – Beneš, Smutmy, Lord Moran, Tommy, John Martin, Sarah, Joe Hollis.

Thursday, January 6th

A small picnic: P.M., Mrs C., Tommy, self. We went back to the scene of our first picnic, a stream running over multi-coloured pebbles between hills on which stood a Jewish village to the right and to the left the house of the local Caid and an old French fort. The P.M. had painted the scene when last he was at Marrakech and the picture hangs in the passage at the Annexe.

The Glaoui of Marrakech, a dignified chieftain in white robes, came to tea. The P.M. thrilled him by showing him the strategic layout in the map-room (which had just been established in the room next to the P.M.'s bedroom by Captain Pim and staff, who had flown out for that purpose).

Again visited the Medina with Lord B., Mrs C. and Sarah. We saw the dancers, the snake charmers and the eloquent story tellers who stand surrounded by a crowd of squatting listeners. The Beaver, watching their gesticulations, said that oratory was the same the whole world over.

Friday, January 7th

First came General Maitland Wilson, and after lunch Alexander, Sir J. Cunningham (C. in C., Med.), Devers, Bedell Smith, Gale and a host of others for a great SHINGLE conference. I dined with the Generals' satellites at the Mamounia hotel. Fitzroy Maclean, Brigadier accredited to Marshal Tito, and Randolph arrived.

Maclean and R. are to parachute into Yugoslavia, taking with them a letter from the P.M. to Tito. Next to SHINGLE and landing craft, the Yugoslav problem, with its intricacies about abandoning Mihailovitch[1] and reconciling King Peter to Tito, has been our chief interest out here.

Saturday, January 8th

There was a further vast conference in the dining-room, and then the tumult and the shouting died as the military departed leaving Maclean and Randolph behind.

After dinner the P.M. and Randolph had a bickering match over the qualities of the Foreign Secretary and in spite of Lord Beaverbrook's efforts, Randolph, having drunk too much whisky, could not be stopped. Fitzroy Maclean says, however, that all will be well in Yugoslavia owing to the absence of whisky and a diet of cabbage soup. Moreover Randolph will be a subordinate officer under his command.

Monday, January 10th

Lord Beaverbrook took Joe and me on a shopping expedition in the Medina. Joe and I had meant to go alone, buying cheap goods for our relatives, but the Beaver led us at breakneck speed from shop to shop in search of dress materials for Joe's family. He finally bought yards of very expensive but quite useless gauze and presented it to Joe. Then he took us through by-ways to an antique shop off the beaten track where we were received by a patriarchal old Moor who gave us mint tea and revoltingly scented quince jam which the Beaver refused for himself but, to our disgust, accepted for Joe and me.

On returning to the villa Lord B. rushed inside to greet Duff Cooper and Lady Diana, who had just arrived by air from Algiers (where Duff Cooper is the newly appointed Ambassador to the Free French) and then dragged me off in a car to the French quarter of the town. There he bought me a magnificent white leather bag to give to whomsoever I wished.

At dinner Lady Diana made a dead set at the P.M. and fascinated him. "There," Lord Moran whispered to me, "you have the

---

[1] Royalist Yugoslav General who was the first to organise resistance to the German invaders, but soon resolved that the Communist partisans, led by Tito, were an even greater evil. Some of his followers therefore collaborated with the Italians, and even in a few cases with the Germans. He was, all the same, a true patriot. After the war, declining to flee from Yugoslavia, he was tried by Tito and, most disgracefully, hanged. His last words at his trial were: "I have been blown away by the gale of the world."

historic spectacle of a professional siren vamping an elder statesman." And it certainly was.

Tuesday, January 11th

After dinner all except the P.M. and the Beaver went to a
reception given by General de Villate in honour of M. Puaux, the
Resident General of Morocco. There was Berber music and
Berber dancing in the garden and much French conversation in
the house.

De Gaulle was due tomorrow. He was to lunch with the P.M.
and it was hoped that a prolonged coolness between them would be
terminated. But there was nearly a disaster. General de Lattre de
Tassigny had, on the advice of Mr Macmillan (Resident Minister in
Algiers) been invited to dine and stay the night on Thursday. A
message from Algiers, given to me over the telephone by Duff
Cooper's Counsellor (Kingsley Rucker), said that General de L.
de T. had felt he should ask de Gaulle's permission. De Gaulle had
said it would be "most inopportune" for him to accept at present.

The P.M. was furious and said in that case he would not see de
Gaulle. Duff Cooper with difficulty pacified him, and the conversation merely became a heated discussion between Mrs C. (very
anti-French), the P.M. (temporarily anti-French) and the Duff
Coopers arguing the other way.

Wednesday, January 12th

At 8.00 a.m. Sawyers, the P.M.'s butler (slightly swollen headed
since Stalin drank his health at Teheran) said the P.M. wanted to
see me. I went in my dressing-gown, was asked to repeat the
message about de Lattre de Tassigny and was told that a message
should be sent to the airfield to tell de Gaulle, on arrival, that the
P.M. did not wish to waste his valuable time. Duff, summoned in
haste from the Mamounia, managed to pacify the P.M. once more.

De Gaulle arrived for lunch, at which I was not present, and
spent the afternoon in conversation with the P.M. who told him, in
a firm but friendly way, just where he got off and remonstrated
about the recent arrests of Flandin, Boisson, etc., at Algiers.

After dinner, in an expansive moment, the P.M. promised I
could rejoin my Squadron for OVERLORD. I got Lord Moran to bear
witness to this and went jubilant to bed.[1]

---

[1] "You seem to think," Churchill said to me, "that this war is being fought for
your personal amusement." There was a pause. "However, if I were your age I
should feel the same, and so you may have two months' fighting leave. But no
more holidays this year."

Thursday, January 13th

There was a review of French troops at which the P.M., in his Air Commodore's uniform, and de Gaulle stood side by side at the saluting base. The rest of us, with French and Moorish dignitaries, were in the stand behind. I was particularly impressed by the Spahis and the Zouaves – less so by the formation "shoot-ups" undertaken by the local French Flying Training School.

We had a picnic in glorious country at a place called the Pont Naturel. There was a deep gorge through which a stream ran, falling from rock to rock into limpid blue pools. Lady Diana gave one look at it and said Alph![1] The P.M. insisted on being carried down and scrambling over the rocks.

Sarah gave a cocktail party for the myriad hangers on – American officers, W.A.A.F. cypherers, the crew of the York, etc. There were Berber dances. Harold Macmillan arrived.

Friday, January 14th

The party flew, in four aeroplanes, to Gibraltar. We made a detour to fly over Casablanca and lunched admirably en route.

At Gib. there was a further SHINGLE conference while Mrs C., Sarah, John Martin and I were taken up to the top of the rock and through some of the tunnels. Embarked on H.M.S. *King George V* for home. Very comfortable cabins, the officers having turned out of theirs for us. The P.M. slept in the Admiral's sea cabin and there was a "High Table Mess" in the Petty Officers' quiet room.

Saturday, January 15th

At sea. Sunshine and gentle breezes as we steamed westwards towards the Azores. Paced the quarter deck and explored the ship, which is an exceedingly overheated one. All the arrangements were admirably conceived and nothing was left undone – even Marines to precede and escort us down the passages.

There was ear-splitting battle practice – including the 14-inch guns – after lunch with our escorting cruiser, *Mauritius*. Each ship fired at the other at an angle off. In the evening we all dined excellently at a Mess dinner in the Ward Room.

---

[1] In Xanadu did Kubla Khan
A stately pleasure-dome decree;
Where Alph, the sacred river, ran
Through caverns measureless to man
Down to a sunless sea.
                    Coleridge.

Sunday, January 16th

Divine service, very well conducted, in the Ward Room. All present except the P.M. and the Beaver. Sea still calm, but we had turned north and the skies were grey.

Monday, January 17th

The P.M. went all Harrovian after lunch and said that the lines "God give us bases to guard and beleaguer, etc." had always inspired him greatly, despite the fact that he detested football. He spent an hour or more in the gun-room answering questions from the delighted Subs and Midshipmen.

We landed at Plymouth at 11.00 p.m. and boarded the train. Found many letters awaiting me, including the news that Terence O'Neill was engaged to Jean Whitaker and that poor Dick Bock, nicest of 168 Squadron, had been shot down in the sea and died of exposure last Friday.

Thursday, January 18th

At Paddington the Churchill family and the Cabinet awaited the train and greeted us effusively.

The P.M. made a dramatic entry into the House of Commons – the real reason for his hastening home – and was loudly cheered. He answered his Questions and then held a Cabinet meeting in his room at the House, leaving at 1.28 to lunch with the King at 1.30! *Plus ça change, plus c'est la même chose*, I observe.

After dinner I took some oranges and lemons (of which rare luxuries I have brought back a large number) to Argyll House. Mother and I spent half an hour with Grandfather, who is in bed but looking well and cheerful in spite of having now gone all but stone blind. Peggy, returning from dinner at the Spanish Embassy, said she heard we had returned by sea – which shows how well that secret was kept!

Wednesday, January 19th

Put on civilian clothes; the first time I have done so for more than a few hours since 1941.

After returning from a meeting on Far Eastern Strategy in the C.W.R. the P.M. told me his heart was giving him trouble. He ascribed it to indigestion, but evidently he must now go warily.

Thursday, January 20th

The P.M. saw the Poles about frontiers. The problem is a hard one and the Soviet Government are ungracious bargainers. Negotiations proceeding on basis of the Curzon line.

Saturday, January 22nd

Operation SHINGLE – landings by Anglo-American force behind the enemy forces in Italy with the object of capturing Rome – has started well and General Alexander seems confident.

A good deal of work and kept up late with telegrams.

Tuesday, January 25th

Lunched with the P.M. and Mrs C. in the downstairs dining-room at No. 10. Other guests: Mrs Romilly,[1] Mrs Henley, Pamela Churchill, Lord Portal. One of the worst phrases of the official jargon today is an "overall strategic concept". The P.M. said that he has an "underall strategic concept". The people of this country are becoming dangerously over confident. There is, after all, a risk that we may suffer serious defeats this year, since the Hun is still very tough and his morale has not seriously deteriorated. The P.M.'s "concept" is therefore to capture Rome, as a result of SHINGLE ("too many pebbles on the beach", John Peck says), and then while the cheering is still loud to make the most depressing speech of his career.

The Cabinet decided in favour of asking the King to make Princess Elizabeth Princess of Wales when she comes of age next April. The King did not favour the idea.[2]

Our policy with regard to Russo-Polish frontiers, about which the P.M. is going to telegraph to Stalin (with whom he now maintains a voluminous telegraphic correspondence) and also about Palestine and Greater Syria was thrashed out in Cabinet.

After dinner the operations in Italy monopolised attention.

Wednesday, January 26th

Italian operation going well; build-up ashore quicker than had been expected.

Thursday, January 27th

Lunched with Geoffrey Lloyd at Claridges; he wants a seat on a Ministerial Committee and thinks I can help.

---

[1] Clementine Churchill's sister. Her elder son was one of the prisoners of war selected by Hitler as hostages in case things should go badly for him. Her younger son, Esmond, fought for the Spanish Republicans in the Civil War, joined the Communist Party, married Jessica Mitford and was killed in action in the R.A.F.

[2] For Accession purposes she came of age at eighteen, though everybody else still attained their majority at twenty-one. Presumably the Prime Minister put the suggestion to the King at his audience that evening.

Monday, January 31st

The P.M. was much disgruntled by a very ungracious telegram from Stalin about Russia's share in the Italian navy and said many harsh things about S., who is obviously less amenable on paper than in conversation.

23

Anzio and the Blitz Renewed

February–March 1944

Tuesday, February 1st

Went to the House with the P.M. whose replies to Questions, re-drafted by himself last night, were in a witty vein and delighted everybody.

A reply from Tito, very different in tone from Stalin's, arrived.

Lunched with David Margesson at Ciro's.

Dined with Gay in Baker Street and spent the rest of the evening at the Ritz with Diana Harvey and Zara Strutt (the latter in plaster of Paris). Talked to Zara in her bedroom (she pointed out that the plaster of Paris was a kind of *ceinture de chasteté*).

Friday, February 4th

Terence O'Neill's wedding to Jean Whitaker at the Guards' Chapel.

Left with the P.M. for Chequers. He went to bed for dinner and Tommy and I dined alone. The P.M. is suffering from indigestion and also very perturbed by SHINGLE's lack of success. It was strategically sound and it had a perfect beginning. He cannot understand the failure to push inland from the beach-head. While the battle still rages he is refraining from asking Alexander the questions to which the P.M. can find no answer, but his great faith in A., though not dissipated, is a little shaken.

Saturday, February 5th

General Donovan (U.S. Army), General Eastwood (to be vetted for Governorship of Gibraltar), and Mrs Churchill came in time for lunch. General Donovan, though straight from the SHINGLE area, can throw no light. (Operationally they have great courage; administratively none, said the P.M.)

Sunday, February 6th

The Polish Prime Minister (Mikolajczyk),[1] Foreign Secretary (Romer) and Ambassador (Raczynski) came to lunch. Also Mr Eden, Sir Owen O'Malley[2] (our Ambassador to the Polish Government), Lord Cherwell and Raymond Guest.[3] Except for the latter, all were present afterwards at a conference on Russo-Polish relations, at which I took notes and subsequently made a record. The Eastern frontier is the main difficulty, and the fact that the Poles do not believe in Stalin's good faith.

It was the first time I had sat all through a conference at which the P.M. was in the chair. He was certainly most effective as chairman.

O'Malley stayed to dine. He told me that the Balkan and East European countries still feel that Germany is their only hope of protection against Russia.

Monday, February 7th

Dined at the Savoy, in a private room, in a party given by Victor Rothschild to celebrate Judy Montagu's twenty-first birthday. There were present: the P.M., Mrs Churchill, Mary, Brendan Bracken, Mr Harcourt Johnston, Mrs Montagu, Judy and Mrs Laycock (Angela Dudley Ward). Dinner was excellent and the wine, from the Tring cellars, included Pol Roger 1921, the Rothschild Château Yquem and a remarkable old brandy. There was an extremely good conjuror who appeared at the end of dinner and whom the P.M. declared to be the best he had ever seen.

Wednesday, February 9th

Lunched at No. 10 with the P.M. and Mrs Churchill. The other guests were the Duchess of Buccleuch,[4] the C.I.G.S. and Lady Brooke, James Stuart, Mother, Mr Irving Berlin (the American song writer and producer), and Juliet Henley. After lunch the P.M. forestalled Irving Berlin asking leading questions by himself addressing them to his potential interlocutor (e.g. "When do you

---

[1] After General Sikorski's death he became Prime Minister of Poland. A man of high principle and determination, he was subjected to strong pressure by the British and Americans and finally deceived and cheated by Stalin and Molotov.

[2] British diplomat, married to the author Ann Bridge, he narrowly escaped involvement in the "Franc scandal" which shook the Foreign Office to its foundations in the 1920s. In consequence he lost seniority. Ended his career as a not very good Ambassador in Lisbon, but on Polish affairs he took a firm and praiseworthy stance.

[3] An American descendant of the 1st Viscount Wimborne and a cousin of Churchill.

[4] Mary (Molly) Lascelles, well-known and widely admired wife of Walter, 8th Duke of Buccleuch.

think the war will end, Mr Berlin?"). This I thought was ingenious technique. Berlin said he thought Roosevelt would get in at the coming presidential election, and in this his name should help him because in all Republican systems human nature triumphed over constitutional principle and the hereditary system came into its own. This also applied to our own Labour Party in which the wife or son of a well known M.P. was always in demand as a parliamentary candidate.

It later transpired that the reason why Mr Irving Berlin had been bidden to lunch was a comic misunderstanding. There are sprightly, if somewhat over-vivid, political summaries telegraphed home every week from the Washington Embassy. The P.M., inquiring who wrote them, had been told by me, "Mr Isaiah Berlin, Fellow of All Souls and Tutor of New College." When Irving Berlin came over here to entertain the troops with his songs, the P.M. confused him with Isaiah and invited him to lunch – and conversed with him, to his embarrassment, as if he had been Isaiah.

The new Health Service is under discussion. Brendan and Lord Beaverbrook came round to persuade the P.M. against the decision taken in the Cabinet this evening which had been in favour of the Minister of Reconstruction's [Lord Woolton] proposals. To bed at 2.40 a.m.

Thursday, February 10th
Submitted a letter to Stalin, thanking for the music of the new Soviet anthem, and got it signed unamended. I think this is the first letter the P.M. has ever written to S. (as opposed to telegrams).

Gave Cynthia Keppel lunch at the Churchill Club,[1] in Dean's Yard, of which I have just been made a member. A lovely building and a good lunch.

Took Cynthia to the first night of Priestley's play *Desert Highway*, which Mrs Churchill wanted vetted before she went herself. It was a singularly bad play about soldiers in the desert.

Friday, February 11th
It being my week-end off I went to North Weald, where No. 168 Squadron is, to fly. Arrived for dinner and slept in a room in the Mess.

Saturday, February 12th
168 today lost their Mustang I As to No. 2 Squadron and received in exchange 2 squadron's dreary Mustang Is. But I borrowed one

---

[1] A fine hall of Westminster School (evacuated from London) which was used as a luncheon club for the higher echelons working in Whitehall.

of the I As and flew for one and a half hours in the morning. I tried to find Chequers, but the visibility was shocking and I failed. Not realising there was wireless silence I demanded a homing and an added stir was caused by the fact that I gave my old call sign "Floral 51" – a number which no longer exists. I was homed through a balloon barrage but arrived safely.

Sunday, February 13th
Flew with Johnny Low,[1] an Australian. We did some close and wide formation and a little air combat, during which I blacked out with surprising facility. Ended with a perfect three-point landing. Returned to London after lunch.

In a book I am reading Princess Lieven quotes Madame de Sevigné on sight-seeing: "What I see tires me, and what I don't see worries me." At the rate things are going in Italy I don't suppose there will remain much sight-seeing to be done after the war.

Monday, February 14th
The Polish question is coming to a head. Some people think that our attitude is a little reminiscent of Munich, but I am sure that the Poles' right course is to accept what they can get while still maintaining their right to fuller claims. O'Malley, our Ambassador, is evidently very much against selling out the Poles and points out that "What is morally indefensible is always politically inept".

Tuesday, February 15th
The Anzio bridgehead hangs fire, the Polish Government seems about to resign and Brendan says the home front is becoming seriously war-weary. Meanwhile we are approaching, in his view, one of "the most desperate military ventures in history" – about which too many people are far too confident. Cabinet approved new Health scheme. (Brendan opposing it violently.)

Wednesday, February 16th
To the House for Questions. The P.M. answered an inspired question about British casualties in Italy so as to give some ammunition for countering the American view that American troops are doing all the fighting. Actually it is the unenterprising behaviour of the American Command at Anzio that has lost us our great opportunity there.

---

[1] A man of stirling qualities and an excellent pilot. On returning to my squadron in May 1944, I travelled to Odiham with him and the pretty Australian W.A.A.F. to whom he was engaged. He was shot down and killed three weeks later, one of those war-time tragedies which dented the callous skin we had all temporarily grown.

We sent 900 bombers over Berlin last night and lost five per cent.

Friday, February 18th
Gave Gerry Fitzgerald's[1] Polish Jew friend, Flaisjer,[2] lunch at the Travellers. On saying goodbye he said: "You have not changed very much, Mr Colville, but you are, allow me to say, perhaps more majestic." I don't know whether this is a compliment or not, nor whether the reference is to increased physical majesty (due to the chef at Marrakech) or otherwise.

After lunch the results of the West Derbyshire by-election came through: Lord Hartington[3] lost to Mr White, the Independent, by 4,500 votes. This caused a pall of the blackest gloom to fall on the P.M. who is personally afflicted by this emphatic blow to the Government in view of the *verbosa et grandis epistola* which he wrote to Hartington, in which he lauded the political record of the Cavendish family. Moreover there was trouble at Brighton a fortnight ago when he wrote another long letter and, in the event, Teeling, the Government candidate, only scraped home in the safest of Tory seats.

Sitting in a chair in his study at the Annexe, the P.M. looked old, tired and very depressed and was even muttering about a General Election. Now, he said, with great events pending, was the time when national unity was essential: the question of annihilating great states had to be faced: it began to look as if democracy had not the persistence necessary to go through with it, however well it might have shown its capacity for defence. In sombre state he went off to Chequers.

Sunday, February 20th
In the evening there was a short, sharp blitz. Incautiously I walked out of the Annexe to look at the rockets and flares, but a disturbance in the atmosphere immediately above my head warned

---

[1] My mother's first cousin, cultured, insatiably thirsty for knowledge and a devout Roman Catholic bachelor with whom I often stayed in Cambridge. He failed by a few weeks to span two hundred years from his grandfather's birth to his own death, a record to which he was keenly looking forward.

[2] A brilliant Polish Jewish historian whom Fitzgerald housed as a non-paying guest throughout the war after his narrow escape from the Gestapo. Became a senior university professor in Israel.

[3] Eldest son of the 10th Duke of Devonshire. Married after a major religious controversy Kathleen Kennedy, daughter of Joseph P. Kennedy. She was viciously attacked for agreeing that any children of the marriage should be brought up as Anglicans. He was killed in action in 1944 and she died in an aircraft accident a few years later.

me that something was amiss and, showing great speed, I reached the brick blast screen just as a stick of three bombs straddled the Horse Guards Parade. No. 10 was superficially damaged: all the windows and window frames were blown in and large pieces of plaster came down from the ceilings in the drawing-rooms, leaving gaping holes. Downing Street is carpeted with glass, a bomb at the corner of the Treasury (which killed several people in Whitehall) burst a large water main, and generally speaking the atmosphere is quite 1940-like. The glow of fires in the sky shows that the damage was widespread, though the Duty Group Captain tells me only sixty aircraft were over.

Monday, February 21st
The Ministry of Works and Buildings, under Lord Portal's personal supervision, cleared up the debris with amazing speed and boarded up all the windows (at No. 10).

Tuesday, February 22nd
The P.M. made a speech on the war situation in the H. of C. and it went very well.

David Margesson dined with me in the Mess and was afterwards invited to see the P.M., who is a bit worried about the Home Front and the future of the Tory party. The P.M. told me it was a great effort to him to make these speeches now.

Wednesday, February 23rd
Took Mary Churchill to see Terence Rattigan's new play [*While the Sun Shines*] and to dine at the Coq d'Or. Bombs fell in St James's Street and shook us in Stratton Street. The effort is small on the Luftwaffe's part but the results are considerable.

Thursday, February 24th
London seems disturbed by the raids and less ebullient than in 1940–41.

Tuesday, February 29th
Stalin has answered, unhelpfully, the proposals for a solution of the Polish problem. If he had been willing to give a little he could still have won for Russia the substance of everything he required, and could have inspired new confidence and readiness to co-operate in the U.S.A. and this country. When I look back at Russian diplomacy during these last five years, it seems to me sadly inept. A little courtesy and a little generosity could have achieved

much. As it is the establishment of really close relationships with the U.S.S.R. looks like being very hard to attain.

Thursday, March 2nd

Accompanied Mrs Churchill to see Bevin's "Back to Work" Exhibition at Burlington House. It shows how disabled men can be taught useful trades. I was impressed by the way in which Mrs C. talked to all the men there and did the whole thing with real thoroughness.

Friday, March 3rd

President Roosevelt's sudden announcements at a press conference of the recent negotiations with Stalin about Italian ships came as a bombshell just before we left for Chequers, but the P.M. finally reached the conclusion that this gaffe was due to a blunder and not to malice aforethought. Still, he said some hard things to Winant.

Air Marshal Coningham[1] was at Chequers. In commenting on the Anzio bridgehead the P.M. said, "I thought we should fling a wild-cat ashore and all we got was an old stranded whale on the beach."

Saturday, March 4th

The P.M. in benevolent but sombre mood. He is disturbed by the attitude of Russia – Stalin refuses to be moderate about the Poles – and many other matters, political and strategic. He said that he felt like telling the Russians, "Personally I fight tyranny whatever uniform it wears or slogans it utters."[2]

Late at night, after the inevitable film, the P.M. took his station in the Great Hall and began to smoke Turkish cigarettes – the first time I have ever seen him smoke one – saying that they were the only thing he got out of the Turks. He keeps on reverting to the point that he has not long to live and tonight, while the gramophone played the "Marseillaise" and "Sambre et Meuse", he told Coningham, Harold Macmillan, Pug, Tommy and me that this was his political testament for after the war: "Far more important than India or the Colonies or solvency is *the Air*. We live in a world of wolves – and *bears*." Then we had to listen to most of Gilbert

---

[1] "Mary" Coningham commanded the 2nd Tactical Air Force (in which I served). A forceful and flamboyant New Zealander, he did not co-operate wholeheartedly with the army and was a severe critic of Field Marshal Montgomery's strategy and personality. Killed when a Tudor passenger aircraft crashed in the Atlantic shortly after the war.

[2] A statement he embodied in a speech over a year later, on March 15th, 1945.

and Sullivan on the gramophone, before retiring at 3.00 a.m.

Coningham is most obliging about promising me information about the future of 168 and 268 squadrons and today the P.M. renewed his promise that I might return to active service for the coming offensive.

Sunday, March 5th
After lunch, at which the shortcomings of General Maitland Wilson (Jumbo) were discussed with Harold Macmillan, the P.M. settled down to bezique with Pamela Churchill, and I went for a walk with the Prof., who talked like the gloomy dean. He foresees a crushing defeat for the Conservative Party at the next election and its possible collapse like the Liberals after the last war. He says that there is much annoyance in Government circles because Brendan and Lord B. attempt, by using their influence with the P.M., to sabotage measures such as the new health proposals about which they are hopelessly ignorant but which have been worked out by experts, with great pains and hard work, over a long period. Moreover he sees great danger in the efforts of Hudson, Amery, Lord B., etc., to sabotage agreement with the Americans over Article VII, which is intended to be an international measure to regulate the trade cycle. To oppose this in order to please the farmers, and thus retain the agricultural vote, would be wrong and perhaps politically disastrous too. Late in the day when the latter topic arose again the P.M., who is inclined to the Beaverbrook camp on this matter, quoted Bonar Law and applied the quotation to the Prof: "It is no use arguing with a prophet; you can only disbelieve him."

The P.M. has now taken to sitting in the Private Secretary's room in the evening for long periods. This makes it hard to work, unless feeding him with telegrams, and impossible to telephone. We got to bed about 2.00 a.m.

Monday, March 6th
Moved to 55 Chester Square where I am going to live, as a P.G., with Lady Ampthill.[1]

---

[1] Tall and imposing, she was the daughter of the 6th Earl Beauchamp, a sister of Lady Maud Hoare (Sir Samuel's wife) and the mother of four tall, stalwart sons. She was a lady-in-waiting to Queen Mary and in both World Wars held the same position as head of the organisation for tracing British prisoners of war. She fought a stern, and expensive, rearguard action in the "Russell Baby" case, endeavouring to prove the illegitimacy of her eldest son's child. Another of her sons, Admiral Sir Guy Russell, commanded H.M.S. *Duke of York* when she sank the German battleship *Scharnhorst*.

Charles Ritchie dined with me in the Mess. He says that 14,000 members of the Canadian forces over here have married English wives.

Tuesday, March 7th
The P.M. says this world ("this dusty and lamentable ball") is now too beastly to live in. People act so revoltingly that they just don't deserve to survive.

Monday, March 13th
Brendan is very down on the President whom he suspects of being more interested in his own re-election than the common struggle.

There are signs of disquiet about the Atlantic Charter, to which the P.M. maintained in the House the other day Germany had no claim by right. I foresee that after the war is over the Germans will make the same play with alleged breaches of the Charter as they did after the last war with the repudiation of the Fourteen Points.

Tuesday, March 14th
Dined with the Hollonds[1] at Whitehall Court. We discussed the inaccuracy of history: every event appears different to different spectators and gains or loses colour and accuracy if described after the passage of time.

A violent raid. Bombs fell in Eaton Square and shook No. 55 Chester Square. Much impressed by the demeanour of Lady Ampthill's four old servants who showed great phlegm. I was really quite frightened.

Wednesday, March 15th
A problem is whether to go on supporting the King of Italy and Badoglio[2] or to accept the claims of the so-called "Six Parties" at Naples. The P.M. is adamant in support of the former policy, largely because he thinks any new régime would try to court favour from the Italian populace by standing up to the Allies. Roosevelt now seems to be veering in the opposite direction.

Tito is telegraphing most politely and shows every sign of wishing to be amenable.

---

[1] H. A. Hollond, Dean and subsequent Vice Master of Trinity College, Cambridge.
[2] Marshal Badoglio, loyal subject of King Victor Emmanuel III, became head of the Italian Government when Italy sought an armistice in September 1943, and Mussolini was arrested.

Friday, March 17th

Montgomery lunched with the P.M.; his car is as ostentatious and covered with emblems as himself.

The P.M. did not go down to Chequers. I dined with Rosemary and Hinch at Boulestins. An air-raid warning sounded and the P.M. dashed off in his car to Hyde Park to see Mary's battery at work.

Saturday, March 18th

The P.M. finally went off to Chequers at 5.30 p.m. after having King Peter* to lunch and cajoling him to do as we want in the Yugoslav imbroglio (but he won't take any action until after he has married Princess Alexandra of Greece on Monday). He also received a disagreeable note from U.J. [Stalin] about Poland. It is quite obvious that the Bear proposes to reach no agreement and accept no compromise and is fabricating all sorts of excuses to this end. His latest pretence is that there have been leakages (which are in any case almost certainly known to have come through the Soviet Embassy) about his correspondence with the P.M. and that therefore he cannot continue it. The P.M. took all this philosophically, but said that it was now obvious our efforts to forge a Soviet–Polish agreement had failed and that he would soon have to make a cold announcement in Parliament to this effect. It all seems to augur ill for the future of relations between this country and the U.S.S.R.

Tuesday, March 21st

This war would be much easier to conduct without Allies. I wonder if we shall ever reach a form of international organisation which will not be made a mockery by the fact that national policies are always self-interested and thus conflicting.

Wednesday, March 22nd

A debate in the House on the 1939–43 and Africa Stars. The P.M. spoke. M.P.s seem deeply interested in these trifling matters at a time when all the major issues of winning the war and the peace ought to be in their minds. Brendan tells me that the P.M. is seriously thinking of becoming Foreign Secretary himself, so that Eden may concentrate on the House of Commons and Home Affairs. The P.M. doesn't want Lord Cranborne as Foreign Secretary because he fears he might quarrel with him, Lord C. being obstinate.

Thursday, March 23rd
The P.M. did not go to the Cabinet this morning and, cause and effect, it completed its deliberations in half an hour. Instead he went off by train with General Eisenhower to look at American troops.

Monday, March 27th
During the week-end the P.M. had a really rude telegram from Stalin and it seems that our efforts to promote a Russo-Polish understanding have failed.

Tuesday, March 28th
The Government were defeated in the H. of C. by one vote (Harvie-Watt was in his bath) over a clause of the Education Bill. Great political excitement; the P.M. welcomes this chance of hitting back hard at his critics and proposes to have the clause reinstated, making the matter a vote of confidence.

Wednesday, March 29th
Education Bill to the fore; P.M.'s box accumulating monstrous pile of urgent and unsettled matter.

Thursday, March 30th
Rode before breakfast, on General Eisenhower's horse, with Bridget and Jean [Greig]. Very refreshing.

The Government got its majority of over 400 and the P.M. was radiant. I thought it was cracking a nut with a sledgehammer.

At midnight we left King's Cross by train for Yorkshire. The party was the P.M., Jack Churchill, Tommy and self. The P.M. worked till 3.00 a.m.

Friday, March 31st
Left the train at Driffield. Inspected R.A.S.C. and corps troops, to whom the P.M. made a speech, and then the 5th Guards Armoured Division. Saw a tank display and the P.M. went for a ride in a Cromwell. General O'Connor (who was captured in N. Africa and escaped when Italy fell), Sir Harry Floyd[1] (B.G.S.) and Brigadier Mathews accompanied us everywhere. The Guards, with their Shermans, were very smart indeed. Before lunch we saw an exhibition of lorry driving through water at Kirkham Abbey and there we met an old and very decrepit man, Colonel Wormald, with whom the P.M. charged at Omdurman.

[1] In civilian life Chairman of Christies.

Rejoined the train at Malton, lunched on it and de-trained at Harrogate where the population gave the P.M. a rousing reception. Inspected the 15th Scottish Division and saw some battle practice.

In the train, on the way back to Chequers, the P.M., who had seen a note in the box referring to staff rearrangements necessitated by my departure for the coming offensive, said I couldn't go. This, however, is not the last word.

At dinner he spent most of the time repeating the *Lays of Ancient Rome* and *Marmion*, which was a remarkable feat of memory but rather boring. Brendan was at Chequers, a rare event as he hates the place.

24

Count-down to Overlord

April–May 1944

Saturday, April 1st
It was Mrs Churchill's birthday and the party was a family one,
consisting of Duncan and Diana, Sarah, Mary and Jack. I rallied
first Mary and then Mrs C. in support of my plea to rejoin the
R.A.F. in accordance with the P.M.'s promise. The clocks were
advanced to double summer time and we sat up till 4.30 while the
P.M. worked, Duncan read important papers not intended for him
to see and I played Gilbert and Sullivan and old music-hall songs
(which are the P.M.'s choice of music) on the gramophone.

Sunday, April 2nd
Monsieur Emanuel Astier de la Vigerie, (a French Resistance
leader) and Mr Garvin [former editor of the *Observer*] came to
lunch with his wife. The P.M. came out with the supreme blas-
phemy that "every nation creates God in its own image". He gave
Astier a bit of his mind about de Gaulle and the French National
Committee (whose execution of Pucheu[1] has done them very great
harm here and above all in the United States).

Mr and Mrs Attlee came to dinner. Cabinet changes are under
discussion owing to Eden wanting to give up the Foreign Office as
he doesn't feel he can manage it as well as the Leadership of the
House. At dinner the P.M. talked of the old order changing and
said, "The pomp and vanity must go; the old world will have had
the honour of leading the way into the new" – by which I daresay he
meant a reference to himself. Even if he did not, it applies.

---

[1] Vichy Minister of the Interior 1941–42 and alleged to be responsible for the
shooting of hostages by the Germans.

Monday, April 3rd
Up from Chequers in time to lunch with Mother and Philip at the Guards Club. P.'s brigade look like being disbanded to provide reinforcements for the Guards division, though the P.M. has sent minutes to Montgomery and to P. J. Grigg protesting.

Tuesday, April 4th
On late duty. Cabinet reconstruction: Eden, James Stuart, Donald Somervell[1] and Edward Bridges present. Former proposals (Cranborne to F.O., Brendan to Dominions Office, Gwylym Lloyd George to Ministry of Information and Shinwell to Ministry of Fuel and Power) superseded by: Eden, Leader of H. of C. and Lord President of the Council; Cranborne, Foreign Secretary and Leader of House of Lords; Attlee, Deputy P.M. and S. of S. for Dominions. The Labour leaders were against Shinwell, who is a party rebel; and many people thought Brendan would be a disaster at the Dominions Office with the meeting of the Dominions Prime Ministers pending.

At 2.00 a.m. the P.M., having done a little work, said "I am now more dead than alive" and retired, very conversationally, to bed. The prospect of the Second Front worries him though he says he is "hardening to it".

Thursday, April 6th
P.M. very excited about financial scandal in Air Ministry connected with breeding pigs. Instigated by Lord Beaverbrook, of course. Lord B. stayed till 2.00 a.m.; we went to bed after 3.00.

Good Friday, April 7th
Spent the Easter week-end at Madeley, recovering from the effects of a very hectic ten days. I read part of *Paradise Lost* from the first edition there.

Tuesday, April 11th
The P.M. has saved Philip's brigade, which General Montgomery and the War Office wanted to disband and use as reinforcements for the Guards' Armoured Division. I sent him a minute on the subject after Montgomery's reply, saying that an officer of the brigade (i.e. Philip) had told me of the deplorable effect it would have on the men's morale and fighting spirit. The P.M. wrote: "Let me see this when the War Office reply comes in. We can then take them both on at once."

[1] Attorney General. Briefly Home Secretary in 1945. Churchill always declared that his father was the master at Harrow who taught him to write good English.

Wednesday, April 12th

Struck by how very tired and worn out the P.M. looks now.

He marked my *cri de coeur* about rejoining my squadron: "C.A.S. What can be done?" This is most inappropriate, as it is purely a question of internal administration in this office.

Thursday, April 13th

The P.M. saw King Peter, whose chances of regaining his throne are visibly shrinking, and, it seems, persuaded him to dismiss his Government.

We have been unnaturally busy for the last three weeks and the position is not improved by the P.M. assuming control of the F.O. while Eden is away on leave.

Friday, April 14th

The P.M. did not leave London for Chequers till nearly 8.00 p.m. and the afternoon at No. 10 was both hectic and annoying. Moreover I have let myself in for making all the arrangements for the visits of the Dominion Prime Ministers, and their entertainment, next month.

Inoculated for T.A.B., typhus and tetanus. At dinner, Desmond Morton was very gloomy. Everybody is nowadays. It all seems like the last act of a Greek tragedy. In the first act one can stand Agamemnon being murdered in his bath; in the last, such an atmosphere of gloom and doom prevails that the audience sit in solemn dejection. Now, in the shadow of an impending struggle which may be history's most fatal, a restless and dissatisfied mood possesses many people in all circles and walks of life. And over everything hangs the uncertainty of Russia's future policy towards Europe and the world.

Thursday, April 20th

The P.M. has apparently now reconciled himself to my rejoining my squadron. After lunch he asked me what date I thought of going and then, in the copy of *My Early Life* which he was signing for the American, Mr McCloy,[1] he drew my attention to the passage on page 180 in which he describes his own difficulties in getting out to the Omdurman campaign.

Commiserating with the enemy on having their backs to the wall,

---

[1] American Under Secretary for War, later American High Commissioner in Germany and finally Chairman of the Chase Bank. Brother-in-law of Lewis Douglas who succeeded Winant as American Ambassador in London.

the P.M. said to me, "I'd run like Hell to help Hitler, if I were a Hun!"

After dinner, reverting to the possibility of replacing Eden by Cranborne, the P.M. said that the trouble about the latter was that when he wasn't ill he would be obstinate. It would be a question of a fortnight's illness alternating with a fortnight's obstinacy.

Friday, April 21st
We spent the day at the House of Commons while the P.M. listened to the debate on Empire affairs and prepared his own speech. He re-wrote it in a last-minute feverish rush and wasn't even able to have his afternoon sleep in the bed which he had had specially installed in his room at the House. Nevertheless he made a good speech, showing more vigour than he has of late and presenting a fine apologia for the British Commonwealth and Empire. The House approved.

Monday, April 24th
Eden, looking scarlet with sunburn, stayed talking to the P.M. till 2.00 a.m. Anyhow the P.M. is no longer acting Foreign Secretary which is a merciful dispensation. To bed at 3.15 in spite of recent resolutions by the P.M. to make 1.30 his bedtime.

Tuesday, April 25th
The P.M. told me that I could have six weeks' operational flying and that he was feeling the same way himself. He would be among the first on the bridgehead, he said, if he possibly could – and what fun it would be to get there before Monty.

Wednesday, April 26th
The P.M. made a fiasco of Questions. He lost his place, answered the wrong question and forgot the name of the Maharajah of Kashmir. He announced a rise in service pay.

Thursday, April 27th
Question of bombing French targets, with consequent high civilian casualties, much to the fore. The P.M. and most of the Cabinet strongly against continuing.

Went in the car with Mrs Churchill to Regent's Park and walked across to Gloucester Gate discussing the war and admiring the cherry blossom.

Friday, April 28th
Motored down to Chequers with Mrs C. Field Marshal Smuts and his son, Jan, arrived shortly afterwards and we went for a walk with them up the hill, through flowering gorse bushes to the South African War Memorial. Smuts was very attentive to the wild flowers and the birds.

The P.M. arrived alone in his car, fast asleep with his black bandage over his eyes and remained asleep in the stationary car before the front door. At dinner Smuts said that order and discipline were the first essentials of a democracy; in these days too much was said of rights and too little of duties. There was a film, Smuts went to bed, and the P.M. worked till 1.30, when the combined efforts of the Prof., Tommy and myself got him to bed too.

Saturday, April 29th
The P.M. did not awake till 11.35, which was strange. After lunch Jan Smuts and I walked up Beacon Hill while the P.M. and the Field Marshal discussed the future world order in the orchard. The Prime Minister of New Zealand and Mrs Fraser and the First Sea Lord[1] and Lady Cunningham arrived at tea-time.

At dinner Smuts said, "You must speak the language of the Old Testament to describe what is happening in Europe today." There was another film, *Fanny by Gaslight*, after which all but the P.M. went to bed. I nearly put my foot in it by admitting that most of my operational activities in a Mustang would be photographic. The P.M. was indignant, said he understood my wanting to kill Huns, but really wouldn't let me go just to take photographs.

Sunday, April 30th
Colonel Hudson, just back from Yugoslavia where he was with Mihailovitch's people, swelled the party at luncheon. Mary also came and sat between Smuts and me. We had a three-cornered conversation. Smuts said Hitler was not a great man: he was utterly undistinguished though he had the capacity of spell-binding. It was a great disappointment to him to see how a civilised nation like the Germans could fall beneath that spell. It seemed to show that human nature was only capable of so much and no more; it must give beneath a certain strain. What the world needed was something more fundamental. We should all re-read the New Testa-

---

[1] Admiral of the Fleet Sir Andrew Cunningham (Viscount Cunningham of Hyndhope).

ment, not so much for the theology, which was out of date, but for the psychology. (I disagree.)

I sat in the sun in the orchard – it was almost too hot – talking to Jan Smuts who has the materialist outlook, the worship of science and progress which I found almost universal among young South Africans.

The Smuts and the Cunninghams left after tea. While the P.M. worked, I drove with Mrs C., Mr Fraser, Jack and Mary some way from Chequers and we walked home, in the most perfect spring evening, pausing to see the tiny thirteenth-century church at Little Hampden, with its ancient frescoes, and to drink some draught cider at "The Rising Sun". There never was a more glorious evening: the beeches just bursting out in pale spring green, the sun slanting through the leaves in the woods and the bluebells coming out. I walked ahead with Mary who was a gay and sympathetic companion.

Mr Fraser told a number of boring stories about New Zealand at dinner, though he is really a nice enough old Scot with a good head on his shoulders. There was the usual film: excellent American fighter combat films and a weird ghost story called *Halfway House*. The evening was finally marred by the arrival of an offensive telegram from Molotov, who quite unjustifiably claimed we were intriguing behind the back of the Russians in Roumania. This set the P.M. off on his gloomy forebodings about the future tendencies of Russia and, as he looked at his watch just before 2.00 a.m. and dated the last minute awaiting his signature, he said, "I have always not liked the month of May; this time I hope it may be all right." Curiously enough almost the first remark he ever made to me, four years ago exactly, was about the 1st of May.

Monday, May 1st
A mad rush to get to London by 12.00 noon in time for the opening of the meetings with the Dominion Prime Ministers at No. 10. The P.M. was late, of course, but the opening ceremony went off all right and afterwards there were the photographs in the garden.

Tuesday, May 2nd
A hectic day, mostly concerned with petty affairs. To add to the chaos caused by the presence of our Dominions guests, General Wilson, Fitzroy Maclean and Averell Harriman have all arrived. I had a talk with Fitzroy who seems to find Tito congenial and says he has a sense of humour.

Thursday, May 4th
Afternoon party at No. 10 in honour of the Dominion P.M.s. Weather not suitable for the garden, as had been proposed, so a vast concourse assembled in the rooms upstairs and it was all a great success. Archie Sinclair button-holed me about going back to the R.A.F. and said it was dangerous from the security angle. But I have the P.M.'s puissant support and he says he thinks Archie and the C.A.S. are being silly.

Friday, May 5th
More nonsense about my departure, Brendan and the C.I.G.S. lending a hand; but, with the P.M.'s support, I got my way.
    Went to Odiham for a week-end's flying.

Sunday, May 7th
Flew over Chequers, rocking my wings, and then on a cross-country down to Cornwall.
    Returned to London in time to go down to Cherkley for the night to stay with Lord Beaverbrook. Colonel Llewellyn[1] (Minister of Food) was there, Mr McCulloch (Canadian newspaper owner), Pamela Churchill and Mrs Richard Norton.[2] Excellent wines, accompanied by indifferent food, followed by a rather poor film, and spiced throughout by Lord B.'s very entertaining conversation.

Monday, May 8th
Lord B. wished us all farewell, gracefully, in his bedroom, talked about the decline of true Tory principles, told me I ought to stand for Rugby, and dismissed Llewellyn, McCulloch and me to London.
    Gave lunch to the Archduke Robert[3] of Austria who wants to get a job in the R.A.F.

Friday, May 12th
The P.M. left on a tour of inspection with some of his Dominion colleagues. I visited the head of Air Ministry Intelligence, and decided not to assume a false name when I go on Ops (in spite of the fact that I have been photographed with the P.M. and in

---

[1] Jay Llewellyn, Conservative Minister of dynamic ability who was later the first Governor General of the Rhodesian Federation.

[2] Daughter-in-law of Lord Grantley. Deeply cherished friend and mistress of Lord Beaverbrook.

[3] Younger son of the last Emperor, Karl, of Austria-Hungary and of the Empress Zita.

uniform): and had tea with Mrs Churchill to meet Monsieur Vienot, the Ambassador of the Free French.

Saturday, May 13th.
Reading the full reports of the Imperial Conferences (written by Sir Gilbert Laithwaite[1] almost verbatim), I am impressed (i) by the great tributes paid by the Dominions P.M.s to our own Prime Minister's leadership; (ii) the unanimity with which they praise our conduct of foreign policy during the last five years – in contrast to the prevalent criticism of it which one hears and reads in England.

Whatever the P.M.'s shortcomings may be, there is no doubt that he does provide guidance and purpose for the Chiefs of Staff and the F.O. on matters which, without him, would often be lost in the maze of inter-departmentalism or frittered away by caution and compromise. Moreover he has two qualities, imagination and resolution, which are conspicuously lacking among other Ministers and among the Chiefs of Staff. I hear him much criticised, often by people in close contact with him, but I think much of the criticism is due to the inability to see people and their actions in the right perspective when one examines them at quarters too close.

Sunday, May 14th
When I survey the vast amount of paper: Chiefs of Staff papers, Cabinet conclusions, memoranda circulated for various ministerial and inter-departmental committees, records of the European Advisory Commission, Foreign Office print, etc., etc. – papers full of interesting facts and suggestions among the inevitable verbiage – I pity the lot of the future historian. To summarise briefly what passed before my eyes every day would take pages of this diary.

Tuesday, May 16th
Went for the night to Mentmore, where Grandfather and Peggy are living in the gaunt and almost deserted house, crammed with evacuated treasures from museums and galleries. Grandfather, racked with sciatica, was lying dressed in a chair. Though physically worn, he is still very much alert mentally and was full of political conversation.

Wednesday, May 17th
The last meeting of Dominion P.M.s took place yesterday and now the field is clear.

---

[1] Eminent civil servant. Deputy Under Secretary at the India Office and Burma Office. Afterwards High Commissioner in Pakistan and Permanent Under Secretary at the Commonwealth Relations Office. Learned and wise.

Dined with Mary Churchill, very pleasantly and well, at l'Ecu de France. Agreeable conversation is a far better entertainment than one which is ready made.

Thursday, May 18th
Lunched with Mrs Churchill alone at No. 10.

Presented the P.M. with a memorandum about this new book *Your M.P.*,[1] which is similar to *Guilty Men* in tone and may well have an equally wide effect. I feel that if we are returning to an age of politics by pamphleteers, the Right should show as much energy as the Left. The Conservatives have the funds at their disposal and they certainly have the material for an inquest into the past speeches and policy of their opponents. It should not be difficult to find publicists as clever – and as vituperative – as Cato, Cassius, Gracchus and Cassandra.

The P.M. was greatly interested in the book and had to be left to himself, fuming and muttering with rage, to read it after dinner in the dining-room.

Brendan came in with a declamation against the F.O., but seemed to have his facts muddled. The Italian offensive goes well.

Saturday, May 20th
Today I rejoin my squadron, which is at Odiham. Concerted efforts have been made to prevent my going, by people as various as the S. of S. for Air and Lord Cherwell. But the P.M. has held firm and, in order to meet the security point, it has been agreed that I am not to fly over enemy territory until D-day, after which my knowledge of the time and place of the Second Front would not be dangerous, should I be taken prisoner by the enemy.

The world is hushed and expectant. Nobody thinks of anything but the coming event – and I for my part am glad to have an opportunity of taking an active part in what may well be the most decisive of the decisive battles of the world.

---

[1] Sequel to Michael Foot's and Frank Owen's *Guilty Men*, written as Labour Party propaganda for the next General Election. Conveniently omitted all reference to the Labour Party's pre-war opposition to rearmament, conscription and the doubling of the Territorial Army.

25

Operational Interlude

May 20th–August 2nd, 1944

At Odiham 168 Squadron of the 2nd Tactical Air Force were living in tents near the perimeter of the airfield. When not flying we were given a great deal of exercise, including fifteen mile route marches along peaceful Hampshire lanes where the beechtrees were wreathed in those pale green leaves that are among the special pleasures of an English spring. In a remarkably short time all flabbiness had vanished and remembering how I had collapsed after racing Mary Churchill up Beacon Hill, I felt that now I could have run up and down twice without the smallest physical discomfort.

We were the sole R.A.F. unit in a four squadron Canadian Mustang Wing, and our strength of twenty-eight pilots included a number of dashing, and without exception likeable, officers of the Royal Australian Air Force. They wore dark-blue battle dress and were locked in endless good-natured banter with their "Pommy" colleagues and our one rotund, gallant and consistently good-natured New Zealander. There was, I remember, little or no squabbling or back-biting, for human beings can live in harmony if they have one primary objective in common. It was so in war, at any rate in those sections of the R.A.F. I knew; but war is a heavy price to pay for harmony.

I was attracted by the individualist personalities of the Australians. Many of the Canadians, brave, friendly and resourceful though they were, seemed by contrast to have a rubber-stamped outlook and upbringing. Moreover, it was irritating to find that they regarded our French Canadian ground-staff, all volunteers since there was no conscription in French Canada, as second-class citizens. When it came to censoring the ground-staff's letters, their own officers were unable to perform the duty, for scarcely any of them could speak or even read French. A naturalised Czech, a Pole and I had to fill the gap. I found our ground-staff obliging and most anxious to serve us well, even though their peculiar French *patois* was a little difficult to understand. I had no doubt that the evident lack of sympathy between them and their English-speaking officers boded ill for the tranquillity of post-war Canada.

When I rejoined the squadron, on May 20th, 1944, they were operating vigorously, with many cross-Channel flights every day. Because I knew the place of the landings and the intended date, I was not allowed to venture beyond the British coastline until D-day; but on that memorable day I did take part in two reconnaissance flights deep into France, one over Falaise and one south of Bayeux. The Channel was bathed in sunshine, but there was thick cloud over northern France. We therefore flew low over the countryside, down the main streets of towns and villages (where the inhabitants waved ecstatically if there were no Germans about) searching far and wide, on that day fruitlessly, for signs of enemy troop movements.

It was thrilling as we crossed the Channel to look down on a sea boiling with ships of all kinds heading for the landing beaches. It was thrilling, too, to be part of a vast aerial armada, bombers and fighters thick as starlings at roosting-time, all flying southwards. Off the Normandy coast, where our troops and the Americans were forcing their way ashore, lay a semi-circle of grey battle-ships. Some, like *Rodney* and *Warspite*, were immediately recognisable, and as we flew over them at some 2,000 feet (for it was no longer necessary to skim the waves to outwit enemy radar) we could see their huge guns belching flame and smoke as they fired at targets inland. On a return flight that morning one popular member of our squadron, Flying Officer Barnard, was by a million to one chance, struck by a 15-inch shell from *Warspite*. He and his Mustang disintegrated.

The German fighters seldom appeared over the beaches, but inland it was a different matter and though I never personally became involved in a dog-fight, it was soon a common event to meet Focke Wulf 190s or Messerschmitt 109s in squadron strength. On one occasion, near Lisieux, I was chased by nine of them. As our sorties consisted of only two or four aircraft, we found the tactics of Lord Thomas Howard as described by Tennyson in *The Revenge*, preferable to those of Sir Richard Grenville. This did not prevent our losing nearly a quarter of our pilots by the end of June.

I had three lucky escapes, two from German anti-aircraft fire and one from the Americans. On June 13th, over Carpiquet aerodrome, outside Caen, which was strongly held by the enemy, a shell blew a large circular hole in my port wing, missing both the vital aileron cable and the flap by a hair's breadth. Had the damage been half an inch further to one side or the other, my aircraft would undoubtedly have spun into the ground and as I was flying low I could not have baled out.

When I left Downing Street to rejoin my Squadron, the Prime Minister had asked me to write and let him know how I fared. So on June 14th, shortly before the squadron moved to France, I sent him an account of my adventures on the previous day:

The weather had been unfavourable all day and when, in the afternoon, it cleared over here it was reported to be still poor over the operational area in Normandy. However at 4.30 p.m. there was a demand from the Ops. room for four pilots from 168 Squadron and we were told that photographs were urgently required of the road and stream southwest of Caen where the Germans are firmly ensconced and where an intense concentration had been encountered earlier in the day. F/O Stubbs, an Australian pilot, was to lead the formation and to take the photographs at the highest level permitted by cloud. Dickson and I, without cameras, were to provide support and fighter cover for the other two.

When we took off, just before 6.0 p.m., the English skies were clear except for broken cloud and there was a 40 m.p.h. westerly wind. We crossed the coast at Selsea Bill, climbed to 7000 feet and flew over a cloudless channel in which I could see the usual stream of convoys and of small vessels, which, from the airman's point of view, have been the most impressive feature of the invasion. We made landfall at Ouistreham after about 20 minutes, but a bank of low cloud, not great in depth but obviously thick, made it necessary to dive to less than 2000 feet over the beaches and the estuary of the Orne. I was on the extreme left as we turned to starboard round the southern outskirts of Caen, where the smoke of battle lay thick, and I had to open the throttle wide to keep up with the others. Then, as we approached the aerodrome south west of the town, the flak came up, concentrated, intense and accurate. Stubbs, who has long experience, says he has never seen it more accurate. We dived and writhed, slipped and skidded, but we could not shake the gunners' aim. White puffs of 20 mm., grey puffs of 40 mm. and the black puffs of heavy 88 mm. appeared above, below and on each side of my aircraft and the paths of tracer were too close to be comfortable. It was difficult to keep with the others: they were weaving, diving, climbing like things possessed; wispy low cloud came between us; and I had to take avoiding action myself besides keeping a weather eye open for enemy fighters. Suddenly there was a metallic sound and the aircraft shuddered. I was not quite sure whether I had been hit or whether the pace, the boost, and the high revs had been too much for the engine and something had given. Then I saw a gaping hole in the port wing where a 20 mm. shell had struck. Fortunately it was exactly between the aileron and the flap, damaging only the latter as far as I could see.

We finished the run just short of Villers Bocage and Stubbs circled southwards, returning to Caen to repeat the performance as he was by no means sure that the first run had been adequate. Flak followed us the whole way and I saw big black bursts above me. A tracer shell flashed past a few feet in front of the engine. But my aircraft was still flying smoothly in spite of periodic shocks which threw me out of my seat against the straps and were due either to atmospheric bumps or, more probably, to shells bursting immediately below me. So I decided to press on and, opening the engine fully, I was level with the others when we approached Villers Bocage again and when Stubbs, observing noxious rockets ahead, turned sharp left to complete our task by means of a tactical reconnaissance of the roads south eastwards to Thury Harcourt, Falaise and back to Caen. I was still on the left, a couple of hundred yards from Dickson, and we were flying through gaps in the cloud, the base of which was still low, climbing to a safer height.

The flak had stopped, but my wireless had failed and I could not communicate with the others. I saw them turn towards me, but a cloud separated us and when I emerged I could see no Mustangs. They were not far away, but the loss of lift in my port wing meant that the pace was a strain on the engine and I could not be sure whether the radiator and other vital parts were still intact. So I turned northwards, climbed to 7000 feet (which is well above the light flak level) and set course for home. I crossed out between Bayeux, peaceful and apparently intact, and Courseulles and flew home at a good height in case I should have to bale out, scanning the skies behind for Focke-Wulfs most assiduously. Instead I ran head on into a formation of highly suspicious Typhoons.

The aircraft shewed no signs of lassitude, however, and the shadowy outline of the Cherbourg peninsula soon gave way to the familiar shape of the Isle of Wight. I crossed in at Selsea unmolested by friendly fighters (who have recently shown a conspicuous inability to distinguish friend from foe – at least so it appears to us) and, after "shooting up" the aerodrome control at Odiham to warn them that something might be amiss, I was relieved to find that my undercarriage and flaps both went down without trouble. I landed just as the other three, who thought I had come to grief, appeared in a faultless formation over the aerodrome.

After all this a technical failure in the camera, which seldom happens, made the photographs worthless. Moreover the intensity and width of the flak, combined with the necessity of constant evasive action and the speed with which it was expedient to pass through the area, had made it impracticable for any of us to empty our eight machine guns into an enemy gun position. I was sorely tempted to do so – it only meant diving 1000 feet, but I was told later that to dive straight for an enemy gun position, with others bringing lateral fire to bear, is the surest method of suicide.

I had a responsive feeling this morning when the B.B.C. announced: "Yesterday evening many of our aircraft encountered unusually heavy anti-aircraft fire south west of Caen."

I wrote again several times and received in Normandy a note from Churchill to the Private Office saying: "Good. Tell him how much interested I have been in reading his letters. W.S.C. 10.7.44." In sending me this message John Martin added: "We heard good news of you via Louis Greig and Archie [Sinclair], who had run into you during their visit to Normandy. As someone unkindly commented: It shows what a small part of France we have conquered so far."

On July 17, sent to take line-overlap photographs of the railway running south-east from Caen, I had to fly straight and level to obtain results. A fragment of 88 millimetre shell penetrated my petrol-tank which fortunately did not explode. Thanks to the self-sealing device, it retained enough fuel for me to limp back home.

My third escape from injury came when, with three comrades, I was returning from a low-flying reconnaissance of Sees and Argentan and we passed over the Forêt de Cerisy in the American sector of the bridgehead. Failing to distinguish Mustangs from Messerschmitts, the Americans greeted us with a storm of machine-gun bullets. One passed through my tail-plane, two through a wing, but fortunately none through the cockpit. One of my companions, whose aircraft was alongside me, had bullets through both his feet but contrived to hold on long enough to make a landing. When our Group Captain telephoned to remonstrate, the American commanding officer said that he really must get round to having his gun-crews brush up their aircraft recognition.

It was, of course, easy to cast blame on the American gunners, but I fear that some of it attached to me. Our formation was off course, though since I was not leading it that was not my fault, and I did not realise we had entered friendly territory. A few minutes before, we had seen and attacked some German staff cars. When I noticed some more, which were in fact part of an American armoured division, I was flying on the right of our formation. I made a steep turn towards them for identification purposes. No doubt they should have recognised a Mustang which was, after all, an American aircraft, but my sharp turn in their direction must have seemed menacing and they had to make up their minds quickly as we were flying low.

It is not, in any case, for me to complain of poor aircraft recognition, for some days later I missed my only opportunity of shooting down a German fighter. I was returning alone to base having parted company with my companion in cloud, when I saw approaching, almost head-on, an American Thunderbolt. I waved cheerfully to the pilot as he passed and then, far too late for action, saw the black German cross on the fuselage. It was a Focke-Wulf 190 flying for dear life from some pursuing Spitfires. If I had made a sharp turn on to his tail he would have been easy prey. In retrospect, though certainly not at the time, I am glad I do not have his death on my conscience.

At the end of June we had moved to a landing strip in Normandy, a few miles north of Bayeux. Our tents were pitched in an orchard which despite a good deal of rain and low cloud was pleasant enough. There were dawn sorties, which at least for me had a romantic appeal; there were mid-day excursions to investigate or photograph something in which the Guards Armoured Division, whose servants we were, were interested; there were dusk sorties when the German flak seemed heaviest; and there were occasional treats when, usually contrary to orders, we would sweep down on German trucks, petrol bowsers or staff cars and riddle them with shot and shell. It was like an enjoyable day's rabbit shooting: nobody gave much thought to the human suffering we caused, for we had been at war for nearly five years and our sensitivities were dulled, at any rate in battle. It would have been hard to survive if they had not been. When it was all over we shed quicker than might have been expected the hard skin of callousness

The author on the wing of a Mustang with Flying Officer John Low, R.A.A.F., Odiham, Hampshire, June 1944.

The Prime Minister away from 10 Downing Street. TOP: Inspecting the Guards Armoured Division, Yorkshire, March 31, 1944. ABOVE: as Colonel of the 4th Hussars, with Eisenhower at the crossing of the Rhine, Operation *Plunder,* March 24, 1945. RIGHT: Leaving H.M.S. *Ajax* for the Conference with the Greek ELAS rebels, Boxing Day, 1944. In the cockpit of the naval pinnace (L. to R.), the author, the Prime Minister in his uniform as Hon. Air Commodore No. 615 Squadron R.A.F., Commander Thompson.

The Quebec Conference, September 1944. ABOVE: arrival at Quebec. Mr. Mackenzie King stands beside Mrs. Churchill. BELOW: the Chiefs of Staff at the Citadel, Quebec. L. TO R.: Field-Marshal Sir John Dill, Admiral of the Fleet Sir Andrew Cunningham, General Sir Alan Brooke, Air Chief Marshal Sir Charles Portal, General Ismay.

A picnic among the prickly pears. Marrakech, January 1944.

Goodbye to 10 Downing Street, July 1945. Mr. and Mrs. Churchill. The author and Mary Churchill.

with which, quite naturally it seemed, most of us had so long covered our emotions.

The dawn patrol usually consisted of four aircraft flying to such towns as Lisieux, Argentan and Alençon and scouring the country as we went. We almost always came back over Villers Bocage and in the first hours of daylight I used to look down with delight on the elegant church and the little houses with red-tiled roofs, apparently still wrapped in sleep. It seemed to me to have a special charm. Then one morning, instead of the familiar quiet scene – for nobody ever shot at us from Villers Bocage – there was an ugly splurge of upturned clay and shattered walls. The small town, scene of a fierce tank battle the previous day, had been totally obliterated by Bomber Command during the night.

I was delighted to be back on French soil and in the evenings, when I was not flying, I often called on local farmers, bringing them chocolates, cigarettes and soap and being presented, in exchange, with Camembert cheeses and flagons of raw cider. The mayor of Magny, the nearest village, was welcoming and hospitable, but I was slightly pained by a white-haired lady who owned a small Louis XVI chateau and who told me that the Germans billeted on her had been *beaucoup plus correct* than the allied soldiery. Doubtless she thought she had been tactless, because she then insisted on giving me a bottle of well matured Calvados, upon which I saluted smartly and said *Vive la France*.

Seeking a change from exclusively male society, we gave a dance in our large mess tent, importing a bevy of nurses from Bayeux. The nights could be unpleasant, for after dark German fighter-bombers usually raided the bridgehead. Our guns would open up and pieces of shell fragment would strike, though not penetrate, our thick canvas tent coverings. However, on the night of our dance all was quiet except for a Doodle Bug (V.1 pilotless aircraft), of which scores were already assailing London. Presumably due to the failure of its automatic compass it passed overhead on a semi-circular course and, to resounding cheers from all of us, sped southwards to the German lines.

The officers of our Wing outnumbered the girls who came to the dance by ten to one; and so I was lucky to engage the attention of a pretty nurse during a full half-hour. Our conversation was not what it might have been in other places and at other times, for in that Normandy orchard war was the only topic that obsessed us all, male and female alike. My temporary partner – I did not even ask her her name, nor she mine – had been ministering that day to wounded young fanatics of an S.S. Hitler Youth brigade which had been in the forefront of the battle. She told me that one boy of about sixteen had torn off the bandage with which she had dressed his serious wound, shouting that he only wanted to die for the Führer. Another had flung in her face the tray of food she brought him. She had quelled a third by threatening, on sudden inspiration, to arrange for him to have a blood transfusion of Jewish blood. "Rather awful of me," she said, "but he at once became a whimpering child and begged pitiably for mercy." It is remarkable in retrospect how many of those apparently incorrigible young demons did, years later, evolve into decent, respectable German citizens; but probably the most fanatical sacrificed themselves on an altar of Mars already dripping with blood, for dictators well understand how to use and pervert the generous instincts of youth.

Leaving aside the besotted, and in reality tragic, Hitler Youth, I think the victorious Allies have seldom paid adequate tribute to the bravery and resilience of the German soldiers. They were fighting for an iniquitous cause, to which many of them had at one time or another been wrong-headed enough to offer faith and enthusiasm. Now, however, in 1944, they were fighting for their country's survival. They stood boldly against the combined might of the whole British Empire, of the United States and of the Soviet Union, with inferiority in the air and without the invaluable foreknowledge which the decrypts of the German ciphers from Bletchley gave to their enemies. Their population was less than one seventh of the countries ranged against them, all of which benefited from the unrivalled productive capacity of the United States. It is no slur on the gallantry and toughness of the British, American and Russian troops to assert that in World War II, as indeed in World War I, the German soldiers were the best in the world.

Once or twice I was given a lift into Bayeux, which was thronged with British soldiers, airmen and even sailors. One afternoon I watched an open lorry drive past, to the accompaniment of boos and cat-calls from the French populace, with a dozen miserable women in the back, every hair on their heads shaved off. They were in tears, hanging their heads in shame. Presumably they had not been sufficiently beastly to the Germans, although I have little doubt that some other citizens, far guiltier than those poor women, subsequently served the Republic in elevated spheres. While disgusted by this cruelty, I reflected that we British had known no invasion or occupation for some nine hundred years. So we were not the best judges of *résistance* emotionalism.

No doubt the unhappy occupants of the lorry would gladly have accepted the advances of the newly arrived liberators; but they and those of their sisters who escaped persecution did not reckon with

General Montgomery, whose puritan zeal led him to decree that all the brothels should be closed. Military police were posted to ensure the order was obeyed. Undeterred and unabashed, several of the deprived ladies (though not, of course, the hairless ones) presented themselves in a field adjoining our orchard. Lines of airmen, including, I regret to say, the worthy Roman Catholic French Canadians, queued for their services, clutching such articles as tins of sardines for payment. We, the officers, watched this sordid display with a mixture of amusement and revulsion, but we took no deterrent steps for, after all, our lives depended on the goodwill of the ground crews; and it may perhaps be that through our daily flying duties we had temporarily sacrificed our own sexual energies to the god of war.

Constant operations were indeed tiring, mentally as well as physically, and so we were allowed an occasional day off. Strange though it may seem, our idea of a holiday was to go as close as we could to the front line. One evening a thousand guns battered three villages north-west of Caen, still held by the Germans weeks after the planned date of capture, as the preliminary to a raid by hundreds of Lancasters and Halifaxes of Bomber Command. Several of us set off along the road to Caen in our commanding officer's jeep and from a vantage point well in front of our own guns watched an apocalyptic spectacle. While the guns thundered, waves of huge aircraft came in just as the sun was setting. We saw three or four Lancasters shot down, one quite close to where we sat, and the crash of falling bombs, added to the ceaseless boom of the guns behind us, was at once hellish and enthralling. It was only when several of our own shells, falling short, exploded uncomfortably near our small group of awe-struck pilots that we beat a retreat to safety.

On one "rest-day" I was even more foolhardy. I had a number of friends in the Guards' Armoured Division and 6th Guards' Tank Brigade with whom I used to go and dine when duty permitted; for after daylight operations the evening was often my own once I had censored a batch of French Canadian letters. With my cousin Terence O'Neill, many years later Prime Minister of Northern Ireland but at that time a Captain in the Irish Guards, I planned a day's sight-seeing. He borrowed his Brigadier's jeep and together with an Australian brother officer of mine, we set off for the front line.

We lunched off Camembert in a cornfield and then walked to Carpiquet airfield, where I had so nearly met my doom. Heavy shelling drove us into a front-line trench held by a Canadian unit. As we crouched there a whole squadron of Messerschmitts flew over our heads in a suicide raid on the Mulberry Harbour at Arromanches. With untypical accuracy our anti-aircraft gunners shot down three. Two parachuting pilots landed a few hundred yards from us, and I subsequently heard that not one of the remainder escaped the ravenous, watchful Spitfires.

It was a striking display of German courage. We thought the Canadian soldiers would fire on the parachuting pilots, because a few days earlier the German S.S. had killed several Canadian prisoners in cold blood and in vengeful fury their comrades had resolved to take no Germans prisoner. However, on this occasion, with praiseworthy restraint they held their fire. By contrast one of the pilots in my squadron was used for target practice as he parachuted down over a German S.S. Panzer division, who only had to await his landing in order to take him prisoner. He was dead long before he reached the ground.

After being unceremoniously ejected when we ventured into Caen, of which our troops only held half, we crossed the Orne at Benouville, were shelled again and were within a mile of the factory at Colombelles, still held by the enemy, when we all but stumbled into a minefield. We were saved in the nick of time from driving straight into the enemy lines by a soldier with a blackened face who leaped out in front of our jeep. Terence O'Neill, totally unperturbed, went into reverse and drove backwards to the Orne bridge singing, in his excellent tenor voice, "*Tout va très bien, Madame la Marquise.*"

After this foolish escapade we went back to dine at Terence's Brigade Headquarters, disguising from the Brigadier how nearly he had lost both his jeep and his Intelligence officer. Accustomed to the dull and repetitive "compot" meals provided by the R.A.F., my Australian friend and I were astonished at the banquet Terence O'Neill offered us. In addition to his other duties he was a catering officer with a flair and had imported, as a useful addition to more war-like equipment, a poultry farm. It had crossed the Channel in the recesses of a L.S.T. (landing craft for tanks). The Brigade of Guards, as magnificent fighters as any in the world, saw no virtue in austerity on active service.

On the few occasions I was shelled on the ground, twice in France and once, later on, in Germany, I found it a great deal more alarming than being shelled in the air. Of course on the ground I was taking no part in the action, but was simply an inquisitive spectator. In the air I was involved personally and was intent on diving, climbing and twisting to confuse the gunners' aim. All the same the shuddering of the earth as shells burst on land did induce fear, at any rate in me, whereas the black but silent puff of an exploding anti-aircraft missile was an instant inducement to self-protective energy. Safety lay in the speed of my own reactions and I was too busy to be afraid. I think, too, that with no feet on the ground, and no sound from the exploding shells, I was in a strange way insulated from fear.

I therefore conclude, though doubtless many aircrew, and especially those who served in Bomber Command, would disagree profoundly, that it required greater courage to be a soldier than an airman. That only applies to being shelled from the ground: I was one of the few in my squadron who had no experience of aerial combat, exhilarating though that may have been for those who survived it.

Early in August my "two months' fighting leave" (extended from six weeks with Prime Ministerial consent) expired. I made my last operational sortie and was flown back to England in a Dakota which inadvertently flew over Havre, still in German hands, and was welcomed by a burst of mercifully inaccurate anti-aircraft fire. A fellow passenger was Lord Reith, disguised as a captain R.N.V.R. Much better, he said, than being in Churchill's Government. How glad I must be to have got away from him. "On the contrary, Sir," I replied, "I am on my way back to him."

I had at least flown on more than forty operations and could tell myself that my training as a pilot had not been wasted. Back in London I went to see the Prime Minister, who gave me an affectionate welcome, and then found a comfortable spare bedroom on the top floor of the Travellers Club where I sank into such an exhausted sleep that I was unaware of the record number of Doodle Bugs which harassed London that night.

26

Second Quebec Conference

August–September 1944

A few days after I came home, three more pilots in my squadron were casualties and two of my closest friends were killed when the 6th Guards Tank Brigade went into action at Caumont. I had dined with the Grenadier battalion, of which my brother Philip was adjutant, on the night at the end of July when the brigade was ordered to move and had watched their Churchill tanks rumble off towards the scene of action.

August 8th–14th
I spent a week's leave at Madeley.

On the 11th came the sad news of Anthony Coates' death, broken to Aunt Celia in a letter from Philip. We were all plunged in gloom and mine was still further thickened by confirmation of a previous report, given me at Ardley by Bobby Rivers Buckley, that Sidney Cuthbert too had been killed. Both Sidney and Anthony had admirable qualities and no ordinary charm. So had a long list of my air force friends who have died in the last year. It is indeed uncanny how the best go. It is as if they had reached the standard set for us in this world, and need undergo no further trials, while the more imperfect live on, requiring more time and further chances. In no other way can I explain this constant decimation of the best; but how ill can we spare those qualities of unselfishness, common sense, good humour which would have been so valuable in a world and a generation devoured by rapacity and self-indulgence. It now begins to look as if the war will last but a few more weeks or months at the outside. If so the process may be halted in time. If not, it seems that the future is heavily weighted in favour of the cold, the calculating and the second best who have stayed behind the lines or have survived the risks of war.

Monday, August 14th
Returned to a sunbaked London from Madeley. The P.M. is in
Italy, having Leslie Rowan and John Peck with him. John Martin
and I are alone at No. 10 where hopes run high as Monty's trap
seems to be closing on the Germans near Falaise and Argentan.
Sleeping in the Central War Room as an insurance against Doodle
Bugs.

Tuesday, August 15th
Operation DRAGOON (ex-ANVIL) took place this morning when
American and French troops landed on the south coast of France.
The Americans insisted on it; we were against it, considering that
the troops could much better be employed by General Alexander
in strengthening and hastening his drive northwards from Flor-
ence. The P.M., it seems, used all his powers against it; but the
Americans were adamant. They shouldn't meet great opposition in
view of the drain on the German strength in Normandy.

The weather remains hot and clear. It has been so for a fortnight
now, atoning for June and July.

Long talks in the C.W.R., with Attlee and others. Attlee,
though not impressive, is very pleasant when not being official.

Wednesday, August 16th
Saw Mary Churchill who has been shooting down Doodle Bugs at
Hastings. She has grown much fatter, but looked gay and handsome. She is very distressed about Anthony. A patch discovered
on the retina of one of my eyes.

Friday, August 18th
Dined at Mentmore. Saw Grandfather, who now looks very frail
and seems to have shrunk away but who still talks gaily of anything.
I told him of my French experiences and he told me of past visits he
had paid to Lisieux (in connection, I gathered, with racing stables
rather than with St Thérèse). Peggy and I dined alone with a bottle
of 1921 champagne and she confided to me that Grandfather had
not sciatica but cancer and could hardly live long. The Battle of
Normandy is won.

Saturday, August 19th
Went to Chequers for the night. Mrs C., with whom I played much
backgammon, Mrs Romilly, Jack Churchill with Johnny[1] and his
wife, Mary, were there.

[1] Major Jack Churchill's elder son. A talented artist who painted the frescoes
adorning the summer-house at Chartwell. Married at this time to Mary Cook-
son.

Sunday, August 20th
Spent the morning at Halton[1] and returned to Chequers for the afternoon – a long walk with Mrs C. in pouring rain – and the night.

Monday, August 21st
Returned to London from Halton for lunch and settled in at No. 10.

Read an interesting paper on Europe after the war in the form of a despatch (dated May 31st) from Duff Cooper. "Mortal hatred," he wrote, "now divides Russia from Germany, but human emotions, whether of love or hate, of gratitude or revenge, have seldom proved durable in politics and have played but a small part in the affairs of nations." In the margin the P.M. has written against this sentence: "*Gratitude* perhaps may fade but revenge does not. Cf. France 1870–1914, Germany 1918–1939."

Duff's thesis is that we can never allow one power to predominate in Europe, whence our wars against Philip II, Louis XIV, Napoleon, Kaiser Wilhelm and Hitler. In case Russia should take her place in the long line of states which have aspired to this role we should insure ourselves by creating a "Bund" of Western European States under our aegis and, it might well be, within the framework of the British Empire which has so successfully contrived to combine federations and the retention of state sovereignty. It would be fatal to ally ourselves with the potential dominator because "the alliance of the wolf and the lamb is ever an uneasy partnership and the advantages accruing to the lamb are apt to prove temporary". In his reply Eden points out that to erect such a "Bund" would be to invite Russian animosity and a counter alliance in Eastern Europe. Frank co-operation and friendship with Russia is the proper course.

Against a reference by Duff to "the Prime Minister's proposal of a Union of England and France in 1940" ("Frangland", Michael Grant and I proposed to call it!) the P.M. wrote: "I had very little to do with this. It was a wave of Cabinet emotion."

Toulon has fallen, we are across the Seine, and in the Falaise pocket the carnage of Huns is said to be horrific.

Wednesday, August 23rd
An exciting day outside – Paris fell and Roumania capitulated – and a busy one in the Private Office where, John Martin going on leave and Tony being away, I was in sole charge. A message from the P.M. intended for the President of Brazil was sent (not by me) to President Roosevelt in error and President Roosevelt thanked for it. Much consternation.

[1] R.A.F. hospital.

Thursday, August 24th

In sole charge and very much snowed under. Talks with Eden, Brendan and the Prof. The last very much belittles the power and danger of V.2, the rocket. He says they will have a warhead of only a ton or so and will be less frequent or alarming than the Doodle Bug.

The Polish rising in Warsaw is a grim problem. They are fighting desperately against fearful odds. We and the Americans want to help in every way possible; in sending supplies we have been losing up to 30 per cent of our aircraft. The Russians are deaf to all pleas and determined to wash their hands of it all. They have even refused to let American bombers land and refuel on Russian airfields if their purpose is to help Warsaw. Explanations: (1) Pique at the fact that they were seriously checked at the gates of Warsaw, (2) According to Prof., a curious pride which makes them determined that other powers shall not do what they cannot do, (3) Fury at finding that the population of Warsaw and the underground movement are behind the Polish Government in London and do not support the puppet Moscow Polish National Liberation Committee.

Saturday, August 26th

England bathed in heat and sunshine and in consequence a pleasing absence of Doodle Bugs. Lay in the sun in the garden at No. 10 for an hour, admiring the very presentable flower border and a fine array of tortoiseshell butterflies. I shall always associate that garden in summer, the corner of the Treasury outlined against a china blue sky, with 1940 and the Battle of Britain.

Sunday, August 27th

Less busy. Alexander is attacking northwards against the Gothic line and the P.M. has prolonged his stay in Italy to be present in the initial stages. Meanwhile under the clear skies – I again made use of the garden at No. 10 – the Germans are reeling backwards in retreat across the Seine, making for the Somme, the Marne and the Jura.

Lord Beaverbrook asked me to Cherkley for the night, but there was too much doing for me to get away.

Monday, August 28th

Accompanied Mrs Churchill to a service in the crypt of St Paul's to celebrate the liberation of Paris. Cabinet and Chiefs of Staff attended as well as Diplomatic Corps. Rather embarrassed, therefore, to find myself in front row with Mrs C., the Edens and Sir

John and Lady Anderson. Service simple but impressive, particularly when the band of the Irish Guards played the "Marseillaise" and none could prevent their cheeks going red with emotion. Yesterday General de Gaulle attended a Te Deum in Notre Dame and the occasion led to shooting actually inside the Cathedral. In St Paul's the emotion was less obvious, and the accompanying circumstances fortunately less dramatic, but there was the same feeling that the end of a long, tragic period was symbolised in the fall of Paris. Perhaps it was a bit ironical that the service took place in front of the Duke of Wellington's tomb and ornate hearse.

Lunched alone with Mrs Churchill at the Annexe. Spent the afternoon in discussions about the plans for the coming conference at Quebec, difficult in view of the P.M.'s indecision whether he will travel by sea or air.

Tuesday, August 29th
Rose at 4.00 a.m. in order to meet the P.M. at Northolt; but his arrival was postponed owing to the weather and so Barker and I walked round Covent Garden instead.

The P.M. did arrive by York[1] at 6.00 p.m. and the Chiefs of Staff, Mrs C. and I were there to meet him. Lord Moran emerged from the aircraft looking agitated and we found that the P.M. had a temperature of 103 degrees, developed since luncheon. He was rushed home and put to bed, nurses and doctors appearing as if by magic. Small patch on lung.

Wednesday, August 30th
The P.M. was better and did a certain amount of work in bed. He also saw Eisenhower about the change in the scheme of command in Normandy.[2]

Thursday, August 31st
A very marked improvement and it was agreed that the arrangements for OCTAGON, the coming conference with the President, should be allowed to stand. The P.M. asked me if I wished to accompany him.

The King came for an hour and signed a submission creating Montgomery a Field Marshal. The P.M. intends this to show that

---

[1] A four-engined high-wing passenger plane, one of which was at the P.M.'s disposal.

[2] By this arrangement General Bradley assumed command of the American armies in Normandy and Montgomery ceased to command all the land forces. Hitherto Bradley, whom Montgomery tended to denigrate, had commanded the American First Army.

he is not being demoted by being made co-equal with General Bradley.

On looting: the P.M. told me that while at General Alexander's H.Q. in Italy he was given a caravan in which he observed two Louis XVI chairs. When he asked where they came from, he was told they had been "liberated".

Friday, September 1st

The P.M., with temperature normal, is in tearing form. He has entirely emptied his box. With regard to the progress of the war he says that he thinks the grand strategy will be highly approved, though there may be an undistinguished minority who proclaim we ought to have invaded in 1943. He told me it had been like a bullfight: TORCH, HUSKEY, etc., were like the preliminaries, the Picadors, the banderillas, etc. Then came OVERLORD, the Matador coming at the crucial moment to make the kill, waiting till the bull's head was down and his strength weakened. But DRAGOON, the landing in the South of France, has been a pure waste: it has not helped Eisenhower at all and, by weakening Alexander's armies, has enabled the Germans to withdraw troops from Italy to Northern France.

Meanwhile our armies are racing to the Belgian frontier, faster by far than went the Panzers in 1940. There is a feeling of elation, expectancy and almost bewilderment and it may well be that the end is now very close.

Saturday, September 2nd

Took train to Slough at lunch-time and was there picked up by Sir Owen Morshead[1] who motored me to Badminton. We stopped for tea at Bristol with the Dean and Mrs Blackburne, a charming and most Christian pair. She was not, perhaps, so quick on the uptake as her husband and when, in discussing Buchmanism, I told her the limerick about the young man of Pretoria (whose confessions grew gorier and gorier, but by sharing and prayer, and some *savoir faire*, he arrived at the Waldorf Astoria) she said: "Oh, but I think it was Brown's hotel where they usually met."

We arrived at Badminton in time for dinner. I sat between Queen Mary and the Duke of Beaufort. The others in the party were the Duchess of Beaufort, Sir Owen Morshead, Miss Wyndham[2] and Major Wickham.[3] After dinner I went with the

---

[1] Librarian at Windsor Castle. Erudite, sensitive and delightful companion.

[2] One of the nine children of the 2nd Lord Leconfield, and a niece of the Prime Minister Rosebery. Trenchant, assertive and often witty. Appointed lady-in-waiting after King George V died.

[3] Private Secretary to Queen Mary.

Queen to her sitting-room and had a long talk about politics and the war. For her seventy-seven years she is most uncommonly alert, quick and unbowed. Never have I seen a woman who carries so much jewellery so well.

Sunday, September 3rd
Said goodbye to the Queen at 9.00 and flew from Hullavington to Hendon in a Proctor piloted by a Dutchman, arriving at No. 10 before noon.

Lunched at the Churchill Club, where I found Hinch,[1] in a high state of indignation about the inadequacy of the morning service at Westminster Abbey today, a day of National Prayer. Leslie Rowan and I went at 3.00 p.m. to Evensong and formed the same opinion. A small male choir of ten monopolised the singing and the character of the service was very unsuitable. The vast congregation took little part and can hardly have been inspired. Only the sermon, by Canon Don, was good.

Messages poured in to the P.M. on the fifth anniversary of the outbreak of war and I drafted rhetorical replies to Chiang Kai-Shek, the Dutch, the Belgians, etc., all of which were accepted. Meanwhile the P.M. was greatly upset by a telegram from our legation at the Holy See containing the text of a message from the women of Warsaw – which still holds out – to the Pope. It was truly pathetic and the P.M. drafted a telegram to the President containing it and suggesting that we might inform Stalin that in default of assistance to Warsaw we should take certain drastic action in respect of our own supplies to Russia.

Monday, September 4th
Dreary drizzle, but that means nothing with the news of British troops in Brussels. People are expecting the armistice any day now (though the Huns show no signs of offering to sue) and there have been no flying bombs for four days. The Cabinet considered the problems of Warsaw, in connection with which much bitterness is arising against Russia, and sent a joint telegram to Molotov and to Roosevelt. It is a black cloud in an otherwise azure sky.

Tuesday, September 5th
Left Addison Road[2] at 9.40 for Greenock. Travelled in the P.M.'s train with him and Mrs Churchill, the three Chiefs of Staff, Lord Moran (plus wife and child), John Martin and Tommy. After a

---

[1] Viscount Hinchingbrooke, M.P. for Dorset. Succeeded his father as 10th Earl of Sandwich, but later renounced his peerage in the hope of being re-elected to the House of Commons.

[2] Now called Kensington Olympia Station.

luxurious journey we reached Greenock at 7.00 p.m. and were transferred by tender to the *Queen Mary*. I found a large and spacious cabin and devoured an even larger and more spacious dinner (oysters, champagne, etc.) in the P.M.'s dining-room. There were just eight of us, the P.M., Mrs C., their immediate entourage, Lord Moran, Lord Leathers and Lord Cherwell. Talking about a coming election the P.M. said that probably the Labour Party would try to stay in the Government (though the rank and file might not let them) until a year or so after the armistice so that they might profit from inevitable disillusionment at the non-appearance of an immediate millennium and might give time for the glamour to fade from a Government which had won the war. But if after that there was a great left-wing majority, let it be so: "What is good enough for the English people, is good enough for me."

After dinner I played three games of bezique with the P.M.

Wednesday, September 6th
A quiet day, the P.M. being still rather under the weather as a result of the substantial doses of M. & B.[1] he has been given during the last week. I lunched and dined with the P.M. and Mrs C., lunch being a small *en famille* affair, and General Ismay and Brigadier Whitby (the blood-transfusion expert) being invited to dinner. Both meals were gargantuan in scale and epicurean in quality; rather shamingly so.

The OCTAGON[2] party on board this ship is a vast one and its members fill a huge dining-room and more than the whole of the main deck. The Chiefs of Staff proceed with their normal deliberations, but as the P.M. did nothing today but read *Phineas Finn*, there is a certain air of tranquillity. I am trying to master the rudiments of the papers on finance in the post-war period which is one of the main subjects for discussion with the President.

The P.M. says that after all he will not "beat up" the Americans about DRAGOON. He will suggest that the controversy be left to history and add that he intends to be one of the historians. More talk about a coming election. If the Opposition tried to sling mud about the past, they would be warned that the other side, though preferring a truce to recrimination, had a full armoury of mud to sling back. The P.M. would not regret the loss of any of his Labour colleagues except Bevin, the only one for whose character and capacity he had any real esteem. The others were mediocrities.[3]

---

[1] Antibiotic drug in its earliest form.
[2] Code-name for the Conference.
[3] Yet some years later he told me he thought Attlee his outstanding Labour colleague.

On another subject, he said that of all the paper and the theories one reads it was wise to pick out certain firm principles (e.g. milk for babies!) and pursue them actively. One of his major tenets was this: we did not enter this war for any gain, but neither did we propose to lose anything through it.

Thursday, September 7th

Another quiet day, devoted by the P.M. to *Phineas Finn* and by me to walking about the deck and swopping "lines" with Liberator pilots on their way home. I also ploughed through the many files, political and economic, we have brought with us.

> *One friendly American pilot, returning after an operational tour of which he and his crew were among the few survivors, told me he had much enjoyed his stay in England and thought it right that his Government should have paid us the tribute of calling this magnificent ship after one of our Queens.*
>
> *"But it's a British ship."*
>
> *"No, no. It's the biggest and fastest in the world."*
>
> *"That doesn't alter the fact that it's British. If you lean over the side – be careful not to fall overboard – you'll see the ensign on the stern."*
>
> *He gasped, "You mean this really is British? And the* Queen Elizabeth *too?"*
>
> *"Yes, I do."*
>
> *"But they're the biggest in the world. How could our Government have let themselves be out-smarted like that?"*

We are racing, at twenty-eight knots, through the mid-Atlantic in the latitude of Cap Finisterre.

Lords Cherwell and Moran were invited to dine. The P.M. produced many sombre verdicts about the future, saying that old England was in for dark days ahead, that he no longer felt he had a "message" to deliver, and that all that he could now do was to finish the war, to get the soldiers home and to see that they had houses to which to return. But materially and financially the prospects were black and "the idea that you can vote yourself into prosperity is one of the most ludicrous that ever was entertained".

The menu for dinner was: Oysters, consommé, turbot, roast turkey, ice with canteloupe melon, Stilton cheese and a great variety of fruit, petit fours, etc.; the whole washed down by champagne (Mumm 1929) and a very remarkable Liebfraumilch, followed by some 1870 brandy: all of which made the conversation about a shortage of consumers' goods a shade unreal.

Friday, September 8th

We are in the Gulf Stream (to which our national debt has never been sufficiently acknowledged) and the weather is very hot, very sticky and cloudy like at the Equator. The P.M., who has finished *Phineas Finn* and taken to *The Duke's Children*, which I myself read in Normandy, feels the heat acutely, says the ship has been abominably routed, and is definitely not his brightest and best.

I spent a good deal of time on deck, conversing agreeably with Antony Head, various W.A.A.F.s and other representatives of the mixed bag which comprises this OCTAGON party.

Lords Leathers and Cherwell dined. The P.M. said he thought the Joint Planners, etc., were being too optimistic about an early victory. It was even money the Germans would still be fighting at Christmas and if they did collapse the reasons would be political rather than military.

Saturday, September 9th

The P.M., feeling more or less himself again, did a considerable amount of work, mostly connected with the strategic questions at the coming conference. He has not yet given his mind to the complicated problems connected with finance and the future of Lease-Lend, and Lord Cherwell is in despair.

The Gulf Stream heat, which the P.M. has found quite over-powering, persisted until midday when there was a sudden fall of about 20 degrees in temperature, accompanied by clear skies and a fresh breeze. I spent much time on deck and, going up to the bows, was greatly impressed by the sight of this great ship cleaving the waveless sea at some thirty m.p.h.

The P.M. had a slight temperature again and was highly iras-cible. Lord Moran does not think seriously of it – probably it is the heat – but he told me that he does not give him a long life and he thinks that when he goes it will be either a stroke or the heart trouble which first showed itself at Carthage last winter. May he at least live to see victory, complete and absolute, in both hemi-spheres and to receive his great share of the acclamations. Perhaps it would be as well that he should escape the aftermath.

I am reading Vita Sackville-West's *The Eagle and the Dove*.[1] The descriptions of Lisieux evoke strong aerial recollections of that town, so familiar to me from 5,000 feet during June and July.

Perhaps foolishly, I took the P.M. a telegram from Attlee about the proposals for increasing service pay in the Japanese war. The

---

[1] The story of St Teresa of Avila (the Eagle) and St Thérèse of Lisieux (the Dove).

P.M. thinks these proposals inadequate and ill-conceived and has said so. This telegram announced the War Cabinet's intention, notwithstanding, of publishing them before his return. He was livid, said Attlee was a rat and maintained there was an intrigue afoot. He dictated a violent reply (which was never sent) full of dire threats. Having no pencil or paper with me, I borrowed the P.M.'s red ink pen and scrawled it on the back of another telegram. To my horror he insisted on reading the production as it was and proceeded to correct what I thought was an illegible semi-shorthand with equal illegibility.

Sunday, September 10th
I had my first glimpse of the New World at about noon. After lunch we moored against the quay at Halifax and, amidst cheers from the troops on board, the party landed and walked to the train. Malcolm MacDonald and some Canadian dignitaries greeted us and the Mounties were there in full regalia. While the luggage was being put on the train the P.M. stood on the balcony at the rear of his "car" while the crowd sang patriotic songs, very well in tune. He made them a short speech.

The train was highly comfortable, the P.M.'s drawing-room car, in which I spent part of the evening, being particularly well appointed. Dinner was rather too much of a good thing – some ten courses. I sat next to Bob Laycock, the Chief of Combined Operations, who was very pleasant.

Monday, September 11th
We arrived at Wolfe's Cove, Quebec, at 10.00 a.m. The sun was shining brightly. The President and Mrs Roosevelt had arrived just before us and he was sitting in his car waiting to greet the P.M. Princess Alice[1] and Lord Athlone were also at the station.

We all drove across the Plains of Abraham to the Citadel, where we are staying. I have got a most comfortable room and we have a spacious office. The main body of the Staffs are at the Château Frontenac. I went up to the main drawing-room where the principal personages were assembled and talked to Lord Athlone, who strangely enough recognised me, but did not have a chance of being introduced to the President.

---

[1] Princess Alice of Albany, Queen Victoria's grand-daughter, married to Queen Mary's younger brother Prince Alexander of Teck, created Earl of Athlone, who won the D.S.O. in the Boer War and was Governor General of both South Africa and Canada. Princess Alice was an energetic and stimulating person who lived frugally (usually travelling round London by bus) and was much loved by all and sundry for her natural simplicity and pleasant disposition.

The Governor General and Princess Alice gave a large dinner party, but as there was no room for me I dined at the Château Frontenac with Buster Long[1] (née Marling), Mrs Hill and Barker.

The Russians have climbed down about Warsaw, but it may be too late.

Tuesday, September 12th

At 11.30 the Governor General and Princess Alice, the President and Mrs Roosevelt, the P.M. and Mrs Churchill faced a huge battery of photographers on the terrace outside the sun room.

At the end of a Chiefs of Staff meeting, over which the P.M. presided, I heard him say to Portal that he might discuss with the President this evening the vexed "Zones of Occupation" question. Knowing he had not read the briefs on the subject and that there was no time for him to do so before dinner, I volunteered to read them aloud to him in his bath. This bizarre procedure was accepted, but the difficulties were accentuated by his inclination to submerge himself entirely from time to time and thus become deaf to certain passages.

The P.M. told me he fears the President is now "very frail".

The original plan was for the British to occupy the south of Germany, the Americans the north and the Russians the east. For shipping and commercial reasons we were anxious to persuade the Americans to agree to a swap with us, since we wished to control Hamburg and other North German ports. We also thought it right that the French should have a zone, carved partly out of ours and partly out of the Americans'. Berlin was a separate problem which would have to be resolved later. We expected American opposition to our proposals, but in the event (and much to our surprise) they accepted them without demur, provided they had passage rights to the port at Essen. At first they resisted the proposal for a French zone. This was only finally agreed, under British pressure, at Yalta the following February.

Wednesday, September 13th

The fine weather gave way to rain and cloud. There was a Plenary Session of the Conference at 11.30, before which the P.M. presented me to the President. As the Combined Chiefs of Staff were assembled when he did so, and as he included in the presentation a brief biographical sketch, I was acutely embarrassed.

[1] Daughter of Sir Charles Marling, former Minister at The Hague. She was in the A.T.S. and was working in the office of the Minister of Defence and Chiefs of Staff secretariat.

As I had been away in the R.A.F. during Churchill's various visits to Washington, and had missed the Casablanca, Cairo and Tehran conferences, I was the only one of the Prime Minister's secretaries who had never met the President.

Seeking to remedy this, and because my R.A.F. adventures had endeared me to him, he insisted on making the presentation before a whole gallery of war leaders while I, disguised as a Flying Officer and feeling exceedingly foolish, stood first on one leg and then on the other.

When the P.M. had finished, the torture for all present was prolonged while the President addressed me for several minutes in flowery language as if I were a public meeting. Subsequent encounters with Roosevelt at the conference were more relaxed, but I heard him say nothing impressive or even memorable and his eyes seemed glazed.

We were fairly busy all the afternoon. We had a party in the Household dining-room at which Bob Laycock, Reggie Winn,[1] Antony Head, Charlesworth[2] and three American officers were present. Geoffrey Eastwood, the Governor General's Controller, who is the only member of H.E.'s staff left behind now that the Athlones have gone off on a tour, did the honours. The food here is quite unusually good.

After dinner the P.M. saw Pug, who is in trouble about strategic matters in S.E. Asia Command, and subsequently Dick Law, who arrived by train from Montreal.

Thursday, September 14th

Rain and mist again which made exercise difficult, though I did stroll up to the Heights of Abraham, and owing to the excessively good food I am feeling rather gross. Eden and Cadogan arrived during the afternoon and Mrs Roosevelt left. The Conference has been going exceedingly well from our point of view and the Americans are being amenable both strategically and financially.

After a vast Household dinner to which Admiral Leahy, deserting the Presidential fold, came, there was a shockingly bad film chosen by the President. The P.M. walked out halfway through which, on the merits of the film, was understandable, but which seemed bad manners to the President. At dinner Lord Moran gave me a dissertation on the poor use we have made of our great

---

[1] Hon. Reginald Winn, A.D.C. to Sir John Dill.
[2] Likeable A.D.C. to the C.I.G.S., Sir Alan Brooke, killed in the York aircraft which crashed on the way to the Yalta Conference (see footnote, p. 556).

scientific brains and resources during this war; they have not been well co-ordinated or exploited. Though Moran is vain, egotistic and exceedingly indiscreet, his judgment of people is often shrewd, though by no means always. He has a low opinion of Anthony Eden, simply based on his handling of the Turks in Cairo, (and also of Pug). I cannot quite make up my mind whether he is right about Eden. He is certainly wrong about Pug.

While going to bed the P.M. told me some of the financial advantages the Americans had promised us. "Beyond the dreams of avarice," I said. "Beyond the dreams of justice," he replied.

Friday, September 15th

The day was taken up with the discussion of outstanding points and was crowned with further successes as far as our desiderata, political, financial and strategic go.

I shopped in Quebec in the afternoon, started a feverish cold, used the P.M.'s penicillin upon it, dined in a gargantuan way, talked to Admiral Wilson Brown (the President's Secretary) and went to bed early, leaving John Martin to cope with an after-dinner meeting about service pay.

Sat next to Eric Speed[1] at dinner. He is a very good conversationalist. He came the whole way out here with Eden in order to help set at rest the P.M.'s worries about this pay question. So did representatives of the Ministry of Labour and the Admiralty.

Saturday, September 16th

The Conference ended and the skies cleared for the occasion, hot sun burning down on the terrace and roof of the citadel. There was a Plenary meeting at noon. After lunch the Chancellor of McGill University and the Senate arrived to confer honorary degrees on the President and the P.M. They, with the Athlones who today returned from their tour, assembled on the roof outside the sunroom for the ceremony. Both the P.M. and the President, the latter wheeled along in his chair by his black servant, were strange spectacles in their academic dress. They both made speeches. Lord Athlone said that both he and the P.M. had been educated "by Degrees".

Then, still on the sun roof, there followed a joint press conference. The battery of photographers and reporters was formidable indeed. The scene was as follows: in the background rose the great

---

[1] Private Secretary to David Margesson at the War Office and then Permanent Under Secretary. Quick-witted and always well-informed, he was later Chairman of Dalgety and Co.

bulk of the Château Frontenac; at the end of the parapet hung the flags of the three countries; below ran the St Lawrence, with a few white sails; and around clustered a great crowd, mostly journalists but, interspersed among them, the members of McGill Senate in their academic robes, the Athlones and their Household, Mrs Churchill, Mr Eden, Lord Leathers and the Prof. Facing the mob sat the President, the P.M. and Mackenzie King flanked by splendid mounties and leering G-men. The President spoke first, scarcely audible above the clicking cameras, and then the P.M. gave an impromptu talk which was truly remarkable for its force and eloquence. It was important that he should say nothing which the Republicans could construe as aid for Roosevelt in the forthcoming Presidential elections (they are already playing that tune) and I do not think he did.

The President left Quebec shortly afterwards, taking with him Admiral Leahy, to whom I had talked at lunch. Under a forbidding exterior the Admiral possesses an attractive personality. His pro-Vichy views were interesting if unacceptable.

The King sent a most cold message in reply to the P.M.'s requests for a fraternal greeting to the Duke of Windsor, whom the P.M. is to see at Hyde Park[1] on Monday. The P.M. dictated to me rather a crushing answer, but, as often, he subsequently had it destroyed and replaced by one more conciliatory.

Sunday, September 17th
Our luncheon party in the Household dining-room included Cruikshank, the P.M.'s press representative on this party who was formerly Editor of the *Star*, and also Nicholas Lawford. Upstairs the Archduke Otto,[2] intent on Legitimist intrigue, lunched with the P.M.

In the afternoon I walked round the Citadel ramparts which offer a magnificent series of views of the St Lawrence, the Île d'Orléans, Quebec and the Plains of Abraham. The P.M. suggested I should fly over Niagara tomorrow, but finding the distance great and the R.C.A.F. not altogether enthusiastic I finally cancelled the arrangements as I think the authorities would have thought it something of an imposition.

We all dined upstairs in the sunroom. Malcolm MacDonald was there and so was Mackenzie King, next to whom I sat. The P.M. launched a diatribe against de Gaulle. Mackenzie King told me that when a celebration of the capture of Quebec was held here the

---

[1] President Roosevelt's family home in New York State.
[2] Eldest son of the former Emperor of Austria and King of Hungary.

descendants of Wolfe and Montcalm were invited. They met in the Château Frontenac. They were in adjoining suites and the occasion of their meeting was in a dispute for the bathroom.

The P.M., Mrs C., John and Tommy left after dinner for Hyde Park. Lord Moran and I, remaining behind, had a long talk which rendered nugatory his preliminary dissertation on his own taciturnity.

Monday, September 18th

Quiet reigned at the Citadel. In the morning Geoffrey Eastwood and I went shopping. I bought a selection of books for the P.M. to read on the voyage, *Jane Eyre*, Lytton Strachey, etc., with some difficulty as most things in Quebec are French and as a pre-requisite was large print.

After lunch Lord Moran, Geoffrey Eastwood and I drove through fine wooded hills, with the maple just beginning to turn red, to a fishing camp on the Valcartier river belonging to some people called Kernan. It was a lovely wild spot with adequate civilised comforts provided. Lord Moran and I put out in a canoe and fished for trout. We were both strangely inexpert.

Tuesday, September 19th

By train from Quebec to New York. I first set my foot on United States soil at a place appropriately called Whitehall. We passed, in a luxurious drawing-room car attached to a special train, through Montreal, Saratoga, Troy and so along the shores of Lake Champlain and the Hudson to New York. The so-called "dim-out" seems very unconvincing to English eyes accustomed to five years of Stygian blackness. Boarded the *Queen Mary* at 10.00 p.m.

Wednesday, September 20th

Sailed at 7.30. The New York skyline only just emerged from the mist through which a very sallow sun was struggling. This was disappointing. The P.M. and the Hyde Park party came aboard by tender from Staten Island, the P.M. looking far, far better – indeed, as John Peck would say, "in rude health".

Lord Leathers, Sir Andrew Cunningham and Pug were among those at lunch, the P.M. being in the best of humours and form. He only clouded over once, when he spoke of de Gaulle and said that of recent years "my illusions about the French have been greatly corroded".

It was again hot and cloudy, as on the voyage out. The P.M. slept for three hours in the afternoon, an all-time record, and I snoozed in a deckchair on the sports-deck. There are some 9,000 American troops on board, but the sun-deck is reserved for the OCTAGON party which has shrunk somewhat in size owing to the return of many of its members by air.

General Laycock, Antony Head and Lord Moran were invited to dinner, which as usual started with oysters and kept up to form. Antony Head was very good with the P.M. He argued and put his case well. Lord Moran (who is so critical that he runs down everybody in the party, especially the P.M., and so indiscreet that he does so indiscriminately) was obviously much put out by the course of the discussion on morale and courage, the P.M. being vicious in his attacks on the military psychoanalysts and declaring that it was more important to win victory by deploying the maximum number of men in the line than to waste thousands in rearward services for increasing the men's comfort.

Two noteworthy points which came out in discussion were (i) on the Russian front the Germans had to cover about twelve miles on a divisional front whereas in Normandy they had only had to cover four miles. Thus their effort against the Americans and ourselves was more concentrated than against the Russians; (ii) in Europe as a whole we had as many fighting men employed against the enemy as had the Americans. From the American papers one would scarcely suppose any British troops were fighting.

Thursday, September 21st

The usual round of alternating walks on deck and sessions in our rather stuffy office, together with periodic games of bezique and backgammon with Mrs Churchill. The First Sea Lord, Leathers and Whitby came to dinner, conversation ranging from a vivid picture of Edward VII receiving homage from a bishop the day before he died (the P.M. being Home Secretary then) to naval reminiscences which included personalities such as Fisher, Tug Wilson, Henry Oliver and Troubridge, and battles such as the Falkland Isles, Jutland and, in this war, Matapan. Cunningham gave an exciting account of Matapan and described how the only three Italian cruisers which had armour thick enough to withstand any of our cruisers ran straight into the 15-inch guns of the *Warspite*, etc. He also told us of the "limpet" bomb attacks on the *Queen Elizabeth* and the *Valiant* in Alexandria harbour, and said that he was himself thrown six feet into the air when that beneath the *Q.E.* exploded.

The P.M. finished the evening by challenging me to bezique and by insisting on continuing playing until 3.00 a.m. He says he will only ask for a six months' extension of Parliament's life in November so as to take the wind from the Labour sails.

Friday, September 22nd
After lunch I accompanied the P.M. and Mrs C. to a film, in Technicolor, about the life of President Wilson. He thought it very good; I thought it deplorably sentimental. Then we all went up on the bridge.

Just as last night I was required for bezique and played, with unvarying success, until 3.00 a.m.

Saturday, September 23rd
Proceeding at some thirty knots in a cool breeze and pleasant sunshine. Again accompanied the P.M. to the cinema, which was in the lounge, and afterwards lay in a deckchair on the sports deck between Buster Long and Joan Bright[1] with both of whom I had pleasant converse. At 6.30 General Ismay gave a cocktail party in his suite.

Sunday, September 24th
Went to church with Mrs C., the First Sea Lord, Lords Leathers and Moran, etc., at 10.30. The padre, an American, preached a most eloquent sermon about Amaziah and said that after this war we must be careful not to bring back with us, and worship, the gods of our enemy, as Amaziah did the gods of the Edomites. But he would refer to Amaziah as "the hero of our text".

Mrs Churchill gave a cocktail party at 6.30. It was quite beautifully executed by the ship's stewards. This was followed by a domestic dinner party, about which the chef took special trouble and at which the P.M. and Mrs C., Tommy, John and myself, Joe Hollis, Lord Moran and Brigadier Whitby were present. The P.M. regained some of his old spontaneous form and did not depend on reminiscences as much as he usually does now. He said that when he was Home Secretary his nerves were in a very bad state and he was assailed by worries in a way he never has been in the war. He then discovered that the best remedy was to write down on a piece of paper all the various matters which are troubling one; from which it will appear that some are purely trivial, some are irremediable, and there are thus only one or two on which one need concentrate one's energies.

Lord Moran said that when deterioration in a man set in the first things that went from him were those he had most recently learnt.

Played bezique with the P.M., who was in very mellow mood, till 2.30 a.m.

---

[1] Trusted personal assistant to General Ismay, who thought the world of her. Married Colonel Philip Astley.

Monday, September 25th

We had hoped to land at Fishguard but the weather was against it and so we plodded on up the Irish Channel to the Clyde. This disappointed and annoyed the P.M., especially as his own most comfortable train awaited him at Fishguard.

We entered the Clyde in the afternoon and reached Greenock about 5.00. Mist and rain gave way to a glorious evening of sun-pierced cloud. David[1] came aboard with his C. in C. and after the P.M. had broadcast a brief address to the troops the party went ashore in a tender.

The First Airborne Division has been wiped out at Arnhem.

Wednesday, September 27th

Went down to the House with the P.M. who delivered the first half of his speech, on military matters, before lunch. He delivered it well and as it contained many new facts it was well received, though M.P.s, who are the worst mannered of men, began to troop out as lunch-time approached without waiting for the interval.

I lunched with John Martin at the Reform Club and returned to the House for the second, less acclaimed, part of the speech on foreign affairs. I then corrected the whole thing in the Official Reporters' Gallery.

Dined with Rosemary and Hinch in Great College street. Alastair Forbes and Nicko Henderson were there, also a woman novelist, and conversation was on a fairly high level.

Friday, September 29th–Sunday, October 1st

Spent the week-end at Stansted. It was hot and sunny, like June, and we sat out of doors. Marie Lou Rothschild[2] was there. On Sunday the Bishop of Chichester (notorious for his anti-bombing speeches in the House of Lords) and Mrs Bell, and Sir Richard Livingstone came over to tea. The last is Vice Chancellor of Oxford, a great educationalist, and I found him most agreeable. He thinks that every Secondary School should have teachers expressly for the purpose of inculcating some knowledge and appreciation of art and literature.

---

[1] My eldest brother.
[2] Gentle and lovable French wife of Lionel de Rothschild.

27

Victory Deferred

October–November 1944

Monday, October 2nd

Returned from Stansted. The P.M. was back from Chequers in time to have General Eisenhower to lunch.

A long Cabinet during which I talked to Colonel Llewellyn,[1] who is perturbed about our intention of winning favour from the Americans by refusing to take Argentine meat, just when we have landed a good contract.

The P.M. tells me he agrees with the Russian desideratum about future world organisation (which the F.O. oppose), namely that parties to a dispute should, if members of the Council and one of the Big Four powers, be allowed to vote in that dispute.

There is great trouble over recognition of the French Provisional Government, which the U.S.A. will not admit at any cost. De Gaulle has an excellent platform in demanding the restoration of France's position as a great power.

Tuesday, October 3rd

The toughening resistance of the Germans is damping unduly high spirits a little and, inevitably, reflecting on our future strategic designs.

Dined with Lady Ampthill. Guy, Leo and Phyllis Russell were there. Leo told me he had resigned from Monty's staff in France (a) because of the bombing of French towns, much of which he had reason to think unnecessary from the military standpoint, (b) because Monty allowed his own staff to loot and rejected Leo's protests, (c) because Monty was at heart "a fascist".

---

[1] At this time Lord Woolton's successor as Minister of Food, having previously been President of the Board of Trade and Minister of Aircraft Production.

Wednesday, October 4th

While I was talking to the P.M. as he dressed after his afternoon sleep, preparatory to going to see *Richard III*, he quite seriously said that there ought to be some new hair brushes in the washing place below because those now there (which are in fact excellent) had black bristles which hid the dirt and because "in view of all the recent victories" the War Cabinet might really be entitled to have some new ones! Being a great man his approach to trivial matters is often an unusual one.

Thursday, October 5th

In conversation with Eden the P.M. said that Bevin was "far the most distinguished man the Labour Party have thrown up in my time".

He made a statement, very insipidly, about the gallant but now, alas, overwhelmed insurrection in Warsaw. It lasted sixty-three days with scarcely any help. Mikolajczyk and Raczynski[1] came up to the P.M. in the lobby and thanked him for his words. The words, produced by the F.O., were good; the delivery, due to the P.M. being too long in his bath and having to rush, was poor.

Friday, October 6th

Having lunched with Buster Long at the Churchill Club I was hoping for a reasonably quiet afternoon, but the Government got into difficulties over the Town and Country Planning Bill and the P.M. had to rush down to the House after lunch, hastily dictate a speech in the Foreign Secretary's House of Lords room and enter the lists. There followed two hours of Parliamentary knock-about to which I listened with enjoyment – Aneurin Bevan and the P.M. alternately bowing and biting, Buchanan[2] being interrupted constantly and accepting the fact with great wit and good humour, Pethick Lawrence[3] (for the respectable Opposition) being constructive, Lord Winterton declaiming that "Never in my forty years' experience of the House . . . etc.", and Sir Percy Harris's[4] rising being a signal for the House to empty. Hore-Belisha made a smooth speech in support of the Government, causing Gallacher[5]

---

[1] Polish Ambassador in London before and during the war. Still living there in 1985.
[2] Labour M.P. for the Gorbals division of Glasgow. Originally a member of the left-wing I.L.P., he was a stalwart patriot.
[3] Ancient and stooping product of Eton and Trinity, ennobled and appointed Secretary of State for India in 1945.
[4] Stolid but dull leader of the Liberal Party in the House of Commons.
[5] The only Communist M.P. His son was killed in the war and he wrote a moving reply to Churchill's sympathetic letter of condolence. Churchill rather admired him.

to congratulate him "on the assiduous way in which the Rt Hon. Member is working his passage home".

There followed a late night chiefly devoted to new ministerial appointments (Swinton* to Civil Aviation and Jowitt to Social Insurance), and to attempts to find a new Chairman of the Tory Party. David Margesson refused all blandishments to accept this and James Stuart failed in an intrigue to get Duncan Sandys appointed and thus clip his wings.

Saturday, October 7th

An exceedingly busy day, being almost single-handed. In the afternoon the P.M., while signing photographs (including one for Stalin) and books, began reading Vol. I of Marlborough aloud to me and continued about Sir Winston Churchill's home life and passion for heraldry for nearly an hour. At the end he said that as I had been subjected to this ordeal he would give me a copy for Christmas. He then worked till dinner, seeing various people and every now and then telling me I ought to read the leading article in today's *Manchester Guardian*.

At 11.30 p.m. the P.M., accompanied by John Martin, left for Northolt to enter the York and fly, via Naples and Cairo, to Moscow. At one moment he talked of taking me, but having had a very exhausting week I am not altogether sorry he did not.

Sunday, October 8th

Calm should have descended had not there been trouble about the drafting of guidance to the press in connection with the new Ministerial appointments. It being necessary to satisfy the opposing views of Archie Sinclair (who wants to be sure control of Civil Aviation is kept by the Air Ministry during the war) and Brendan (who wants to be sure it is not), I had to go and see Sinclair and telephone repeatedly to Brendan. Finally I produced a document which, like the second Prayer Book of Edward VI, satisfied both parties and was issued to the press.

The P.M.'s visit to Moscow, which is really very dangerous to his health, is, he assured me yesterday, entirely because he wants to discourage any idea that the U.K. and the U.S.A. are very close (as exemplified by the Quebec Conference) to the exclusion of Russia. His visit will make it quite clear that our counsels with Russia are close too, and that there is no tendency to leave her in the cold.

Miss Helen Waddell[1] has sent these verses to the P.M.:

[1] Daughter of a presbyterian missionary in Japan. An eminent scholar, expert on medieval Latin lyrics and author of *Peter Abelard*, which was translated into nine languages.

The Polish Eagle, nailed to the barn door,
Torn wings outstretched, bedaubed with blood and turd;
Beneath in German and in Russian script,
"So perish all who trust in England's word".

She wrote it in 1939; she sent it now.

Monday, October 9th

On the way to bed I looked in as usual at the C.W.R. Mess and talked to Edward Bridges and Colonel John Bevan[1] (the Cover Plan Expert). We discussed the increasingly well authenticated number of German atrocities against our soldiers (John Hussey[2] had told me of some of the results actually seen by members of 168 Squadron) by members of S.S. divisions. The question is whether or not some strong threat of retaliation should be made. Both Bevan and Bridges feared it would incite the Germans to yet worse. But we must exterminate the S.S. The next generation, tired of war reminiscences and probably as full of illusions as we were, is so likely to forget and, of course, those of our enemies who have the cunning to turn their coats in time will probably get away with it – at least in the lower ranks and especially if post-war Russian imbroglios lead some people to think Germany must be utilised as a buffer state. I become more and more persuaded that something drastic should be done about the youth such as taking all children under eight from their parents and constructing vast state nurseries for them in South Germany. But who shall be responsible for their upbringing; who shall select their guardians; and *quis custodiet ipsos custodes*?

A disturbed night owing to demands from Moscow that the Polish Ministers shall at once fly there for conversations; and the Poles don't want to do so except on conditions.

Tuesday, October 10th

Things much quieter and nothing startling from Moscow. The P.M.'s daily post shows a strong body of feeling (a) demanding a war correspondent for the *Daily Worker* (refused by the Cabinet owing to its poor record in this war); (b) protesting against the release from internment of Captain Maule Ramsay, M.P.; (c)

---

[1] Head of the Cabinet Office section responsible for schemes to deceive the enemy. In private life senior partner of the Stockbrokers Bevan Simpson and married to Field Marshal Alexander's sister-in-law, Lady Barbara Bingham (aunt of the missing Lord Lucan).

[2] Rotund and invariably affable New Zealand pilot in No. 168 squadron. Correctly guessed in advance the date and place of the OVERLORD landing.

outraged because there is a shortage of housing and yet houses are being used to billet Italian prisoners of war.

Brendan says the Government will fall over housing and that Lord Portal [of Laverstoke] is in a state of hysteria, punctuated with frequent tears.

Wednesday, October 18th
The Moscow conversations seem to be going well and some progress has been made even on the vexed Polish problem, though there is a hitch about the definition of the Curzon line frontier.

Together with Mrs Churchill and Mary I went to Claridges to dine with the Bessboroughs in a private room there. Others present were Lord Linlithgow, Oliver Stanley, Tommy Lascelles (just back from visiting the front with the King; he agrees with Leo Russell that Monty is one of nature's fascists), Mrs Euan Wallace,[1] Lady Dorothy Charteris[2] and Rosemary,[3] Sammy Hood, etc. A good dinner, but the prevalent fashion of not dressing for dinner in London rather spoils the effect.

After dinner Mary and I joined a peculiar party at the Dorchester. It contained Sarah Oliver, Ann O'Neill, Pat Wilson (ex-Jersey) whose husband was only killed a few days ago, and several American officers; also Mrs William Randolph Hearst, Jnr., formerly of the Ziegfeld Follies. Many of them were drunk and Mrs Hearst paid for the champagne which flowed. Most of us then repaired to the Milroy, a new night club, from which Mary and I walked home at 2.00 a.m. Mary is being urged by Lord Beaverbrook to stand at the next election and is thinking seriously of so doing.

Thursday, October 19th
Represented the P.M. at a service at St Paul's in celebration of the Liberation of Athens. A large throng headed by the King of Greece* was there and the service, partly in English and partly in Greek, was conducted by the Bishop of London jointly with the Archbishop Germanos, both in mitres and full regalia. I sat immediately behind King George who, poor man, is faced with great difficulties in regaining his throne. The Bishop of London preached a polished but dull sermon. Perhaps the most stirring

---

[1] Barbara, widow of Euan Wallace, former Minister of Transport.
[2] Daughter of the Earl of Kenmare, sister of the well-known columnist Lord Castlerosse and married to Sir Evan Charteris, K.C., who had been a prominent member of the "the Souls".
[3] Pretty daughter of Lady Dorothy Charteris by her first marriage. Later married the Hon. George Dawnay.

thing was the singing, by the Greek choir, of their national anthem.

Friday, October 20th

Mrs C. has asked my advice on some papers sent by the Duchess of Atholl.[1] They show a horrible picture of the treatment of the Poles, especially the children, deported to Russia by the Soviet Government in 1939–40. If the Poles, taken thus for labour, were so abominably treated, what will be the fate of the Germans whom the victorious Russians will surely deport? But the more one hears of Teutonic atrocities, of which so many are well authenticated now, the less one can feel pity for the fate in store for them.

During dinner a V.2 rocket landed at South Norwood. It was the first I had heard. Its explosion was a long, rumbling roar.

Sunday, October 22nd

I went to Northolt to meet the P.M. on his return, via Cairo and Naples, from the very successful Muscovite conference. He arrived, well and cheerful, in the York and I accompanied him to Chequers, whither Duncan and Diana, Sarah, Brendan and Jack came. After dinner there was a film *The Hitler Gang*, in which the leading Nazis were represented in a most lifelike way. After it the P.M. cleared his box and then went into the Great Hall where Brendan and Duncan told him he ought to take more interest in the Home Front. There followed a violent discussion, though very good-natured, during which the P.M. said that if a majority of the Tories went into the Lobby against him during the coming debate on Town and Country Planning (the Tories oppose the Government plan for compensating owners of requisitioned land on the basis of 1939 prices), he would resign the leadership of the Conservative Party.

Thursday, October 26th

Princess Beatrice[2] and the Archbishop of Canterbury[3] died. The latter's demise caused the P.M. no sorrow. In fact he was quite

[1] Though a Conservative M.P., she was known as "Red Kitty" on account of her support of the Republican cause in the Spanish Civil War. She had a fine intellect, held honorary degrees from seven universities and was the aunt of Professor Sir James Butler of Trinity College, Cambridge.

[2] Youngest of Queen Victoria's nine children and Governor of the Isle of Wight.

[3] William Temple, previously Bishop of Manchester and Archbishop of York. A scholar of distinction and profound philosopher. Churchill, who as far as clerics were concerned had a touch of King Henry II about him, disliked Temple's left-wing tendencies and outspoken political comments.

ribald about it. Nairn, from Marrakech, and Joe Hollis dined with me.

The P.M. gave up working on tomorrow's speech at 11.40 and went to bed at this record early hour.

Friday, October 27th–Monday, November 20th
I listened to the P.M.'s speech, about foreign affairs, corrected it for Hansard and then went off to Madeley with Mother in order to collect some winter clothes. On Sunday I felt odd, took my temperature (102°) and retired to bed with chicken pox, which was accompanied by a recurrence of last year's impetigo. I stayed in bed ten days and read *Mansfield Park* and *Dombey and Son*. While I was in bed Shane O'Neill[1] was killed in Italy, a tragedy which Aunt Nancy took with her usual philosophy. In the world outside, the P.M. visited Paris and had a triumphal reception,[2] Lord Moyne was assassinated in Cairo, and the public were at last told about the V.2 rocket (of which everyone in England had long known unofficially).

When I could go out, I visited the Madeley P. of W. camp to look at the German prisoners. I also grew a moustache.

Tuesday, November 21st
At No. 10 I found Government changes in progress, Duncan Sandys replacing Wyndham Portal at the Ministry of Works. The Cabinet met at 6.00 and as they were already assembled in the Cabinet Room, the P.M. saw two M.P.s, Brabner and Wilmot, in our room in order to offer them Under Secretaryships. He turned us out and then, of course, the telephones began ringing. When I came back he said, "A lady with a foreign accent was asking for you." I replied, speciously, "Monsieur Massigli's secretary, I expect." Oddly enough it was.

Wednesday, November 22nd
Two long Cabinets took up most of the day. Reconstruction matters have now grown from a stream to a flood.

During the evening Duncan Sandys, who has in his great ambition been pressing for the Ministry of Works and Buildings, came

[1] Eldest son of my mother's sister Lady Annabel Dodds and first husband of Ann Charteris. He was second in command of the North Irish Horse and by a strange coincidence his commanding officer was Colonel David Dawnay. Their respective fathers had been killed in the First World War, standing side by side as first and second in command of the 2nd Life Guards. On this occasion Dawnay had only just moved a few yards away when a shell struck Shane.

[2] I had been going to accompany him, had not chicken pox struck.

to peruse with the P.M. the comments on his appointment in the early editions of tomorrow's newspapers. Brendan says that Duncan S. may do the job well because he is ruthless, but that unfortunately he is not good with subordinates and has adopted too much of the *Führerprinzip*. Certainly he is very unpopular. To bed after 3.00 a.m.

Thursday, November 23rd
The P.M. has taken exception to my moustache, which he told John and Leslie was "the worst thing that has happened since Randolph's beard"; so, in spite of the Atlantic Charter and the Four Freedoms, I suppose it will have to go.

In a minute about Spain (where the F.O. want to upset Franco's régime and to incite the U.S.A. thereunto) the P.M. says that his three cardinal tenets are (i) opposition to Communism; (ii) non-intervention in the internal affairs of other countries; (iii) prevention of one power dominating Western Europe by armed force, but reliance on a world organisation.

Friday, November 24th
Lunched at New Court with Tony Rothschild. General Sir Hubert Gough, Commander of the 5th Army in the First World War, and General Sir Clive Liddell were there.

To Chequers. Duncan Sandys came to dinner. We saw a French film called *Ignace* and the P.M. worked till 3.00 a.m.

Saturday, November 25th
Winant came with a letter containing a telegram from the President about civil aviation. It was pure blackmail, threatening that if we did not give way to certain unreasonable American demands, their attitude about Lease-Lend supplies would change. Winant was shame-faced about presenting it and didn't want to stay to lunch, but the P.M. said that even a declaration of war should not prevent them having a good lunch. The rest of the week-end was largely devoted to concerting, by telephone with Beaverbrook, a long reply. The Americans are also being tough, and even threatening, about a number of other things and the P.M. is disturbed at having to oppose them over so many issues. The President wanted to make a declaration to the Germans about our good intentions: it was a silly idea, ambrosia for Goebbels, and the P.M. turned it down flat. And there is a sharp wrangle about our imports of Argentine meat, the Americans being anxious to bring economic pressure on the Argentine.

Lord Woolton also came to lunch and talked about housing.

In the evening Mrs C. and Sarah came and we saw the film of *Henry V* in Technicolor, with Laurence Olivier. The P.M. went into ecstasies about it. To bed at 2.30.

Sunday, November 26th

Very busy all day with civil aviation and Argentine meat, while the P.M.'s box is hopelessly overcrowded with more or less urgent papers.

General Maitland Wilson, Lord Cherwell and General Ismay came for the night. Jumbo Wilson has little pig's eyes in his huge face. Saw *Left of the Line*, a film about the British and Canadian armies in OVERLORD. Not as good as *Desert Victory*, though the terrain was more familiar to me. To bed at 2.45 a.m.

Monday, November 27th

The P.M. had four meetings today, beginning with a Cabinet at 12.00 about his civil aviation telegram to the President. Lunched with Alexander Hood,[1] wrestled with some differences of opinion between the F.O. and the Defence Office (who always malign each other) and went to see Aunt Celia in hospital. She had a V.2 near her on Saturday. The same day one at Deptford fell on the local Woolworth's and killed over 150 people.

The P.M. said on Saturday that his election programme would be: free enterprise for the individual provided that (i) there were no big monopolies or cartels allowed (Lord Woolton cited as an iniquitous example the case of electric light bulbs, which he tried to assail by manufacturing and selling them for 1/- instead of 2/6); (ii) high taxation – though less high than at present – was retained.

Wednesday, November 29th

Rushed to the House at 2.00 and heard William Sidney[2] make his maiden speech in moving the Loyal Address which was seconded by a young Labour Scottish miner, Tom Fraser.[3] William spoke well and was loudly applauded for his eloquence as well as for his gallantry. The P.M. spoke later but I didn't wait for that.

Thursday, November 30th

The P.M.'s seventieth birthday brought such a spate of letters and telegrams as never was seen. Everybody, from the Shah of Persia

---

[1] One of my oldest friends. Served in the R.N.V.R. After the war a director of Schröder Wagg and Chairman of Tanganyika Concessions. Married Diana Lyttelton and succeeded his brother as 7th Viscount Hood.

[2] M.P. for Chelsea. Later Lord De L'Isle.

[3] Labour M.P. for Lanarkshire. Joint Parliamentary Under Secretary for Scotland in the 1945 Labour Government.

to Harry Lauder, from Queen Mary to Rosa Lewis, sent their good wishes. With Leslie on leave, John Peck retiring early with a headache and Tony Bevir away I found the combination of ordinary work and the birthday almost unmanageable. Meanwhile the P.M.'s box is in a frightful state, with scores of urgent papers demanding a decision. He has frittered away his time in the last week and has seemed unable or unwilling or too tired to give his attention to complex matters. He has been reading the first paragraph or so and referring papers to people without seeing what is really required of him. Result: chaos.

28

Drama in Athens

December 1944

Friday, December 1st
Another exhausting morning, the P.M. having many engagements and much untouched work awaiting him.

He went to Harrow for a school concert, accompanied by Mrs Churchill, Jack, Donald Somervell, Amery, Geoffrey Lloyd, Paul Emrys Evans[1] and McCorquodale.[2] The Songs were good except for the "school twelve" which was lamentable. A small boy, with a magnificent treble, sang "Five Hundred Faces". Afterwards there was a sherry party in the Headmaster's House, where the P.M. talked long and charmingly to the school monitors, such as he did to the midshipmen on the *K.G. V* last January, enthralling but never patronising.

Saturday, December 2nd
Like an ostrich I dug my head in the pile of birthday greetings and remained oblivious to telegrams to Tito, Stalin and the rest. At Chequers great upheavals were going on as the P.M. delved industriously into the accumulated masses of the last ten days.

There has been much excitement about the Duke of Sutherland, whose matrimonial delinquencies made it necessary for him to resign the Lord Lieutenancy of Sutherland. He refused to do so and thus a notice was published in the Gazette "determining his appointment". This morning *The Times* and the *Daily Telegraph*

---

[1] Conservative M.P. for South Derbyshire, friend of Anthony Eden and Lord Cranborne. Formerly in the Foreign Office.

[2] Malcolm McCorquodale, M.P. for Epsom. Chairman of the well-known printing firm. Chosen to be Chairman of the Conservative Party in 1952 when Lord Woolton was thought to be dying, but Woolton recovered and so McCorquodale was given a peerage to compensate him.

decided this meant that the Duke had been *appointed* Lord Lieutenant and said so. Fur flies.

Sunday, December 3rd
After an industrious morning I went down to Trinity for the night,
staying with Winstanley. I was present at a carol service in Trinity
Chapel which was well attended and impressively conducted. All
the bells of Cambridge ringing out struck me as a cheerful sound as
I walked to Chapel with Winstanley across the Great Court; but he
said that he always found church bells melancholy; they brought
down upon him the burden of sorrows he had never felt and sins he
had never committed.

Monday, December 4th
Lunched at No. 10 with the P.M. The other guests were M. Paul
Boncour,[1] Harold Macmillan and Harold Balfour,[2] who is going
out to West Africa as Minister Resident, having just given up the
Under Secretaryship of the Air Ministry. Paul Boncour is described in the Foreign Office "Personalities Report" as assiduously
cultivating the appearance of Robespierre, but, though perhaps
Sea Green, certainly not incorruptible. I found him a crashing bore
with his moans about the hard lot of the French people and his
ceaseless reversion to the topic of arms for the French army. Also
he spat while talking to an extent unusual even in France. The P.M.
found him tedious too and spoke in French more execrable than
usual, frequently calling upon me to translate and more frequently
still turning to address Harold Macmillan in English, which Paul
Boncour cannot understand, about the iniquities of the Communists in Greece and of Sforza[3] in Italy. The P.M. becomes more and
more vehement in his denunciation of Communism, and in particular of E.L.A.S. and E.A.M.[4] in Greece, so that before lunch today
Mrs C. had to send him a note begging him to restrain his
comments.
    Crisis in Greece where E.L.A.S., the left-wing organisation, is
getting out of hand. The P.M. stayed up till 4.00 a.m. dictating

[1] Constantly recurring Minister in the Third Republic. Prime Minister 1932–33.
Foreign Minister 1932–34 and for one month in 1938.
[2] Won M.C. and bar as a pilot in the First World War. Conservative M.P. for the
Isle of Thanet. A man of vigour and determination. Created Lord Balfour of
Inchrye in 1945.
[3] Italian politician of ancient descent and mushy liberal sentiment. Weak,
vacillating and incompetent.
[4] The Greek guerilla organisation which had seized most of the country after the
Germans left and was intent on imposing a Communist one-party régime.

telegrams, and reading tomorrow's newspapers. Bob Dixon[1] came over from the F.O. and he and I remained with the P.M. while he dictated, but these late hours do not improve the quality of his work. ("Treat Athens as a conquered city", he wrote in his telegram to Scobie.[2])

As the Combined H.Q. at Caserta contained both British and American officers, we had a convention that telegrams we did not wish the Americans to read, because they were concerned with purely British matters, should be headed "Guard". Owing to the late hour at which the telegram to Scobie was being dictated, and the fact that at 4.00 a.m. the Prime Minister wanted it despatched immediately, I forgot to write the word "Guard" at the top. This had unfortunate results, because the Americans at Caserta telegraphed the text to Washington and the resulting leak to the press, from either the White House or the State Department, lent fuel to the explosive campaign against our Greek policy which was launched both in the American and British press. After this leakage I remember confessing my delinquency and Churchill saying kindly that it was his fault for keeping me up so late.

Tuesday, December 5th

In the House the P.M. made a statement about Greece and this was followed by clamorous demands from Aneurin Bevan, Buchanan, Gallacher and Haden Guest[3] for an immediate adjournment and debate. The left wing see a heaven-sent opportunity for saying that we are supporting by our arms the forces of reaction in Italy and Greece.

Returned to the Annexe to find that the State Department in the U.S. had published a statement which could be interpreted as nothing but an attack on our Greek and Italian policies. Angry telegram from the P.M. to the President.

Thursday, December 7th

The chief topic is still the Greek crisis. The general public have no idea of the true nature of E.L.A.S., which they believe to be a heroic left-wing resistance movement.

---

[1] Pierson Dixon, Principal Private Secretary to Anthony Eden. Greek scholar. Wise, soft spoken and universally liked. Eventually Ambassador in Paris.

[2] Lieutenant General Sir Ronald Scobie, G.O.C., Malta, 1942 and Commander of the British Troops in Greece from 1944 to 1946.

[3] Dr Haden Guest, Labour M.P. for Islington North.

Friday, December 8th

The P.M. spoke in the House of Commons, in reply to an amendment to the Gracious Speech about Greece and Italy. He was very telling and, as there was a good deal of interruption, had a good opportunity for showing his quickness in debate.

Evidently this Greek trouble is causing widespread criticism here and in America. I am sure the P.M. is in the right, and the inability of these Levantine bandits to postpone their internecine feuds until Germany is defeated is nauseating; but nevertheless there may be something in Desmond Morton's thesis that if the P.M. falls it will be over his handling of foreign policy. Moreover the belief, now current, that we support the monarchies of Europe as a matter of principle – whatever the will of the people – will not, in the long run, be to the good of the Crown in this country.

The P.M. did not go off to Chequers which upset everybody else's week-end arrangements.

Sunday, December 10th

The P.M. is at Chequers, swamped with papers which now fill three boxes, and still preoccupied with the military problems of Greece. Whatever their vices and their political asininity, the Greeks can certainly fight.

Monday, December 11th

I think the P.M. and the Government are, quite unjustly, losing stock over Greece.

Tuesday, December 12th

The Isles of Greece, indeed. I shall never feel any sentiment towards them again. All the afternoon there were Cabinets on the subject, interspersed with visits from the King of Greece. He came three times altogether and proved very obstinate to the Cabinet's wish that he should appoint the Archbishop of Athens Regent. He told me that he was sure this rising was organised and inspired by the Germans.

At 6.00 the P.M. saw Eisenhower and Tedder. The former is having a disagreement with Monty about future strategy.

I dined at the Ritz with Lady Constance Milnes Gaskell.[1] The other guests were Mr and Mrs Douglas Woodruff,[2] Miss Freya Stark[3] (the Middle Eastern expert), Mother and an

---

[1] Daughter of the Earl of Ranfurly and one of Queen Mary's ladies-in-waiting.

[2] Chairman and Editor of the Roman Catholic paper, *The Tablet*.

[3] Celebrated traveller and writer on Persian and Middle-Eastern affairs.

U.N.R.R.A.[1] expert called Rattigan. I thought Douglas Wood-ruff interesting, even though his political prejudices are very Roman. He said that the Church in Spain had suffered because the King had appointed the bishops and had taken care not to appoint anything but mediocrities. He also said that in 1934 the Left had revolted in Spain because Gil Robles and the Right won the elections and the democratic Left thought resort to force justified in order to prevent the Opposition getting into power.

Worked at No. 10 with the P.M. who was incensed, not unnaturally, at the discovery that one of his personal telegrams to General Scobie in Athens had been seen and published by the notorious anti-British American columnist, Drew Pearson.[2] It had reached the State Department without authorisation, through A.F.H.Q. Italy and somebody in the State Department had given it to Pearson. That such a thing could happen is incredible.[3]

Wednesday, December 13th

What with the leakage and the Greeks, no ordinary work is being done at all. And these Balkan monarchs do not make things easier; today it was Peter of Yugoslavia's turn.

I lunched with Flaisjer, a Polish Jew of no mean intelligence, at the Café Royal. He says that the guerilla Freedom movements in Belgium, France, Yugoslavia, Greece, etc., which are giving so much trouble, are a legacy of fascism. They form themselves into a party and adopt the totalitarian thesis that the party has a right to dominate the State.

Thursday, December 14th

The King of Greece is being very obstinate, sincerely upholding what he believes to be the principles involved against the combined pressure of the War Cabinet and President Roosevelt to seek a solution of the Greek crisis by having the Archbishop of Athens appointed Regent.

The P.M. dictated part of his speech on Poland for tomorrow. He couldn't think of anything new to say on the subject and so inserted long quotations from his own earlier speeches and a certain amount of padding about the Sybilline Books and the

---

[1] The United Nations organisation for the relief of refugees.

[2] Journalist on the *Washington Post* with a source either in the White House or the State Department from whom he obtained secret or sensitive material. This was the telegram to Scobie mentioned on Dec. 4th.

[3] It was at this stage that the absence of the word "Guard" on the telegram was disclosed.

Liberum Veto.[1] Then he was persuaded not to speak at all, but after dinner Anthony Eden came to No. 10, where the P.M. had returned from dinner with the Liberal Nationals at Claridges, and undid all the good work. This was mischievous as a speech is unnecessary and the P.M. is very tired.

Friday, December 15th

The P.M. made his speech – most of which he composed between 9.00 and 10.30 a.m. – at 11.00 and it went well in spite of his interposing an imaginary clause from the Atlantic Charter which led Kenneth Pickthorn[2] (who hates the P.M. because he has never been offered a job in the Government) to say that he doubted whether the P.M. had ever read the Atlantic Charter. The speech was a sensible lead towards a *via media*, though there now seems little hope of this.

Tuesday, December 19th

The P.M. apparently did badly over Questions in the House, especially about Greece. The Chief Whip says it is the first time he has seen the House really irritated and impatient with him. The P.M., who disagrees with Eden about Greece (Eden wants to over-rule King George and get the Archbishop of Athens appointed Regent), said he would intervene tomorrow in the debate on the adjournment. The Foreign Office are terrified of what he may say and James Stuart, who thinks he has been speaking too much lately, did his utmost to dissuade him. But he insisted that he would make a short, gay and impromptu speech. He stayed up till 3.00 a.m.

Wednesday, December 20th

To the House for Questions which were uneventful. The P.M. did not intervene about Greece. Another over-burdened afternoon – there is so much happening, Greece, Poland, a powerful German counter-attack on the Luxembourg frontier which has thrown the Americans some twenty miles back (Monty, who is suffering from personal pique as a result of a difference of opinion with Eisenhower about questions of command, is very gloomy about it all); and in addition to all this the usual mass of amorphous trivialities such as Honorary Fellowships of French institutions, the breaking up of

---

[1] In the Polish Diet, before the eighteenth-century partitions of the country, each member had a free right of veto so that legislation became a practical impossibility.

[2] Fellow of Corpus Christi and one of the two Cambridge University M.P.s.

battalions in which the P.M. has an interest (the Oxfordshire Hussars this time), etc., etc.

Thursday, December 21st

I met Alec Cadogan in the park. He said the P.M. was creating a deplorable impression in Cabinet now because he would not read his papers and would talk on and on. It is very distressing and unless he will delegate much of his work I see little hope of a change. Obviously he is hopelessly overtired and at seventy his powers of recuperation may not be very good.

There are signs of an impending quarrel between the P.M. and Eden about the Regency in Greece.

Friday, December 22nd

After the P.M. had lunched (having Mervyn Haigh, Bishop of Winchester, to be vetted for the Archbishopric of Canterbury; afterwards he told me he liked Haigh but thought Fisher, the Bishop of London, the tougher of the two), he again had interminable discussions with the King of Greece and Eden. Eden says the King keeps on telling lies.

Then the P.M. sent for P. J. Grigg and rammed down his throat an announcement about additional manpower for the army. This was subsequently rammed down the throat of others (including Bevin, who was snatched from the stalls of the Coliseum) and given to the press and the B.B.C., the idea being that at this moment when the German thrust has broken through Eisenhower's too dispersed strength, an announcement of our determination to raise a further 250,000 men would arouse the country from its present victory-complex and stimulate the Americans, who always want to go one better, to call up another million.

The P.M. dilly-dallied so much in the Defence Map Room that it was too late to go to Chequers and he dined at the Annexe. He talked to John Martin and me interminably after dinner about his differences of opinion over Greece with Eden, his intention of flying to Athens to settle the matter, and the fact that the English people throughout their history always turned on those whom they thought had served them well in hard times (e.g. Marlborough, Wellington, Lloyd George). So long did he talk that he became too tired, and it became too late, to go down to Chequers at all, and so, in spite of Sawyers and the luggage having gone ahead, we remained at the Annexe.

Saturday, December 23rd
The P.M. spent most of the day in bed at the Annexe and had lunch in his room. At 5.00 we left for Chequers, where we found Mrs Romilly, Jack, Clarissa and the Sandyses. After dinner the P.M. spoke of flying to Athens tomorrow, but though I made the preliminary arrangements I did not think seriously that he would.

Sunday, December 24th
The Cranbornes, Prof. and Horatia Seymour came to lunch. I sat between Lady Cranborne, who is one of the world's most attractive conversationalists, and Horatia Seymour. After lunch it seemed that Lord Cranborne and others had dissuaded the P.M. from his proposed venture and those whom I had warned by telephone were in a state of miserable uncertainty. However at 5.30 the P.M. agreed with Eden by telephone that both should go tonight though neither were at all clear what they should find in Athens when they got there. A chaotic evening ensued, with the P.M. telling the King, Attlee, Bevin, Beaverbrook on one telephone and me warning the C.A.S., Admiralty, Tommy, etc., etc. on the other. Mrs C. was greatly distressed but resigned herself to the inevitable. I had had my uniform sent down from London and at 11.30 p.m. we were all dressed and ready to depart, though it was difficult to drag the P.M. from the sofa in the Great Hall where he was reading telegrams, dictating manuscript comments, and carrying on a conversation with Mrs Romilly (who was most outrageously reading the telegrams too) all at the same time.

Christmas Day, Monday, December 25th
We took off from Northolt, seen off by the C.A.S., Duncan Sandys and the Prof., at 1.00 a.m. It was the first journey of the P.M.'s new C.54, a beautifully appointed aircraft provided by General Arnold. The party consisted of the P.M., Anthony Eden, Bob Dixon, myself, Tommy Thompson, Miss Layton and Miss Holmes (the P.M.'s two most attractive typists), a detective and Sawyers, the P.M.'s servant. Also Lord Moran.

The best record I can give of the next two days is contained in the following letter I wrote to John Martin on Boxing Day and in a description I wrote of the meeting at the Greek Ministry of Foreign Affairs:

Athens,
December 26th, 1944

Dear John,

I think you will be interested to have some sort of background to the official telegrams about our activities which will be reaching you.

Our journey went without a hitch. The C.54 is remarkably comfortable and very quiet. We had to climb to 13,500 feet over France and as no one but the P.M. was awoken for oxygen we all arose with splitting headaches. However these passed off very quickly. At Pomigliano we did not go more than 100 yards from the aircraft, having breakfast in a rather bare building which had only slightly recovered from the many bombardments it had had to withstand. We wasted but little time there but at breakfast the Prime Minister had a talk with the C. in C., Mediterranean, Slessor and Harding.[1] We found that the C.54 would be able to get into Athens, so did not change aircraft. We flew over Taranto, where I took over the controls without in any way endangering the passengers and thence across the Adriatic, past Cythera and Ithaca (which was "cloud-capped" in the best Homeric tradition) and flew up the Gulf of Corinth past Patras. We lunched in the air.

At the aerodrome Alexander, Macmillan and Leeper[2] came on board. We had a conference lasting two hours in the aircraft itself. At this conference the plan of campaign was worked out and just before dark we set off on a long drive in armoured cars to the quay. The driver of my armoured car encouraged me greatly by beginning the conversation with "The last man who sat where you are sitting died yesterday morning." However nobody sniped at us on the way, although at one point we passed a place which E.L.A.S. had been mortaring during the morning.

We boarded *Ajax* just after sunset and were received with astonishing hospitality. Shortly afterwards Leeper, Macmillan and Scobie arrived bringing with them Papandreou[3] and the Archbishop. While the Prime Minister and the rest saw Papandreou, we entertained the Archbishop, who is a magnificent figure and obviously has a great sense of humour. The Admiral

---

[1] Chief of Staff to Alexander. After the war he was appointed C.I.G.S. and was Governor of Cyprus during the E.O.K.A. troubles. Made a Field Marshal in 1953 and a peer in 1958.

[2] An Australian who joined the British Diplomatic Service in 1918. Ambassador in Athens, 1944–46, and afterwards in Buenos Aires. Subsequently a most effective Chairman of the British Council.

[3] Prime Minister of King George's Greek Government and father of the republican Andreas Papandreou who came to power in the 1980s.

cleverly produced a bottle of ouzo, a nauseating Greek liqueur tasting like a cheap cough mixture. It is the colour of water, and Tommy, thinking it was water, obligingly filled up a glass of whisky with it and handed the contents to me. I have never felt nearer death.

The Archbishop impressed the Prime Minister as much as he had the rest of us and we are now in the curious topsy-turvy position of the Prime Minister feeling strongly pro-Damaskinos (he even thinks he would make a good Regent) while the S. of S. is inclined the other way.

Ajax is temporarily the Flagship of Admiral Mansfield, who is a man of great charm. The Captain, Cuthbert, was in the Cabinet Office early in the war and greeted me as an old friend. One or two of the complement of *K.G. V.*, who brought us home last January, are also on board. The ship's company celebrated Christmas in a big way and the Archbishop's arrival coincided with a deafening rendering of "The First Noel" by the ship's carol party. This seemed very appropriate. Parties in the various Messes continued until a very late hour.

This morning the sun is shining brightly and I have just persuaded the P.M. to get up and go out on the quarter-deck. From the bridge one can see the smoke of battle in the street fighting west of the Piraeus, and there is a constant noise of shell-fire and machine-guns. We had a splendid view of Beaufighters strafing an E.L.A.S. stronghold on the side of one of the hills surrounding Athens. Four of them went round and round, diving with all their cannons blazing and then joining in behind the tail of the preceding aircraft to continue the process. As E.L.A.S. seem to be deficient of flak, however well provided they may be with other weapons, the Beaufighters seem to be having a very pleasant time.

There is no nonsense about fraternising among the troops here, who, to a man, consider E.L.A.S. and all their works utterly loathsome. I have spoken to several and I gather that there is a general sense of anger at the attitude of the British press and certain elements of the Labour Party. Nobody here has any illusions about the real character of the rebels. On the other hand E.L.A.S., in spite of their diabolical activities, have a strangely obliging side to them. For instance, the telephone exchange is in the hands of E.L.A.S. but they have never yet made any difficulties about our telephoning messages from the aerodrome to G.H.Q., even though these, in the form sent, provide them with no useful information. Macmillan says that they possess many of the qualities and defects of the Irish.

The above was written after lunch and it is now 11.45 p.m. with the bag almost closing. This afternoon's events were the purest melodrama. Just before we left the ship we were straddled by shells and another fell quite close as we landed. The meeting with the Greeks was preceded by long sessions at the Embassy, in which the Archbishop figured prominently. There were photographs in the garden and the Prime Minister made a stirring speech to the staff of the Embassy thanking them for their excellent work in arduous conditions. This gave enormous pleasure both to Leeper and to the staff. It looked as if E.L.A.S. would not turn up for the meeting and the Archbishop had made his opening speech and the P.M. was halfway through his, when there were noises off and three shabby desperadoes, who had been searched and almost stripped before being allowed to enter, came into the dimly-lit conference room. All the British delegation, the American, the Russian and the Frenchman, rose to their feet, but the Greek Government remained firmly seated. The P.M. was only prevented from rushing to shake the E.L.A.S. people by the hand by Field Marshal Alexander's bodily intervention.

The proceedings then began all over again and, with the sound of rocket-firing Beaufighters, and bursting mortar shells without, the light of a few Hurricane lamps within and the spectacle of what was surely the oddest galaxy of stars ever assembled in one place, one had continually to rub one's eyes to be sure one was not dreaming. Osbert Lancaster,[1] who sat near me, has promised to send me a second carbon of his first cartoon on the subject.

Since the meeting broke up life has been pretty hectic. Miss Holmes[2] and I, who stayed behind at the Embassy to clear some things up, had a most harrowing return journey. First we fell into the hands of some Greek Home Guards, who viewed my blue uniform with deep suspicion which was, alas, confirmed when I tried to speak to them in German; then as no boat was waiting for us from *Ajax*, and as we were both going the way of Captain Oates, we finally begged a lift from the launch of a Greek destroyer. This was a precarious undertaking and I began to regret it when for the fifth time we failed to come alongside the ship properly and appeared in imminent danger of capsizing. There is no time for more now, but even Lord Moran admits that

---

[1] Writer of books on architecture, which he illustrated, and producer of hilarious "Pocket Cartoons" for the *Daily Express*.

[2] One of the most attractive shorthand-typists at 10 Downing Street whom Churchill sometimes annexed to help with his personal work.

this is an unusual expedition and it is certainly not one which will be forgotten in a hurry.

We are all tired and bewildered but generally speaking happy, and the Prime Minister is in the best of health and spirits, which is the most important thing of all.

Yours ever,
Jock.

On the way home, three days later, I wrote the following as an official record:

DESCRIPTION OF THE CONFERENCE OF GREEK PARTIES
CONVENED BY THE PRIME MINISTER ON TUESDAY,
DECEMBER 26th, 1944

The Conference was due to start at 4.00 p.m., but there was doubt whether the E.L.A.S. representatives, who had been offered a safe conduct through the British lines, would come and several postponements had to be made. Shortly after five o'clock, in the gathering darkness, the Prime Minister, Mr Eden and the remainder of the British party left the Embassy in armoured cars and drove a few hundred yards down the street to the Ministry of Foreign Affairs. The security officials had had a field day: tanks patrolled the streets, an armed cordon surrounded the building, and the passes of everybody approaching the Ministry were closely scrutinised.

The Ministry of Foreign Affairs must at best be a gloomy building, and with the electricity cut off its dinginess was accentuated. Followed by the rest of the party, the Prime Minister was ushered through a seething mob of Greek politicians, of all ages and parties, of security officials and of heavily-armed soldiers, into a large rectangular room devoid of all furniture except an immense table about which some thirty chairs had been placed. The room was lit by hurricane lamps, of varying degrees of brightness, placed on the table, and was heated by evil-smelling oil stoves. Apart from a yellow glow thrown by the lamps on the faces of those seated round the table, darkness prevailed. It was a scene such as would normally be associated with the meeting of some hunted band of conspirators and this no doubt helped the E.L.A.S. delegates, when they finally arrived, to feel at ease and at home.

No seating arrangements had been made, but the Archbishop, who was Chairman of the Conference, sat down in the centre of the table on the right-hand side of the door. Mr Churchill sat on his right with Mr Eden next to him, and on the left of the Archbishop sat Field Marshal Alexander. The other British representatives spread themselves on either side facing members of the Greek Government. Monsieur Papandreou sat opposite Mr Churchill and next to him was General Plastiras,[1] whose fierce mien and waxed moustaches were the cynosure of all eyes. At the end of the table facing the door were the American Ambassador, Mr Mac-Veagh, the French Minister, Monsieur Beynet, and the Soviet Military representative, Colonel Popoff.

Room was left at the other end of the table, near the door, for the representatives of E.L.A.S., should they decide to come. But as time passed and they made no appearance, it was decided to begin the Conference. The Archbishop rose to his feet, a tall and impressive figure in his black robes and high black hat. His speech welcoming the Prime Minister and Mr Eden was admirably interpreted, sentence by sentence, by Major Matthews and when he sat down Mr Churchill, who was also interpreted with great fluency, began his address.

He had not, however, been speaking for more than four or five minutes when noises without heralded the belated arrival of the E.L.A.S. delegates. They were first well searched, and General Mandakas, who had brought with him a Mauser rifle and large quantities of ammunition, was required to lay them aside. He refused on principle to hand his weapons over to British troops but eventually a compromise was reached whereby the arms were placed in an empty room, the door locked and a guard placed outside. The Conference waited patiently while all this took place, and then the three E.L.A.S. leaders, dressed shabbily in khaki battledress and glancing furtively around as if they expected a trap, shuffled into the room. Following the Prime Minister's example, the British representatives and the Allied observers rose to their feet with one accord and bowed to the new arrivals. The Archbishop followed suit, but the members of the Greek Government remained firmly seated and did not so much as turn their heads to the door. The E.L.A.S. delegates sat down, Monsieur Partsalides on the right, Monsieur Siantos, the Secretary and brains of the rebel committee, in the middle and General Mandakas on the left.

It was decided to begin the proceedings again. The Archbishop repeated his speech and Mr Churchill then spoke for half an hour addressing his remarks largely in the direction of the E.L.A.S.

---

[1] The Prime Minister would insist on referring to him as General Plaster-arse.

delegates. Gradually, as Mr Churchill proceeded, the three rebel leaders lost their look of intimidation and seemed to abandon their suspicion of an intended "*coup de main*". Perhaps it was wholesome that whenever they raised their eyes from the table they looked straight into the glittering spectacles, spotless uniform and impeccable bearing of Colonel Popoff, whose appearance was every inch that of an officer and a gentleman.

While the Prime Minister was speaking, the sound of gun-fire went on ceaselessly without, and at one moment the roar of descending rockets, launched by Beaufighters at some nearby enemy position, almost drowned his words. Field Marshal Alexander followed with a short but powerfully-reasoned speech which clearly left its effect on his audience. When he had finished, the Archbishop enquired whether any of the Greek representatives had questions to ask. There was an awkward pause and it was evident that a difference of opinion existed in the E.L.A.S. ranks. However just as the Prime Minister was suggesting that the British representatives should depart and leave the Greeks to their own deliberations, an aged Royalist, Monsieur Maximos, rose to his feet and, instead of asking a question, made a short and highly-coloured speech of welcome. He was followed by Monsieur Papandreou, whose speech was equally ponderous but a great deal longer, and who spoke with evident shyness and embarrassment. Then Monsieur Partsalides of E.L.A.S. arose and, beginning with the utmost diffidence, his eyes bent downwards, paid a glowing tribute to Mr Churchill. However as he warmed to his subject, his excitement got the better of him, he raised his eyes which flashed in the lamp-light and spoke with such speed and vehemence that the interpreter was unable to get a word in edgeways and was obliged to give up the unequal task. As it was clear that his speech was largely based on a misunderstanding of the intention of the Conference Mr Eden said a few words of explanation.

The time had now come to leave the Greeks to their own devices and so, headed by the Prime Minister, the British representatives walked out of the room, shaking hands as they left with members of the Greek Government and lastly with the delegates of E.L.A.S., whose bows could not have been lower, handshakes warmer nor protestations more friendly had they been ambassadors of a party under the deepest obligation to Great Britain.

On the steps of the Ministry of Foreign Affairs, while Mr Churchill was entering his armoured car. there was a further alarum, and indeed excursion, as various Greeks, headed by the eighty-four-year-old Liberal leader, Monsieur Sophoulis, made a desperate effort to flee from the Conference chamber. They were however firmly held and persuaded to return to their places at the council table.

So ended the opening session of what must surely be the strangest conference which a British Prime Minister and Foreign Secretary have ever attended.

Wednesday, December 27th

They treated us with great kindness and hospitality on board H.M.S. *Ajax* but what with the depth charges exploding by way of precaution all night and bluejackets continually bringing telegrams into my cabin I had very little sleep.

Today it was colder on the quarter-deck and the clouds obscured the sun. We lay in Phaleron Bay, with a fine view of Athens, the Piraeus, Mount Hymettus and, on the other side, Aegina and Salamis.

Eden and Dixon went ashore early to see the Archbishop and hear the result of last night's inter-Greek discussions. The P.M., Lord Moran, Tommy and I followed at noon. The rest of the party drove to the Embassy in an enclosed armoured car, but I followed behind in a smaller one with an open turret and, clutching a Tommy gun in my hands, was able to look out upon the crowds in the streets, the Acropolis, the Temple of Zeus, etc. I had last seen Athens in 1934.

There was excitement before lunch when, as the P.M. was about to set off with General Scobie for a review of our military dispositions, a burst of machine-gun fire, coming from well over a mile away, struck the wall of a house some thirty feet over his head. Several bursts were fired and a woman in the street was killed. I was amused by our troops whose first reaction was to fix bayonets. We lunched at the Embassy. I sat between Mrs Leeper and Osbert Lancaster, now press attaché to the Embassy.

After lunch the P.M. saw MacVeagh, the American Ambassador, and gave him a piece of his mind about the very inadequate support the U.S.A. have given us in this affair. He then held a press conference, speaking to the dirtiest and most unreliable collection of "news hawks" ever assembled. The P.M. was not at his best, but the conference was not unsuccessful and the press, so I gathered from Osbert Lancaster, were pleased. It was bitterly cold in the Embassy, there being no coal for heating, and we all felt rather worried about the P.M. The Chancery, in which Osbert L. and I spent hours correcting Miss Layton's shorthand report of the P.M.'s speech to the press, was warmer; but we were all chilled to the marrow when, at about 7.30 p.m. we left to return to the ship.

The Embassy is not a gay place and I thought the Ambassador, Leeper, rather grim.

On board all was light, warmth and comfort again. F.M. Alexander and Macmillan were there. The P.M. said he regretted having refused to see the E.L.A.S. delegates, but the Archbishop as well as his own colleagues had been against it.

Thursday, December 28th

There was a last-minute possibility of our staying for another session of the conference, but finally it was decided against and we went ashore at lunch-time, after the P.M. had addressed the ship's company on the quarter-deck.

We flew away from Kalamaki airfield at 2.00 and lunched as we flew westwards down the Gulf of Corinth. Attica and the islands, Parnassus and the Peloponnese crowned with snow, were glorious in the sun and the unbroken visibility.

Alexander and Macmillan flew back with us. When we reached Pomigliano, just before dusk, we got into cars and drove through Naples to the Field Marshal's guest villa. I drove with Air Marshal Slessor who is a charming companion.

We dined at the villa as Alexander's guests. Sir John Cunningham, C. in C., Mediterranean, was there and so were Slessor and General Harding, Alexander's Chief of Staff. I sat next to the latter and had an amusing three-cornered conversation, largely about Parliament, with him and Eden. After dinner we sat about in the drawing-room and the C. in C.'s A.D.C.s joined us.

Friday, December 29th

Rising at 6.00 a.m. we flew away from Pomigliano at 8.00 a.m. The weather, as throughout the expedition, was glorious. We saw Rome and Ostia below us to starboard, with the Tiber winding its way inland, and then it was Corsica, crowned with snow, the Mediterranean, deep blue, Toulon, Narbonne, and the Pyrenees on our left. There was no cloud, as we flew northwards at between six and eight thousand feet, until we had crossed the Loire. We lunched aboard and when I saw Mt St Michel I started a hare by pointing out that the Channel Isles were still in German hands; but we were assured that our course went far eastwards of them. In the air I dictated a description of the conference at Athens.

It was fine over England and one could see the ground white with frost, but there was thick fog over London itself and so we landed on an American aerodrome at Bovingdon near Watford. Mrs C., Jack, John Martin, John Peck and Lady Moran were there to greet us. Lord M. had, incidentally, shamelessly unfolded to me during the morning his plan for becoming Provost of Eton, an appointment for which he would in every way be unsuitable. It is a Crown appointment so he wanted my advice whether he should go straight to the P.M. and ask for it. I said, very definitely, no. All this was wrapped round with protestations of having no ambitions but of this being forced on him by friends, etc.

Sunday, December 31st
At Ardley. A long and undisturbed sleep, the first for some days, was very refreshing. Went to church with Joan and the children. Clear blue skies and a hard frost under foot – weather which has lasted since before Christmas.

Listened to the B.B.C. broadcast ushering the New Year in (very ineffective) and then to the opening of a broadcast by Hitler, who seemed in low spirits.

29

Build-up to Yalta

January 1945

Monday, January 1st
Sunshine and frost at Ardley. Bicycled to Middleton with Ann[1] and drank rum with Diane Maxwell.

Returned to No. 10 in the evening to find the P.M. ice-bound at Chequers and a pile of work awaiting me.

Tuesday, January 2nd
Admiral Sir Bertram Ramsay was killed in an air crash. The P.M. composed a crushing letter to Barrington-Ward[2] about *The Times'* attitude on the Greek question, but after consultation with Eden, Brendan, etc., decided not to send it. Meanwhile letters, etc., from British troops in Greece show them 100 per cent behind the Government.

Wednesday, January 3rd
The P.M. went off to Versailles to visit SHAEF and subsequently Monty. He spurned the company both of the Defence Office and the Private Office and took with him a strange trio, Commander Thompson, Kinna[3] and Sawyers.

Thursday, January 4th
It transpires that Archbishop Damaskinos' name is also Papandreou. As Regent he has now appointed General Plastiras Prime

---

[1] Ann Elliot, formerly Child-Villiers.
[2] Geoffrey Dawson's successor as Editor of *The Times*.
[3] One of the clerks at No. 10 next in seniority to Charles Barker. Bright, intelligent and alert, he could take shorthand and sometimes, when Churchill was going somewhere where he judged "the young ladies" might be in danger, Pat Kinna accompanied him on his journeys.

Minister. Leeper says in a telegram: *"Papandreou est mort; vive Papandreou."*

I heard with sorrow that Derek Dickson, Joe Stubbs and Gibbons, all of 168 Squadron, together with several others, have been killed in the last few days. The R.A.F. had a rough time on New Year's morning, the Luftwaffe coming over in strength at 0 feet and destroying many aircraft on the ground.

Friday, January 5th

The P.M. returned from France, confident about the position on the northern flank of the German breakthrough, where Monty is in command, but less sure of the southern sector.

Things are in something of a trough; Stalin has recognised the Lublin Poles, in face of our and U.S. requests that he should not; de Gaulle is throwing his weight about in military affairs; Drew Pearson, the most venomous of American columnists, has published another of our secret documents (about Italy this time) which he has procured from the State Department somehow or other; and V.2 rockets are falling like autumnal leaves.

Stole away after lunch to Hendon and flew an elegant M.38[1] put at my disposal by Commander Brabner, Under S. of S. for Air.

The P.M. says that sending Tedder to Moscow to talk about purely military affairs is like asking a man who has learned to ride a bicycle to paint a picture.

He is also incensed with Stafford Cripps for making a speech about brotherly feelings for the Germans. He says he might agree with such sentiments when victory is won, but not with a great battle raging and the Huns shooting captured soldiers in cold blood. (Eisenhower tells him they have shot 130 prisoners of war.) To bed at 2.45 a.m.

Sunday, January 7th

Went to the early service at Westminster Abbey which looks very romantic by candlelight on a dark morning.

Spent the evening and the night with Tommy Lascelles and his family at their house in Windsor Castle.

Monday, January 8th

A cold and very frosty morning. Windsor looked magnificent. Returned to London where rockets are becoming much too frequent and where the Mean Point of Impact seems to be moving westwards.

---

[1] Single-engined two-seater aircraft.

The P.M. returned from Chequers rather depressed, in spite of reassuring news from Monty. His prevalent feelings were shown in a letter to someone to whom he sent best wishes for this "new, disgusting year". John Peck thinks the prospect of the end of the war and the problems it will bring with it are depressing the P.M.; but John's view is that that is a cheap price to pay for the end of the war. Dictated myriads of letters, some harsh, some sloppy, but all dull. Jasper Ridley,[1] intelligent, experienced and wise, dined in the Mess. Snow falling and lying deep.

Tuesday, January 9th
The P.M. has a cold which, he says, is attacking on a broad front. So he saw the King of Yugoslavia in bed and told him in terms of no uncertainty how his only hope lay in consenting to the agreement reached between Subasic[2] and Tito and in agreeing to a Regency. After the King had gone, the P.M. and Eden said that if they were him they would do just the opposite to what they had been advising him and snap their fingers at Tito.

It would be hard to find two worse advertisements for hereditary monarchy than George of Greece and Peter of Yugoslavia.

About midnight, while Lord Beaverbrook and Brendan were closeted in the P.M.'s bedroom, having come no doubt on some nefarious intrigue (anti-Bevin, whom the P.M. cherishes above all Labour Ministers, I suspect), Anthony Eden rang up in a storm of rage. It was about a minute from Lord Cherwell, forwarded by the P.M. to the F.O., in which Eden's assertions about the starvation confronting Europe were flatly denied. Eden told me he would resign if inexpert, academic opinions were sought on subjects to which he had given so much thought. I put him through to the P.M., to whom he ranted in a way in which neither the P.M. nor I (who was listening in) had ever heard him before. The P.M. handled the storm in a very adept and paternal way, said he would take the Prof.'s paper back and go into it himself, protested at Anthony vexing himself with such matters at the end of a long, weary day, and said there was only one thing he could and would not allow: the feeding of Europe at the expense of an already hard-rationed England.

Monty's triumphant, jingoistic and exceedingly self-satisfied

---

[1] The Hon. Sir Jasper Ridley, erudite trustee of the British Museum and Chairman of the Tate Gallery. For many years executive Chairman of Coutts and Co.

[2] Dr Subasic, the Ban (Governor) of Croatia was envisaged as a new head of the Royal Yugoslav Government who might be found acceptable to Marshal Tito, himself a Croat.

talk to the press on Sunday has given wide offence. Now that he is in command of the northern part of the salient, where things are going well, he has won his point – or part of it – over Eisenhower and is indecently exultant. The P.M. has countered, to soothe the Americans (who are also rather worked up by an outspoken attack on American complacency and superiority in the *Economist*, written by Geoffrey Crowther) by means of a published telegram of congratulations to Omar Bradley.

At 1.00 a.m. came telegrams from Athens to the effect that E.L.A.S. were asking for a truce, good news which caused the P.M. to expatiate on the wisdom of holding firm. To bed at 2.00.

Wednesday, January 10th

Snow deep on the ground and bright sun. The P.M. remained in bed. He is disgusted that the President should want to spend only five or six days at the coming meeting between "the Big Three" and says that even the Almighty required seven to settle the world. (An inaccuracy which was quickly pointed out to him. Viz. Genesis I.)

Lunched at the Reform with Nicko Henderson who says that H.M.G. are assuming the role of Metternich in the concert of Europe, a demonstrably unfair historical parallel.

Thursday, January 11th

It looks as if our policy in Greece is going to triumph, to the discomfiture of critics here and in the U.S.A. The Greek Socialist Party and Trade Unions have passed powerful resolutions in support of H.M.G. and denouncing E.L.A.S.; E.L.A.S. at Salonica have surrendered; General Scobie's new and enlarged terms in Attica look like being accepted. The P.M. therefore thinks he will have a debate next week instead of the following week so as to strike in the House of Commons while the iron is hot.

King Peter of Yugoslavia has rejected the P.M.'s and Foreign Secretary's advice and has issued an announcement refusing to accept certain parts of the Tito-Subasic agreement and the establishment of a Regency (unless he chooses the Regents). He has acted against the advice of his Prime Minister, but on that of Princess Aspasia[1] of Greece and probably of Derek Mond (Melchett's son). So H.M.G. are going to drop his cause.

Archie Sinclair is in a tangle about scandals concerning the R.A.F. pig farm at Regent's Park and the administration of

---

[1] Widow of King George's brother Alexander who had been King for a short time but had been poisoned by the bite of a pet monkey. Her daughter married King Peter of Yugoslavia.

B.O.A.C. General Critchley[1] is at the bottom of both. Archie is despondent.

The P.M., who was angry because I carried no revolver when we were in Athens, reverted to the subject tonight and said if I did not procure one he wouldn't take me on any further trips. So I shall.

Friday, January 12th

Minor Greek crisis owing to the fact that Scobie has signed a truce with E.L.A.S. without first stipulating the release of the hostages.

To Stansted for the week-end. Lord and Lady Bessborough, Moyra and George were there. There were two other guests, Oswald Normanby,[2] for three years a prisoner of war and now P.P.S. to Lord Cranborne, and a Canadian soldier called Maxwell Bruce.

Saturday, January 13th

Shot in the morning, walking round clumps of trees and a duck pond with Normanby and George Ponsonby.[3] We killed five cock pheasants, three duck, a partridge, three rabbits, two grey squirrels and a green woodpecker (for which I was guilty – it flew like a teal). Among the duck was a Golden Eye, which I shot.

Monday, January 15th

The P.M. received, very formally, a Labour Deputation about Greece. He insisted on my having them all seated in the Cabinet Room before he came up from luncheon so that he might avoid shaking hands with Aneurin Bevan.

Tuesday, January 16th

The P.M. has something of a sore throat and so, after taking Questions (the House reassembled today), he retired to bed and spent the day there, composing his speech on the war for next Thursday and emptying his box.

---

[1] Brigadier A. C. Critchley, M.P. A soldier in the First World War who joined the R.A.F. in the Second World War and was much engaged in business deals.

[2] Oswald, 4th Marquess of Normanby. Taken prisoner in 1940 when serving with the Green Howards, he was justly praised for organising the return home, with German consent, of a number of gravely wounded British prisoners. Married Lord Moyne's daughter, Grania Guinness, and became Chairman of King's College Hospital and the National Art Collection Fund. Lord Lieutenant of North Yorkshire.

[3] Youngest son of Lord and Lady Bessborough, accidentally killed shortly after joining the 9th Lancers. Another of the Bessboroughs' sons had been killed many years before in a riding accident.

Looking at the messages and letters that go out from this office under the P.M.'s signature, I often think how difficult it will be for future historians to know what is "genuine Churchill" and what is "school of". We are all fairly good imitators of his epistolary style now, and though his speeches are of course all original, as are most of his minutes, only a few of his letters and messages are. But I defy anyone to trace a bar sinister in my message to Papandreou signed today or in recent letters I have composed for the P.M.'s signature to M. Lebrun, Mrs Philip Guedalla, Mrs Wendell Willkie, Mrs Denys Reitz, etc.

Wednesday, January 17th
The Russian offensive, which began last week, proceeds with great éclat. Today Warsaw was taken and spirits, depressed by the German success against the Americans, are again soaring in the belief the war may yet end in a comparatively short time.

I lunched with the P.M. and Mrs C. at the Annexe to meet the new South African High Commissioner, Mr Heaton Nicholls, and his wife. Others present were Brendan, Lady Ismay, Cousin Nellie Graham, Edward Bridges and Mary, who is off to Antwerp shortly in command of the A.T.S. in her battery. I sat between Mary, looking very pretty, and Cousin Nellie. When the Heaton Nichollses were leaving, the P.M. said to him, "Smuts and I are like two old love-birds moulting together on a perch but still able to peck."

Attended a meeting at the F.O., with Alec Cadogan, Edward Bridges and Gilbert Laithwaite about the publication of Keith Feiling's biography of Neville Chamberlain. Agreed that Feiling should be pressed to postpone publication; the matter, much of it based on official papers, is too controversial and Neville's comments, especially on the Americans and the Russians, too caustic.

Thursday, January 18th
In spite of a cold and sore throat, which had kept him in bed some days, the P.M. gaily opened the debate on the war situation in the House. He spoke for over two hours, dividing his speech for luncheon. He was in great form, both witty and combative. Before lunch he spoke of foreign politics and particularly Greece, trouncing Gallacher, Aneurin Bevan and other interruptors. His allusion to *The Times*' deplorable attitude to the Greek crisis – he referred to a "time-honoured" newspaper – evoked a roar of laughter and applause such as I have seldom heard. In the afternoon his speech was less pugnacious, but very eloquent. Indeed, rhetorically, it was the best effort I have heard him make since 1941 or even 1940.

Friday, January 19th

The P.M. stayed in bed, but rushed down to the House at 4.00 to hear Eden wind up the debate and to vote in the division (which was brought about by that ass, Sir R. Acland, leader of the New Commonwealth Party).[1]

Saturday, January 20th

Snow again. The P.M. is spending the week-end in London, because of his cold. So as it is my "Chequers week-end", I am in attendance. The Annexe is gloomy and one has all the hard work of Chequers, and the late hours, without any of the perquisites.

Attlee has written a very blunt letter to the P.M., protesting (i) against the P.M.'s lengthy disquisitions in Cabinet on papers which he has not read and on subjects which he has not taken the trouble to master; (ii) against the P.M.'s undue attentiveness to Brendan and Lord Beaverbrook, whose views, often entirely ignorant, are apt to be thrown into the scale against the considered opinion of a Cabinet Committee when that Committee brings its views to the War Cabinet. This has happened several times recently. Greatly as I love and admire the P.M. I am afraid there is much in what Attlee says, and I rather admire his courage in saying it. Many Conservatives, and officials such as Cadogan and Bridges, feel the same. However, the P.M. exploded over Attlee's letter, drafted and redrafted a sarcastic reply, said it was a socialist conspiracy, harped on nothing but the inadequate representation of the Tories in the Cabinet, in spite of their numerical weight in the House (which is beside the point), and worst of all, finally read Attlee's very personal letter – poorly typed by his own hand so that none of his staff should see it – to Beaverbrook on the telephone, having first of all discussed it with Mrs Churchill. As John Martin said, "that is the part of the P.M. which I do not like."

However, what of it? The Russians sweep gaily on, past Lodz, past Cracow, over the Silesian border. The war, once again, enters a fast-moving, thrilling phase and hopes rise high.

After dinner there was a film in an air-ministry room on the ground floor in King Charles Street. The P.M. bid us all cast care aside and "not bother about Atler or Hitlee", and so all the typists, drivers, servants, etc., saw first of all a first-class newsreel of the Luftwaffe attack on our airfields in Holland on New Year's Day and then Bette Davis in *Dark Victory*, a brilliantly acted film and one of the few I have seen end as a tragedy.

---

[1] A short-lived experiment to found a new left-wing party. It won by-elections at Gravesend and Chelmsford, presumably a rebellion by the local electorate against the "Party Truce"; but it received only temporary support.

Sunday, January 21st
Snow lying deep, but a bright sun. The P.M. having worked till
2.30 a.m. did not wake till 11.30, when he said he felt recovered
and that life had returned.

Walked in St James's Park with Mrs Churchill, who says that she
thinks Attlee's letter of yesterday both true and wholesome. The
last straw – to the P.M. – was when Lord Beaverbrook, against
whom it was partly aimed, said he thought it a very good letter after
seeing it at luncheon today. Finally the P.M., still sorely piqued but
probably in his heart of hearts not unmoved by the arguments, sent
Attlee a short, polite acknowledgment.

Another film after dinner, a very good thriller about blackmail,
Edward G. Robinson in *The Woman in the Window*. The P.M. said
that Robinson "is just like Max".

Monday, January 22nd
Things have slackened off a little, at any rate in comparison with
the frenetic rush before Christmas.

The Russians are within 165 miles of Berlin and still advancing.
King Peter, in the hands of his mother-in-law, has dismissed his
Government and burnt his boats. We proceed without him.

Tuesday, January 23rd
The snow is still lying and more seems to be on the way. The P.M.
sat up late with Harry Hopkins, who arrived yesterday from
Washington. Brendan, who in 1941 said Hopkins was the finest of
men, said tonight he was weak, useless and only courted because of
his probably illusory influence with the President.[1]

When going to bed the P.M. said to me, "Make no mistake, all
the Balkans, except Greece, are going to be Bolshevised; and there
is nothing I can do to prevent it. There is nothing I can do for poor
Poland either."

It seems that on the Eastern Front the Russians, whose spectacular advance continues, have a superiority of: 12–1 in tanks, 12–1 in
aircraft and 7–1 in men.

Wednesday, January 24th
The P.M. told me that today was the fiftieth anniversary of his
father's death. It is a strange descent, Lord Randolph, Winston,
Randolph, with many characteristics in common, such as a capacity for being utterly unreasonable, but great differences of personality.

---

[1] Cf. Brendan Bracken's comments to me on January 10th, 1941 (Chapter 13).

Thursday, January 25th
With snow lying and persistent hard frosts it looks as if there is to be a recurrence of the 1940 conditions.

Went to the House with the P.M. who lost his temper with Lord Winterton over the question of an enquiry about alleged irregularities in the administration of B.O.A.C. He then couldn't open his box, so we had to force it in an ante-room. Finally he made quite a good impromptu speech about the rebuilding of the House of Commons.

Friday, January 26th–Sunday, January 28th
Went to Ardley with Mother. David was on leave and I celebrated my birthday delightfully in the bosom of my family. All the same I don't feel thirty.

The weather was bitterly cold. Snow covered the fields and roads and the temperature remained doggedly below freezing point. But the January sun shone every day and the trees, white with snow, glistened entrancingly. On Saturday night David and I shot pigeon. In my R.A.F. "escape-boots" the cold was of no significance and the scene was like fairyland. In church, on Sunday, the pale sunlight streamed on to a scanty congregation and overhead, ceaselessly, we heard the drone of many Fortresses on their way to the battle line.

Meanwhile, in this unusually bitter month, the Germans are fleeing from their homes in East Germany and themselves experiencing the miseries which, albeit in summer, others suffered at their hands in 1940.

Monday, January 29th
After a two-hour wait on Bicester platform I returned to London, feeling myself like a refugee from Breslau.

In the evening the P.M., accompanied by John Martin (Leslie Rowan will follow; he has flu), left for Malta, whither Eden and the Chiefs of Staff have preceded him, en route for Yalta in the Crimea where ARGONAUT, the conference between Stalin, Roosevelt and the P.M., will take place. The conditions there sound ghastly and I am glad not to be going.[1]

---

[1] Churchill invited me to go, but it would have upset office arrangements in London and John Martin (to my disappointment) dissuaded him. This saved my life, for there was no more room in the Prime Minister's C.47 and I should have been in the York which crashed off Pantelleria, having lost the way to Naples, killing all but one of the passengers.

Wednesday, January 31st
All very dreary and wet. Moreover Guy Millard at the F.O., being quite unable to draft a telegram to Turkey to warn the Turks that the P.M. would be flying over Turkish territory, I had to send for the F.O. file and do it myself which was annoying.

The Russians took Landsberg, the key point in what is thought to be the last line of defences before Berlin. *Sieg Heil!* Last night I listened in to the Führer, broadcasting on the twelfth anniversary of his accession to power. He was gloomy but more eloquent than of late.

30

Appeasing Stalin

February 1945

Thursday, February 1st
I went to see Ralph Assheton, Chairman of the Conservative
Party, about my adoption as a candidate at the next election. He
seemed to favour the idea, but the difficulty is bread and butter. If I
resign from the F.O. I must find some alternative means of
subsistence. Journalism seems a possibility, and the kind offices of
Lords Kemsley or Camrose might be solicited. The Beaver would,
I think, be very ready to help, but nothing would induce me to put
myself under such an obligation.

Dined at the Reform with Nicko Henderson and Frank
Pakenham.[1] We discussed foreign policy. Frank P., who is standing for Oxford against Quintin Hogg[2] at the next Election, is full of
theories, the main one being the importance of directing policy by
principles rather than *"raison d'état"*. His admiration for De
Valera is profound.

Friday, February 2nd
A York, containing some of the ARGONAUT party, crashed in the sea
off Lampedusa. Several members of the Foreign Office, including
Peter Loxley, were killed and also one of the officers, Newy by
name, from the Defence Map Room.

Rosemary Hinchingbrooke took me to dine with Miss Joan

---

[1] Afterwards 7th Earl of Longford. As a Labour Minister, he later held many
offices including the Admiralty and the leadership of the House of Lords. Also
Chairman of the National Bank and of Sidgwick and Jackson (publishers).
[2] Learned lawyer, Fellow of All Souls and Q.C. First Lord of the Admiralty at the
time of the Suez affair in 1956 and twice Lord Chancellor. Witty, explosive and
a genuinely devout Christian who combined ambition with good nature,
kindness and scrupulous honesty.

Haslip[1] in a flat in Carrington House. The other guests were the Archduke Robert of Austria, Mrs Simon Harcourt Smith[2] (gay, attractive, *bas bleu* and a shade Rodd-ish) and Baron Gondalfieri, a courteous man with polished manners and half closed eyes who represents the Italian Government in Dublin. The Baron said that whether or not Italy went Communist was a question of food. The Archduke said that Berchtesgaden should be given to Austria as an attraction for tourists (all Germans being forbidden entry) and a source of income to the Austrian State. Mrs Harcourt Smith told diplomatic stories in a drawl and waxed eloquent about the art of cooking. Miss Haslip attacked the left-wing prejudices of the B.B.C. staff, among whom she works. Rosemary, who expects a child any moment, looked delightful but said little.

Tuesday, February 13th

The Prof., who is very much of a Jeremiah these days, tells me that nobody realises the horror of our financial prospects. We are facing an Economic Dunkirk. It is no use Amery, etc., talking about our having "a splendid market"; one might as well say that he, Prof., was a great asset to Claridges merely because he had a splendid appetite. We could only hope to survive if we took the German and Japanese pre-war markets, and as for Germany she must not be allowed to export but must live on an autarchic system and accept a low standard of living.

I know nothing of economics, but instinctively I feel the Prof.'s views to be both immoral and unsound.

Wednesday, February 14th

Ash Wednesday and St Valentine's day, an inharmonious combination. Blue skies and sunshine which enabled the air forces to destroy Dresden. The P.M. stopped in Athens to receive an ovation from the populace, freed from fear if not from want.

Everybody is furious that the British offensive near Cleves is being called Canadian and British troops are getting hardly any kudos. This is because the "1st Canadian Army" is the unit, but practically all the divisions taking part are British. Such self-effacement, which has characterised our publicity throughout the war, gives great offence and makes many people adopt a very jingoistic attitude in conversation.

I saw a V.2 airburst – a loud explosion and a cloud of white

---

[1] Well-known author and broadcaster.
[2] Daughter of the former Ambassador to Rome, Sir Rennell Rodd (1st Lord Rennell).

smoke – in the blue sky to the north-west. It seemed to be over Sloane Street but was in fact over Finchley.

Thursday, February 15th

Read the full and interesting records of the Plenary Conferences at the Crimea. We seem to have won most of our points and the P.M. has won another great personal success. He was tireless in pressing for this conference, in spite of Roosevelt's apathy, and deserves most of the credit for what has been achieved.

Before going to bed in the C.W.R., Brendan waxed eloquent on the solid, unshakeable qualities of old Sir Dudley Pound, and Johnny Bevan gave a vivid description of F. M. Alexander when he first saw him: last man in for Harrow at Lords in 1910, a dramatic occasion on which Alex's defiant attitude was very impressive.

Sunday, February 18th

For dinner in the Mess, being short of food, we had to borrow and devour the whole of the P.M.'s and Mrs C.'s meat ration for next week.

Monday, February 19th

The ARGONAUT party was due to return. At the last moment a landing at Northolt was found to be impossible and so they put down at Lyneham. Having myself been all the way to Northolt in vain I then set off for Reading with Mrs C. and found the P.M., Eden and Sarah awaiting us in a hotel (where the management were very startled) while the rest of the retinue were bumping crossly towards London in a Green Line bus.

I drove to London wedged between Eden and Sarah and heard a good deal about the Conference. Eden said that he thought the Tories had no right to complain about Poland. The P.M. had not sold the pass. On the contrary the Curzon line was a boundary proposed as fair by H.M.G. after the last war; we had not committed ourselves to accepting any specific western frontier for Poland; and finally we had only undertaken to recognise a new Polish Government in Poland if and when we were satisfied with its composition.

The P.M. had been very persuasive about the Dumbarton Oaks compromise (voting in the Security Council) and the Russians would have been quite happy to agree to none of their constituent states belonging to the Assembly, had not the Americans foolishly acquiesced. Finally the Americans had been very weak. The President looked old and ill, had lost his powers of concentration and had been a hopelessly incompetent chairman.

It is often forgotten that a primary objective of the British and Americans at Yalta, in days when the successful development of an atomic bomb was still far from certain, was to induce the Russians to join in the war against Japan. It was feared this might last another eighteen months or two years and cost half a million Anglo-American casualties when the main Japanese Islands were assaulted. Stalin's agreement to declare war at the appropriate time (which in the event was only a few days before the Japanese surrender) was regarded as an important achievement. So was the apparent willingness of the Russians to co-operate with the projected United Nations' Organisation and to agree to a "free and unfettered" election in Poland.

Athens had been inspiring and at Corinth, which Eden visited, he had been impressed by the keen interest taken by the British soldiers in the comments of Parliament and the press – a great contrast to the last war. In Cairo Ibn Saud had been magnificent, Shukri Quwaitli (the President of Syria) a shrewd advocate for his case, and the Emperor of Abyssinia had demanded Eritrea and several other territories but had had to be content with a couple of aeroplanes.

When we reached No. 10 the whole Cabinet was waiting to receive the P.M. in the hall and they followed him in to the Cabinet Room to hear an account of his Odyssey.

After dinner James Stuart came in. The P.M. said he was very sorry to hear that William Sidney was likely to oppose the Government over Poland as he was one of those to whom office would be likely to be given. We wanted to put V.C.s in power. Though I like William, I do not agree with this principle – nor, emphatically, does James Stuart. Incidentally I have told Ralph Assheton, with whom I have been discussing my possible parliamentary future, that I would like to be considered for Chelsea when William succeeds to the peerage.

Tuesday, February 20th
Accompanied the P.M. to the House for Questions. He· was received with cheers.

Lunched at the St James's Club with the Archduke Robert and Count Seilen and listened to a diatribe against the Czechs.

Wednesday, February 21st
After lunching with Zara at the 500 Club in Albemarle Street, I returned to the Annexe to receive General Anders[1] who has come

---

[1] Gallant Commander in Chief of the Polish divisions fighting under Alexander's command in Italy.

from his Polish Corps in Italy, black with gloom about the Crimea Conference decision like most of his fighting compatriots. After he had arrived I went to fetch the P.M. from the dining-room where I found Lady Diana Cooper and Venetia Montagu arrayed in the magnificent robes presented to the P.M. by Ibn Saud in Cairo, Lady Diana in purple and striking a dramatic pose.

Thursday, February 22nd
Lunched with John Cairncross, who is less of a bore than he used to be and talked with sense about the barrenness of German philosophy – an imposing façade of a building which had no interior decoration or furnishings.

Went with Betty Montagu to see Flanagan and Allen, etc., at the Victoria Palace and afterwards to dine at Boulestins. It was a beautiful night and we walked back along the Embankment by the misty river.

Friday, February 23rd
The P.M. accepted the draft message which I composed to Stalin on Red Army Day, which is today.

To Chequers. The P.M. dictated his speech for next Tuesday on the way down. As he got out of the car at our journey's end he was still dictating. He paused on the steps of the house and said "whose-whose-whose history has been" (looking up at the house) "chequered and intermingled".

Edward Bridges came to dine and sleep and also Sir Arthur Harris,* C. in C., Bomber Command. The P.M. was rather depressed, thinking of the possibilities of Russia one day turning against us, saying that Chamberlain had trusted Hitler as he was now trusting Stalin (though he thought in different circumstances), but taking comfort, as far as Russia went, in the proverb about the trees not growing up to the sky.

Before dinner, while waiting in the Great Hall for the P.M. to come down, I asked Sir Arthur Harris what the effect of the raid on Dresden had been.

"Dresden?" he said. "There is no such place as Dresden."

Though the obliteration of Dresden later became a topic which aroused widespread indignation, it was not at the time regarded as different from previous "saturation" bombing attacks on Hamburg, Cologne and, above all, Berlin. A principal reason for the Dresden raid was the intelligence report, received from the Russians, that one or possibly two German armoured divisions had arrived there from Italy on their way to reinforce the defence of the eastern front. Churchill was on his way back from Yalta when the raid took place and since it was in accord with the general policy of bombing German towns massively, so as to shatter civilian morale, I do not think he was consulted about the raid. He never mentioned it in my presence, and I am reasonably sure he would have done so if it had been regarded as anything at all special.

With regard to Spaatz,[1] the American air C. in C., the P.M. said, "He is a man of limited intelligence." Harris replied, "You pay him too high a compliment."

At dinner I asked the P.M. if he had read Beverley Nichols' *Verdict on India* which I had urged him to take to Yalta. He said he had, with great interest. He had been struck by the action of the Government of India in not removing a "Quit India" sign which had been placed in a prominent place in Delhi and which Nichols had seen on arrival and on departure a year later. He seemed half to admire and half to resent this attitude. The P.M. said the Hindus were a foul race "protected by their mere pullulation from the doom that is their due" and he wished Bert Harris could send some of his surplus bombers to destroy them. As for Lord Wavell, and his Anthology of Poetry,[2] he thought him "mediocrity in excelsis".

After dinner we saw an amusing film: Bob Hope in *The Princess and the Pirate.* Then we sat in the Great Hall and listened to the *Mikado* played, much too slowly, on the gramophone. The P.M. said it brought back "the Victorian era, eighty years which will rank in our island history with the Antonine age". Now, however, "the shadows of victory" were upon us. In 1940 the issue was clear and he could see distinctly what was to be done. But when Harris had finished his destruction of Germany, "What will lie between the white snows of Russia and the white cliffs of Dover?" Perhaps, however, the Russians would not want to sweep on to the Atlantic or something might stop them as the accident of Ghenghis Khan's death had stopped the horsed archers of the Mongols, who retired and never came back.

Bert Harris: "You mean now they will come back?"

W.S.C.: "Who can say? They may not want to. But there is an unspoken fear in many people's hearts."

---

[1] General Spaatz was asked to dine by the Prime Minister at Carthage in December 1943. Churchill told John Martin to find out how his name was pronounced. "Like S.P.O.T.S.," said the General's A.D.C. So Martin, failing to make allowance for the American pronunciation, was responsible for us all, including the Prime Minister, calling him General Spots throughout the evening.

[2] *Other Men's Flowers.*

After this war, continued the P.M., we should be weak, we should have no money and no strength and we should lie between the two great powers of the U.S.A. and the U.S.S.R. If he lived, he should concentrate on one thing: the air. Harris replied that it would have to be rockets: "The bomber is a passing phase and, like the battleship, it has nearly passed." "Then," said the P.M., "you mean we must make our island into a volcano."

Finale: The P.M. quoted "Ye Mariners of England" at length.

Bert Harris: "That was written before the invention of the 12,000 lb. bomb."

The P.M.: "Ye Doodle Bugs of England . . ."

Saturday, February 24th

President Beneš, who returns to Czechoslovakia to set up his Government next week, came to lunch and was received by a Guard of Honour. Masaryk, the Czech Foreign Secretary, also came, and Phil Nicholls, our Ambassador to the Czechs. Beneš said he had learned much during his six years in England, not least the truth of what President Masaryk had said to him in the last war, that America might be materially far more powerful than England but that England's cultural dominance was supreme and unchallenged. The P.M. said that a small lion was talking between a huge Russian bear and a great American elephant, but perhaps it would prove to be the lion which knew the way.

Duncan and Diana Sandys arrived for dinner, Duncan being in disgrace over a statement he made about housing without first consulting the P.M. or the Cabinet.

Sunday, February 25th

Winant and Prof. came to lunch. After lunch the P.M. said that he would like to make many bitter remarks about the Government if he were not head of it. "There never has been a Prime Minister who has kept up such a steady stream of corrective sneering and jibing against the Government departments" (this apropos of an Air Ministry proposal to employ 1,000 men in an analysis of our bombing results in Germany).

Dinner was very gay and cheerful, the P.M. being at the top of his form. Sarah was there and Diana was at her best. Duncan was cheerful and Winant benevolent though sickening for flu and consequently rather dull.

Monday, February 26th

Returned to London at breakneck speed so that the P.M., who

always starts late, should not keep M. Bidault[1] waiting for lunch. Spent the evening and night with the Greigs at Richmond.

Tuesday, February 27th
Galloped round Richmond Park. The going was good and the weather fine. Sorely in need of air and exercise.

The P.M. made a speech in the House about the Crimea Conference and in particular about Poland. I did not listen. He is trying to persuade himself that all is well, but in his heart I think he is worried about Poland and not convinced of the strength of our moral position.

Wednesday, February 28th
Moley Sargent tells me that the Polish Government's propaganda against the Crimea Agreement has been both extensive and effective. In fact they have been driving home the lesson which Goebbels has sought to instil: Russia is the danger, Russia will seize Poland, Russia wants to dominate Europe; Germany is the only bastion.

I went to the House with the P.M. after lunch. The debate was in full swing on a Conservative amendment in favour of Poland. The level was high. Harold Nicolson's voice was croaky but his delivery good; Manningham Buller was staid and statesmanlike; Willoughby de Eresby a bit like Bertie Wooster; Raikes sincere and eloquent. Eden wound up very well, putting the Government's case most effectively. 396 voted for the Government and twenty-five Tories against. A number abstained. One of them, William Sidney, dined with me afterwards.

In the evening came sinister telegrams from Roumania showing that the Russians are intimidating the King and Government and setting about the establishment of a Communist minority government with all the technique familiar to students of the Comintern. The P.M. was dining at Buckingham Palace, but Eden rang me up and said he viewed these events with great concern because Vyshinski, who was their executor, had come fresh from the understanding and undertakings of Yalta. When the P.M. came back, I spoke to him of the position and he said he feared he could do nothing. Russia had let us go our way in Greece; she would insist on imposing her will in Roumania and Bulgaria. But as

[1] Foreign affairs representative of the French National Committee and later, for many years, Foreign Minister. Some fifteen years earlier he had, as an inconspicuous professor, taught Sarah Churchill when she was at Mademoiselle Ozanne's finishing school for young ladies in Paris.

regards Poland we would have our say. As we went to bed, after 2.00 a.m., the P.M. said to me, "I have not the slightest intention of being cheated over Poland, not even if we go to the verge of war with Russia."

31

Across the Rhine

March 1945

Thursday, March 1st
A quiet day, the P.M. spending the afternoon at the House where the three-day debate ended in a thumping vote of confidence in spite of some Tory abstentions.

Friday, March 2nd
The P.M., accompanied by the C.I.G.S., Pug Ismay, Tommy and John Peck left for a tour of the front, and Mrs Churchill and I accompanied them to Brussels. We left from Northolt in the C.54 at 11.00, a glorious day, and flew over Dungeness, St Omer and Lille (seeing some of the flying bomb sites en route). At Brussels "Mary" Coningham and Mary Churchill met us and we all lunched at Coningham's sumptuous villa, where massed flowers, expensive furniture and rare foods combine to create an effect too luxurious for the H.Q. of an operational commander. Monty's Chief of Staff, Sir Frederick de Guingand was there and I sat next to him – not a very striking man.

After lunch the P.M. and his party left for Monty's H.Q. at the front and Mrs C. and I, whose visit is to Brussels, went to the Embassy with Mary to greet the Knatchbull-Hugessens. He is delightful but seems weak;[1] she is called "Lady Frigid" in Brussels, but beneath a forbidding exterior I found her *"sympathique"* and easy to talk to. There was a large cocktail party at the Embassy.

Mrs C. and Mary dined quietly together at the Embassy. I went back to the Air Marshal's palazzo, where I was staying, and dined

---

[1] Sir Hughe Knatchbull-Hugessen was, when Ambassador in Turkey, the unfortunate victim of his valet, code-named CICERO, who was in the pay of the Germans and was in the habit of removing secret papers from the Ambassador's official box when he was in his bath.

with his S.A.S.O. (A.V.M. Victor Droom) and his P.A., S/Ldr. Fielding Johnson, who has been operational, and decorated, in both wars and who in this war had a son on ops. in the same Group as himself. The son, whom I remember in 170 Squadron at Sawbridgeworth, was missing in a Mosquito last week. We dined well and saw a film (Laurence Olivier and Penelope Dudley Ward in *Demi Paradise*, about a Soviet engineer who came to England).

Saturday, March 3rd

A day spent touring the Y.W.C.A.s, Y.M.C.A.s and service clubs of Brussels. Never can the welfare of the troops have been so lavishly and painstakingly cared for. We saw the magnificent Montgomery Club, in the palace of the Princesse de Ligne, and Mrs C. could not have done her job better or spoken more effectively when called upon to do so. She looked ravishing, was always interested and never condescending.

We lunched at the Embassy and in the afternoon, when the last function was over, Mary and I walked through Brussels, fighting our way through the throng of soldiers on forty-eight hours' leave, walking into shops and visiting the great church of St Gudule with its rugged gothic façade and its grey pillars within. Then we went to have a drink at 2nd T.A.F. H.Q. with Fielding Johnson and some of the crew of the C.54. Mary was, as ever, a great success. She told me of her passion for a French parachutist, de Gannet by name, and her thoughts of becoming a R.C. if she were going to marry him when he returns from the Far East.

There was a dinner party at the Embassy at which was present the new Belgian P.M., Van Acker and his wife, the Foreign Minister and Mme Spaak, the Canadian Ambassador, Aveling (the Counsellor), and la Baronne Boël, a remarkable old lady who spent most of the last war in a German cell and had a pretty hard time in this one. She told me that when she heard of Brest Litovsk[1] from her prison she had despaired and thought that all was lost; remembering this she had never despaired in 1940. After dinner I had a talk with the Ambassador who could not have been more affable. It was strange to see footmen in livery again.

Sunday, March 4th

In the large Daimler which the Air Marshal had put at my disposal I picked up Mary at the Embassy and went with her to the early

---

[1] Treaty of peace between Imperial Germany and Bolshevik Russia at the end of 1917. It was a black day for the Western Allies as the Germans were able to move to the Western front most of their divisions which had been fighting the Russians.

service at the Garrison Church, where, amongst others, was Jean Greig.

During the morning I went for a walk with Mrs C. and we visited the beautiful Grande Place with its Hôtel de Ville and old houses with gilded fronts.

Mrs C. and Mary and the Knatchbull-Hugessens lunched with the Queen Mother at Laeken. I lunched with the Air Marshal who let himself go about Monty who, he said, was the most egotistic man he had ever met. Moreover he was indiscriminate in his ruthlessness and in Normandy had made demands for the elimination of French towns and villages which were unnecessary and many of which Coningham had refused. He aped the Americans who loathed him. Finally his handling of the recent operations, Operations VERITABLE and GRENADE, to clear the west bank of the Rhine, had been slow and, considering the paucity of the opposition, very inadequately executed. After the war Coningham understood that Monty proposed to settle down and write his history of the war and C. had little doubt what sort of bombastic and highly coloured account that would be. Further, Coningham told me he was in favour of dismembering Germany as a means of incapacitating her. Personally I am doubtful and inclined to the view that dismemberment would neither pay nor be permanent.

After lunch Mrs Churchill and I flew back to England in a Dakota. The visibility was poor and the passage bumpy. Returned to find that flying bombs had begun again, from fixed bases in the Netherlands, and that German bombers, for the first time since last spring, had been over England. On the other hand Monty's operations, if they have been slow, are now showing great success and we have reached the Rhine in many places. Everybody is worried about the fate of our prisoners.

Tuesday, March 6th
The P.M. and party returned from General Eisenhower's H.Q. at Rheims in the C.54. I met them at Northolt and drove back with the P.M. who told me he had had a great reception in Holland, at Hertogenbosch, and had spent a good deal of time in Germany itself. He also launched an invective against General Plastiras, P.M. of Greece, who has surrounded himself with an authoritarian and anti-British clique in Athens. He must go.

Wednesday, March 7th
In the evening I accompanied the P.M. to the House to hear him answer Lord Winterton's motion on the adjournment about the right of Members to demand a Select Committee and to obtain it

from the Government. The question at issue was Austin Hopkinson's allegation about irregularities at the Air Ministry (the "Pig Farm") at Regent's Park and B.O.A.C. (in both of which General Critchley is involved). We had to wait till 8.40 p.m. before the debate on the Naval Estimates was finished. I went to the bar to have a drink with Harvie-Watt and talked to Lionel Berry and Johnny Gretton[1] then listened to Pilkington[2] winding up for the Admiralty, an inexpert performance no doubt made more embarrassing for him by the presence of the P.M. since he had deliberately abstained from voting for the Government over the Yalta Conference (Poland) and has offered his resignation as Civil Lord of the Admiralty. Eventually Winterton spoke, convincingly I thought, and then the P.M. made a slashing reply which won applause and laughter too, though I did not think he quite answered Winterton's point.

During dinner I showed the P.M. a telegram from Roumania reporting that the new Russian-sponsored Roumanian Government may forcibly remove Radescu, the late Prime Minister, from the sanctuary which has been given him by the British Military mission. This inflamed the P.M. who saw that our honour was at stake. He subsequently spoke to Eden on the telephone. It seems that we may be heading for a show-down with the Russians who are showing every sign of going back on the Yalta agreement over Poland and of enforcing aggressive Communism on an unwilling Roumania. The P.M. and Eden both fear that our willingness to trust our Russian ally may have been vain and they look with despondency to the future. The P.M. is prepared to put the issue to the House and the Country with confidence in their support, but Eden, though nauseated, still hopes the Russians will not face an open breach with ourselves and the Americans. It looks as if Dr Goebbels' disciples may still be able to say "I told you so"; but, God knows, we have tried hard to march in step with Russia towards the broad and sunlit uplands. If a cloud obscures the sun when we reach them, the responsibility is with Moscow and the bitter, though for the Germans empty, triumph is with Berlin.

---

[1] M.P. for the Burton division of Staffordshire. His father, Chairman of Bass, Ratcliffe and Gretton, owned three yachts including the magnificent ketch, *Cariad*, which won the King's Cup at Cowes six times. He several times lent her to my father.

[2] Having served in the Coldstream Guards and won the M.C. in the Dunkirk campaign, he was appointed Civil Lord of the Admiralty in 1942.

Thursday, March 8th

Went to the House with the P.M. who made a statement about war gratuities and saw various ministers in his room at the House. The war goes better and better: the Americans are over the Rhine north of Coblenz and both we and the Americans are rapidly clearing the west bank of the river. ? The end in April.

Saturday, March 10th

After a heavy day, in the lighter parts of which I devoted myself to writing a memorandum on the acquisition of English pictures and furniture for our Embassies and Government Houses during the inevitable sales of private collections after the war, I went down to Mentmore. Talked to Grandfather before dinner. Though very old, blind and in constant pain, he keeps up a gay demeanour and talks with grasp, wisdom and concentration of the present as of the past. He says he thinks the continuation of a coalition Government after this war will prove to be essential in some form. He told me Lord Randolph Churchill had more charm than Winston but, if that were possible, worse manners.

Sunday, March 11th

Spent the morning reading some of Lord Rosebery's essays and walking round Mentmore. A long talk with Grandfather before lunch. After lunch Sybil Smith[1] came in for a little, then Peggy showed me some of the treasures stowed at Mentmore (including the vast gold lamps from the *Bucentaur*, used when Venice wed the sea and now suspended in the hall). In the house are effigies from Westminster Abbey and pictures from public galleries; in the garden is Le Sueur's Charles I, better visible there than on his pedestal in Trafalgar Square. It really is a magnificent statue, showing so well Charles's obstinate forehead, the strained muscles of his horse's arched neck and even the veins on the animal's left fore-leg. The general effect does not suffer from the wealth of detail. I take pride in having instigated Winston to order its removal from Trafalgar Square. Shortly afterwards a bomb fell a few yards away.

In the riding school is the Speaker's gilded coach, together with more effigies from St Paul's and Westminster and carved choir stalls. A veritable treasure house.

Returned to London in time to dine quietly at the Travellers,

---

[1] Daughter of Lord Rosebery and niece of Lady Crewe.

where I sat with Nigel Ronald[1] who thinks (i) we shall be able to work with the Russians provided we do not expect them to use Western methods of thought and codes of behaviour; (ii) the Roumanians do not expect anything other than what they are at present experiencing from their Soviet conquerors. The Balkan mind does not work like ours.

Monday, March 12th
The P.M. and Mrs C. want me to accompany the latter on her coming tour of Red Cross Centres in Russia, but it would upset the working of the office and also my plans for moving into Mulberry Walk[2] and so I am contracting out, even though six weeks' travel in Russia, in conditions of great comfort and with no work to do, is an attractive idea.

Lunched with Sir David[3] and Lady Kelly at the Ritz. Others present were the Italian representative (Carandini), Chips Channon, Mrs Corrigan,[4] Derek Hoyer Millar,[5] Mrs Leo Lonsdale, the new Dutch Ambassador in Paris (Witz?) and his very pretty wife. I sat between Mrs Lonsdale and Carandini. The latter, an enlightened man, said that Grandi[6] (who has recently been publishing his apologia in the *Daily Express*) was a black-hearted fascist and a double-crossing blackguard. He had said he thought it a distinction to have been condemned to death by Mussolini; he would soon have the double distinction of being condemned to death by the present Italian Government also.

Tuesday, March 13th
Brilliant summer sunshine of the last few days makes one long to be over the hills and far away.

The P.M. was largely occupied with writing his speech for next Thursday's Conservative Party Conference.

The feeding of liberated Europe looms up as one of the most

---

[1] Sir Nigel Ronald, after the war British Ambassador in Lisbon, where I was his Head of Chancery. Seriously wounded in World War I and thereafter always frail, he was immensely well-read and had an encyclopaedic knowledge of music. He was also an expert gardener who delighted in rare and by no means always colourful shrubs.

[2] A house my mother had just bought in Chelsea.

[3] Ambassador to the Argentine in the war and subsequently to Turkey and the Soviet Union. His wife, Marie Noele, was a Belgian.

[4] Rich and socially ambitious American who entertained lavishly in London.

[5] Afterwards Lord Inchyra and Permanent Under Secretary at the Foreign Office. Invariably wise and charming.

[6] Italian Ambassador in London before the war. Too much trusted by those holding office and also by Churchill.

serious problems to be faced. S.H.A.E.F.[1] seem to have made a mess of things and the liberated peoples will soon be saying openly that they were materially better off under the Germans. The reason, apart from S.H.A.E.F.'s incompetence, is partly due to the great diversion of shipping resulting from MacArthur's and Nimitz's unexpected progress against the Japanese in the Pacific.

Thursday, March 15th
The Cabinet talked lengthily about the now serious food supply prospects. After the Cabinet, which is held in the C.W.R. nowadays because of V.2s, the P.M. sits in a chair and is carried upstairs backwards by three stalwart marines. The Cabinet trail behind and the general effect of the procession is utterly ludicrous.

Aunt Addy[2] rang me up during dinner to say that Alick[3] had been killed in a flying accident. I gathered from the Admiralty that it happened yesterday on take-off at the airfield in the Azores. He was a simple, honest and lovable character, genuinely good and in many ways gifted. He was gauche and very shy, but he could be amusing and his gentle, unassuming character made him beloved by the small circle who knew him.

Tuesday, March 20th
Cocktail party given by Harvie-Watt – chiefly politicians and Lobby correspondents. Eddy Marsh[4] dined in the Mess, also an officer in the Welsh Guards, called Hardy, whom I met in the train last Sunday.

The P.M. corrected very considerably the text of a speech Anthony Eden is to make at Glasgow tomorrow, grumbling much about it and saying that Eden was only half educated and had not added to it by subsequent reading. He evidently thought very poorly of the speech. He corrected it at the dining-room table (when he dines alone with Mrs C. at the Annexe they use a small

---

[1] Somewhat over-staffed Supreme Headquarters of the Allied Expeditionary Force under Eisenhower.

[2] Lady Adelaide Colville, daughter of Admiral of the Fleet the Earl of Clanwilliam, sister of Admiral Meade-Fetherstonhaugh and widow of my father's brother, Admiral Sir Stanley Colville.

[3] Viscount Colville of Culross, my first cousin and godfather. He had been a career naval officer in his youth and fought at the battle of Jutland. In 1939 he rejoined and as a Captain R.N.V.R. commanded the naval station in the Azores. He married late in life and had three sons.

[4] Churchill's Private Secretary almost continuously from 1905 to 1929 and his intimate friend. An aesthete, with a prodigious memory, he spoke in a high-pitched squeaky voice and was popular in intellectual circles, not least with "The Souls". A close friend of the poet Rupert Brooke.

circular table in the drawing-room) while I sat opposite him, assented silently to his comments, which were penetrating and to the point, and sipped brandy. Most of the rest of the evening was devoted to Under Secretarial appointments, caused by recent resignations over Poland. The Chief Whip came and Brendan arrived in time to upset the whole apple cart just as everything had been settled. At one moment, in order to check Brendan, the P.M. proceeded to give me a vivid description of the German attack on March 21st, 1918 as he had seen it from 10,000 yards behind the 5th Army front.

The more I contemplate the present trend of opinion and of events, the more sadly I reflect how much easier it will be to forgive our present enemies in their future misery, starvation and weakness than to reconcile ourselves to the past claims and future demands of our two great Allies. The Americans have become very unpopular in England; the Russians are losing their glamour and a few publicised examples of their incorrigibly bad manners and brutal methods of getting their own way will awaken that dread of their future intentions which twenty-five years of Red Bogy propaganda (preceded by a century of the Eastern Question) has left close to the surface in most Englishmen's minds. So far only a few, stirred by the wrongs of Poland and the Baltic States, have given vent to their uneasiness. It is, as Grandfather would say, all very "vexatious".

Mainz and Worms were captured.

Leslie Rowan thinks the P.M. is losing interest in the war, because he no longer has control of military affairs. Up till OVER-LORD he saw himself as Marlborough, the supreme authority to whom all military decisions were referred. Now, in all but questions of wide- and long-term strategy, he is by force of circumstances little more than a spectator. Thus he turns his energies to politics and the coming General Election, varying the diet with occasional violent excursions into the field of foreign politics.

Friday, March 23rd[1]
After a quick lunch with Zara at the Churchill Club I accompanied the P.M., C.I.G.S. and Tommy to Northolt, boarded a Dakota and flew slowly (so slowly that the accompanying fighter escort were reduced to going around in circles) over Dungeness, Gris Nez and Brussels to Venlo, where we landed on a heavily bomb-scarred

---

[1] The entries for this and the next three days are written on paper headed "21st Army Group Headquarters". I had thought it wiser not to take my diary too near the front line.

aerodrome. The others in the party were Colonel Charrington (successor to Barney Charlesworth as A.D.C. to Sir Alan Brooke), Kinna and the inevitable, egregious Sawyers (the valet).

In a few miles we were over the German frontier, whence we could see Monty's great smokescreen over the Rhine. Most of the houses, except for solitary farms, were wrecked. Slogans such as *"Sieg od. Siberien"* were written on the walls.

Charrington and I went to 2nd Army H.Q. at Walbeck, where we sleep in the Visitors' Mess, a *"Gasthaus der Drei Kronen"* renamed "The Savoy". The P.M., C.I.G.S. and Tommy are at Monty's Tac H.Q. some six miles away, living in caravans. Monty's camp surrounds a rectangular clearing (formerly a riding school) in the middle of a pine forest. The P.M. has two caravans, one for work and one for sleep. Monty has several of various nationalities and designs: one, in which he works, belonged to General Berganzoli (Electric Whiskers), another in which he sleeps belonged to General Messe, a third, filled with canaries, is fitted up as a map room. All are replete with photographs, mostly of Monty himself, but three large ones of Rommel are included and one of Rundstedt.

The 6th Guards Tank Brigade are not far from 2nd Army, at a place called Pont. I dined there, not wisely but very well, at the H.Q. of the 4th Grenadiers and sat between Charlie Tryon[1] and Philip at a long table in a German mill-house, laden with fine china and glass. Filled with champagne and brandy, I went by jeep to Monty's camp after dinner and took the P.M. some important telegrams, including a venomous one from Molotov who, on the eve of what may well be our war-winning operation, had the impudence to say that the Russians were bearing the main brunt of the war. Germany's internal structure and economic position have in fact been brought to the verge of collapse as much by Bomber Command and the U.S. Army Air Corps as by the Russian advances – perhaps more so.

Saturday, March 24th

Today is D-day for Operation PLUNDER – the crossing of the Rhine. It was clear, cloudless and sunny, conditions for which we had prayed. Together with Colonel Charrington and two young liaison officers called Bullit (an American) and Gill (English) I set out by jeep from 2nd Army H.Q. at 7.00 a.m. and drove to a high wooded

---

[1] Brigadier Lord Tryon, commanding the 4th Battalion Grenadiers, son of the Conservative Minister who died in 1940. After the war he was Keeper of the Privy Purse and responsible in addition for the Queen's racing establishment.

hill (the Staatsforst) S.S.W. of Xanten and about 1½ miles from the town. We took up our position so that we could see a great expanse of country, the Hochwald to our left, Xanten, in ruins and with one of its church spires missing, before us, and the Upper Rhine and Wesel to our right. We were there before eight and we had a long time to wait. The rising sun began to disperse the mists over the Rhine, fighters flew ceaselessly backwards and forwards above our heads; and nearly 2,000 guns, of which we could see many batteries below and to the left of us, thundered away in a gigantic barrage, which sometimes alternated with minutes of complete silence. Suddenly, far away to the north-east, a trail of white smoke or condensation began climbing skywards. It seemed to travel very slowly, but I watched its vertical path up to 30,000 or more and realised that it was a V.2, presumably en route for Antwerp or perhaps even London.

At 9.50 – the guns had been silent for twenty minutes and the dust on the other side of the Rhine was settling – we saw what we were awaiting. A host of Dakotas, flying low and in close formation, the doors in the fuselage open and a parachutist standing ready in the aperture, came over the hills behind and passed before us, right over Xanten. A solitary Flying Fortress accompanied them. To our left appeared another fleet and behind yet another. They vanished in the haze across the Rhine and, dimly, I saw parachutes beginning to open. More and more fleets of Dakotas came on, while the first lots streamed back empty overhead. The Flying Fortress reappeared, on fire, and the occupants baled out one by one as the aircraft flew steadily on, the flames spreading towards the tail. The endless stream continued and soon there were fleets of gliders too. We could see many of the gliders released while their tugs turned steeply away for home. There seemed to be but little flak, and very few failed to return. However a few returning Dakotas were in trouble and several crashed before our eyes, bursting into flames as they struck the ground. One, struggling low over Xanten, lost height irrecoverably and there was a great flash and explosion as it crashed just below us, apparently on top of one of our heavy gun positions. For two and a half hours the Armada came, but Gill and I, having seen much of it, left our hill which was now shared by many officers, press correspondents and photographers, re-entered our jeep and pushed on into Xanten itself and thence to the banks of the Rhine.

It seemed a very peaceful river and we quickly yielded to the temptation to cross to the other bank. We found room in a small launch and shortly after 11.00, long before the airborne operation was complete, we stood on the eastern bank. There were mines everywhere and we watched the sappers exploding them. Prisoners, newly taken, came marching towards us, their hands clasped behind their heads, their faces a mixture of relief and despair. We walked up a road towards the little village of Marwick, where on a bluff above the river stood a *Gasthaus* in process of being turned into a first-aid post. It was full of German prisoners keeping a strained and rather depressed *Wacht am Rhein*.

I was talking to Gill in front of the house. The Colonel of an Airborne Regiment arrived, in claret-coloured beret, with jeep and driver. I stared through the windows at the prisoners. They stared back, one young man with his cap aslant, very defiantly. Suddenly a shell exploded in the river, then another, another and another. A fifth hit the bank eighty yards from us. A sixth struck the opposite shore. Gill said it would be fun to talk to the prisoners and find out their impressions. I agreed. We moved towards the front door to ask the officer in charge if he had any objection. As we reached the door an 88 mm shell landed just where we had been standing and about ten yards from where we then were. The airborne Colonel's driver, standing beside me, was hit. An artery was cut and I was drenched in blood. Another shell brought down a tree by the corner of the house. The Germans were by now lying flat on the floor. The wounded man and the rest of us moved to the cellar, which seemed solid, and a few minutes later another shell landed a few yards from the house, wounding a second soldier. We waited for things to quieten down and then crawled out from among the debris, making our way northwards to the village of Bisslich.

We joined up with some tank officers, who gave us eggs they had just collected from a trans-Rhenanian farm and told us that the enemy were less than a mile away, not five or six as we had supposed. Then we all re-crossed the river in a Buffalo, which failed, the first time, to negotiate the steep western bank and flung us all in a heap, including the poor man with the severed artery, who, since it was in his arm, could nevertheless walk.

Back we went through devastated Xanten, where the children seemed well-fed and the population curious rather than resentful, while the sun beat down as it should in July and the dust was nearly as thick as in Normandy. We had a picnic lunch by the side of a quiet lane near Geldern.

The P.M. was thrilled by our adventures and, while pretending to disapprove, was in fact rather pleased, though Monty was not. I took Bullit to dine with the 4th Grenadiers, where we both enjoyed ourselves, and then returned to the P.M.'s caravan at Monty's

H.Q. where he was working. "Sleep soundly," he said to me. "You might have slept more soundly still."

Sunday, March 25th
Still bright and clear though not quite yesterday's imitation of mid-summer.

Attended the P.M., C.I.G.S. and Monty to church parade, at which a Clydeside Church of Scotland padre preached a moving and rarely eloquent sermon. I think it is the first time I have known the P.M. go to church. After the Blessing and the National Anthem he presented some Good Conduct Certificates and then more or less preached a sermon himself, on his theme, which he often expounds, of an Influence, supreme and watchful, which guides our affairs and of the Almighty's Great Design into which all our human actions fit if we do our duty.

After church the P.M., in his 4th Hussars uniform which he has worn throughout the visit, set off to visit Eisenhower. I let Kinna go off sight-seeing with a liaison officer and myself spent the day sitting in the sun outside the P.M.'s caravan or writing all this disjointed description. I lunched in Monty's Mess with some of his staff.

De Guingand (Chief of Staff) told me yesterday that he thought the Western Front should crumble in three weeks. Mathematically it seemed certain. He also described the immense planning necessitated by Operation PLUNDER and the great pains taken to neutralise the German defences before the airborne landing. First they had bombed, with the maximum weight available, all the German fighter airfields; then they had put every gun they possessed, including ack-ack, on to the flak positions; finally, in the last half hour, when the guns stopped to let the dust settle, all the fighter bombers had been turned on to prevent the flak positions from recovering.

Dined again in the Grenadiers Mess, which is wonderfully luxurious for a combatant one, with Dresden china, white table-cloths and candles.

Returned to Tac H.Q. where the P.M. worked till after 1.00 a.m. on the Russian situation, which is murky. Molotov is playing a foul game. The P.M. said he hardly liked to consider dismembering Germany until his doubts about Russia's intentions had been cleared away.

Monday, March 26th
The P.M. set out with Monty for another tour across the Rhine. When he had gone I went with Gill, my bear-leader and a charming

fellow, to Monty's air strip nearby and flew in an Auster. First of all we prospected, at low level, a new site for Monty's H.Q. near Xanten. Then we flew over the wreckage of Xanten, northwards along the Rhine, over fields pitted with thousands of shell holes and large bomb craters (sometimes filled with the carcasses of dead cows), past tented camps near Calcar where homeless German civilians were congregated, in sight of the smoke of battle beyond Rees and Emmerich, over devastated Cleves, the great Reichswald, Goch and so on. Germany has indeed paid dearly and except for a few isolated farms I scarcely saw a single house unscathed by war.

Gill and I called on Philip's battalion to say goodbye (they go into battle tomorrow) and stayed to lunch. Motoring back I noticed one or two flags hung out – the red, black and gold of the Weimar Republic. Some of the leopards will no doubt be quick to change their spots. The children looked well-fed and healthy, but the P.M. told me this afternoon that he thought their faces very strained and that for his part what he had seen of the German civilian population had moved and upset him. I think this is his reaction to the apparently sinister designs of Russia who – in addition to obvious moves against the spirit of the Yalta agreement – have now decided not to send Molotov to San Francisco but to send three subordinate officials. And yet they complained bitterly when we only sent William Strang and some military delegates to Russia in the summer of 1939, subsequently alleging that to be one of the causes of the breakdown of Anglo-Soviet talks and of their August alliance with Germany.

We said goodbye to Monty and his staff at 4.15 p.m. (Winston giving him a fine edition of Marlborough, a long inscription for his autograph book and a heap of compliments) and took off from much bombed Venlo in a Dakota escorted by twelve Spitfires. The P.M. worked in the plane, which was alternately too hot and too cold, and we landed at Northolt after an exciting week-end in glorious weather, much the better in health and temper.

Tuesday, March 27th
The newspapers have won the war already, but it certainly seems that the map of Germany is being rolled up. The 6th Guards Tank Brigade are in the van. I am glad not to be accompanying Mrs Churchill who left for Russia in the C.54 tonight. It is better to miss the Kremlin than the victory celebrations. Mrs C. gave a small party, for the office and a few personal friends, such as Archie Sinclair, the Beaver and C.A.S., before her departure.

Wednesday, March 28th

Accompanied the P.M. to the House. Jimmy Rothschild, answering his first questions since his recent appointment as Under Secretary, was jeered and hooted. It was in deplorable taste but he took it very well. The P.M. says that if the House treats him like that again he will make him a Privy Councillor!

After Questions the P.M. announced the sad loss of Rupert Brabner, one of the most attractive younger Tories, who is missing on a flight to Canada where he was to represent H.M.G. at the winding up of the Empire Air Training Scheme.

Then the P.M. paid his tribute to Lloyd George,[1] eloquent in parts and well delivered but not, I thought, as good as that he paid to Neville Chamberlain in 1940. He was followed by Greenwood, Percy Harris (who is always effective in emptying the House), Geoffrey Shakespeare, old George Lambert (elected only a year after L.G. in 1890), Aneurin Bevan (who was generous to the P.M.'s qualities for once), W. J. Brown, Lady Astor, Thelma Cazalet and Gallacher, who said that Lenin had advised him to study L.G., as the greatest statesman England ever had.

Thursday, March 29th

The British and American armour is racing deep into Germany. The P.M. went off to Chequers for Easter.

Good Friday, March 30th

Went to Westminster Abbey at 10.00. Ante-Communion and the Litany.

Spent Easter at Stansted, where March went out like a lion, a strong gale and fine rain making outdoor exercise unpalatable. Besides the Bessboroughs, Moyra and George, Arthur[2] and Pat Ponsonby were there. Played much bezique and backgammon and read a little Creevey. As our headlong advance into Germany continues, the 6th Guards Tank Brigade, leading into Munster, are much in the news.

---

[1] He died on March 26th.

[2] Lord Bessborough's nephew. Served in the Welsh Guards. His first wife, Pat, who died suddenly when still young, was an American with an exceptionally attractive personality.

32

Victory and Chaos

April 1945

Monday, April 2nd
Returned to London, where the Dominions representatives are assembling for a preliminary canter over the Dumbarton Oaks ground prior to the San Francisco Conference. However the Russians are being so objectionable diplomatically, and so utterly unco-operative about Poland, that hopes are low.

Tuesday, April 3rd
The P.M. spent the day at No. 10 – since V bombs are apparently finished[1] – for the first time since Christmas. It is a great deal pleasanter to work there than at the musty Annexe.

Dined with Will Codrington[2] to meet Ivone Kirkpatrick, head of the political section of the German Control Commission. Kirkpatrick is a man about whom opinions differ. I found him strikingly agreeable and his wits are certainly quick. He gave a damning account of the inefficacy of both S.O.E. and P.W.E.[3], both of which have been loud in self-advertisement during the war. As regards S.O.E., he said that they had not even been able to organise their own communications with the French on D-day and had had to rely upon code messages from the B.B.C. The more he saw of them, the more convinced a parliamentarian he became: the

---

[1] The last V.2. rocket to fall on England was on March 27th.
[2] Son of General Sir Alfred Codrington, Colonel of the Coldstream Guards. Won the M.C. in the First World War and was for six years in the Foreign Office before going into business. From 1940 he was made responsible for Foreign Office security and was invited to be a member of the No. 10 Mess.
[3] Political Warfare Executive, responsible for anti-Nazi propaganda. Richard Crossman was one of its leading lights, thereby avoiding active service. It was not considered a very effective organisation.

open investigation of such organisations by Parliament was invaluable. He also condemned loudly, as does the P.M. very frequently, the Foreign Office addiction to the principle of "Buggins' turn" which made the selection of the best men for important posts quite impossible.

Wednesday, April 4th

The P.M. spent most of the afternoon with the King at the Houses of Parliament discussing the plans for a State Opening of Parliament. The P.M. seems to visualise the end of the German War before this month is out. He gave a dinner to Bernard Baruch* at No. 10 and then worked in the Cabinet Room while I sat beside him and acted as a salvage dump.

Thursday, April 5th

The P.M. has put in writing a very apt comment on the State Department who suggested our consulting the Soviet Government about the rearming of the Greeks: "This is the usual way in which the State Department, without taking the least responsibility for the outcome, make comments of an entirely unhelpful character in a spirit of complete detachment."

In the middle of the morning came a bombshell – a telegram from the President containing one from Stalin which accused us and the Americans of making a deal with the Germans at Berne for the purpose of holding the Eastern Front while the West was thrown open. There is no atom of truth in this, though we did inform the Soviet of certain approaches for a purely military surrender in Italy which had been made to Alexander. These in any case came to nothing but it looks as if the Germans had succeeded in persuading the Russians that something sinister was afoot. Herein may lie an explanation of the very unsatisfactory attitude adopted in recent weeks by Stalin and Molotov and, in their simplicity, no doubt they really have been taken in by the Germans. Nevertheless their accusations are entirely unjust and, to us, unthinkable. I am glad to see that the President has reacted violently; and the P.M. spent all the rest of the day – with Cabinets and Chiefs of Staff Meetings – doing the same. He was even half an hour too late for lunch with the King of Norway[1] as nothing would move him from his bed until he had finished dictating the first draft of a counterblast to Stalin.

[1] Haakon VII, formerly Prince Charles of Denmark and married to a sister of King George V. Chosen and crowned King of Norway when that country separated from Sweden in 1905. His was the last Scandinavian Coronation. Spent the war in England with his exiled Government.

Dined at the Dorchester to meet some of the lesser Dominions' luminaries (the major ones were dining at No. 10 with the P.M.) at the expense of H.M.G. Paul Emrys Evans presided. I sat next to an Australian, Professor Bailey (personal assistant to Evatt)[1] who is an expert on constitutional law and gave me an interesting exposition of Australian federalism. I then talked to General Cawthorne[2] of the Indian Army (now Director of Military Intelligence in India) who says that we are too frightened of loosening our grip on India and of showing the Indians that we trust them. We ought to prove our confidence by some great gesture such as the appointment of an Indian Viceroy.

The Japanese Cabinet resigned. I have always felt one might back worse outsiders than the possibility of Japan succumbing before, or as soon as, Germany.

Friday, April 6th

To Chequers. Field Marshal Smuts, Janny Smuts and Sarah were there. Talk was of the Americans, the P.M. saying that there was no greater exhibition of power in history than that of the American army fighting the battle of the Ardennes with its left hand and advancing from island to island towards Japan with its right. Smuts said the Americans were certainly very powerful, but immature and often crude. We dined off plovers' eggs sent by Lord Portal and the finest South African brandy brought by Smuts.

After dinner we saw the Russian film *Koutusov* presented to the P.M. by Stalin. The P.M. is greatly impressed by the unprejudiced attitude shown in the film to the Tsarist régime. Smuts said that after 1815 Russia sank into the background for a generation in spite of her victories (my recollections of the Rev. F. A. Simpson's[3] lectures on the Eastern Question don't bear this out altogether) and when Stalin died the same might well happen again.

Saturday, April 7th

The old Jewish American financier, Bernard Baruch, six foot five with thick white hair and almost deaf, arrived before lunch. So did

[1] Minister for External Affairs in Australia. Self-assertive and devoid of charm.
[2] Australian officer who transferred to the Indian Army. One of the Indian delegation to the San Francisco Conference.
[3] Brilliant but idle historian, given a Fellowship at Trinity, Cambridge, on account of two excellent books about Napoleon III. He never finished the proposed trilogy. As a priest he was eccentric but his occasional sermons in Trinity Chapel attracted congregations from far and wide. His comment on one essay I wrote was: "Never write that something was inevitable. Only death is inevitable." Since then I have avoided the word.

Sir Richard Hopkins[1] and Sir Robert Knox,[2] to talk about campaign stars.

At luncheon there was a heated debate on gold and its future. Smuts said gold was like the British Monarchy: it must cease to rule but must remain as a constitutional, stabilising influence. The P.M. became passionate in support of a currency based largely on commodities and only partly on gold; he also made great play with the American gold dug into the earth at Fort Knox. Baruch said gold always had been paramount and given people confidence. Anybody would take gold rather than paper. It had been so in the time of Alexander the Great and, whatever the P.M. and Smuts said, so it would remain.

Went for a brief walk with Sarah after lunch. After dinner – at which the themes were diamonds, cartels and butterflies, and in particular the Cullinan diamond – we saw various films including the Russian one of the Yalta Conference, which was very long and almost incredibly detailed. The P.M. worked on his box in the White Parlour till 2.30 a.m., waxing very contemptuous of the F.O. who, he said, always had to be active and never could see when it was wise to do nothing. *Mise en demeure* was a very good diplomatic phrase, but he never saw it used nowadays.

This reference to the Cullinan diamond reminds me that Churchill told us a story, which Smuts, who said he had entirely forgotten it, confirmed as true. Shortly after the treaty with South Africa in 1906, when we gave the defeated Boers back their freedom, the Cullinan diamond was discovered and was presented as a mark of loyalty and appreciation to King Edward VII. Since the King designated it part of the Crown Jewels, and not his personal property, the Government assumed responsibility for cutting it. It was so large that it had to be divided into two stones, one of which is now at the top of the sceptre and the other in one of the crowns. The Cabinet decided that it should be cut in Amsterdam, which was the traditional centre for diamond cutting. They also told the Dutch diamond cutters that they might keep the chips as payment for their work, although the diamond cutters declared with commendable honesty that the value of the chips was far greater than the cost of the work. His Majesty's Government, however, cared nothing for that, provided they did not have to foot any bill. When

---

[1] Permanent Secretary to the Treasury, head of the Civil Service and a Privy Councillor. Churchill had an affection for him dating from his years as Chancellor of the Exchequer, and insisted on addressing him as Sir Richard Valentine Nind Hopkins! Nind fascinated him as a Christian name.

[2] Remarkably obstinate Secretary of the Honours Committee.

this became known, Generals Botha and Smuts organised a
public subscription in the Union of South Africa to purchase the
chips from Amsterdam and re-present them to the British Crown.
Years later I repeated this story to Queen Elizabeth II who said
that she often wore a brooch made from the chips of the Cullinan
diamond, which Queen Mary had left to her, but that she had not
had any idea of their origin.

Churchill, when he told the story, said that he thought it a
shameful episode in British Cabinet history.

Sunday, April 8th

Mr Peter Fraser, the New Zealand P.M., came for luncheon and to
stay the night. There was a vast luncheon party including, in
addition to all those staying here, the Deputy P.M. of Australia
(Mr Forde), the Australian Minister of External Affairs and his
somewhat faded, blonde Mrs Evatt, the Duchess of Marlborough,
Blandford[1] (on leave from an O.C.T.U.) and Lord Cherwell. The
P.M. posed the question: "What is now Hitler's best course?" and
answered it by suggesting a repetition of the Hess trick on the lines
of "I am responsible; wreak your vengeance on me but spare my
people". The Duchess of Marlborough suggested that in such a
case the only course would be to take him back and drop him by
parachute over Germany. Smuts said that if he were Hitler he
would fight on, to the last, in the mountain redoubt near Berchtesgaden.

After lunch I showed Forde the house. He was ill-at-ease in
strange surroundings and among people with unfamiliar habits – a
great contrast to Menzies. While we stood in the rain on the
croquet lawn looking at the west front of Chequers, which is its best
side, Mr Forde asked me what this type of architecture was called. I
said it was Elizabethan. "Well," he replied, "in Melbourne we
have a lot of fine residences of the same type of architecture, but
out there we call them Tudor."

The Smuts family left, after the Field Marshal had inspected a
Guard of Honour of Welsh Guards in front of the house, and so did
the Australians. The sun was shining brilliantly and the P.M. went
off to his revolver pit in the woods for a shooting match with
Blandford. I took Mr Fraser for a walk up Beacon Hill and found
him full of conversation, though much saddened by the loss of his

---

[1] Afterwards 11th Duke of Marlborough. He, Freddy, 2nd Earl of Birkenhead,
and my daughter Harriet were Winston Churchill's only three godchildren – so,
at least, Mrs Churchill said.

wife. He fears, as do I, that San Francisco and the World Organisation may never come to much on account of the vetos of the Great Powers and the impossibility of holding the world together if the Big Three fall asunder. Personally I feel strongly that the whole subject should have been approached much more humbly, starting with regional associations at the bottom instead of a glittering World Council and Assembly at the top. However Mr Fraser was too captivated by the sight of some cherry blossom against the blue sky, and by asking me about the recent Greek imbroglio, to pursue this unsettling topic further.

Before dinner I sat on a seat above the croquet lawn writing to Mary, in Brussels. Judge Rosenman, Roosevelt's representative in Europe to investigate the problem of supplies for liberated Europe, came to dine and sleep, but though he had much of the former he had little of the latter as the P.M. kept him up till 3.00 a.m. on the theme that Britain shall not starve or lower her exiguous rations still further to feed Axis satellites while the American army and civil population live on their present gigantic diet. There was also talk about housing, from which emerged the astonishing fact that we were in fact the best housed country in the world before the war. Lord Cherwell said we had three per cent slums. The U.S.A. had less than two-thirds of their population properly housed.

Monday, April 9th
During the weekend Bevin made a strong political speech attacking the Conservatives. The P.M. said to me while he was dressing at Chequers that if the Labour Party were going ahead on those lines, he thought the time had come for him to *brusquer les affaires* – i.e. to hasten the departure of the Opposition groups from the Government.

He and Sarah went off to Chartwell for lunch, to profit from the warm sun and to investigate the mysterious theft of the P.M.'s favourite goldfish from the upper pond there. I returned to London.

Brendan made a slashing reply to Bevin. The Coalition is nearing its end, though in matters of foreign and military policy it is still solid.

Tuesday, April 10th
A brisk canter in Richmond Park where I examined a large V.2 crater near White Lodge. There have been no V.1s or V.2s for over a week.

Stalin has answered the P.M. both about Poland and the accusations he made about negotiations with the Germans. He has climbed down, ungraciously, in his own way about the latter. It boils down to this: the Russians are jealous of our rapid successes in the West while, on the Oder at any rate, they are stuck. The explanations are briefly:

i   Our weapons are better and man for man our soldiers more efficient;

ii we have massive air superiority and they have none;

iii the Germans view our advance with less horror than they do that of the Russians – and not without reason.

Wednesday, April 11th

There is a good deal afoot. In the military field we still race towards the Elbe, from which we are not now far. In the political field, Poland and the coming conference at San Francisco, France's place in the sun and the problem of supplying food to liberated areas are all pressing matters. Internally, the shadow of the return to party politics means constant sessions of the P.M. with James Stuart, Ralph Assheton, Brendan, Lord Beaverbrook, and the canvassing of non-party members of the Government to remain when it is re-formed.

Von Papen[1] has been captured in the Rühr, the first of the war criminals to be taken alive.

In the car, on the way back from No. 10 to the Annexe at 2.30 a.m., the P.M. told me that in July 1940 a number of Tories had tried to break up the Government and to engineer the formation of a kind of dictatorial triumvirate consisting of L.G., himself and Bevin. The instigators had been Amery, Harold Macmillan, Boothby and P. J. Grigg. The P.M. had suggested to Amery there and then that he should resign and make his explanations to Parliament. He gave me a lifelike account of the speech he would have made in reply.

The Americans have reached the Elbe.

Thursday, April 12th

President Roosevelt died in the afternoon. The news did not reach the P.M. till midnight, but I gather he was very distressed. It is a bad moment for the removal of America's one great international figure.

---

[1] Franz von Papen. Adroit and slippery politician who was Hitler's predecessor as Chancellor of the Reich. Narrowly escaped death in the 1934 "Night of the Long Knives" and ended as German Ambassador to Turkey during the war.

Friday, April 13th
The President's sudden death has caused a great stir though his appearance in recent months has been a warning to many. The P.M., after much deliberation, decided not to fly over to Washington today for the funeral tomorrow.

Went with Jock Gibb[1] to stay with him and Elizabeth at their house, Mousehall, in Sussex.

Saturday, April 14th
Sat about in the garden most of the day, reading the P.M.'s copy of Arthur Bryant's *The Years of Victory*, or sauntered through country lanes ablaze with blossom and wild flowers. It is a very early year, owing to weeks of sunshine, and the primroses are Brobding-nagian, but the cowslip, like the musk before it, seems to be losing its scent year by year. This spring only a very faint scent remains. The oak is coming out before the ash.

Today, over this part of England where the Battle of Britain raged hottest and the Flying Bombs did their worst, the sky was black with Fortresses and Liberators returning from the bombardment of the German pocket on the Gironde. Meanwhile in Germany things move at a great pace and very soon the Russian and the Western armies will have linked up. Only a hundred miles separates them and the Americans are securely over the Elbe.

Sunday, April 15th
Lunched at the Turf, with Hinch, and then proceeded to Cambridge to stay with Winstanley. After tea we went to the Fellows' Garden. Surely there has never been such a spring. Its earliness and its beauty have made me quite botanically minded. The cherries are weighed down with blossom. The chestnuts and the lilac are already out, as is the wistaria in Great Court, before the daffodils have faded. In the Fellows' Garden Wilderness there is a fantasia of blossom, tulips, daffodils, lilac (mauve and white) and berberis, while the tall avenue of elms wears its early coat of distinctive pale green. And all beneath a china blue sky. We walked back through the garden of Johns, along the path where three and a half years ago I drilled as an A.C.2, now banked with cherry and with tulips, along the avenue of limes and cherries that leads over the Cam to Trinity, and through to the Bowling Green. Winstanley said it had been nearly as beautiful in 1940, but then it

---

[1] Son of Sir Alexander Gibb, the celebrated engineering contractor. He was a publisher, beginning his career with the well-known firm of Methuen and Co. He was kind enough to publish a travel book I wrote when I was only nineteen.

had been quite painful to enjoy the peaceful seclusion; in fact to enjoy it had been impossible. To me the memories of that spring and summer are different: excitement of a new and almost delirious kind was my predominant emotion.

Winstanley told me three stories worth recording:

i. Lord Acton, whom he had consulted about studying Luther's works, had said that he would find him difficult to comprehend because he would never understand the deep strain of brutality in the German character. Lord A. was, of course, himself half German and brought up in Germany.

ii. At Hatfield Gerald Balfour told a man he was a Philistine. The man replied, "What is a Philistine?" Old Lord Salisbury said from afar, "A Philistine is a man who is killed by the jawbone of an ass."

iii. An American, dining at Pembroke, told many long and improbable stories. After one of them had been doubted he turned to Professor Whibley and said, "Won't you bear me out, young man?" Whibley replied, "It was a young man who bore out Ananias."

Dined in Hall. Afterwards repaired to the Vice Master's rooms, with their magnificent Elizabethan ceiling, with Sir William Clark (formerly High Commissioner to South Africa and P.S. to Lloyd George), Bernard Darwin, Prince Obolensky and Dennis Robertson, now Professor of Economics in the University. We talked of Russia. Obolensky said he doubted the theory that Russia had gone wholly nationalist. He thought there were still two forces in the country, of which that of pure Communist doctrine was not much the weaker.

Monday, April 16th
Returned to London which is unnaturally sweltering in mid-summer heat. Judging from the week-end's telegrams the P.M. seems to have started famously with President Truman.

Tuesday, April 17th
After an early lunch at the Travellers I returned to the Annexe where the P.M., just back from the memorial service for President Roosevelt at St Paul's, was feverishly composing over the luncheon table his tribute to the President. I thought it adequate but not one of his finest efforts, or in any way comparable to his epitaph on Neville Chamberlain in 1940.

I went down to the House with him. Proceedings were greatly delayed by the behaviour of the recently elected Scottish Nationalist member for Motherwell (Dr McIntyre) who insisted on making his bow to the Speaker without sponsors, thus contravening a resolution of the House dating from 1688. The Speaker sent him back behind the bar and there ensued an hour's debate on the subject, ending in a division. It all seemed very trivial when the galleries were packed to hear the P.M.'s tribute to Roosevelt, but Labour members insisted that if McIntyre did not choose to have sponsors, since no other Member agrees with his Scottish Nationalist views, then it was right on principle for him to refuse to have any.

The P.M. spoke well, his voice thrilling with emotion when he quoted Longfellow's lines "Sail on, O ship of state", which the President sent over by the hand of Wendell Willkie during one of our darkest hours.

The P.M. worked in bed, in the best of spirits and temper. He talked, most unwarily, across the open Atlantic telephone to Anthony Eden (in Washington on his way to San Francisco); he had a long session with Moley Sargent, of whom he thinks highly, partly because I once told him of Moley's disparaging remarks on the F.O. balcony during the hysterical scenes when Chamberlain came back from Munich; he read the early editions of tomorrow's newspapers (an ancient vice now only pursued when he has made a speech); and reverting, for the fifteenth time, to my escapade during the Rhine crossing, he said, apropos of the airborne soldier who was wounded beside me, that one could say everyone had been in it, "airborne and chairborne side by side".

In September 1938, when I was working in the Foreign Office, I walked out on to the balcony overlooking Downing Street to watch the scenes of joy and emotion when Mr Chamberlain returned from Munich. The Foreign Office as a whole was strongly anti-Munich and nobody joined me for a long time. Eventually one of the French windows opened and Sir Orme Sargent (Deputy Under Secretary) strolled out on to the balcony. "You might think," he said, "that we had won a major victory instead of betraying a minor country. But I can bear anything as long as he doesn't talk about peace with honour." A few minutes later Mr Chamberlain appeared at a first-floor window in No. 10 and told the crowd that he had brought back not only peace, but peace with honour.

Wednesday, April 18th
It is so hot and sunny the dog-days might be here. Nobody seems to remember such weather in April before.

Thursday, April 19th

The P.M. is annoyed with Tito who now looks almost exclusively to Russia, oblivious of past favours from us. He feels we should now back Italy (from whom Tito will claim Trieste, etc.) and thus aim at splitting the Italian Communist party.

At Mulberry Walk where the floors were filthy and we could get no charwomen, Mother spent the evening on her knees scrubbing the kitchens and I handled a broom in the other rooms. I then dined with Bob Coates at Pratts. Those at dinner talked of classical education, India, the merits of respective Dominions, and German atrocities. The papers are full of the latter, with stomach-turning photographs, consequent on the Allied armies overrunning Buchenwald and other German concentration camps. Proof is now supplied that the stories of the last ten years have not been just propaganda, as were many of the last war's atrocity stories.

Eisenhower told the P.M. the other day that when the Mayor and Mayoress of Weimar were shown Buchenwald they went home and hanged themselves.

Friday, April 20th

Before dinner the P.M..recorded, in my presence, a message which, with those of Stalin and President Truman (who seems to be showing great good sense and to be earning golden opinions), will be broadcast when the armies of Soviet Russia and the Western Allies link up. He then dined alone with Lady Lytton[1] whom, he told me, he once nearly married. At midnight he left for Bristol to present honorary degrees – in very different circumstances from when I accompanied him there in the spring of 1941 while the fires of the previous night's blitz still burned.

Saturday, April 21st

I am impressed by the weakness of American foreign policy: in Greece, as in Roumania, the State Department are petrified of associating themselves with any démarche which might be ill-received by the American press or by Congress. Fear of popular criticism hamstrings diplomacy.

Monday, April 23rd

Very busy at the office. The P.M.'s box is in a ghastly state. He does little work and talks far too long, as he did last December

---

[1] Pamela, Countess of Lytton, born Pamela Plowden. Churchill told me he proposed to her in a punt when they were both staying at Warwick Castle. She said no; but their affection for each other survived.

before his Greek adventures refreshed him. This time, I think, it is the Polish question and the unsatisfactory conversations proceeding on that subject at Washington between Eden, Stettinus[1] and Molotov that are weighing him down.

Tuesday, April 24th
The P.M. is now becoming an administrative bottleneck. He persists in thinking he can be Foreign Secretary as well as P.M. and Leader of the House, and in addition to everything else proposes to take the chair at the Lord President's Committee.

Wednesday, April 25th
Lunched with Moyra Ponsonby at the Churchill Club. Returned to find a telegram from Stockholm reporting Himmler's wish to surrender to the Western Allies and the fact that Hitler is moribund with cerebral haemorrhage. This may be a last-minute attempt to separate us from the Russians but the P.M. immediately summoned a meeting of the Cabinet and the C.O.S. and sent off the whole story to Stalin. At any rate it shows that, as the P.M. said to me, "they are done".

Dined with Mrs Henley and Juliet Daniel.[2] We talked a lot about these German atrocities, as everybody in England has been talking since the publication of the photographs and accounts of Buchenwald, Belsen, etc.

Thursday, April 26th
At No. 10 there is a feeling of expectancy, based on yesterday's telegram but damped by the continued impasse over Poland (Stalin, by telegram, and Molotov in the U.S., keep on insisting that the re-organisation of the Polish Government should be on the Yugoslav model – which has in fact been a complete victory for Russia in that benighted land). We are also damped by the amount of work pouring in and the failure of the P.M. to deal with it.

After lunching with Buster Long, I went to No. 10 where the P.M. had Baldwin and the Archbishop of York[3] lunching with him. I was left with the Archbishop (whom I thought saintly, sensible and of great charm as well) while the P.M. darted off to the House. I followed him there but half missed Questions. Back at the Annexe the P.M. dictated a long and masterly telegram to Stalin, one of his very best efforts. He also despatched a telegram against

---

[1] American Secretary of State after Cordell Hull and before James Byrnes.
[2] Formerly Juliet Henley.
[3] Cyril Garbett, previously Bishop of Winchester.

the F.O. tendency of bullying the Hapsburgs, in which he said that if we had been a little less hasty in overthrowing the ancient dynasties after the last war, but had left a "crowned Weimar Republic" with which to co-operate, there might well have been no Hitler. He instructed me to see that this telegram was given wide distribution inside the F.O. which he accuses of republicanism.

The P.M. returned from dining with Massigli, the French Ambassador, to find a nice telegram from Stalin, indeed the most friendly U.J. has ever sent. This quite fascinated him and I sat beside him in his room at the Annexe while he talked of nothing else, first of all to Brendan for one and a half hours and then to me for another one and a half. His vanity was astonishing and I am glad U.J. does not know what effect a few kind words, after so many harsh ones, might well have on our policy towards Russia. My suggestion that this telegram – thanking the P.M. for his attitude and his frankness over the Himmler-Bernadotte[1] business – might be prompted by a certain shame over the unworthy suspicions entertained over the earlier German approach to us (operation CROSSWORD[2]) was impatiently swept aside. Further joy was caused by a generous message from de Gaulle. But no work was done and I felt both irritated and slightly disgusted by this exhibition of susceptibility to flattery. It was nearly 5.00 a.m. when I got to bed.

Friday, April 27th

The P.M. was in benign mood. I had to stand behind him in the Cabinet and show him just which telegrams were where when he read them, purring with pleasure, to a Cabinet which had already seen copies.

However after lunch the clouds descended with the announcement of a smashing Commonwealth victory over the Conservative at Chelmsford, a Conservative seat. The Beaver, Brendan, James Stuart and Ralph Assheton were at once summoned for a lengthy conclave.

Saturday, April 28th

A heavy day, moving into Mulberry Walk the second van-load of furniture from Madeley and coping, for the first time in my life,

[1] Count Bernadotte, a cousin of the King of Sweden, acted as a go-between for the Germans and the Western Allies. He had reported Himmler's willingness to arrange the surrender of all his troops in north Germany to the Anglo-Americans. Churchill not only declined, but immediately informed Stalin of the approach.

[2] Secret plan for the surrender of the German armies in Italy, instigated by Alan Dulles who had talks in Zurich with S.S. General Wolff on behalf of O.S.S. without first letting the President or the State Department know he was doing so.

with a boiler (success limited). The house begins to look habitable and all we now need is a cook.

Sunday, April 29th

Charles Barker drove round to tell me that CROSSWORD had at last succeeded: the Germans had accepted unconditional surrender on the Italian front. He stayed to help cope with the blinds. Betty Montagu called to see the house and I then had lunch with her at the Churchill Club.

So far succeeded with the boiler as to have a hot bath.

Monday, April 30th

The newspapers are full of "Victory any minute now", and so indeed are we all. But opinion remains sober and I doubt there being the same jubilation or the same illusions as in 1918.

A hectic two hours when the P.M. returned at 6.00 from Chequers, matters being complicated by the shocking mess in which John Peck had left the box and by the endless telephone calls from the press.

33

Party Politics Renewed

May–June 1945

Tuesday, May 1st

Feverishly busy. After lunch the P.M. took Questions and told a House full to overflowing with people expecting a victory announcement that he had no statement to make about the war situation except that it was much better than it was five years ago.

On the way out we met the Duke of Norfolk. The P.M. said how glad he had been to see him at the Cabinet yesterday (when the arrangements for a State Opening of Parliament were discussed). It was such an agreeable change to see an Earl Marshal there instead of all the usual Air Marshals.

Back at the Annexe I sat in on a conference with Moley Sargent, Pug and Joe Hollis about zones of occupation in Vienna, the desirability of Alexander getting Venezia Giulia before Tito, and other kindred questions. The whole proceedings bore out a remark of Pug's, made later tonight, that the P.M. can be counted on to score a hundred in a Test Match but is no good at village cricket. The most recent example of the Test Match style is a long and masterly telegram to Stalin, a final appeal to resolve the Polish impasse.

As Lord Beaverbrook is being too high-handed about the Tory Party and the coming election, the P.M. saw him before dinner and protested. He then had a political dinner party, to discuss election propaganda to which, in addition to Lord B., Oliver Lyttelton, James Stuart and Ralph Assheton were bidden. Brendan was not included, as the P.M. is well aware that people, and particularly the Tory Party, are beginning to look askance at the Brendan–Beaver combination.

In the middle of dinner I brought in the sensational announcement, broadcast by the Nazi wireless, that Hitler had been killed today at his post at the Reichs Chancery in Berlin and that Admiral Doenitz was taking his place. Probably H. has in fact been dead several days, but the 1st May is a symbolic date in the Nazi calendar and no doubt the circumstances ("fighting with his last breath against Bolshevism") were carefully invented with an eye to the future Hitler Myth and Legend. The P.M.'s comment over the dinner table was: "Well, I must say I think he was perfectly right to die like that." Lord B.'s reply was that he obviously did not.

The party caucus stayed till 3.00 a.m. and the P.M. then dawdled over a few telegrams until after 4.00 a.m. I am writing this at that unseemly hour, cursing politics and all politicians, staring with exasperation at a box crammed with important unlooked-at papers and rather hoping that at the coming election the sovereign people follows the recent example of the electors of Chelmsford. At least socialism should not prevent one going to bed at a respectable hour.

Wednesday, May 2nd

While the last remnants of Axis power are tottering, the leaders of Germany and the Quislings engaged in flight or self-destruction, whole armies surrendering in Italy and on the Elbe, and a new era being vaporously discussed in San Francisco, the British Government machine is partly occupied by a threatened clash of arms between British Honduras and Guatemala. A cruiser is steaming westwards at full speed from Gibraltar; British bomber squadrons are bombing up; anxious glances are cast towards Washington. Then comes the news that the whole story is a mare's-nest and that fighting which had been observed from the air was really a forest fire. *Parturiunt montes et nascitur ridiculus mus.*

After last night's orgy I felt tired and irritable and overwhelmed by the gigantic heaps of paper in the box, on my table and indeed everywhere in the office. So I went home early and thereby missed the P.M.'s 7.30 p.m. dash to the House of Commons to announce unconditional surrender of the German forces in Italy to Alexander's armies. However, all is not well in that part of the world: Tito has beaten us in the race for Trieste and Venezia Giulia and, backed as he is by Russia (which has also, unilaterally, established its own puppet government in Vienna) it is hard to see how he can ever be dislodged. Still by backing Italy against Tito's claim to possess Trieste we may split the Italian Communist party and thus at least save Italy from the Russian imperialist clutches. As it is, the Soviet looks like dominating Europe east of a line drawn from the North Cape to Trieste and soon the pressure will be turned on Turkey. Our only entry on the credit side is that the Americans occupy *de facto* great parts of Germany which belong *de jure* to the Russian zone of occupation. Hamburg and Lübeck are ours.

Went home to find the married couple whom Mother has engaged had arrived and also that she had since discovered that the man had just completed a three-year sentence for fraud and embezzlement. This was something of a shock, but we decided, after dining at the *Good Intent*, that we ought to give him a chance to make good. Besides his wife seems honest and hardworking. All the same, an "old lag" for a butler, with several other previous convictions, is something of an experiment. Mulberry Walk now begins to look charming.

Thursday, May 3rd
The press and Parliament all on tenterhooks. They are even drawing startling deductions from the negative fact that the P.M. (who stayed in bed till 6.00 p.m.) did not go to the House to answer his Questions.

Poland and the stupid bellicosity of the French towards Syria and the Lebanon chiefly to the fore. The P.M. drafted some masterly telegrams on both subjects.

My démarche about St James's Park is bearing great fruit. Iron railings are appearing to preserve the grass and the unsightly paths trodden by the side of the lake are being dug up and resown. The Ministry of Works, in obedience to a minute which I submitted to the P.M., have taken rapid action.

The P.M. sat up till 3.30 and actually worked.

Friday, May 4th
It looks as if the Germans opposite Monty may surrender en masse, but there is a threat of the Russians trying to get to Denmark first by parachute, and thus control the Kattegat. Meanwhile it seems that Alexander did reach Trieste before Tito, but the latter announced he was there, no doubt to try and establish a prior claim. Now he is protesting vigorously.

Lunched at New Court with Tony Rothschild, arriving scandalously late owing to the Cabinet failing to rise till 1.50. Lord Bennett,[1] Sir Basil Brooke[2] and Colonel Vickers were the other guests. In conversation it was pointed out that in the former occupied countries, the underground organisations have necessarily

[1] Portly, unpopular Conservative Prime Minister of Canada, 1930–35. Restored the acceptance of titles in Canada and was himself made a Viscount in 1941.
[2] Nephew of Field Marshal Lord Alanbrooke. Prime Minister of Northern Ireland for twenty years from 1943. Leader of implacable Ulster Unionists, he first promoted and then undermined his successor, Terence O'Neill. Created Lord Brookeborough in 1953.

been built up on a basis of lies and intrigue. It will be very difficult to ensure that this does not become the tradition of public life and, on the children in particular, the effect may be very noxious.

Left St Pancras by 9.15 p.m. train for St Boswells with the luxury, rare in these days, of a first-class sleeper.

Saturday, May 5th–Saturday, May 12th
At Floors, staying with Mary Roxburghe. The Border was at its best and bathed in sunshine. On Sunday, May 6th, the French Ambassador and Madame Massigli came to luncheon and also Monsieur Rocher.[1] Lord and Lady Minto came to meet them. I was much taken with Lady Minto.

The Coldstream Guards being at Hawick, we saw a good deal of them. Bob, Bill and Ronnie Dawnay came for the week-end and Hugh Norman, Andrew Cavendish and David Chetwode came to dinner. Others who dined were Elizabeth Dunglass, Lord Robert Innes Kerr and Jimmy Coats (who expected to talk of nothing but racing and fishing and was terrified when Mary and I talked enthusiastically about obscure non-conformist sects we had discovered in *Chambers Encyclopaedia*).

Tuesday, May 8th, was V.E. Day. Mary and I lunched with the Balfours at Newton Don where we played bridge and listened to the Prime Minister announcing the end of the war against Germany. In the evening, after attending a packed service in the kirk, we went into Kelso to see the great bonfire. Mary, being recognised, was clapped by the populace.

I spent the days shooting pigeon, browsing in the magnificent library (chiefly on Captain Gronow's memoirs:[2]) or walking with Mary by the Tweed and through the glorious country round Floors. On Friday, May 11th, we bicycled over to lunch near Coldstream with Elizabeth Dunglass (who is vivacious, competent and agreeable) and then went with her to see Lord Home's remarkable rhododendron wood at the Hirsel. In the evening we motored over to Mellerstain, one of the Adam brothers' proudest achievements, to dine with Lord and Lady Haddington. Lady Haddington is as fascinating as her sister Lady Minto.

Returned to London by train, arriving at Mulberry Walk at 11.30 on Saturday, May 12th.

Sunday, May 13th
Went with Mother to a solemn thanksgiving at St Paul's. In the afternoon Betts and I watched the King and Queen and the

[1] Member of the French Embassy Staff.
[2] Memoirs of the Napoleonic Wars.

Princesses drive through Trafalgar Square on their way to St Paul's and then sat gossiping between the Lions at the foot of the Nelson Column under a poster which said in large yellow letters "Victory in Europe – 1945".

Monday, May 14th

At No. 10 I found everybody looking rather strained after a week of violent rejoicing and tumult. Mrs Churchill was just back from Russia where her tour has been a remarkable success.

The volume of work is if anything more pressing than when I left. Victory has brought no respite. The P.M. looks tired and has to fight for the energy to deal with the problems confronting him. These include the settlement of Europe, the last round of war in the East, an election on the way, and the dark cloud of Russian imponderability. In Venezia Giulia we stand on the brink of an armed clash with Tito, secure of Russian support, who wishes to seize Trieste, Pola, etc., from Italy without awaiting the adjudication of the Peace Conference. The Americans seem willing to stand four square with us and Truman shows great virility; but Alexander has alarmed them – and incensed the P.M. – by casting doubts on the attitude of the Anglo-American troops, should there come an armed clash with the Yugoslavs. Equally, as regards the Polish question, Russia shows no willingness to compromise and storm clouds threaten. Finally, as if we had not enough, de Gaulle sends a cruiser full of troops to Syria, where the position is delicate and the feeling against French domination strong, and there is a possible threat of a show-down, with British troops involved, in the Levant.

At 2.30 the P.M. went to bed, leaving almost untouched the voluminous weight of paper which awaits his decision. He told me that he doubted if he had the strength to carry on.

Tuesday, May 15th

Another very heavy day. I feel as if all the benefit of a week's leave has been almost sapped already.

Thursday, May 17th

The P.M. tells me he feels overpowered by the prospect of a meeting of the Big Three, which is imminent and which in view of the clash of interests over Poland, Venezia Giulia and Austria is vitally important, coinciding with a General Election which also ought not to be postponed. He is weighed down by the responsibility and the uncertainty. *Bellum in Pace.*

Friday, May 18th

The P.M. and Mrs C. set off for Chartwell and I went to Chequers to dine and await them. Meanwhile, after a Conservative meeting at No. 10, the P.M. has written to Attlee, Sinclair and Ernest Brown, saying that he hopes they will agree to preserve the Coalition till the end of the war with Japan but that he cannot agree to fixing a date for an election in the autumn since that would mean an attempt to carry on the Government in an atmosphere of faction and electioneering. Attlee came to see the P.M. at the Annexe and was favourably disposed to trying to persuade his party to continue at its Whitsun Blackpool conference. He has Ernest Bevin with him in this.

The P.M. was so pleased with Chartwell that he stayed, leaving me in comfortable solitude at Chequers.

Saturday, May 19th

A lovely hot day. Went for a long walk and did my best to put the great array of papers in the box, most of which have been unlooked at for many days, in some order.

Harold Macmillan, summoned from Italy because of the Venezia Giulia crisis, arrived at tea-time with Robert Cecil,[1] who is acting as his A.D.C. The P.M. was still loitering with his geese and goldfish ponds (recently plundered of their, to him, precious occupants by a thief or an otter – it was long before anyone dared break the news) at Chartwell and so I took Macmillan and Robert up to Beacon Hill. I don't like the would-be ingratiating way in which Macmillan bares his teeth.

The P.M. arrived for a late dinner and after it we saw a film. Then a very little work was done, in the Private Secretary's room, and a good deal of aimless discourse took place.

Sunday, May 20th

Whitsunday. The P.M. can't get the political prospect out of his head and all day the conversation was on a coming election, occasionally varied with fears of the Russian peril or a diatribe against those who wish to treat all leading Germans as war criminals and to leave none with authority to administer that battered and disordered land.

General Auchinleck and his wife, whom I thought frightful and the P.M. thought attractive, came to lunch. Prof. and I devoted

---

[1] Conservative M.P. for Bournemouth, 1950–54. Only surviving son of Lord Cranborne and himself eventually 6th Marquess of Salisbury.

great energies to eradicating many of the P.M.'s papers and we did contrive to get some of the remainder dealt with.

Bert Harris, C. in C., Bomber Command, came to dinner.

Monday, May 21st

In the afternoon Randolph arrived and Harold Macmillan, who had left yesterday, returned. Just as the Prof. and I had all but reached our goal of getting "the box" dealt with, Attlee rang up from his Blackpool conference and gave his reply to the P.M.'s letter which was negative. At once all was swept aside and electioneering became the only topic, while the P.M., Macmillan and Randolph all tried their hands at drafting a reply to Attlee. They think they have manoeuvred skilfully, by placing on the Labour Party the onus of refusing to continue and of preferring faction to unity at a time when great dangers still remain. I don't think the P.M. is quite happy about this, but for all the other Tory politicians the time has now passed "when none were for the party and all were for the state". The most assiduous intriguer and hard-working electioneer is Lord Beaverbrook. Brendan, who is offended with the P.M. over a number of minor slights, is sulking in his tent.

Tuesday, May 22nd

Remained at Chequers till 5.00 p.m. when we returned to London in time for the P.M. to preside over a meeting of Tory ministers. At Chequers the P.M. stayed in bed. He wrote an admirable letter to the King, for the archives he said, and brought to fruition one to Mr Attlee, for publication. Lord Beaverbrook persuaded him to leave out the last paragraph, which had contained generous references to the help of his late Labour colleagues.

I read the letter to Attlee to him on the telephone, as the P.M. wanted it published on the 6.00 news. It took me about forty minutes to do as Attlee insisted on copying it down himself, in long hand, word by word on a very indistinct line.

So tomorrow the P.M. resigns and the Government which has won the war is at an end.

Wednesday, May 23rd

The P.M. went to the Palace at noon, as pre-arranged, and asked to resign. Then there was a pause, as the P.M. was anxious to emphasise to the public that the King has the right to decide for whom he shall send, and at 4.00 he returned to be invited to form a new, and a Conservative, Government. On the whole I think the people are on the P.M.'s side in this preliminary skirmish and it is generally supposed that many will vote for the Conservatives merely out of personal loyalty to W.S.C. Parliament will be dissolved in three weeks and the election will be on July 5th.

At No. 10 no work is being done by the P.M. We are all having to deal ourselves with many papers which ought to be submitted to him and I have persuaded the Foreign Office to send us the very minimum of minutes. I "weed" every day some sixty per cent of the Foreign Office telegrams. I suppose that three times as much paper comes to us now as in 1940 and that the P.M. sees half as much. But, of course, the problems, though more immediately grave then, were simpler in that the machinery of Government was far less elaborate and we had no Allies. Now there are boards and committees without number and two mighty Allies to be considered at every turn, apart from the host of lesser concerns such as French tactlessness in the Levant, Greek claims to the Dodecanese, internal Italian feuds, etc., etc. In 1941, when I left to join the R.A.F., I used often to be comparatively idle for days at a time and to think we were overstaffed. Now, apart from the Prof., Desmond Morton and Harvie-Watt we are six Private Secretaries (of whom Anthony Bevir, concentrating on Patronage, and Miss Watson on Parliamentary Questions, take no part in the routine of the office in current affairs) three male clerks, three eminently efficient women who look after the vast files of secret papers, and about sixteen typists, etc. Yet we seem to be understaffed.

Thursday, May 24th
The P.M. devoted the day to the formation of what the press calls a "Caretaker Government". Brendan has refused the Admiralty, though he thinks it the most attractive of offices, and is aiming for a combination of the Ministry of Production and the Board of Trade.

With politicians coming and going – glints in all their eyes – and the Chief Whip in constant attendance, no work was done, even in regard to a telegram from Stalin demanding a third of the German Navy and merchant fleet (all of which have surrendered to us).

I was interested by some of the bombing figures showing our and the American share of the bombing of Germany:

| R.A.F. | 678,500 tons | on Germany only. |
| U.S. Army Air Force | 684,700 | |

Total for both forces everywhere in Europe: 2,170,000 tons.

| Losses in Europe: | R.A.F. | 10,801 aircraft |
| | U.S.A.A.F. | 8,274 aircraft. |

Friday, May 25th

More Government making. Brendan has now taken the Admiralty and Harold Macmillan the Air Ministry. Alex Dunglass becomes an Under Secretary at the F.O. and William Sidney at the M. of Pensions.

Saturday, May 26th

Joan[1] lunched with me and we went together to a memorial service for Alick[2] at Holy Trinity, Brompton, at the unsuitable hour of 1.30. It was his birthday. There were but few people there, but the choir were good and the service adequate.

Am reading Trevelyan's *Social History of England*. Denis Speares[3] brought round after dinner his brother, just released from an *Oflag*, who gave a remarkable description of an attempted escape and his subsequent adventures at the hands of the Gestapo.

Sunday, May 27th

Went to Cherkley for the night to stay with Lord Beaverbrook. He was alone when I arrived and he took me for a long walk to see his chickens, to look at the little house he gave Mrs Norton (whose death last winter was a great blow to him), and back through the woods and valleys. He told me at length the story of Bonar Law's resignation and Lord Curzon's disappointment and then switched off to sing the praises of Brendan (whom he is backing against Eden for the Leadership of the Tory Party) and to complain that the P.M. had maltreated him in a number of ways over appointments.

When we got back to the house Harold Balfour, just returned from West Africa and about to become a peer, arrived, followed by Lord Queensberry[4] and Brendan.

Before dinner there was an incident which was indicative of the strong social chip on Lord Beaverbrook's shoulder. In the course of attacking Eden he said that the latter owed his success to his birth and education. He then turned on the assembled company and said that true men of quality, like Harold Balfour, Brendan and himself had worked their way up from nothing by sheer hard work and ability, whereas Lord Queensberry and I were like Anothony Eden and had only got where we were because of the

[1] My sister-in-law, Joan Colville.
[2] Lord Colville of Culross.
[3] A fellow pilot in the R.A.F.
[4] 11th Marquess of Queensberry. Married at this time to the elegant portrait painter Cathleen Mann. Himself a dedicated clubman (he was a member of ten), he ran a successful and popular one for the armed forces during the war.

circumstances in which we were born. Having made this attack, with flashing eyes, he then proceeded to send for the Scottish Psalter and read aloud to us several of the metrical Psalms. I think he did this as a form of grace before dinner and a possible means of making amends to the Almighty.

We had an excellent dinner with a magnum of champagne and lots of brandy, followed by a rotten film. When Balfour and Queensberry had gone, there followed a long political conversation, with attacks on Bevin and praise of Morrison (the Beaverbrook–Bracken theme), abuse of Eden and Anderson and of the recent appointment of Dunglass (who is pro-Pole while they are violently pro-Russian) as Under Secretary at the F.O. The evening was fun, with a real buccaneering, racketeering atmosphere. Of course, they are both utterly mischievous and will do the Conservative Party countless harm, at this election and afterwards.

Monday, May 28th
Awoke to a glorious view through the Dorking Gap, a bath in a fantastically over-luxurious bathroom, and a single poached egg accompanied by the *Daily Express*. Brendan had said he would be ready to leave for London at 9.30 but was not in fact ready until 11.30. Meanwhile I sat in the sun and poked about in Lord B.'s library, in the belief that books often tell one much of their owner. His were mostly dull, the lesser novelists and the standard biographies. But on a reading desk, by the side of two dictaphones, stood the Bible, open at the Psalms and in a nearby bookshelf was Wilkes's notorious *Essay on Woman*, an obscene parody of Pope's *Essay on Man*, which on publication was burned by the public hangman. Copies are therefore rare.

Lord B. came down, sat beside me in the sun, carried on some politico-journalistic intrigue by telephone, told some unknown caller that he would surely try and get him the Financial Secretaryship of the War Office (which he subsequently made no attempt to do), blackguarded James Stuart to somebody else as a Highlander, at once treacherous and loyal (James stands up against the Beaver–Brendan schemes and wields too much influence over appointments for their liking), discoursed to me cheerfully on various subjects, and finally, after a debunking description of Charles Dickens' private life, presented me with one of the maligned author's first editions.

Brendan came down and talked politics for an hour, saying that the socialist plot was to nationalise only the mines, the Bank of England and electricity, but that if they nationalised the last they controlled industry as a whole and the second would tie finance to their apron. Eventually we left in Brendan's car and he talked the whole way up to London in an absolutely sane and sensible way.

Later in the day Lord B., who had argued with me that the Prof. had been utterly wrong about the V-weapons (the Prof. opposes him about the Bretton Woods financial project) sent me part of his dossier on the matter, each page taking one instance in which the Prof. could be shown to have been utterly wrong. He must be an uncomfortable colleague.

Lunched with Robert of Austria at the St James's Club. At 4.30 p.m. the P.M. gave a party at No. 10, to which I went, for the outgoing members of the Government and the new Cabinet. Conservative, Liberal and Labour met on most friendly terms.

More Government appointments (minor offices), the dissolution Honours List, satisfactory telegrams from Truman and Uncle Joe about a Big Three meeting in Berlin, and bed at 3.00 a.m.

Tuesday, May 29th
The House of Commons met, with the Labour Party in Opposition. I was not there, but gather there was a good deal of noise.

Opinion seems to be that in the election the forces, particularly the army, will vote left. Lord Queensberry told me that eighty per cent of the soldiers coming through his club say they will vote Labour. On the other hand it is thought the P.M. will counter-attract many votes purely on personal grounds and the Tories, apart from Brendan, are confident. Today I bet Leslie Rowan five shillings that Labour will get in, or rather that the Government (Conservative, Liberal National and Independent) will not get a majority.[1]

Wednesday, May 30th
The new Cabinet met for the first time. No. 10 is being refurbished and made ready for constant use and we may soon be able to leave the dismal Annexe for good. Immersed in rather interesting problems and papers. In the Levant the threatened storm between the French and the Syrians has broken and my sympathies are not with the French. War has made people too "trigger-happy" as the Americans call it.

John Martin tells me he is leaving No. 10 at the end of June for the Colonial Office.

---

[1] I later hedged my bet by wagering Nicko Henderson ten shillings that the Tories would win. So I was down five shillings.

Thursday, May 31st
Dined at Pratts with Bob Coates. Mother returned from Badminton, for the last time, as Queen Mary is about to return to Marlborough House.

*   *   *

On Friday, June 1st, I went down to Chequers with the Prime Minister and the week-end was largely devoted to the preparation of the first political broadcast of the series which members of all parties are making before the General Election on July 5th. The P.M.'s, the first of four which he is to make, was a fighting and provocative effort, mentioning the necessity of a political police to a really socialist state. He delivered it on the evening of Monday, June 4th, in the little study, hung with small Constables, at Chequers. I sat in the room with him while he delivered the broadcast and was amused to note that his gestures to the microphone were as emphatic as those he uses in a political speech to a large audience and far more pronounced than those he employs in ordinary conversation. The speech, in which, contrary to general supposition, neither Brendan nor the Beaver had a hand, aroused widespread criticism and did not really go down well, at any rate with the educated classes. For the first time he was speaking against the clock which made him hurry unduly.

And now, a few weeks after the war in Europe is over, I bring to an end this diary which is essentially a war-time measure and which began a week after hostilities broke out. Those sunny days of September 1939 seem to belong to a past life. The whole face of Europe has changed, physically and spiritually also. For us the great problem is Russia, whose intentions we cannot with certainty fathom and whose more sinister designs seem to be crystallised in the Polish question, as far from solution as ever. "The Big Three" are to meet in Berlin on July 15th and after their conference we may see more distinctly the shape of things to come.

Elsewhere Europe is in no happy state. France is ruled by a hyper-sensitive autocrat whose foolish and impetuous actions – in the Levant, and in the Val d'Aosta where he ordered his troops to resist the orders of the Supreme Commander, Eisenhower – effectively block the close friendship with the Western Powers which all thinking Frenchmen and all their friends abroad see to be indispensable to the recovery of France and to the restoration of Europe.

In Italy six weak parties conduct their petty intrigues while

Allied Military Government keeps the peace and the partisans of the north commit their counter-atrocities against fascism in the same spirit that originally produced the worst fascist excesses. In the Balkans, apart from Greece and Turkey, Russian puppets rule unhampered by free elections and the system of "rule by the Party" is established. In Spain Franco holds precarious sway, reviled by the outside world and threatened by Spanish republican concentrations behind the Pyrenees. He seems to be toying with the idea of restoring the monarchy in order to present an appearance of respectability.

Germany hangs her head, bewildered and disgraced, while the Russians vary in their zone between fraternisation, to counteract the prevailing preference for the English and Americans, and a policy of rape, murder and arson. Whether Austria is to be free is problematic and at present the Russians have set up a government, headed by an octogenarian Social Democrat (to give it respectability) but boasting Communists in the Ministries of the Interior and Education which are the Ministries that matter. Over all Europe hangs the cloud of insufficient supplies, disjointed distribution, lack of coal and a superfluity of destitute and displaced persons. The situation is no easier, nor are the prospects apparently brighter, than before the first shot was fired.

At home the first intoxication of victory is passing. The parties are creating bitterness, largely artificial, in their vote-catching hysteria. Brendan and the Beaver are firing vast salvos which mostly, I think, miss their mark. Labour propaganda is a great deal better and is launched on a rising market. Without Winston's personal prestige the Tories would not have a chance. Even with him I am not sanguine of their prospects, though most of their leaders are confident of a good majority. I think the service vote will be Left and the housing shortage has left many people disgruntled. The main Conservative advantage is the prevailing good humour of the people and the accepted point that Attlee would be a sorry successor to Winston at the meeting of the Big Three and in the counsels of the Nations.

I have written a great deal in these pages, much that I ought not to have written and much that was not worth writing. I have omitted many of the details, as indeed many of the great or significant events, which would have made it easier to recall the scenes as they passed before me. But however great or little its value may be to me in the years to come, it records one fact for which I have good reason to be thankful. I have lived as interesting and as varied a life as could be conceived, and I have experienced things which the ordinary course of events would never have brought my way, during five and a half years in which the rest of humanity has suffered the extremes of boredom and depression only alternating with those of grief, horror and fear. If I have not profited, then there is none but myself to blame.

J.R.C.
June 18th, 1945
4 Mulberry Walk.

34

End of War Coalition

Having written this rather sententious farewell to my diary, I nevertheless kept brief notes of my activities for the next four months from which this chapter is constructed. Early in October, I rejoined my parent department, the Foreign Office, after six years' secondment.

When William Sidney succeeded his uncle as Lord De L'Isle and Dudley I applied for the nomination in his Chelsea seat, strongly supported by both Winston Churchill and Brendan Bracken. However, a matter of hours before my application was received the Conservative Association had already selected another candidate. My strongly Liberal mother, and her equally Liberal step-mother, Peggy Crewe, showed no inclination to condole with me.

On June 20th my grandfather died at his home at West Horsley. I went straight from the funeral in the lovely red sandstone church at Barthomley on his remaining Crewe estate to join Winston Churchill's train at Leeds; for though he was on an electioneering tour in which it would have been improper for officials to take part, he was still Prime Minister, required to deal with the daily business of Government.

He addressed vast and enthusiastic crowds at Leeds, Bradford and Preston. The train moved on to Glasgow where he made about ten speeches to deafening applause. He drove to Edinburgh along roads thronged with cheering men, women and children, and when he finally returned to the train, after a reception in Edinburgh as warm and moving as in Glasgow, he said to me that nobody who had seen what he had that day could have any doubt as to the result of the coming election. I said that I would agree if it were a presidential election.

July 5th was polling-day. The Conservative Central Office and

Lord Beaverbrook both forecast a majority of at least a hundred seats for the Government. Winston Churchill decided to take a fortnight's holiday, the first he had had since war began. A hospitable Canadian, Brigadier-General Brutinel, who owned the Château Margaux vineyard, offered his house, Bordaberry, near Hendaye. The General had somehow contrived to remain in France throughout the German occupation and had been a leading conspirator in arranging for escaping Allied airmen and prisoners of war to cross the Pyrenees into Spain.

So on July 7th Mr and Mrs Churchill, Mary, Lord Moran and I flew to Bordeaux. The Prime Minister devoted most of the time to painting. He was accompanied and advised on his artistic expeditions by a talented artist, Mrs Nairn, wife of the British Consul at Bordeaux, who had been at Marrakech when we were there in January 1944 and had won Churchill's esteem. The rest of us walked, visited Biarritz, St Jean de Luz and Bayonne, watched Basque dancing at Hendaye and drank the finest clarets. We were joined for a day or two by Duff Cooper.

In the mornings we bathed from a sandy beach. The Prime Minister floated, like a benevolent hippo, in the middle of a large circle of protective French policemen who had duly donned bathing suits for the purpose. His British detective had also been equipped by the thoughtful authorities at Scotland Yard for such aquatic duties. Round and round this circle swam a persistent French Countess, a notorious *collaborateuse* who hoped by speaking to Winston Churchill to escape the fate which the implacable *résistance* were probably planning for her. It reminded me of the mediaeval practice of "touching for the King's evil". The encircling gendarmes, patiently treading water, thwarted her plot, but she did entrap me on the beach. Looking at her golden locks I felt pity and hoped she would not suffer the fate of those shorn girls I had seen at Bayeux the preceding summer. I believe that in the end her good looks, and no doubt her influential connections, saved her from anything worse than a short prison sentence.

Before we left for France Churchill asked President Truman to telegraph the result of the test of the first atomic bomb shortly due to take place in the Nevada desert. "Let me know," he had signalled, "whether it is a flop or a plop." When we were about to leave Bordaberry a telegram came from the President to the Prime Minister. It read: "It's a plop. Truman." A new, glaring light was shed on the future of the war against Japan.

On July 15th Churchill left for a meeting of the Big Three at Potsdam where my colleagues Leslie Rowan and John Peck awaited him, together with the whole British delegation and, by Churchill's special invitation, the leader of the Opposition, Clement Attlee, for whom he had even been thoughtful enough to provide a valet. It was, Attlee told me afterwards, the first and last time he ever had a valet.

I returned to No. 10 with Mrs Churchill and acted as the rearlink until, ten days or so later, the Potsdam Conference adjourned so that Churchill, Eden and Attlee might fly back to London for the declaration of the polls. This had been delayed three weeks so that the service voting papers could be flown home from distant parts of the world and added to the votes cast in Britain.

Early on July 26th the Prime Minister, Beaverbrook, Brendan Bracken and David Margesson seated themselves in Churchill's own map-room, opposite the entrance to the Annexe in the Office of Works building. Special arrangements had been made for the results to be flashed on a screen as each was announced. After half an hour it was evident there was going to be a landslide to the Labour Party. Nobody was more surprised than Attlee who, driving to Chequers three weeks later, told me that in his most optimistic dreams he had reckoned that there might, with luck, be a Conservative majority of only some forty seats.

That evening Churchill resigned and the King sent for Attlee. There was world stupefaction, not least at Potsdam, where Stalin supposed that Churchill would have "fixed" the results.

It was surprising to find myself on July 27th, 1945, Private Secretary to Mr Attlee. It was still more surprising to read the letters from people, many of them in high official places and apparently devoted to Churchill, who wrote to Attlee saying how much they rejoiced in the election result. Prominent among these was General Sir Archibald Nye, Vice Chief of the Imperial General Staff, a post he owed to Churchill personally. He wrote to say how delighted he was by the election result both on political and personal grounds. Having read his letter I was astonished to travel up in the lift with him to attend a party Duncan Sandys gave that evening for the outgoing Conservative administration.

When I said to Dr Dalton that he must indeed be gratified, he replied that while the Tories had left the constituencies untended, their agents being for the most part away fighting, he, like Herbert Morrison, had spent much time and effort in ensuring that the Labour electoral machinery was in good order. However, Sir Edward Bridges and Sir Alan Lascelles persuaded the King to suggest to Attlee that Bevin should be Foreign Secretary rather than Dalton who had originally been intended for the post.

Attlee and Bevin returned to Potsdam, with, to the astonishment of the Americans and Russians, exactly the same team as had ministered to Churchill and Eden. Meanwhile I was lent to Churchill to help him clear up his affairs. Chequers was placed at his disposal for the week-end after the election and I went with him. There was a large family party and we drank a Rehoboam of champagne for dinner. I recorded that Churchill said it was fatal to give way to self-pity, that the new Government had a mandate which the Opposition would have no right to question, and that in matters of national as opposed to party interest, it was the duty of everybody to support them, facing as they were the most difficult task of any peace-time Government in modern times. In foreign affairs, at any rate, he stuck to that resolution.

Nevertheless internal political bickering began soon enough. It started with a severe letter from Churchill to Attlee complaining of an injudicious statement Professor Harold Laski had made during the election campaign. As I was spending part of my time at No. 10 and part of it at Claridges, where the Churchills were temporarily installed, I helped draft both the charges and counter-charges in the ensuing correspondence. It was a wholly Gilbertian situation, especially as neither Churchill nor Attlee saw any objection to the role I was expected to assume.

On August 2nd the new Prime Minister returned from Potsdam, with all too little settled by the Big Three, and completed the formation of his Government. He thought he should acquire a sober "Anthony Eden" black Homburg hat and asked me where to buy one. With deliberate irony I took him to Lock's in St James's Street, the most aristocratic hat-maker in London. He bought a hat that suited him well.

A few days later I made this brief diary note: "*August 6th.* The first atomic bomb was dropped on Hiroshima and a new terrifying era begins. I had known of the project since 1941, but had never fully realised its implications until now. The startling news was, at Winston's express request, broken to an unprepared England by W.'s statement (drafted last week-end at Chequers) with a preface by Attlee."

The mood was one of elation; for a long drawn-out end to the war, with hideous further casualties, now seemed certain to be avoided and few people paused to contemplate the subsequent implications.

On August 15th I saw on the tape-machine at No. 10 that Japan had surrendered. I brought the news into the Cabinet room where Attlee was closeted with Lord Louis Mountbatten* who was professing Labour sympathies. Such is the fallibility of great men's memories that Mountbatten subsequently averred he had heard the news at the Admiralty and had darted across the Horse Guards

Parade to tell the Prime Minister. I am quite sure my own recollection is correct. Not, of course, that it matters in the least except as a minor indication of the inaccuracies of history.

My diary note for August 15th reads: "The Japanese, conquered by the atomic bomb, accepted the Potsdam terms of surrender and, after several days of uncertainty, Mr Attlee announced the news last night at midnight. V.J. Day.

"The King and Queen opened Parliament in state. I drove to the house with Mr Attlee through exuberant crowds. Winston received the greatest ovation of all. Debate on the Address. I listened to Attlee and to Winston."

Attlee lent Churchill the Prime Ministerial C.54 aircraft to fly to the northern Italian lakes for a painting holiday; and on August 17th I went to Chequers with the Attlees for a long week-end. I was "greatly attracted by his simple charm and lack of ostentation or ambition".

The contrast with my previous week-ends at Chequers was, however, notable. Mrs Churchill's superb cook had vanished and the A.T.S. replacement, though she did her best, was not in the same class. The new Labour Prime Minister was more formal in his dress and behaviour than his Conservative predecessor. At dinner a starched shirt and stiff butterfly collar was the order of the day. Mrs Attlee, distinguished looking and clearly a beauty in her youth, was welcoming and friendly, but Mrs Churchill's sometimes caustic comments and unflagging perfectionism were missing.

Attlee asked me what I thought of Geoffrey de Freitas who was there to be vetted as a candidate for Parliamentary Private Secretary. Charming, I said, and highly intelligent. "Yes," replied Attlee, "and what is more he was at Haileybury, my old school." Churchill, though he sometimes said nice things about me, never included in his recommendations that we were both Old Harrovians. I concluded that the old school tie counted even more in Labour than in Conservative circles.

None of this detracted from Attlee's virtues of total honesty, quickness, efficiency and common sense. He was an outstanding manager of an often difficult team; and he was the only Prime Minister of the United Kingdom in the twentieth century, apart from Sir Alec Douglas-Home, who had no shred of either conceit or vanity. In the mornings he tended to be a little astringent: after luncheon he was invariably mellow and most approachable.

On August 21st, the day after we left Chequers, Ernest Bevin, Anthony Eden's replacement as Foreign Secretary, made a speech on foreign affairs which caused dudgeon in left-wing continental circles and caused Oliver Stanley to comment on "The Importance of being Anthony". As for me, the time soon came to go to a farewell luncheon which the Attlees gave for my mother and myself, to say goodbye and to leave 10 Downing Street, as I wrote in my diary, "for the third and presumably the last time".

Part Three

October 1945–October 1951

35

Pastures New

October 1945–October 1951

In the Southern Department of the Foreign Office, where I arrived in October 1945, the country allotted to my care was Yugoslavia, about which I already knew a certain amount owing to Winston Churchill's frequent preoccupation with Tito, King Peter and the Ban of Croatia (Dr Subasic).

My predecessor at this desk was John Addis, who now succeeded me at No. 10, thus continuing a policy which began with my own appointment in 1939, and has persisted ever since, that there should be a member of the Foreign Service among the Prime Minister's secretaries. However, John Addis had been on leave for three weeks before I took his chair so that I was faced with a gargantuan pile of papers awaiting attention, was obliged to take bags full home at night and found myself working fifteen to sixteen hours a day.

I was not amused when a few days after establishing myself in the Southern Department I received a sharp note from Addis enquiring why a question from the Prime Minister about Yugoslavia had not been answered. On searching through the heap of papers in my in-tray I found that the question was contained in a letter *I* had written weeks before we changed places. I hope he showed Mr Attlee my caustic reply.

Relations with Tito were no longer what they had been a few months earlier. He was now, and for four years to come, firmly in the Stalinist camp; he had tried to seize the Italian territories of Trieste and Venezia Giulia; and he had even contemplated occupying Austrian Carinthia. Part of my job was to compose in flowery prose indignant despatches to our Ambassador in Belgrade instructing him to complain, in the name of His Majesty's Government, of the tyrant's behaviour. As exercises in composition they were enjoyable; as protests they were ineffective. Another of my duties was to pronounce whether Yugoslavs captured by our forces in Italy and demanded by Tito should or should not be returned to Yugoslavia for probable execution. As a rough and ready rule it was agreed that no Chetniks, loyal supporters of King Peter but at one time prone to collaborate with the Italians, should be sent back to Tito-land. On the other hand, the leaders, though only the leaders, of the Croat terrorist Ustasi, who were guilty of many atrocities, should be surrendered. Few of them were caught. This policy, especially as it related to the Chetniks, infuriated Tito; but Ernest Bevin stood no nonsense from the Yugoslav Ambassador when he called to protest. Bevin never did stand any nonsense, from Members of Parliament, Trade Unionists, foreigners or his own colleagues.

In due course I was promoted assistant head of the department, which meant that the misdeeds of the new Communist régimes in Hungary, Roumania, Bulgaria and Albania were added to my Yugoslav responsibilities, as was the shilly-shallying of the recently elected Greek Government and their increasingly vociferous claim to Cyprus.

All this meant hard labour, and most of it was depressing because not only did Molotov persistently say No on behalf of the Soviet Union to every proposal we made for some semblance of democracy in the Balkans, but also because Britain was subjected to an economic stringency still grimmer than in the war. It was galling to watch living conditions improve month by month in France and Italy while we, the victors, languished in bleak monotony. Gloom reigned in the bomb-devastated streets of London and the provincial cities. The winter of 1946–47 was the worst for fifty years. The Thames froze at Westminster Bridge and in Chelsea I often had to dig thick snow from round the wheels of my car after a stationary hour or two. There was a fuel crisis and domestic coal supplies were severely rationed. All my girl-friends were platonic; London was grey; life was grey.

A change of occupation, and an unexpected one, came my way in the spring of 1947. Sir Alan Lascelles invited me, in the King's name, to become Private Secretary to the twenty-one-year-old Heiress Apparent, Princess Elizabeth. I did not want to abandon my diplomatic career for too long, but I said yes with alacrity on the basis of a two-year secondment, spurred on by Winston Churchill who pronounced: "It is your duty to accept." It was in the event a greater pleasure than a duty, for I served a young lady as wise as she was attractive. She already had three hard-working ladies-in-waiting, who dealt with her heavy load of correspondence from the general public; but I was the first male member of her Household. They were for me two wholly enjoyable years beginning, four months after my appointment, with Princess Elizabeth's marriage to Lieutenant Philip Mountbatten, an event which with nation-wide rejoicing, splendid decorations and the re-emergence of State carriages and the Household Cavalry in full-dress uniform, helped to lift the encircling gloom.

Food parcels from the United States and the Dominions, which were doing so much to alleviate the austerity in thousands of British homes, had been matched by hundreds of tons of tinned food of every variety, given by British communities abroad as wedding presents for Princess Elizabeth to distribute as she saw fit.

How to distribute them was a problem. I consulted Stella, Lady Reading. She had been secretary to Lord Reading, who rose from cabin-boy to Viceroy of India, and when his first wife died he married her. Realising that there were many tasks for women to perform which were not the responsibility of established organisa-tions such as the Red Cross, St John of Jerusalem or the women's uniformed services, she had brought her natural organising gifts to fruition by founding the Women's Voluntary Service, with its headquarters in Tothill Street and its activities projected through-out the country. She and her devoted volunteers found no chal-lenge unacceptable in war or peace.

Up till then those whom I consulted had said with one accord: "Hand it all over to the Ministry of Food." Princess Elizabeth was far from content with this unimaginative proposal, well knowing how unlikely the donors were to be gratified; and that was why I suggested confiding in Lady Reading.

She mobilised a hundred or so willing members of the W.V.S. They, with the King's permission, took over the large kitchens at Buckingham Palace during the Royal Family's holiday at Balmoral the following year. By the end of September 1948, thousands of beautifully packed and well assorted food parcels had been de-spatched to widows and old-age pensioners throughout the king-dom, each containing a message from Princess Elizabeth personal-ly. Thanks to Lady Reading and the agreement of the Post Office to send the parcels free of charge, the whole operation cost almost nothing.

This is but one example of the drive, the willingness to leap any hurdle, which Lady Reading inspired in a body of selfless women volunteers who worked so hard and whose praises have not been adequately sung.

One of Princess Elizabeth's ladies-in-waiting, Lady Margaret Egerton, endowed with a beautiful voice, had been wont to sing a metrical psalm, "The Lord's my Shepherd" (Crimond), in the heather at Balmoral and had taught the two princesses a little-known descant. Princess Elizabeth decided to have this at her wedding, but nobody could find the score of the descant. Lady Margaret, tunefully accompanied by the two princesses, therefore sang it to the Organist and Precentor of Westminster Abbey who took down the notes in musical shorthand and taught it to the Abbey Choir. On the wedding day nobody was more surprised than the composer of the descant who, far away in Stirling, listened to the service on his radio. Since then both the metrical psalm to the tune Crimond and the descant have been consistently popular in churches throughout the British Isles and the Common-wealth.

Before the wedding there was a magnificent evening party at Buckingham Palace for which sparkling tiaras and orders emerged from long years of storage. The guests were as various as half a dozen foreign Kings and Queens on the one hand and Beatrice Lillie and Noël Coward on the other. The Roumanian Govern-ment took advantage of King Michael's presence in London to declare a republic, something they had not dared to do while he was still in Bucharest because of his popularity with his people. An Indian Rajah became uncontrollably drunk and assaulted the Duke of Devonshire (who was sober), but otherwise there were no untoward events. However, Queen Mary, scintillating as ever in a huge display of jewellery, without giving the least impression of vulgarity or ostentation, was somewhat taken aback when Field Marshal Smuts said to her, "You are the big potato; the other Queens are all small potatoes."

Apart from the colour and national jubilation which marked the royal wedding, the outlook was black as the country stumbled through a rough economic blizzard. After talking to Winston Churchill at his birthday dinner party on November 30th, 1947, at 28 Hyde Park Gate, I made this gloomy entry in my diary:

Winston is in sombre mood, convinced that this country is destined to suffer the most agonising economic distress. He says that the anxiety he suffered during the Battle of the Atlantic was "a mere pup" in comparison. We could only get through if we had the power of the spirit, the unity and the absence of envy, malice and hatred which are now so conspicuously lacking. Never in his life had he felt such despair and he blamed it on the Government whose "insatiable lust for power is only equalled by their incurable impotence in exercising it". The phrases and epigrams rolled out in the old way, but I missed that indomitable hope and conviction which characterised the Prime Minister of 1940–41.

While the Princess and the Duke of Edinburgh were away on their honeymoon the King gave a party for the Foreign Ministers of Britain, the United States and Russia who abandoned their squabbles at Lancaster House to come to Buckingham Palace and drink champagne cocktails. Winston and Molotov talked like old friends and Princess Margaret engaged Vyshinski[1] in a twenty minutes' argument which much impressed him. He said to me that if only she had not been a Princess she would assuredly have made a most formidable Advocate. The Foreign Secretary, Ernest Bevin, who for all his virtues liked to take personal credit for most things, told me – when I said at the end that the party had done more good than any number of meetings at Lancaster House – that he was glad I thought *he* had organised it well. Hector McNeil,[2] Minister of State at the Foreign Office, asserted that photographs of Molotov's earnest conversations with the King and Winston Churchill would have been powerful diplomatic weapons.

My duties as a courtier did not hinder excursions into other circles. Once or twice, with Peter Townsend,[3] Meg Egerton and my Communist friend Janet Margesson (beginning to lose her faith in the Kremlin), I spent an evening at the Dockland Settlement and, as the following extracts from my diary show, I sometimes strayed into more rarefied atmospheres:

Friday, December 19th
Dined at the French Embassy to see Elizabeth Chavchavadze,[4] who is staying there. Lady Cunard, Lulu de Vilmorin,[5] Peter Quennell, Garrett Moore, Violet Trefusis, Hugh Ross and Gerard

[1] Andrei Vyshinski, hard-line Soviet prosecutor of Stalin's victims, with special responsibility for the imposition of Communist régimes on the Balkan countries.

[2] At one time journalist on the *Daily Express*. Labour M.P. for Greenock. Able and faithful supporter of Ernest Bevin who much preferred him to his predecessor, Philip Noel-Baker.

[3] Group Captain Peter Townsend, D.S.O., D.F.C. and bar. Gallant Battle of Britain pilot. Equerry to the King and Deputy Master of the Household.

[4] Heiress to an American Loyalist family settled in France after American Independence. First married the Comte de Breteuil and then the talented and charming Russian pianist Prince George Chavchavadze. She had a fine *hôtel* in Paris and rented the Palazza Polignac in Venice where I stayed with her for three idyllic weeks in the hot summer of 1947. Her figure was deplorable, but her wit and culture enchanting.

[5] Much admired French novelist. Intimate friend of the Duff Coopers in Paris.

Andre[1] were the other guests. A wonderful dinner, and conversation ranging from gossip to Baudelaire. Lady Cunard, who is always original, said that Lord Louis Mountbatten* was one of the most tedious men she knew; he thought a mask of superficial charm could compensate for never having read a book.

Nineteen forty-eight began with dark prospects internationally and serious economic prospects at home. Luckily it was a singularly warm winter so that there was no repetition of the previous year's desperate coal crisis. Food parcels poured into many homes from generous people in the Dominions and the U.S.A., horrified that the British, who had given so much in lives and treasure, should still be victims of shortages and drab austerity.

Friday, February 6th, 1948
Queen Mary took Lord Cambridge, Lady Helena Gibbs and me to see *Annie Get Your Gun*. It was my fourth time. H.M. revelled in it, and in addition she received an overwhelming and most touching ovation from the actors and the audience. After the song "I'm an Indian too, a Sioux", she turned to me and asked, "Is *that* one of the songs Margaret sings?" I said it was, to which she remarked, "What a pity!" I thought I had said the wrong thing and done Princess Margaret ill-service, but a minute or two later her grandmother reverted to the subject and said, "What a pity I have never heard her!"

Saturday, February 7th
Stayed the week-end with Tony and Yvonne Rothschild at Ascott.[2] Tony has a magnificent library and some admirable pictures. The house is certainly as comfortable as could be wished, but overheated bedrooms always give me restless nights.

Sunday, February 8th
After Tony, Ann and I had been for a seven-mile walk (very hard going on the high road) we returned to tea where we found that agile conversationist Princess Marthe Bibesco[3] whom I had met dining with David[4] and Jean Lloyd. We discoursed till dinner.

---

[1] Popular member of the French Embassy in London for many years. Eventually French Ambassador in Finland and Thailand.

[2] At Wing in Buckinghamshire.

[3] French writer who married a Roumanian. An internationally known "bluestocking".

[4] Son of George Lloyd, distinguished proconsul and Secretary of State for the Colonies. Himself Under Secretary of State at the Home Office and then the Colonial Office, 1952–57. Married Lady Jean Ogilvy.

Speaking of the institution of monarchy she said that when the King is no more *"les termites se désinterressent de la termitière"* – a fact to which she ascribes the political maladies of France.

We spent most of the evening after dinner trying to persuade Madame Laffon, an attractive French friend of Yvonne, who has three children at school in England, that English schools were not riddled with homosexuality and that incessant and brutal corporal punishment was not an invariable feature of the curriculum. Such are the curious conceptions which one race forms of another.

Thursday, February 19th
Sorine, the Russian artist who is painting Princess Elizabeth and being given innumerable sittings, told me I had a very interesting head. I should have been more flattered had he not told Jean Elphinstone precisely the same last week!

Meanwhile I had fallen head over heels in love with one of Princess Elizabeth's ladies-in-waiting, Meg Egerton. As she was strikingly good-looking, and no less strikingly vivacious, she had many suitors. I had an unfair advantage because my office, on the second floor of Buckingham Palace, was next to the lady-in-waiting's suite of rooms. So she found it hard to escape.

Saturday, May 1st
I arrived last night at Chartwell Farm to stay with Mary and Christopher Soames.* Tonight we dined with Winston at Chartwell. Sarah and Bill Deakin[1] made up the party. Dinner began badly, with reading of the newspapers and monosyllabic answers; but when the champagne had done its work, Mr C. brightened up and became his brilliant, gay and epigrammatic best. He gave me the proofs of Volume II of his book, May 1940 to the end of that year, to read and comment on.

Sunday, May 2nd
Six weeks of warmth and sunshine have given way to cold and rain. Christopher had tummy trouble; Mary a vile carbuncle which gave her great pain. In the evening we went to Winston's private cinema, saw an exceptionally good film called *To Be Or Not To Be*, and dined most agreeably. Winston, who had been busy all day painting a red lily against the background of a black buddha,

---

[1] A distinguished historian who helped Churchill on his life of Marlborough and *History of the English-Speaking Peoples*. The first British liaison officer with Marshal Tito in Yugoslavia and after the war Master of St Antony's College, Oxford.

switched from art to Operation TIGER,[1] and rather to my embarrassment told in great detail the story of my trouble with Monty when
he took me out to Germany for the crossing of the Rhine in March
1945. He was scathing about Monty's self-advertising stunts and
said he presumed British soldiers would soon have to be called
"Monties" instead of "Tommies". Speaking of the Anglo-
American disputes over the question of a Second Front in the
Cotentin in 1942, Winston said, "No lover ever studied every whim
of his mistress as I did those of President Roosevelt."

Monday, May 10th
Princess Elizabeth and Prince Philip, attended by Meg and myself,
dined at the French Embassy. After dinner I talked to Hector
McNeil who said that if the Russians were sly enough to make some
conciliatory gesture, with the object of appeasing popular sentiment in the democracies, the F.O. would not know how to deal
with the situation. But he said it would not be in accordance with
the way their minds worked to do so.

*　　*　　*

Early in 1948 I had suggested to the Foreign Office that it would be
good for Anglo-French relations if Princess Elizabeth and Prince
Philip, whose wedding had been romanticised and enthusiastically
covered in every country outside the Soviet bloc, were to visit
Paris. I approached Ernest Bevin who said he wholeheartedly
applauded the suggestion provided it was not in March. "Lent?" I
queried. "No," he replied, "because I expect a Communist drive in
Paris then and because the Government's ban on foreign travel
won't be raised till May 1st." The King approved, and so the first
royal visit to France for nine years took place in May during
probably the hottest Whitsun week-end ever known.

It was exhilarating, if exhausting. The Princess won Parisian
hearts on the very first day, because the quality of her French
accent and the contents of a speech broadcast from the steps of the
Musée Gallièra were an astonishment to those who had been
expecting a dull oration and a heavy English accent. Nothing
enchants the French so much as foreigners with a fluency in their
language, especially if the speaker is a pretty girl and a Princess
into the bargain. With a calmness which has always been one of her
characteristics, she refused to be disconcerted by the constant

[1] Transport of tanks for Wavell's army through the Mediterranean in 1941.

Princess Elizabeth and Prince Philip at the
Paris Opera, May 1948.

Lady Margaret Egerton, who before her
marriage to the author was a Lady in Waiting
to Princess Elizabeth.

Lady Margaret Colville with the godparents outside St. Peter's, Eaton Square, after the christening of her daughter Harriet in February 1953. L. TO R.: The Queen, Mrs. William Whitelaw, Lady Margaret, Lord Home, the Prime Minister.

The Churchills at St. Margaret's, Westminster, after the author's wedding, October 20, 1948.

'This is interesting. It will suit Meg no doubt to get home' – King George VI's comment on a note from Sir Alan Lascelles with the news that the author would be joint principal private secretary (with David Pitblado) to the Prime Minister following the Conservative victory in the General Election, October 1951.

On June 23, 1953, the day he had his stroke, Churchill greets the Italian Prime Minister, de Gasperi.

clicking of cameras and the loud ringing of nearby church bells while she was speaking.

We drove to Versailles. All the fountains, including those in the woods, were playing in shimmering heat, and we lunched at the Grand Trianon. The tablecloths and napkins, with delicately embroidered E's, P's, and roses, had been specially woven for the occasion. We made a triumphal journey down the Seine, all the banks lined by enthusiastic crowds, to the Hôtel de Lauzun where de Gaulle's brother, Pierre, President of the Paris Municipal Council, gave a greatly overcrowded reception in dripping heat. There was a dinner-party of sixty-four at the Embassy, followed by a still larger reception, at which the Princess glittered in the diamond tiara and necklace the Nizam of Hyderabad had given her as a wedding present. On Whit Sunday we all walked to a special early service at the Embassy church, followed by Mattins at 10.30. Nobody could say that the future Supreme Governor of the Church of England was neglecting her duties. Prince Philip looked and felt ill, but with characteristic determination he insisted on going through with the heavy programme. Indeed he made a major contribution to the successful fulfilment of more than usually arduous duties during the whole time we were in Paris.

We went to Fontainebleau, lunched at Barbizon and visited Vaux-le-Vicomte. Princess Elizabeth said she thought it the most perfect house she had ever seen. Everywhere, at Fontainebleau, at Barbizon, at Vaux, there were cheering crowds on the roads and in the streets, and as we re-entered Paris the throng was so great that the cars had difficulty in moving. That night, after a visit to the Opera, it was the same story as the Prince and Princess stood floodlit at the top of the steps. In four hectic days Princess Elizabeth had conquered Paris.

I was gratified when President Vincent Auriol kissed me on both cheeks and made me an Officer of the Légion d'Honneur, but I was brought down to earth by my mother when I returned home. "That," she said, "is what used in my youth to be called a dinner medal."

The crowds were as dense and the plaudits just as loud in Britain as Princess Elizabeth, accompanied by Prince Philip whenever his naval duties allowed, travelled far and wide throughout the kingdom. Her speeches were usually reported on the front pages of the national newspapers. Quite mysteriously, a visit by a young princess with beautiful blue eyes and a superb natural complexion brought gleams of radiant sunshine into the dingiest streets of the dreariest cities. Princes who do their duty are respected; beautiful

Princesses have an in-built advantage over their male counter-parts.

Falling in love coincided with a relaxation from travel, for the Princess was expecting her first child and had cancelled her engagements. It was also a distraction from unsavoury world events. I had no inclination to brood on the international situation which was dominated by the dangerous crisis arising from the refusal of the Russians to allow the Western powers to feed the people in their zones of Berlin. I wrote: "We have taken a very firm line and cannot go back on it. The Russians may find it difficult to climb down without losing face, especially as they have a serious problem with Marshal Tito who has deviated from the Party line. The question of 'face' has caused so many wars." In the event the Russians were forced to climb down as a result of the brilliantly executed Berlin air-lift. Interference with that would have meant war; and at that time the Russians had no atom bomb.

> Whatever happens we have got
> The Maxim Gun and they have not.

For another year or two that late Victorian verse was still quotable.

At the end of July Meg Egerton and I became engaged and for me everything, even Berlin air-lifts and Molotovian intransigence, was bathed in the rosiest of hues. We were married at St Margaret's, Westminster, on October 20th, 1948, causing a traffic jam in Parliament Square of major inconvenience to the public.

In September 1949 my two years of secondment from the Foreign Office expired and after a farewell visit to the King and Queen at Balmoral, we sailed for Lisbon where I had been appointed Head of Chancery in the Embassy. If I had been thrilled by my time as a courtier, it was not just on account of the glamour, considerable though that was. A lasting impression was the dedication and total honesty of those for whom and with whom I worked, qualities I have not seen excelled.

We were two years at the Embassy in Portugal, during the course of which I spent a month in the beautiful but scantily developed colony of Angola, then firmly controlled from Lisbon. I also had an unexpected two hours with Doctor Salazar. He seemed to me an idealist of genuine personal humility. Many, though probably not at that time a majority, of the citizens of Portugal would have disagreed with me sharply; but if he ruled his fellow-countrymen severely, he did on the whole rule them well, at least until he became obsessed with the preservation of the Portuguese Colonies in total contradiction to the new spirit of the times. The two Iberian dictators, Franco and Salazar, used methods that were sometimes harsh; but they were cast in a finer mould than their contemporary tyrants in Germany, Italy and Russia, and their government was a great deal more beneficent. The ordinary citizen in Spain and Portugal had no need to lower his voice or look anxiously over his shoulder when talking politics in a café.

The time, however, was approaching for me to regard foreign policy from a less parochial viewpoint.

Part Four
October 1951–April 1955

36

"Churchill is Back"

We went home from Lisbon on leave in October 1951, just before the General Election. Mr Attlee, having won a majority of only six seats at the election held eighteen months before, concluded that he must try again. We were invited to an election night party given by Lord Camrose at the Savoy. In days when television sets were still comparatively rare, there was no quicker or pleasanter way of hearing the results. Those at the Savoy included Sir Norman Brook,[1] successor to Sir Edward Bridges as Secretary to the Cabinet. "Hello," he said. "Back on leave?" It was an innocent enough question.

The Conservatives had a majority of sixteen, marginally better than that of the outgoing administration. Having absorbed the fact, we set off on the following day to stay, en route for a holiday in Scotland, with my mother-in-law near Newmarket. It was the Cesarewich meeting. As I watched the races and contemplated my losses (endemic, as far as I am concerned, on a race-course) an agitated official emerged from the Jockey Club Stand and asked if I was Mr Colville. When I assented, he said, "It's the Prime Minister wants you on the telephone." "Whatever he asks you to do," advised my innately cautious wife, "Say No."

I heard a familiar voice: "Norman Brook tells me you are home on leave. Would you, if it is not inconvenient (but do pray say if it is), take a train to London and come to see me?"

"Tomorrow morning?"

"No, this afternoon."

Of course I did, and was invited to be the new Prime Minister's Principal Private Secretary. I was, by Whitehall standards, some

---

[1] Later Lord Normanbrook.*

ten years too young for such an appointment. There were two more potent objections. The first was that although I knew a certain amount about foreign affairs and could doubtless get by on Commonwealth, Colonial and Defence matters, and perhaps with luck on Education and Trade, I was abysmally ignorant of the Treasury, of economics generally, of Housing, Local Government, Transport, Pensions, Industry and Agriculture. Secondly, Mr Attlee had appointed to the job, only a month or so previously, David Pitblado,[1] a competent and knowledgeable Treasury official. If Pitblado were now required to make way for me, it would smack of favouritism and those who mattered in Whitehall would resent the imposition of a largely unqualified incumbent to replace a highly qualified one. Moreover, it would be grossly unfair to David Pitblado.

I made these points to Churchill and said that although deeply gratified by the invitation, I felt I must decline. "Rubbish," he replied. "Pitblado is doubtless an excellent man, but I must have somebody I know. Go and talk to Edward Bridges."

Bridges said that if this was what the Prime Minister required, I must do as I was told. I argued and said it would not be regarded as a good start for the new Prime Minister. So he eventually proposed a solution whereby David Pitblado and I should be Joint Principal Private Secretaries. It should have been a recipe for ill-will and mismanagement, but in the event it worked well. I was close to the Prime Minister personally, despite an age gap of forty years, for one of Churchill's endearing and enduring characteristics was to treat young men as if they were his contemporaries. I became a frequent channel of his communication with other Ministers, many of whom I already knew well. Pitblado for his part handled with exemplary skill the Treasury, the Civil Service and economic affairs.

There were many, including his wife, who did not think Churchill should return to office a month short of his seventy-seventh birthday. At first he himself, as he told me when I rejoined him, intended to remain Prime Minister for one year only, and then hand over to his invariably loyal lieutenant, Anthony Eden, whose courage, energy and integrity, though not always his judgment,

---

[1] Had been a delegate to the San Francisco Conference in 1945. In 1951 he was an Under Secretary in the Treasury whereas I was only a First Secretary in the Foreign Service (who saw no reason whatever to promote me to equal status). Afterwards he was economic Minister at the Embassy in Washington, Permanent Secretary at the Ministry of Power and thereafter at the Ministry of Technology and the Civil Service Department. A civil servant of high ability and unfailing efficiency.

Churchill consistently respected. He just wanted, he said, to have time to re-establish the intimate relationship with the United States, which had been a keynote of his policy in the war, and to restore at home the liberties which had been eroded by war-time restrictions and post-war socialist measures.

Circumstances in 1951 were totally different from those existing in 1945, but Churchill began by trying to re-create the situation as he had left it six years before. His faithful associates, General Ismay and Lord Cherwell, were brought into the Cabinet against their own better judgment. Lords Woolton and Leathers were recalled for an unsuccessful experiment as Overlords of clutches of government departments. For a few months Churchill combined, as he had in the war, the office of Minister of Defence with that of Prime Minister; but then it occurred to him that Field Marshal Alexander, of whom he had the highest opinion, would be excellent for the post, oblivious of the fact that Alexander, while a soldier of indisputable gallantry and an excellent emollient as Supreme Allied Commander in Italy, had no experience of Whitehall or of Parliament. So the poor Field Marshal was withdrawn from the Governor Generalship of Canada, in which he was both happy and successful, to become an unhappy and unsuccessful Minister of Defence. General Sir Ian Jacob, by then Director of Overseas Services at the B.B.C., was conscripted to be Alexander's Chief Staff Officer. When Winston Churchill wanted something and chose to exercise his persuasive gift, there were few who found it possible to refuse. Thus Auld Lang Syne was ringing out along the Whitehall corridors and I suppose that I myself was a small part of the refrain.

Yet if some were disturbed by this attempt to revert to the past, others were not. In Britain, and perhaps still more in other countries of the free world, the signal "Churchill is back" carried some of the nostalgic appeal that it had for the Royal Navy on September 3rd, 1939. His name was a household word far beyond the shores of the British Isles. Roosevelt was dead; Stalin was now recognised to be an ogre; Churchill alone of the world's political leaders was placed by millions of people on a pedestal wearing a halo. His return to power seemed to many to presage the recovery of hopes tarnished by the dismal aftermath of the war.

If those hopes, like almost all human hopes, fell short of complete fulfilment, it is nevertheless true that in the three and a half years of Churchill's last administration, there was a shedding of austerity, a return to comparative prosperity and a temporary restoration of peace on earth. This was not so in the first year when, as my diary illustrates, the financial situation remained bleak and rationing was as severe as ever. However, late in 1952 the clouds began to lift and by the time of Queen Elizabeth II's Coronation in June 1953, the prospects were brighter than they had been for many years past.

The tones of Auld Lang Syne were gradually muted and in due course the Overlords, Field Marshal Alexander and Lord Cherwell thankfully departed. General Ismay became Secretary General of N.A.T.O. Sir Ian Jacob, to his great relief, returned to run the B.B.C. Lords Beaverbrook and Bracken, by this time inseparable allies, seldom crossed the threshold of 10 Downing Street, though Bracken's devotion to Churchill did not waver. The Korean war ended; the Coronation was an occasion for even greater national enthusiasm than the royal wedding six years before; Mount Everest was conquered by a British expedition; rationing was a misery soon forgotten; larger foreign travel allowances were granted; and though Churchill's last ambition, to bring the Cold War to an end after Stalin's death, was frustrated, the early 1950s do in retrospect seem like a golden summer.

All this is the more remarkable in that the new administration inherited both a war in the Pacific and an alarming economic crisis at home. It may not be altogether extravagant to suggest that the figure of Winston Churchill brooding benevolently over the scene and, as his eightieth birthday approached, as much cherished by the Labour Party and the Liberals as by his own side, made a significant contribution to the sense of well-being which briefly filled the hearts of men in the United Kingdom and far afield.

With the strain of war-time leadership relaxed, he was now less irascible and impatient than of old and readier to be convinced by argument, provided the right moment was chosen for the exercise. The charm and the lovable qualities were undiminished and at Chartwell, now a more frequent week-end resort than Chequers, he was a solicitous host.

At least until the midsummer of 1953 his mind was as clear and his reactions almost as prompt as in former days. He still dictated incisive minutes, though the menacing red labels, ACTION THIS DAY (carefully hoarded by the messengers at No. 10 and placed on the Cabinet Room table the very day of his return) were no longer in use. His speeches were heard with attention in the House of Commons, reported at length by the press and seldom interrupted except by cheers. He still dominated the Cabinet, now more like Buddha than Achilles, but not with the long monologues, product of weariness, which had irritated his colleagues during the last year of the war.

Like most elderly people, he was bad at remembering names. It had not been one of his more notable gifts ten years previously. When Sir Norman Brook brought Sir Thomas Padmore on to the scene as probationary Deputy Secretary to the Cabinet, Churchill persisted in referring to him as Potsdam; and he said to me one morning, "I don't think much of that fellow Shorthorn." It required ingenuity to discover that the object of his temporary dissatisfaction was General Sir Nevil Brownjohn.

If his memory had lost some of its sharpness, that was only by contrast with its unusual, indeed phenomenal, strength in former days. In lighter moments he could, and did, still quote verses of poetry, sing the music-hall songs of the 1890s and discourse learnedly on the American Civil War or the campaigns of Marlborough and Prince Eugene. He abandoned his war-time practices of an hour's sleep in the afternoon and perusing the first editions of the following day's newspapers before going to bed; but the number of cigars he smoked remained constant and, although he was never inebriated (or, indeed, drank between meals anything but soda-water faintly flavoured with whisky), he would still consume, without the smallest ill-effect, enough champagne and brandy at luncheon or dinner to incapacitate any lesser man.

As far as current affairs were concerned, he was as attentive to Parliament as ever, but in the ordinary day's business he concentrated his thought on those issues, mainly in the foreign field, that interested him. From time to time this led to clashes with the Foreign Secretary, Anthony Eden, who objected to Prime Ministerial interference in his diocese. Churchill was content to leave much of the rest, except where housing, food and labour relations were concerned, to Ministers and officials whom he no longer pursued on points of detail. He made greater use of his Private Office to handle relationships with his colleagues; he was influenced by the sensible and usually moderating opinions of his new son-in-law and Parliamentary Private Secretary, Christopher Soames; and he listened to the advice of the Secretary to the Cabinet, Sir Norman Brook, whose wisdom and diligence he esteemed and whose company he found so agreeable that he elected him to the Other Club. That was the highest personal honour he could confer, and not one offered to either of Norman Brook's predecessors.

The diary I kept during Churchill's second administration was spasmodic, and latterly confined largely to foreign journeys; for though marriage is an honourable estate, it is seldom a tonic for diarists unless they behave like Pepys.

On November 25th, 1951, I made the following note of a dinner-party conversation at Chequers. There was present Richard Casey, Australian Minister of Foreign Affairs, at one stage of the war a much praised Minister of State in Cairo and a future Governor General of Australia.

> The Prime Minister said that he did not believe total war was likely. If it came, it would be on one of two accounts. Either the Americans, unable or unwilling any longer to pay for the maintenance of Europe, would say to the Russians you must by certain dates withdraw from certain points and meet us on certain requirements: otherwise we shall attack you. Or, the Russians, realising that safety did not come from being strong, but only from being the strongest, might for carefully calculated and not for emotional reasons, decide that they must attack before it was too late. If they did so their first target would be the British Isles, which is the aircraft carrier. It was for that reason that Mr Churchill was anxious to convert this country from its present status of a rabbit into that of a hedgehog.
>
> Mr Casey said that there was an ancient Lebanese proverb to the effect that one did not cut a man's throat when one had already poisoned his soup. Mr Churchill said he agreed: it was a matter of supererogation. Mr Casey thought that until the sores in Malaya, Indo-China and the Middle East had been cured, the Russians might consider that the soup was poisoned.

Churchill wasted no time in setting forth for America. There were defence matters to discuss and the progress of the Korean War. The Americans were bearing the brunt of the fighting, but there was also a sizeable British contingent, including the gallant Gloucestershire Regiment, and representative forces from other members of the United Nations. At the Potsdam Conference Churchill thought well of Truman who had assumed Roosevelt's mantle with shrewdness and determination. Since then there had been the Truman doctrine, relieving Britain of her burden in liberated Greece; and the two men had established an immediate friendship in 1946, travelling together by train to Fulton, Missouri, where Churchill roused the world with the eloquent warning he gave in his Iron Curtain speech.

On returning home in January 1952, I wrote this account of our journey to North America:

> On Boxing Day I went with John[1] to shoot at Lennoxlove and caught the night train to London in order to prepare for departure to America with Mr Churchill. We boarded the *Queen Mary* on New Year's Eve, a party of thirty in all which included Eden,

---

[1] My brother-in-law, John, Earl of Ellesmere, later 6th Duke of Sutherland.

Ismay, Cherwell, Slim[1] (C.I.G.S.), McGrigor[2] (First Sea Lord), Roger Makins, Norman Brook and David Pitblado. The *Queen Mary*'s anchor was found to be fouled and so we had to spend the night on board, alongside the quay at Southampton. Lord Mountbatten came from Broadlands to dine and talked arrant political nonsense: he might have learned by heart a leader from the *New Statesman*. The P.M. laughed at him but did not, so Pug Ismay thought, snub him sufficiently. He caused much irritation to the Chiefs of Staff. I escorted Mountbatten off the ship. As we walked down the corridor he put his arm on my shoulder and said: "Without you, Jock, I should feel no confidence, but as you are back I know all will be well." It was, of course, intended as a friendly remark, but flattery, especially when so exaggerated, makes one wonder why one should be thought so naive.

During the crossing we worked on our briefs: oh, the amount of paper that even a small conference evokes! It was very difficult to get the P.M. to read any of it. He said he was going to America to re-establish relations, not to transact business. Fellow passengers included Hector McNeil, Ruth Draper[3] and Priscilla Tweedsmuir[4] – of all of whom we saw a good deal.

On January 3rd we steamed into New York and our party was taken ashore by special arrangement on the Brooklyn shore. The reception was on a huge scale but ill-organised and Pug Ismay and I got separated and all but lost. There followed a flight to Washington and four nights in that city, with conferences at the White House, two of which I attended. Churchill stayed at the British Embassy with the Ambassador, Sir Oliver Franks.* President Truman was affable but not impressive and I did not think Acheson[5] or Lovett[6] anything out of the way.

[1] Field Marshal Viscount Slim, Commander of the 14th Army and hero of the campaign in Burma. C.I.G.S., 1948–52. Governor General of Australia, 1953–60.

[2] Admiral of the Fleet Sir Rhoderick McGrigor, C. in C., Home Fleet, 1948–50. First Sea Lord, 1951–55.

[3] Celebrated American whose impersonations held audiences sometimes in helpless laughter and sometimes close to tears.

[4] Priscilla Thomson by birth. Her second husband was John Buchan's eldest son. She was the slim, attractive and quick-witted Conservative M.P. for South Aberdeen. Minister of State in the Scottish Office and then in the Foreign Office in Edward Heath's 1970 Conservative Government.

[5] Dean Acheson served in Roosevelt's administration and was Secretary of State in Truman's. Respected and liked by Anthony Eden. It was he who said, "Britain has lost an Empire and has not found a rôle."

[6] Robert A. Lovett, a partner in Brown Brothers Harriman. Influential member of Roosevelt's war-time Government and Secretary for Defense in Truman's Cabinet from 1951 to 1953.

There was an embarrassing incident at the first White House meeting. The President and the Prime Minister sat facing each other, flanked by their respective Chiefs of Staff, and one of the main topics for discussion was naval command of the NATO forces, to which we laid claim since the Americans were in command on land. It fell to the First Sea Lord, the diminutive but intelligent Sir Rhoderick McGrigor, to present our case. He went red in the face, large drops of perspiration appeared on his brow and he was too overawed to do more than stutter a few disjointed words. The C.I.G.S., General Slim, stepped into the breach and presented the naval case coolly and calmly. It was a magnificent *tour de force* by the representative of another service and it was evident that the Americans were as impressed as we were. They agreed to the British proposal.

On January 9th we listened to the President address Congress on the State of the Union and then went by train to New York. Before we left the Embassy the Prime Minister, at Sir Oliver Franks' request, agreed to address the staff assembled in the garden. When he walked out on to the terrace for this purpose, he gasped with astonishment. In front of him, filling the entire garden, was a crowd not, as he had expected, of some fifty or sixty people, but, including the wives and children, the best part of a thousand. The service departments in particular were grossly overmanned. He addressed the huge gathering most affably, but he instructed me to procure a detailed list of the officers attached to the Embassy. I did so when we returned to London and discovered that there were, amongst many others, forty-seven lieutenant-colonels and forty-three wing commanders. Evidently nobody had given thought to reducing the vast staffs established in a war which had ended six and a half years previously. The Prime Minister then issued a peremptory order, in his capacity as Minister of Defence, and a drastic reduction was effected.

The P.M. stayed with Bernie Baruch at his flat in E. 66th Street and I with the Henry Hydes in their house on E. 70th Street. On Thursday, January 10th, the Hydes[1] took me to dine with Mrs George Widener and on to the Metropolitan Opera where, in the interval, I met the Duke and Duchess of Windsor and the latter's friend, Mr Donoghue.

Late that night we entrained for Ottawa, where the P.M. had a

---

[1] Henry Hyde, brought up in France and educated in England, was my greatest friend at Cambridge. In the war he joined General Donovan's O.S.S. and was responsible for its effective operations in France. He became a successful international lawyer in New York. At this time he was married to an extremely pretty French wife, Mimi de la Grange.

great reception. We stayed with the Alexanders at Rideau Hall, Christopher Soames having meanwhile joined the P.M.'s party in New York. We were exceedingly comfortable at Government House, and nobody could have been more charming than the Alexanders. Moreover I was pleased because I wrote a speech for the P.M. to use at a banquet for both houses of Parliament, in respect of which he said: "This is very good; too good. I may feel bound to use it in which case it will be the first time in my career I have ever used somebody else's speech." In the event he did not; but I was flattered.

While we were at Rideau Hall, Churchill discussed with Alexander the unsatisfactory situation in Malaya where Chinese Communist guerillas were attacking troops and British-owned plantations. A new energetic and resourceful Commander in Chief was required, and Churchill ordered Sir Gerald Templer[1] to be flown out to Ottawa for inspection and interrogation by himself and Alexander. The latter's high esteem of Templer, who was then unknown to Churchill, carried weight, but on arrival at Ottawa Templer himself so impressed Churchill that he offered him the command right away.

On the 15th we left by train for Washington and on the 17th the P.M. made a great speech to Congress, which I attended on the floor of the House. Lord Knollys,[2] Bill Elliot[3] and other Embassy people present thought it had had a chilly reception; but we were quite wrong. Congress reacted slowly, but the subsequent praise was generous – except at home where the Labour Party asserted that the P.M. had committed us to a more active part against China.

Churchill had been still in bed putting the finishing touches to his speech when Sir Roger Makins came into the room to say the cars were at the door and we ought already to be leaving for the Capitol. In the Prime Minister's speech it was essential to refer to Britain's contribution in the Korean War, which had been raging since 1950. "If the Chinese cross the Yalu River, our reply will be – what?" "Prompt, resolute and effective," suggested Roger Makins on the spur of the moment. "Excellent," said Churchill. He wrote these

---

[1] Field Marshal Sir Gerald Templer. Brought the Malayan operations to an entirely successful conclusion.

[2] 2nd Viscount Knollys. Won a D.F.C. in the First World War. Was Governor of Bermuda, 1941–43, Chairman of Vickers Ltd, and of several insurance companies. Public spirited and a delightful personality.

[3] Air Chief Marshal Sir William Elliot, Chairman of the British Joint Services Commission in Washington.

words in the text of his speech, got up, dressed and reached the Capitol with two minutes to spare.

It was these words with no special significance except to declare that the Allies would react strongly to such an attack, which the Labour Opposition interpreted to mean that an atomic bomb would be used. Such a thought had not crossed Churchill's mind nor, I believe, President Truman's.

We returned to New York on the 19th and though the P.M. caught a cold which prevented a triumphal drive down Broadway, we had a gay time. Then on January 23rd we sailed in the *Queen Mary* and reached Southampton on my thirty-seventh birthday, January 28th. Meg had come down with Mrs Churchill, Mary, Lady Brook, Lady Moran and Mrs Pitblado to greet us and they all had luncheon with us on board.

A few weeks later I wrote this further narrative:

On February 5th there began a foreign affairs debate in the House. I heard Anthony Eden make a somewhat insipid speech and then the Opposition put down a vote of censure on the P.M. personally. He prepared to answer it on the following day by a fighting speech revealing the dramatic fact that the Labour Government had gone further in committing us to bomb China in certain circumstances than anyone supposed and that he had entered into no new commitments.

On the morning of February 6th I arrived at No. 10 early and asked the Private Secretary on duty for the text of the speech. He said that there was no need to think of it further: Edward Ford[1] had just been round from Buckingham Palace to announce that the King was dead.

When I went to the Prime Minister's bedroom he was sitting alone with tears in his eyes, looking straight in front of him and reading neither his official papers nor the newspapers. I had not realised how much the King meant to him. I tried to cheer him up by saying how well he would get on with the new Queen, but all he could say was that he did not know her and that she was only a child. He summoned a Cabinet that morning and he insisted on my attending it. It was, I think, the only time I attended a whole Cabinet meeting.[2]

---

[1] Served in the Grenadier Guards. Second Private Secretary to George VI and Elizabeth II. Secretary to the Pilgrim Trust, 1967–75, and Registrar of the Order of Merit. Married Virginia, the daughter of Lord Brand.

[2] It was not until after Churchill resigned that officials, apart from the Cabinet Office Secretariat, were admitted to Cabinet meetings.

For a week all normal business came to a standstill, while the world showed a large and genuine measure of grief, the new Queen returned from Kenya and the Government dealt with all the ceremonial and constitutional matters attendant on a Demise of the Crown. All had in fact been prepared the previous September when the King had his serious lung operation.

On Friday, 15th February, Meg and I went to the King's funeral at St George's, Windsor, on a bright, cold day, and were moved by the sound of the pipes drawing closer and closer as the funeral cortège approached the Chapel. I remembered so vividly sitting in the nave on a warm June evening in 1947 when the King and Queen took their guests there to hear Dr Harris play the organ.

During the next weeks much happened. First there was trouble over the name of the Royal House. Prince Philip wrote a strongly, but ably, worded memorandum protesting against a proposed Proclamation saying that the House remained the House of Windsor. This annoyed the P.M. and on his behalf I attended two meetings of the Lord Chancellor, Lord Privy Seal, Home Secretary and Leader of the House of Commons (Crookshank)[1] to draft a firm, negative answer. In the end I had more or less to recast it myself and the P.M. accepted it in final form on March 12th. This had all arisen because Queen Mary sent for me on February 18th to say that Prince Ernst August of Hanover had come back from Broadlands and informed her that Lord Mountbatten had said to an assembled house party of royal guests that the House of Mountbatten now reigned. The poor old lady, who had spent a sleepless night, was relieved when I said that I doubted if the Cabinet would contemplate such a change. Indeed when I told the P.M. he had at once consulted the Cabinet who said unanimously that they would tolerate no such thing.

The name of Windsor had been adopted by a decree of King George V in 1917. It was alleged, apocryphally or not, that on hearing the news the Kaiser, not usually renowned for his wit, said: "Well then, let us have tonight at the Opera a performance of the Merry Wives of Saxe-Coburg-Gotha." The name Mountbatten was also new, having replaced Battenberg at the same time as the Royal House, which had no generally accepted name after the death of Queen Victoria (the last of the Hanoverians), became Windsor and Queen Mary's family, the Tecks, became

[1] A Grenadier officer in the First World War. M.P. for the Gainsborough division of Lincolnshire. In February 1952 he was Minister of Health and Leader of the House of Commons.

Cambridges. Prince Philip had logic on his side when he sug-
gested that his children should be the House of Edinburgh; but the
trouble was caused by Lord Mountbatten's tactless assertion
which put both the Cabinet and the leaders of the Opposition up in
arms.

Then came the foreign affairs debate which had been adjourned. The P.M. made a good but much interrupted speech, discrediting Attlee and Morrison and dumbfounding his attackers. He followed it up the next week with a speech in the Defence Debate, two days after handing the Ministry of Defence over to Lord Alexander. This was followed by a clever Budget, slashing the food subsidies but providing new incentives for hard work and overtime by lowering the bottom rates of income tax.

But all this had been a severe strain on the P.M. On Friday, February 22nd, Lord Moran came to me with the news that on the previous evening the P.M. had had a small arterial spasm. This might be the precursor of an immediate stroke; if not, it was at least a plain warning that if the pressure was not relaxed dire results would follow in six months or less. He wanted political advice and so we went to see Lord Salisbury and Tommy Lascelles. The former thought W. might go to the Lords, leaving Eden to manage the Commons, and thus remain P.M. till after the Coronation in May 1953. Nowadays a repetition of the Salisbury–A. J. Balfour[1] partnership would normally be impracticable; but Winston is not an ordinary person, the country as a whole would not like to see him go, and with America as with the continent of Europe he is far our greatest asset.

We kept our counsel until the debates and the budget were over, but on March 13th Lord Moran, having first consulted Mrs Churchill, wrote him a letter – which did not, however, tell quite the whole story. He took it, so I gather, with sang-froid; but he does not know that anyone apart from Mrs C. knows of this matter.

Friday, March 14th
I was on duty this week-end. Instead of staying at Chartwell as usual, Meg and I both went to spend the week-end with Mary and Christopher Soames and were lodged in the cottage in the garden which Winston himself built.

After dinner I went up to the big house. I scored a success –

[1] From 1895 to 1902, while his uncle, Lord Salisbury, was Prime Minister, A. J. Balfour was First Lord of the Treasury and Leader of the House of Commons, becoming Prime Minister himself in 1902.

for the Admiralty – in putting W. off Admiral Vian,[1] whom he was contemplating forcing the Admiralty to send as C. in C., Portsmouth instead of Edelston, by telling him the deplorable impressions Vian created at Lisbon.

Saturday, March 15th

Quite busy all day. The Mark Wyndhams came to lunch with the Soameses. They are obviously *not* on good terms with John and Pamela (whom I like very much and with whom we stayed at Petworth a few weeks ago).[2] After luncheon Winston and I saw a film on guided missiles, explained by a brilliant man called Mitchell from the Ministry of Supply. These will evidently revolutionise defence in war and may go some way to neutralise the atomic bomb.

Sunday, March 16th

At 6.00 we all went to a film (*Edward and Caroline* – French and admirable) at Chartwell, where we dined afterwards. W. liked Meg (who was petrified of him) and told me he found her charming indeed. He is worried about Egypt, where he thinks Eden is throwing the game away; irritated with the Prof. who is being tiresome about atomic matters; and disturbed by the thought that the old-age pensioners may suffer in consequence of an otherwise admirable Budget.

Saturday, March 22nd–Sunday, March 23rd

Drove to Chequers with the P.M. Meg was invited for the week-end and other guests were the Salisburys, the Alexanders and the Soameses. Lord Montgomery and the Prof. came to luncheon on Sunday – Monty, mellow and in good form but, as ever, trying to lobby the P.M. about matters in which he is but slightly interested (this time Greece and Turkey) or on which he hardly thinks Monty an expert. The P.M. is angry, almost to breaking point, with the Prof. who is digging in his toes over the control of atomic energy. In the long gallery on Sunday night, after the rest had gone to bed, he

---

[1] As Captain of H.M.S. *Cossack* he had by a daring raid into a Norwegian fjord, in March 1940, rescued the British merchant seamen held prisoner on the German ship *Altmark*. However, as C. in C. of the Home Fleet in the early 1950s he was much criticised by the officers of his flagship, *Vanguard*, and he was disliked both in naval and civilian circles.

[2] John Wyndham, later Lord Egremont, was Mark Wyndham's elder brother. Much cherished private secretary to Harold Macmillan, he married the exceedingly beautiful Pamela Wyndham-Quinn and inherited Petworth and Cockermouth from his uncle.

told Christopher and me that the programme of the Tory Party must be: "Houses and meat and not being scuppered." He didn't feel quite happy about the latter though he does not himself think war probable unless the Americans lose patience. As he subsequently added, perhaps "not being broke" is going to be our major difficulty and preoccupation.

Quite favourably impressed by Alex this time. He is not original or clever, but I thought he showed common sense on most things, even though he usually took the obvious line. Surprisingly he feels strongly about class distinction: he loved Canada for its absence and is alarmed by it in his own Brigade of Guards.

Friday, April 4th
Last Monday we moved into 60 Westminster Gardens and we are now in a state of chaos. This morning the results of the L.C.C. elections, which went strongly for the socialists, were published. The P.M. took them well though he found them a shock. The reason, I have no doubt, is that the country hoped a Tory Government would mean relaxations and more food: in fact it has meant controls as stringent as ever and severer rationing.

Tonight Meg and I dined with Joey[1] and Sarah Legh to meet the Queen. Jamie Leveson[2] was the sixth. It was the first time I had seen her since her Accession, though I had lunched with her at Clarence House just before Christmas. She looked handsome in black with two strings of huge pearls, seemed animated and gave us both the impression that she was at ease and self-possessed.

Saturday, April 5th
Meg has been feeling more than usually unwell of late. She had a pregnancy test this morning and it was positive.

Monday, April 7th
A tedious Honours Committee this morning. Some of the P.M.'s wishes cause consternation – especially baronetcies for "Bomber Harris" and Louis Spears.

Tuesday, April 8th
Trouble with the Ministry of Transport which has been brewing for long came to something of a head. The P.M. wants to denationalise

---

[1] Hon. Sir Piers Legh, Master of the Queen's Household. He had an apartment in St James's Palace.
[2] Later 5th Earl Granville, M.C. A first cousin of the Queen.

road haulage as quickly as possible. Personally I think that undoing what the last government did, in the certain knowledge that they will re-do it when next they come into power, is folly; and this applies more to iron and steel than to road transport.

There is also trouble with Eden over the Egyptian situation, the P.M. wishing to take a much stronger line with the Egyptians than Eden does. The latter is rather discredited in the P.M.'s eyes at present. I don't myself quite see how he can prove a very good successor to Winston when he has no knowledge or experience of anything except foreign affairs.

Wednesday, April 9th

This afternoon Queen Mary, who had been ill, asked me to come and see her and received me in bed (looking very regal all the same in a vast bed, with a monogrammed back, an embroidered quilt of extraordinary beauty and a huge canopy). She kept her eyes closed throughout the conversation but in spite of feeling wretched, and constantly complaining how tiresome it was to be old, she was very determined in what she said and more than usually downright on the subject of her relations.

Lunched today at the French Embassy, a party in honour of Pug Ismay who is going – strongly against his original wishes – as Secretary General of N.A.T.O.

Saturday, April 19th

W.S.C. has been at Chartwell over Easter with a heavy cold and I have been moving things in and out of Westminster Gardens, Meg being not allowed to do anything strenuous. I went down to Chartwell for the night and was alone with the P.M. who is greatly exercised over the position of nationalised transport which is now in the home fore-front, the real problem being how to denational-ise the road transport, open it to free competition and yet prevent the railways from becoming insolvent. The position as far as I am concerned is getting a little difficult: W. complains he sees very little of me, but I can't push myself more to the front without hurting my colleagues' feelings. But W. says he has nothing in common with any of them (they haven't the same friends and don't play Oklahoma![1]) and won't have them to Chartwell if he can avoid it.

Am in correspondence with George Trevelyan, the Lord Chancellor and Tommy Lascelles about a book called *The Daughter of*

---

[1] A two-handed card game popular at the time.

Time[1] which seeks to prove that the Princes in the Tower were murdered not by Richard III but by Henry VII.

Saturday, April 26th–Sunday, April 27th
Went to Chartwell for the week-end. The P.M. plans to sack Lord Woolton and make "Mr Cube" (Lord Lyle) Chairman of the Tory Party.[2] He also revealed to me a private project for getting the Queen Mother made Governor General of Australia. We went through the Honours List during the week-end and I was pleasantly surprised to find the P.M. amenable to my views on most points.

On Sunday evening Lord and Lady Donegall[3] came bringing a Russian film called *The Fall of Berlin*. Russia, it seems, won the war single-handed and now breathes nothing but peace.

I gave Christopher Soames a lecture on not appearing to have too much of the P.M.'s ear. It is dangerous for his future. I like him increasingly, though his manners can be coarse. Brendan Bracken, with whom I had a drink the other day, says that Eden is violent against Christopher.

Tuesday, May 6th
Tonight I went with the P.M. to dine with the Massiglis[4] at the French Embassy. The others at dinner were Eden, Alexander, General Juin[5] and Gérard André also Madame M. who couldn't bear to be out of it but left us at the end of dinner. General Juin was inhibited by his bad English. The P.M. said Germany must be given fair play: if France would not co-operate we, America and Germany must go forward without her. He wanted to see British, American, German and French contingents march past him at Strasbourg, each to their own national songs: in creating international unity, national marching songs could play a great part.

When Juin said that General Koenig had now gone into politics

---

[1] A book by Josephine Tey (Elizabeth Mackintosh) who also wrote (as Gordon Daviot) the play *Richard of Bordeaux*. She argued for the theory that Henry VII, not Richard III, murdered the Princes in the Tower. This fascinated Sir Alan Lascelles, the Lord Chancellor (Lord Simmonds) and me. I persuaded Churchill to read the book: he said he still thought Richard III was the villain.

[2] He afterwards preferred the idea of Malcolm McCorquodale.

[3] 6th Marquess. Born when his alleged father, the 5th Marquess, was eighty-one. His heir and cousin (b. 1861) was probably in fact his father, but had to be content with remaining the heir for as long as he lived. Donegall wrote articles for the *Sunday Despatch*.

[4] One of de Gaulle's right-hand men and a powerful force for moderation. A successful French Ambassador in London after the war.

[5] Marshal of France. Joined the Allies in 1942 and commanded Free French troops in North Africa and in Italy.

the P.M., looking at Alexander, said far be it from him to run down soldiers turned politician. Look, he said, at Napoleon. Wellington, too, I ventured. No, he replied, Wellington was a politician turned soldier. A totally invalid statement.

Alexander, next to whom I sat, said to me that war was a tradition among men. As Clausewitz had put it, it was a way of pursuing national policy "by other means". But he thought the atomic bomb might well put a stop to all that: it might be the end of war by making war impossible. He thought, too, that now was the time to show an imaginative policy to Germany: we should lose all if we niggled.

Massigli said that Pinay, the new French P.M., had come to stay. He believed a new political stability was dawning in France.

Thursday, May 15th
Tonight the P.M. and Mrs C. gave a farewell dinner for the Eisenhowers at No. 10, on the eve of his departure from S.H.A.P.E. to become a candidate in the Presidential Election. There were thirty-two to dinner, including most of the war-time Chiefs and the present Service Ministers – Alexanders, Tedders, Alanbrookes, Portals, Jumbo Wilson, Attlees, etc. Both the P.M. and Ike made admirable speeches. When Ike left he said that if he were elected he would pay just one visit outside the U.S.A. – to the U.K. – in order to show our special relationship. The atmosphere could not have been more cordial – though things almost started badly with neither the P.M. nor Mrs C. knowing that it was white tie and decorations.

Friday, May 16th
Went to Chartwell this evening. Alone with the P.M. who is low. Of course the Government is in a trough, but his periods of lowness grow more frequent and his concentration less good. The bright and sparkling intervals still come, and they are still unequalled, but age is beginning to show. Tonight he spoke of coalition. The country needed it he said, and it must come. He would retire in order to make it possible; he might even make the demand for it an excuse for retiring. Four-fifths of the people of this country were agreed on four-fifths of the things to be done.

Saturday, May 17th
A heatwave. I lunched alone with W. who recited a great deal of poetry. While he slept in the afternoon I bathed in the swimming pool, and then we drove for two hours to Chequers. On the way he dictated notes for a speech to wind up the transport debate next

Wednesday. He says he can only dictate in a car nowadays. His theme seems a good one: the nationalisation by the socialists of only 41,000 vehicles was for doctrinaire, not practical motives, and they need 80,000 people, including 12,000 clerks, to run them. Private owners [of transport for hire] to a total of 800,000 have been driven to the most uneconomic measures to survive. When he had finished he said to me: "It is a great mistake to be too mechanically minded in affairs of State."

At Chequers were Lord Montgomery, Duchess of Devonshire (Moucha), Antony and Dot Head, Marques and Marquesa de Casa Valdes and their pretty daughter Maria.

The men sat up till 2.30 gossiping about strategy and Generals in a lively manner.

Sunday, May 18th
Heatwave intensified. Worked with W. all the morning; sat on the lawn and gossiped most of the afternoon: walked on the monument hill (the whole party went, notwithstanding all the picnickers) after tea. Monty in role of grand inquisitor: how did the P.M. define a great man? Was Hitler great? (P.M. said No – he made too many mistakes). How could P.M. maintain that Napoleon was great when he was the Hitler of the nineteenth century? And surely the great religious leaders were the real great men? The P.M. said their greatness was indisputable but it was of a different kind. Christ's story was unequalled and his death to save sinners unsurpassed; moreover the Sermon on the Mount was the last word in ethics.

Monty has become a mellow, lovable exhibitionist; tamed but lonely and pathetic. He is not afraid of saying anything to anybody. But Maria de Casa Valdes scored (to Monty's great delight) when she asked him: "But you tell me you don't drink, and you don't smoke: what *do* you do that is wrong? Bite your nails?"

Monday, May 19th
Drove to London in shimmering heat with Antony Head. Attended the first meeting of the Coronation Joint Executive Committee at St James's Palace, Bernard Norfolk presiding over a large mixed Commonwealth gathering most competently.[1]

Tuesday, May 20th
This evening Brendan, with whom I had a drink, was very gloomy about the Government's prospect, doubtful about W.'s ability to

---

[1] The Duke of Norfolk, Earl Marshal, was in over-all charge. At this and subsequent meetings the Committee recommended that the Coronation should not be televised. The Cabinet accepted this recommendation, but the Queen did not.

go on and highly critical of R. A. Butler whose financial policy he has been attacking vigorously in the *Financial Times*.

Wednesday, May 21st
Transport debate in House of Commons. W. who spoke fifth made a good impression, but I cannot help feeling it is both wrong and foolish to denationalise transport and steel, however doctrinaire may have been the motives of the late Government in nationalising them. When the Labour Government get back they will be re-nationalised and this political game is not only unsettling for the economic life of the country but a blow to the constitutional "Gentleman's Agreement" that one Government did not normally set about undoing the work of its predecessor. It is clear that a large element in the Tory party feel the same.

Friday, May 23rd
W., who had been at Chartwell all day, came up to speak at a Tax Inspectors' dinner with a speech almost entirely written by me. This is indeed a sign of advancing senility – and it wasn't nearly as good as the one I wrote for him in Ottawa.

Friday, May 30th
The country is in a bad way. It is difficult to see how our economic ills can be cured and at the moment nothing that is done seems to be more than a short-term palliative. The remedy for 50 million people living in an island which can maintain 30 million and no longer leads the world in industrial exports or in capital assets invested abroad is hard to find. Harold Macmillan said to me at the Turf yesterday that he thought development of the Empire into an economic unit as powerful as the U.S.A. and the U.S.S.R. was the only possibility. At present this seems to be neither pursued nor envisaged.

The Government is in a bad way too. Their popularity has fallen owing to bad publicity, rising prices and a silly policy of denationalisation. Winston is, I fear, personally blamed both in the country and by his own party in the House. Mrs Churchill does not think he will last long as Prime Minister.

Saturday, May 31st
Went to Milton[1] to stay with Tom Fitzwilliam[2] for Whitsun.

[1] The Fitzwilliams' house near Peterborough.
[2] 10th and last Earl Fitzwilliam, owner of Wentworth and Milton. He married Joyce, widow of Lord Fitzalan of Derwent, was renowned as a judge of fox-hounds, and was a kind and generous host.

There was a Conservative Fête on the Monday, addressed by Miss Patricia Hornsby Smith[1] who was staying in the house.

The Duke of Rutland, Elizabeth Ann Naylor-Leyland and I judged a beauty competition.

Friday, June 13th–Sunday, June 15th

I spent the week-end at Chartwell. Last Friday and Saturday I went racing with the P.M. at Lingfield. On Saturday evening Lord Cherwell and Bill Deakin came to stay. We did little work, but W. was in better form than of late, though still depressed. He told me that if Eisenhower were elected President, he would have another shot at making peace by means of a meeting of the Big Three. For that alone it would perhaps be worth remaining in office. He thought that while Stalin lived we were safer from attack than if he died and his lieutenants started scrambling for the succession.

He also elaborated his theme of "the commodity sterling dollar" – an international medium of exchange based on the world price of, say, fifteen commodities over a period of three years. This year, for instance, the years chosen would be 1948, 1949, 1950; next year 1949, 1950, 1951; and so on. The Prof. said that such a scheme had possibilities if the Americans would lend it their support and their material backing.

Feeling wearied by the prospects of the future I wrote the following in the early hours of the morning:

It is foolish to continue living with illusions. One may bury one's head in the past, reading James Boswell or the privately printed letters of Labouchere to Lord Rosebery; or one may talk of forcing reality on the people by a slump with the accompaniment of hunger and unemployment and the consequent acceptance of a lower standard of living. But the facts are stark. At the moment we are just paying our way. A trade recession in America will break us; the competition of German metallurgical industries and the industrialisation of countries which were once the market for our industrial products will ruin our trade sooner or later and sap the remaining capital on which our high standard of living is based.

It costs too much to live as we do. The price of keeping a man in hospital is more than £700 a year. To send an individual to settle in the Commonwealth costs £1,000 a head.

What can we do? Increasing productivity is only a palliative in

---

[1] Conservative M.P. for Chislehurst. Under Secretary at the Ministry of Health and later at the Home Office. Made a peeress in 1977.

the face of foreign competition. We cannot till sufficient soil to feed 50 million people. We cannot emigrate fast enough to meet the danger, even if we were willing to face the consequent abdication of our position as a great power and even if there were places for two-fifths of our population to go.

The British people will face war or the threat of invasion with courage. It yet remains to be seen if they will accept a lower standard of living.

Lord Cherwell sees hope in the union of the English Speaking World, economically and politically. He thinks that just as the Scots complained of Union with England but ended by dominating Great Britain, so we in the end should dominate America. He thinks that Roosevelt, had he lived, and Winston, had he remained in power in 1945, might have led us far along the road to common citizenship. They often spoke of it. But now England, and Europe, distrust, dislike and despise the United States.

Some pin their faith in the development of the Empire as a great economic unit, equal in power to Russia and the U.S.A. We have left it late. Ambitious efforts, such as the groundnuts scheme, have failed.

It is easier for the old. Their day is almost over. Meg and I hope for a child in November. It should be easier for him or her if neither hunger nor nuclear fission cut life short, because the child will grow into a new world. We are the transitional generation, who have climbed to the watershed and will soon look down the other side, on a new world. It will be wiser neither to think nor to speak too much of the past.

The Prime Minister is depressed and bewildered. He said to me this evening: "The zest is diminished." I think it is more that he cannot see the light at the end of the tunnel.

Nor can I. But it is 1.30 a.m., approaching the hour when courage and life are at their lowest ebb.

Friday, June 20th

I again went to Chartwell. Alone with the P.M. but joined by Norman Brook in the evening.

After we had fed the fish – indoors and out[1] – and driven away the horses which were eating the water lilies in the lake, we had lunch together. W. greatly exercised by the economic prospects. He said: "I can assure you it is the most horrible landscape on

[1] Apart from his outdoor ponds, full of large golden orfe, Churchill established in his working library at Chartwell tanks full of brightly-coloured small tropical fish, each tank supplied with an elaborate oxygen apparatus. Feeding the fish was a frequent diversion from serious work.

which I have ever looked in my unequalled experience." But when champagne and brandy had done their work he talked of the Chamberlain family – Joe the greatest of the three; Austen, generous and gallant but whose whole work came to nothing; Neville who was not above scheming to ruin Baldwin at the time of the Duff Cooper–Petter[1] election in the St George's Division of Westminster so that Neville might profit by his fall.

After the usual film, Christopher and Mary dined and Norman, who wanted to talk confidentially about the weak position of sterling and suggest changes in the Government, was irked because Christopher would not leave us. However he did tell the P.M. that Woolton should give up the Home Affairs Committee and that Eden should take it over, relinquishing the F.O. The P.M. also thinks Eden should have a change but says he is "Foreign Officissimus" and doesn't want to go.

Saturday, June 21st

A somewhat wasted morning (much more fish-feeding); luncheon with W. and Norman devoted to desultory discussion of the Treasury, of Defence and of the economic position; and returned to London with Norman, leaving the P.M. to go to Chequers.

Monday, June 23rd

This afternoon Sir Oliver Franks* came in, like a breath of fresh air from the U.S.A. He thought everybody too gloomy. We must edge our way out of this crisis: the balance of payments had begun to improve, as he had said it would, in May; time was needed for remedial measures to take effect. People talked a lot of the popular insensitiveness to our plight; but as four-fifths of the population had known seven years of prosperity and a standard of living higher than ever before, it was not surprising they paid little attention to cries of economic alarm. Successive Chancellors of the Exchequer spoke as if the impoverishment felt by one-fifth of the people was an experience shared by all.

I gathered he would not consider the chairmanship of the Governors of the B.B.C. which W. had hoped he would take.

Went to see Brendan. Discussed the same theme as with Franks. He thinks the Overlords should go, especially Woolton, Leathers and the Prof. He says Eden's small coterie of advisers and friends don't want him to leave the F.O.: they think he might mar his reputation in other fields.

---

[1] Sir Ernest Petter was put up by Lords Beaverbrook and Rothermere as an anti-Baldwin candidate.

Monday, August 11th

Returned from Chartwell after a long week-end. I have been particularly slothful about this diary of late, partly because it has been such a hot summer.

The session ended in heated feelings, partly engendered by the Government's forecast of important decisions to announce, coupled with their failure in the event to do so – and one of the worst speeches I have ever heard W. make about defence.

Now the Churchills are at Chartwell. Just before he went (Mrs C. being at Capri) W. took Meg and me to see *The Innocents*, a stage version of Henry James' *The Turn of the Screw*. He got a great welcome but embarrassed us by being unable to hear and asking questions in a loud voice.

Philip's Dragon *Orthos* sank under him at Cowes last Saturday; King Farouk has abdicated; the Persian situation deteriorates with the return of Mossadeq[1] to power; Anthony Eden and Clarissa Churchill are engaged. Clarissa, who was at Chartwell for the week-end, is very beautiful but she is still strange and bewildering, cold if sometimes witty, arrogant at times and understanding at others. Perhaps marriage will change her and will also help to calm the vain and occasionally hysterical Eden. W. feels avuncular to his orphaned niece, gave her a cheque for £500 and told me he thought she had a most unusual personality.

Friday August 15th–Monday, August 18th

Meg and I spent the week-end at Chartwell. Montgomery was the other guest, with his persistent but oddly endearing egotism (even on the croquet lawn). He and I and Sarah were godparents to Jeremy Soames, christened in Westerham Church on Sunday, 17th. On the 18th Christopher and I shot duck at Sheffield Park and lunched there; in the evening Churchills, Soameses and Colvilles went to see *The Yeomen of the Guard* at Streatham. The P.M. was received with immense acclamation by the audience.

Friday, August 22nd–Monday, August 25th

Again to Chartwell with Meg, this time alone with the Churchills except for Horatia Seymour and in glorious sunny weather. There is a slight drama. W. has persuaded Truman to join with him in sending a message, signed by them both, to Mossadeq in Tehran about the Persian oil question. W. himself did it and the F.O. and

---

[1] Democratic but nationalist Prime Minister of Persia, who quarrelled with the Shah, sought to nationalise the British oil installations at Abadan and invariably fainted at awkward moments.

oil people agreed. It is the first time since 1945 that the Americans have joined with us in taking overt joint action against a third power. Fear of ganging up has hitherto prevented them. But Anthony Eden, completing his honeymoon in Lisbon, is furious. It is not the substance but the method which displeases him: the stealing by Winston of his personal thunder. Moreover, should Eisenhower be elected President of the U.S.A. in November – an event thought to be decreasingly probable – there will be further trouble on this score, because W. has several times revealed to me his hopes of a joint approach to Stalin, proceeding perhaps to a congress in Vienna where the Potsdam Conference would be reopened and concluded. If the Russians were unco-operative, the cold war would be intensified by us: "Our young men," W. said to me, "would as soon be killed carrying truth as death."

Meg and I spent all September at Mertoun.[1] When I returned to London at the end of the month I accompanied the Prime Minister to Balmoral where he went in his capacity as Prime Minister at his own suggestion. The Queen and Prince Philip, who had a very young party staying with them, may have been a little reluctant, but the visit went off well and was in the event enjoyed by both sides, although Winston (aged nearly seventy-eight and not having touched a gun for years) complained to me on the way home that he thought he should have been asked to shoot!

Sunday, November 9th
I have not written this for many weeks, partly from laziness, partly because living in flats, with a shared writing table, militates heavily against keeping a diary. I have been to Chartwell numerous weekends, but although much has been said and a few things done there is nothing especially noteworthy. However, I do record that last Wednesday evening, November 5th, after Eisenhower's victory in the American Presidential Election had been announced, Winston said to me: "For your private ear, I am greatly disturbed. I think this makes war much more probable."

He (W.) is getting tired and visibly ageing. He finds it hard work to compose a speech and ideas no longer flow. He has made two strangely simple errors in the H. of C. lately, and even when addressing the Harrow boys in Speech Room last Friday what he said dragged and lacked fire. But he has had a tiring week, with speeches, important Cabinet decisions, etc., so that I may be unduly alarmist.

[1] My brother-in-law's house in Berwickshire.

On Friday, November 7th, Ashley Clarke[1] lunched with me at the Turf and offered me the post of Counsellor and head of Chancery in Washington next summer if I can escape from No. 10 then.

Dreadfully tied up with the Coronation arrangements.

Meg's baby, approaching delivery, has turned the wrong way up and now the right way up again. It appears to be a most energetic child.

Sunday, November 30th
Winston's seventy-eighth birthday. Meg and I entertained him, Mrs Churchill, Mary and Jane Portal[2] to lunch in the Ladies' Annexe of the Turf Club.

We then had tea with the Lascelles at St James's Palace and when I got home I felt unnaturally cold.

Monday, December 1st
Retired to bed with a temperature of 103.

Tuesday, December 2nd
Meg, to avoid my flu, was packed off to the Nursing Home at 31 Queen's Gate.

Wednesday, December 3rd
At 2.45 a.m. Harriet Jane was born. Her mother had a disagreeable time; her father languished anxiously in bed. Visited Meg and the child briefly after luncheon. Harriet did not look beautiful.

Her Christian names were subsequently re-registered as Elizabeth Harriet, because the Queen offered to be a godparent. So did the Prime Minister, and they came to the Christening. This led to a curious historic coincidence because having no Christening robe we borrowed one from Lord Jersey. It had been made over a hundred years previously for the baptism of the then Lord Jersey's son, my sister-in-law's grandfather. On that occasion, in 1845, Queen Victoria and Sir Robert Peel stood sponsors in person.

[1] Afterwards Ambassador in Rome. His knowledge of both music and Italian was such that he was able to give a lecture to an enthralled audience of cognoscenti from the stage of the Scala in Milan. On retirement he was the prime mover in the steps taken to preserve Venice from decay and destruction.

[2] One of Churchill's personal secretaries. Attractive niece of Rab Butler and Marshal of the R.A.F. Lord Portal. After her second marriage to Charles Williams she was a magistrate, a member of the Parole Board and secretary of the Other Club.

Thus, quite fortuitously, the same robe came to be used on the next, and probably only other, occasion that a Sovereign and her Prime Minister both attended a Christening as godparents.

Thursday, December 4th
Harriet's looks improved. Meg says she has a will of iron.

Friday, December 5th
Harriet almost beautiful, except for abominable squint. Left for Arundel to stay with Bernard and Lavinia Norfolk.

Saturday, December 6th
While I shot in bright sunshine, Meg, Harriet and London were enveloped in one of the worst fogs ever.

Sunday, December 7th
Returned to London and the fog. Meg has had no less than forty bunches of flowers sent to her.

37

New York and Washington
January 1953

Saying farewell to the outgoing President Truman and greeting the incoming President Eisenhower was an excellent excuse for a further journey to the United States. Sir Roger Makins had been appointed British Ambassador in Washington, in succession to Sir Oliver Franks, and he and Lady Makins travelled with us. Fortunately they knew the Embassy well, for they had but a few days after their arrival to prepare for the reception of the Prime Minister and for his Washington programme. I took a Stationery Office note-book with me and wrote as follows:

Tuesday, December 30th, 1952
The Prime Minister, Mrs Churchill, Mary and Christopher Soames and I left Waterloo at 7.30 p.m. bound for Southampton and the *Queen Mary*. We dined on the train and talked of many things, from the War of 1812 to the future of Pakistan. We went on board about 9.45 and occupied a series of eminently luxurious cabins.

Wednesday, December 31st
We sailed at 10.15 a.m. I worked with the P.M. for most of the morning and lunched *en famille* in his dining-room, with the usual gastronomic excellence associated with these liners. At Cherbourg we sent off a bag. Christopher and I had a Turkish bath.

Sir Roger and Lady Makins to dinner. The P.M. said he thought the recent treason trials in Prague, with so many Jews among the condemned, indicated that the Communists were looking towards the Arab States, Persia and North Africa and were deliberately antagonising Israel. He also said he would preach to Eisenhower the vital importance of a common Anglo-American front "from Korea to Kikuyu and from Kikuyu to Calais".

Saw the New Year in at a somewhat amateurish ceremony in the main lounge.

Thursday, January 1st, 1953

A quiet day on board with sunshine and smooth seas. We all lunched and dined in the Verandah Grill. During the evening Winston told me several things worth remembering. He said that if I lived my normal span I should assuredly see Eastern Europe free of Communism. He also said that Russia feared our friendship more than our enmity. Finally he lamented that owing to Eisenhower winning the presidency he must cut much out of Volume VI of his War History and could not tell the story of how the United States gave away, to please Russia, vast tracts of Europe they had occupied and how suspicious they were of his pleas for caution. The British General Election in June 1945 had occupied so much of his attention which should have been directed to stemming this fatal tide. If F.D.R. had lived, and had been in good health, he would have seen the red light in time to check the American policy: Truman, after all, had only been a novice, bewildered by the march of events and by responsibilities which he had never expected.

Friday, January 2nd

Life flows evenly on this great Cunarder and one feels detached from the speed and flurry of the world. Therefore the irruption of one or two short cypher telegrams, one of which was wholly corrupt, was irritating; but the food in the Verandah Grill, walks on the Sunshine Deck and the pleasures of a Turkish bath soothed away all irritation. We had warning of a Force 12 hurricane, but we altered course and evaded it.

Saturday, January 3rd

Sunshine and Mediterranean blue seas on the Great Newfoundland Banks. The P.M. gave a cocktail party before dinner to which, amongst others, the Munsters, Makinses, Lord Listowel, Lord Birdwood, Admiral Johnston (U.S.N.), Sir E. Hall Patch, Lord Iliffe, J. Wilson Broadbent (*Daily Mail* Diplomatic Correspondent in Washington and very charming) came.

After dinner, in the Verandah Grill, I was left alone with the P.M. and fired at him about thirty questions which he might be asked at his press conference on arrival in New York. He scintillated in his replies, e.g.:

Qn: What are your views, Mr Churchill, on the present stalemate
     in Korea?
Ans: Better a stalemate than a checkmate.
Qn: How do you justify such great expenditure on the Corona-
     tion of your Queen, when England is in such financial straits?
Ans: Everybody likes to wear a flower when he goes to see his girl.
Qn: Is not British policy in Persia throwing Persia into the hands
     of the Communists?
Ans: If Britain and America refuse to be disunited, no ill can
     come.

And there were many others as good or better. I wished so much
I had had a microphone.

Sunday, January 4th
Last day at sea. Read briefs and papers relating to the Eisenhower
talks with the P.M. The Makinses to lunch. All pleasantly quiet.
P.M.'s bill for Verandah Grill and for wines, and private telephone
calls – £83.10.0.

Monday, January 5th
Docked in New York at 8.15 a.m. Pandemonium let loose. Mr
Baruch, high dignitaries, low officials, Embassy people, pressmen
swarmed on board. The P.M. saw the press in the Verandah Grill
and answered questions well; but perhaps less well than the night
before last.

When we disembarked we went to Baruch's flat and thence I
drove to Henry and Mimi Hyde's house on E. 70th Street, where I
am staying.

General Eisenhower arrived amid the flashing of bulbs at 5.00
p.m. and greeted W. with: "Well, the one thing I have so far learnt
in this damned game of yours is that you have just *got* to have a
sense of humour." After a blinding photographic session, Baruch
and I withdrew leaving the two to talk of many things (papers about
which I deposited on a table beside W.).

Returned for dinner at which Eisenhower, Baruchs (father, son
and daughter), Sarah, Christopher, Mr and Mrs C. and Miss
Navarro[1] were present. Winston said that a protoplasm was sex-
less. Then it divided into two sexes which, in due course, united
again in a different way to their common benefit and gratification.
This should also be the story of England and America. Ike talked
about Cleopatra's Needle (how the Egyptians raised it), the charm

[1] Bernard Baruch's secretary and mentor to whom he left quite a large part of his
  wealth.

of the Queen, the intelligence of the Duke of Edinburgh, and a few war-time indiscretions.

After dinner I listened to the P.M. and the President elect talking: Winston made one or two profound observations. For instance, "I think you and I are agreed that it is not only important to discover the truth but to know how to present the truth"; and (apropos of the recent treason trials in Czechoslovakia) "That they should think it good propaganda is what shows the absolutely unbridgeable gulf between us."

Bernard Baruch, next to whom I sat at dinner, told me that he thought European unity, in some striking form, was essential if America was not to tire of her efforts – and only Winston (who, he said, was deaf to his pleas on the subject) could bring it about. England now had three assets: her Queen ("the world's sweetheart"); Winston Churchill; and her glorious historical past. I said there was a fourth: her unrivalled technical ability. But his pleas for rapid action were met by the following remark of Winston's: "It may be better to bear an agonising period of unsatisfactory time . . . You may kill yourself in getting strong enough."

Tuesday, January 6th
A day of unrelenting activity. After a hideous morning, during which Mrs C. and Mary left for Jamaica, I lunched at the Knickerbocker Club with Gladwyn Jebb.

At 2.30 I went to the Commodore Hotel with a letter and Cabinet Paper for Ike from the P.M. Ike kept me twenty minutes, talking about Persia, and John Foster Dulles* was with him too, in a rather bare hotel room which is his office until he moves to the White House on January 20th. He was very genial and talked a great deal. Has a bee in his bonnet about "collusion" with us: is all in favour of it clandestinely but not overtly. Dulles said little, but what he did say was on our side. Ike struck me as forceful but a trifle naive.

At 6.00 John Foster Dulles came for a conversation with the P.M. He brought with him Winthrop Aldrich, the new American Ambassador in London. He began by saying that 1953 was a critical year: if the new administration did not get off to a good start, and the American people lost faith in it, who could say what might happen. W. said that he, for his part, thought nothing should be done for some four months: "the trees do not grow up to the sky"; we should let events in many places – Korea, Persia, Egypt – take their course and see where we found ourselves. At this point I left them. Subsequently W. told me what passed and I made a record for the F.O.

Wednesday, January 7th

Wrote a document about Anzus[1] and Anzam for the P.M. to give Ike this evening.

At 4.30 the Duke of Windsor, Duchess of Windsor, Mrs Luce[2] (a beautiful woman shortly to be appointed American Ambassador in Rome on account of Luce's support of the Republicans in the recent Election), Mrs Philip Reid,[3] Mr Swope,[4] Sarah and another Baruch daughter came to drinks. Mrs Luce tried to cross-question W. about the *Tory* antagonism to Chiang Kai-shek, but W. (a) thought she said *socialist* (b) wasn't playing! The Windsors would not go, and Eisenhower arrived at 5.00. So Ike and Winston went to another room. The only remark of Ike's I overheard was: "we must not make the mistake of jeopardising big things by opposition to little". This seems to be one of the bees in his bonnet.

The P.M. told me, after Ike had left, that he had felt on top of him this time: Ike had seemed to defer to his greater age and experience to a remarkable degree. I made a record of what W. told me had transpired.

Governor Dewey[5] came to dinner. The others present were Baruch, W.S.C., Christopher and myself. For a lawyer Dewey seemed to have a remarkably inaccurate memory for dates and places, but otherwise he talked well and made himself agreeable. All was quiet until towards the end of dinner John Foster Dulles arrived, by invitation. He had come, at Ike's suggestion, to say what he felt about a project of W.'s for not returning to England in the *Queen Mary* on January 23rd but remaining another fortnight in Jamaica, going to Washington for three or four days on February 1st or 2nd, being joined there by Rab (who would stay on for the economic discussions arising out of the recent Commonwealth talks) and returning home on February 7th. Dulles said he thought this would be most unfortunate, whereupon W. sat up and growled. He explained that the American public thought W. could cast a spell on all American statesmen and that if he were directly associated with the economic talks, the fears of the people and of Congress would be aroused to such an extent that the success of the talks would be endangered. W. took this very reasonable state-

---

[1] Establishing military co-operation between the United States, Australia and New Zealand.

[2] Clare Booth, a beautiful actress who married Harry Luce, founder and owner of *Time* and *Life*.

[3] Owner of the *Herald Tribune*.

[4] A financier who was Baruch's closest friend.

[5] Thomas Dewey, Republican candidate in the 1948 Presidential Election.

ment ill, but Christopher and I both took pains to assure Dulles afterwards that we thought he was absolutely right.

Irritated by this, W. let fly at Dewey after dinner and worked himself into a fury over certain Pacific Ocean questions. Christopher and I again applied soft soap subsequently. We told Dewey that a sharp debate was the P.M.'s idea of a pleasant evening and assured him that he would only have spoken thus to a man whom he trusted and looked upon as a friend.

But, alas, this was not so. W. was really worked up and, as he went to bed, said some very harsh things about the Republican party in general and Dulles in particular, which Christopher and I thought both unjust and dangerous. He said he would have no more to do with Dulles whose "great slab of a face" he disliked and distrusted.

For what it is worth my impressions of the leading New Men is that they are well intentioned, earnest, but ill informed (which can be remedied) and not very intelligent – excepting Dulles – (which cannot). Ike in particular I suspect of being a genial and dynamic mediocrity.

Thursday, January 8th
We took off from La Guardia airport at 11.15 a.m. in President Truman's magnificently fitted aircraft "The Independence". At Washington, after a brilliant landing with a 400-foot cloud base, we were met by Dean Acheson, Roger Makins and others.

Luncheon at the Embassy, Kit Steel[1] and wife and Bernard Burrows[2] being present. Talk ranged from what has gone on in New York to the war of 1812 and the responsibility for it of slow communications.

At 4.00 the P.M. went to the White House. At 5.30 the following came for cocktails to the Embassy: Vice President Barkley, Senator Bridges, Senator Taft, Senator Johnson, Senator Wiley, Senator Millikin and Senator George; Representative Martin (Speaker of the House) and Representatives Halleck and Rayburn. I talked to Millikin, Barkley and Rayburn (whom I liked) and to Halleck (whom I thought abominable).

My luggage had been left in New York so I had to borrow divers garments for dinner from divers people, including the P.M.'s very shabby second pair of evening shoes. It is the first time I have actually found myself standing in his shoes!

---

[1] Minister at the Embassy. Afterwards Ambassador in Bonn.
[2] Head of Chancery, whose successor I was invited to be. Afterwards Ambassador in the Persian Gulf.

The President arrived for dinner at 9.00. Others at the dinner party were: Dean Acheson, Snyder, Averell Harriman, General Marshall, General Bradley, General Bedell Smith,[1] "Doc" Matthews,[2] the Ambassador, the P.M., Kit Steel, Sir E. Hall Patch, A.C.M. Sir William Elliot, Christopher, Dennis Rickett.

I sat between General Bradley[3] and "Doc" Matthews. We had very agreeable conversation until the P.M. and the President decided to hold the table. This happened after the P.M. had, quite wrongly, proposed the Queen's health. The President later said, quite rightly, that this was for him to do and so we had to drink it twice.

There was some talk about Stalin. Truman recalled how at Potsdam he had discovered the vodka Stalin drank for toasts was really weak white wine, and how when W.S.C. had said the Pope would dislike something, Stalin had answered "How many divisions has the Pope?" W. said he remembered replying that the fact they could not be measured in military terms did not mean they did not exist.

After dinner Truman played the piano. Nobody would listen because they were all busy with post-mortems on a diatribe in favour of Zionism and against Egypt which W. had delivered at dinner (to the disagreement of practically all the Americans present, though they admitted that the large Jewish vote would prevent them disagreeing publicly). However, on W.'s instructions, I gathered all to the piano and we had a quarter of an hour's presidential piano playing before Truman left. He played with quite a nice touch and, as he said himself, could probably have made a living on the stage of the lesser music-halls.

When he had gone, the political wrangle started again, this time between W. (unsupported) and Dean Acheson (supported by Harriman, Bedell Smith and Matthews). The main bones of contention were the European Defence Community,[4] which the P.M. persists in describing as "a sludgy amalgam" infinitely less effective than a Grand Alliance of national armies, and the situation in Egypt where Acheson and Co. have far greater hopes of General

[1] Eisenhower's Chief of Staff during the 1944–45 campaign. After the war a power in the State Department.
[2] Influential official in the State Department, much esteemed by the British Embassy.
[3] Omar Bradley, commander of the American forces in France and Germany in 1944–45, initially under Montgomery. Appointed to command S.H.A.P.E., the peacetime successor to S.H.A.E.F. in Europe.
[4] The proposed European army.

Neguib[1] (our last hope, they say) than has W. The Americans, apart from Truman and Marshall, stayed till 1.00 a.m. I had an uneasy feeling that the P.M.'s remarks – about Israel, the E.D.C. and Egypt – though made to the members of an outgoing administration, had better have been left unsaid in the presence of the three, Bradley, Bedell Smith and Matthews, who are staying on with Ike and the Republicans.

Friday, January 9th
We left the Embassy at 9.30 a.m. and boarded "The Independence" for Jamaica. We had a very rough flight until we were south of Florida and both Christopher and I were a little worried about the effect of the bumps on W. However he ate a huge steak for lunch and had his usual brandy and cigar, so I concluded he must be looking worse than he felt.

We flew over Cuba, bathed in sunlight, to Montego Bay, where we landed in the presence of a guard of honour, a band and Mr Bustamente.[2] We drove through the town, W. sitting up on the back of an open car, and thence for two and a half hours in the dark to Prospect, a house near Ocho Rios lent to the P.M. by Sir Harold Mitchell.

Saturday, January 10th
Overcast, cloudy and hot. Bathed in the morning. In the afternoon the Governor's A.D.C. drove the Soameses, myself and a girl called Daphne Walthall to see local sights, including a "pub crawl" of the best known hotels (of which I thought Jamaica Inn the most fabulous).

Sunday, January 11th
Not good weather. Lord Beaverbrook to luncheon. He spoke very disparagingly of Anthony Eden. Then all drove to the Brownlows' house, Roaring River, for drinks. The P.M. (who last night said he would give £10,000 to be back at Chartwell) is cheering up a bit.

Monday, January 12th
Bathed by myself at Laughing Water Beach (a superb mixture of salt and fresh water against a background of golden sand and waving palms). A golden retriever stole my towel.

Went with Christopher and Mary to lunch with Lord

---

[1] Leader of the officers who deposed King Farouk and established a republic in Egypt. Later deposed and succeeded by Colonel Nasser.

[2] Prime Minister of Jamaica (which was still a British colony).

Brownlow,[1] whose house is marvellous (with lovely furniture brought from Belton, wide verandahs and a spreading view of the park and the sea beyond). His daughter, Caroline Cust (vivacious and agreeable), his son Edward and a painter called Hector Whistler were there.

After dinner, *en famille* at Prospect, W. attacked Christopher and me violently for criticising one of his literary assistants. I told him, after the tirade, that I thought he had been guilty of the most unprovoked aggression since September 1939. He said of Ike that he was "a real man of limited stature" – which, I think, about sums the new President up.

Everybody very nicely says they wish I were not going home so soon and W.'s goodnight words were: "If I didn't admire Meg so much, I wouldn't allow you to go."

Tuesday, January 13th
Christopher and I got up at 5.00 a.m. to go deep-sea fishing with Ernest Hemingway's brother, but the weather was bad and the sea rough so we had to abandon the plan.

Sarah[2] and Lady Foot arrived for luncheon and about 4 p.m. I drove away with Lady F. for Kingston, taking with me the last three chapters of Winston's war memoirs which he had been correcting.

Stayed the night at King's House with the Governor[3] and Lady Foot. Very agreeable dinner party at which two highly cultivated negroes were present: Mr Grantly Adams, Chief Minister of Barbados, and a man of remarkable intelligence called Springer who is attached to the University at Kingston. Sir Hugh Foot spoke of the evils of ju-ju in Africa and we had a long and learned argument about the merits of dealing with evil by the old and sharp puritanical approach or by the modern psychological method which seeks to explain and justify actions however wicked. Foot gave most interesting examples, from his own experiences as a Colonial administrator. In Palestine collective punishment, by fine, had been wholly efficacious in stopping the 1,000-year-old

---

[1] "Perry", 6th Lord Brownlow, owner of the magnificent Belton House near Grantham and an intimate friend of the Duke of Windsor, whom he conducted to exile in December 1936.

[2] Sarah Beauchamp, formerly Churchill, had divorced Vic Oliver and remarried.

[3] Hugh Foot, afterwards Lord Caradon, most of whose life was spent in the Colonial Service, holding important posts in many countries, including the Governorship of Cyprus at the start of the E.O.K.A. terrorism. Minister of State in the Foreign and Commonwealth Office and permanent British representative at U.N.O., 1964–70.

feuds which took the form of cutting down a neighbour's tree; in Cyprus the administration had encouraged villagers to take collective action, *by voting*, against the tough herdsmen from the hills who brought down their goats to feed on and ravage the valley pastures; in Jamaica the Government was just taking measures against predial theft by forcing the guilty to sit in their own doorways from sunset to sunrise for a period of weeks or even months – a modern version of the stocks and an attempt to use public humiliation as a deterrent.

Wednesday, January 14th
Rose at 5.15 a.m. and was taken by the A.D.C. to Palisadoes airport, whence I flew in a Viking to Montego Bay. Changed there into a Stratocruiser for Nassau and New York.

Was met at N.Y. by a representative of the U.K. Delegation and by the Manager of B.O.A.C. Changed into a London-bound Stratocruiser which, after stopping at Gander (temperature 10°F in contrast to 80°F at Jamaica this morning), deposited me in a fog at London Airport at 12.00 noon on Thursday, January 15th, thus bringing to an end this brief American journey.

38

The Prime Minister's Stroke

On May 11th, 1953, the Prime Minister, who was acting as Foreign Secretary in Anthony Eden's absence on protracted sick-leave, opened a foreign affairs debate with a well thought out and equally well delivered speech, partly about our relations with Egypt, but ending with the offer of an olive branch to the Soviet Union. He made this speech wholly contrary to Foreign Office advice since it was felt that a friendly approach to Russia would discourage the European powers working on the theme of Western union. However, Selwyn Lloyd,* the Minister of State, was personally enthusiastic about it, as were most of the Tories and the Opposition. I thought it a statesmanlike initiative and knew it to be one which was entirely Churchill's own.

There followed the Coronation of the Queen with all the attendant gaieties and celebrations, of which I wrote an account at the time and now attach as an appendix to this volume. For two cheerful months flags flew, bands played and party spite was muted, though the Scottish Nationalists continued to make an absurd fuss about the Queen being Elizabeth II rather than Elizabeth I. They had stolen the Stone of Scone from Westminster Abbey and blown up pillar boxes with EIIR on them. They were satisfied (at least for the time being) when the Queen and Parliament agreed that any future sovereign should take whichever was the higher number stemming from English or Scottish history. Thus a new King James would be James VIII, but a new King Henry would be Henry IX. Charles I and Charles II were Kings of both England and Scotland; so Charles III would satisfy both.

While this peculiar royal arithmetic and other matters of scarcely greater significance were being debated, an unexpected event occurred. I wrote the following in my diary early in July 1953:

On June 23rd Meg and I dined at No. 10 for a big dinner in honour of the Italian Prime Minister, de Gasperi. Meg sat between Hector McNeil and Lord Rennell of Rodd, I next to Kenneth Clark. At the end of dinner W. made a little speech in his best and most sparkling form, mainly about the Roman Conquest of Britain! After dinner he had a stroke, which occurred while he was in the pillared room among the guests. He sat down and was almost unable to move. After the guests had left, he leant heavily on my arm but managed to walk to his bedroom.

The next day he presided at the Cabinet, but his speech was slurred and his mouth drooping.[1] It was obvious that the Bermuda Conference with Eisenhower and *a* French Prime Minister (France had been without one for a month) must be postponed. We were to have sailed in H.M.S. *Vanguard* the following Tuesday.

On Thursday, June 25th, I went to Chartwell with W. and Lady C. I stayed nearly a fortnight. To begin with he went downhill badly, losing the use of his left arm and left leg. At this stage Lord Moran told me he did not think Winston would live over the week-end. It looked as if he would have to resign and I was in constant touch with Tommy Lascelles, Lord Salisbury, Eden and Rab Butler. A Caretaker Government under Lord Salisbury for six months, until the Conservative Party could choose between Eden (now convalescing in America from a gall-bladder operation) and Butler, was mooted. But W.'s recuperative powers, both physical and mental, invariably outstrip all expectation and after a week he began rapidly to improve, though his powers of concentration appeared slight and he preferred Trollope's political novels to work. Butler presided at the Cabinet and Salisbury went to Washington to meet the Americans and the French.

Meanwhile the Princess Margaret–Peter Townsend story broke in the press when his appointment as Air Attaché in Brussels was announced. The subsequent publicity was most distasteful.

The staff at No. 10, Christopher Soames and myself in particular, were in a quandary. Two days after his stroke, when I drove down to Chartwell alone with the Prime Minister (Lady Churchill having gone on ahead to prepare the household), he gave me strict orders not to let it be known that he was temporarily incapacitated and to ensure that the administration continued to function as if he were in full control. We realised that however well we knew his

---

[1] Nobody seemed to notice that he did not stand up to say goodbye to de Gasperi or any of the ladies. Equally Rab Butler later told me that nobody at the Cabinet table on June 24th noticed anything strange except that the Prime Minister was more silent than usual.

policy and the way his thoughts were likely to move, we had to be careful not to allow our own judgment to be given Prime Ministerial effect. To have done so, as we could without too great difficulty, would have been a constitutional outrage. It was an extraordinary, indeed perhaps an unprecedented, situation.

I could not obey Churchill's injunction to tell nobody. The truth would undoubtedly leak to the press unless I took immediate defensive action. So I wrote urgently and in manuscript to three particular friends of Churchill, Lords Camrose, Beaverbrook and Bracken, and sent the letters to London by despatch rider. All three immediately came to Chartwell and paced the lawn in earnest conversation. They achieved the all but incredible, and in peace-time possibly unique, success of gagging Fleet Street, something they would have done for nobody but Churchill. Not a word of the Prime Minister's stroke was published until he himself casually mentioned it in a speech in the House of Commons a year later.

A second factor of great help to us was the wisdom and coolness of the Secretary of the Cabinet, Sir Norman Brook, whom I consulted as soon as the crisis occurred. My colleagues and I had to handle requests for decisions from Ministers and Government departments entirely ignorant of the Prime Minister's incapacity. Discussion of how best to handle such enquiries, whether by postponement, by consultation with the Minister or Under Secretary responsible or, in some cases, by direct reply on the Prime Minister's behalf were the subject of daily discussion with the Secretary of the Cabinet. It was the more difficult for us because Anthony Eden, the second in command, had his operation on the very day Churchill had his stroke, and because although R. A. Butler took charge of the Cabinet with tact and competence, we knew that Churchill was unwilling to delegate his powers to anybody.

This situation lasted the best part of a month. It was eased for Pitblado and me by a third factor, the sense of responsibility and the down-to-earth intelligence of Churchill's son-in-law, Christopher Soames, Member of Parliament for Bedford. He had over the previous five years won the affection and trust of his formidable and, in the first instance, somewhat doubtful father-in-law. He now held the place in Churchill's heart so long reserved for Randolph who had been incapable of filling it. As Parliamentary Private Secretary, Christopher was in a curious position. He grew closer every month to Churchill, whom he even lured into owning racehorses (and was accordingly dubbed "The Master of the Horse" by Randolph); but he was not in principle supposed to see

Cabinet Papers or secret documents. That indeed had accounted for Sir Norman Brook's worries described in my entry for June 20th, 1952. However, in the unusual circumstances prevailing, it seemed to me that, whatever the rules might be, Christopher should be given access to many papers he was not supposed to see, including Cabinet papers. In the event the shrewdness of his comments, combined with his ability to differentiate between what mattered and what did not, was of invaluable help in difficult days.

Before the end of July the Prime Minister was sufficiently restored to take an intelligent interest in affairs of state and express his own decisive views. Christopher and I then returned to the fringes of power, having for a time been drawn perilously close to the centre. For the next two years the distance between the fringes and the centre was far shorter than it had once been.

Wednesday, July 15th

To Glyndbourne with the Normanbys. Went by train, a party of fourteen including Fritzy[1] and Bridget of Prussia, Howard de Waldens,[2] Cyril Egerton,[3] the Dunboynes,[4] Mary Roxburghe, John Lewis. Saw *Cosi fan Tutte* admirably performed.

Thursday, July 16th

Meg gave away prizes to the nurses of St Giles' hospital and made a short speech admirably. Then to the garden party at B.P. Pouring rain. We inadvertently got mixed up with Sherpa Tensing[5] and the Everest party.

Saturday, July 18th

To Cherkley for tea and dinner. The main object was to show Lord Beaverbrook some papers about the Duke of Windsor's activities in Spain and Portugal[6] during 1940 and to ask his opinion. He was in good form and the party, consisting of Lord B.'s granddaughter,

---

[1] Prince Frederick of Prussia, son of the German Crown Prince and married to a daughter of Lord Iveagh.

[2] John, Lord Howard de Walden, famous in the racing world.

[3] First cousin of my wife.

[4] Patrick, Lord Dunboyne, a contemporary of mine at Cambridge. Became a Q.C. and in due course a judge.

[5] On Coronation Day the news had broken of Edmund Hillary and Sherpa Tensing reaching the summit of Everest.

[6] The so-called Marburg papers, found in the German Government files, related in detail the German attempt in 1940 to persuade the Duke of Windsor to stay in Portugal. Ribbentrop hoped to make use of him after a successful invasion of Britain.

Jean Campbell,[1] Sir Patrick Hennessy,[2] Lord B.'s French mistress and Mr Junor[3] of the *Evening Standard* was entertaining. Lord B., who has given me a good many first editions, presented me with one of *The Jungle Book*.

Sunday, July 19th
By way of contrast lunched at Stratfield Saye to look at a house which the Duke of Wellington offers to let to us. We thought it most attractive.

Went to Chartwell for dinner as R. A. Butler was to be there, with his speech for the foreign affairs debate. W. much improved in powers of concentration. He did a little work before dinner (including approval of my draft reply to a tricky P.Q. about the Regency Act – made tricky by the Pss Margaret–Townsend explosion); he sparkled at dinner; and after dinner he went carefully and meticulously through Rab's speech.

Drove back to London with Rab, who is very, very smooth, though oddly enough an agreeable companion. He says he will serve loyally under Eden and that anyhow some of the Conservative Party might not want him (Rab) as P.M. because of Munich. We discussed potential troubles when Anthony Eden returns next week fully expecting that he is shortly going to form a new administration. But there is no certainty that the P.M. intends to give up: on the contrary I surmise that he still hopes to bring off some final triumph, like Disraeli at the Congress of Berlin in 1878, and perhaps light the way to the end of the Cold War. Rab says he hopes his end will be like that or, if it cannot be so, like Chatham's[4] end.

Tuesday, July 21st
Listened to Rab open the foreign affairs debate. It was a dull speech, yet more dully delivered. He is certainly no orator. And it left the Opposition, and indeed most of his hearers, with the thought: where is Winston's great peace initiative of May 11th? It is entombed in a guarded oration inspired by Frank Roberts[5] (now a

---

[1] Lady Jean Campbell, daughter of Beaverbrook's daughter Janet and the Duke of Argyll. She was a first-class journalist who wrote accounts of U.S. affairs for the *Evening Standard*. One of her husbands was Norman Mailer.
[2] Chairman of the Ford Motor Company in Britain. A long-standing friend of Beaverbrook and Bracken and of mine.
[3] Sir John Junor, afterwards Editor of the *Sunday Express*.
[4] Lord Chatham fell back in a fit during a fiery speech in Parliament opposing the British withdrawal from the American Colonies and died shortly after.
[5] There were few cleverer or more conscientious members of the Foreign Office. His strong inclination to the Eden rather than the Churchill theme of foreign policy accounts for my acid comment on a man I respect.

great power in the F.O. who dislikes the P.M. and all his policies and who sat smiling contentedly beside me in the official box while Rab unfolded his dismal and pedestrian story).

Friday, July 24th

Lunched alone with W. at Chartwell. He is now amazingly restored, but complains that his memory has suffered and says he thinks he probably will give up in October or at any rate before the Queen leaves for Australia in November. Still very wrapped up with the possibility of bringing something off with the Russians and with the idea of meeting Malenkov[1] face to face. Very disappointed in Eisenhower whom he thinks both weak and stupid. Bitterly regrets that the Democrats were not returned at the last Presidential Election.

Monday, July 27th

At Chequers. Anthony and Clarissa Eden came to luncheon, the former thin and frail after his three operations but in good spirits. He is, of course, thinking above all of when he will get the Prime Ministership, but he contrived to keep off the subject altogether today and to talk mainly of foreign affairs. He thinks the fall of Beria three weeks ago may have been a defeat for moderation. The signs, flimsy though they be, do seem to point that way.

Gave Winston *Candide* to read. He has had a surfeit of Trollope's political novels.

Today the Korean War ended – after months of infuriating haggling over the terms of the armistice.

Friday, July 31st–Tuesday, August 4th

To Chequers again. Lord Beaverbrook came on Friday night, in disgrace because of an unpleasant cartoon of Lord Salisbury in the *Daily Express*. Winston has seen more of Lord B. since his illness than at any time since he formed the present administration. Junor, of the *Evening Standard*, told me when I lunched with him last Wednesday, that the Labour Party saw in an (imaginary) split between W. and the rest of the Cabinet over four-power talks with Russia their best propaganda line for many a day. The *Daily Express*, because of Lord B.'s hatred of Lord Salisbury (and of the nobility in general) seems to be playing roughly the same hand. However, at Chequers Lord B.'s charm soon thawed the resentment – though Winston had the Visitors' Book removed so that Lord B.'s signature should not be visible when Lord Salisbury arrived next day!

---

[1] Stalin's successor who, in the event, had only a short tenure. His colleague at the top of the Politburo, Beria, was executed.

The Edens, the Salisburys, Meg, Mary and Christopher were there for the week-end. Randolph, Sarah and Duff Cooper came over on August Bank Holiday. The underlying interest was two-fold. First of all the two invalids: Winston and Eden. The latter was burning with the big question-mark: "When do I take over?" The former had told me in private that if asked he would say that the more he was hustled, the longer he would be. However, Eden (warned by Patrick Buchan-Hepburn,[1] Brendan and, I expect, Rab – with all of whom I have discussed the problem in recent weeks) said nothing. He looked very frail and probably realises he must first prove that he will be fit to be P.M. himself.

The second drama is our attitude to Russia. Winston is firmly hoping for talks which might lead to a relaxation of the Cold War and a respite in which science could use its marvels for improving the lot of man and, as he put it, the leisured classes of his youth might give way to the leisured masses of tomorrow. Eden is set on retaining the strength of N.A.T.O. and the Western Alliance by which, he believes, Russia has already been severely weakened. W. is depressed by Eden's attitude (which reflects that of the F.O.), because he thinks it consigns us to years more of hatred and hostility. Still more depressing is that Lord S. says he found Eisenhower violently Russophobe, greatly more so than Dulles, and that he believes the President to be personally responsible for the policy of useless pinpricks and harassing tactics the U.S. is following against Russia in Europe and the Far East.

On Sunday I went with W. to Royal Lodge where he had an audience of the Queen. He said that he had told her his decision whether or not to retire would be made in a month when he saw clearly whether he was fit to face Parliament and to make a major speech to the Conservative Annual Conference in October. He also asked, and received, permission to invite Eisenhower here on a State Visit in September or October. He has learned from Winthrop Aldrich (U.S. Ambassador) that Eisenhower would do this for him but for nobody else – after he retired there would be no question of it. It would be a great event, because U.S. Presidents seldom if ever go abroad and none has been here since Woodrow Wilson at the end of World War I.

Meg and I left Chequers on Tuesday, August 4th.

[1] Conservative Chief Whip. Created Lord Hailes. Governor General of the short-lived West Indies Federation established by Harold Macmillan. An outstandingly good amateur artist.

Thursday, 6th–Sunday, 9th August

At Chequers again. Meg, Nanny and Harriet came over for the day on the 9th and I drove them home. On the 8th, Lord Salisbury, Rab Butler and William Strang came for a meeting at 12.00 noon about the reply from Russia to the three-power note sent after the Washington Conference. The P.M. took the meeting in the Hawtrey room, the first time he has presided at a meeting since the Cabinet on the morrow of his stroke. The line he had proposed was accepted: namely to ask the Americans a lot of questions and leave them the burden of drafting the answer: this in spite of contrary and long-winded drafts prepared by the F.O. The old man still gets his way: usually because it is simple and clear, whereas the "mystique" of the F.O. (as Selwyn Lloyd calls it) tends to be pettifogging and over detailed. After the meeting we had a most agreeable luncheon party, the P.M. in sparkling mood. He said that all his life he had found his main contribution had been by self-expression rather than by self-denial. And he has started drinking brandy again after a month's abstinence. Apart from his unsteady walk, the appearances left by his stroke have vanished, though he still tires quickly. However Lord Moran told me he thought there might be another stroke within a year. Indeed it was probable.

On the afternoon of the 8th Monty came for the week-end. I walked up Beacon Hill with him (the weather for the last week has been gorgeous). He volunteered the opinion that Frank Roberts was a menace to the country with his "rigid constipated mentality". After dinner we talked, the P.M., Monty and I, till late about the two world wars. Monty and the P.M. said the Americans had made five capital mistakes in the military field in the last war:

i. They had prevented Alexander getting to Tunis the first time, when he could easily have done so.

ii. They had done at Anzio what Stopford did at Suvla Bay: clung to the beaches and failed to establish positions inland as they could well have done. The P.M. said he had intended it to be a wholly British expedition.

iii. They had insisted on Operation ANVIL, thereby preventing Alexander from taking Trieste and Vienna.

iv. Eisenhower had refused to let Monty, in OVERLORD, concentrate his advance on the left flank. He had insisted on a broad advance, which could not be supported, and had thus allowed Runstedt to counter-attack on the Ardennes and had prolonged the war, with dire political results, to the spring of 1945.

v. Eisenhower had let the Russians occupy Berlin, Prague and

Vienna – all of which might have been entered by the Americans.

Monty told me he had got Ridgway[1] sacked from S.H.A.P.E. He had gone off to America specifically to tell Ike that this was necessary and had found Ike alive to the fact. But Ridgway, who had been made American Chief of Staff, still thought he had been promoted and not sacked!

He inclines to agree with Lord Salisbury about Ike's present political ineptitude but says he is the prisoner of Congress.

Tuesday, August 11th–Wednesday, August 12th
At Chequers again, alone with the P.M. and Norman Brook. Talk about reconstituting the Cabinet. Possibly Eden Leader of House and Lord President, Salisbury Foreign Secretary; or Harold Macmillan Foreign Secretary, Eccles Minister of Housing, Patrick Buchan-Hepburn Minister of Works. But all depends on W.'s own future and he gives himself till the end of September to decide.

Much talk about Russia: the P.M. still inclining to think we should have another shot at an understanding. He said, "We must not go further on the path to war unless we are sure there is no other path to peace."

Wrote a Cabinet Paper, which the P.M. accepted, about the Windsor papers (relating to the Duke's activities in Spain and Portugal in 1940). The P.M. still set on suppression.

Friday, August 14th–Saturday, August 15th and Monday, August 17th
At Chartwell. P.M. coming round towards resignation in October. Says he no longer has the zest for work and finds the world in an abominable state wherever he looks. Greatly depressed by thoughts on the hydrogen bomb. He had a nightmare on Thursday, dreaming that he was making a speech in the House of Lords and that it was an appalling flop. Lord Rothermere came up to him and said, "It didn't even *sound* nice."

He made a good pun at luncheon on Monday. We were talking about a peerage for Salter, who is to be removed from the Ministry of Materials. Christopher asked whether he could not also get rid of Mackeson[2] from Overseas Trade, but said he didn't merit a peerage. "No," said W., "but perhaps a disappearage."

---

[1] Successor to Eisenhower as Supreme Commander in Europe.

[2] M.P. for the Folkestone and Hythe division of Kent. A Conservative Whip, 1947–52, and then Secretary for Overseas Trade. He was given a baronetcy in 1954.

When the explosion of the first hydrogen bomb was announced in an after-dinner speech in the United States, the only English paper to carry the news was the Manchester Guardian. *The Prime Minister read it in bed at 10 Downing Street and immediately telephoned to the Chiefs of Staff and everybody else in Whitehall who might know about the matter. Nobody did. The account in the* Manchester Guardian *described in some detail the effect of exploding a thermo-nuclear bomb and the P.M. said to me that we were now as far from the age of the atomic bomb as the atomic bomb itself from the bow and arrow. His subsequent reaction, which he fully maintained over the rest of his Prime Ministership, was that this ghastly invention might perhaps present humanity with a real chance of lasting peace, since war would now be impossible.*

Tuesday, August 18th

W. came to London to hold his first Cabinet since June. After it he discussed Cabinet changes further. Eccles may now be given Overseas Trade and Cabinet rank; or he might be Minister of Education. I said to the P.M. that I shouldn't like to be educated by Eccles. "Oh," he said, "I don't know. Good taste is not part of the curriculum."

*   *   *

Meg and I were leaving for the South of France on Wednesday, but the hotel at Beauvallon has closed because of the French strikes. We have sent Harriet off by train to Ladykirk and shall now go northwards ourselves by car.

We left on August 21st, staying at Stretchworth[1] for two or three days and then going to Scotland until September 20th. We stayed at Ladykirk with the Askews, at Drummond with the Ancasters, at Douglas with the Homes, at Gartshore with the Whitelaws and at Mertoun.

Harriet divided her stay between Ladykirk and Gartshore.

On September 24th I flew out to the South of France to be with Winston at Cap d'Ail, near Monte Carlo, where Lord Beaverbrook lent him his villa, La Capponcina, for a recuperative holiday, and where Meg joined us. There were two episodes I found entertaining.

Beaverbrook had provided his guest not only with a chef of

---

[1] Near Newmarket. My mother-in-law, Violet, Lady Ellesmere, lived there after her husband died.

quality and a judiciously stocked cellar, but also with a small black Fiat car which had known better days. It was not in much demand, for we seldom ventured beyond the garden or the rocky shore where Churchill, with his detective, Sergeant Murray (who was also an artist), spent hours painting the rocks and pine trees. However, Churchill had never been averse to casinos, and one evening he thought it would be fun to go to Monte Carlo and try his luck at the tables. I said firmly that I thought it a most unsuitable expedition for a Prime Minister shortly to preside over a Party Conference at Margate, since he was bound to be recognised, photographed and thereafter severely criticised. When I eventually succeeded in dissuading him, he insisted I should go in his place. From the recesses of his private black box he extracted several 20,000 Italian lire notes, relics of a painting holiday by Lake Como some years previously. He endowed me with them, declaring that if I won we should share the winnings, but that if I lost his lire nest-egg he would bear no grudge.

So, after dinner, while Meg and the Prime Minister settled down to play Oklahoma (still one of his favourite card-games) I drove the battered Fiat to Monte Carlo in this unusual representative capacity and entered the flamboyant, late Victorian Casino. I played Chemin de Fer with conspicuous ill-luck and quickly lost the French franc equivalent of all the Prime Ministerial lire. I was then informed that the notes I had proffered in payment for the chips received in exchange were found to be an extinct issue, no longer legal tender. I escaped, with some difficulty, on the strength of an I.O.U. and drove back, much dejected, to La Capponcina. Churchill said that somebody should have told him the Italians had changed their currency; but he did subsequently take steps to redeem my I.O.U.

A day or two later we had an outing which I have recorded in less detail elsewhere.[1] Churchill recalled something Mrs Reggie Fellowes had told him. Daisy Fellowes was a wicked but attractive lady, French by origin, who, according to Clementine, tried to seduce Winston at the Ritz Hotel in Paris shortly after the Churchills were married. It was an unsuccessful effort and she had been forgiven, even by Clementine.

This notorious lady had recently been to a restaurant in the Italian resort of San Remo where she was shown a remarkable crustacean called a sea-cricket. The Prime Minister, always fascinated by birds, beasts and fishes, now suggested that we should dine at San Remo and examine this unusual creature.

[1] In *The Churchillians* (Weidenfeld & Nicolson, 1981).

Lord Beaverbrook's chef was given a night off and Sergeant Murray informed the French police of our intention. In pitch darkness and pouring rain we entered the two-doored Fiat, Meg and I cramped uncomfortably behind and Churchill sitting in front beside Sergeant Murray, who acted as chauffeur as well as artistic adviser and detective. When our shabby little car emerged from the drive we found two shiny black limousines and a posse of police motorcyclists waiting to escort us. We set off at speed, but had not gone far before the window next to Churchill came adrift. Meg leant forward, the rain and cold night air rushing in upon her, and held it partially closed. A few minutes later we reached the Italian frontier where guards of honour, alerted that the famous British Prime Minister would be passing by, presented arms as this strange procession tore through the open barriers.

At San Remo the alleged abode of the sea-cricket proved to be a dark and ramshackle *estaminet* by the quay-side with bare wooden tables. It was empty, and the *patron* was astonished by the arrival of a large motorised police force and a battered little Fiat from which emerged a figure whom he evidently recognised.

"Where," asked Churchill, "is the sea-cuckoo?"

"Sea-cricket," said Meg by way of explanation.

"I have come," said Churchill, quite unabashed, "to see the sea-cuckoo."

Round the *estaminet* stood glass tanks, which must normally have been replete with every kind of crustacean awaiting death for the gastronomic pleasure of customers. But an equinoctial gale had been raging for several days and even the most intrepid fisherman had declined to put to sea. So all that was visible in the tanks was one jaded langouste and a few prawns. San Remo was searched from east to west for a sea-cuckoo or cricket, and a disappointingly ugly crustacean was finally produced. We ate spaghetti and *prosciuto con melone* at the bare boards with a grumpy Prime Minister who should have learned by experience to disregard suggestions made by Mrs Reggie Fellowes.

The next day Meg had a temperature of 103 degrees. Churchill returned to Downing Street accompanied only by his valet and Sergeant Murray. One of the shiny French police cars transported him to Nice airport, and I stayed for almost a week's extra holiday with my convalescent wife, well cherished by Lord Beaverbrook's chef. Working for Churchill could be pyrotechnic; it was seldom dull.

*   *   *

October 1953

Winston cannot make up his mind whether or not to go on as P.M. On the whole he inclines to do so or at any rate to see what he can do. He certainly wants to, but is a little doubtful of his capacity to make long speeches. He thinks he will take the big one he has to make on October 10th, at the Conservative Conference at Margate, as the test. His conversation at Cap d'Ail was of little else, apart from the tragedy that the Bermudan Conference had not taken place and the desirability of him and Eden meeting Malenkov and Molotov face to face.

Eden, of course, longs for him to go; and Patrick Buchan-Hepburn, with whom I had a talk before going to France, thinks there will be trouble in the House and in the Conservative Party if he does not.

On October 9th I went to Margate with W. for the Conservative Conference. He made a big speech the following day and did it with complete success. He had been nervous of the ordeal: his first public appearance since his stroke and a fifty-minute speech at that; but personally I had no fears as he always rises to occasions. In the event one could see but little difference, as far as his oratory went, since before his illness.

Meanwhile a sudden scheme for a meeting with the President at the Azores next week (we going in *Vanguard*) has been turned down by Eisenhower. The blunt truth is that E. does not want to meet him as he knows he will be confronted with a demand for a conference with the Russians which he is unwilling to accept. W. was for pursuing the matter but was stopped by a chance remark of mine on Friday evening when I said to him, "What subjects are you going to discuss when you get there?" It suddenly dawned on him that everything he might say to the President would necessarily be met with a negative response and that on other topics, such as Egypt, he (W.) would have nothing to offer but criticisms and complaints of the U.S. attitude. To bring the President 1,000 miles for that seemed discourteous and unfair.

Eden, who though still thin looks a great deal better, also had his success at Margate. On the surface he seems resigned to W. remaining in power (W. told me, after his speech, that he now hoped to do so until the Queen returned from Australia in May). There are two potential causes of friction: (i) Egypt. If W. and Eden fall out over that – assuming the Egyptians agree to our terms – W. would have the support of the Conservative Party against

Eden but not of the Opposition. (ii) A visit to Malenkov. Here W. would have the support of the country and the Opposition against Eden, backed by the Foreign Office and a section of the Conservatives. W. thinks a meeting, of an exploratory kind, might do good and could do no harm. The F.O. think it might lead to appeasement and would certainly discourage our European allies who would relax their defence efforts if even the shadow of a detente appeared. The Foreign Office and the U.S.A. are at one in thinking that Russia's slightly more reasonable attitude of late is due less to Stalin's death than to the success of our own constant pressure and increased strength.

On Saturday night we got back to London from Margate and I dined at No. 10 with W. and Clemmie and Duncan and Diana Sandys. W. very elated by his success, but more tired than one might have hoped.

*   *   *

At this stage I abandoned keeping a diary, in the main because living in the country, and above all moving to a new home at Stratfield Saye, absorbed such energy as might otherwise have been left to me by the end of the day. I did, however, keep detailed accounts of two more journeys to America, which were written at the time.

39

The Bermuda Conference

Once again I purloined a small Stationery Office note-book.

Tuesday, December 1st, 1953
Tonight we left Heathrow for Bermuda in the B.O.A.C. aircraft Canopus, which took the Queen to Bermuda last week. Our party included the P.M., Mr Eden, Sir N. Brook, Sir P. Dixon, Sir F. Roberts, Denis Allen,[1] Evelyn Shuckburgh,[2] John Priestman,[3] Christopher Soames, David Pitblado, Lord Cherwell and Lord Moran, with not too numerous assistants and ancillaries.

Strong headwinds obliged us to land at Shannon. Thence to Gander, where snow was lying on the ground and so, after about seventeen hours of journeying, to Bermuda where the Governor (Sir A. Hood), the foremost citizens, and a Guard of Honour of the Royal Welch Fusiliers, complete with goat and white "hackles", greeted us.

The main party stayed at the Mid-Ocean Golf Club and at the Castle Harbour Hotel. I have been lent Henry Tiarks'[4] villa "Out of the Blue" and have invited Lord Cherwell, Norman Brook and Christopher Soames to share its luxurious comfort and beautiful view.

---

[1] An Under Secretary in the Foreign Office, subsequently Commissioner General in S.E. Asia and Ambassador to Turkey.
[2] Principal Private Secretary to Anthony Eden. Afterwards Ambassador to N.A.T.O. (in Paris) and to Italy.
[3] Assistant Private Secretary to Anthony Eden. Later joined the Council of Europe and became Clerk of the European Parliament.
[4] A senior director of Schröders, the merchant bank, and a man of great generosity.

Thursday, December 3rd

This morning went to the airport with the P.M. for the ceremony of receiving the French Prime Minister, M. Laniel,[1] and the Foreign Secretary, M. Bidault. Last time this conference was proposed, the French could not form a Government and the meeting had to be postponed week after week until just as we were packing to leave the P.M. had his stroke.

Lunched in the P.M.'s dining-room at the Mid-Ocean with Eden, Cherwell, Brook, Bob Dixon and Christopher as the other guests. An undistinguished conversation. Rushed away to see the Governor and the Speaker of the Assembly, both of whom are exercised over the colour question. There was a row because when the Queen was here last week no coloured guests were invited to the banquet at Government House. The P.M. has insisted that two should be asked to the Governor's banquet tomorrow. This meant tampering with the precedence list (oh horror!) and leaving out three most important local guests. I solved the problem by dropping instead three of our delegation.

Bathed twice today in a limpid blue sea (temperature nearly 70 degrees) and dived by the rocks to look at black and yellow striped fish shaped like melons.

Dinner with the P.M., Prof., Lord Moran, Brook, Christopher and Pitblado. The P.M. got going well after dinner, but the room was too small and we were all but perishing from the heat. The P.M. said, "It may be that we are living in our generation through the great demoralisation which the scientists have caused but before the countervailing correctives have become operative."

First prize to the Prof. who began illustrating a point with the following words: "I was told by a Russian waiter at Los Angeles in 1912 . . ."

Delicious balmy night and the noise of the tree frogs is far better than that of crickets. We sat outside on the terrace at midnight with no discomfort.

Friday, December 4th

Went to a delegation meeting with N. Brook at the Castle Harbour Hotel and escaped in time to bathe before luncheon, while the P.M., who had met Eisenhower and Dulles on their arrival at the airport, pirated the former and took him to lunch privately in his room. This greatly disturbed both Dulles and Eden who neither of them trust their chief alone. However, the P.M. seemed, from what he told me, to get a good deal out of Ike including some

---

[1] Short-lasting and by no means memorable French Prime Minister.

alarming information about tough American intentions[1] in certain circumstances.

When Ike had left, the P.M., Christopher and I walked to the beach and the P.M. sat like King Canute defying the incoming tide (and getting his feet wet in consequence) while C. and I bathed naked and I swam out to fetch Winston some distant seaweed he wished to inspect.

At 5.00 there was the first Plenary Meeting, of which I made a record. There were memories of former conferences. The Big Three first sat on the porch in wicker chairs and were photographed in a manner reminiscent of Tehran. Then, when the conference started, all the lights fused and we deliberated by the light of candles and hurricane lamps as in Athens at Christmas 1944. After a turgid if quite intelligent speech by Bidault, the P.M. (who had not prepared anything to say) launched forth into a powerful disquisition on his theory – which he calls a "double-dealing" policy – of strength towards the Soviet Union combined with holding out the hand of friendship. He spoke of contacts, trade and other means of infiltration – always provided we were united and resolute in our strength. Only by proving to our peoples that we would neglect no chances of "easement" could we persuade them to go on with the sacrifices necessary to maintain strong armed forces. This, coming after an intransigently anti-Russian speech by Bidault ("the only decent Frenchman" as Evelyn Shuckburgh called him to me), upset the Foreign Office representatives except for Denis Allen who thought the speech statesmanlike and constructive. Frank Roberts and Shuckburgh said it was a disaster. I gather Eden felt the same. But I think Allen was right.

Ike followed with a short, very violent statement, in the coarsest terms. He said that as regards the P.M.'s belief that there was a New Look in Soviet Policy, Russia was a woman of the streets and whether her dress was new, or just the old one patched, it was certainly the same whore underneath. America intended to drive her off her present "beat" into the back streets.

I doubt if such language has ever before been heard at an international conference. Pained looks all round.

Of course, the French gave it all away to the press. Indeed some of their leakages were verbatim.

To end on a note of dignity, when Eden asked when the next meeting should be, the President replied, "I don't know. Mine is with a whisky and soda" – and got up to leave the room.

Busy with Norman Brook doing the record of the meeting, while

[1] Of an atomic nature.

the P.M., Eden, Cherwell and Lord Moran went to the dinner at Government House. We all (the rest of us) dined in the P.M.'s private dining-room where we thought the food would be a good deal better than in the Grill Room.

Saturday, December 5th
To the British delegation suite at the Castle Harbour for a briefing meeting. Everybody greatly perturbed by the American attitude on (a) the prospects (b) their action, in the event of the Korean truce breaking down. This question has such deep implications that it is undoubtedly the foremost matter at the conference – though it has to be discussed behind closed doors with the Americans. No atomic matters can be talked about to the French who are very sensitive at having no atomic piles or bombs. The P.M., Ike, Lord Cherwell and Admiral Strauss[1] discussed the matter in the President's room from 11.30 till lunch-time.

This afternoon, while standing on the beach, I talked to Douglas MacArthur of the State Department. He said that the French system was hopeless, though Bidault was doing all he could. If E.D.C. [the European Defence Community: a plan for a European army] were not ratified, the American administration could ask for no appropriations from Congress and would have to re-orientate their whole policy to Europe.

I did not go to the Plenary Meeting – leaving David Pitblado to do this. Instead I went with Christopher to Government House for a quarter of an hour as the Governor was giving a cocktail party.

We gave a dinner party at "Out of the Blue" for Pug Ismay who arrived today. Meanwhile the P.M. and Eden were dining alone with Eisenhower and Dulles and were engaged in grim conversations about the future actions to be taken in the event of a breach of the truce in Korea. Eden was most particularly perturbed by this and by the effect on public opinion in England. There was also discussion of a draft speech, mainly on atomic matters, which Eisenhower wants to deliver next week at the General Assembly of the United Nations. Christopher read it aloud in the P.M.'s bedroom, while I sat in a chair and the P.M. and Eden, still fully dressed in dinner jackets, lay side by side flat on the P.M.'s bed. The Americans had of course gone to their own apartments by then.

---

[1] Head of the American Atomic Energy Commission. He worked closely with Lord Cherwell.

Sunday, December 6th

This morning everybody was in rather a state. First there is the momentous matter of last night's discussion[1] which far outstrips in importance anything else at the conference. Secondly there is E.D.C. The Americans are disgusted with the French but nevertheless convinced that E.D.C. is the only alternative for them to withdrawing to the periphery of Europe. The French, wily diplomats that they are, have at least this card to play: Bidault and the Quai d'Orsay are all for E.D.C. and have done everything possible to meet the American point of view. Therefore, say the Americans, it is the British who must satisfy the French Chamber of Deputies by guaranteeing to leave their troops on the continent for a defined number of years or even by actually joining the E.D.C. Thus it is we who are to suffer on account of French weakness and obduracy. Of course, the obvious answer is (i) we will keep our troops on the continent as long as the Americans agree to do so, (ii) we could not possibly get our Parliament and people, or the Commonwealth, to accept our actual membership of E.D.C.

The Prime Minister, when first I went to see him this morning, was engaged in writing a letter to Ike approving, apart from one or two points, the text of his draft speech to U.N.O. I took it down to the beach to show Eden who was lying there with Dulles, engaged in a mixture of bathing and negotiation. Anthony Eden at once said that in view of what we knew from yesterday's private talks with the Americans, approval of the terms of the speech in all its aspects would make us accessories before the act. He proposed the insertion of a statement that in view of our exposed position, we had to make reservations. This the P.M. accepted and sent me down with the letter to give it to the President.

Eisenhower was in his sitting-room, cross-legged in an armchair, going through his speech. He was friendly, but I noticed that he never smiled: a change from the Ike of war days or even, indeed, of last January in New York. He said several things that were noteworthy. The first was that whereas Winston looked on the atomic weapon as something entirely new and terrible, he looked upon it as just the latest improvement in military weapons. He implied that there was in fact no distinction between "conventional weapons" and atomic weapons: all weapons in due course became conventional weapons. This of course represents a fundamental difference of opinion between public opinion in the U.S.A. and in

---

[1] The American inclination to use the atomic bomb in Korea if the Chinese came to the aid of the Communist North Koreans, a suggestion strongly resisted by Churchill and Eden.

England. However, he said that America was prepared to be generous in the sacrifice of fissionable material to an international authority that she was willing to make.

I told him that a reference to "the obsolete Colonial mold" contained in his draft speech would give offence in England. He said that was part of the American philosophy. I replied that a lot of people in England thought India had been better governed by the Viceroy and the British Government of India than at present. He said that as a matter of fact he thought so himself, but that to Americans liberty was more precious than good government.

W. saw him for half an hour before lunch and he agreed to remove the obnoxious phrase about colonialism and to substitute for the United States being "free to use the atomic bomb" a phrase about the United States "reserving the right to use the atomic bomb".

It has been a gloriously sunny day. I bathed twice and lunched out of doors.

After luncheon there was trouble because the Foreign Ministers had sent off to Adenauer the text of their proposed reply to the Soviet Government, accepting a conference at Berlin in January, without showing it to Ike or W. (Laniel retired to bed yesterday with pleurisy and a temperature of 104 degrees). W. remonstrated strongly with Eden and wanted to have left out the reference to German reunification, on the grounds that you couldn't confront the Russians at Berlin with both our determination that Western Germany should be an armed member of E.D.C. *and* a demand that Eastern Germany be united to it. Eden enlisted the support of Dulles (even heavier and more flabby now than last January) and after pointing out that German reunification had figured in all the previous notes, and that Adenauer expected it, they won their case. In the confusion Frank Roberts, who was in a state of fury with the P.M., was mistaken by the latter for one of Dulles' advisers and treated to a homily as such.

During the Plenary Conference, which centred on E.D.C. and which again Pitblado attended, Christopher and I entertained to drinks at "Out of the Blue" Alastair Buchan,[1] Wilson Broadbent (*Daily Mail*), Ed. Russell,[2] and one or two members of the delegation.

Dined at the "Pink Beach" with Christopher, Ed. Russell, and

---

[1] Younger son of John Buchan, Lord Tweedsmuir. An energetic journalist and writer.

[2] American provincial newspaper owner, always friendly and forthcoming, married to the Duke of Marlborough's eldest daughter, Sarah, not to be confused with Winston Churchill's daughter.

two particularly glamorous American women called Mrs Steele and Miss Jinx Falkenburg. The latter is the sister of the Wimbledon champion and obviously a champion herself in other ways. There is no doubt that American women are supreme in the art of flattering the male ego.

Dragged self away to return to the Mid-Ocean and put a thoughtful P.M. (unconscionably bored by a dinner given in his honour by the French) to bed. He said, as I have been feeling for the past forty-eight hours, that all our problems, even those such as Egypt, shrink into insignificance by the side of the one great issue which this conference has thrown up.

A snake runs away from you because it is frightened. But if you tread on its tail it will rear up and strike you. This is to me an analogy with Soviet Russia. I put it to Eden who agreed most heartily.

Before going to bed the P.M. told me that he and Ike had agreed to treat forcing through the ratification of E.D.C. as a combined military operation. If it does not go through, the Americans do not agree with the P.M. that Germany must be invited to join N.A.T.O. On the contrary they talk of falling back on "peripheral" defence, which means the defence of their bases stretching in a crescent from Iceland via East Anglia, Spain and North Africa to Turkey. This, in the P.M.'s view, would entail France becoming Communist-dominated (and finally going the way of Czechoslovakia) while the Americans sought to rearm Germany sandwiched between the hostile powers of Russia and France. Frank Roberts thinks that we shall in the event just get over the E.D.C. hurdle. If we don't, the P.M. intends to go all out to persuade the Americans to work for the Germany-in-N.A.T.O. alternative. This is a precarious situation.

Monday, December 7th
Today there were endless Plenary Meetings, three in all. I attended two of them and recorded the talks about Egypt and about Indo-China. Most of the morning meeting was *in camera* – discussing the one thing of importance that has arisen at this conference. The last, about the Communiqué (which was bound in any case to be colourless and uninformative) lasted till 1.30 a.m. The real mistake was having the French, with whom none of the things we mind most about can be discussed and who, at the Plenary Meetings, insist on making long formal statements (e.g. on Indo-China) explaining the situation at length – as if we didn't know the facts (rather than the remedies) already.

Eden told me that the P.M. did really well at the meeting *in camera* and turned the minds of the Americans.

Tonight I dined in Hamilton with Mrs Steele, Ed. Russell and Christopher but returned at 10.30 to the Mid-Ocean where discussions on the Communiqué were in full swing – the French being adamant about some reference to E.D.C. It was curious that Eden, not Bidault, went up to seek agreement from the bed-ridden Laniel.

Tuesday, December 8th
This morning I strolled down to bathe with John Foster Dulles, who said that the presence of the French, and the constant need for interpretation, had greatly hampered the conference. Since it was the Americans who insisted on the French being invited, I thought this indeed ironical. The surf was heavy on the beach and Dulles was twice capsized.

The P.M. went to see Ike at 10.00 and told me that he said to him that the Americans sending arms to Egypt after January 1st would have no less effect in the U.K. than the British sending arms to China would have in the U.S.A. The President, he said, took this seriously.

Eisenhower also told him that he was in favour of International Conferences provided there was no agenda *and* no communiqué. The press here (nearly 200 of them) are furious at the scanty information they have received. Alastair Buchan had the impudence to tell me that conferences such as this should be arranged for the convenience of the press.

The President left before lunch, and Bidault with Parodi and de Margerie came to take leave of the P.M. before their departure. W. said to Bidault that if he had been rough on the French it was not because he loved them less than formerly, but because he wanted to urge them to save themselves and not, in consequence of refusing E.D.C., to force the Americans to fall back on a "peripheral" defence of Europe. It was not the French Government which was "bitching" (a word de Margerie found difficulty in translating!) it all but the French parliamentary system. With this Bidault heartily concurred.

This evening the Speaker (Sir John Cox) gave a dinner for the House of Assembly in the Mid-Ocean – the Conference Room having rapidly been converted for the purpose. The P.M. was the principal speaker and did it very well. The Governor, Sir Alexander Hood, was outstandingly eloquent; the Speaker outstandingly turgid.

I sat between two members of the Assembly. Bermuda has a

parliamentary system in which there are no parties but each member votes according to his conscience. This is simplified by property qualifications for the franchise which means that out of 35,000 inhabitants only 5,000 can vote. One of my neighbours was gravely annoyed that the P.M. should have insisted on two coloured men being asked to the banquet which the Governor had given for the Big Three. No black men had been asked to the banquet given for the Queen a fortnight ago and there had been a fuss both in the House of Commons and in the British press which had prompted the P.M.'s action.

Wednesday, December 9th
A day of rest and glorious sunshine. Played golf in the morning with Norman Brook on the Mid-Ocean golf course which is both good and beautiful. Saw a number of strange birds – bright blue and bright red, also a long-legged white bird like a crane. The cedar trees all over the island have died of a blight and present a strangely funereal effect.

Lunched with the P.M., Eden, the Governor, the Speaker, Pug Ismay, Lord Cherwell and Christopher. Then drove with Christopher to Hamilton where the P.M. inspected the Bermuda Regiment.

Christopher and I entertained Evelyn Shuckburgh, John Priestman and Denis Allen to dinner at the villa. They went for a midnight bathe while I went to collect Mrs Steele at the Coral Beach Club and went with her to hear calypsos at the Elbow Beach. Returned to the villa at 3.30 a.m. and found myself locked out. Prof.'s valet/secretary, the admirable Harvey, saved the situation.

Thursday, December 10th
Bathed in the morning and attended to the P.M. who was in a cantankerous frame of mind. I, too, was mentally dyspeptic.

In the afternoon drove with Norman Brook to St George's, the old capital, to see the beautiful seventeenth-century colonial style church, white without and roofed with delicious-smelling cedar beams within. The early colonial stone memorial tablets are particularly delightful. It is notable how many Governors and eminent citizens were carried off by yellow fever in comparatively early youth. Observed, with amusement, that the vain Lord Moran had contrived to have his signature, solitary on a large sheet of writing paper, inserted in the treasure chest, among seventeenth-century silver, with those of the Queen, Mr Eden and M. Bidault.

Boarded the B.O.A.C. aircraft Canopus at 8.00 p.m. with the

rest of the British delegation and the now recovered M. Laniel. The P.M., who didn't want to have to talk French, contrived to have him sent straight to his bunk on Lord Moran's advice, after arranging for him to dine before we left. Heavily drugged, the unsuspecting M. Laniel went to sleep and did not disturb the dinner party on board.

The four-hour difference of time between Bermuda and London rather puts one out for eating and sleeping purposes.

John Priestman stood on his head in the main cabin saying that he wanted to be the first Englishman who had ever done so in mid-Atlantic.

Friday, December 11th

We reached London after a wonderfully smooth flight at 11.30 a.m. G.M.T. Before landing I dictated a long letter descriptive of the Bermuda Conference for the P.M. to send to the Queen, who is shortly due at Fiji in the *Gothic*.

We reached Downing Street 12½ hours after leaving the Mid-Ocean Club. Magic carpet indeed. And so the £2. 2. 6. I had spent on insuring my life was fortunately wasted.

After luncheon I took the train to Woking, with Mama and Violet Bonham Carter[1] as travelling companions. The latter very incensed with W.S.C. who, she says, promised her that there should be a free vote in the House on the vexed question of sponsored television. She asked me to tell him that she was affectionate but disaffected!

Met by Meg, looking very well, and found Harriet enchanting though aloof, and suffering from a whooping cough injection.

[1] Lady Violet Bonham Carter, daughter of Asquith by his first marriage. A leading Liberal protagonist and first-class public speaker. Very old friend of Churchill.

40

Visit to the U.S.A. and Canada
June 1954

Thursday, June 24th
At 7.45 p.m. we took off from Heathrow, the following party:
  The Prime Minister
  Mr Eden
  Lord Cherwell
  Lord Moran
  Sir Edwin Plowden
  Sir Harold Caccia
  Denis Allen
  Anthony Rumbold
  Christopher Soames
  Me (or perhaps it should be I) plus
  an unusually small body of ancillaries.
The journey was planned by the Prime Minister as long ago as last April, but its purposes have varied as the weeks went by. Primarily it was to convince the President that we must co-operate more fruitfully in the atomic and hydrogen sphere and that we, the Americans and British, must go and talk to the Russians in an effort to avert war, diminish the effect of Cold War and procure a ten years' period of "easement" during which we can divert our riches and our scientific knowledge to ends more fruitful than the production of catastrophic weapons. Now, owing to Anglo-American disagreement over S.E. Asia, reflected very noticeably at the Geneva Conference, the meeting has become in the eyes of the world (and the Foreign Secretary) an occasion for clearing the air and re-creating good feeling. The main topics are to be: Indo-China, Germany if E.D.C. fails, Egypt and atoms.
  We had a prosperous flight in the Canopus, landing for an hour

at Gander. It only became bumpy when we approached the American coast (which was, of course, the moment I chose to write this).

Friday, June 25th

On arrival at Washington we were met by Nixon, the Vice President, and Foster Dulles. Winston and Christopher are staying at the White House; I at the Embassy. I spent most of the day at the White House where, on arrival, W. at once got down to talking to the President. The first and vast surprise was when the latter at once agreed to talks with the Russians – a possibility of which W. had hoped to persuade the Americans after long talks on Indo-China, Europe, atoms; on all these the first impressions were surprisingly and immediately satisfactory while the world in general believes that there is at this moment greater Anglo-American friction than ever in history and that these talks are fraught with every possible complication and difficulty.

The White House is not attractive; it is too like a grand hotel inside. Moreover all the lights burn all the time which is extremely disagreeable at high noon – particularly as the sunshine is bright and the temperature in the 90°s.

This evening, after the official conversations – at which Eden and Dulles were present – the President gave a dinner for the P.M. to meet the American Cabinet. I was not bidden and went instead to dine with the Empsons,[1] in their garden, by the light of candles and fireflies. To bed, very tired, at 11 p.m.

Saturday, June 26th

After a comfortable and delicious breakfast, to the White House for the morning. The P.M. was closeted with the President, again to his great satisfaction. Christopher and I made the acquaintance of his large staff and also swam in the indoor pool (water temperature 86 degrees). The P.M. met the leaders of Congress at lunch and (according to his own account) addressed them afterwards with impromptu but admirable eloquence! I lunched at the Embassy with the Makinses. They have delicious food provided by a French chef.

At the White House all the afternoon. Good progress, this time on Egypt. The P.M. elated by success and in a state of excited good humour. In the middle of the afternoon meeting, while Christopher and I were sipping high-balls and reading telegrams in his

---

[1] Sir Charles Empson, Commercial Minister in Washington. He and his wife, Monica, had been hospitable to my wife and me on our honeymoon, when he held a similar post in Rome. He was later Ambassador to Chile.

sitting-room, he suddenly emerged and summoned us to go up to the "Solarium" with him so as to look at a great storm which was raging. I can't imagine anybody else interrupting a meeting with the President of the United States, two Secretaries of State and two Ambassadors just for this purpose. The Russian visit project has now been expanded (by the President, so the P.M. says) to a meeting in London, together with the French and West Germans, at the opening of which Ike himself would be present.

Dined with Rob Scott[1] and his wife. Interesting conversation with several State Department officials, especially Merchant and Byroade, about recognition of Communist China.[2] Their reasoning is ruled far more by sentiment than by logic. No answer to my question whether we should have been well advised to break off relations with Yugoslavia in 1947 because our feelings towards Tito's régime were so bitter.

Sunday, June 27th
All day at the White House except for luncheon at the Embassy. At 10.30 a.m. the President, in his luxurious cinema, showed us *The White Heron*, a film of the Queen's tour.

The Russian project has shrunk again as Dulles has been getting at the President. W. still determined to meet the Russians as he has now an assurance that the Americans won't object.

Invited to dinner with the President. Others there were, besides the P.M. and Eden, Dulles, Bedell Smith, Winthrop Aldrich, Roger Makins, Merchant, Christopher Soames. Very gay dinner, during which the P.M. and the President spoke highly of the Germans and in favour of their being allowed to rearm. The President called the French "a hopeless, helpless mass of protoplasm". Eden took the other line, with some support from Dulles, and ended by saying he could not be a member of any Government which acted as Ike and Winston seemed to be recommending. After dinner we adjourned to the Red Room and worked collectively and ineffectively on the draft of a Declaration – a kind of second Atlantic Charter – which the P.M. and the President propose to publish. It seems to me a very messy affair.

The P.M. went to bed at 12.00 elated and cheerful. He has been buoyed up by the reception he has had here and has not as yet had one single afternoon sleep. His sole relaxation has been a few games of bezique with me. Roger Makins said he never remembered a more riotous evening.

---

[1] Minister at the British Embassy.
[2] Which the British had done and Americans had not.

Monday, June 28th
Meeting in the President's office at 10.00 to discuss the Declaration (in which the P.M. had suddenly espied some Dulles-like anti-colonial sentiments) and the draft minutes on Indo-China, E.D.C. and Egypt. This was a much more orderly affair and was satisfactorily concluded.

At 12.30, having issued a separate and rather colourless communiqué on the subjects that have been discussed, we all set off for the Hotel Stattner to lunch with the Washington Press Club. A disgusting luncheon after which the P.M. answered written questions that had been handed in with his best verve and vigour. Everybody greatly impressed by the skill with which he turned some of the most awkward. Himself so pleased by his reception that when I leant over to collect his notes he shook me warmly by the hand under the impression that I was a Senator or pressman endeavouring to congratulate him.

After lunch the P.M. and Eden drove to the Embassy, whither they move their headquarters this afternoon. I played bezique with a highly contented Winston (in spite of the fact that I won 26,600 in one solitary game), but at 6.00 he was still fresh enough to address, first, the Commonwealth Ambassadors and after them the British press representatives. This was followed by a huge dinner at the Embassy, from which I mercifully escaped. I dined with Ed. and Sarah Russell at the Colony restaurant. Meanwhile at the Embassy the P.M. was holding forth about the Guatemala revolution (a current event) and, according to Tony Rumbold,[1] making the Foreign Secretary look rather small in argument (the F.S. being all for caution and the P.M. being all for supporting the U.S. in their encouragement of the rebels and their hostility to the Communist Guatemalan régime). I talked to the P.M. as he went to bed and he said that Anthony Eden was sometimes very foolish: he would quarrel with the Americans over some petty Central American issue which did not affect Great Britain and could forget about the downtrodden millions in Poland.

Tuesday, June 29th
A hectic morning for me at the Embassy mainly concerned with arrangements for the publication of the Eisenhower–Churchill Declaration of principles, to which the Cabinet had suggested a few amendments. The P.M. went down to the White House at 11.30 to settle this and to take leave.

---

[1] Sir Anthony Rumbold, Bt., Evelyn Shuckburgh's successor as Principal Private Secretary to Anthony Eden.

Luncheon party at the Embassy. The American guests were Dean Acheson, Eugene Meyer, Senator Hickenlooper, Mr Sterling Cole (Chairman of the Atomic Energy Commission), Mr Whitelaw Reid, Ed. Russell. I sat between the latter and Edwin Plowden.[1] After lunch the P.M. became jocular. He said that if he were ever chased out of England and became an American citizen, he would hope to be elected to Congress. He would then propose two amendments to the American Constitution: (i) that at least half the members of the U.S. Cabinet should have seats in Congress (ii) that the President, instead of signing himself Dwight D. Eisenhower a hundred times a day should be authorised to sign himself "Ike".

At 3.30 we left the airfield, seen off by the Vice President and Dulles, in a Canadian aircraft for Ottawa. Mike Pearson,[2] Canadian Foreign Minister, travelled with us. I played bezique with the P.M. most of the way.

We reached Ottawa at 5.45 p.m. Guards of Honour of all three Services – the band in scarlet and bearskins – "Rule Britannia" played as a special tribute to the P.M., a short broadcast message (written by me), and a slow drive to the Château Laurier Hotel.

Dinner in the P.M.'s suite: St Laurent,[3] Howe (Minister of Defence), the Prof., Sir A. Nye (High Commissioner), Christopher and self. Dinner excellent (caviare, etc.). Nye most interesting and agreeable, also Howe. St Laurent dumb and a little glum – possibly even a bit shocked. A most secret subject[4] discussed with apparent success. Left the party as soon as I could get away in order to record this and to draft a speech for the P.M. to broadcast tomorrow.

Wednesday, June 30th

The P.M. and Anthony Eden went to a meeting of the Canadian Cabinet and at 12.00 noon the former addressed the press correspondents. He did not do it as well as in Washington, but it went down all right. Tony Rumbold and I then lunched with Nicholas Monsarrat, author of *The Cruel Sea*, and now Information Officer in the High Commissioner's Office. A gentle intelligent man, he prophesied that in South Africa it might well be that when Malan[5]

---

[1] Afterwards Lord Plowden. Held numerous appointments of great importance including Chairmanship of the Atomic Energy Commission.
[2] Later Prime Minister of Canada.
[3] French-Canadian Liberal Prime Minister.
[4] The American threat to use the atomic bomb in Korea.
[5] Nationalist Prime Minister who had beaten Smuts in a General Election.

went, the extremists (Strydom and Donges) would get the upper hand. A republic would be declared, Natal would secede and out of the resulting civil war would come a great native uprising.

The P.M. would spend most of the afternoon reading the English newspapers so that he started his broadcast (to which I contributed a few sentences) very belatedly, recorded it after we were supposed to have left for the Country Club and in consequence made everything late throughout the whole evening. Our drive to the Country Club, in huge open Cadillacs, was impressive because of the affectionate cheering crowds. The dinner there, given by St Laurent, was also impressive, partly on account of two moving speeches made by the two Prime Ministers and partly because all the Canadian Ministers, etc., present were so delightful. I sat between Compney, from Vancouver, who becomes Minister of Defence tomorrow, and Mr Beaudouin, the Speaker. The latter, a French Canadian, was voluble, sentimental and rather a bore, the former interesting and redolent of that enthusiasm tempered by modesty which distinguishes the Canadians from their southern neighbours.

After dinner we had a tumultuous ovation at the airport and flew in a Canadian aircraft to New York, I playing bezique with a somewhat tired but very triumphant P.M. Boarded the *Queen Elizabeth* at 1.00 a.m.

Thursday, July 1st

A milling crowd came on board, Baruch, Giraudier (a Cuban who keeps Winston supplied with cigars and brandy at home) to see the P.M., Roger Makins, etc., to see Eden, Henry and Mimi Hyde to see me. Bags, newspapers, letters succeeded each other at confusing speed and all in a heat and humidity which seemed, if anything, to increase as we sailed away at noon, past Manhattan and down the Hudson River.

Lunched with the P.M. in the Verandah Grill. Oh, the changes that have taken place, in order to please the great dollar-producing clientele, since last we sailed on the *Queen Mary* in January 1953! The Verandah Grill food, which formerly equalled or surpassed many famous French restaurants, has become Americanised and has sunk to a level of ordinariness, if not tastelessness, which bewilders and disappoints. The same applies in lesser degree to the service and the appearance of the ship's company.

We went on the bridge after lunch and then I played bezique with the P.M. till dinner-time. Dined in the Verandah Grill with Lord Moran and Tony Rumbold. Afterwards we saw a series of short films – all American. It is a pity, and rather a humiliating pity, that the Cunard line must go to these lengths to de-Anglicise themselves.

Friday, July 2nd
Still very hot. Indeed today and yesterday are more oppressive than any day in Washington. The broken ice has moved further south than usual this year and we are taking the southern Gulf-Stream route.

The P.M. told me this morning he was decided on an expedition to Russia, where he would ask freedom for Austria as an earnest of better relations. Meanwhile Anthony Eden, who has only come back by sea because he wants to talk over future plans and to get a firm date for Winston to hand over to him, is feeling bashful about choosing the right moment and last night consulted me about this. I thought, and said, how strange it was that two men who knew each other so well should be hampered by shyness on this score. This morning the opportunity came and W. tentatively fixed September 21st for the hand-over and early August for the Moscow visit. Returning to his cabin he then dictated to me a long telegram to Molotov proposing talks with the Soviet leaders in which the U.S. would not, indeed, participate but could, W. thought, be counted on to do their best with their own public opinion.

We all had a gay luncheon in the P.M.'s dining-room, but after luncheon the fun began over the Molotov telegram. Eden went on deck to read; Winston retired to his sitting-room and had the telegram shortened and amended. He asked me to take it to Eden and to say he now intended to despatch it. Eden told me he disliked the whole thing anyway: he had been adding up the pros and cons and was sure the latter (danger of serious Anglo-American rift, effect on Adenauer and Western Europe, damage to the solid and uncompromising front we have built up against Russia, practical certainty that the high hopes of the public would be shattered by nothing coming of the meeting) far outweighed the pros. However, what he really disliked was Winston's intention of despatching the telegram without showing it to the Cabinet. Why couldn't he wait till we were home and let A.E. deliver the message to Molotov when he saw him at Geneva? Would I tell W. that if he insisted, he must do as he wished but that it would be against his, Eden's, strong advice.

I imparted this to W. who said it was all nonsense: this was merely an unofficial enquiry of Molotov. If it were accepted, that was the time to consult the Cabinet, before an official approach was made. I represented, as strongly as I could, that this was putting the Cabinet "on the spot", because if the Russians answered affirmatively, as was probable, it would in practice be too late for the Cabinet to express a contrary opinion. W. said he would make it a matter of confidence with the Cabinet: they would have to choose between him and his intentions. If they opposed the visit, it would give him a good occasion to go. I said this would split the country and the Conservative Party from top to bottom. Moreover if he went on this account, the new administration would start with a strong anti-Russian reputation. After a great deal of talk Eden was sent for and eventually agreed to a compromise which put *him* "on the spot". The P.M. agreed to send the telegram to the Cabinet provided he could say that Eden agreed with it in principle (which of course he does not). Eden weakly gave in. I am afraid the P.M. has been ruthless and unscrupulous in all this, because he must know that at this moment, for both internal and international reasons, Eden cannot resign – though he told me, while all this was going on and I was acting as intermediary, that he had thought of it.

Bezique with W. till dinner, which Charles Moran, Tony Rumbold and I had downstairs. Then a film, followed by drinks with Gavin[1] and Irene Astor who are travelling home on board.

Saturday, July 3rd
Cooler. Atlantic breezes instead of the Gulf Stream. Worked with W. most of the morning and composed telegrams, descriptive of the Washington talks, to Menzies and Holland[2] which the P.M. accepted. Drinks with the Astors before luncheon, which we had in the P.M.'s dining-room with Charles Moran, Christopher and the Prof. The latter was in his best anecdotal form. I liked his apocryphal story of Victor Cazalet and Lady Colefax[3] having a race after an electric lion. Victor won because Lady Colefax would keep on stopping to tell the public she had known the lion as a cub.

After lunch I succeeded in getting away with only one game of bezique and making Christopher take over. Saw Eden this morning. Got the impression that he was aggrieved with W. which I don't find surprising. W., on the other hand, complains to me that he was trapped into sending the telegram to the Cabinet, had forgotten it was the week-end, and now he wouldn't get a reply till Monday. So he telegraphed to Rab saying that he assumed the telegram had already gone on to Moscow.

[1] 2nd Lord Astor of Hever, married to Field Marshal Earl Haig's daughter, Irene (Rene).
[2] Prime Minister of New Zealand.
[3] Well-known London hostess who collected everybody of political and intellectual importance at her dining-room table, fed them well and amused them.

Dined in the Verandah Grill with the Astors and Tony Rumbold. Then joined the P.M. and Eden. The former was now quite reconciled to the Cabinet having been consulted about the Molotov telegram because Rab had telegraphed suggesting only one or two small amendments and had appeared generally satisfied with the main idea. So everybody went to bed happy and W. and I played bezique, to my great financial advantage (six grands coups!) till nearly 2.00 a.m.

Sunday, July 4th
The P.M. deep in Harold Nicolson's *Public Faces* and greatly impressed by the 1932 prophecy of atomic bombs. Went to church, which was packed. Then descended to the profane and played bezique till luncheon. The Astors, Christopher and I lunched with the P.M. who was in splendid form, describing the heart trouble he developed in consequence of dancing a *pas seul* after dinner at Blenheim some fifty years ago, elaborating the desirable results which would come from re-establishing the Heptarchy in England (so as to ease the pressure on Parliament) and teaching Gavin, a non-smoker, to smoke cigars.

A Turkish bath this evening, followed by dinner with the Astors and Adrian Bailey in the Verandah Grill, a cinema and a blood row between Winston and Anthony Eden. This arose in the following way. I went down about 11.30 to see how their dinner party (W.S.C., A.E., the Prof., Moran, Christopher) was getting on. Everybody very jovial when suddenly Miss Gilliatt[1] brought me a telegram from Roger Makins about the effects in America of a speech made by Senator Knowland,[2] who has evidently implied that we have been pressing the Americans to let Red China into U.N.O. and has said that if this happens, the United States will leave the Organisation. Eden read the telegram first and said that he objected to H.M.G. saying anything in reply to Knowland: it looked as if we minded. The P.M. then read it and wanted to issue a statement from this ship to the effect, first, that the matter had not been seriously discussed during the Washington talks and secondly that there was no question of our recognising Red China while she was still in a state of war with the United Nations.

Eden said that if we made any such statement it would destroy all chance of success at Geneva: we ought to keep entry into U.N.O.

---

[1] Elizabeth Gilliat, daughter of the leading gynaecologist Sir William Gilliatt, was one of Churchill's personal secretaries.

[2] Right-wing Republican senator and strong support of Chiang Kai-shek against the Chinese Communists.

as a reward for China if she were good. The P.M. looked grave: he had not realised, he said, that what Knowland said was in fact the truth – Eden *did* contemplate the admission of China into U.N.O. while a state of war still existed. Eden got red in the face with anger and there was a disagreeable scene. They both went to bed in a combination of sorrow and anger, the P.M. saying that Anthony was totally incapable of differentiating great points and small points (a criticism that has an element of truth in it).

Christopher and I then went to the Verandah Grill with Gavin and Rene, Tony Rumbold and two American girls. We danced and drank champagne till nearly 4.00 a.m.

Monday, July 5th
The P.M. looked still grave and depressed this morning and dictated to me a minute about the Knowland question. Anthony Eden did not wake up till 12.00, but he seemed to have recovered his equanimity and was cheerful when I handed the minute to him. We lunched in the P.M.'s dining-room (he staying in bed). In the afternoon I talked to Rene on deck, played bezique and at 6.30 there was a small cocktail party for fellow passengers given by the P.M. and Mr Eden.

We all dined in the P.M.'s dining-room. It was a most amicable occasion, last night's differences resolved and the P.M. saying that provided A.E. always bore in mind the importance of not quarrelling violently with the Americans over Far Eastern questions (which affected them more than us) a way ought certainly to be found of bringing Red China into the United Nations on terms tolerable to the U.S.A. This was followed by much quoting of Pope, Shakespeare and others on the P.M.'s part and a dissertation on Persian and Arabic poets and writing by Eden (who apparently got a First in Oriental Languages at Oxford). To bed at 2.00.

Tuesday, July 6th
Cherbourg at 9.00 a.m. and a swift passage homewards. We docked at Southampton just before 5.00 p.m. after a passage which scarcely a ripple had disturbed – at any rate as far as the sea was concerned. Meg met me and drove me to the Old Rectory at Stratfield Saye with the disconcerting news that the Italian cook whom we have just imported at great expense from Treviso is six months pregnant. Up till the present a series of disasters has accompanied our "moving in".

I told Winston that I believed the cook's downfall to have been brought about by a man in a street in Verona after dark. "Obviously not one of the Two Gentlemen," he commented.

*   *   *

The following day, July 7th, there was a Cabinet in the course of which W.S.C. revealed his intention to meet the Russians and also another even more startling decision recently taken by the Defence Committee and communicated to St Laurent and Howe in Ottawa at dinner last Tuesday. In the evening I heard from Lord Swinton the reactions of the Cabinet, underlined even more forcibly by Harold Macmillan after dinner at No. 10 (an official dinner for Ismay in his capacity as Secretary General of the United Nations, during which I sat next to Sir W. Haley, editor of *The Times*). In consequence of all this Lord Salisbury said he must resign. I became much involved in the subsequent activities, being approached separately by Lord Swinton and the Lord Chancellor and asked by them to explain all the circumstances to Sir M. Adeane for the information and (as the Lord Chancellor thought) possible intervention of the Queen. Salisbury both dislikes the Russian project and objects to the P.M.'s action in approaching Molotov without consulting and obtaining the agreement of the Cabinet. Lord Swinton has represented to him, first that this is the "end of a voyage" with Winston and that a similar case is therefore unlikely to occur; secondly, that his resignation will do great harm to Anglo-American relations because it will be greatly played up by those who, like Senator Knowland, will cry out against the Russian talks and will be represented as a revolt by Lord Salisbury against an anti-American move on the part of Winston and Eden. Also, of course, it will be highly embarrassing to Eden.

*   *   *

Friday, July 16th

Things came to a head today, at any rate within 10 Downing Street. Before luncheon Harold Macmillan came to see Lady Churchill and told her that the Cabinet was in danger of breaking up on this issue. When he had gone she rang me up and asked me to come and see her. I in fact knew more about the situation than she did and since she proposed to "open" the matter to Winston at luncheon, I suggested I should stay too.

She began by putting her foot into it in saying that the Cabinet were angry with W. for mishandling the situation, instead of saying that they were trying to stop Salisbury going. He snapped back at her – which he seldom does – and afterwards complained to me that she always put the worst complexion on everything in so far as it affected him. However, he did begin to see that Salisbury's resignation would be serious on this issue, whereas two days ago when I mentioned the possibility to him he said that he didn't "give a damn". On the other hand it became clear that he had taken the steps he had, without consulting the Cabinet, quite deliberately. He admitted to me that if he had waited to consult the Cabinet after the *Queen Elizabeth* returned, they would almost certainly have raised objections and caused delays. The stakes in this matter were so high and, as he sees it, the possible benefits so crucial to our survival, that he was prepared to adopt any methods to get a meeting with the Russians arranged.

*   *   *

I wrote the following in August:

It ended thus. There was a crucial Cabinet on Friday, July 23rd, at which Lord Salisbury threatened to resign and was supported by Harry Crookshank. W. did not therefore send off the telegram he had drafted to Molotov, more especially as he had received from Eden a cold and almost minatory minute just before the Cabinet began. The matter was adjourned till Monday, with the threat of Lord S.'s resignation hanging over everybody and the still more alarming possibility that Winston, if thwarted, would resign, split the country and the party and produce a situation of real gravity.

We went to Chequers for the week-end. It was a stag-party: Lord Goddard, [Lord Chief Justice] Lord Swinton, Oliver Lyttelton, Walter Monckton, Prof., Brendan Bracken, Desmond Morton and me, with Christopher arriving for dinner on Sunday night. There was much laughter, many anecdotes (at which Lord Goddard excels) and prodigious feats in the repetition of verse. But the air of crisis permeated it all and Oliver Lyttelton, who is in any case resigning the Colonial Office next week to go back to business, was positively alarmist. However, on Sunday a note from the Russians was published, answering one of ours dated May 7th and demanding a meeting of thirty-two powers to discuss the Russian European Security plan. "Foreign Secretaries of the World unite; you have nothing to lose but your jobs," was the P.M.'s first comment on this proposal. It was nevertheless clear that we could hardly go forward with the P.M.'s plan for bilateral talks in the face of this new Russian proposal and so the critical Cabinet on Monday morning passed off without dispute. A new telegram to Molotov was decided upon and the text of it agreed by the P.M. and Eden on Monday afternoon. Unless the Russians react strongly in favour of a meeting, the prospective visit to Russia is likely to be postponed *sine die* and the P.M., feeling that he has at least made the effort and is justified as far as his frequent policy statements over the last two years are concerned, is content – at least on the surface. Lord Salisbury is smiling again.

But the P.M., in spite of his undertaking to Eden on the *Queen Elizabeth* that he will resign about September 20th, is showing new signs of irresolution on that issue. The thought of abandoning office grows more abhorrent as the time comes nearer. I doubt if he realises what trouble is in store for him from his Cabinet colleagues if he stays on. But I think he does realise how difficult it would be for them to *turn* him out without ruining their chances at the next election.

The Cabinet went away for the recess, some of them glum, some of them bewildered. Winston retired to Chartwell where I spent much of August with him. As the days went by he became less reconciled to giving up office and adumbrated all sorts of reasons why he should not. Never had a P.M. been treated like this, that he was to be hounded from his place merely because his second-in-command wanted the job. And what was there in the argument that the new régime needed a year to take over before an election? On the contrary there was little for a new Government to offer and as an election drew near it would be a target for abuse by half the country. Eden had far better start an entirely new deal after a General Election. It looks like a terrible and painful struggle and Anthony, of course, will say: I was promised July, then September 20th; why should I now believe he will even hand over at the next election? Meanwhile the Russian visit, not over-enthusiastically received by Molotov, seems to have sunk into the background.

41

The Prime Minister's Resignation

[Written in two parts: the first six days before
the resignation, the second immediately after it]

March 29th, 1955
When he asked me to rejoin him, in October 1951, Winston said it
would probably be only for a year. He did not intend to remain
long in office but wished to initiate the recovery of the country
under a Conservative Government. However, although many
people, recalling Baldwin's action after the Coronation of King
George VI, predicted that Winston would make way for Anthony
Eden after the Coronation, he never had any intention of so doing.
The Margate speech, in October 1953, satisfied him that he could
still dominate the scene; but, of course, in the winter of 1953–54
Eden's "hungry eyes", as Winston called them, became more
beseeching and more impatient.

During the spring of 1954, when Eden went to Geneva for the
Five-Power Conference, he had extracted what he thought a
promise – and what almost certainly was a half promise – that W.
would go at the end of the session. On a Sunday at Chequers (in
March or April) he had a long talk with W. in the small sitting-
room across the passage from the dining-room and emerged with
sparkling eyes to tell me that he was doubtful whether he ought
to form his Government at the beginning of the summer recess.
Ought he not to meet Parliament with it at once and not wait for
that till October? He asked me to look up the precedents. I did so
and wrote to him in manuscript, when he was at Geneva, to the
effect that there were no clear precedents one way or the other; but
in 1905 Campbell Bannerman had certainly governed quite a time
before presenting himself and his Government to Parliament. In

spite of this he foolishly wrote to Winston saying that he attached importance to this point and hoped W. would go in the middle of July so that A. could form his Government before the House rose. Winston replied that he had given no promise and had in any case now decided not to resign at the end of the session.

Under pressure Winston next said that he would go on September 20th, 1954. The fact that Eden only came back with him on the *Queen Elizabeth* in order to settle the issue, had occurred to W. just before we embarked and almost induced him to fly home instead.

But in August 1954 the Prime Minister again changed his mind. Why should he resign? He wrote to Anthony, who was on holiday in Austria, a masterly letter which went through about six drafts during the week of August 10th–18th. He emphasised the folly of taking over the end of an administration and becoming the target for electoral abuse, and he said that he intended to reconstitute the Government and remain in office. He reminded him of the dismal careers enjoyed at No. 10 by Rosebery after Gladstone and by Balfour after Salisbury. Eden was dejected, but there was in fact nothing he could do about it, and the P.M. had a great personal success at the Conservative Conference in October 1954 at Blackpool.

Even the press now began to be tired of speculating on W.'s resignation, except for the *Daily Mirror* which has a personal vendetta against him. But Winston himself, seeing the hopes of a Top Level meeting deferred owing to Eisenhower's unwillingness to meet the Russians, began to tire of his position. During the winter months, alone with him at the bezique table or in the dining-room, I listened to many disquisitions of which the burden was: "I have lost interest; I am tired of it all." So he finally decided to go at the beginning of the 1955 Easter recess and, after he had ruminated on this for some weeks, he told A.E. and Rab Butler. He also invited the Queen to dine on April 4th, 1955, the eve of his resignation. The secret was closely guarded.

On Friday, March 11th, I set off with Winston for Chequers in a Rolls Royce he contemplated buying. On the way we went to the Zoo to see his lion, Rota, and his leopard, Sheba. Shortly after we had reached Chequers, and had settled down to bezique, there arrived a minute from Anthony Eden covering a telegram from Makins in Washington which described various manoeuvres suggested by the Americans for inducing the French to ratify the London–Paris Agreements which have taken the place of the European Defence Committee as the basis of Western European Defence. These included a suggestion that Eisenhower should go to Paris on May 8th, 1955, the tenth anniversary of V.E. Day, and solemnly ratify the agreements in company with President Coty, Adenauer and Sir Winston Churchill. W. did not take in the implications at once. Lord Beaverbrook came to dinner (the first time for many months) and it was not until he had gone that W. re-read the telegram and the somewhat discouraging and disparaging minute which accompanied it. Of course, he said to me, this meant all bets were off: he would stay and, with Eisenhower, meet the Russians. I pointed out that no suggestion of meeting the Russians was made, but he brushed this aside because he saw a chance of escape from his increasingly unpalatable timetable.

The next morning he had not changed his mind and wrote to A.E., who was at Dorneywood, to tell him. Not surprisingly this produced an infuriated reply and there was every sign of trouble. It happened on Monday in the Cabinet. Anthony had been warned by Norman Brook and by me (I had given the P.M. and Norman dinner at the Turf on Sunday night) to stick entirely to the merits of the American proposal. But at the end of the Cabinet he raised the personal issue, and W., in the face of silent and embarrassed colleagues, said coldly that this was not a matter on which he required guidance or on which Cabinet discussion was usual. Eventually, when it was established that Eisenhower did not contemplate a meeting with the Russians (and to this end there were quiet talks between the American Ambassador, Aldrich, and Sir Ivone Kirkpatrick – of which the P.M. knew nothing and of which I only heard by accident), Winston gave way and announced he would still go as planned.

The ensuing days were painful. W. began to form a cold hatred of Eden who, he repeatedly said, had done more to thwart him and prevent him pursuing the policy he thought right than anybody else. But he also admitted to me on several occasions that the prospect of giving everything up, after nearly sixty years in public life, was a terrible wrench. He saw no reason why he should go: he was only doing it for Anthony. He sought to persuade his intimate friends, and himself, that he was being hounded from office.

The truth was this. He could still make a great speech, as was proved in the defence debate on March 1st. Indeed none could rival his oratory or his ability to inspire. But he was ageing month by month and was reluctant to read any papers except the newspapers or to give his mind to anything that he did not find diverting. More and more time was given to bezique and ever less to public business. The preparation of a Parliamentary Question might consume a whole morning; facts would be demanded from Government departments and not arouse any interest when they arrived (they would be marked "R" and left to moulder in his black box); it was becoming an effort even to sign letters and a positive condescension to read Foreign Office telegrams. And yet on some days the old gleam would be there, wit and good humour would bubble and sparkle, wisdom would roll out in telling sentences and still, occasionally, the sparkle of genius could be seen in a decision, a letter or a phrase. But was he the man to negotiate with the Russians and moderate the Americans? The Foreign Office thought not; the British public would, I am sure, have said yes. And I, who have been as intimate with him as anybody during these last years, simply do not know.

Like the fish which is almost landed, he made the last struggle to escape from the net when the day of his resignation was only a week off. At least I *think* it is the last struggle, because at the time of writing it is not over. On Sunday, March 27th, he learned that Bulganin [Soviet leader] in spite of the fact that the French Senate had ratified the agreements, had spoken favourably of Four-Power talks. On the evening of March 28th, after W. had dined with Rab and discussed the forthcoming Budget, he told me that there was a crisis: two serious strikes (newspapers and docks); an important Budget; the date of the General Election to be decided; the Bulganin offer. He could not possibly go at such a moment just to satisfy Anthony's personal hunger for power. If necessary he would call a party meeting and let the party decide. This latter threat was one he had made during the March 11th–15th crisis and I had said that it would indeed make an unhappy last chapter to his biography if it told how he had destroyed the party of which he was the leader. However, I took all this to be late-night fantasy, a rather pathetic indication of the grief with which he contemplated the approach of his political abdication.

It was not. In the morning he was coldly determined not to go. He sent for Butler and despatched him as an emissary to Eden to say that the proposed timetable must be changed. As for me I preached to Tony Rumbold that for Eden "Amiability must be the watch-word". The Prime Minister thrived on opposition and show-downs; but amiability he could never resist.

Tonight he and Lady C. dine with the Edens who are giving a supposedly farewell dinner in their honour. During the day A.E. has at least had the good sense not to say or write anything.

Written shortly afterwards, but not dated:

On the morning of the 30th W. told me that the dinner-party had been agreeable, but that previously, at his audience, he had told the Queen he thought of putting off his resignation. He had asked her if she minded and she had said no! However he had had a very good night and felt peacefully inclined: he did not really think there was much chance of a top-level conference and that alone would be a valid reason for staying. At 6.30 p.m. he saw A.E. and Rab to tell them his decision. Before the meeting he said to me, "I have been altered and affected by Anthony's amiable manner." This proved to me that the advice I had given was right and I am sure that the result, though pathetic, is in the best interests of all.

When the meeting was over, W. was a sad old man. He asked me to dine with him, but I could not on account of Sheran Cazalet's[1] twenty-first birthday party. All he said was: "What an extraordinary game of bezique we had this afternoon. I got a thousand aces the very first trick and yet in the end you rubied me."

On April 4th the Queen and Prince Philip dined at No. 10. It was a splendid occasion. The party consisted partly of the Senior Cabinet Ministers, partly of Grandees like the Norfolks and partly of officials and family friends – some fifty in all. Lady Churchill took special pains about the food and 10 Downing Street can seldom if ever have looked so gay or its floorboards (soon due to be demolished)[2] have groaned under such a weight of jewels and decorations. There were incidents: the Edens, whose official precedence was low, tried to jump the queue advancing to shake hands with the Queen and the Duchess of Westminster put her foot through Clarissa's train ("That's torn it, in more than one sense," said the Duke of Edinburgh); Randolph got drunk and insisted on pursuing Clarissa with a derogatory article about Anthony Eden he had written for *Punch*; Mrs Herbert Morrison became much elated and could scarcely be made to leave the Queen's side; and I had a blazing row at dinner with Patrick Buchan-Hepburn because I had persuaded Lady Churchill to ask Alec and Elizabeth Home (he being Minister of State for Scotland) while James Stuart, the Secretary of State, had not been invited.

When they had all gone, I went up with Winston to his bedroom. He sat on his bed, still wearing his Garter, Order of Merit and knee-breeches. For several minutes he did not speak and I, imagining that he was sadly contemplating that this was his last night at Downing Street, was silent. Then suddenly he stared at me and said with vehemence: "I don't believe Anthony can do it." His prophecies have often tended to be borne out by events.

---

[1] Daughter of Peter Cazalet by his first wife. Later married Simon Hornby, Chairman of W. H. Smith.

[2] The decision had been taken to pull down Nos. 10, 11 and 12 Downing Street and rebuild them.

The next evening Winston put on his top hat and frock coat, which he always wore for audiences, and went to Buckingham Palace to resign. Having ascertained from him some days before that if he were offered a Dukedom he would refuse, I pressed Michael Adeane to persuade the Queen to make the offer. Michael asked if I was absolutely sure it would be declined and I said that I was. Nevertheless I had qualms while the audience lasted and was relieved when Winston told me, on his return from the Palace, that the Queen had said she would be happy to make him a Duke and that though he had been tempted for a moment, he felt he would prefer to remain in the Commons till he died. Besides, he said, what good would a Dukedom be to Randolph; and it might ruin his and little Winston's political careers.

The following day we left in a special plane for Syracuse: Winston and Lady Churchill, Lord Cherwell and I. Meg was invited but she was soon to have another baby and did not feel up to it. In Syracuse it rained almost solidly for a fortnight. Winston painted one of the caves and we entertained Harry and Clare Luce who descended on us from Rome. The Prof. talked much of the crying need for higher technological education and I volunteered to try to raise the money for a new institute or college, to be inspired and promoted by Winston. [It was thus that Churchill College had its origins.]

Our visit, intended for three weeks, was cut short because of the cold and wet and we came home about April 20th. I had decided to leave the Foreign Service, in spite of flattering offers to be Head of Chancery in Washington, Paris and Bonn from Roger Makins, Gladwyn Jebb and Derick Hoyer Millar, the respective Ambassadors in those posts, and I had done so because I had been so long out of that world. Indeed out of eighteen years in the Diplomatic Service I had only served six directly under the Foreign Office, two abroad and four at home. So I had accepted an invitation to join Philip Hill,[1] instigated by my cousin Bill Cavendish-Bentinck. Accordingly there I went, at the beginning of June 1955, about a fortnight after my elder son, Sandy, was born.

[1] Philip, Hill, Higginson, merchant bankers; subsequently Hill Samuel and Co.

Appendices

Appendix I
The Coronation of Queen Elizabeth II

Sunday, May 31st, 1953
The newspapers are saying that the lavishness, the popularity and the magnificence of the Coronation are due to the inspiration of Sir W. Churchill. Some Labour supporters doubtless think he will have an election on the emotional proceeds. All this is far from the case. Indeed he thinks it is being overdone, particularly by the newspapers, and he has had little or nothing to do with the preparations. But it is certainly a gay time and the country has gone wild with delight, showing its enthusiasm by decorations which are far more elaborate than those of 1937.

Meg and I, living temporarily at Chobham, have neither the energy nor indeed the strength to go to all the parties and the celebrations to which we have been invited. We went to the Coronation Ball at the Albert Hall on Wednesday last, May 27th, after a dinner-party of sixteen at 10 Downing Street (W.S.C. resplendent in his Garter, with the diamond star that belonged to Castlereagh); and on Friday (after I had spent an agreeable but exhausting twenty-four hours alone with W. at Chartwell) we went to the Household Brigade's Ball at Hampton Court. That was a splendid affair. The whole Palace was floodlit and the fountains were surrounded by massed flowers. Every man wore a tailcoat and decorations, the Knights of the Garter in knee-breeches. Almost every woman wore a tiara and a dress worthy of the occasion. We danced in the Great Hall and supped in the orangery. A world that vanished in 1939 lived again for the night, which obliged by being a fine and balmy one. The Queen, dancing with the Duke of Edinburgh and looking as beautiful as the people imagine her to be, stopped to ask us how her god-daughter did and whether she was yet out of control. She must, I thought, have wished she lived at Hampton Court rather than Windsor.

On Saturday and Sunday we recovered, with the help of some strenuous gardening, and eschewed the garden party at Hatfield with the prospect of so much before us in the coming week. Meanwhile in London Coronation fever grew, the crowds milling through the streets to see the banners and the arches, to catch a glimpse of the arriving celebrities among whom the most famous, such as Nehru and General Marshall, pass for nothing among so many. Practically all traffic was stopped and the police were near to being overwhelmed. Never has there been such excitement, never has a Monarch received such adulation, never has so much depended on the weather being kind for the great day.

Thursday, June 4th

But the weather on June 2nd was certainly not kind. Meg and I left at 7.15 a.m. for Westminster Abbey under skies cold, grey and threatening. I wore the full-dress uniform of the Diplomatic Service, with white knee-breeches; Meg her wedding dress with tiara. We sat in the Queen's box, to which she had kindly invited us, immediately above the Queen Mother and the Princesses. We were seated next to the Count and Countess of Barcelona[1] and to Porchy.[2] Though we saw little of the procession entering the Abbey, we saw every movement of the Queen, including the anointing, better than ninety-five per cent of the people in the Abbey, and looked straight at the massed peeresses whose robes and jewels sparkled with unique magnificence and whose movement as, with white gloved hands, they put their coronets on was aptly compared to the corps de ballet in *Lac des Cygnes*. Before the service began I walked out into the road between the Abbey and Westminster Hall and there, with some fifty peers in their crimson robes and others in pre-war full dress uniforms, I watched the Prime Ministers in their clarences and the Queen Mother's procession drive past towards the entrance of the Annexe. The skies were grey but the downpour did not come until well after the Coronation service had begun.

We lunched, rather poorly, in Westminster Hall. My mother, also in the Queen's Box, rushed home, took off her tiara and set off by underground to some evening festivity in Shoreditch. Meg and I, members of a less stalwart generation, went to bed till dinner.

[1] Parents of King Juan Carlos of Spain.
[2] Lord Porchester, son of the Earl of Carnarvon, and a close friend of the Queen, whose racing manager he became.

Then, with Owen[1] and Ruth Gwynedd, we joined the Prime Minister in a room in the Ministry of Materials from which to see the great fireworks display on the Thames. We returned with difficulty through the crowds to No. 10 and thence to the Soames' house in Eaton Place for a delicious midnight feast with them, the Westmorlands, the Rupert Nevills, Sarah Beauchamp and a couple of totally fish-out-of-water American actors.

Written later in June
On Friday, June 5th, we went, again in full dress uniform, to the Foreign Secretary's banquet to the Queen, given by Sir W. Churchill in the absence through illness of Anthony Eden. It was at Lancaster House, just restored to its ancient glories at phenomenal expense, and while the tables were bright with the Duke of Wellington's famous "Ambassador's Service" of gilt plate, the walls and the rooms were decorated by Constance Spry with flowers. Over 150 people sat down to dinner. Meg was between Prince Jean of Luxembourg and the Sheikh of Kuwait (the richest man in the world, but apparently a very grumpy magnate) and I between the representative of San Marino (in a magnificent uniform) and the soberly clad Icelander. W.S.C. was in his full dress of Lord Warden of the Cinque Ports, the Duke of Edinburgh in naval full-dress which had been temporarily revived for the Coronation, and almost everybody resplendent in seldom-seen uniforms and jewels. After it was over we drove down the illuminated Mall – an unforgettable sight – to a reception at Buckingham Palace where again unwonted brilliance reigned.

On June 6th we went to the Derby, driving behind Winston's car at breakneck speed on the wrong side of the Kingston by-pass. We saw Gordon Richards win his first Derby on Pinza, beating the Queen's Aureole, from Sybil Grant's[2] box and afterwards dined at the Durdans.[3]

On Monday, June 8th, we went to Covent Garden to see the gala performance, before the Queen, of Benjamin Britten's opera *Gloriana* written for the occasion. Oliver Messel's decor was superb, and the audience – well dressed at Covent Garden for a change – matched it. But the music was above our heads and the

---

[1] Grandson of Lloyd George, married to Ruth Coit with whose parents we were staying.

[2] Wife of General Sir Charles Grant and sister of Lord Rosebery and Lady Crewe. Extraordinary to behold, but as witty and entertaining a woman as I have ever known.

[3] House at Epsom bought by Lord Rosebery, the Liberal Prime Minister (1892–1895) and bequeathed to his daughter, Lady Sybil Grant.

episode depicted by the opera, Elizabeth's squalid romance with Essex, totally unsuited to the occasion.

On Tuesday, June 9th, there was a vast Commonwealth dinner at No. 10 for the visiting Prime Ministers, followed by a reception which, thanks to lavish supplies of good champagne, was far superior to normal occasions of this kind. The Queen of Tonga stole the show.

On Friday, 12th, I escaped the Banquet to the Queen at the Guildhall and went to Chartwell. On the following day Tommy Lascelles drove down to tell the P.M. and me of Princess Margaret's wish to marry the recently divorced Peter Townsend – a pretty kettle of fish.

The Prime Minister's first reaction after Lascelles had left was to say that the course of true love must always be allowed to run smooth and that nothing must stand in the way of this handsome pair. However, Lady Churchill said that if he followed this line he would be making the same mistake that he made at the abdication.

This gave me an opportunity of asking him what he had really intended at the abdication. Had he contemplated the possibility of Mrs Simpson as Queen of England? He said that he had certainly not. He was, however, loyal to his King whom he wrongly believed to be suffering from a temporary passion. His scheme, and that of Lord Beaverbrook, had been to frighten Mrs Simpson away from England. When she was gone he hoped the King would retire to Windsor and "pull up the drawbridge, post Lord Dawson of Penn[1] at the front gate and Lord Horder at the back gate", and let it be announced that he was too ill to undertake public business.

Winston said that great measures were taken to frighten Mrs Simpson away. Bricks were thrown through her windows and letters written threatening her with vitriol. "Do you mean that you did that," I said, aghast. "No," he replied, "but Max did."

Years afterwards I told this story to Lord Beaverbrook who said that he certainly did not, but it was possible somebody from the Daily Express *might have! He also said that whereas it was probably true that Winston's principal motive had been loyalty to the King, his had been that it was all a lot of fun.*

I omit accounts of the lavish balls and other festivities which followed the Coronation – the Naval Review, magnificent fireworks at a great Windsor Castle ball, visits to Sutton to stay with the Sutherlands and many other purely social activities, all of

[1] Lord Dawson and Lord Horder were the best-known London doctors.

them in sparkling contrast to the constraints of the previous years and seeming to usher in a period of prosperity and relaxation. They may have been, for a privileged few, the bubbles on the surface; but the surface itself was for the next ten years much less troubled than would have seemed credible twelve months previously.

One of the last emblems of austerity to vanish was sugar and sweet rationing. Churchill had, against the advice of the Minister of Food, insisted that this be abolished before the crowds assembled, from home and abroad, for the Coronation. He was warned that such action might lead to a chaotic shortage. In fact, by the autumn of 1953, there was a glut of sugar.

Appendix II
The Suez Crisis
1956–57

On Friday, October 26th, 1956, Meg and I went to a cocktail party given by the Duchess of Kent at Kensington Palace. The Edens came and I had a long talk with Anthony. The Hungarian revolt had just begun and he was elated by the apparent split in the Communist empire. I found him cheerful and apparently exhilarated.

The following week Britain and France intervened against Nasser and landed troops at Suez. Most people were a bit doubtful of the morality, but assumed that at least we were sure of success. What they criticised subsequently (apart from the Labour Party which persisted in mouthing pious but unconvincing platitudes about the United Nations) was our failure to finish the job and the slowness of our military action. The Americans, at the climax of a Presidential Election, took immediate umbrage and voted at U.N.O. with Russia against us. Anglo-American relations sank to a level unknown in recent history.

On Tuesday, November 20th, I dined with Winston and urged that as he was the only Englishman to whom Eisenhower would listen he should write to him and ask him to put events in their proper perspective. He was reluctant, but finally agreed that I should prepare a draft of what I suggested he might say. This I accordingly did and he despatched it, almost unaltered, through the U.S. Embassy, showing it to nobody in H.M.G., but sending a copy to the Queen.

Draft letter for W.S.C.   November 22nd, 1956
to send Eisenhower

There is not much left for me to do in this world and I have neither the wish nor the strength to involve myself in the present political stress and turmoil. But I do believe, with unfaltering conviction, that the theme of the Anglo-American alliance is more important today than at any time since the war. You and I had some part in raising it to the plane on which it has stood. Whatever the arguments adduced here and in the United States for or against Anthony's action in Egypt, it will now be an act of folly, on which our whole civilisation may founder, to let events in the Middle East come between us.

There seems to be growing misunderstanding and frustration on both sides of the Atlantic. If they be allowed to develop, the skies will indeed darken and it is the Soviet Union that will ride the storm. We should leave it to the historians to argue the rights and wrongs of all that has happened during the past years. What we must face is that at present these events have left a situation in the Middle East in which spite, envy and malice prevail on the one hand and our friends are beset by bewilderment and uncertainty for the future. The Soviet Union is attempting to move into this dangerous vacuum, for you must have no doubt that a triumph for Nasser would be an even greater triumph for them.

The very survival of all we believe in may depend on our setting our minds to forestalling them. If we do not take immediate action in harmony, it is no exaggeration to say that we must expect to see the Middle East and the North African coastline under Soviet control and Western Europe placed at the mercy of the Russians. If at this juncture we fail in our responsibility to act positively and fearlessly we shall no longer be worthy of the leadership with which we are entrusted.

I write this letter because I know where your heart lies. You are now the only one who can so influence events both in U.N.O. and the free world as to ensure that the great essentials are not lost in bickerings and pettiness among the nations. Yours is indeed a heavy responsibility and there is no greater believer in your capacity to bear it or well-wisher in your task than your old friend Winston S. Churchill.

Ike's immediate reaction on receiving this letter was to make public a friendly reference to this country and to say that he would see we did not suffer as far as oil supplies were concerned. He sent W. a long answer (obviously written by himself because expressed in so woolly and unscholarly a way). He admitted that Anglo-American solidarity in the face of Soviet Russia was far more important than any of the present issues, but he made it plain that he had been deeply offended by Anthony Eden's failure even to inform him of what we proposed to do. The reply showed at once his sincerity and his smallness of mind. I think it also showed that W.'s letter had taken effect.

In Egypt things went from bad to worse, and together with many others I formed the view that Eden ought to go and that, however, indisputable both his courage and his integrity, one could never again feel confidence in his judgment. The senior members of the Foreign and Civil Services were outspokenly hostile to the whole performance. Conservative Members of Parliament with whom one talked were very lame in the defence of their Chief. Nigel Birch (S. of S. for Air) and Christopher Soames (Under S. of S. for Air) were frankly hostile to Eden in their private comments to me and accused him of having decided insanely on war against Nasser as soon as he heard the news, at the end of July, of the nationalisation of the Suez Canal. They also maintained that we had intervened when we did, rather than let the Israelis themselves carry their attack as far as the Canal, because (albeit indirectly, through the French) we were committed in advance to help Israel by destroying the Egyptian Air Force.

About this time John Junor, Editor of the *Sunday Express*, and I formed a luncheon club. It had nine argumentative members and five rules. The former were:

John Junor and me.
Sir Walter Monckton, Chancellor of the Duchy and Member of the Cabinet.
Lord Hailsham, First Lord, but not in the Cabinet.
Mark Bonham Carter.
Edgar Lustgarten.
Ian Gilmour (Owner of the *Spectator*).
Woodrow Wyatt (former Labour Secretary of State for War)
Roy Jenkins (Labour M.P.).

The latter were:

1. The laws of libel and slander shall not apply.
2. The Official Secrets Act shall be treated with contempt.
3. Physical violence shall as far as possible be avoided.
4. There shall be no sneaking.
5. Mr Randolph Churchill shall not in any circumstances be admitted.

We had our first luncheon on December 11th and it was clear to me that Walter Monckton had been opposed to the whole Suez venture. He ought no doubt to have had the courage to resign, but I suppose he did not want to give the Labour Party an important handle to their propaganda (which seemed, in these weeks, to be directed far more to the interests of the party than the welfare of the nation).

On Thursday, November 29th, Winston had told me in reply to a direct question that he thought the whole operation the most ill-conceived and ill-executed imaginable. It was at luncheon at 28 Hyde Park Gate. I had begun by asking him if he would have acted as Eden had if he had still been Prime Minister. He replied, "I would never have dared; and if I had dared, I would certainly never have dared stop." He also said that if Eden resigned he thought Harold Macmillan would be a better successor than R. A. Butler.

The departure of Eden, taken suddenly ill, to Jamaica seemed to many people a disastrous decision from the point of view of his own political future. It was an island much patronised by tax evaders and affluent idlers, and with petrol and oil rationed again in England, the retreat of the Prime Minister to a parasite's paradise seemed to rank prominently in the annals of ministerial follies.

After Christmas with the children at Ladykirk,[1] Meg and I went to stay at Sandringham for the New Year. We travelled to Wolferton on the afternoon of December 31st with the Salisburys, and in the train we discussed the whole Suez affair in great detail. Lord Salisbury said he was still convinced that some action had been necessary and that to do nothing would have led to still greater disaster. There was a bubble, or a boil, which had to be pricked or else we should have had a far greater explosion in the Middle East at a later stage. It might, however, be that mistakes had been made in the way we carried out our plan. It might indeed have been better not to proclaim that our objective was to divide the two combatants (which meant we had to stop when we did) but to say frankly that we were driven to take action against the Egyptian dictator. I gathered that he himself had been ill when the fateful decision was taken, and it was while in bed at Hatfield, with more time than usual to read Intelligence Reports, that the magnitude of the Soviet aid to Egypt and Syria had become clear to him. Immediately he recovered he made a speech in the House of Lords on this subject (and I must say it was the first statement on the Government side, albeit made several days after our ultimatum, which made me feel there might be some real justification for what they had done). In reply to a question he said he had no idea why this aspect of the affair had been allowed to go by default in the initial stages. He did *not* contradict me when I said I suspected Eden's personal pique against Nasser had had a lot to do with our precipitate action. The reason for this pique is not hard to find if one remembers Eden's passionate defence, against Winston's obstinate distaste, of the 1954 treaty with Egypt – to which I have referred earlier in this diary [page 679].

[1] Home of Major John and Lady Susan Askew, my wife's sister.

I told Lord S. frankly that like many others I could never again have confidence in Eden's judgment or handling of affairs, however much I might admire his courage and integrity. He seemed a little ill at ease when he said that he could see nobody to take his place. Why not Macmillan, I asked? His reply was, both Meg and I thought, evasive: he said something about Macmillan being a very tired man.

Incidentally, on the way up to Ladykirk on December 20th, I had put the same point to Alec Home (S. of S. for Commonwealth Relations). He, too, had not demurred at my suggestion that Eden must go, and had rather grudgingly agreed that Harold Macmillan would be the preferable successor. He also said he had never been through such a period: Munich had been nothing to it.

On January 9th the news broke that the Queen was returning to London and Eden was going to resign. The world seemed to think that Rab Butler would succeed. Personally I felt sure Macmillan was the man and I was confident that both Winston and Bobbety Salisbury would be asked and would recommend Harold M.

Randolph "scooped" the situation by an article in the *Evening Standard* on the night Eden resigned. He was guilty of a "chronological inexactitude" in saying that Lord Salisbury had been with the Queen at Sandringham on the night of Monday, January 7th. From this inaccurate statement a lot of rumour grew about Lord S. paving the way with the Queen, etc.; and the Labour Party impudently questioned the accepted constitutional convention that the sovereign chooses the Prime Minister. They overlooked similar occasions in 1931 and 1940.

Appendix III
Postscript to Suez

On April 7th, 1957, I flew home from New York after a week in America in connection with Winston's and my technological scheme, which was the basis for the establishment of Churchill College, Cambridge.

Air Chief Marshal Sir William Dickson,[1] formerly C.A.S. and now Chairman of the C.O.S. Committee, was on board. We talked for hours, and after he had told me how much he and his military colleagues disapproved of Alanbrooke's diaries, recently published, and after we had both consumed several whiskies and sodas, he dilated with considerable frankness on Suez. The following points emerged:

1. Anthony Eden's personal rage and animosity against Nasser. This made him beside himself on many occasions, and Dickson had never been spoken to in his life in the way the P.M. several times spoke to him during those tempestuous days. (Freddy Bishop, Eden's Principal Private Secretary, had previously told me the same, adding that he had finally given up making allowances for A.E. or feeling sorry for him.)

2. The French were convinced that nothing but Nasser's fall could save Algiers for them. Eden thought highly of Mollet and Pineau[2] and considered that no other French Government could be as good. When they came to London they made an impassioned plea for common action and said that otherwise they must resign. They said that in 1940 W.S.C. had offered France union with England. Now, on behalf of France, they would like to repeat the offer. Eden and Selwyn Lloyd said this

---

[1] Later Marshal of the Royal Air Force.
[2] French Prime Minister and Foreign Minister.

was impossible at present, but they evidently felt still more beholden to the French on account of this offer.

3. The French had definitely "colluded" with Israel, and all parties to the attack were agreed that it had to be before the U.S. Presidential Election. If it were left till afterwards, Eisenhower would checkmate it. The U.S. were not told of our intentions because Eden and Eisenhower had had a long exchange of letters on the subject and the latter had refused to be moved by any of Eden's arguments, some of which (e.g. the reactions of the Arab world) were shown by subsequent events to be fallacious. Eden was convinced, by much past experience, that American thought and policy over the Middle East was both ill-informed and impractical.

4. Eden during the final days was like a prophet inspired, and he swept the Cabinet and Chiefs of Staff along with him, brushing aside any counter-arguments and carrying all by his exaltation.

5. Monty and Winston (influenced, I think, by Monty) had thrown spanners into the military wheel by pressing for a landing at Mersa Matruh and an armoured sweep on Cairo. This, in Dickson's view, was absurd. Monty himself had told me this would have been the right course when he lunched with us at Stratfield Saye in December. The Chiefs of Staff, however, intended to hold the Canal with three divisions, plus some troops along the Mediterranean coast as far as Tel el Kebir. Apparently they and the Cabinet thought they would not have to stay there long before Nasser fell from loss of face. In my opinion this showed a most improvident assessment of Egyptian and Arab nationalist feeling.

6. We gave way on economic grounds alone. At a 10 p.m. Cabinet in the P.M.'s room at the House, it being clear that the U.N. Assembly was going to vote for sanctions against us and probable that the U.S. would vote with the majority, the Chancellor of the Exchequer (H. Macmillan) said that although he had been greatly in favour of the action we took, he must tell the Cabinet that if sanctions were imposed on us, the country was finished. There was therefore nothing for it but to climb down. The Russian threats had not been taken into serious consideration.

And in New York, Wall Street financiers and taxi-drivers alike had said to me: you were right to go in, but why on earth didn't you finish the job? They did seem to admit a certain U.S. responsibility and it was evident that in the space of a few months Eisenhower's vast domestic prestige had sunk far. Of Dulles I did not hear one good word.

Postscript: April 6th, 1966
At lunch today at Windsor Lord Caccia[1] told me he had been present in Washington shortly after Suez when Dulles asked Selwyn Lloyd why on earth we did not go through with the operation!

---

[1] Harold Caccia, British Ambassador in Washington, 1956–61, and Permanent Under Secretary of State at the Foreign Office, 1962–65.

Biographical Notes

Biographical Notes
(Indicated by * in the text)

Alanbrooke, Field Marshal, 1st Viscount, K.G., G.C.B., O.M., G.C.V.O., D.S.O. (1883–1963)
Uncle of Sir Basil Brooke, Prime Minister of Northern Ireland, he was educated mainly in France and distinguished himself as a gunner in World War I. He went from being G.O.C., Southern Command, in 1939 to lead the 2nd Corps in Lord Gort's British Expeditionary Force, and he fought a successful holding action against the advancing Germans on the eastern flank in May 1940. He was briefly in command of the troops sent to northern France after Dunkirk, but returned home to be once again in charge of Southern Command and, thereafter, of Home Forces. From the end of 1941 he was C.I.G.S. for five years, at once spellbound and exasperated by Churchill and gravely disappointed not to be given command of Operation OVERLORD. He was an admirer and faithful supporter of Montgomery. After the war he was appointed Lord Lieutenant of London, the Master Gunner of St James's Park, Chancellor of Queen's University, Belfast and Constable of the Tower. He was a keen naturalist with a passion for bird-watching.

Alexander of Hillsborough, Albert Victor Alexander, 1st Earl, K.G., C.H. (1885–1965)
Fought in World War I, first in the ranks and then as an officer, and was elected Labour M.P. for Sheffield (Hillsborough division) in 1922. In Ramsay MacDonald's 1929 Government he was First Lord of the Admiralty, the office to which he returned in May 1940. Good-natured, friendly but distastefully egotistic, he was regarded with affection rather than admiration by the Admirals and also by Churchill who always referred to him as Albert Victor. He was a Baptist lay preacher and a dedicated Non-Conformist. From 1946 to 1950 he was Minister of Defence and after 1955 Leader of the Opposition in the House of Lords. A Viscount in 1950, an Earl (on Conservative recommendation) in 1963, he was made a Knight of the Garter just before his death.

*Alexander of Tunis, Field
Marshal, 1st Earl, K.G., G.C.B.,
G.C.M.G., C.S.I., D.S.O., M.C.
(1891–1969)*
Harrovian cricket hero, wounded
three times in World War I and
noted for his courage under fire,
he was engaged in operations in
Russia (1919) and on the Indian
North-West Frontier. By 1930 he
had already been mentioned in
despatches for gallantry seven
times and had commanded his regiment, the Irish Guards. He was
given the 1st Division in the British
Expeditionary Force, 1939–40,
and Lord Gort having been
ordered to hand over command to
him to avoid capture, he was put in
charge at the end of the evacuation
and was among the last to leave the
Dunkirk beaches. After holding
Southern Command in the inva-
sion-threatened summer of 1940,
he commanded the British forces in
Burma in 1942 and presided coolly
and competently over the retreat
before the numerically superior
Japanese. At the end of 1942 he
was made Commander in Chief in
North Africa, with Montgomery
commanding the 8th Army, and
thence he went to Sicily and Italy
as Supreme Allied Commander.
After the war he was Governor
General of Canada, 1946–52, to
the entire satisfaction of both the
Canadians and himself, until Churchill hauled him back to Britain in
1952 to be an inadequate and far
from happy Minister of Defence.
He was Churchill's *beau idéal* of a
soldier and the admiration was
mutual.

*Amery, the Right Hon. Leopold
C.H. (1873–1955)*
Harrow, Balliol and All Souls between them produced this prodigy
of energy, mental and physical,
minute in height but vast in intellect. He professed to speak seventeen languages, but was never put
to the test. He worked for ten years
at *The Times*, and became a Birmingham M.P. in 1911. For part
of World War I he was assistant
secretary to the War Cabinet and
made such an impression on the
leading politicians that he was
soon, in succession, First Lord of
the Admiralty, Secretary of State
for the Colonies, for the Dominions and finally, from 1940 to 1945,
for India. There were those who
thought he was *too* clever and there
were others who objected to his
casting his net a little far outside his
own waters. He was, however, certainly one of the best-known political figures in the first half of the
twentieth century.

His elder son Jack, who was at
school with me and had considerable charm, unfortunately became
a fascist, broadcast enemy propaganda from Italy during the war
and was hanged for treason after it.
So excessive a retribution would
surely not have been his fate had
his father not been eminent. His
other son, Julian, who strove valiantly to save his brother, went into
politics early, married Harold
Macmillan's daughter and held
several ministerial offices.

*Auchinleck, Field Marshal Sir
Claude, G.C.B., G.C.I.E., C.S.I.,
D.S.O. (1884–1981)*
A man who gave immediate con-
fidence. From Wellington and
Sandhurst he went into the
Indian Army and fought in Egypt
and Mesopotamia in World War I.
After a spell in England in 1940

as G.O.C., Southern Command (when he greatly impressed Churchill), he was appointed C. in C. in India. Then for two depressing years he commanded in North Africa, while Rommel swept all before him and Auchinleck, excellent soldier though he was, was let down by his army commanders. An unsuccessful general has to be replaced whether or not personally at fault, and "the Auk", as he was called, took his failure with dignity and without reproach. He returned to India as C. in C. for four years and was appointed, in 1947, Supreme Commander in India and Pakistan. The Indians loved him as did all who served under him, and though he retired to live in Marrakech he came back to England in 1974 when the Army Council gave a huge luncheon party in the Royal Hospital at Chelsea, to celebrate his ninetieth birthday. He outlived all his contemporary Generals.

Avon, Anthony Eden, 1st Earl of, K.G., M.C. (1897–1977)
From Eton and Christ Church, Oxford (where he won a First in Oriental Languages), and after three years' active service with the King's Royal Rifle Corps, he went into Parliament at the age of twenty-six as Conservative Member for Warwick and Leamington. He became Parliamentary Private Secretary to Sir Austen Chamberlain at the Foreign Office and then, cherished by Stanley Baldwin, he rose quickly in the ministerial hierarchy. He was Lord Privy Seal with responsibility for League of Nations affairs and, in 1935, Foreign Secretary. Objecting to Neville Chamberlain's interference, and to the general belief that

Sir Robert Vansittart was *de facto* Foreign Secretary, he shunted the latter sideways and resigned from the former's administration in January 1938. When war broke out he returned to office as Secretary of State for the Dominions, was given the War Office by Churchill in May 1940, and was back at the Foreign Office the following December. Despite frequent efforts to provide him with experience in home departments, he remained firmly attached to the Foreign Office until he became Prime Minister in 1955. He and Winston Churchill sometimes squabbled, but until Churchill's last year in office they were good friends and faithful colleagues. Indeed Eden, who was a man of the highest integrity, was never anything but faithful. By his first wife, Beatrice Beckett, he had two sons, one of whom was killed in Burma, flying in the R.A.F. His second wife was Clarissa Churchill.

Baruch, Bernard (1870–1965)
This veteran Jewish financier rose from humble origins by his financial acumen, persistence and capacity for impressing prominent American politicians. Churchill first met him in 1919 at the Paris Peace Conference where he had acquired from President Wilson a post in the American delegation. On Churchill's visits to America he gave him useful financial advice and after the Wall Street Crash of 1929, when Churchill, who loved a gamble, was most ill-advisedly playing the market, Baruch saved him from disaster by quietly selling every time Churchill bought and vice versa. He was adviser to numerous American Presidents

and wrote frequently to Churchill on political matters for which he had no flair at all. His financial flair occasionally deserted him too, as when in 1955 he advised me to put all I had into South America, the El Dorado of the future. Luckily I had nothing to put there. Churchill, though grateful to him and often his guest in New York, found endless letters containing his views on political and strategic matters a burden. He usually answered five or six together.

Beaverbrook, Maxwell Aitken, 1st Lord (1879–1964)
Many people thought he was evil. He was, in fact, impish and he was capable of great kindness. Born a son of the Manse (all influential Canadians seem to have been sons of the Manse), he made a fortune at an early age by deals which, whether or not actually dishonest, were certainly "borderline". He came to England in 1910, basking in the friendship of the Conservative leader Bonar Law, himself a Canadian, and within six months was Conservative M.P. for Ashton-under-Lyne of which he had never heard a few months before. He bought the derelict *Daily Express* in order to provide an organ for the Conservative Party and he bought and sold, at a profit, the Rolls Royce Company. Between the wars he became a highly successful press lord, circulation being his prime objective. He had a genuine enthusiasm for the British Empire, but he was an arch-appeaser of the dictators. Yet when he was made Minister of Aircraft Production in May 1940, he performed miracles of production and made a major contribution to

winning the Battle of Britain. Later in the war he was markedly unhelpful, upsetting any apple-cart in sight, becoming infatuated by Stalin and urging a Second Front in totally unsuitable conditions. He opposed the planning of a Welfare State, and as the end of the war drew near he was more excited by the prospect of a return to party strife than by possible methods of winning the peace. After 1945 his influence on politics was muted, and his relationship with Churchill became distant though always amiable. In 1953, when Churchill had his stroke, nobody rallied more whole-heartedly to his help.

Bevin, Rt. Hon. Ernest (1881–1951)
This unwieldy, unlettered Trade Unionist, formerly General Secretary of the Transport and General Workers' Union, Chairman of the General Council of the Trade Union Congress and a leader of the 1926 General Strike, was a splendid Minister of Labour during the war, an undaunted tower of strength both to Churchill and to Attlee. In 1945 he became Foreign Secretary, in preference to Hugh Dalton whom Attlee had originally intended for the post, and it fell to him to confront Molotov and the intransigent Soviet delegations, when they threw heavy spanners into the works at every conference assembled to negotiate peace treaties. The Foreign Service, whose members all came from backgrounds totally different from his, were devoted to him. Indeed, it may be doubted if there was ever a more loved and respected Foreign Secretary.

Bevir, Sir Anthony, K.C.V.O.,
C.B.E. (1895–1977)
Scholar of Eton and Hertford College, Oxford, he was badly gassed
when serving with the King's Liverpool Regiment in World War I. He
worked in the Colonial Office between the wars, was transferred to
the War Cabinet Office in 1939 and
thence, in 1940, to succeed Cecil
Syers (q.v.) at No. 10. He was
not ideally suited to cope with
Churchill's unusual régime, and so
all patronage matters, apart from
the Honours' List and the appointment of Lord Lieutenants, were
placed in his hands. He worked in a
room of his own (previously Sir
Horace Wilson's) and there was
not a bishop or dean in England
whom he did not know. He held
this post for twenty-five years, took
large quantities of snuff, occasionally lost the office keys and was
always at hand to give wise and
practical advice to anybody who
applied to him. He was among the
kindest of men.

Boothby, Lord, K.B.E. (b. 1900)
In his early parliamentary days
many people thought him a future
Prime Minister. Elected for Aber-
deenshire as a Conservative in
1924, he started well as Parliamentary Private Secretary to Winston
Churchill when Chancellor of the
Exchequer. He was much influenced by Lloyd George,
but not by that elder statesman's
strange addiction to Hitler and
Mussolini, and he became an energetic member of the pre-war anti-
appeasement group in the Commons. His appointment by Churchill in 1940 as Parliamentary
Secretary to the Minister of Food
was brought to a dramatic end in
1942 when he was accused, doubtless falsely, of improper dealings
over some Czechoslovak gold.
After the war he was one of the
leading exponents of a united
Europe and became a well-known
figure on television.

Bracken, Brendan, 1st and last
Viscount (1901–1958)
His rise in the world was astonishing. An unruly, truant boy-
hood in Ireland, adolescent years
spent with an uncle in Australia,
education sought and obtained
from an imaginative headmaster of
Sedbergh when he pretended to be
three years younger than he was:
all this was the prelude to being
Member of Parliament for Paddington at the age of twenty-nine,
having in the meantime forced
himself on Winston Churchill as a
disciple, founded The Banker,
bought The Economist and become
Chairman of The Financial News.
Underneath a mop of wiry, uncon-
trolled red hair, behind thick
glasses and a pretended ruthlessness, lay a heart of gold; and he had
a memory so remarkable, for people, events and the architecture of
houses, that when Brendan was
available no books of reference
were required. In the years immediately before the war, and during the war itself, he was a bright
comet sweeping across the skies,
afraid of nobody, jolting Churchill
out of melancholy or intemperate
moods, and proving a strikingly
successful Minister of Information,
in contrast to his three predecessors in the post. Yet he was a lonely
man, disguising the fact with incessant and, latterly, repetitive
conversation, but genuinely loved

by all who dug beneath the physically unattractive façade.

Bridges, Edward, 1st Lord, G.C.B., G.C.V.O., M.C., F.R.S., (1892–1969)
Son of the Poet Laureate, Robert Bridges, he was educated at Eton and Magdalen College, Oxford. He won the M.C. in World War I and then served in the Treasury until in 1938 he was appointed Secretary to the Cabinet in succession to Sir Maurice Hankey, the first holder of the office. Throughout the war he and General Ismay, on the military side, were the twin pillars on which the Prime Minister rested for they were first rate administrators. From 1945 till his retirement in 1956 he was Permanent Secretary of the Treasury and a great power in the land. Friendly, apt to give one a playful punch in the tummy on meeting, he was a forceful and outspoken man with a high sense of public service and propriety.

Butler of Saffron Walden, Lord, K.G., C.H. (1902–1982)
Son of a distinguished Indian civil servant who became Master of Pembroke College, Cambridge, R. A. Butler, always known as "Rab", was President of the Cambridge Union in 1924 and went on to be one of the most eminent British statesmen of the mid-twentieth century. A staunch supporter of Munich, appeasement and Neville Chamberlain, he became in due course a loyal colleague and admirer of Churchill, though to some extent a rival of both Anthony Eden and Harold Macmillan, with neither of whom he was on anything more than polite terms. He was the leading influence in reviving the fortunes of the Conservative Party after its defeat in 1945 and the policies he advocated, not far different from those of the Labour leader Hugh Gaitskell, were known as "Butskellism". He held every senior ministerial post, including the Home Office, Foreign Office and Exchequer, and as Minister of Education in 1944 he gave his name to an Education Act of lasting importance; but twice, in 1957 and 1963, he failed to be chosen Prime Minister. He ended his career, happily, as Master of Trinity College, Cambridge.

Cadogan, Right Hon. Sir Alexander, O.M., G.C.M.G., K.C.B. (1884–1968)
A younger son of the 5th Earl Cadogan, he was at Eton and Balliol and passed top into the Diplomatic Service in 1908. He was Ambassador to China, 1933–36, and when Anthony Eden managed to dispose of Sir Robert Vansittart in 1936, he was appointed Permanent Under Secretary. Calm, sage in counsel and the very reverse of "flashy", his diaries, published after his death, caused astonishment by their outspoken and sometimes vituperative comments. From 1946 to 1950 he represented Britain at the Security Council of the United Nations and in 1952 Churchill appointed him Chairman of the B.B.C., an office he fulfilled admirably in spite of knowing nothing about radio or television. His wife, Lady Theodosia, daughter of the 4th Earl of Gosford, had rather too forceful a character and an idiosyncratic personality.

Camrose, William Berry, 1st Viscount (1879–1954)

The prime builder, with his brother Lord Kemsley and Lord Iliffe, of a great newspaper empire, of which the brightest stars in the constellation were the *Daily Telegraph* and the *Sunday Times*. Good-tempered, wise and strictly honourable in all his dealings, he was much liked by Churchill to whom he gave great financial assistance by combining with others to buy Chartwell and present it to the National Trust (on condition that Churchill should have it for his life-time), and still more by buying the Churchill papers, with which the *History of the Second World War* was composed and, after publication, giving them back to Churchill. He felt that Parliament should have shown the nation's gratitude by a substantial grant, such as was made to Lloyd George after 1918, and he did his generous best to remedy its failure to offer one.

Chandos, Oliver Lyttelton, 1st Viscount, D.S.O., M.C. (1893–1972)

An engaging buccaneer, son of a Cabinet Minister and educated at Eton and Trinity, Cambridge, he had an excellent record as a Grenadier in World War I and then made large profits in tin. Brought into the Government in 1940 as President of the Board of Trade, partly by the influence of Brendan Bracken, he was prominent in governmental deliberations but a surprisingly poor performer in the House of Commons. He was Minister of State in Cairo in 1941, with a seat in the War Cabinet, and dealt patiently with the explosive tantrums of General de Gaulle. Minister of Production, 1942–45, he was Secretary of State for the Colonies in the 1951 Government, but retired in 1954 to be Chairman of Associated Electrical Industries. Married to Lady Moyra Osborne, a daughter of the Duke of Leeds, he had two sons and a daughter. He was a rumbustiously agreeable companion, primed with entertaining political and commercial gossip, and he wrote two books in faultless English prose.

Channon, Sir Henry (1897–1958)

An American who went to Christ Church, Oxford, married Lord Iveagh's daughter, Honor, and became Conservative M.P. for Southend in 1935. He was Parliamentary Private Secretary to R. A. Butler when Under Secretary at the Foreign Office (1938–41) and he entertained splendidly and amusingly at his house in Belgrave Square, where both R. A. Butler and, later, Lord Wavell used to stay. He was a leading light in London café society, a great friend of Lady Cunard, of Prince Paul of Yugoslavia and of his neighbours, the Duke and Duchess of Kent; but his main claim to fame is that he wrote with great elegance. *The Ludwigs of Bavaria* is an entertaining book of quality and his diaries are an enthralling peepshow of certain elements of London society between the wars. His only child, Paul, became a Minister in Mrs Thatcher's Government of the 1980s.

Charteris of Amisfield, Lord, G.C.B., G.C.V.O., Q.S.O. (New Zealand) (b. 1913)

The younger son of Lord Elcho

(killed in 1916) and Lady Violet Benson, daughter of the 8th Duke of Rutland, he went to Eton and Sandhurst and fought in the war with the 60th Rifles. Attractive, energetic and the best of good company, he married in 1944 Gay, younger daughter of David, Viscount Margesson. In 1949 he became Private Secretary to Princess Elizabeth, in succession to the author of these diaries, and in due course (1972–77) was a much liked Private Secretary to the Queen. On retirement he was chosen as Provost of Eton, the statutes having to be amended by the Privy Council since, having been to Sandhurst, he had no university degree. He was also appointed Chairman of the National Heritage Memorial Fund, an assignment he performed with diligence and good taste. Under the tuition of Mr Oscar Nemon he developed great aptitude as a sculptor.

Cherwell, Frederick Lindemann, 1st and last Viscount, C.H. (1886–1957)
To those he liked the Prof., as he was called, was generous, helpful and entertaining. Against those who had displeased him he waged a vendetta. He inherited a fortune arising from waterworks in Germany, studied physics in Berlin under the great Professor Nernst and became a friend of Einstein. He was a keen tennis-player (tennis champion of Sweden), he was always immaculately dressed and had a liking for high society. Two of his claims to enduring fame are that he revived the moribund Clarendon Laboratory at Oxford, which under his direction became the foremost centre of low-temperature research in physics; and that throughout the war he was Churchill's interpreter in all technical matters, whether scientific or economic. He had the capacity to explain the most difficult problems in clear, simple, well-expressed English. He detested Germans (despite his successful years of study in Berlin) and ruthlessly, though unavailingly, plotted the destruction of their trade and industry. He looked with contempt on Jews and coloured people: he was arrogant and impervious to argument when his mind was made up. Yet he was good company when in the mood, never boastful of his achievements, and a loyal friend to Churchill and to many others. He was an acquired taste, but a pleasing one, despite his obvious faults, to those whom he found acceptable.

Churchill, Hon. Randolph (1911–1968)
Born with numerous golden spoons in his mouth: outstandingly handsome in his youth, a natural orator, an original wit, showing a mastery of language and the son of an already famous father. Most of these gifts he dissipated, disappointed in his political ambitions, making friends easily but losing them more easily still. His father, determined that his only son should be more cherished than he had been, eagerly introduced him, when he was still a boy, to the stimulating company of such men as Lloyd George and Lord Birkenhead. As a result he was unnaturally precocious and found most of his contemporaries dull. He was imaginative and original in his ideas, but he became self-

indulgent, excessively addicted to drink and, when he felt like it, inexcusably abusive. Yet when he exerted his charm, those who had vowed never to let him over their threshold again almost invariably relented. He was a talented journalist, and some of the books he wrote won acclaim; but his early promise came to little, both his wives were tried too hard, and the efforts of his mother to counteract her husband's excessive indulgence of their son won Randolph's seldom relenting hostility. Latterly, too, he squabbled with his father, devoted though he was to him. He grew up in the shade of a giant of the forest, and that may have inhibited his own development. Perhaps Winston Churchill himself would have been a less bright meteor in the sky if his own father, Lord Randolph Churchill, had not died young.

Colville, Lady Cynthia,
D.C.V.O., D.B.E., F.R.C.M.
(1884–1968)
Twin daughter, with Lady Celia Coates, of the Marquess of Crewe, by his first marriage to Sibyl Graham of Netherby, and granddaughter of Richard Monckton-Milnes. Married in January 1908, the Hon. George Colville. From her early married days she became deeply involved in the affairs of the desperately poor borough of Shoreditch, where she started a school for mothers, a home for babies and other welfare schemes. She was a staunch Liberal, with a large number of socialist friends, Chairman of a Juvenile Court and President or Chairman of numerous charitable organisations. She was a dedicated Anglo-Catholic, a long-serving member of the Church Assembly, an outstandingly good public speaker and a woman who took endless pains for others without ever thinking of herself. From 1923 till 1953 she was a lady-in-waiting to Queen Mary on whom she had great influence. Despite her sometimes radical views George V was fond of her and used to ask her to race on his famous cutter *Britannia*.

Colville, David (b. 1909)
Eldest son of the Hon. George and Lady Cynthia Colville. Educated at Harrow and Trinity College, Cambridge; joined Lloyds Bank in 1931 and was Treasurer of the Bank when war was declared. Married, 1933, Lady Joan Child-Villiers, daughter of the 8th Earl of Jersey, with magnificent Titian-red hair. After five years' service in the R.N.V.R. he was invited by Mr Anthony de Rothschild to join the Rothschild bank, of which he became the first non-member of the family, and the first Christian, to be a partner. He had a high reputation in the City.

Colville, Hon. George
(1867–1943)
Youngest son of the 1st Viscount, 11th baron, Colville of Culross K.T. (who was Chief Whip in the House of Lords in the Derby and Disraeli administrations, Chairman of the Great Northern Railway and Lord Chamberlain to Queen Alexandra) by the Hon. Cecile Carington. A mathematician of some ability, his Wykehamist education convinced him that ambition was, if not a sin, at least an error. So he was content to be, after a few years at the Bar, Secre-

tary of the Institute of Chartered Accountants, a post he held till his retirement. He was a carpenter of exceptional ability making, amongst much else, a fine copy of a Jacobean chair from an oak tree he had himself planted at the age of three. He was a skilful helmsman in small boat racing, a pillar of the Royal Yacht Squadron and Commodore of the Island Sailing Club, Treasurer of King's College Hospital and Chairman of the Professional Classes Aid Council. He had an attractive simplicity of character and a total integrity which made him many friends.

Colville, Philip (b. 1910)
Second son of the Hon. George and Lady Cynthia Colville. Educated at Harrow and Trinity College, Cambridge. Joined Cazenove and Ackroyd, stockbrokers, but accepted a partnership in R. Nivison and Co. shortly before the war. He enlisted in the Grenadiers, fought in France in May/June 1940, became adjutant of the 4th battalion and served with the 6th Guards' Tank Brigade from the summer of 1944 to the final defeat of Germany. A keen yachtsman, owning a *Dragon* class boat for over thirty years, he was at one time rear-Commodore of the Royal Yacht Squadron. Also a first-class bridge player and an unconscionably lucky card-holder. He is Treasurer and financial adviser to King's College Hospital and a member of the Council of the Royal National Lifeboat Institution.

Crathorne, Thomas Dugdale, 1st Lord (1897–1977)
A wise and much loved habitué of No. 10, who had formerly been Parliamentary Private Secretary to Lord Swinton and to Stanley Baldwin. Conservative M.P. for Richmond (Yorks.), he was an almost daily caller when I first went to Downing Street. He went with the Yorkshire Hussars to fight in the Middle East, and came back in 1942 to be Chairman of the Conservative Party. In 1951 he was Minister of Agriculture, but in 1954 he felt obliged to resign because of the mishandling by his department of the Crichel Down affair. Ennobled in 1959.

Crewe, Robert Crewe-Milnes, 1st and last Marquess of Crewe, K.G. (1858–1945)
Son of the celebrated man of letters, Richard Monckton-Milnes, Lord Houghton, and Annabel, sister and heiress of the last Lord Crewe, whose great estates in Cheshire and Staffordshire he inherited as well as his father's house and land at Fryston, near Ferrybridge, with a famous library.

After Harrow, while still at Trinity College, Cambridge, he became engaged to Sibyl Graham, daughter of Sir Frederick and Lady Hermione Graham of Netherby. She died suddenly after seven years of marriage, a sorrow he described poignantly in verse (for he wrote good poetry), leaving him disconsolate with four children under six. A Liberal follower of Mr Gladstone, in 1892 he was appointed Viceroy of Ireland at the early age of thirty-four. In 1895 he inherited the Crewe estates, was created Earl of Crewe and three years later married Lady Margaret Primrose, aged eighteen, younger daughter of the former Prime Minister, Lord

Rosebery. He was tall, handsome and a well-informed, attractive talker: she fell in love with him across the dining-room table at Mentmore.

When the Liberal Government of 1905 was formed, he was given high Cabinet office, being Secretary of State for the Colonies, and later for India, Lord President, and Leader of the House of Lords, with the unenviable task of taking the Parliament Bill, limiting the Lords' powers, to the Upper Chamber. Mr Asquith is on record as saying that there was no member of his Cabinet on whom he relied so much. His speeches read well, but were poorly and hesitantly delivered, reflecting the caution with which he chose his words. In 1911 he was given the Garter and created a Marquess.

He was briefly President of the Board of Education and, surprisingly enough, Chairman of the L.C.C.; but although he was for six years Ambassador in Paris (1922–28), Lord Lieutenant of London, leader of the Liberals in the Lords and Secretary of State for War in the 1931 National Government, his political career effectively ended when Lloyd George succeeded Asquith as Prime Minister in 1916.

His tastes were catholic, though his religion was Anglican. Of scholarly inclination, well-read in all branches of literature, a good historian and a competent classicist, he was at the same time devoted to the Turf, a breeder of racehorses, and a lavish host, perhaps the last of the Whig grandees. There was no better company when he was in expansive mood, but he nevertheless seemed detached from human beings, except for his wife, and was dutiful rather than affectionate to his daughters. He lost both his sons, one by each marriage, when they were still young and this heart-breaking experience probably accounted for his apparent lack of interest in other people, masked though it was by unwavering courtesy.

Cripps, Hon. Sir Stafford, C.H., F.R.S., K.C. (1889–1952)
Product of Winchester College and University College, London, he was a son of the 1st Lord Parmoor. His wife, Dame Isabel, was an intelligent Eno's Fruitsalts heiress. He did well at the Bar, became steadily more radical in politics and was elected Labour M.P. for Bristol East in 1931, standing on the far left of the party. He was a devout Christian, a vegetarian and a foe to alcohol. He moderated his political views considerably after being Ambassador in Moscow, 1940–42, and returned to London to a seat in the War Cabinet and the leadership of a House of Commons which had a vast Conservative majority. From 1942 to the end of the war he was Minister of Aircraft Production.

In the post-war Labour Government he was, first, President of the Board of Trade and from 1947 Chancellor of the Exchequer, the very emblem of austerity. Austere he may have been, but he was honest through and through and nobody had a more kindly smile. He was clever, but not always sensible.

Daladier, Edouard, G.C.M.G. (1884–1970)
One of the leaders, with Léon Blum, of the French Front Popu-

laire in the early 1930s, he moved steadily to the right. He was French Prime Minister at the time of Munich and an ardent appeaser of Germany. He reluctantly led France into war in September 1939; but two months before the German offensive of May, 1940, resigned in favour of Paul Reynaud and became Minister of Defence in an unstable Cabinet. After the collapse of France, he might have been willing to carry on the war from North Africa, but he was incarcerated in a ship by the supporters of Pétain and all efforts to communicate with him were frustrated. After the Munich Conference in September 1938, which gave Hitler his way with Czechoslovakia, Neville Chamberlain asked the King to confer on Daladier the Grand Cross of the Order of St Michael and St George.

Dalton, Dr Hugh (1887–1962)
Labour M.P. for Bishop Auckland, educated at Eton and King's College, Cambridge, he was a leading light in the Labour Party, Minister of Economic Warfare in the war and Chancellor of the Exchequer (he had hoped for the Foreign Office) in Attlee's 1945 Government. However, in 1947 he had to resign on account of a Budget leak for which he was not responsible; for though sharp, he was honest. He had a first-class brain, but never quite lived down Queen Victoria's reference to him as "Canon Dalton's horrid little boy".

Darlan, Admiral J. F. (1881–1942)
As Commander-in-Chief of the French Navy before the war he made it an efficient fighting force. Although jealous of the Royal Navy and at heart anti-British, he co-operated loyally until the fall of France. He then became a leading appeaser of the victorious Germans and his Anglophobe sentiments were strengthened by the sinking of the French fleet at Oran in July 1940. By then he was Minister of Marine and in 1941 he rose still higher to become Pétain's Vice President and Foreign Minister. He put Syrian airfields at the disposal of the Germans when, in May 1941, they planned to bring military aid to Rashid Ali's anti-British insurrection in Baghdad. Yet in November 1942, happening by accident or design to be in North Africa when the Anglo-American Operation TORCH took place, he made an agreement with the American General Mark Clark and gave orders, in Marshal Pétain's name, for the French military commanders to stop resisting the Allied landings. Without these orders the operation would have been far more costly. This sudden turn of coat led Vichy and the Germans to denounce him, but it also aroused indignation in England and the United States where a deal with this friend of Germany was regarded with horror. The problem was resolved when a young royalist Frenchman assassinated him on Christmas Eve 1942.

De La Warr, Herbrand Sackville, 9th Earl, G.B.E. (1900–1976)
Always known as Buck, he was a man of great good looks, irresistible to women. He declared himself a conscientious objector on reaching military age, but since he was no coward he served before the

mast in a minesweeper. Joining the Labour Party, he held office in Ramsay MacDonald's Governments of 1924 and 1929–31 and then, having followed MacDonald and Snowden into a National Labour Party, he was Parliamentary Secretary in several departments before becoming Lord Privy Seal in 1937, President of the Board of Education and First Commissioner of Works. In 1951, by which time he had become a Conservative, he was appointed Postmaster General and he had the task of piloting through Parliament the bill establishing Independent Television of which he personally (like Churchill and Eden) strongly disapproved. Apart from being Chairman of the Royal Commonwealth Society and other multifarious activities, he was, with Brendan Bracken, co-secretary of the Other Club. One of his sisters, the glamorous Lady Idina, had five husbands, including the Lord Erroll who was murdered in Kenya in 1941.

De L'Isle, Viscount, V.C., K.G., G.C.M.G., G.C.V.O. (b. 1909)
Educated at Eton and Magdalene College, Cambridge, he was a Chartered Accountant and worked in Barclay's Bank. Having joined the supplementary reserve of the Grenadier Guards, he fought with the regiment in the war, won the V.C. by a feat of gallantry at Anzio and married Jacqueline, daughter of Field Marshal Viscount Gort, V.C. He was elected M.P. for Chelsea in 1944 and deplored the Yalta agreement on Poland. Succeeding his uncle as Lord de L'Isle and Dudley, he inherited the mediaeval Penshurst Place with its fourteenth-century hall and cherished it with the utmost care all his days. In 1951 he was Secretary of State for Air, a task he performed efficiently till Churchill resigned, and from 1961 to 1965 he was Governor General of Australia. A right-wing Tory, dedicated to duty, his kindliness and generosity won him many friends. Apart from Lord Roberts, also a winner of the V.C., he was the only Knight of the Garter ever able to put any letters in front of K.G. after his name.

Dill, Field Marshal Sir John, G.C.B., C.M.G., D.S.O., D.S.M. (U.S.) (1881–1944)
There were few more likeable human beings. Hailing from Co. Armagh, he went to Cheltenham College and Sandhurst, and fought with the Leinster Regiment in the South African War. He was a staff officer in France for most of World War I, but took part in several engagements, was wounded and won the D.S.O. He acquired such a reputation in the army that he was disappointed not to be made C.I.G.S. by Hore-Belisha in 1937, and again not to be C. in C. of the B.E.F. in 1939. In both cases Lord Gort, his junior in rank, was preferred and he had to be content to command I Corps under Gort from September 1939 to April 1940. He was then recalled to the War Office to be Vice Chief of the Imperial General Staff. On May 27th, at the climax of the Dunkirk evacuation, he succeeded General Ironside as C.I.G.S.

Neither the Secretary of State, Anthony Eden, nor Eden's successor, David Margesson, had anything but praise for him. However, he was a tired man and Churchill found him unsufficiently vigorous. So after the Atlantic Charter meeting with Roosevelt in August 1941, he was left behind to be the British representative with the Combined Chiefs of Staff in Washington. It was here that he came into his own, performing an invaluable service for his country, winning golden opinions from the Americans, forming a strong personal friendship with General Marshall, and finally, when he died in Washington, being given the high American distinction of burial in Arlington Cemetery.

Dodds, Lady Annabel (1881–1948)
Eldest daughter of the Marquess of Crewe and Sibyl Graham of Netherby. In 1902 she married the Hon. Arthur O'Neill, M.P. for Mid-Antrim, who was the elder son and heir of Lord O'Neill. He died at Ypres, while serving with the 2nd Life Guards, the first M.P. to be killed in World War I. She had five O'Neill children. In 1922 she married Major Hugh Dodds and had two more sons. She had the capacity of making her companions feel more intelligent and amusing than they really were, and she was a "great lady" without being at all arrogant or ostentatious. When her father died in 1945 she changed her name to Dodds-Crewe.

Dowding, Air Chief Marshal Hugh, 1st Lord, G.C.B., G.C.V.O., C.M.G. (1882–1970)
Educated at Winchester and the Royal Military Academy, Woolwich, he was a Lieutenant Colonel in the Royal Artillery in World War I before joining the Royal Flying Corps. A member of the Air Council, 1930–35, and then appointed C. in C., Fighter Command. A principal architect of victory in the Battle of Britain, and a decisive influence in the decision not to send additional fighter squadrons to France in June 1940, which would have dangerously denuded the home defences, he was retired by the Air Ministry with much tactlessness in the following November. This was done on the doubtless true grounds that he was exhausted. He was justifiably hurt at not being promoted to Marshal of the R.A.F. but Churchill made him a peer.

Dulles, John Foster (1888–1959)
He was a successful lawyer, but personal charm was not among his attributes. Eisenhower appointed him Secretary of State in 1952. His grasp of foreign affairs was slight and he directed American foreign policy insensitively. During the run-up to the 1956 Suez operation, he was guilty of inconsistencies and changes of mind which infuriated both the French and the British and had a significant bearing on the whole unfortunate episode. It would have been better if he had stuck to the law. He was an intelligent man of high moral character and deeply serious intent. His fate was to be the wrong man in the wrong place at the wrong time. His brother, Alan, of the Office of Strategic Services under General Donovan, and later head of the C.I.A., was a more cosmopolitan and sophisticated operator.

Duncan-Sandys, Lord, C.H. (b. 1908)
Son of a Conservative M.P. with

a New Zealand wife, he was educated at Eton and Magdalen, Oxford, before passing into the Diplomatic Service in 1930. He served at the Embassy in Berlin in the last days of the Weimar Republic and was elected Conservative M.P. for Norwood in 1935, the year in which he married Winston Churchill's eldest daughter, Diana. In 1936, having learned from a brother territorial officer details of the shortage of anti-aircraft guns, he raised the matter in the House of Commons. Hore-Belisha, Secretary of State for War, sought to court-martial him, but parliamentary privilege as well as family loyalty were at stake and his father-in-law came powerfully to his rescue in debate. "The Sandys Case" was headline news.

From 1941 onwards his political career blossomed. He held at different times the portfolios of Works, Supply, Housing and Local Government, Defence, Aviation, the Colonies and Commonwealth Relations. Hard-working, imaginative, humorous and, as far as I was concerned, pleasant company, he was almost always at odds with the civil servants in his various departments, disliking some and distrusting most.

He was, in the years after the war, a leading proponent of European Unity and instigated Winston Churchill to make the United Europe movement a crusade.

He was made a peer in 1974, and became president of the Civic Trust, which he had founded, and Chairman of Lonrho Ltd.

Eisenhower, General Dwight D. (1890–1969)
Although his military career had not progressed far when he was promoted to dizzy heights, and although he had little experience of tactics and strategy, there can be no doubt that Eisenhower's generosity of character, constant good nature and keen sensitivity in handling people were major factors in the Allied victories of 1943–45. His headquarters, containing an equal number of British and American officers, may not always have been efficient, but it was a model of Anglo-American cooperation, and his personality radiated optimism and goodwill. In that sense he was a good politician, but when it came to international politics he was less sure-footed, indeed disastrous in 1945 at the time of the German surrender. He could have taken Berlin and Prague: he deliberately let the Russians occupy them, despite Churchill's protests, and so ensured that the Iron Curtain clamped down with greater ease than was necessary.

After the war he converted S.H.A.E.F. into S.H.A.P.E. with the same goodwill as in war-time. Then he became a politician and the slogan "I like Ike" captivated America. Elected Republican President in 1952, he was not as amenable as Churchill could have wished, and he developed a passionate dislike of the Russians, to whom he had been so helpful in 1945. Despite a heart-attack he stood for the Presidency again in 1956 and was re-elected. He was a man with real goodness of heart and totally honest; but he was a better Supreme Allied Commander than President of the United States.

Franks, Oliver, 1st Lord, O.M.,
G.C.M.G., K.C.B., C.B.E.
(b. 1905)
If ever there was a man for all seasons it was Oliver Franks. When he came back from the Embassy in Washington in 1952, he was pursued with earnest invitations to be Editor of *The Times*, Chairman of the B.B.C., Headmaster of Harrow and numerous other offers which he politely declined. He was first and foremost a University man, a Fellow, and eventually Provost, of the Queen's College, Oxford, a lecturer in philosophy and finally, at the end of his career, Provost of Worcester College. In the war he shone so brightly as a temporary civil servant that he finished his Whitehall stint as Permanent Secretary, Ministry of Supply. He became, after four critical years in Washington (which included the Berlin air lift and the Korean War), Chairman of Lloyds Bank and an obvious candidate for the Governorship of the Bank of England. Every Royal Commission wanted him to be Chairman and his last appointment of this kind was the Review Committee set up after the Falklands War. Despite the eagerness with which his patronage was sought, by government departments and industrial companies, his lasting preference was to sit smoking his pipe in philosophic contemplation and conversation at Oxford.

Gamelin, General Maurice
Gustave (1872–1958)
He hoodwinked both his own countrymen and the British into believing him a great General. The man who did not think so was his second in command, General Georges, who would have had his place had he not been gravely wounded in the bomb attack which killed King Alexander of Yugoslavia at Marseilles in 1934. His claim to fame arose from his having been on Marshal Joffre's staff in 1914 and written the directives at the battle of the Marne. He had also defeated a Druse rebellion in Syria and been Inspector General of the Army. He was interned by the Vichy Government and incarcerated by the Germans at Buchenwald Concentration Camp in 1943.

Gaulle, General Charles de
(1890–1970)
Few men in history have risen to the pinnacle of power so fortuitously. An unknown brigadier who had made a profound study of tank warfare and been taken up, right at the end of the day, by Paul Reynaud, he came to London without expecting to lead a Free French movement. Nor would he have done so if any leading French politician had been available. However, Winston Churchill saw in him the very reverse of the defeatism which he had found in France and, once he had made his choice, he did not go back on it, though he was often tempted to do so by de Gaulle's arrogance, suspicions and ingratitude. De Gaulle was a patriot; but he was also a nationalist, and to him the erasure of the 1940 shame and the recovery of French greatness were all that mattered. Churchill protected him from the dislike and distrust of the Americans, but he was exasperated when de Gaulle took steps, often not in

the general Allied interest, without consultation; nor could he stomach the General's absurd conviction that the British wished to seize the French colonies, notably Syria and the Lebanon (which the British would have paid any price *not* to possess). All the same, even when de Gaulle, as President of the Republic, was giving rein to his Anglophobe instincts by blocking British entry to the Common Market, he did on several occasions make it clear that he recognised the debt he owed Churchill.

Geoffrey-Lloyd, Lord
(1902–1984)
After Harrow and Trinity, Cambridge, he was private secretary to both Sir Samuel Hoare and Stanley Baldwin before being elected in 1931 Conservative M.P. for the Ladywood division of Birmingham. He then became Parliamentary Private Secretary to Baldwin as Prime Minister. On Baldwin's retirement he was promoted to be Under Secretary at the Home Office and in 1939 was Secretary for Mines and later for Petroleum. In this capacity, and as Chairman of the Oil Control Board, he was responsible for PLUTO, the pipeline under the Channel required for Operation OVERLORD. In 1951 Churchill made him Minister of Fuel and Power and under Harold Macmillan he was Minister of Education. A gentle, unassertive man of ability, he was made a peer in 1974 and devoted his retirement to the brilliant organisation of the Leeds Castle Foundation, bequeathed by his great friend and constant hostess Olive, Lady Baillie, daughter of Lord Queenborough and owner of the castle.

George II, King of Greece
(1890–1947)
Son of King Constantine I, he succeeded to the throne when his pro-German father abdicated in 1922 after the Greek defeat by the Turks in Asia Minor. He was deposed by the republicans two years later. However, the Greek parliamentarians were so undisciplined and the state of the country so chaotic that sentiment began to flow in the ex-king's favour. A strong man, General Metaxas, seized power and the king was restored to the throne in 1934. He had to retire to London when the Germans occupied Greece in 1941, but he never again ceased to be King and, despite the E.L.A.S. revolt and the wrangles over the appointment of Archbishop Damaskinos as Regent, his reign was endorsed by an overwhelmingly favourable plebiscite in 1945. He married a most unsatisfactory Roumanian princess and had no children, being succeeded by his brother, Paul.

Goering, Field Marshal Hermann
(1893–1946)
He had a way of persuading foreigners, including Lord Halifax, that he was "a good chap", whereas he was in fact ruthless, egotistic and "kinky" to boot. He won fame as an airman by taking command of "the Richthofen Circus" after Richthofen was killed in World War I. One of Hitler's earliest followers, he was wounded in the abortive Nazi "putsch" at Munich in 1923, after which he was air adviser to the Danes and Swedes. In 1932 he became President of the Reichstag, which he probably arranged to have burned down, and Prime Minister of Prussia.

Because of his record he was appointed Commander in Chief of the Luftwaffe in 1933 and presided over the air-raids on Britain in 1940–41. Sentenced to death at Nuremberg in 1946, he cheated the hangman by taking an anally secreted cyanide pill.

Gort, Field Marshal John Standish Vereker, 6th Viscount, V.C., G.C.B., D.S.O. (and 2 bars), M.C. (1886–1946)

When the American General Patton visited him in Malta in 1943, he said he had come to see the bravest man in the British army. Gort was indeed brave, with a V.C., three D.S.O.s and a M.C. to his credit in the 1st World War. He served in India and in Shanghai, and was Commandant of the Staff College. Hore-Belisha picked him in 1937, junior though he was to many other generals, to be C.I.G.S. He was not the ideal choice, hard though he worked, and he was soon at daggers drawn with Hore-Belisha who nevertheless recommended him for command of the B.E.F. He had two generals senior to himself, Dill and Alan Brooke, as his Corps Commanders. When the crunch came in May 1940, with the B.E.F. cut off and almost surrounded, it was Gort who took the decision to withdraw to Dunkirk for embarkation. Had he not done so, almost every trained officer and N.C.O. in the British army would have been lost and it is doubtful whether Britain could have fought on. So it may well be that he changed the course of history. To his disappointment he was never again given an active command, but after a year as Governor of Gibraltar, where he extended the small airfield with most beneficial consequences for the 1943 campaigns, he was Governor and Commander in Chief of Malta, during much of the Island's terrible siege. His organisation of the defence was masterly. His last appointment was High Commissioner in Palestine in 1944 and there, by sheer force of personality, he preserved the peace between Jews and Arabs. But cancer struck, and he returned home to die in 1946, his services inadequately recognised.

Graham, Lady Helen, D.C.V.O. (1879–1945)

Eldest daughter of my mother's aunt the Duchess of Montrose, who was born Violet Graham of Netherby. Lady Helen was President of the Y.W.C.A. and was the first lady-in-waiting to the Duchess of York (Queen Elizabeth, the Queen Mother) of whom, and of whose children, she became an intimate friend. Well-read, a watercolourist of distinction, a frequent contributor of short stories to *Blackwood's Magazine*, a dedicated Scot though never a nationalist, she was withal humble and unself-assertive. There was no better advertisement for the schoolroom, governess-controlled upbringing of Victorian young ladies at its best.

Greig, Group Captain Sir Louis, K.B.E., C.V.O. (1880–1953)

As a young man played Rugby Football for Scotland, became a doctor, and was appointed medical officer at Osborne, the junior college for naval cadets. Among them was the then delicate Prince Albert, afterwards Duke of York and King George VI. In the war Greig fought with the Royal Marines, was taken prisoner by the Germans and then joined the R.A.F., becoming a Wing Commander in record time. He became Comptroller and Equerry to the Duke of York whom he partnered at tennis at Wimbledon (without notable success). He married Miss Phyllis Scrymgeour, was appointed deputy-ranger of Richmond Park and resided there, at Thatched House Lodge. In World War II he was personal assistant to Sir Archibald Sinclair, Secretary of State for Air.

Grigg, Sir Percy James, K.C.B., K.C.S.I. (1890–1964)
Educated at Bournemouth School and St John's, Cambridge, he was Private Secretary to Churchill at the Exchequer (1924–29). He was always known as P.J. After being Chairman of the Board of Inland Revenue, he went to India as financial member of the Viceroy's Executive Council. Thence, in 1939, he arrived in Whitehall, like an explosive rocket, as Permanent Under Secretary at the War Office. He had no opinion of Hore-Belisha, his Secretary of State, or of most other people's Secretaries of State. He said exactly what he thought and did not care a fig for those superior to him except, on occasions, the Prime Minister. Clever and hard-working, though holding truthfulness to be a cardinal virtue, he thought tact a social affectation.

To everybody's surprise, includ-

ing his own, Churchill found him a parliamentary seat at Cardiff and in 1942 made him Secretary of State for War to replace David Margesson who was sacrificed as a scapegoat after the fall of Singapore.

He left politics when the war ended, became Deputy Chairman of the National Provincial Bank, a director of I.C.I. and other leading companies and Chairman of Bass.

Halifax, Edward Wood, 1st Earl of, K.G., O.M., G.C.S.I., G.C.I.E. (1881–1959)
A Fellow of All Souls who was also a M.F.H., a devout practising Anglican, Viceroy of India, Foreign Secretary, British Ambassador in Washington at a crucial period in Anglo-American relations, and the holder of eighteen honorary degrees is a subject worthy either of Dryden or of W. S. Gilbert. Calm and unhurried, he shared Neville Chamberlain's dedication to peace at almost any cost, and although capable of cunning in his diplomacy he was taken in by Goering. He went so far as to suggest that *we* might satisfy the Germans by letting them have the *Portuguese* colonies. He was, all the same, a good and fascinating man, who was a great success in Washington with Roosevelt, Cordell Hull and Harry Hopkins. He was much helped in Delhi as well as in Washington by his admirable wife, born Lady Dorothy Onslow. Of their three sons one was killed in action, but another, though severely maimed, held many political offices and was himself made a peer.

Hankey, Sir Maurice, 1st Lord,
G.C.B., G.C.M.G., G.C.V.O.
(1877–1963)
This long-standingly eminent Civil
Servant went from Rugby and the
Royal Naval College at Greenwich
to be a Captain in the Royal
Marine Artillery; but several years
before World War I he became
Secretary of the Committee of Imperial Defence and in 1916 Lloyd
George, with whom he worked
closely, made him the first Secretary of the Cabinet. He combined
these two key functions between
the two world wars, but still found
time to be Secretary at the Versailles Peace Conference, Clerk of
the Privy Council and Secretary to
five Imperial Conferences. In 1938
he thought it time to retire, but
Neville Chamberlain made him a
peer and inveigled him into the
War Cabinet as Minister Without
Portfolio. At Chamberlain's request Churchill, who had been the
object of Hankey's deep suspicion,
retained him in office, first as
Chancellor of the Duchy of Lancaster and then as Paymaster General and Chairman of the Scientific
Advisory and Engineering Advisory Committees. He continued
busily to take the chair of numerous other governmental and semi-
governmental committees after the
war.

Harriman, Hon. W. Averell
(b. 1891)
Son of the fabulously rich American railway king, E. F. Harriman,
Averell struck out on his own at an
early age, founding the successful banking enterprise Brown
Brothers Harriman, and excelling
at everything, from polo to croquet, to which he set his hand. In

1941 he came to Britain, as President Roosevelt's special envoy,
to organise the supply of equipment. He became a friend of the
Churchills and a frequent visitor
to Chequers until, in 1943, he was
sent as Ambassador to Moscow
and formed an amiable personal
relationship with Stalin. After the
war he was Governor of New York
and adviser to successive Democrat
Presidents. When Mrs Harriman
died, he married Randolph Churchill's first wife, Pamela, who became in her own right a significant
feature in the Democrat Party in
Washington. As late as 1983, when
he was over ninety, the Harrimans
visited the Kremlin and had an interview with Brezhnev in the hope
of improving Soviet-American relations. By 1985 Averell Harriman
and Molotov were the last survivors of the men of power in
World War II.

Harris, Marshal of the R.A.F. Sir
Arthur, Bt., G.C.B., A.F.C.,
O.B.E. (1892–1984)
Having joined the Royal Flying
Corps in 1915 and served in India,
Iraq and the Middle East, he was
promoted from the command of a
bomber group in 1940 to be deputy
Chief of the Air Staff and head of
the R.A.F. delegation in nominally
neutral Washington. In 1942 he became A.O.C. in C. Bomber Command and held that vital post till
the end of the war. He was a controversial figure in R.A.F. circles
where some thought him too ruthless, though he did not lose the
respect of his sorely tried bomber
crews in the costly strategic bombing raids he directed. In OVERLORD
he resented the insistent demands
of the army for area bombing, thus

deflecting him from his principal objective of flattening German factories and towns. After the war Attlee did not recommend him for a peerage. Feeling slighted he went to live in South Africa and was managing director of the South Africa Marine Corporation. On returning to office in 1951 Churchill made him a baronet and was only deterred from recommending him for a peerage by the vehement opposition of the Air Ministry. He went back to England and lived to a great age, possessed of many more foreign than British decorations, and most carefully cherished by his second wife.

Head, Antony, 1st Viscount,
G.C.M.G., C.B.E., M.C.
(1906–1983)
Behind a humorous, almost "Bertie Wooster", exterior lurked a keen intelligence, administrative competence and innate common sense. After Eton and Sandhurst, he joined the Life Guards but found time for adventurous activities, including a voyage to Australia before the mast in a windjammer. Having won a Military Cross in France in 1940, he joined General Ismay's staff and worked for "the Joint Planners" while his bosom friend and companion in adventure, Robert Laycock, became Chief of Combined Operations. Elected Conservative M.P. for Carshalton in 1945, he did so well in opposition that he was chosen as Secretary of State for War in 1951 and appointed Minister of Defence a few days before the Suez operation in 1956. In 1960 he was the first British High Commissioner in the newly independent Nigeria (sensibly making his acceptance dependent on the provision of a swimming pool, a tennis court and a launch with a uniformed crew). He was subsequently High Commissioner in Malaysia, and was appointed in 1968 Colonel Commandant of the S.A.S. He married a skilled portrait painter, Lady Dorothea Ashley-Cooper, daughter of the 9th Earl of Shaftesbury, K.P., and they were both honest, outspoken and the best possible company.

Henderson, Sir Nicholas,
G.C.M.G. (b. 1919)
Son of a well-known economist, he was educated at Stowe and at Hertford College, Oxford, where he belonged to a set of fashionably pink Fabians, such as Anthony Crosland, and became a friend of Hugh Gaitskell, Roy Jenkins and Frank Pakenham (Longford). Prevented by a tubercular infection from joining the armed forces, he was a temporary Private Secretary to Anthony Eden, after serving in the Minister of State's office in Cairo. He quickly made his name in the Foreign Office and was established as a full member of the service after the war. He was Private Secretary to five Secretaries of State, establishing a specially close friendship with Ernest Bevin, and went on to be British Ambassador in Warsaw, Bonn and Paris where he was much esteemed for his sartorial eccentricity as well as for his diplomatic skill. After his retirement in 1979, on reaching the age of sixty, Lord Carrington offered him the Embassy in Washington. He was notably successful in stating the British case, orally and on television, during the Falklands campaign of 1982. He married Mary

Cawardias, daughter of a Greek doctor with a high reputation in London. She had two claims to fame. She was an intrepid leader of Greek guerillas during the war, and she was such a superb mistress of the culinary art that in all their posts the British Embassy dining-room was a centre of attraction.

Hollis, General Sir Leslie, K.C.B., K.B.E. (1899–1963)
The son of a clergyman, he was educated at St Lawrence College, Ramsgate, and joined the Marines in 1915. He was on the foretop of H.M.S. *Edinburgh*, the sole ship of the 1st Cruiser Squadron not to be sunk at the Battle of Jutland. A man of notable charm, if not as clever as Sir Ian Jacob, he became an Assistant Secretary of the Committee of Imperial Defence in 1936 and thence passed on to General Ismay's staff as his senior assistant. He remained in the office of the Minister of Defence throughout the war, liked by all and often accompanying Churchill on his travels. He remained at his post till 1948 and was then promoted to full General and appointed Commandant General of the Royal Marines.

Home of the Hirsel, Alexander Douglas Home, Lord, K.T. (b. 1903)
Eldest son of the 13th Earl of Home and Lady Lilian Lambton, daughter of the 4th Earl of Durham. Educated at Eton and Christ Church, Oxford, he was elected, as Lord Dunglass, M.P. for South Lanark in 1931 and became Parliamentary Private Secretary to Neville Chamberlain in 1937, accompanying him to the Munich meeting with Hitler in 1938. He married Elizabeth, daughter of the Headmaster of Eton and Dean of Durham, the Very Revd C. A. Alington. He was incapacitated during the war by spinal tuberculosis, but in 1951 he became Minister of State at the Scottish Office and succeeded his father as Earl of Home. He was soon promoted to be Secretary of State for Commonwealth Relations, Leader of the House of Lords, Lord President and, from 1960–63, Foreign Secretary. In 1963, on Harold Macmillan's retirement, he renounced his peerage and became Prime Minister. He lost the 1964 General Election by four seats and the Conservative Party, in their folly, replaced him as leader by Edward Heath whom he nevertheless served faithfully as Foreign Secretary, 1970–74. A man universally loved and admired, by political opponents as well as supporters, he was devoid of vanity and did not know the meaning of rancour or jealousy. A lover of the countryside, he was happiest watching birds, catching salmon at his home on the Tweed or shooting grouse at his other home, Douglas in Lanarkshire.

Hopkins, Harry L. (1890–1946)
He came from a humble home, the son of a harness-maker in Sioux City, and his sympathies were always for the poor and down-trodden. Thin, with wispy hair, always untidy and obviously frail, he nevertheless had piercing, intelligent eyes, a winning smile and a slow, impressive way of speaking. He worked for welfare organisations in the New York slums until he became a friend of Averell

Harriman and, through him, of President Roosevelt. The President appointed him Secretary of Commerce in 1938 and he was soon established in the White House as Roosevelt's intimate friend and adviser. The British had represented everything he disliked, especially their far-flung Empire; but he was captivated by Queen Elizabeth when she and King George VI went to Washington in the spring of 1939, and in January 1940, he fell beneath the spell of Winston Churchill, whom he had expected to dislike. After France fell in 1940, he had recognised the British to be the sole active champions of a free world. He used his influence with the President to accelerate the provision of supplies for Britain. He worked closely with Lord Halifax. Later on he became an equally strong partisan of Russia, was foolish enough to advocate a Second Front in 1942 and at the end of the war trusted the word and goodwill of Stalin to an imprudent extent, as did Roosevelt and the State Department. He was much hampered by recurring ill-health, but he was always an honourable man and a sincere idealist.

Hore-Belisha, Leslie, Lord
(1893–1957)
Educated at Clifton, St John's, Oxford, Paris and Heidelberg, and President of the Oxford Union after a respectable war record, he aspired to be a second Disraeli. So he fought and won the Devonport division of Plymouth for the Liberals in 1923, spoke fluently in the House, was Parliamentary Secretary to the Board of Trade in 1931, Financial Secretary to the Treasury a year later and then (1934–37)

Minister of Transport. There he became a national figure by introducing pedestrian crossings lit by Belisha beacons. The publicity he received did him no good, for he pursued it too diligently when, in 1937, Chamberlain gave him the War Office.

He did much for the welfare and comfort of the troops. However, on matters of army organisation and future strategy he fell foul of the military establishment, tending to consult his unofficial adviser, Liddell-Hart, rather than the Army Council. His fall came when on visiting the British Expeditionary Force in France in November 1939, he crossed swords with the Commander in Chief, Lord Gort, over a matter of pill-boxes. At home Sir Horace Wilson, Sir Edward Bridges, Sir Alexander Hardinge (the King's Private Secretary) and his own new Permanent Under Secretary, P. J. Grigg, all turned against him. In January 1940, Chamberlain demanded his resignation and offered him instead the Board of Trade, which Churchill advised him to accept, but which he foolishly declined. His political career was at an end, though he was briefly Minister of National Insurance in Churchill's caretaker government of 1945. In 1954 he was made a peer.

Ironside, Field Marshal 1st Lord,
G.C.B., C.M.G., D.S.O.
(1880–1959)
Having fought in the South African War (where his adventures supplied John Buchan with the portrait of Richard Hannay in *The Thirty-Nine Steps*), and been a gunnery officer in the 1st World War, Edmund Ironside was given

command of the British forces at Archangel in 1919. His career thereafter was a varied one, but it included three years as Commandant of the Staff College, and, in 1936, Eastern Command. Distraught by obsolete equipment and by governmental inactivity, he paid visits to Churchill at Chartwell and declared that the army was unprepared for war. He was informed by Lord Gort in the summer of 1939 that he was the C. in C. designate of the British Expeditionary Force. In the event, on September 3rd the Secretary of State, Hore-Belisha, obtained Cabinet approval for Gort to be C. in C. and for Ironside to replace him as C.I.G.S. He was not a success in the post and was succeeded in July 1940, by Sir John Dill, being compensated by a brief command of Home Forces and the rank of Field Marshal. The next year he was given a peerage.

Ismay, General Lord, K.G., G.C.B., C.H., D.S.O. (1887–1965)
Son of a senior Indian civil servant, he was educated at Charterhouse and Sandhurst, joining the army in 1905 and winning his D.S.O. in a campaign against the Mad Mullah who dominated Somaliland for more than twenty years. He had long service in India, on the North-West Frontier as a young officer and at headquarters later, being Military Secretary to the Viceroy, 1931–33. He transferred to the Committee of Imperial Defence in London in 1936 and became its Secretary, in succession to Sir Maurice Hankey, in 1938. He was thus the natural choice to be Chief of Staff to Churchill, as Minister of Defence, in 1940. He was the main channel of communication between Churchill and the Chiefs of Staff, of whose committee he was a full member, and he was equally trusted by both. Nobody did more to oil the wheels on the sometimes bumpy road between the service chiefs and the politicians and it was due to him more than anyone else that the confrontations between the two in World War I were avoided in World War II. His ability and dedication to hard work was matched by his personal charm. He was universally known as Pug, for he looked like one and when he was pleased one could almost imagine he was wagging his tail.

He had married a well-endowed wife and after the war he looked forward to a peaceful life, caring for his herd of Jersey cows. It was not to be. In 1951 Churchill inveigled him, against his wishes, into becoming Secretary of State for Commonwealth Relations and in 1952 he was elected, for five years, Secretary General of N.A.T.O. Honours and directorships were heaped on him, but he remained what he had always been, a straightforward, hardworking and totally honourable army officer.

Jacob, Lieutenant General Sir Ian, G.B.E., C.B. (b. 1899)
Son of Field Marshal Sir Claud Jacob, educated at Wellington, the Royal Military Academy, Woolwich, and King's College, Cambridge. A man of tireless industry (nicknamed "Iron Pants" by Antony Head), he was far above the average in both intelligence and common sense. As one of

General Ismay's two principal lieutenants in the Office of the Minister of Defence, he was liked and respected by Churchill as a true professional and accompanied him on several of his foreign tours and visits. After the war he was Director of Overseas Services at the B.B.C. until summoned by Churchill in 1952 to be Chief Staff Officer to Field Marshal Alexander as Minister of Defence. He was released after a brief interval and was Director General of the B.B.C., 1952–60. Invariably public spirited and obedient to duty, and a sharp observer of people and events.

Kennedy, Joseph P. (1888–1969)
As Kennedy knew all the tricks of the financial trade, and had himself made a fortune by dealing, President Roosevelt chose him to be the first Chairman of the S.E.C. (Securities Exchange Commission) established to control Wall Street under Roosevelt's "New Deal". A Boston Irishman and an uncompromising Roman Catholic, he brought his eight children with him when he came to London as Ambassador in 1937. They were all enthusiastically received, but in the war Kennedy advised his government that Germany would win, and when the bombs began to fall on London, the American Embassy was, to Roosevelt's disgust, the first to flee from the capital. He was withdrawn by the President at the end of 1940, but had the satisfaction, and then the sorrow, of watching the career of two of his brilliant sons, Jack and Bobby. The eldest, Joe, was killed in action in the air force.

Keyes, Admiral of the Fleet Lord, G.C.B., K.C.V.O., C.M.G., D.S.O. (1872–1945)
Nobody would stint praise to Roger Keyes for the dash and gallantry with which he commanded the raid on the U-boat bases at Zeebrugge and Ostend in 1918. Indeed his entire naval career was a distinguished one, recognised by Parliament in 1919 with a vote of thanks and a cheque for £10,000. Of courage and of drive he had plenty: of modesty he had scarcely any.

That was the root of the trouble in 1940. On May 7th he went down to the House of Commons (to which he had been elected in 1934 for North Portsmouth) in uniform and wearing rows of medals, to speak against Chamberlain. He then rushed off to Belgium to support King Leopold and returned to England bristling with indignation against the Chiefs of Staff, bombarding the Prime Minister with demands for action, combined with his own advancement, and causing the maximum irritation in Whitehall with the minimum of useful results. He asked to preside over the Chiefs of Staff; he even asked to be Deputy Prime Minister; and Churchill, still under the spell of Keyes' record in World War I, did go so far as to appoint him Director of Combined Operations, though he was tactfully removed in 1941 to make place for Lord Louis Mountbatten.

Kirkpatrick, Sir Ivone, G.C.B., G.C.M.G. (1897–1964)
This forthright Roman Catholic from Downside and Balliol fought throughout World War I with the Inniskillings and entered the Dip-

lomatic Service in 1919. As First Secretary at the Embassy in Berlin, 1933–38, he was convinced that the Nazis intended war and he wholeheartedly disliked the policy of his appeasing chief, Sir Nevile Henderson, and of the Munich Settlement. Returning to Whitehall, he was made director of the foreign division of the Ministry of Information, where he was contemptuous of Duff Cooper's activities, and then controller of the European Services of the B.B.C., a function he performed with energy and fruitful results. In 1949 he was permanent Under Secretary of the German Section of the Foreign Office, from 1950 to 1953 British High Commissioner in Germany and finally, from 1953 to 1957, Permanent Under Secretary of State. On retirement he was appointed Chairman of the Independent Television Authority.

Laval, Pierre (1883–1945)
Between the wars he was always to the fore in French politics, sometimes Prime Minister and sometimes Foreign Minister. His views were extremely right wing and he sympathised with the fascists. When France fell in 1940 he was the most outspokenly pro-German member of the Vichy clique, often causing embarrassment to Marshal Pétain, to whom the Germans appointed him Vice President in 1942. After the war he was tried for treason and executed in October 1945.

Leathers, Frederick, 1st Viscount, C.H. (1883–1965)
Chairman of William Cory and Son Ltd, and a man of power and influence in the shipping world, he was selected by Churchill (who had sat on one of his boards and been impressed by his qualities) to be Minister of War Transport in 1941. He performed his task, an onerous one during the Battle of the Atlantic, with such quiet efficiency that he won the admiration of all his Cabinet colleagues. He was liked and respected even though he was not given to sparkle in company. Churchill thought so well of him that he insisted on recalling him in 1951 to be Secretary of State for the Co-ordination of Transport, an office of Overlord which served no useful purpose and was abolished in 1953. He had been created a Baron in 1941, so as not to need a seat in the House of Commons, and was made a Viscount in 1954.

Liddell-Hart, Sir Basil (1895–1970)
Undoubtedly a great military historian and invariably helpful to students, though his teaching that in any future war defence must have the advantage over attack lost him his prestige in 1940, as did his belief that Britain would lose the war. He had been military correspondent of *The Times* and was Hore-Belisha's unofficial adviser, to the fury of the Generals, when Belisha was Secretary of State for War. He left a library of great importance to students of military history and after the war became a friend and frequent companion of Field Marshal Montgomery.

Lloyd of Dolobran, George, 1st Lord, G.C.S.I., G.C.I.E., D.S.O. (1879–1941)
Educated at Eton and Trinity College, Cambridge, he worked at the British Embassy in Constantinople

and in the Middle East before becoming a Conservative M.P. in 1910. He was much concerned with the Arab revolt and with Lawrence of Arabia. In 1918 he was appointed Governor of Bombay, an office he held for five years. He was the creator of the Lloyd barrage across the Indus, which irrigated thousands of square miles. In 1925 he succeeded Field Marshal Lord Allenby as High Commissioner in Egypt and was made a peer. However, he fell into disfavour at home and resigned in 1929.

He was a resolute man, unbending in his views, but dynamic both in speech and action. Unlike Churchill, he was an unwavering supporter of the Arab cause, but they joined forces in opposition to Baldwin's Government of India Bill, in demanding rapid rearmament and in opposing Neville Chamberlain's foreign policy. He was an active and enthusiastic Chairman of the British Council and President of the right-wing Navy League. There was no more dedicated imperialist. Churchill, who respected his energy and intelligence, made him Secretary of State for the Colonies in 1940. Seeing a certain amount of him socially as well as officially, I was deeply impressed by the brilliance of his conversation and the shrewdness of his judgment. In January 1941, he became Leader of the House of Lords, but died a few weeks later. He married a sister of Sir Alan Lascelles and his son, David, held ministerial office under Churchill and Eden from 1952 to 1957.

Maclean, Sir Fitzroy, Bt., C.B.E. (b. 1911)
A man of action who is also a master of the English language. Joining the Diplomatic Service in 1933, he wrote a highly acclaimed account of an adventurous journey through little visited southern provinces of the Soviet Union made when he was on the Embassy staff in Moscow. Transferred back to London in 1939, he decided to take an active part in the war. He escaped from his reserved occupation in 1941 by declaring himself a parliamentary candidate, joined the Cameron Highlanders as a private (and, in 1942, the S.A.S.) after being elected Conservative M.P. for Lancaster, a seat he held till 1959. In 1943 he was promoted to Brigadier and chosen to lead the British mission to Tito, with whom he worked closely for two years of guerilla warfare, establishing a most friendly personal relationship. He was from 1954 to 1957 Financial Secretary at the War Office and he wrote a series of excellent books of which the best-known is *Eastern Approaches*. He married the delightful and intelligent daughter of the 16th Lord Lovat, widow of Sir Eric Phipps' younger son, Alan, a naval officer killed in the war.

Margesson, David, 1st Viscount, M.C. (1890–1965)
After Harrow and Magdalene College, Cambridge, he joined the 11th Hussars and won the Military Cross in World War I. Entering the House of Commons in 1922, he became a Whip in 1926 and Chief Whip in 1931. He controlled the Government majority in the House with exemplary skill, employing a mixture of charm (with which he was exceptionally endowed), disciplinary threat and organising

ability. Loyal to Baldwin and Chamberlain, he was equally so to Churchill when circumstances changed, and no member of the 1940 Coalition Government, Conservative, Liberal or Labour, thought ill of him. Churchill made him Secretary of State for War in December 1940. He gave every satisfaction, being on most amicable terms with the C.I.G.S., Sir John Dill; but in 1942, after the fall of Singapore, he was thrown to the wolves as a scapegoat, albeit an entirely unblemished one. In 1916 he married an American heiress, Frances Leggett, by whom he had three intelligent children; but he and his wife lived separate lives.

Martin, Sir John, K.C.M.G., C.B., C.V.O. (b. 1904)
A first-class classical product of the Edinburgh Academy and Corpus Christi, Oxford, he had a shy and retiring disposition combined with a ready wit, a delectable sense of humour and a conscientious devotion to the public service. Coming to No. 10 from the Colonial Service, with the secretaryship of the Palestine Royal Commission and the admiration of Chaim Weizmann behind him, he quickly won favour, went with the Prime Minister to the Atlantic Charter Meeting, the Casablanca, Tehran, Cairo and Quebec conferences and on several visits to Washington and Moscow; but he was too law-abiding to keep a diary. That is a pity as his writing is as agreeable as his conversation. After the war he was deputy Under Secretary of State in the Colonial Office and High Commissioner in Malta, 1965–67. His wife, Rosalind, is a daughter of a former Provost of Oriel, Sir David Ross.

Mary, Her Majesty Queen (1867–1953)
Tall and regal, with a magnificent presence. Her mother, Princess Mary of Cambridge, immensely fat and adored by the populace, was a grand-daughter of King George III; her father, the Duke of Teck, was the morganatic child of Duke Alexander of Württemberg and Countess Rhédey. The Tecks were poor, and the Duchess extravagant, so that Princess Mary of Teck seldom had new clothes and lived in strained circumstances at the White Lodge in Richmond Park, placed at the family's disposal by Queen Victoria. She was selected, doubtless with little enthusiasm on her part, to marry the heir to the throne, the Duke of Clarence. He died while they were engaged and her tryst was, with Queen Victoria's approval, transferred to George, Duke of York, whom she much preferred, though when he became King George V she held him in awe and was unsuccessful in mitigating his authoritarian treatment of their children. Queen Alexandra, her not very intelligent but strikingly beautiful mother-in-law, never liked her; but Queen Victoria, conscious of the fact, went out of her way to provide affectionate compensation. As Queen Mother she was an immensely popular figure. She had a sense of humour, a social conscience and an unswervingly rigid sense of duty. She was a discriminating collector of jade and objets d'art and catalogued, with minute attention to detail, many of the royal possessions.

*Meade-Fetherstonhaugh, Admiral
the Hon. Sir Herbert, G.C.B.,
C.B., D.S.O. (1875–1964)*
An Admiral of no great brains, but
of charm, gallantry and fine sea-
manship. He commanded the constantly active flotilla of destroyers
at Harwich in World War I. He was
always known as Jimmy Meade.
Although in 1940 he was sixty-five,
nothing would induce him not to
serve again. So he became second
mate in a coastal trader and was at
one stage, in the interval of commanding the Houses of Parliament
Home Guard, Commodore of a
convoy of merchantmen sailing
through U-boat infested waters.
One of his sisters married my
father's second brother, also an
Admiral, so that there was a family
connection.

Molotov, Vyacheslav M. (b. 1890)
His face was not his fortune, for it
portrayed intransigence and the
conviction that there was only one
side to every case, namely that
which represented Soviet policy.
He was Chairman of the Council of
People's Commissars and effectively Foreign Minister. One of the
few high-ranking officials who
lasted the course with Stalin into
whose disfavour he never seemed
to fall and whose moods he
reflected faithfully. His name is for
ever attached to the infamous
Molotov–Ribbentrop Pact of August 1939 which allied Nazi Germany to Soviet Russia and provided for the partition of Poland as
well as the seizure by Russia of the
democratic Baltic States, Latvia,
Lithuania and Estonia. After the
war his consistently negative attitude destroyed all hope of a harmo-
nious settlement with the Western

Allies and of a generally acceptable
German peace treaty. He was
still alive in the mid-eighties, a
nonagenarian relic of past misdeeds.

*Monckton of Brenchley, Walter,
1st Viscount, K.C.M.G.,
K.C.V.O., M.C., K.C.
(1891–1965)*
He may not have been a strong
man, but he was most intelligent
and never anything but well-liked,
whether by the Duke of Windsor,
whose intimate adviser he was, by
Arthur Deakin, Secretary of the
Transport and General Workers
Union, or by Winston Churchill.
He played for Harrow, in company
with Field Marshal Alexander,
in the famous "Fowler's Match"
against Eton, and his sporting
activities included a Mastership of
Fox Hounds. After going to Balliol, he served in the army throughout World War I, winning the
Military Cross, and then became a
barrister at the Inner Temple. His
charm and his ability brought him
important clients. He was a member of the Bar Council as well as
standing Counsel to Oxford University. In 1940 he was Director
General of the Ministry of Information and thereafter went to
Cairo as Oliver Lyttelton's head of
propaganda. In 1951 he was
elected M.P. for Bristol West and
joined the Cabinet as Minister of
Labour, basking continuously in
Churchill's favour. He declined the
Home Office in 1954, but Eden
made him Minister of Defence a
year later. Disapproving of the
Suez venture he resigned shortly
before the operation started. After
retirement from politics he was
Chairman of the Midland Bank

and the Iraq Petroleum Company, and President of the M.C.C.

Montgomery of Alamein, Field Marshal, 1st Viscount, K.G., G.C.B., D.S.O. (1887–1976)
Inspired trainer of men though he was, and much applauded for his handling of the 3rd Division in 1940, it was purely by the accident of General Gott's death in an aeroplane crash that in 1942 he was given command of the 8th Army in North Africa. With remarkable flair he restored the wilting morale of the troops and after winning the battle of El Alamein he became a national hero. In command of all the Allied ground forces in the Normandy invasion (June 1944), he moved slowly but surely, but too slowly to hamper the build-up of the German defence. However, once his armies had broken through, he led the British 21st Army Group the whole way across the Rhine to the German surrender at Luneberg Heath. On the way he quarrelled persistently with the American Generals Eisenhower and Bradley, resented having the American troops removed from his command in August, objected to being denied the concentration of stronger forces under his command on the left wing and formed the unattractive habit, then and after the war, of denigrating all the American commanders. He was undoubtedly a great General, if a cautious one, and although egocentric, and indeed vainglorious, he developed in his old age a mellowness and charm, occasionally marred by deplorable tactlessness. He was C.I.G.S., 1946–48, causing Mr Attlee much irritation, and deputy Supreme Commander at the Supreme Headquarters, Allied Powers in Europe (S.H.A.P.E.), 1951–58. In retirement he lived benignly in Hampshire, his war-time caravans open to inspection, his garden planted in military order and rice-pudding offered to his guests.

Moran, Charles Wilson, 1st Lord, M.C. (1882–1977)
He had a distinguished medical career, during which he was Dean of St Mary's Hospital Medical School for twenty-five years and President of the Royal College of Physicians from 1941 to 1950. He was recommended to Winston Churchill by Lord Beaverbrook in 1940, but did not see much of the Prime Minister until at Christmas, 1941, after America had entered the war, Churchill had a minor heart disturbance in Washington. Thereafter, Wilson, whom Churchill recommended for a peerage in 1943, accompanied the Prime Minister on most of his foreign travels and made notes of the views suppressed by the galaxy of stars whose acquaintance he in consequence made. Highly intelligent though hypercritical, he was usually a pleasant companion and he wrote extremely well. He seldom treated Churchill's ailment himself but always knew the right specialist to summon. *The Anatomy of Courage*, which he published in 1945, shows depth of insight and an understanding of fear; but after Churchill's death he infuriated his family and was severely criticised by the medical profession for writing *Winston Churchill, The Struggle for Survival*, excusing himself on the fallacious grounds that Churchill's health affected the out-

come of the war. It was President Roosevelt whose powers were failing, not Churchill. In reviewing this book, I wrote unkindly but truthfully: 'Lord Moran was never present when history was made, though he was quite often invited to luncheon afterwards.'

Morrison of Lambeth, Herbert, 1st Lord, C.H. (1888–1965)

Riding on the crest of a wave, as a result of his much praised leadership of the London County Council (1934–40), he became a powerful influence in the Labour Party, in and out of Parliament. He had been its Chairman in 1928. Having been Minister of Transport for two years in Ramsay MacDonald's 1929 Government, his next taste of office was in 1940 when the Labour Opposition joined Churchill's Coalition. He began as Minister of Supply, frequently thwarted by Lord Beaverbrook whose piracy for aircraft production purposes made a heavy dent in the goods Morrison could produce. In October 1940, he was moved to the Home Office and the new Ministry of Home Security, and there he remained till 1945, being admitted to the War Cabinet in 1942, but never taking his eye off the preparation of Labour's next election campaign. He was dynamic, he was tireless and with both fascists and Communists he was ruthless; but he and Ernest Bevin formed a bitter rivalry and hostility.

In 1945 he was the leader of those in the Labour Party who opposed the continuation of the Coalition till after the defeat of Japan and demanded a return to party politics. He became Lord President, was for a time respon-sible for economic planning and led the House of Commons, through which he piloted the various nationalisation measures. In 1950, when his adversary, Bevin, fell ill, he was for a year an incompetent and unpopular Foreign Secretary; but his eye had long been fixed on ousting Attlee and becoming Prime Minister, for he was not short of ambition. In the end it was Hugh Gaitskell, and not Morrison, who succeeded to the leadership of the party.

Morton, Major Sir Desmond, K.C.B., C.M.G., M.C. (1891–1971)

A devout Roman Catholic, educated at Eton and Woolwich, he was shot through the heart in World War I but miraculously survived, though he always looked pale and ill. He ended that war as A.D.C. to Field Marshal Haig.

He lived at Edenbridge and was thus a neighbour of the Churchills at Chartwell. He had become head of the Industrial Intelligence Centre and, whether with or without authority is uncertain, he supplied Churchill with much information valuable to him in the 1930s when he was trying to warn the government and the country of the danger ahead.

In May 1940 Churchill brought him to 10 Downing Street and sought to use him as his liaison with the Foreign Office, an experiment much resented in that quarter. He was at an early stage involved with de Gaulle and the Free French and later became the Prime Minister's contact with the Allied governments in London and some branches of the Secret Service. However, his usefulness declined and the Prime Minister, though certainly not wishing to be unkind, made less and less use of his services. He resented this the more because he had given the impression in many quarters that he was the Prime Minister's right-hand man. Churchill did procure a K.C.B. for him and in 1946 persuaded Attlee to appoint him U.K. delegate to the Inter-Allied Reparations Agency; but because he had been over-ambitious he died a sad and embittered man.

Mountbatten of Burma, Admiral of the Fleet, 1st Earl, K.G., G.C.B., O.M., G.C.S.I., G.C.I.E., G.C.V.O., D.S.O. (1900–1979)

Younger son of Admiral of the Fleet Prince Louis of Battenberg (1st Marquess of Milford Haven) and Princess Victoria of Hesse, a great-grandson of Queen Victoria and godson of both Queen Victoria and the Tsar Nicholas II. He had an illustrious naval career, including the command of H.M.S. *Kelly* in the battle of Crete, and he married Sir Ernest Cassell's energetic heiress, Edwina Ashley. He was Chief of Combined Operations, 1941–43, Supreme Allied Commander in South East Asia, 1943–46, Viceroy and Governor General of India, 1947–48, C. in C., Mediterranean, 1952–54, First Sea Lord, 1955–59 and Chief of the Defence Staff, 1959–65. Churchill admired his courage, but mistrusted his judgment and deplored his outspoken support, while still a serving officer, of the Labour Party. He therefore declined to agree to his being First Sea Lord until a week before his own resignation. His was the unique case in modern times of a member of the Royal Family actively involved in major political and operational affairs. He was murdered by the I.R.A. while on holiday in Ireland.

Moyne, Walter Guinness, 1st Lord, D.S.O. (and bar) (1880–1944)

Third son of the 1st Earl of Iveagh, he entered the House of Commons in 1907 as Member for Bury St Edmunds, won a D.S.O. and bar in the 1st World War, fought at Gallipoli and was seriously wounded. He was Under Secretary for War in Lloyd George's Coalition Government, Financial Secretary at the Treasury when Churchill was Chancellor and then for four years Minister of Agriculture. In the Second World War he succeeded Lord Lloyd as Secretary of State for the Colonies, was for a time Leader of the House of Lords and was sent out to Cairo as Resident Minister in the Middle East. In Cairo he was callously assassinated by the Jewish Stern Gang. He was a man of courage and ability owning, in more peaceful days, a fine steam yacht *Rosaura* in which Clementine Churchill went for a long Pacific cruise shortly before the war. He married Lady Evelyn Erskine, daughter of the 14th Earl of Buchan, and had two sons and a daughter. The daughter, Grania, married Lord Normanby.

Normanbrook, Norman Brook, 1st Lord, G.C.B. (1902–1967)

From Wolverhampton School and Wadham College, Oxford, he entered the Home Office in 1925. After being Principal Private Secretary and personal assistant to Sir John Anderson, he was a Deputy

Secretary to the War Cabinet in 1942. Five years later he succeeded Sir Edward Bridges as Secretary to the Cabinet, the third man to hold that key post. Prime Ministers – Attlee, Churchill, Eden, Macmillan – had implicit trust in him and his recommendations were seldom turned down. Indeed, whether on appointments or on matters of home policy his influence was all but paramount, and he was the very model of a good administrator. He advised and acted with discretion, for he was by temperament reserved and entirely unostentatious. He never put a foot wrong. When Churchill decided to show his appreciation for the man he considered the most meritorious of civil servants by making him a Privy Councillor, I objected that such discrimination would be unfair to Sir Edward Bridges. So he put forward both their names. In 1956 he was appointed joint Permanent Secretary to the Treasury and Head of the Civil Service; in 1963 he was made a peer; and although he became ill from sheer overwork he accepted the Chairmanship of the B.B.C. in 1964.

Norwich, Alfred Duff Cooper, 1st Viscount, G.C.M.G., D.S.O. (1890–1954)
His claim to fame stemmed at least in part from being married to the beautiful Lady Diana Manners. In the Foreign Office before the First World War, a brave Grenadier Officer during it and a Tory M.P. after it, he was a witty speaker, an interesting conversationist and the owner of an excellent prose style; but he was idle as a Minister. As Secretary of State for War, and then First Lord of the Admiralty in

the 1930s, he was regarded as a light-weight, but he did have the courage of his anti-Nazi convictions when he resigned at the time of Munich.

He could scarcely have been worse as Minister of Information (though, as successor to Lord Reith, he did wear a temporary halo), and when sent to Singapore at the end of 1941 to report on the defences he suggested no useful palliatives. However, as Ambassador to the Free French, first in Algiers, and then in Paris at the end of the war and for two years after it, he helped to restore Anglo-French relations and his letters and despatches home often brimmed over with useful analysis and intelligent anticipation.

O'Neill of the Maine, Terence, Lord (b. 1914)
Youngest son of the Hon. Arthur and Lady Annabel O'Neill. Educated at Eton. After war service with the Irish Guards, he entered Northern Irish politics as a Unionist, was Deputy Speaker of the Stormont Parliament, 1953–56, then Minister of Home Affairs, Minister of Finance and finally, from 1963 to 1969, Prime Minister. He came nearer than anybody before or since to creating an understanding between Protestants and Catholics in Ulster and actually dared visit the Irish Prime Minister in Dublin and receive him on a return visit to Belfast. His liberalism was distasteful to the leaders of the Unionist Party, including his predecessor Lord Brookeborough. He was defeated in his constituency by the rampant Paisley and stabbed in the back by his own party. Mr Harold Wilson recom-

mended him for a peerage in 1970. He married Miss Jean Whitaker.

Pétain, Marshal Philippe (1856–1951)

The victor of Verdun and suppressor of the French army mutinies in 1917, he ended the First World War as Commander in Chief, was for ten years Vice President of the Supreme War Council and in 1934 Minister for War. Ambassador in Madrid in 1939, he returned to France when the fighting began and joined Paul Reynaud's government, becoming himself Prime Minister on June 16th, 1940. The French, in defeat, distress and despair, needed a father-figure to whom to turn. They had not had one since Clemenceau in World War I. Pétain filled that rôle during the German occupation, but both he and Weygand believed that France had sinned and must expiate her sin by suffering. So although he was not such an ardent collaborator with the Germans as Laval, Darlan and Baudouin, and considered it his main duty to ensure strict adherence to the terms of the armistice with Germany, he made no effort to help the Western Allies and actually condemned de Gaulle to death. Such was the prestige of the father-figure that French officers and colonial officials obeyed instructions from Vichy without hesitation, whatever their personal predilections. After the war he was sentenced to death, but the sentence was commuted to imprisonment on an island off the coast of France.

Peter II, King of Yugoslavia (1923–1970)

Son of King Alexander, assassinated during a state visit to France when Peter was only eleven. His father's first cousin, the Regent Prince Paul, who was married to the Duchess of Kent's beautiful sister and much preferred collecting pictures to governing Yugoslavia, was overthrown by General Simovic when the Germans invaded the country in March 1941, and King Peter, aged seventeen, was proclaimed ruler. He only ruled a few days before having to flee to London with his government, while General Mihailovic did his best to maintain the royalist cause in the forests and mountains. George VI was his "Koum", or godfather, and Churchill saw that the only way for Peter to retain his throne was by an agreement with Tito and the victorious partisans. To that end he tried to persuade Peter to reconstitute his royal government in London under Dr Subasic, the Ban (Governor) of Croatia. Under the influence of his mother-in-law, Princess Aspasia of Greece, Peter insisted on maintaining an uncompromising attitude, but it is clear that Tito would not in any case have agreed to preserve the monarchy.

Portal of Hungerford, Marshal of the R.A.F., 1st Viscount, K.G., G.C.B., O.M., D.S.O., M.C. (1893–1971)

Educated at Winchester and Christ Church, Oxford, he joined the R.F.C. in 1915 and was a skilful, daring pilot. He rose steadily to the top of the R.A.F., was A.O.C. in C., Bomber Command, for most of 1940 and Chief of the Air Staff for the rest of the war. Quiet, unforthcoming and not easy to converse with, he was shrewd in his judgment and seldom averse to risk and adventure. Churchill told me that of the three Chiefs of Staff it was on Portal that he relied most. After the war he was Controller of Atomic Energy at the Ministry of Supply, 1946–51, and then Chairman of British Aluminium, of the British Match Corporation and of the British Aircraft Corporation. Although he displayed no goods in his shop window, he was universally respected and admired.

Portal of Laverstoke, Wyndham, 1st and last Viscount, G.C.M.G., D.S.O. (1885–1949)
Son of Sir William Portal, whose family, of Huguenot descent, made paper for £5 notes at the Laverstoke mill. Wyndham struck out from the family mould and was Chairman not only of Portals, but of Wiggins Teape and the Great Western Railway. Most agreeable in conversation and an affable host, he was ruthless to those who worked for him. After success as a war-time Regional Commissioner, he developed political ambitions and, with the help of Brendan Bracken and Oliver Lyttelton (Viscount Chandos), he obtained a ministerial post as Minister of Housing. He won incidental Prime Ministerial favour by sending both Churchill and Attlee (to whom he sucked up shamelessly, despite his Conservative affiliations) baskets of plovers' eggs from Laverstoke every spring.

Pound, Admiral of the Fleet, Sir Dudley, O.M., G.C.B., G.C.V.O. (1877–1943)
He wore a lugubrious air and his mere entry into the room made the occupants feel grave. Yet, off duty he was said to be cheerful and sometimes almost garrulous. Originator of the Directorate of Plans at the Admiralty, former Chief of Staff to Sir Roger Keyes in the Mediterranean and finally C. in C., Mediterranean, himself, he was recalled to London to be First Sea Lord only six weeks before the outbreak of war. Slow, but sure, he seemed the very antithesis of the new First Lord, Winston Churchill; but in fact they worked well together and Churchill developed an affection for Pound, criticise him though he often did for his cautious approach to problems. He overworked consistently and died, still in harness, after the first Quebec Conference in 1943.

Reith, John, 1st Lord, G.C.V.O., G.B.E., C.B. (1889–1971)
Founding father and, indeed, Dictator of the B.B.C. after a youthful apprenticeship in engineering and a short, sharp interlude on the Western Front. In 1938 he was made Chairman of Imperial Airways. He gave the impression of ruthless efficiency, but the efficiency seemed to desert him when, ennobled for the purpose, he entered the Government. It is hard to say whether he was worse as Minister of Information or as Minister of Transport, but whatever his failures his achievement at the B.B.C. is a claim to enduring fame. His Scottish dourness appealed to some, who thought it a sign of his honesty and virtue (which it probably was). He loathed Churchill, whom he found insufficiently Puritan; but Churchill, who had other worries, took no notice of the fact.

Reynaud, Paul (1878–1966)
A prominent politician of the French Third Republic who, after holding the usual assorted collection of Cabinet offices, went from the Ministry of Finance to succeed Daladier as Prime Minister two months before the German offensive of May 1940. He had a majority of only one in the Chamber and a divided Cabinet. On May 9th he offered his resignation, but withdrew it the next day when the battle started. He tried to keep France in the war, fighting if necessary from North Africa, and Charles de Gaulle was his special protégé. However, he was overwhelmed by his defeatist colleagues, Pétain, Weygand, Baudouin and others, and resigned in favour of Pétain on June 16th. After arrest by the Vichy Government and two years' imprisonment in Germany, he was again French Minister of Finance in 1948 and took a leading part in drafting the new constitution of the Fifth Republic.

Ribbentrop, Joachim von (1893–1946)
Subservient satellite of Hitler who was a champagne salesman in Canada before World War I, in which he won the Iron Cross. He reverted to wine salesmanship from 1920 until elected a Nazi member of the Reichstag in 1933. In 1936 his subservience gained him the German Embassy in London, where he hit the headlines by giving a Nazi salute to King George VI at a St James's Palace levée and busied himself, not at all effectively, in trying to implant pro-Nazi sentiment in important people. Recalled to Berlin in 1938 to be Foreign Minister, he obeyed his master's voice unquestioningly, gave his name to the infamous Molotov–Ribbentrop Pact and after the Nuremberg Trials was hanged (very clumsily by the American hangman) as a war criminal. When he was captured in 1945, he wrote a crawling and obsequious letter to Churchill attempting to exonerate himself from all blame for the war. Churchill was revolted by his cringing words and sent no reply.

Rowan, Sir Leslie, K.C.B., C.V.O. (1903–1972)
He came to No. 10 from the Colonial Office, via the Treasury, and was one of the ablest and most endearing men I have known. He had played hockey for England, had been well grounded in the classics at Tonbridge and had shone at Queen's College, Cambridge. Of the brightest intelligence, he was serious of purpose but possessed a rollicking sense of fun. In due course he was Principal Private Secretary, first to Churchill and then to Attlee, ministering to them both at the Potsdam Conference. He returned to the Treasury to be Second Secretary and worked with Sir Stafford Cripps as Chancellor. Why he was not promoted to be head of the Treasury is one of Whitehall's unsolved mysteries. He left to become Managing Director, and in due course Chairman, of Vickers Ltd and died too soon.

Rucker, Sir Arthur Nevil, K.C.M.G., C.B., C.B.E. (b. 1895)
Son of a Fellow of the Royal Society, and educated at Marlborough and Trinity College, Cambridge, he entered the Civil Service after

three years in the trenches and was Private Secretary to several Ministers of Health. In 1939 he became Neville Chamberlain's Principal Private Secretary and was wholly uncritical of his policies. He remained with Chamberlain, by then Lord President of the Council, throughout the summer of 1940 and subsequently returned to the Ministry of Health as Deputy Secretary. A man of great goodness, with a sparkling sense of humour, but sometimes blinded by his loyalty.

Salisbury, Robert Cecil, 5th Marquess of, K.G. (1893–1972)
Grandson of a Prime Minister, descendant of Queen Elizabeth I's all-powerful minister, Lord Burleigh, and owner of Hatfield House, he was a political figure of major importance for some twenty years. Having fought as a Grenadier in the First World War, he was, as Lord Cranborne, elected Conservative M.P. for South Dorset in 1929. Representing, with Anthony Eden, the younger element in the Tory Party, he was Parliamentary Under Secretary at the Foreign Office, 1935–38, but resigned with Eden in protest against Neville Chamberlain's interference in foreign affairs. Back in office in 1940, he was soon Secretary of State for the Dominions, and at one stage for the Colonies, Lord Privy Seal and Leader of the House of Lords. On two occasions Churchill had his name on the list to be Foreign Secretary. His influence in the Conservative Party, in and out of office, was dominant and he held a series of high offices between 1951 and 1957 when he resigned on the Cyprus issue. He and his wife

Betty, daughter of Lord Richard and Lady Moyra Cavendish, were on the closest terms of friendship with both the King and Queen and the Churchills; but "Bobbety" Salisbury was interested in everybody and was as ready to listen to the views of unimportant people as to those of Kings and Cabinet Ministers.

Selwyn-Lloyd, Lord, C.H., C.B.E., Q.C. (1904–1978)
Elected to Parliament for the Wirral division of Cheshire in 1945, he held all the important portfolios – Defence, Foreign Affairs (at the time of the Suez episode), the Exchequer (from which he was unceremoniously ejected by Harold Macmillan in 1962) and the leadership of the House of Commons. He was not, however, adequately respected and applauded until he became Speaker of the House of Commons (1971–76). He could be biting; he could appear supercilious; but often his least appreciated remarks were induced by a deadpan sense of humour which, like claret, improved as the years went by and made him an increasingly pleasant companion.

Sherfield, Roger Makins, 1st Lord, G.C.B., G.C.M.G. (b. 1904)
There have not been many diplomats or civil servants to rival Roger Makins in distinction and intelligence. From Winchester he went to Christ Church, Oxford, won a first in "Greats" and was elected a Fellow of All Souls. Years later his elder son did the same, so that, perhaps uniquely, father and son were Fellows of All Souls at the same time.

Rising rapidly in the Diplomatic

Service, which he entered in 1928, he married Alice, daughter of Dwight D. Davis of Davis Cup fame. Anthony Eden was greatly impressed by his abilities; and so was Harold Macmillan, after he had served as his No. 2 in North Africa. So, too, was Winston Churchill in his dealings with him at the British Embassy in Washington.

He had already served twice on the staff at the Washington Embassy when, in 1953, he was appointed Ambassador. Thence he was wafted by Harold Macmillan in 1956 to be Joint Permanent Secretary of the Treasury, which was not a post for which his experience, wide though it had been, qualified him; but from 1960 to 1964 he was a successful Chairman of the Atomic Energy Commission. In so-called retirement he was amongst much else Chairman of Hill Samuel, of the Industrial and Commercial Finance Company (I.C.F.C.), of A. C. Cossor, of Raytheon International and of Wells Fargo Ltd. He was also Chancellor of Reading University, a superb ballroom dancer and the owner of one of the loudest and most totally sincere laughs in the United Kingdom.

Simon, John, 1st Viscount, G.C.S.I., G.C.V.O., K.C. (1873–1954)
The son of a Congregational minister, he was educated at Fettes and Wadham, Oxford, and was a Fellow of All Souls. A brilliant advocate, he was not popular with his fellow barristers who proclaimed, "There'll be no moaning at the Bar when he puts out to sea." Shattered by the death of his first wife for whom, before he made a for-

tune at the Bar, he could not afford the medicaments she needed, he went in to Parliament as a Liberal in 1906, was Solicitor General and then Attorney General in Asquith's pre-war Government, was one of the Ministers originally opposed to Britain entering the war, but became Home Secretary, 1915–16. After the war he was Chairman of the Simon Commission sent to India in 1928 to study constitutional reform when Lord Irwin (later Lord Halifax) was Viceroy. In 1931 he led a section of the Liberal Party into Ramsay MacDonald's National Government, was a most unpopular Foreign Secretary (1931–35), a somewhat more esteemed Home Secretary (1935–37), and Chancellor of the Exchequer with great influence (1937–40). In 1940 Churchill made him Lord Chancellor, but did not put him in the War Cabinet. He was capable of taking great trouble to help people in distress, but he never succeeded in overcoming the dislike of those who worked for him.

Soames, Christopher, Lord, G.C.M.G., G.C.V.O., C.H., C.B.E. (b. 1920)
From Eton and Sandhurst, he joined the Coldstream Guards in 1939 and when the war ended became assistant military attaché at the Embassy in Paris. There he met Mary Churchill and after a short, whirlwind romance they were married in 1947. His parents-in-law knew nothing about him, but he quickly established an excellent relationship with Winston Churchill who delighted in his company. He was elected Conservative M.P. for Bedford in 1950, was Parliamen-

tary Private Secretary to Churchill 1951–55, and thereafter, beginning as Under Secretary at the Air Ministry, he was Financial Secretary at the Admiralty, Secretary of State for War and Minister of Agriculture in Macmillan's and Douglas Home's Cabinets. In 1968 Harold Wilson sent him as Ambassador to Paris for four years, when his impeccable knowledge of French was invaluable, but "the Soames affair" with General de Gaulle, due to leakages in London, caused him embarrassment. From 1973 to 1977 he was the senior British E.E.C. Commissioner in Brussels, and in 1979 Lord Carrington gave him the task, as Governor of Rhodesia, of presiding over the transfer of power to a black government. He got on well with Mr Mugabe. He returned to London to be Lord President and Leader of the House of Lords for two years, but left after disagreement over a settlement of a Civil Service strike. He and Mrs Thatcher were not birds of a feather.

Spears, Major-General Sir Edward Louis Bt., K.B.E., C.B., M.C. (1886–1974)
Bilingual in English and French, he made his name as British liaison officer with the French armies in World War I. Between the wars he was Conservative M.P. for Carlisle and a strong supporter of Churchill, who always thought well of him. At Bordeaux in 1940 he did his best to rally the French and it was he who brought de Gaulle to England. He later quarrelled with that emotional general over the affairs of Syria and the Lebanon. He also quarrelled with the French

authorities in Beirut when he was British Ambassador to Syria and the Lebanon in the last years of the war. After the war he was Chairman of Ashanti Goldfields. His first wife was the gentle American authoress, Mary Borden, author of *Jane Our Stranger*.

Spears wrote beautiful English and explained his subject with clarity. Churchill once told me that to understand the history of World War I, I need do no more than read two of Spears' books, *Liaison 1914* and *Prelude to Victory*.

Stanley, Col. Right Hon. Oliver, M.C. (1896–1950)
Second son of the 17th Earl of Derby. A master of epigram inside and outside the House of Commons and much sought after as a wit. He fought throughout the First World War, married Lord Londonderry's daughter and was elected Conservative M.P. for Westmorland in 1924. He held many portfolios, Transport, Labour, the Board of Trade and, from January to May 1940, the War Office. However, he was more impressive in debate than in administration, and Churchill did not offer him an office he thought acceptable when the 1940 Government was formed. He did, however, return to the Government in 1942 as Secretary of State for the Colonies. In opposition, after the war, his rapier thrusts in debate were of value to the Conservative Party.

Stockton, Harold Macmillan, 1st Earl of, O.M. (b. 1894)
Educated at Eton and Balliol, he fought with distinction as a Grenadier officer in World War I, married the Duke of Devonshire's

daughter, Lady Dorothy Cavendish, in 1920 and became Conservative M.P. for Stockton-on-Tees in 1924. Being a consistent critic of the Baldwin and Chamberlain Governments, he was not given office till 1940; but he made his reputation as British Minister-Resident in North Africa where, although removed from the mainstream of political and military policy at home, he dealt imaginatively with the vagaries of the Free French and the imbroglios in Italy after the Allied landings. He was prominent in opposition from 1945 to 1951 and then won great acclaim, as Minister of Housing and Local Government, by fulfilling the Tory promise to build 300,000 houses in a year. Thereafter he was in rapid succession Minister of Defence, Foreign Secretary and Chancellor of the Exchequer until, in January 1957, he succeeded Sir Anthony Eden as Prime Minister. The Macmillan years, following on the 1956 Suez fiasco, were years of prosperity and in the 1959 General Election he increased his parliamentary majority. He also inaugurated the Wind of Change, which led to the dismantling of the British Empire. Retiring in 1963 because of ill-health, he resumed the chairmanship of his family publishing firm, Macmillan and Co., and remained for over twenty years a much sought-after elder statesman. In 1960 he was chosen to be Chancellor of Oxford University.

Strakosch, Sir Henry. G.B.E. (1871–1943)
By birth an Austrian, he was naturalised in 1907 and in due course was Chairman of Union Corporation and of *The Economist*. Business relationship with Brendan Bracken turned into personal friendship. He was a financier of unusual skill, responsible for the foundation of the Central Banks of both India and South Africa. He reorganised the currency of several European states and dominated the Financial Committee of the League of Nations. At Bracken's instigation he gave Churchill, often short of money before the war, investment advice and Churchill felt under an obligation to him. He also found his views on international financial matters valuable.

Stuart of Findhorn, James Stuart, 1st Viscount, C.H., M.C. and bar (1897–1971)
Third son of the 17th Earl of Moray, married Lady Rachel Cavendish and was Harold Macmillan's brother-in-law and M.P. for Moray and Nairn, 1923–59. Outstandingly handsome and no less outstandingly downright, he was Deputy to Captain David Margesson whom he succeeded as Chief Conservative Whip in 1940. He was respected, though not particularly liked, by Winston Churchill to whom he had once been most abusive before the war. He was one of Lord Beaverbrook's pet aversions, but Churchill always listened to his sound political advice. Secretary of State for Scotland, 1951–57.

Swinton, Philip Cunliffe-Lister, 1st Earl of, G.B.E., C.H., M.C. (1884–1972)
He was born Philip Lloyd-Greame, but changed his name on marrying an heiress. After fighting bravely in World War I, he became M.P.

for Hendon and held minor office as early as 1918. Thereafter he figured, sometimes largely, in every post-war Coalition or Conservative Government, his shrewdness and drive making him indispensable. He became Secretary of State for the Colonies in 1931, but perhaps his most notable achievement was, as Secretary of State for Air from 1935 to 1938, to preside with enthusiasm over the development of the two great war winners, the Hurricane and the Spitfire. Having been closely associated with Baldwin and Chamberlain, he did not receive high office in Churchill's war-time Coalition Government, but was sent to administer West Africa. He came into his own again in 1951, winning Churchill's confidence, though mistrusted and disliked by Anthony Eden. As Secretary of State for Commonwealth Relations he was frequently consulted on matters having nothing to do with the Commonwealth, and he was made an earl in 1955. Imperious, intolerant of lesser men and with a keen eye to the main chance, he was nevertheless a man who made a mark on the history of his times.

Syers, Sir Cecil, K.C.M.G., C.V.O. (1903–1981)
A Dominions Office official who was Private Secretary briefly to Stanley Baldwin as Prime Minister and then, from 1937 to 1940, to Neville Chamberlain. He went on to be Deputy High Commissioner in South Africa under Lord Harlech and High Commissioner in Ceylon, 1951–57, ending his career as Secretary of the University Grants Committee. Intelligent, efficient, a trifle jaunty, but an admirable colleague with a well-developed sense of the ridiculous.

Tedder, Marshal of the R.A.F., Arthur, Lord, G.C.B. (1890–1967)
Educated at Whitgift School and Magdalene, Cambridge, he joined the Colonial Service but switched to the Dorsetshire Regiment in 1914 and a year later to the Royal Flying Corps. In the 1930s he played an important part in the vital modernisation of the Royal Air Force. As Air Officer C. in C. of the Desert Air Force in 1943 he was justly praised for his tactics and success; but as Deputy Supreme Commander of OVERLORD under Eisenhower, he was given a task less suited to his talents and he did not get on well with some of the army commanders, notably Field Marshal Montgomery. After the war he was Chief of the Air Staff and in 1950–51 Chairman of the British Joint Services Mission in Washington. Good-natured, quick in his reactions, with an unusual, occasionally twisted, sense of humour, he divided his retirement between the assorted occupations of Chancellor of Cambridge University and Chairman of the Standard Motor Company. He was made a peer in 1946.

A month before Churchill's illness at Carthage in 1943, Tedder married Mrs Black, his first, Australian, wife having recently been killed in an air accident. He thereby unwittingly caused consternation to the British representative in Tunisia, Mr Consul General Moneypenny, into whose idyllic garden he had asked leave to have his caravan towed for the wedding night. Unfortunately Mrs Black's estranged naval husband, believing the divorce not to be absolute, arrived at Mr Moneypenny's Consular palace in the middle of the night in search of his wife and sought refuge from a storm. "Go away, go away," cried the distraught Moneypenny, who had put on his dressing-gown to answer the insistent ringing of the doorbell. "You cannot stay here: try the Desert Air Force Headquarters up the road."

Templewood, Samuel Hoare, 1st and last Viscount, G.C.S.I., G.B.E., C.M.G. (1880–1959)
It was not without justification that he was called "Slippery Sam". The son of a Norfolk baronet, his intelligence was matched, or even surpassed, by his natural bent for intrigue. Educated at Harrow and New College, Oxford, he married Lady Maud Lygon, daughter of the 6th Earl Beauchamp, and when presenting to the House of Commons his apologia for the Hoare–Laval Pact of 1935 (which would have given part of Abyssinia to Italy) he brought the House down by declaring that in his hurry to report to them he had "left Lady Maud and the luggage" in Paris. M.P. for Chelsea, he was Secretary of State for Air in 1922, and subsequently for India and for Foreign Affairs, First Lord of the Admiralty and Home Secretary. It was in this last office, which he combined with Lord Privy Seal, that in 1937–39 he was a powerful, influential and strongly appeasing member of Chamberlain's Cabinet. There was a dire moment in 1939 when, had anything happened to Chamberlain, he might well have been Prime Minister. His own great

ambition was to be Viceroy. In 1940 Churchill, who was not one of his admirers, sent him as Ambassador to Madrid where he performed a most useful service in countering the pro-German influence of General Franco's supporters.

Thurso, Archibald Sinclair, 1st Viscount, K.T., C.M.G. (1890–1970)
Head of the Caithness Sinclair clan, he went to Eton and Sandhurst and, although an officer in the Life Guards, became Winston Churchill's second in command of the 6th Royal Scots Fusiliers in 1916. He stayed with Churchill, whom he worshipped, as Personal Secretary at the War Office, 1919–21, and then at the Colonial Office. However, in 1922 he was elected Liberal M.P. for Caithness and Sutherland. When the National Government was formed in 1931, he did not join those Liberals who, under Sir John Simon, remained loyal to Ramsay MacDonald and Stanley Baldwin. After a brief tenure of the Scottish Office, he and his chief, Sir Herbert Samuel, left the National Government on the issue of Free Trade. In 1935 he succeeded Samuel as Leader of the Opposition Liberals, vigorously opposed Chamberlain, Munich and appeasement, declined to bring his party into the Government in September 1939, but became, to his great satisfaction, Churchill's choice as Secretary of State for Air in 1940. He retained that office, in constant controversy with Lord Beaverbrook, till the end of the war. His wife, Marigold, daughter of the notoriously flighty Lady Angela Forbes, had a stronger

character than her husband and was a pleasant, if alarmingly determined, woman.

Tree, Ronald (1897–1976)
Affable and public-spirited owner of Ditchley Park, possessed of a substantial Marshall Field fortune from Chicago, he was a British subject, educated at Winchester, and was elected Conservative M.P. for a Leicestershire constituency. His first wife was a stimulating niece of Lady Astor, with exquisite taste, and his second, Marietta, daughter of the Bishop of Syracuse, was a trusted friend of the Democrat Presidential Candidate, Adlai Stevenson, and works hard in political and social service activities in America.

Wavell, Field Marshal, 1st Earl, G.C.B., G.C.S.I., G.C.I.E., C.M.G., M.C. (1883–1950)
This well-read Wykehamist, who loved poetry, was considered by many the finest soldier in the British Army. In 1937 Lord Gort, as Military Secretary, was about to put forward his name to be C.I.G.S. when Hore-Belisha surprisingly chose Gort himself instead. Having commanded in Palestine and Transjordan, he was G.O.C., Southern Command, before being sent in 1939 to take charge of the British Army in Egypt. When Italy came into the war Wavell won two successful campaigns against General Graziani, but in 1941 the arrival of Rommel and the Germans on the scene changed the situation. His handling of the Greek and Crete campaigns that spring was not adept, at least so Churchill thought, and he was badly checked in the Western Desert, despite the arrival of many new tanks and guns by means of Operation TIGER. So at the end of 1941 he was relieved of his command and sent off to India, first as C. in C. and then, from 1943 to 1947, as Viceroy until Mountbatten came out to replace him and organise Indian independence. He was shy and not good at expressing himself orally so that Churchill never grasped his best qualities. He did, moreover, preside over a grossly overmanned H.Q. in Cairo and he seemed to Churchill more interested in building up a large body of supporting personnel in Egypt than in taking offensive action.

Waverley, Sir John Anderson, 1st Viscount, G.C.B., O.M., G.C.S.I., G.C.I.E., F.R.S. (1882–1958)
His company and his appearance were pontifical. Brendan Bracken, who had a *penchant* for creating nicknames, called him God's Butler, but he was on a par with Lord Hankey as one of Britain's greatest twentieth-century administrators.

Of comparatively humble origin, but with a distinguished academic career at George Watson's College and Edinburgh University, he passed top into the Civil Service in 1905 and quickly rose to be Chairman of the Board of Inland Revenue, Under Secretary in Ireland during the distressing Black and Tans period, and, from 1922, Permanent Under Secretary at the Home Office. There he made necessary preparations to deal with a General Strike and established the basis of air-raid precautions. Ten years later he was appointed Governor of Bengal and narrowly escaped two terrorist attempts on his life. Back in England he became independent M.P. for the Scottish Universities, and in 1938, at the time of Munich, was Regional Commissioner for London and the Home Counties. Neville Chamberlain appointed him Lord Privy Seal, responsible for manpower and civil defence, and in 1939 he was promoted to be Home Secretary. Later in the war he was Lord President of the Council and from 1943 till the fall of Churchill's Government Chancellor of the Exchequer. The Lord President's Committee, of which he was Chairman, was the main instrument for regulating home affairs. The smoothness with which the country's civil administration was conducted, and its economic resources maintained, was in large part due to his calm and steady administrative skill. He was also responsible, with Lord Cherwell, for the British contribution to the atomic bomb programme, deadly secret and known as TUBE ALLOYS. At one stage, when the Prime Minister and Eden were setting off together on a foreign journey, Churchill suggested to the King that, should they both be killed, Anderson, as a non-party statesman of proved ability, might be the man to send for as Prime Minister.

After the war he was made a Viscount, and in addition to being Chairman of the Advisory Committee on atomic energy, and Chairman of the Port of London Authority, he threw himself energetically and successfully into reviving the fortunes of the Covent Garden opera. He disliked personal publicity and he was an uninspiring speaker in either House of Parliament, but by his quiet efficiency and capacity for hard work he was a major contributor to winning the war.

Weygand, General Maxime (1867–1965)

He was commanding the French Army in the Middle East when summoned urgently in May 1940 to succeed General Gamelin in charge of the Allied armies in France. Active, apparently tireless and impressive in speech, he owed his high reputation mainly to having been Chief of Staff to Marshal Foch, who was reputed to have said: "When France is in danger, send for Weygand." The mystery of his birth added to his fascination for the French public. Some said his father was the Archduke Maximilian, Emperor of Mexico, others that he was a son of the appalling King Leopold II of Belgium, and yet others that he was the illegitimate offspring of a Jewish businessman in Bruges who had a gardener called Weygand. Whatever the truth, it was too late for him to prove his worth by the time he was called to command in 1940; but he was infuriated by the failure of the British to accept defeat as inevitable once the French Army had been crushed. In September 1940, after three months as Minister of National Defence in the Vichy Government, he was sent to Algeria as Governor General and there were hopes in London and Washington that he might defect to the Allies. The same thought must have occurred to the Germans, for in 1942 they imprisoned him for three years, and so, after the war, did the French.

*Wilson, Sir Horace John, G.C.B.,
G.C.M.G., C.B.E. (1882–1972)*
By nature modest and retiring,
educated at Kurnella School,
Bournemouth, and the London
School of Economics, he was by
the late 1930s one of the most
powerful men in Britain, an *emi-
nence grise* without whose advice
the Prime Minister seldom moved.
This was not his fault, or indeed his
desire. Having been Permanent
Secretary at the Ministry of Labour
before he was forty, he was
appointed Chief Industrial Adviser
to the Government in 1930, imported to No. 10 by Stanley Baldwin in 1935 and retained with ever
increasing influence by Neville
Chamberlain. He knew little about
defence or foreign affairs, but was
plunged into the deep end of both
by the Prime Minister, and in
1939 he was also made Permanent Secretary to the Treasury
and Head of the Civil Service.
Churchill, who regarded him with
aversion, removed him from No.
10, but left him at the Treasury,
where he pursued his duties
efficiently. Kind-hearted, conscientious and a good Christian, he
had much blame heaped on his
head, a good deal of it unjustly.

*Winant, Hon. John Gilbert
(1889–1947)*
A gentle, dreamy idealist, whom
most men and all women loved, he
had been Governor of New Hampshire and looked like Abraham
Lincoln. He came to England, with
President Roosevelt's full confidence, as a welcome contrast to
his defeatist predecessor, Joseph P.
Kennedy. He was soon a personal
friend of the Churchill family and
there was seldom a week-end when

he did not go to Chequers. He fell
in love with Sarah Churchill,
though the relationship was an
innocent one. He was an intro-
spective man, unhappily married.
In 1947, no longer employed, but
renting a house in South Street
where he was only happy talking
about old times, he suddenly returned to America and committed
suicide.

Wood, Sir Kingsley (1881–1943)
Insignificant in appearance, and
considered by some to be a time-
server, he nevertheless carried
weight in the counsels of the Conservative Party. Son of a Wesleyan
minister in Hull, he became a solicitor, set up a thriving practice in
London while still in his twenties,
was elected to the L.C.C. and, in
1918, to Parliament. He was amiable to all and easily accessible;
and even though he was a poor
speaker he was a good manipu-
lator. He had much to do with
establishing a Ministry of Health
and was therefore smiled upon by
Neville Chamberlain. He was also
the most efficient of Postmaster
Generals and made the Post Office
so popular (temporarily) that in
1933 Stanley Baldwin put him in
the Cabinet. In 1938 he became
Secretary of State for Air, which
was an ill-judged appointment as
he knew nothing of the armed services and rearmament was at last
beginning in earnest. Churchill,
with encouragement from Chamberlain and Margesson, sent him to
the Treasury where the poor man
had to bear the odium of the first
swingeing war-time Budget. He
called in Keynes, Brand, Robertson and others to advise him, increased taxation to a scarcely bear-

able extent and balanced his budgets. He adopted the idea of P.A.Y.E. and died, suddenly, on the morning of the day he was to announce it.

Woolton, Frederick Marquis, 1st Earl of, C.H. (1883–1964)
The successful import of non-politicians into the War Coalition included Sir Andrew Duncan, Lord Leathers, Oliver Lyttelton and P. J. Grigg. As successful as any of them was Lord Woolton, who kept the nation wholesomely fed in spite of the devastation of merchant shipping by U-boats. A man with a strong social conscience, he began his adult life with energetic efforts to lessen the impact of poverty and was warden of a settlement in Liverpool dockland. Unfit for military service, he worked as an economist in the War Office during World War I and was involved in commercial and industrial matters. Almost by accident he joined the Liverpool, Manchester and Birmingham retail chain called Lewis, becoming Managing Director in 1928 and later Chairman. He was by then an important industrialist.

He made a favourable impression on Sir Horace Wilson who persuaded Chamberlain to withdraw him from the job of providing clothing for the army and to make him, in April 1940, Minister of Food. He worked miracles of organisation and became a national figure. In 1943 he was brought into the War Cabinet as Minister of Reconstruction. When Churchill was defeated in 1945, Woolton, who had once been a Fabian, was so angry with the electorate that he joined the Conservative Party, and in 1946 Churchill asked him to be Party Chairman. He so remained until 1955 and was in addition made Lord President in 1951. Though an endearing man, he was vain and inclined to be pompous, as well as sometimes indiscreet; but few served their country better.

Glossary

Glossary

A.A. = Anti-Aircraft
A.C.I.G.S. = Assistant Chief of
   Imperial General Staff
A.C.2. = Aircraftsman 2nd Class
A.D.C. = Aide de Camp
A.E. = Anthony Eden
A.E.U. = Amalgamated Engineering
   Union
A.F.H.Q. = Allied Forces
   Headquarters
A.I. = Airborne Interception
A.M. = Air Ministry
A.O.C. = Air Officer Commanding
A.O.C. in C. = Air Officer
   Commanding in Chief
A.R.P. = Air Raid Precautions
A.T.S. = Auxiliary Territorial Service
A.V.M. = Air Vice Marshal

B. 17 = Flying Fortress Aircraft
B. 24 = Liberator Aircraft
B.E.F. = British Expeditionary Force
B.G.S. = Brigadier, General Staff
B.O.A.C. = British Overseas
   Airways Corporation

"C" = Brigadier Menzies, head of the
   Secret Service
C.A.S. = Chief of Air Staff
C.I.D. = Criminal Investigation
   Department
C.I.G.S. = Chief of Imperial General
   Staff
C. of E. = Church of England
C.O.S. = Chiefs of Staff

C.W.R. = Central War Room

D.M.I. = Director of Military
   Intelligence
D.N.I. = Director of Naval
   Intelligence

E-boat = German torpedo boat
E.D.C. = European Defence
   Community
E.A.M. = Political organisation of
   Greek Communists
E.L.A.S. = Combatant organisation
   of Greek Communists

F.O. = Foreign Office
F.W. 190 = Focke Wulf 190 German
   aircraft

G.H.Q. = General Headquarters
G.L. = Radar-controlled searchlight
G.O.C. = General Officer Commanding

H.B. = Hore-Belisha (Leslie)
H.E. = His Excellency
H.E. bomb = High-Explosive bomb
H.M. = His Majesty
H.M.G. = His Majesty's Government
H.M.S = His Majesty's Ship
H. of C. = House of Commons

I.C.I. = Imperial Chemical Industries
I.L.P. = Independent Labour Party
I.O.U. = I owe you
I.R.A. = Irish Republican Army

JU. 88 = Junkers 88 German aircraft

K.G. = Knight of the Garter
K.T. = Knight of the Thistle

L.C.C. = London County Council
L.D.V. = Local Defence Volunteers
(Home Guard)
L.G. = Lloyd George
L.P.T.B. = London Passenger
Transport Board

M. and B. = antibiotic drug
M.A.P. = Ministry of Aircraft
Production
ME. 109 = Messerschmitt 109
German aircraft
M.F.A. = Minister for Foreign
Affairs
M.I.5 = Internal Security Service
M.I.6 = Overseas Intelligence Service
M. of I. = Ministry of Information
M.P. = Member of Parliament
M.T.C. = Military Transport Corps

N.C. = Neville Chamberlain
N.C.O. = Non-Commissioned Officer
N.Z. = New Zealand

O.C.T.U. = Officer Cadet Training
Unit
O.S.S. = Office of Strategic Services

P.A. = Personal Assistant
P.E. = Photo-Electric
P.F. = Proximity Fuse
P.G. = Paying Guest
P.M. = Prime Minister
P. of W. = Prisoner of War
P.P.S. = Parliamentary Private
Secretary
P.Q. = Parliamentary Questions
P.S. = Private Secretary
P.W.E. = Political Warfare Executive

R.A.C. = Royal Automobile Club
R.A.F. = Royal Air Force
R.A.F.V.R. = Royal Air Force
Volunteer Reserve
R.A.S.C. = Royal Army Service
Corps

R.C. = Roman Catholic
R.C.A.F. = Royal Canadian Air
Force
R.D.F. = Radio Direction Finding
(Radar)
R.M. = Royal Marines
R.M.S. = Royal Mail Steamer
R.N. = Royal Navy
R.N.V.R. = Royal Naval Volunteer
Reserve

S.A. = Sturmabteilung
S.A.S. = Special Air Service
S.A.S.O. = Senior Air Staff Officer
S.H.A.E.F. = Supreme Headquarters
Allied Expeditionary Force
S.H.A.P.E. = Supreme Headquarters
Allied Powers Europe
S.O.E. = Special Operations
Executive
S. of S. = Secretary of State
S.S. = Schutzstaffel
s.s. = steam ship
S.W.C. = Supreme War Council

T.A.B. = Typhoid anti-bacillus
Tube Alloys = code name for atomic
research
T.U.C. = Trades Union Congress
T.R.H. = Their Royal Highnesses

U-boat = Untersee-boot (German
submarine)
U.J. = Uncle Joe (Stalin)
U.N.O. = United Nations
Organisation
U.N.R.R.A. = United Nations Relief
and Rehabilitation Administration
U.P. = aerial minefield
U.X.B. = unexploded bomb

V. 1 = Vergeltungswaffe (German
flying bomb)
V. 2 = German rocket
V.C. = Victoria Cross
V.C.I.G.S. = Vice Chief of Imperial
General Staff
V.C.N.S. = Vice Chief of Naval Staff
V.E. = Victory in Europe
V.R.I. = Victoria Regina et
Imperatrix

W.A.A.F. = Women's Auxiliary Air Force

W.O. = War Office

W.V.S. = Women's Voluntary Service

Y.M.C.A. = Young Men's Christian Association

Y.W.C.A. = Young Women's Christian Association

Index

Index

(Names marked with an asterisk * are included in the biographical notes. Married names of women mentioned in the text are placed in brackets after the entry, as are titles subsequently conferred when they differ from the original surname. The title Right Honourable for Privy Councillor has been omitted.)